"For those who fight for it, life has a flavour the sheltered never know."

Pinned to a noticeboard at the US Command Post at Khe Sanh

"Nothing is dearer than independence and liberty."

Ho Chi Minh, former leader of North Vietnam

THE VIETNAM WAR

The illustrated history of the conflict in Southeast Asia

THE VIETNAM WAR

The illustrated history of the conflict in Southeast Asia

PUBLISHED BY
SALAMANDER BOOKS LIMITED
LONDON

A Salamander Book

Published by Salamander Books Ltd,
8 Blenheim Court, Brewery Road,
London N7 9NT, United Kingdom

© Salamander Books Ltd, 1979, 1983, 1987, 1996 and 1999

ISBN 1 84065 108 3

Credits

Editor: Ray Bonds

Colour drawings: Wilf Hardy, pages 20–21, 28–29, 32–33, 38–39, 44–45 (© Salamander Books Ltd.); and John W. Wood & Associates, pages 18–19, 22–27, 30–31, 34–37, 40–43 (© Salamander Books Ltd.)

Maps: Peter Sarson and Tony Bryan (© Salamander Books Ltd.)

Filmset by SX Composing Ltd., England.
Colour reproductions: Process Colour Centre Ltd., Colourcraftsmen Ltd., Positive Colour, Culver Graphics Litho Ltd., Tenreck Ltd., and Adtype Ltd., England.

Printed in Spain.

Editor's Acknowledgements

In the process of preparing this timely volume for publication I have been fortunate in having received the help and advice of very many people and organizations. It is not possible to mention them all here, but I do thank them for their assistance. In particular, I am extremely grateful for all the efforts of and the support from the consultant, Bernard C. Nalty, Charles B. MacDonald of the US Army Center for Military History, Lt. Col. Lane Rogers for much enlightening information, and two other authors, in England, Richard O'Neill and Lt. Col. David Miller.

Each of the US Services has been extremely helpful, and I accordingly thank the offices of information of the Department of Defense, the Army, the Navy, the Air Force and Marine Corps, and other US Government organizations and agencies in the United States and in Europe.

Ray Bonds

Contents

The Consultant

Bernard C. Nalty is a recognized authority on United States military affairs, having served with the Centers of Military History of both the United States Air Force and the United States Marine Corps. He wrote *Air Power and the Fight for Khe Sanh* (US Govt. Printing Office, 1973) was co-author of *Central Pacific Drive*, a volume of the official US Marine Corps operational history of World War II, was co-editor of *Blacks in the US Armed Forces: Basic Documents*. He has contributed many technical articles on military subjects to official US armed forces publications and historical journals, including *Army, Marine Corps Gazette, US Naval Institute Proceedings, American Neptune, Aerospace Historian,* and *American Aviation Historical Society Journal*.

The Authors

William L. Allen is a former military intelligence officer and historian with the US Army. He served a total of five years in Southeast Asia (two years in South Vietnam and three in Thailand) as a Foreign Area Specialist. For some months in Vietnam he was the Military Assistance Command, Vietnam (MACV) Historian. He wrote chapters for two consecutive MACV Histories and for other historical volumes. His last three years in the Army (to 1977) were spent as an historian in the US Army Center of Military History, Washington D.C. He was a major contributor to a recent *Encyclopedia of World War II,* and is author of the book, *Anzio: Edge of Disaster* (1978).

Colonel Ray L. Bowers, USAF (ret.), is a former Chief Navigator with a C-130 squadron in Vietnam. He was an historian with the Office of Air Force History from 1969 to 1977 and is the author of the official USAF history of tactical air transport in Southeast Asia. He has written very many technical articles for professional military journals (including *US Naval Institute Proceedings* and *Defense Management Journal*) and in October 1978 presented a paper, "Air Power in Southeast Asia: a Tentative Appraisal", at the 8th Military History Symposium, US Air Force Academy, Colorado. He is now with the Carnegie Institution, Washington D.C.

Dr. Jeffrey J. Clarke is a former Captain in the US Army, and Commanding Officer, 17th Military History Detachment, Vietnam. He has been an historian with the US Army Center of Military History and is currently an Instructor at the University of Maryland.

Ronald H. Cole is a former Intelligence Officer, US Army, and Intelligence Research Analyst, Defense Intelligence Agency. He also served as historian with the US Air Force History Office, and is currently an historian with the US Army Center of Military History. He has written a volume, *Combat Operations in Southeast Asia, 1968–1973,* for the official series, *The US Army in the Vietnam War,* and is author of a USAF monologue entitled *People's War, Phase II: An American View of the Viet Cong Organization and Doctrine for Revolutionary Warfare, 1960–1964,* and an article, "Victor Michel: The Unwanted Clairvoyant of the French High Command, 1911", for the journal *Military Affairs*.

John T. Greenwood is currently Chief of the Historical Division, US Army Corps of Engineers. He has served as strategic aircraft historian, Headquarters, Strategic Air Command, USAF, Chief Historian, Headquarters, USAF Space and Missile Systems Organization (SAMSO) and also worked on a history of USAF's strategic force at the Office of Air Force History. He has had numerous technical articles published in respected military journals (including *Aerospace Historian*), and has edited/compiled volumes on Soviet military aviation and other military affairs.

Dr. William Michael Hammond is an historian with the US Army Center of Military History, having prepared a volume in the Army's official history of the Vietnam War: *The Word War: Military Relations with the News Media.* He is also author of the article on "Propaganda, World Wars I and II" in Scribner's *Dictionary of American History*.

Richard A. Hunt is a former Captain in the US Army, his last year of service being with the Command Historian's office in the Military Assistance Command, Vietnam (MACV). He is an historian with the Current History Branch, US Army Center of Military History, preparing a major volume on the Pacification Program in Vietnam. He has

contributed to several works, including *Allied Participation in Vietnam, Dictionary of American History, Guide to Military History* and *Encyclopedia of World War II.* He has also delivered papers at American Historical Association and Canadian Historical Association meetings, and has been a participant in panels on the Vietnam War with Dean Rusk (1975) and William Colby (1978).

Charles B. MacDonald is the Deputy Chief Historian for Southeast Asia in the US Army Center for Military History, in which position he supervises the preparation of the US Army's official history of the war in Vietnam. During World War II he served in four campaigns in Europe as infantry rifle company commander at the age of 21, and received the Purple Heart and Silver Star. He wrote two of the US Army's official histories of the European and Meditteranean Theaters, co-authored another and contributed to two more; was author of a book entitled *Company Commander,* based on his experiences in World War II, and regarded as a classic in its subject. He is the author of other books on military affairs and contri-

butor to several military histories and encyclopedias, including the Salamander title *The Encyclopedia of Land Warfare in the 20th Century,* and he assisted General Westmoreland in the writing of the general's memoirs, *A Soldier Reports.*

Lieutenant Colonel David Miller is an officer in the British Army. He has had extensive service overseas and has spent six years in the Far East. He has carried out an in-depth study of Communist revolutionary warfare and has had many technical articles published, many of them on the two campaigns in Indochina, in professional military journals, including *International Defense Review, RUSI Journal, British Army Review* and *Army Quarterly.*

Jacob Neufeld is currently an historian with the Office of Air Force History, and was previously a historian at Headquarters Eighth Air Force. He has written several works on the USAF space and missile programs and is preparing a history of the long range ballistic missiles. He served with the US Army Corps of Engineers as a company grade officer and instructor at the Army Engineer School, and has contributed technical articles to *Air Force Magazine* and *Aerospace Historian.*

Richard O'Neill, having formerly served with the British Army, is a specialist writer on naval warfare and the history of Southeast Asia. He has contributed to many technical military publications and has

also published material on art history and prize-fighting. *Tokko-Tai,* the first volume of his study of the Imperial Japanese Navy's suicide boats and submersibles, was published in 1969.

Lt. Col. Lane Rogers is currently an historian with the History and Museums Division, Headquarters, US Marine Corps. He is a veteran of two tours of duty in Southeast Asia, where he served as Chief of the Laos-Thailand-Cambodia Section of the US Defense Intelligence Agency; as Senior Advisor, 3rd Battalion, Vietnamese Marine Corps; and as the Assistant US Naval Attache to Thailand and Laos. Among his military awards are the Silver Star, Bronze Star w/"V", Meritorious Service Medal, Air Medal (1), Combat Action Ribbon, Vietnamese Cross of Gallantry (Division level), and the Vietnamese Honor Medal, First Class.

Dr. George M. Watson, Jr., served with the US Army for two years, including a year's tour of duty with the 101st Airborne Division in Vietnam, 1969–70. He returned to scholastic pursuits at the Catholic University of America (having previously received the B.A., and M.A.), where he achieved a Ph.D. in Modern European History, in 1974. He worked briefly with the US Army Historical Office, then transferred to the Office of Air Force History, and is currently an historian at the Air Force Systems and Command Headquarters. He has contributed to technical journals and encyclopedias.

Foreword

by General William C. Westmoreland, US Army, Retired

General William C. Westmoreland, USA, here seen greeting newly-arrived US infantrymen at Qui Nhon, South Vietnam, in August 1966, replaced General Paul D. Harkins, USA, as Commander, US Military Assistance Command, Vietnam, on 20 June 1964, serving in this capacity until June 1968. In retirement from 1972, General Westmoreland is a stern critic of the haste with which the US policy of disengagement in Southeast Asia was implemented.

Twenty-five centuries ago a Chinese warrior-philosopher, Sun Tzu, wrote profoundly on the art of war. Fighting, he declared, is the crudest form of warfare. He advised, instead:

Break the will of the enemy to fight, and you accomplish the true objective of war. Cover with ridicule the enemy's tradition. Exploit and aggravate the inherent frictions within the enemy country. Agitate the young against the old. Prevail if possible without armed conflict. The supreme excellence is not to win a hundred victories in a hundred battles. The supreme excellence is to defeat the armies of your enemies without ever having to fight them.

The Communist leader of North Vietnam, Ho Chi Minh, could hardly have been unaware of Sun Tzu's dicta when he devised a strategy both for his war of liberation against France and for his war of aggression against South Vietnam, in which the United States was his principal adversary. Although he was unable to prevail in either conflict without giving battle, he—or his successors—was able in both cases to "exploit and aggravate the inherent frictions within the enemy country" and to "agitate the young against the old", and in the war with the United States he was also able to "cover with ridicule the enemy's tradition". In at least some circles, the North Vietnamese succeeded in changing the long established image of the United States as a champion of liberty into that of a big power interfering harshly and inhumanely in the internal affairs of a small nation. In the process, the North Vietnamese "broke the will of the enemy to fight" and, despite American victory on virtually every battlefield, emerged in the end triumphant.

Therein lies a cardinal lesson for the democracies. No nation should put the burden of war on its military forces alone. It matters not whether a war is total or limited; a nation must be wholly dedicated in its purpose, firm in its resolve, and committed to sacrifice by more than one segment of its society. As the war in Vietnam clearly demonstrated, without that dedication, that resolve, that commitment, no matter what the performance on the field of battle, victory will be elusive.

The interest of the United States in South Vietnam was born in the post-World War II era, when Communist movement into insecure and unstable areas around the world appeared to be a monolithic threat. In that atmosphere, President Harry S. Truman in 1947 pledged the nation to unconditional support of free people who are "resisting attempted subjugation by minorities or by outside pressures". Congress approved that doctrine by a large majority.

President Dwight D. Eisenhower in his turn emphasized that policy of containment in association with a strategy of massive retaliation. With South Vietnam much in mind, the Eisenhower administration sponsored the Southeast Asia Treaty Organization, which the Senate in 1955 ratified with only one dissenting vote.

When John F. Kennedy became president, he developed personal interest in the problem posed by a Communist strategy of small wars of "national liberation". Chastened by failure at the Bay of Pigs in Cuba and by a personal confrontation with Premier Nikita Khrushchev of the Soviet Union, the young president reputedly told a correspondent for the New York *Times*: "We have a problem in making our power pertinent and Vietnam looks like the place."

President Kennedy set the tone of his administration in his inaugural address, pledging the nation "to bear any burden, meet any hardship, support any friend and oppose any foe to assure the survival and success of liberty". To attempt to foil the Communist strategy of wars of national liberation fitted that ideal. President Kennedy thus sharply increased American involvement in South Vietnam, but in his zeal made the unfortunate mistake of approving American participation in the overthrow of South Vietnam's President Ngo Dinh Diem. That action morally locked the United States into Vietnam, and despite political chaos in South Vietnam amply demonstrating a lack of leadership and unity, neither Mr Kennedy nor his successor, President Lyndon B. Johnson, chose to risk the likely domestic political repercussions of pulling out.

While determined to pursue Mr Kennedy's policy in Vietnam, President Johnson was nevertheless obsessed with his program of domestic achievement, the Great Society. Although he expanded American military commitment, he pursued a policy at home of business as usual. Had it not been for the draft, and sensational coverage of the war piped for the first time by television into American living rooms, only those who served and their loved ones would have recognized that the nation was at war.

Despite congressional endorsement for military action as firm as that provided Truman, Eisenhower, and Kennedy, President Johnson was determined to keep the war limited and publicly announced that he would sanction no expansion of it. That locked American military forces into a defensive strategy, and anyone versed in military history knows that a force on the offensive has advantages over one on the defensive; for the force on the offensive possesses the initiative and can mass its strength at the time and place of its own choosing. North Vietnam had the additional advantage of knowing that its operating bases in neighboring Cambodia and Laos and—for the most part—in North Vietnam were virtually inviolate. Although those of us in Vietnam were acutely conscious that a defensive strategy contributed to a prolonged war, and that a prolonged war contributed to the success of the strategy the enemy had borrowed from Sun Tzu, we were powerless, in view of the political restrictions, to shift to an offensive strategy and bring the war to a swift conclusion.

Only in the bombing of North Vietnam did President Johnson sanction an offensive strategy, and even in that he bowed to political advice and accepted a selective, on-again, off-again campaign reflecting political pressures at home and abroad. To North Vietnam it must have been clear that the bombing demonstrated not strength and determination but political weakness and uncertainty. Actions by vocal elements of American society to frustrate the will of the majority, highlighted and sometimes glorified by the news media, no doubt helped convey that message. "Illegal war" and "immoral war" became clichés of the times.

In the Gulf of Tonkin Resolution, passed by the Congress in 1964 with only two dissenting votes in both houses, President Johnson obtained clear authority to commit military forces as he deemed necessary to achieve the national objective of assuring a free and independent South Vietnam; but as the war dragged on without decisive American military action, the mood of the Congress changed, a reflection of public attitudes strongly influenced by the news media, particularly television.

When the war became intensely controversial, the president should have asked for reaffirmation each year of the Gulf of Tonkin Resolution; indeed, congressional leaders should have demanded it. Yet neither the president nor congressional leaders wanted to face open national debate, and a rift between legislative and executive branches of the government was allowed to widen.

Despite dissent at home and restrictions on military operations against enemy sanctuaries beyond the borders of South Vietnam, American and South Vietnamese military forces by the end of 1967 had achieved substantial progress, both on the battlefield and in establishing security for the South Vietnamese people. Then came the enemy's Tet offensive of early 1968. Despite the fact that the North Vietnamese and Viet Cong incurred a military defeat of such proportions that it took them four years to recover, reporting of the offensive by press and television in the United States gave an impression if not of American and South Vietnamese defeat, then of an endless war that could never be won. Even a number of senior officials in Washington were deceived, failing to heed the fact

that historically an enemy who is losing may launch a desperate effort to reverse the tide of battle, as in the German offensives of 1918 and in the Battle of the Bulge. Halting the bombing of most of North Vietnam, President Johnson removed himself from the political arena, which led to political negotiations in Paris; but the negotiations were for long years meaningless, achieving little more than to decide the shape of the conference table. Yet the war went on, and more American soldiers were killed while their enemy ostensibly parlayed peace in Paris than had been killed before the negotiations in Paris began.

Once the North Vietnamese had failed in a major conventional invasion of South Vietnam in 1972 and President Richard M. Nixon had directed a renewed and, finally, intensive bombing campaign against North Vietnam, the Communist representatives in Paris at long last made some concessions, however minor. They might have been compelled to make more, but under ever-mounting political pressure and agitation, Mr Nixon had already begun pulling out American troops, and he underscored his determination to withdraw whatever the cost by making a major concession: to accept a continued presence of North Vietnamese troops inside South Vietnam.

Despite that one-sided concession, the cease-fire agreement reached in Paris early in 1973 was theoretically workable—*if* the threat (and reality) of American airpower remained. By adopting the Case-Church Amendment in the summer of 1973, which prohibited "any funds whatsoever to finance directly or indirectly combat activities by the United States military forces in, over, or from off the shore of North Vietnam, South Vietnam or Cambodia", the United States Senate took away that threat. Subsequent sharp cuts in military aid to South Vietnam must have reinforced the North Vietnamese leaders in their recognition that the United States on its own volition had executed an act of surrender.

By that time there were still weaknesses in the South Vietnamese government, military leadership, and body politic, but the country had made great strides toward becoming a viable nation and could no doubt have handled any threat of internal subversion alone. Yet the country still faced a powerful external military force entrenched within its borders, and the cut in American aid left South Vietnamese military units short of equipment, ammunition, and replacement parts and virtually devoid of air support, severely impairing morale at all levels. The enemy meanwhile was amply equipped and supplied and remained free to concentrate at the time and place of his choosing. Thus South Vietnam was doomed to eventual defeat.

The Leaders in Hanoi had learned Sun Tzu's dicta well. Having achieved ridicule of their enemy's tradition, having exploited and aggravated inherent frictions within their enemy's country, and having agitated the young against the old, they had removed their primary adversary from the fight and were free to exploit their raw military power, with only minimal assistance from the southern revolutionaries, to conquer South Vietnam and impose on the country a harsh Communist regime.

The essays that follow tell in detail the story of the war in Vietnam, from the opening days to the last. They have been written by a diversity of able historians and predictably reflect a diversity of views. Although I cannot in all cases agree with their interpretations and conclusions, the participant in history—whatever his role—must accept the fact that history may not always see events in the same way he sees them. The essays are, in any event, informative and provocative, and thus conducive to helping democratic peoples to learn from the trials, the errors, the failures, and the successes that occurred in the course of a long, frustrating, and tragic war in a little corner of the world known as Vietnam. Unfortunately, the end of that war has, from all accounts, brought no end to the suffering.—*William C. Westmoreland, General, US Army, Retired*

ABRAMS, General Creighton Williams, USA (1914–1994)
Commander, US Military Assistance Command, Vietnam, 1968–72; US Army Chief of Staff, 1972–74.

General Abrams tours a fire support base in Vietnam, 1969

BALL, George Wildman (1909–1994)
US Under Secretary of State, opposed to American military involvement in Vietnam, 1961–66.

BAO DAI (b. Nguyen Vinh Thuy) (1911–)
Last Emperor of Vietnam, 1925–45; "Citizen Prince" under Ho Chi Minh, 1945–46; Premier and "puppet Emperor" under French, deposed after referendum, 1945–55; exile in France.

BIGEARD, General de Corps d'Armée Marcel (1916–)
France's leading airborne officer; served in Indochina, 1945–54; led parachute drop at Dien Bien Phu, 20 November 1953; in Viet Minh captivity, 1954; commander of parachute regiment in Algeria, 1958–60; promoted four-star general, 1974.

BOUN OUM (1911–)
American-backed, right-wing Premier of Laos, 1960–61; member of Souvanna Phouma's National Union government from 1962.

BUNDY, McGeorge (1919–)
US Special Assistant for National Security Affairs under Presidents Kennedy and Johnson, when a major influence on US foreign policy, 1960–66.

BUNDY, William Putnam (1917–)
US Assistant Secretary of State for East Asian and Pacific Affairs, influential on President Johnson's decision to begin bombing North Vietnam, 1965.

BUNKER, Ellsworth (1894–)
US Ambassador to South Vietnam, 1967–73.

CASTRIES, General Christian Marie, Comte de la Croix de (1902–)
French Army commander at Dien Bien Phu, 1954.

CLIFFORD, Clark MacAdams (1906–)
US Secretary of Defense, March 1968–January 1969.

CUSHMAN, General Robert Everton, Jr., USMC (1914–1985)
Commander, III Marine Amphibious Force, Vietnam, 1967–69; Deputy Director, CIA, 1969–71; Commandant, United States Marine Corps, from 1972.

Key individuals in Southeast Asia

These were the men most concerned in the struggle for hegemony in Southeast Asia

DULLES, Allen Welsh (1893–1969)
Director, CIA, 1953–61.

DULLES, John Foster (1888–1959)
US Secretary of State under President Eisenhower, a major architect of US Cold War policy, 19653–59; brother of Allen Dulles.

DUONG VAN MINH, Lieutenant General (called "Big Minh") (1916–)
Led campaign against Binh Xuyen bandits, 1955; Military Adviser to President Diem of South Vietnam, 1962–63; a leader of the coup against Diem, 1963; Chairman, Revolutionary Military Committee government, November 1963–January 1964; head of State, South Vietnam, January–October 1964; in Bangkok, Thailand, 1964–68; as last President of South Vietnam (for two days only) surrendered Saigon to Communist forces, 30 April 1975.

ELLSBERG, Daniel (1931–)
Member of staff of Assistant Secretary of Defense for International Security Affairs, 1964–65; with Department of State staff, Vietnam, 1965–67; Assistant to US Ambassador to South Vietnam, 1967; reported to have leaked the "Pentagon Papers" to the press, published from 13 June 1974; criminal charges against Ellsburg dropped, May 1973.

ELY, General Paul Henri Romuald (1897–1975)
French Commander in Chief, Indochina, supervising withdrawal of French troops after his appeal for US military assistance failed, 1954; Chief of General Staff, 1953–61.

FELT, Admiral Harry Donald, USN (1902–)
US Commander in Chief, Pacific, 1958–64.

FORD, President Gerald Rudolph, Jr., (1913–)
Acceded to US presidency on Nixon's resignation, 1974; continued policy of disengagement in Southeast Asia; ordered refugee airlift and military action in "Mayaguez incident", in 1975; defeated by Jimmy Carter in presidential election, 1976.

GAYLER, Admiral Noel Arthur Meredyth, USN (1914–)
US Commander in Chief, Pacific, from September 1972.

HARKINS, General Paul Donal, USA (1904–)
Chief of US Military Assistance Advisory Group in Vietnam and the first Commander, US Military Assistance Command, Vietnam, February 1962–June 1964.

HARRIMAN, William Averell (1891–1986)
US Assistant Secretary of State for Far Eastern Affairs, playing a leading part in negotiating Geneva Agreements and Laotian settlement, 1961–63; ambassador to Paris peace talks, 1968–69.

HO CHI MINH (b. Nguyen That Thanh) (1890–1969)
Founder of Indochinese Communist Party, 1930; founder of Viet Minh, 1941; leader of North Vietnam until his death.

Ho Chi Minh, wily politician, often called "Uncle Ho".

JOHNSON, President Lyndon Baines (1908–1973)
Acceded to US presidency on assassination of Kennedy, 1963; re-elected, 1964; consistently attacked by "doves" for increasing US commitment to anti-Communist stands in Southeast Asia, refused to seek re-election, 1968; retired from public life, 1969.

KENNEDY, President John Fitzgerald (1917–1963)
Elected US President, defeating Nixon, 1960; pledged increased support for South Vietnam, 1961; assassinated, 22 November 1963.

KHIEU SAMPHAN (1932–)
Cambodian Secretary of State for Commerce, joined Khmer Rouge, 1967–70; named Deputy Premier and Minister of Defense in government-in-exile of Norodom Sihanouk, 1970; Commander in Chief, Khmer Rouge High Command, from 1973; Head of State, 1976–79; Prime Minister of Khmer Rouge Opposition Government fighting Vietnamese forces, from December 1979.

KISSINGER, Doctor Henry Alfred (1923–)
Assistant for National Security Affairs from 1968 and Secretary of State from 1973, when a chief architect of US foreign policy, including initiation of strategic arms limitation talks, 1969, and Paris Agreement on the Vietnam War, January 1973; Nobel Peace Prize, 1973 (also awarded to Le Duc Tho).

KOMER, Robert William (1922–)
Special Assistant to the President for National Security Affairs, 1966–67; Deputy to Commander US Military Assistance Command, Vietnam, for Civil Operations and Rural Development Support, 1967–68; US Under Secretary of Defense, from 1979.

KONG LE, Captain (1924–)
Leader of neutralist military force in Laos, 1960–62; seized control of Vientiane, August 1960.

LAIRD, Melvin R. (1922–)
US Secretary of Defense, January 1969–January 1973; Domestic Adviser to President Nixon, 1973–74.

LANSDALE, Major General Edward G., USAF (1908–)
US counter-insurgency expert, attached CIA and adviser to President Diem, South Vietnam, 1954–66; Special Assistant to US Ambassador to South Vietnam, 1965–68.

LATTRE DE TASSIGNY, Marshal Jean de (1889–1952)
Commander, French First Army, World War II; rallied military and civilian morale during brief period as French Commander in Chief, Indochina, 1950–51; posthumously promoted Marshal of France, 1952.

LE DUAN (1908–1986)
Founder member of Indochinese Communist Party, 1930; member of Central Committee, Democratic Republic of Vietnam, Hanoi, 1945; directed Communist subversion in South Vietnam from 1954; instrumental in forming National Liberation Front, 1960; First Secretary, Vietnam Workers Party from 1959 and Secretary General From December 1976.

LE DUC THO (b. Phan Dinh Khai) (1911–1990)
Founder member of Indochinese Communist Party, 1930; founder member of Viet Minh, 1941; chief North Vietnamese negotiator at Paris peace talks, 1968–73; declined to share jointly awarded Nobel Peace Prize with Henry Kissinger, 1973.

LODGE, Henry Cabot (1902–1985)
Unsuccessful vice presidential candidate on Nixon ticket, 1960; US Ambassador to South Vietnam, 1963–64 and 1965–67; chief US negotiator at Paris peace talks, 1969.

LON NOL, Marshal (1913–1985)
Pro-American Cambodian leader of campaign against Vietnamese Communists; Commander in Chief, Khmer Royal Armed Forces, under Sihanouk's regime; Premier and Minister of Defense, 1969–71; President of Khmer Republic and Supreme Commander of Armed Forces from March 1972 until overthrow and exile in Hawaii, April 1975.

MANSFIELD, Senator Michael Joseph (1903–)
Montana Democrat, Majority Leader of US Senate from 1961, a prominent Vietnam "dove"; US Ambassador to Japan, from 1977.

MARTIN, Graham Anderson (1912–1990)
US Ambassador to Thailand, 1963–67; Special Assistant to Secretary of State for Refugee and Migration Affairs, 1967–69; last US Ambassador to South Vietnam, 1973–75.

McCAIN, Admiral John Sidney, Jr., USN (1911–1981)
US Commander in Chief, Pacific, 1968–72.

McNAMARA, Robert Strange (1916–)
US Secretary of Defense, January 1961–February 1968.

Robert McNamara who proposed the "McNamara wall" concept.

MOMYER, General William Wallace, USAF (1916–)
Commander, US Seventh Air Force, 1966–68, serving also as General Westmoreland's deputy for air operations.

MOORER, Admiral Thomas H., USN (1912–)
US Chief of Naval Operations, 1967–70; Chairman, Joint Chiefs of Staff, 1970–74.

NAVARRE, General Henri (1898–1983)
Commander in Chief, French forces in Indochina, 1953–54.

NGO DINH DIEM (1901–1963)
Minister of the Interior under Emperor Bao Dai before World IWar II; refused office under Ho Chi Minh and went into exile, 1945; US-backed President of South Vietnam from 1954; overthrown and murdered, 1963.

NGO DINH NHU (1910–1963)
Brother and principle adviser of Ngo Dinh Diem; died with him during coup, 1963.

NGUYEN CAO KY, General (or Air Vice Marshal) (1930–)
Former member of French forces and a violent anti-Communist, commander of the South Vietnamese Air Force from 1963; a leader of the military coup against Phan Huy Quat, 1965; Premier of South Vietnam, 1965–67; Vice President, 1967–71; exiled in US from April 1975.

NGUYEN HUU THO (1910–)
Vietnamese nationalist leader, agitated against French and US intervention, 1949–50; imprisoned by Diem, 1954–61; although a non-Communist, President of National Liberation Front, 1961–69; Vice President, Socialist Republic of Vietnam, 1976–80; Acting President, April 1980–July 1981; Vice President, Council of State, from 1981.

NGUYEN KHANH, General (1927–)
Chief of Staff to General Duong Van Minh and associated with him in coup against Diem, 1963; led coup against Minh and was briefly Premier of South Vietnam, 1964; semi-exile from 1965.

NGUYEN VAN THIEU, Lieutenant General (1923–)
Led coup against Diem, 1963; US-backed Head of State of South Vietnam, 1965–67; elected President, 1967; re-elected, 1971; resigned in favor of Tran Van Huong, 21 April 1975; retired to Taiwan, later to UK.

Nguyen Van Thieu inspects ARVN and US Marine troops, 1966.

NIXON, President Richard Milhous (1913–1994)
US Vice President, 1953–61; lost presidential election to Kennedy, 1960; defeated Hubert H. Humphrey in presidential election, 1968; ordered "secret bombing" of Cambodia, 1969–70; implemented "Nixon doctrine" of replacing troops abroad by increased advice and economic aid and progressively reduced US commitment to Vietnam; re-elected 1972; resigned as a result of Watergate scandal, August 1974.

NORODOM SIHANOUK, Prince Samdech Preah (1922–)
King of Cambodia, 1941–55; Premier, 1955–60; neutralist Head of State, 1960–70; overthrown by Lon Noi and formed government-in-exile in Peking, 1970; restored as Head of State, 1075; resigned 1976; Special Envoy of Khmer Rouge to UN, 1979; retirement in Korea, from 1979.

PHAM VAN DONG (1906–)
Co-founder of Viet Minh, 1941; Premier of North Vietnam, 1955–76; Premier, Socialist Republic of Vietnam, 1976–80; Chairman, Council of Ministers, from 1981.

PHOUMI NOSAVAN, General (—)
Pro-US commander of Royal Laotian Army; Defense Minister, 1958; drove Kong Le from Vientiane and overthrew Souvanna Phouma, 1960; went into exile after failure of coup, 1965.

POL POT (also TOL SAUT, POL PORTH) (1925–)
Plantation worker, joined Ho Chi Minh in opposition to French in 1940s; member of Indonesian Communist Party until 1946, thereafter of Cambodian Communist Party, elected Party Secretary, 1963; elected to

People's Representative Assembly of Kampuchea, March 1976; Prime Minister, Kampuchea, April–September 1976; resigned for health reasons, resumed office September 1977; overthrown after Vietnamese invasion and sentenced to death *in absentia* for crimes of genocide, August 1979; leader of guerrilla army, from 1979.

RIDGWAY, General Matthew Bunker, USA (1895–1993)
Commanded US 8th Army, Korea, 1950–51; Supreme Commander, Far East, 1951–52; Supreme Commander, Europe, 1952–53; US Army Chief of Staff, opposed to ground war in support of the French in Indochina, 1953–55.

ROSTOW, Walt Whitman (1916–)
Deputy Special Assistant to the President for National Security Affairs, 1961; Chairman, US State Department Policy Planning Council, 1961–66.

RUSK, David Dean (1909–)
US Secretary of State, a vigorous advocate of US action in Vietnam, 1961–69.

SCHLESINGER, James Rodney (1929–)
Director, Central Intelligence Agency, 1973; US Secretary of Defense, 1973–75.

SHARP, Admiral Ulysses S. Grant, USN (1906–)
Commander in Chief, Pacific, and US Military Adviser to SEATO, 1964–68.

SOUPHANOUVONG, Prince (1902–)
Half-brother of Souvanna Phouma, associated with Ho Chi Minh since before World War II; founder member of Communist Pathet Lao, 1950; vice Premier of Laos, then imprisoned and escaped to lead pro-Communist military faction, 1962; Chairman, Joint National Political Council, 1974-75; President, Lao People's Democratic Republic, from December 1975.

SOUVANNA PHOUMA, Prince (1901–1984)
Neutralist leader, Prime Minister of Laos, 1962–75; Counselor to Government of Laos, 1976.

TAYLOR, General Maxwell Davenport, USA (1901–1987)
Commander US 8th Army, Korea, 1953; US and UN Commander, Far East, 1955; US Army Chief of Staff, 1955–59; Military Adviser to President Kennedy, 1961–62; Chairman, Joint Chiefs of Staff, 1962–64; US Ambassador to South Vietnam, 1964–65; Special Consultant to the President, and Chairman, President's Foreign Intelligence Advisory Board, 1965–69; President, Institute of Defense Analyses, 1966–69.

TRAN THIEN KHIEM, General (1925–)
Co-leader with Nguyen Khanh, of coup against Duong Van Minh, 1964; Defense Minister and Commander in Chief Armed Forces, South Vietnam, 1964' Ambassador to US, 1964–65; Ambassador to Republic of China (Taiwan), 1965–68; Deputy Prime Minister, South Vietnam, 1969; Prime Minister, 1969–75; fled to Taiwan, April 1975.

TRAN VAN HUONG (1903–)
Viet Minh activist against French, Mayor of Saigon, 1954; imprisoned, 1960; Prime Minister, South Vietnam, 1964–65 and 1968–69; Vice President, 1971–75; President, 21–28 April 1975.

VO NGUYEN GIAP, General (1912–)
Co-founder of Viet Minh, 1941; Minister of Interior, 1945; Commander in Chief, Viet Minh armed forces from 1946, victor of Dien Bien Phu, 1954; Deputy Prime Minister, Minister of Defense, and Commander in Chief, Democratic Republic of Vietnam, until 1976; Vice Premier, Socialist Republic of Vietnam, from July 1976; Minister of National Defense, 1976–80.

WALT, General Lewis William, USMC (1913–)
Commander, III Marine Amphibious Force, and Senior Adviser to I Corps Military Assistance Command, South Vietnam, 1965–67; Assistant Commandant, United States Marine Corps, 1968–71.

General Walt, given a "free hand" in 1 Corps Tactical Zone, Vietnam, 1965.

WESTMORELAND, General William Childs, USA (1914–)
Commissioned 2nd Lt., US Army, 1936; Chief of Staff, 9th Infantry Division, 1944–45; Chief of Staff 82d Airborne Division, 1947–50; commander, 187th Airborne RCT, Korea and Japan, 1951–53; Superintendent, US Military Academy, 1960–63; Commanding General, XVIII Airborne Corps, 1963; Commander, US Military Assistance Command, Vietnam, 1964–68; US Army Chief of Staff, 1968–72; retired, 1972.

WEYAND, General Frederick Carlton, USA (1916–)
Commander, US 25th Infantry Division, Vietnam, 1966–68; Military Adviser at Paris peace talks, 1968–70; Deputy Commander, US Military Assistance Command, Vietnam, 1970–72, and Commander 1972–73; Vice Chief of Staff, US Army, 1973; Chief of Staff, US Army, 1974–76.

WHEELER, General Earle Gilmore, USA (1908–)
US Army Chief of Staff, 1962–64; Chairman, Joint Chiefs of Staff, 1964–70.

ZUMWALT, Admiral Elmo Russell, Jr., USN (1920–)
Commander, US Naval Forces, Vietnam, 1968–70; US Chief of Naval Operations, 1970–74.

Chronology of main events

Principal events in Southeast Asia from the Japanese occupation to the present

1945

March 9. An "independent" Vietnam, with Emperor Bao Dai as nominal ruler, is proclaimed by Japanese occupation authorities.
September 2. The Communist-dominated Viet Minh Independence League seizes power; Ho Chi Minh establishes the Government of the Democratic Republic of Vietnam (GRDV) in Hanoi.
September 22. French troops return to Vietnam and clash with Communist and Nationalist forces.

1946

March 6. France recognizes the Democratic Republic of Vietnam as a free state within the Indochinese Federation and French Union.
December 19. The Viet Minh initiate the eight-year Indochina War with an attack on French troops in the north.

1949

March 8. France recognizes an "independent" state of Vietnam; Bao Dai becomes its leader in June.
July 19. Laos is recognized as an independent state with ties to France.
November 8. Cambodia is recognized as an independent state with ties to France.

1950

January. The newly established People's Republic of China, followed by the Soviet Union, recognizes the Democratic Republic of Vietnam led by Ho Chi Minh.
May 8. US announces military and economic aid to the pro-French regimes of Vietnam, Laos, and Cambodia.

1954

May 7. The remnants of the French garrison at Dien Bien Phu surrender.
July 7. Ngo Dinh Diem, newly chosen premier of South Vietnam, completes the organization of his cabinet.
July 20-21. The Geneva Agreements are signed, partitioning Vietnam along the 17th Parallel and setting up an International Control Commission to supervise compliance with the Agreements.
September 8. An agreement is signed at Manila establishing a Southeast Asia Treaty Organization, aimed at checking Communist expansion.
October 5. The last French troops leave Hanoi.
October 11. The Viet Minh formally assume control over North Vietnam.
October 24. President Dwight D. Eisenhower advises Diem that the US will provide assistance directly to South Vietnam, instead of channeling it through French authorities.

1955

March 29. Diem launches his successful campaign against the Binh Xuyen and the religious sects.
May 10. South Vietnam formally requests US instructors for armed forces.
May 16. The United States agrees to furnish military aid to Cambodia, which becomes an independent state on 25 September.
July 20. South Vietnam refuses to take part in the all-Vietnam elections called for by the Geneva Agreements, charging that free elections are impossible in the Communist North.

October 23. A national referendum deposes Bao Dai in favour of Diem, who proclaims the republic of Vietnam.

1956

February 18. While visiting Peking, Cambodia's Prince Norodom Sihanouk renounces SEATO protection for his nation.
March 31. Prince Souvanna Phouma becomes prime minister in Laos.
April 28. An American Military Assistance Advisory Group (MAAG) takes over the training of South Vietnamese forces; the French Military High command disbands and French troops leave South Vietnam.
August 5. Souvanna Phouma and the Communist Prince Souphanouvong agree to a coalition government in Laos.

1957

January 3. The International Control Commission declares that neither North Vietnam nor South Vietnam has carried out the Geneva Agreements.
May 29. Communist Pathet Lao attempt to seize power in Laos.
June. The last French training missions leave South Vietnam.
September. Diem is successful in South Vietnamese general election.

1958

January. Communist guerrillas attack a plantation north of Saigon.

1959

April. A branch of the Lao Dong (Worker's Party of Vietnam), of which Ho Chi Minh became secretary-general in 1956, is formed in the South, and Communist underground activity increases.
May. The US commander in chief, Pacific, begins sending the military advisers requested by the South Vietnamese government.
June-July. Communist Pathet Lao forces attempt to gain control over northern Laos, receiving some Vietnamese Communist assistance.
July 8. Communist South Vietnamese wound American advisers during an attack on Bien Hoa.
December 31. General Phoumi Nosavan seize control in Laos.

1960

August 9. Captain Kong Le occupies Vientiane and urges restoration of a neutral Laos under Prince Souvanna Phouma.
November 11-12. A military coup against Diem fails.
December. The Communist National Liberation Front (NLF) of South Vietnam is formed.
December 16. The forces of Phoumi Nosavan capture Vientiane.

1961

January 4. Prince Boun Oum organizes a pro-Western government in Laos; North Vietnam and the USSR send aid to the Communist

insurgents.
May 16. A 14-nation conference on Laos meets at Geneva.
September 1-4. Viet Cong forces carry out a series of attacks in Kontum province, South Vietnam.
September 18. A Viet Cong battalion seizes the provincial capital of Phuoc Vinh.
October 8. The Lao factions agree to form a neutral coalition headed by Souvanna Phouma.
November 16. President Kennedy decided to increase military aid to South Vietnam, without committing US combat troops.

1962

February 3. The "Strategic Hamlet" program begins in South Vietnam.
February 7. American military strength in South Vietnam reaches 4,000, with the arrival of two additional Army aviation units.
February 8. The US MAAG is reorganized as the US Military Assistance Command, Vietnam (MACV), under General Paul D. Harkins, USA.
May 6-27. Phoumi Nosavan's forces are routed, paving the way for a settlement in Laos.
August. The first Australian Military Aid Forces (MAF) arrive in South Vietnam.

1963

January 2. Battle of Ap Bac: ARVN with US advisers is defeated.
April. Inception of the Chieu Joi ("Open Arms") amnesty program, aimed at rallying VC to support of the government.
May 8. Riots in Hue, South Vietnam, when government troops try to prevent the celebration of Buddha's birthday; country-wide Buddhist demonstrations continue into August.
June 11. The first of seven Buddhist monks to commit suicide by fire in protest against government repression dies in Saigon.
November 1-2. A military coup overthrows Diem; he and his brother Ngo Dinh Nhu are murdered.
November 6. General Duong Van Minh, leading the Revolutionary Military Committee, takes over leadership of South Vietnam.
November 15. Following a prediction by Defense Secretary McNamara that the US military role will end by 1965, the US government announces that 1,000 of the 15,000 American advisers in South Vietnam will be withdrawn early in December.

1964

January 30. A junta headed by General Nguyen Khanh deposes Duong Van Minh in South Vietnam.
June 20. General William C. Westmoreland, USA, replaces General Harkins as Commander, US MACV.
July 2. General Maxwell D. Taylor is named as US ambassador to South Vietnam.
August 2. North Vietnamese torpedo

boats attack the destroyer USS *Maddox*.
August 4. the destroyer USS *C. Turner Joy* reports a similar attack.
August 5. American Seventh Fleet carrier aircraft retaliate by attacking the bases used by the torpedo boats and other military targets in North Vietnam.
August 7. The US Congress adopts the Tonkin Gulf Resolution, endorsing whatever measures the President may consider necessary to repel attacks on American forces and to prevent further aggression.
November 1. After two months of political turmoil, Tran Van Huong becomes South Vietnam's Premier.
December 24. Terrorist bombing in Saigon kills two Americans and injures 52.
December 31. Total US strength in South Vietnam is 23,000.

1965

January 8. Two thousand South Korean troops arrive in South Vietnam.
February 7. Viet Cong attack the US base at Pleiku.
February 8. US Air Force and South Vietnamese planes retaliate by attacking military targets in North Vietnam.
February 10. Viet Cong terrorists bomb a billet a Qui Nhon, killing 23 American soldiers.
March 2. "Operations Rolling Thunder", the sustained aerial bombardment of North Vietnam, gets underway.
March 8. The first US Marine infantry battalion arrives at Da Nang, South Vietnam.
March 30. A terrorist bomb, detonated outside the American Embassy at Saigon, kills two Americans and wounds, among others, Deputy Ambassador U. Alexis Johnson.
May 3. The US Army's 173d Airborne Brigade begins landing in South Vietnam.
June. Nguyen Cao Ky emerges as head of the Saigon government.
June 18. B-52 bombers from Guam make their first strikes of the war against targets in South Vietnam.
June 27. The 173d Airborne Brigade launches a major offensive northeast of Saigon. The number of American soldiers, marines, sailors, and airmen in South Vietnam exceeds 50,000.
October. A South Korean combat division begins landing in South Vietnam.
October 27. American troops launch the month long Ia Drang campaign.
November. Anti-war demonstrations are widespread in the USA.
December 31. Total US strength in South Vietnam is 181,000.

1966

January 31. US bombing of North Vietnam resumes after a 37-day pause.
March. Communists capture a US Special Forces camp in the A Shau Valley, gaining control of this vital access route into South Vietnam.
March 2. Secretary of Defense McNamara announces that American forces in South Vietnam number 215,000, with another 20,000 en route.
April 12. For the first time B-52s bomb targets in North Vietnam, attacking near Mu Gia Pass.
June 23. South Vietnamese troops seize Buddhist headquarters at Saigon, bringing to an end a wave of protest that had begun in March with agitation against military rule.
October. Some 2,000 non-combatant Filipino troops arrive in South Vietnam.

October 24-25. Manila Conference of Free World nations committed to the Vietnam conflict.
December 31. Total US strength in South Vietnam is 385,000.

1967

January 8. American and South Vietnamese forces launch "Operation Cedar Falls", a sustained offensive north of Saigon against the Communist-controlled Iron Triangle.
February 22. "Junction City", largest operation of the war to date, begins in Tay Ninh province.
February 28. The commander, Naval Forces, Vietnam, establishes the Mekong Delta Mobile Riverine Force.
May 1. American military strength in South Vietnam reaches 436,000.
May 4. Ambassador Robert W. Komer becomes General Westmoreland's deputy for Civil Operations and Rural Development Support (CORDS).
September 3. General Nguyen Van Thieu is elected president of South Vietnam; Nguyen Cao Ky is vice-president.
September 29. A contingent of Thai combat troops arrives in South Vietnam.
October 4. The North Vietnamese siege of Con Thien is broken.
December 31. American military strength in South Vietnam is 486,000.

1968

January 22-April 7. The combat base at Khe Sanh sustains a 77-day siege and is successfully relieved.
January 30-31. The Tet offensive erupts throughout South Vietnam, lasting until late February.
March 16. The My Lai massacre takes place.
March 31. President Johnson restricts the bombing of North Vietnam to the panhandle region, he announces that he will not seek re-election.
April 10. President Johnson announces that General Creighton W. Abrams will take over from General Westmoreland as Commander, MACV, in June.
May 3. President Johnson accepts a North Vietnamese offer to conduct preliminary peace discussions in Paris.
May 4-5. A wave of attacks – less severe than those of the Tet offensive – hits 109 cities, towns, and bases in South Vietnam.
May 13. Delegates from the United States and North Vietnam hold their first formal meeting in Paris.
May 31. "Operations Toan Thang" comes to an end: for 60 days, 42 American and 37 South Vietnamese battalions have searched out enemy units near Saigon.
June 23. The Khe Sanh combat base is abandoned.
October 31. President Johnson announces that the bombing of North Vietnam will end the following day, although reconnaissance flights will continue.
November. President Richard M. Nixon elected; he promises a gradual troop withdrawal from Vietnam.
December 31. American military strength in South Vietnam is 536,100.

1969

January 25. Formal truce negotiations begin in Paris.
February 23-24. Communist forces carry out rocket and mortar attacks against 115 bases, towns, and cities in South Vietnam.
June 5. American planes make the first raids against North Vietnam since the bombing halt of 1

November 1968, in retaliation for the shooting down of a reconnaissance aircraft.
June 8. While meeting at Midway Island with President Thieu, President Nixon announces the planned withdrawal of 25,000 American combat troops.
September 4. Radio Hanoi announces the death of Ho Chi Minh.
September 16. President Nixon reveals a plan to withdraw an additional 35,000 men.
September 30. The US and Thai governments announce a planned withdrawal of 6,000 Americans, mostly airmen, from Thailand.
October 8. Souvanna Phouma requests increased American aid to meet heavier Communist pressure in Laos.
November 15. "Moratorium": massive anti-war demonstrations in USA.
December 15. President Nixon announces that an additional 50,000 Americans will be withdrawn from South Vietnam by 15 April 1970.
December 18. Congress prohibits the use of current Department of Defense appropriations to introduce ground combat troops into Laos or Thailand.
December 21. Thailand announces plans to withdraw its 12,000-man contingent from South Vietnam. South Korea will maintain its 50,000-man force. The Filipino non-combatants have already departed.
December 31. US troop strength in South Vietnam is 474,000.

1970

February 10. Souvanna Phouma states that he will take no action against Communist supply activity along the Ho Chi Minh Trail if North Vietnam will withdraw combat troops from Laos.
March 18. General Lon Noi ousts Prince Norodom Sihanouk (who has visited Moscow on 13 March) and seizes power in Cambodia.
March 27. South Vietnamese forces, supported by US helicopters, attack Communist base camps across the Cambodian border.
April 4. An estimated 50,000 persons gather at Washington, D.C., to support President Nixon's conduct of the war.
April 14. Cambodian President Lon Nol appeals for foreign military assistance.
April 29. MACV announce American participation in a South Vietnamese offensive into Cambodia.
May 2. Anti-war demonstrations break out on a number of US college campuses.
May 9. An estimated 75,000 to 100,000 demonstrators gather in Washington to oppose the Cambodian involvement. Protests, exacerbated by the fatal shooting of four Kent State University students by members of the Ohio National Guard during a demonstration against the war, continue at some 400 colleges.
June 29. US ground troops withdraw from Cambodia, President Nixon having declared that their combat role would end by June 30. Air operations continue.
October 15. President Nixon announces that a further 40,000 American troops will be withdrawn from South Vietnam by the end of the year.
December 29. Congress adopts legislation that denies funds for the introduction of ground combat troops into Laos or Thailand but does not include a proposed ban on further operations elsewhere in Southeast Asia.
December 31. Congress repeals the

Tonkin Gulf Resolution. American military strength in South Vietnam is 335,800.

1971

April 7. President Nixon announces at 100,000 American troops will leave South Vietnam by the end of the year.
April 24. Up to 500,000 anti-war protesters converge upon Washington, D.C.; at least 150,000 take part in a similar demonstration in San Francisco, California.
June 13. The New York *Times* begins releasing the Pentagon Papers, a study of the American involvement in Vietnam that was originally prepared for Secretary of Defense McNamara.
August 18. Australia and New Zealand declare that they will withdraw their troops from South Vietnam.
September 9. South Korea announces that most of its 48,000 troops in South Vietnam, will depart by June 1972.
October. Presidential elections result in the confirmation of Nguyen Van Thieu as president of South Vietnam.
November 12. President Nixon states that an additional 45,000 American troops will leave South Vietnam during December and January.
December 26-30. In reaction to a North Vietnamese buildup, American planes attack airfields and other military targets in the southern part of the country – the most extensive air operations against the Communists since the November 1968 bombing halt.

1972

January 13. President Nixon announces withdrawals that will reduce American troop strength in South Vietnam to 69,000 by 1 May.
March 30. North Vietnamese forces invade South Vietnam.
April 3. USS *Kitty Hawk* is the first of four additional aircraft carriers to join the two carriers already on station off Vietnam.
April 5. US Air Force fighter-bombers began reinforcing the units in Thailand.
April 6. Marine aircraft begin landing at Da Nang; the chairman of the Joint Chiefs of Staff, Admiral Thomas W. Moorer, USN, announces the resumption of aerial attack and naval bombardment against North Vietnam.
April 26. President Nixon states that American strength in South Vietnam will fall to 49,000 by 1 July.
May 1. Quang Tri City falls to the North Vietnamese.
May 8. President Nixon announces the mining of North Vietnamese harbors.
June 12. South Vietnamese troops break the siege of An Loc, begun on 5 April.
June 29. General Frederick C. Weyand, USA, replaces General Abrams as commander, US Military Assistance Command, Vietnam.
August 12. The last American ground combat troops leave South Vietnam; 43,500 airmen and support personnel remain.
August 29. President Nixon announces withdrawals that will reduce total US strength in South Vietnam to 27,000 by 1 December.
September 16. The South Vietnamese recapture Quang Tri city, but most of the province remains in Communist hands.
December 18. President Nixon orders the resumption of bombing north of the 20th Parallel, following a two-month pause; the Paris peace talks are suspended until 8 January 1973.

December 30. Bombing north of the 20th Parallel comes to an end after the North Vietnamese agree to negotiate a truce.

1973

January 15. The President suspends American military operations against North Vietnam.
January 27. The Paris peace accord is signed and the Vietnam war is officially ended.
January 28. Lon Nol proposes a cease-fire in Cambodia.
February 12. Five hundred eighty eight Americans being held by the North Vietnamese, Pathet Lao or Viet Cong are released during Operation Homecoming.
February 21. Souvanna Phouma and the Communists conclude a cease-fire in Laos.
March 17. A Cambodian pilot bombs the presidential palace at Phnom Penh in an unsuccessful attempt to kill Lon Nol.
March 29. The last American troops leave South Vietnam, only a Defense Attaché Office remains.
April 1. The last Americans held prisoner in North Vietnam arrive at Clark Air Base, Philippines.
April 9. Prince Sihanouk acting as spokesman for the Cambodian rebels, rejects Lon Nol's truce proposal.
June 29. Congress bans aerial bombing in Cambodia after 15 August.

1974

January 4. President Thieu claims that the war in South Vietnam has resumed; 55 government soldiers are killed in two clashes with Communist troops.
January 15-28. Cambodian rebels inflict large numbers of civilian casualties when shelling Phnom Penh.
January 27. Saigon reports that 13,778 government soldiers, 2,159 civilians, and 45,057 Communists have died in the fighting since the January 1973 truce.
April 5-7. Communist insurgents overrun six outposts protecting Phnom Penh.
July 9. Prince Sihanouk rejects another request by Lon Nol for truce talks.
November 30. Lon Nol again proposes a cease-fire in Cambodia.

1975

April 1. Lon Nol flees Cambodia.
April 9-11. Clashes occur between Communist insurgents and Laos government troops.
April 10-15. After heavy fighting, North Vietnamese troops capture Zuan Loc, 38 miles east of Saigon.
April 12. The US ambassador to Cambodia and his staff leave Phnom Penh.
April 13. The Department of Defense announces that US aircraft are parachuting supplies into Phnom Penh; the airport has been closed by enemy fire.
April 17. Phnom Penh falls to the insurgents.
April 21. President Thieu resigns.
April 28. Duong Van Minh, who helped overthrow Diem in 1963, takes over the government of South Vietnam.
April 30. North Vietnamese troops enter Saigon, as the remaining Americans and many of their South Vietnamese allies are evacuated. President Duong Van Minh announces unconditional surrender.
May 15. US Marines land on Koh Tang Island to free the American
continued overleaf

freighter SS *Mayaguez*, seized by the Cambodian Communists.

May 16. In Laos, the Pathet Lao seize Pakse.

May 20. Savannakhet falls to the Pathet Lao.

June. Pathet Lao troops seize US Embassy property in Vientiane.

August 23. The Pathet Lao consolidates the Communist takeover of Laos.

December 3. The Lao coalition headed by Souvanna Phouma is abolished; Laos becomes a Communist state with Souphanouvong as President.

December. The Congress of the National United Front of Cambodia approves a new, republican constitution; the state is renamed Democratic Kampuchea.

1976

March 26. Dr. Kissinger, US secretary of state, announces that the US is "in principle" prepared to normalize relations with Vietnam.

April 2. Sihanouk resigns as head of state in Kampuchea and Khieu Samphan takes his place; Pol Pot becomes prime minister.

April 25. Nationwide elections are held in Vietnam for a National Assembly of 249 deputies from the North and 243 from the South; it is claimed that 98.7 percent of the electorate votes.

April. It is estimated that 30,000 to 50,000 refugees have entered Thailand from Kampuchea since April 1975.

June 8. The Laotian government claims that dissident Meo tribesmen, who had regained control of Long Chong in January, have been "swept away".

June 24. The National Assembly of Vietnam meets for the first time; the Socialist Republic of Vietnam is proclaimed on 2 July and, among other decisions, Hanoi becomes the capital of united Vietnam and Saigon is renamed Ho Chi Minh City.

September 15. Vietnam is admitted to membership of the International Monetary Fund.

September. Pol Pot temporarily relinquishes the office of prime minister of Kampuchea because of ill-health; Nuon Chea replaces him (until September 1977).

October 6. An anti-Communist regime takes power in Thailand, causing a worsening of relations with Vietnam, Laos, and Kampuchea.

November 15. The US vetoes Vietnam's application for membership of the United Nations on the grounds of the country's "brutal and inhumane" attitude to US servicemen still listed as missing in Vietnam.

November 22. Border clashes occurred between Thai and Kampuchean troops.

December 14-20. The Vietnamese Workers Party, now renamed the Communist Party of Vietnam, holds its Fourth National Congress in Hanoi, electing Le Duan as secretary-general.

December 29. In answer to a petition presented to the UN by 90 former leading US opponents of the Vietnam War, protesting at violations of human rights by the Communist regime, Vietnamese officials claim that 95 percent of soldiers and officials of the former regime now enjoy full civil rights.

1977

February 3. Western embassies in Vientiane are asked by Laos to reduce their staffs by 50 percent; the Laotians suspect the embassies are aiding dissidents, whose activities continue to trouble the Communist regime.

March 12. Meo dissidents attack installations near Luang Prabang, Laos; ex-King Savang Vatthana and Crown Prince Vongsavang are arrested and sent for re-education.

March 14. Kampuchea refuses a US request for a meeting between an American delegation and Kampuchean authorities.

March 16. Refugees report that anti-Communist guerrillas have blown up the Long Binh ammunition dump, near Ho Chi Minh City; similar acts of resistance are reported throughout the year.

March 17-18. The bodies of 12 missing US pilots are handed over in Hanoi as a first move in improving US-Vietnamese relations.

May. The Kampuchean attaché in Moscow is recalled, breaking Kampuchea's last diplomatic link with the USSR. The US announces that it will no longer oppose Vietnam's admission to the UN.

June 30. The Southeast Asia Treaty Organization (SEATO) is dissolved. It is estimated that more than 700,000 people have left Ho Chi Minh city for resettlement in agricultural areas since the beginning of the year.

July 18. Laos and Vietnam sign a treaty of friendship and cooperation; there are an estimated 45,000 Vietnamese troops in Laos.

July. Relations between Vietnam and Kampuchea worsen; there are severe border clashes throughout the year. US estimates suggest that "possibly" 1,200,000 people have died in Kampuchea, many from disease or starvation, since the Communist takeover.

August 6. The prime minister of Thailand announces that there have been 400 border incursions by Kampuchea since the beginning of the year and threatens military action.

August 19. Khmer Rouge defectors to Thailand state that Pol Pot wields almost total power in Kampuchea and that Khieu Samphan is "only a figurehead".

September 23. Following reports that 20 Soviet MiG aircraft have been delivered to Vientiane, Thailand imposes an embargo on oil, food, and "strategic supplies" for Laos.

September 27. The existence of the ruling Kampuchean Communist Party is officially confirmed for the first time; Prime Minister Pol Pot, who resumes office this month, is its secretary.

September. Vietnam is admitted to membership of the UN.

October. Kampuchea's total isolation policy is relaxed when Pol Pot visits Peking and North Korea.

November. Announcement of talks to resolve difficulties between Kampuchea and Thailand.
Meo refugees state that more than 5,000 anti-government guerrillas have been killed in Laos in a major offensive by Laotian and Vietnamese troops near the Plain of Jars.

December 17-22. President Souphanouvong of Laos makes an official visit to Kampuchea.

December 31. Kampuchea accuses Vietnam of "criminal activities" in supporting abortive coupes in Kampuchea in 1975-1976.
Vietnam launches a major offensive into the Parrot's Beak area of eastern Kampuchea; Talks between the US and Vietnam, aimed at stabilizing their relationship, are resumed. The number of refugees leaving Vietnam by sea in late 1977 is estimated at 1,500 per month; about 7,000 Vietnamese have been admitted to Australia since 1975.

1978

January 8. Vietnam states that nearly 1,330,000 people have been resettled in "new economic zones" in 1976-1977.

January 9-12. Vietnam signs an agreement with Thailand on trade and economic and technical cooperation; similar agreements are reached with Malaysia and the Philippines.

January-February. Vietnamese troops establish themselves within Kampuchea's borders; Vietnam calls for a cease-fire and the establishment of a demilitarized zone along the border.

March 3. Vietnam announces that 90 percent of those placed in re-education camps since 1975 (a total variously estimated at between 40,000 and 400,000) have now been released.

June 20. Vietnam agrees that Chinese ships may evacuate members of Vietnam's Chinese minority who wish to leave; the number is estimated at between 30,000 and 300,000. China claims that more than 130,000 Chinese have left Vietnam since the beginning of hostilities with Kampuchea.

June. Refugees from Kampuchea increase as Pol Pot launches a purification campaign. Since 1975, an estimated 2 million Kampucheans have died in purges of disease and starvation, or as a result of forcible resettlement.
Vietnam becomes a member of COMECON, the Soviet-dominated economic alliance. Encouraged by China, Kampuchea refuses a Vietnamese request for an immediate border cease-fire and settlement talks.

June-July. The propaganda war between China and Vietnam escalates as China reportedly moves 15 divisions to the Vietnamese border and Vietnam deploys five divisions to face them.

July. Vietnam launches a major offensive against Kampuchea; US sources estimate that up to 80,000 Vietnamese troops are committed.

September 1-5. Pham Van Dong accuses China of instigating Kampuchean aggression and subverting Vietnam's Chinese minority.
Kampuchea accuses the USSR of supplying arms to Vietnam for the border conflict.

September 17. Following the visit of the UN high commissioner for refugees to Vietnam, Hanoi agrees to allow some of the 150,000 Cambodian refugees received since 1975 to leave for Western countries.

September. Pham Van Dong begins a tour to seek support from the Association of Southeast Asian Nations (ASEAN): Singapore Malaysia, Thailand, Indonesia, and the Philippines.

October. Kampuchean refugees are entering Thailand at the rate of 200 per week; 150,000 have escaped to Vietnam since the beginning of hostilities.

November 3. Vietnam and the USSR sign a mutual defense pact in Moscow; Vietnam accuses China of intensifying its military activities on the Sino-Vietnamese border.

November 9. Ending a five-day visit to Thailand to win support for China's stand against Soviet expansion, Chinese Vice Premier Teng Hsiao-ping denounces the Vietnam-Soviet pact as a "military alliance".

November 21. Sir Robert Thompson, counter-insurgency expert and former head of British Advisory Mission in Saigon, states that "The Vietnam War was lost on the television screens of the US".

November 22. Malaysia states that there are now 37,947 Vietnamese refugees in the country illegally.

November 29. The US announces that it will double the number of refugees admitted for resettlement and that an extra 21,875 refugees – 75 per cent of them "boat people" – will be admitted by spring 1979. Malaysia estimates its refugee population at 42,500 and expresses concern that local hostility will trigger racial violence.

December 1. The newly appointed soviet ambassador to Thailand, Yuri Kuznetsov, accuses China of "interfering in the internal affairs of Vietnam" and fomenting war between Vietnam and Kampuchea, describing China as the foremost threat to peace and stability in Southeast Asia.

December 3. Vietnam announces the establishment of the 'Kampuchea National United Front for National Salvation' (KNUFNS) – a guerrilla organization similar to the Viet Cong – to fight against the Phnom Penh regime. It is the first Communist insurgency ever to seek the overthrow of a Communist government.

December 4. US intelligence reports heavy Kampuchean casualties in large-scale frontier battles.

December 5. The president of the Front for National Salvation is variously identified by Western observers as So Phin, a former commissar of the Kampuchean Communist Party, or Heng Samrin, a former Kampuchean Army officer.

December 7. Kampuchea, still avoiding mention of the Front for National Salvation, alleges that the USSR and Vietnam are conspiring to overthrow the Phnom Penh government. China denounces the Front as a Vietnamese tool to establish a "puppet regime" in Kampuchea, and warns that the effort will be expanded to include other Southeast Asia nations. Western observers report that Vietnam is invading the 'Parrot's Beak' and 'Fish Hook' areas of Kampuchea in strength. The front is seen as a way for Vietnam to avoid international condemnation by portraying the war as a "legitimate" movement by indigenous dissidents rather than an act of aggression by a foreign power.

December 10. Claiming that 40,000 Vietnamese troops have entered Kampuchea from Laos, Thailand places its army on the alert.

December 11. Vietnamese refugees reaching Australia claim that there has been a sharp increase in anti-Communist insurgency within Vietnam.

December 12. Following a clash between a Vietnamese gunboat and a Chinese fishing vessel, Radio Hanoi claims that Chinese troops have made an incursion into Cao Bang province and that China is moving "thousands of reinforcements" to border areas. At a 40-nation conference to discuss the refugee problem, in Geneva, Vietnam denies that it is organizing the flight of refugees by sea and claims that China is inciting the exodus of ethnic-minority refugees from Vietnam. The conference estimates that some 320,000 refugees have now fled from Vietnam, Laos, and Kampuchea; about 150,000 are in camps in Thailand.

December 15. Reports from Peking suggest that Pol Pot has been advised by the Chinese to leave Kampuchean capital, Phnom Penh, though this sprawling city is not

under immediate threat, to wage a protracted guerrilla war from the countryside.
December 25. The anticipated all-out dry-season offensive is launched by Vietnamese-led forces in Kampuchea.
December 27. The master of a Panamanian freighter, *Tung An*, claiming to have saved about 2,500 refugees from the South China Sea on December 10, reported to officials in Manila Bay that 200 other refugees had fallen struggling into the sea and drowned in the panic to board the freighter.

1979

January 1. Kampuchean guerrillas claim in radio broadcasts to have overrun the Mekong River town of Kratie, "effectively placing the country's north-east region under rebel control".
January 2. Kampuchean President Khieu Samphan broadcasts that Vietnamese troops are attacking along a 200-mile wide front.
Radio Hanoi admits there is fighting under way deep in Kampuchea, but claims that KNUFNS guerrillas are acting alone.
January 3. Radio Phnom Penh broadcasts that the Kampuchean forces are abandoning classical warfare tactics for guerrilla operations.
January 4. Radio Phnom Penh claims 14,100 Vietnamese forces killed or wounded and 64 Soviet-built tanks destroyed in the week since the "invasion" began.
January 7. Radio Hanoi reports that the Kampuchean capital "has been successfully liberated".
There are reports that Phnom Penh fell without conflict in the city itself, suggesting that Kampuchean Government leaders have escaped.
January 9. Vietnam is the first country to recognize a provisional revolutionary People's Council set up in Phnom Penh on January 8. Recognition by Laos follows immediately. KNUFNS claims control of all 19 Kampuchean provinces, but heavy fighting is reported still in south-western and western regions.
January 11. Leng Sary, former Kampuchean deputy premier, flies into Hong Kong after Thai government apparently airlifted him from the border town of Pol Pet in an unmarked helicopter.
Radio Hanoi announces that, under the new Phnom Penh regime Kampuchea would now be officially known as the People's Republic of Kampuchea, and assures non-Communist Southeast Asian nations that Vietnam's policies towards her neighbors would not be affected by recent conflict in Kampuchea.
January 15. A UN Security Council resolution presented by seven non-aligned states and supported by 13 other members, calling for a ceasefire in Kampuchea and the withdrawal of all foreign troops, was vetoed by the Soviet Union, whose ambassador, Mr. Troyanovsky, persists in supporting Vietnamese claims that no Vietnamese troops have taken part in the overthrow of the Phnom Penh regime.
January 16. Thai Navy sources reports a naval battle in the Gulf of Thailand between Vietnamese-led forces and units loyal to Pol Pot. At least 22 boats were thought to be involved in fierce fighting, part of a naval, air and amphibious operation by Vietnam/KNUFNS forces to seal off Kampuchea's only stretch of coastline and to take control of Koh Kong island.
January 29. Radio Hanoi says that some 200 Chinese troops have raided the northern frontier province of Lang Son.
Khmer Rouge guerrillas claim to have isolated the Vietnamese garrison in Phnom Penh and say that ten other Kampuchean cities are threatened.
February 6. Heng Samrin, president of the Kampuchean Revolutionary Council, calls on all citizens to oppose the Khmer rouge, who claim 736 Vietnamese killed and 18 tanks destroyed between 26 January-2 February. It is believed that Chinese supplies are reaching anti-government forces by way of Thailand.
February 9. The US State Department expresses "serious concern" at the Chinese buildup on the border with Vietnam, and similar concern at Vietnamese activity in Kampuchea.
February 15. Vietnam says that China is "feverishly preparing for war". Western analysts believe that China now has 19 divisions (150,000 to 160,000 men) and several hundred military aircraft within 40 miles (64km) of the Vietnamese border.
February 16. Vietnamese Premier Pham Van Dong arrives in Phnom Penh for talks with Kampuchean leaders.
Western analysts estimate that Vietnam has 100,000 militia, with artillery and air support, near the Chinese border, and that up to 18 divisions are now committed in Kampuchea.
February 17. Some eight Chinese divisions attack 26 border-crossing points and invade Vietnam. Claiming that in the past six months Vietnam, "emboldened by the support of the Soviet Union", has made more than 700 armed provocations against China, killing more than 300 Chinese, the official Chinese news agency says that, "driven beyond forbearance, Chinese frontier troops have been forced to rise in counter-attack". It is emphasized that China has no territorial ambitions. The US calls for a Chinese withdrawal from Vietnam and a Vietnamese withdrawal from Kampuchea.
February 18. The provincial capital of Mon Cai falls to the Chinese.
In Phnom Penh, Vietnam and Kampuchea sign a treaty of peace, friendship, and cooperation.
February 19. Hanoi claims that the Chinese advance has been checked after maximum penetration of 3 miles (4.8km); 46 Chinese tanks have been destroyed, and "hundreds" of troops killed.
US intelligence suggests that China intends only a "short, punishing" invasion.
The Soviet Union denounces China's "brazen aggression" and "attempts to plunge the world into war".
February 20. Official Chinese sources state that a field army of 30,000 troops – out of 210,000 massed on the border – has penetrated more than 6 miles (9.6km) into Vietnam, inflicting 10,000 casualties. China appears to have halted the advance in order to limit its "punitive action", but denies that withdrawal is imminent.
Vietnam says that China has taken territory in five border provinces and has occupied the provincial capital of Lao Cai: Chinese troops have been given "a bloody nose", losing 5,000 men and 80 tanks. The ASEAN nations condemn both Chinese aggression and Vietnam's commitment in Kampuchea.
Khmer Rouge guerrillas claim to have killed or wounded 1,500 Vietnamese troops in one week and to have forced a Vietnamese withdrawal from key areas of northwest Kampuchea.
February 21. In heavy fighting on a 450-mile (720km) front, Chinese jets are reported to be striking at Vietnamese missile sites well ahead of the main advance.
February 22. It is estimated that 90,000 Chinese in Vietnam are facing some 100,000 Vietnamese militia. Vietnamese regulars are moving up to Lang Son from the Hanoi area. It is thought that the initial failure to engage Vietnamese regulars and the relatively heavy casualties inflicted by the militia have caused the Chinese to prolong the invasion. Vietnam now claims that Chinese casualties total 12,500 killed or wounded, 138 tanks, and 26 other military vehicles.
Yuri Andropov, head of the KGB and a senior Politburo member, warns China to withdraw "before it is too late".
The US states that Soviet troop movement into Vietnam would be viewed with "considerable disfavor and concern".
February 27. Chinese Vice-Premier Teng Hsiao-ping states that 75,000 to 85,000 Chinese troops have entered Vietnam. They are reported to have made spectacular advances of up to 50 miles (80km) into Vietnam, but a Chinese spokesman says that no attacks on Hanoi or Haipong are intended. Radio Hanoi puts maximum penetration at 25 miles (40km) and claims that China has lost 80,000 men.
March 2. Total Vietnamese losses in the border fighting are estimated at 26,800 killed, wounded, or missing.
March 4. Some 220,000 Chinese troops, commanded by Hsu Shihyu, have entered Vietnam since 17 February, penetrating to a maximum of about 25 miles (40km) on the Cao Bang front. Vietnam, claiming to have mobilized 1,500,000 militia, is reported to be moving up three main force divisions – one withdrawn from Kampuchea – for a major offensive. China specifies "disputed areas" on the border, raising speculation that it intends to make claims on Vietnamese territory.
Some 200 Kampuchean and Vietnamese troops attack two villages across the Thai frontier, withdrawing when Thai armor is brought up.
March 5. China, having "dealt devastating blows", officially announces its withdrawal from Vietnam and again calls for talks "to settle the boundary and territorial disputes". Hanoi refuses to talk while Chinese troops remain in Vietnam.
General Krianksak Chomanan, premier of Thailand, announces that the country's armed forces have been placed on alert following Kampuchean-Vietnamese incursions.
Kampuchea announces that, following the fall of Pol Pot, all Khmer Rouge have been driven from the country.
March 7. Vietnam confirms that China is withdrawing, accusing the invaders of "barbarous criminal acts" and promising "punishment". Laos claims that China has massed several divisions on its border.
March 12. Hanoi claims that Chinese troops have moved border markers to new positions deep in Vietnamese territory.
Western analysts estimate that China assembled some 20 divisions for the invasion, using fewer than 15. They deployed three artillery divisions; long-range artillery duels constituted a major part of the conflict. Neither side made significant use of air power.
March 21. Vietnam proposes to begin peace talks on 29 March, provided all Chinese troops are withdrawn.
March 25. General William Westmoreland, former commander, US Military Assistance Command, Vietnam, predicts that a protracted civil war in Kampuchea will extend into Vietnam, where nearly one million ethnic Kampucheans in the Mekong Delta region are in a state of unrest.
March 29. Vietnam announces that Soviet warships have been granted the use of Cam Ranh Bay facilities.
April 2. There are now some 52,000 Vietnamese refugees in temporary camps in Malaysia.
April 10. It is estimated that China hold some 2,000 Vietnamese POWs, and that fewer than 1,000 Chinese POWs are held in Hanoi at the "Peking Hotel" prison.
April 15. US sources claim that Soviet military aircraft are based at Da Nang, Vietnam.
April 18. Peace talks between China and Vietnam begin in Hanoi.
Vietnam claims that China still occupies more than 10 enclaves (totaling some 23 square miles, 60 sq km) inside Vietnam: China claims that Vietnam continues to make cross-border raids.
Vice-President Pen Sovan of Kampuchea states that the Pol Pot regime killed close on 3,000,000 people. Pol Pot himself is now said to be Thailand.
April 27. UN Secretary-General Kurt Waldheim, who has offered to mediate in Sino-Vietnamese talks, is told by Vietnam that Cam Ranh Bay will not become a Soviet base.
April. In Peking, Norodom Sihanouk claims that China plans to back a 2,000-strong, right-wing guerrilla group – the Khmer Serei – to fight in Kampuchea.
May 8. Japanese intelligence estimates that China lost 10,000 men killed in the border conflict, many in "human wave" attacks.
May 13. Refugee administrators estimate that 4,000 Vietnamese "boat people" are landing in Malaysia every week; since the border war, some 50 percent are ethnic Vietnamese.
May 14. Vietnam charges that Thai air and ground forces made 16 incursions into Kampuchea between 27 April and 1 May.
May. China admits to 20,000 casualties in the border war. It is believed that Vietnam now has more than 140,000 troops in the northern border area.
June 16. Thailand begins expelling 40,000 Khmer Rouge refugees back into Kampuchea; many are said to be hard-core Pol Pot followers; many are still armed. Previously, 40,000 Kampucheans, some ethnic Chinese, had been expelled. Almost 160,000 Vietnamese refugees are in 14 UN-supported camps in Thailand.
June 19. Sir Murray Maclehouse, governor of Hong Kong, said over 54,000 Vietnamese refugees had reached Hong Kong, and there were 170,000 to 200,000 at sea; he estimated that at least 150,000 would have arrived by the end of 1979.

1980

January 26. US Department of State expresses concern about Vietnamese reconnaissance probes from Kampuchea into Thailand and calls upon Vietnam and Soviet sponsors to refrain from any actions dangerous to Thai sovereignty.
June 23-24. Vietnamese troops attack Kampuchean refugee camp located in Thailand but retreat across border when Thai troops intervene.
July 1. President Carter accelerates delivery of arms and ammunition already ordered by Thai government.

continued overleaf

1981

May 22. Department of Defense spokesman pledges that US will do "whatever is appropriate" to check reports of American servicemen still alive and held prisoner in Southeast Asia. Previous day, reports had surfaced of covert expedition by Asian mercenaries in an unsuccessful search for Americans believed held in Laos (though DoD withheld confirmation at the time, in 1983 it admitted this had taken place; Reagan administration expressed disapproval).
July. The remains of three Americans are turned over to US officials by the Vietnamese government.
September. General Assembly for third time votes to seat Pol Pot government of Kampuchea rather than the Heng Samrin regime.
October 19. UN General Assembly reaffirms its conviction that foreign troops should leave Kampuchea.

1982

March 11. Representatives of Association of Southeast Asian Nations, (ASEAN) join US officials in pledging continued economic cooperation.
September. Vietnamese Foreign Minister Thach announces agreement to a long-standing US request for regular meetings in Hanoi to resolve the POW/MIA issue.
September 8. Delegation from the National League of Families of American Prisoners and Missing in Southeast Asia begin visit to Laos and Vietnam in search of information on fate of missing US servicemen and women.
October. The government of Vietnam turns over the remains of four Americans and identification data on three others.
November 2. During visit to Southeast Asia, Secretary of Defense Weinberger reaffirms American support of regional efforts to free Kampuchea, by peaceful means, from Vietnamese domination. He also assures Thailand of increased military assistance and American help in the event of Communist attack.
November 13. More than 100,000 veterans of the Vietnam War gather at Washington, D.C., for the dedication of a memorial honoring the dead of that conflict.
December. Congress passes a resolution supporting President Ronald Reagan's efforts on POW/MIAs and encourages the United States and Laos to expedite efforts at cooperation.
December 24. A group of Vietnam veterans begins a round-the-clock candlelight vigil at the site of the Vietnam Veterans Memorial to call attention to US servicemen still missing in action.

1983

January 28. At a meeting of the National League of Families of American Prisoners and Missing in Southeast Asia, President Reagan calls the goal for a full accounting of POW/MIAs a "highest national priority".
February. A US POW/MIA technical team visits Laos for the first time since the war's end.
March 31. Vietnamese troops and artillery assault a refugee camp on the Thai-Cambodian border, forcing thousands of Cambodians into Thailand and causing Red Cross doctors to abandon the camp hospital.
June. The government of Vietnam returns the remains of nine American servicemen.
July. The Vietnamese government suspends technical talks on the POW/MIA issue, citing "hostile statements" by senior American officials of the Administration.
July 5. Documents made public by Federal Judge George C. Pratt Jr. indicate that the Dow Chemical Company knew as early as the mid-1960s that dioxin exposure might cause serious illness or death, but withheld the information from the United States government.
October 29. The Reagan Administration's sharp curbs on press coverage of the action in Grenada are linked to military resentment of Vietnam War reporting, when journalists had freedom of movement within war zones.
December. At Lao government invitation, a US technical team surveys a US crash site in Southern Laos and proposes a joint excavation effort by both governments.

1984

February. A US delegation led by Assistant Secretary of Defense Richard Armitage meets with senior Vietnamese officials, who agree to resume technical meetings and accelerate cooperation on the POW/MIA issue. The remains of five Americans are turned over to US representatives.
May 7. Federal District Court Judge Jack B. Weinstein announces a $180 million out-of-court settlement against seven manufacturers of Agent Orange in a class-action suit brought by 15,000 Vietnam veterans.
May 28. The unknown American service member from the Vietnam war is laid to rest during Memorial Day ceremonies at Arlington National Cemetery, Washington, D.C.
July. The Vietnamese government returns the remains of eight persons, six of whom are later identified as Americans.
July 15. Fighting breaks out along the Vietnam-China border. The Chinese charge that the Vietnamese invaded, first; Vietnam charges the Chinese were the perpetrators, and began it by shelling Vietnamese villages and moving troops into the country.
September 11. Secretary of State George Schultz announces that the United States will ask Vietnam to release about 10,000 political prisoners held in that country. They are to be resettled in the United States along with 8,000 Vietnamese children fathered by US servicemen.
November 11. A statue of three Vietnam war infantrymen is dedicated at the War Memorial on Veteran's Day.

1985

February 22. US and Lao technical personnel conduct the first joint site crash excavation.
March 20. The remains of six American servicemen are repatriated to US officials during ceremonies in Hanoi.
July 7. Indonesian Foreign Minister Mochtar relays a message to the United States from Hanoi of an agreement to reenter into high level discussion with US officials to resolve the POW/MIA issue within a two-year period, beginning January 1, 1986.
August 17. The government of Vietnam turns over to US officials the remains of 26 Americans, the largest effort of its kind since the end of US involvement in Vietnam.
November 17. US and Vietnamese technical officials meet in Hanoi to conduct the first joint excavation of a US crash site in that country.
December 7. The Vietnam government turns over to US technical officials the remains of seven US servicemen.

1986

February 15. During a meeting in Hanoi with a US delegation, Vietnamese officials reiterate their pledge to investigate live sightings and publicly admit the possibility of Americans being alive in remote areas.
February 17. US and Lao technical officials jointly excavate a second crash site in Southern Laos to resolve the status of 14 Americans missing in 1972 incident.
April 10. The government of Vietnam turns over to US officials in Hanoi 21 remains believed to be US personnel.
July 19. President Reagan thanks the governments of Vietnam and Laos for their renewed efforts to help find MIA remains.

1987

January. Retiring US Army General John W. Vessey Jr., former chairman of the Joint Chiefs of Staff, is appointed special presidential emissary for POW/MIA affairs.
April 22. The US says plans to send a special envoy to Hanoi are on hold until that capital indicates an interest in resolving the issue of POW/MIAs.

1988

March 14. Vietnam and China begin three days of military skirmishes over the disputed Spratly Islands.

1989

September 26. Vietnam completes its withdrawal of forces from Kampuchea. Some 23,000 Vietnamese soldiers were killed and 55,000 wounded fighting Pol Pot's regime for 11 years.
December 11-12. Hong Kong authorities forcibly repatriate 51 Vietnamese refugees. Some 2,000 refugees agree to return voluntarily by the year's end.

1990

October. The European Economic Community (EEC) establishes trade relations with Vietnam.
October 1. The Vietnam National Assembly passes a new banking law that allows cooperative businesses to declare bankruptcy.
December 1. The Communist Party of Vietnam (CPV) releases its draft platform for the Building of Socialism in the Transitional Period.

1991

April. The Vietnam National Assembly passes a law that sanctions and protests private businesses in the country.
August. Vietnam resumes diplomatic relations with China following the visit to Beijing by the Vietnamese Premier Vo Van Kiet for talks with the Chinese Premier Li Peng.
October 29. Britain and Vietnam sign an agreement on the repatriation of Vietnam refugees from Hong Kong.

1992

April 13. The US lifts its embargo on Telecommunications links with Vietnam and by the end of April agrees to begin trading such crucial items as medicine and food.

1993

June 4. In a step toward normalizing relations with the US, the Vietnamese government confirms the release of all former South Vietnamese officials being held in re-education camps.
June 15. Soviet President Boris Yeltsin announces that US prisoners of the Vietnamese War had been detained in USSR labor camps, and he promises to return any still there. On 26 June, President Bush's special envoy to Moscow, Malcolm Toon, can find no validity in Yeltsin's claim.
September 19. The Vietnam National Assembly disbands the National Defense Council that played a leading role during the Vietnam War.
October 10. Following an assurance by the US government of resettlement in the States, guerrillas of Vietnam's United Front Liberation of Oppressed Races (Fulro) surrender to United Nations officials, ending their 28-year fight for autonomy.
October 17-19. The US presidential envoy, General John Vessey, visits Vietnam and receives that government's promise to search through records and photographs relating to POW/MIAs.

1993

July 15-17. A US government delegation visits Vietnam and decides to create three temporary posts there for US State Department officials who would help in the search for POW/MIAs.
September 13. President Clinton announces the relaxing of America's trade embargo with Vietnam and says US companies can now bid for Vietnam projects that use funds from international organizations.
November 11. Glenna Goodacre's sculpture, "Vietnam Women's Memorial", is dedicated to those women who served during the Vietnam War. It depicts a Vietnam soldier with three nurses, and is located near the Vietnam Veterans Memorial in Washington, DC.

1994

February 3. The US ends its 19-year trade embargo with Vietnam because, President Clinton states, the Vietnamese have cooperated in searching for the remains of Americans killed and missing in action. Clinton's action prompts the United Nations to begin phasing out its emergency assistance to Vietnam boat people.
February 7. The Vietnamese government hands over the apparent remains of 12 American soldiers to US authorities.
March 20. An exhaustive joint US-Vietnamese search for POW/MIAs ends (which had begun 26 February). It was headed by Lieutenant Colonel John C. Cray from America's MIA office in Hanoi.

1995

January 28. In a move to normalize relationships, the US and Vietnam sign an agreement to reopen diplomatic relations by setting up liaison offices in Hanoi and Washington, DC. James Hall becomes the first consul-general to Vietnam, but the US desires more information about POW/MIAs before exchanging ambassadors.
April. The Vietnamese government publishes casualty figures for the war (1954-75) showing that more than 1 million Vietnamese combatants and some 2 million civilians had been killed.

Weapons and warfare techniques used in Vietnam

by Lt. Col. David Miller

There are many who would claim that the Vietnamese wars suffered from a surfeit of technology and that the French and United States campaigns would have been more effective if they had not tried to use advanced technology as a substitute for deficiencies in manpower and tactical ability. It can also be argued that—especially in the case of the United States—because the technological resources existed, it was virtually impossible not to use them. In the British campaign in Malaya, for example, helicopters were both new and in short supply, so that they were used sparingly and seldom had any effect on either strategy or tactics. For the United States, however, helicopters existed in vast numbers and tactics—possibly even strategy in the years 1965 to 68—tended to revolve round optimising the use of the helicopter, rather than using the helicopter as a mere tactical tool.

It also was true that the United States response to a tactical problem was sometimes so devastating that it was actually counter-productive. The Viet Cong, for example, would deliberately cause an incident in a village, which would then be bombed or shelled by the Americans without anyone actually coming to the scene at all. The inevitable damage, casualties and deaths would simply serve to alienate the population yet further.

Despite all this, however, the Vietnam War acted as a great technological proving ground, where the United States and the Soviet Union tested their latest weaponry and techniques on each other. In general terms, and taking aviation as an example, post-war military equipment has passed through a number of overlapping phases:

1945–1955 World War II equipment remained in use, e.g. piston-engined fighters and bombers, and the very early straight-winged turbojet fighters.

1950–1960 The first "generation" of post-war equipment entered service: swept-wing turbojet fighters and bombers, with the most advanced being capable of Mach 1 in level flight.

1960–1970 The second "generation", with fighter aircraft capable of Mach 2 and all equipped with advanced electronics.

The first post-war generation of equipment had its testing ground in Korea, and it was the last of that generation and virtually the whole of the second generation which was tested in Indochina. Many lessons were learned in the sustained combat environment of Vietnam which simply did not emerge from the shorter conflicts such as those in the Middle East. The value of an integrated missile and gun air defense system caused surprise to those pundits who saw missiles as being the complete answer, while the ability of a civil population to withstand very heavy aerial bombardment was once again demonstrated.

This technology section is, therefore, presented in the full realization that the Indochina war demonstrated on occasions the grave limitations in the ability of technology to affect the political overtone of a war. Nevertheless, the impact of the Indochina experience on many aspects of modern weapons technology will be felt for many years to come. This section highlights the more significant weapons and techniques in the more important fields.

Geographical factors of the Vietnam War

The topography and climate of the different areas of South Vietnam profoundly influenced the nature of the fighting during two wars in the country. The climate is predominantly hot, humid, and tropical, depending largely on the monsoon. The wet seasons occur in the winter months to the north of the mountain area and in the summer months in the piedmont and Mekong Delta to the south. Annual rainfall is very heavy: 80 inches (203cm) in the Mekong Delta; 40 inches (101cm) on the central coast; 102 inches (260cm) in the northern coastal plain (of which 65 inches, 165cm, fall in September–November). During the monsoon visibility is poor, cross-country movement is more difficult than usual, and flying conditions are bad. Health hazards—particularly for non-Asian troops—increase and quartermaster problems of resupply and storage multiply. The North Vietnamese Army and Viet Cong generally tended to reduce their activity levels during the monsoon period.

Republic of South Vietnam

In July 1954, the Geneva Agreements partitioned Vietnam along the line of the 17th Parallel, which became a Demilitarized Zone (DMZ). The Communist Democratic Republic of Vietnam occupied the North; the non-Communist Republic of Vietnam lay to the South.

South Vietnam in 1973

Area: 67,293 square miles (174,289 sq km)
Population (estimated): 19,582,100
Capital: Saigon (3,805,900)
Language: Vietnamese
Religions: Pagan, Buddhist, Confucian, Christian
Monetary unit: Piastre
 On 16 September 1974 the free exchange rate was:
 US $1 = 650 piastres
 £1 = 1,530 piastres
Gross Domestic Product in 1972:
 1,127,000,000,000 piastres

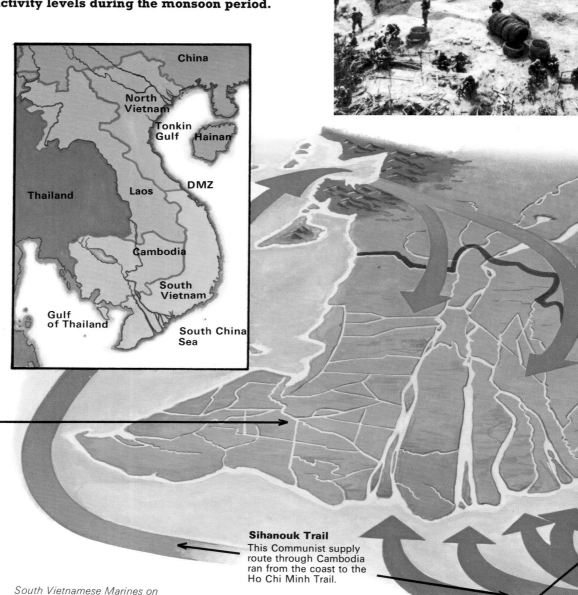

Mekong Delta

This comprises a very flat, low-lying area of extensive rice paddies and swamps, cut by rivers of various widths, streams, and canals. In most areas it is impassable for vehicles and hard going on foot: wet paddies, deep ditches, steep-sided, booby-trapped dikes, and searing heat made life more than usually difficult for the infantryman. The Delta was the scene of "riverine operations", in which shallow-draft gunboats, floating artillery, and hovercraft assisted the infantry against the Viet Cong guerrillas.

South Vietnamese Marines on a sweep in the Mekong Delta.

Sihanouk Trail

This Communist supply route through Cambodia ran from the coast to the Ho Chi Minh Trail.

Piedmont

The piedmont is an area of gently rolling hills and broad plains. The area includes War Zones C and D in its central region—notorious sanctuaries for Communist troops and the scene of many large-scale "search and destroy" operations. It also borders on the main North Vietnamese Army and Viet Cong supply depots in Cambodia. This type of terrain is well-suited to armored warfare—unlike the greater part of Vietnam—and was thus the scene of many "main force" engagements.

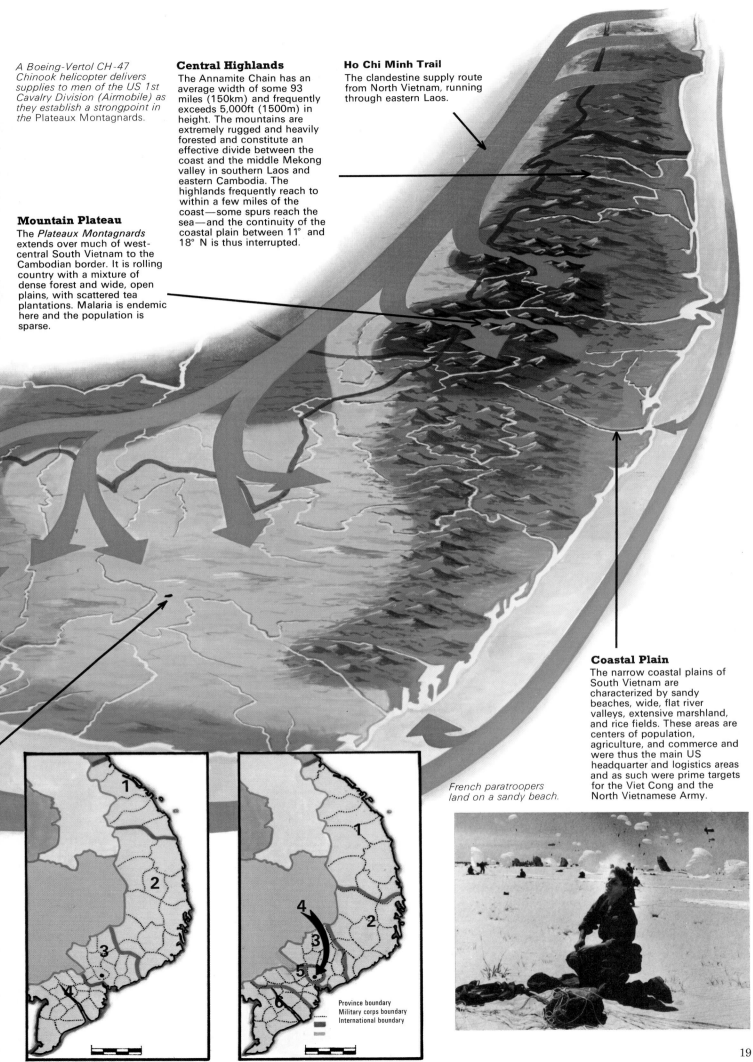

A Boeing-Vertol CH-47 Chinook helicopter delivers supplies to men of the US 1st Cavalry Division (Airmobile) as they establish a strongpoint in the Plateaux Montagnards.

Central Highlands

The Annamite Chain has an average width of some 93 miles (150km) and frequently exceeds 5,000ft (1500m) in height. The mountains are extremely rugged and heavily forested and constitute an effective divide between the coast and the middle Mekong valley in southern Laos and eastern Cambodia. The highlands frequently reach to within a few miles of the coast—some spurs reach the sea—and the continuity of the coastal plain between 11° and 18° N is thus interrupted.

Ho Chi Minh Trail

The clandestine supply route from North Vietnam, running through eastern Laos.

Mountain Plateau

The *Plateaux Montagnards* extends over much of west-central South Vietnam to the Cambodian border. It is rolling country with a mixture of dense forest and wide, open plains, with scattered tea plantations. Malaria is endemic here and the population is sparse.

Coastal Plain

The narrow coastal plains of South Vietnam are characterized by sandy beaches, wide, flat river valleys, extensive marshland, and rice fields. These areas are centers of population, agriculture, and commerce and were thus the main US headquarter and logistics areas and as such were prime targets for the Viet Cong and the North Vietnamese Army.

French paratroopers land on a sandy beach.

Province boundary
Military corps boundary
International boundary

South Vietnamese Military Zones

North Vietnamese Military Zones

The fighting men

The anti-Communist forces in Vietnam included the South Vietnamese (Army of the Republic of Vietnam, ARVN), French, American and Australian. The ARVN were often compared unfavorably with the North Vietnamese Army and Viet Cong, but the ARVN fought well when led well. The French fought in Indochina from 1946 to 1954, losing 94,581 killed and missing, with 78,127 wounded. The US infantrymen bore the brunt of the Second Vietnam War effort; there were more than 500,000 US troops in Southeast Asia in 1968-69. Between 1964 and 1973 45,790 had been killed, making the war increasingly unpopular in the United States. The Australians had 7,672 men committed in 1969.

The Australian
This Australian infantryman carries his squad's 7.62mm light machine gun and two spare ammunition belts. The weight of his web equipment is taken by the belt; the front of his body is clear so that he can lie comfortably in the prone firing position. The Australians were heirs to two generations of jungle warfare, and this experience is shown by his extra waterbottles, the value of which more than offsetting the extra weight involved.

The American
This private in the US Marine Corps during the battle for Hue, February 1968, wears standard olive-drab combat dress and a flak jacket. The bayonet on his M16A1 5.56mm rifle is fixed for house-to-house fighting, and slung around his body is a belt of 7.62mm ammunition for his squad's M60 light machine gun. His pack contains spare clothing and equipment.

20

The Communist forces included the Viet Cong, which was the indigenous national liberation movement of South Vietnam, and the North Vietnamese Army, of which it was nominally independent. There were regular VC units of up to regimental strength and many small, part-time units in villages under Communist control. The North Vietnamese Army at first supplemented and then took over from the VC. The Communist victory in 1975 was the result of a conventional invasion by North Vietnamese armor and infantry.

The Viet Cong soldier

This Viet Cong soldier (below) wears the "black pajamas", which have come to characterize the guerrilla fighter, and a soft kahaki hat and web equipment produced in jungle workshops. His light, open sandals are probably cut from an old truck tire. He carries a Soviet Kalashnikov AK-47 rifle.

The North Vietnamese soldier

This soldier of the North Vietnamese Army wears a green uniform and a cool, practical helmet resembling the pith helmet of earlier European colonizers. The basic personal weapon of the NVA was the AK-47, but this man carries a Soviet-supplied RPG-7 anti-tank missile launcher. His food-tube contains sufficient dry rations and rice to last seven days.

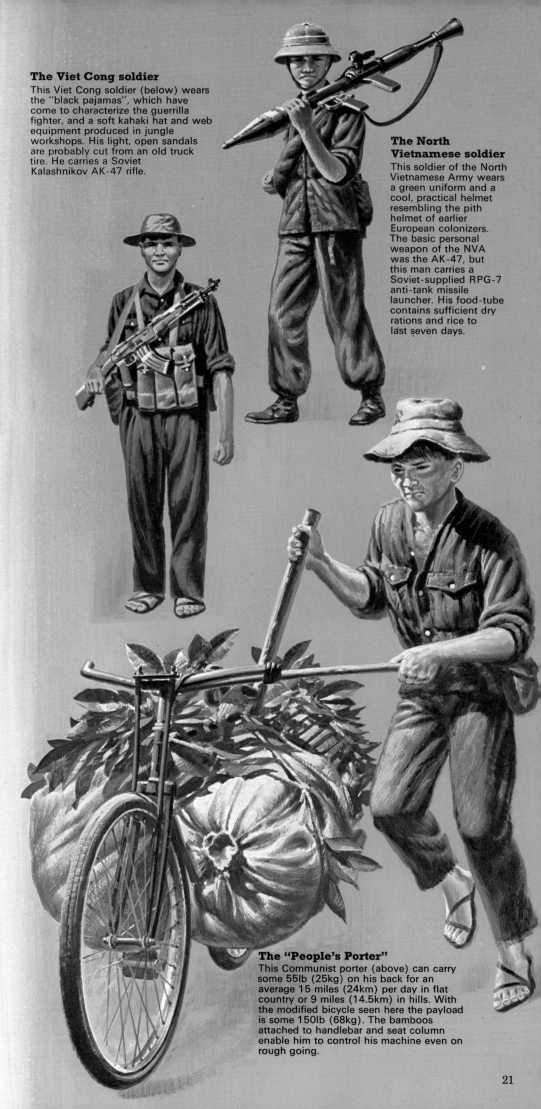

The French soldier

This corporal of a line regiment from Metropolitan France (above) carries the compact, reliable 9mm MAT-49 sub-machine gun. He wears a jungle-green uniform and canvas and rubber jungle boots like those worn by the British in Malaya. His pack is the French canvas and leather pattern; his web equipment and steel helmet are of American manufacture.

The South Vietnamese soldier

This soldier of the Army of the Republic of Vietnam (left) is equipped with US weapon, uniform, webbing, and radio pack. He carries the M16A1 Armalite rifle, which the small-statured Vietnamese found ideally suited to their needs. While his allies came, fought, and left, the ARVN soldier had to live with his successes and failures. When well led he was fully the equal of his enemies: during the Communists' Tet offensive of 1968, for example, despite being caught badly off-balance the men of the ARVN stood firm and defeated the Viet Cong.

The "People's Porter"

This Communist porter (above) can carry some 55lb (25kg) on his back for an average 15 miles (24km) per day in flat country or 9 miles (14.5km) in hills. With the modified bicycle seen here the payload is some 150lb (68kg). The bamboos attached to handlebar and seat column enable him to control his machine even on rough going.

Viet Cong booby traps

The booby trap is a daunting weapon and the Viet Cong became great experts in its use. The most complex component was usually a grenade or a mine, and the only real skill lay in disguising the release mechanism. Most booby traps resulted in an explosion close to the victim, causing severe local destruction of flesh and tissue and forcing large amounts of dirt and debris into the wound, which led to massive contamination. Booby trap injuries almost always necessitated a casualty evacuation operation and led to the unit concerned moving more slowly and cautiously in case there were more traps around. These illustrations show a representative sample from among the many ingenious devices used during the two wars in Vietnam.

Tin-can grenades
Below right: Grenades were often used in booby traps; one of the simplest release mechanisms is shown here. The grenades have been placed in appropriately sized tin cans with the safety-pins removed. A pull on the wire extracts the grenade, which then primes itself and explodes. Placing a grenade at both ends of the wire greatly increases the chances of the trap being effective.

Spiked ball
Far right: Sometimes encountered was this almost medieval device, consisting of a heavy mud ball spiked punji stakes and attached to a tree by an innocuous-seeming jungle vine. When released by the trip-wire, the ball would swing hard across the track.

Punji stake traps

Left: Members of a Viet Cong unit shown laying a series of punji traps. Used for centuries to trap wild game, the punji trap was used by the Viet Cong to wound and harass even bigger game—man.

The punji was a sharpened spike; sometimes steel nails driven through a block of wood were used, but lengths of sharpened bamboo (either raw or hardened in a fire) were almost equally effective. In its simplest form the punji trap comprised a shallow pit with punji stakes embedded upright in the floor (bottom). The length and width of the pit was kept to a reasonable size so that it could be covered with twigs and foliage and take on an innocent appearance. The depth was sufficient for the victim's foot to descend with enough force for the stakes to pierce the sole of his boot. A more sophisticated version (below) was slightly larger and included stakes in the walls facing downwards, making extraction of the foot much more difficult.

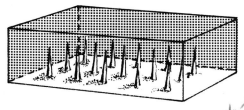

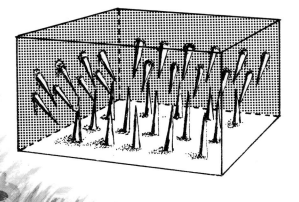

Grenade in stream

US and ARVN patrols frequently traversed streams, minor rivers, and swamps, especially in the Mekong Delta region—so the more obvious crossing points were often booby trapped. Here, a grenade is shown pegged firmly to one bank of a stream with a trip-wire running from its safety-pin to the other bank.

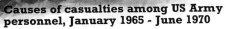

Bow and arrow

Right: This device was used by aboriginal tribes in the highlands to kill animals, but was adapted by the Viet Cong for use in the war. It consisted of a concealed pit containing a bow, with its ends embedded in the sides. An arrow was held under tension in the bow and a simple release mechanism was activated by a trip-wire running across the track.

Hidden mines

Right: In addition to the punji stakes and grenades, many mines were used. A favorite spot for a mine was around a fallen tree or log lying across a track.

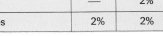

Causes of casualties among US Army personnel, January 1965 - June 1970

The table shows the effectiveness of the booby traps against soldiers of the US Army alone; it may be assumed that similar figures apply to other Free World forces and to the ARVN. Eleven per cent of combat deaths in the US Army amounts to some 4,000 men during the 6½-year period; thus, the simple and cheap booby-trap proved to be a most cost-effective weapon.

Causes	Deaths	Wounds
Small arms	51%	16%
Fragments (mainly from shells and grenades)	36%	65%
Booby traps, mines	11%	15%
Punji stakes	—	2%
Other causes	2%	2%

Weapons of the Communist forces

Against the billion-dollar arsenals of the United States and South Vietnam, with the most sophisticated military equipment in the world, the Communist armies in Vietnam deployed a miscellaneous collection of weapons, some from Communist nations, although even the major suppliers, China and the USSR, refrained from sending their latest and best equipment; some captured from Free World forces; and some manufactured in-country in workshops widely dispersed to escape the effects of US bombing.

130mm M-46 field gun

The Soviet-designed 130mm M-46 field gun fires a 73.6lb (33.4kg) HE projectile to 33,900 yards (31,000m). The M-46 was normally used by the NVA against US Fire Support Bases; it outranged the US M102 105mm howitzer considerably, allowing NVA gunners to operate almost with impunity.

Type 56 assault rifle

A single sniper equipped with this weapon could hold a well-sited position against an entire company.

Type 56-1 assault rifle

The Chinese 7.62mm Type 56-1 assault rifle (above) is a copy of the Soviet AK-47; by 1968 most NVA and VC main force units were equipped with this reliable weapon.

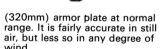

RPG-7 portable rocket launcher

The Soviet RPG-7 replaced the RPG-2 in service with the VC and NVA; small, light, and with a big "punch", it was an ideal weapon for them. The PG-7 grenade is percussion fired; when it has traveled 10.9 yards (10m) the rocket motor fires, propelling the missile out to 328 yards (500m). The warhead can penetrate 12in (320mm) armor plate at normal range. It is fairly accurate in still air, but less so in any degree of wind.

Soviet T-55 tank

The NVA first used the Soviet-supplied T-55 main battle tank in the attack on An Loc in 1972. The 35.9-ton tank mounts a 100mm D-10T gun and two 7.62mm PKT machine guns. It has a range of 310 miles (500km) at a maximum speed of 30mph (48km/h), with a 4-man crew. The NVA initially handled its T-55s most ineptly, but learned very quickly from its mistakes.

7.62mm K-50M SMG

The Type 50 sub-machine gun is a Chinese copy of the Soviet PPSh-41; many were supplied to the NVA and VC and the VC produced their own version—the K-50M, seen above—in jungle workshops. The solid butt of the original weapon is replaced by a French-style sliding wire butt-stock; the barrel jacket is shortened; the muzzle-brake is omitted; a pistol-grip is added; and the foresight is placed on the barrel. The SMG weighs 8.8lb (4.09kg) and has a 35-round magazine.

81mm mortar

This 81mm mortar manufactured in North Vietnam is a copy of the US 81mm M1 mortar. The mortar was a popular weapon with the NVA and VC because it could be broken down to three one-man loads.

Captured US M16 rifles

Despite prolific supplies from the countries of the Communist block, and their own limited production facilities, the NVA and VC were always short of weapons. These female Viet Cong members (right) carry captured US M16 rifles from the scene of an engagement.

7.62 MAT-49 Mod SMG

The Communists captured many 9mm MAT-49 sub-machine guns from the French. These were converted to take the Soviet 7.62 x 25 pistol cartridge by fitting a longer 7.62mm barrel (right).

PT-76 amphibious tank

The USSR supplied the NVA with the PT-76 amphibious tank in 1967. The AFV made its first appearance at the time of the Tet offensive of 1968, when it was used to overrun the US Special Forces camp at Lang Vei, near Khe Sanh, on 7 February. The 13.78-ton tank mounts a 76mm D-56T gun and a 7.62mm SGMT machine gun. It has a range of 155 miles (250km) at a maximum 27mph (44km/h) on land and 62.5 miles (100km) at a maximum 6.25mph (10km/h) on water. It has a crew of three and armor of 11 to 14mm.

75mm recoilless rifle

Recoilless rifles were popular with the NVA and VC because they combined firepower with light weight. The Chinese 75mm Recoilless Rifle, Type 52 (above) was a direct copy of the obsolete US M20, but its performance—firing an HE shell to a maximum range of 7,300 yards (6675m) or a HEAT shell to an effective range of 875 yards (800m)—was quite adequate for the needs of the Viet Cong.

Surveillance of the Communists

The darkness of night was one of the greatest tactical allies of the North Vietnamese Army and Viet Cong; there was at one stage a popular saying: "The night belongs to Charlie". The Communists invariably conducted approach marches, laid ambushes and moved supplies at night, and the United States and other Free World forces devoted great efforts to overcoming this, employing sophisticated surveillance devices including those shown here.

Remote surveillance of the Ho Chi Minh Trail

The Communists moved men and supplies down the Ho Chi Minh Trail (below) to operational areas in the South. The intelligence necessary to interdict this traffic by air attack was largely gathered by the Americans using remote means under the "Igloo White" program, which cost some $1.7 billion over the years 1966–71.

A. Principal means of remote surveillance used was the Air Delivered Seismic Intruder Device (ADSID, bottom right), dropped in planned patterns by F-4 Phantoms (**A**) using radar navigation techniques. The ADSID—36in (91.4cm) long and 6in (15.24cm) in diameter—fell freely and buried itself, leaving visible only a 4ft (120cm) antenna that blended into jungle foliage. It transmitted seismic intelligence automatically, with a battery life of 30–45 days.

B. A linear pattern of ADSIDs could be laid to detect vehicle movement.

C. A square pattern of ADSIDs could be laid to monitor movement in a vehicle park and storage area.

D. ADSIDs transmitted automatically to specially-modified aircraft like the Beech Model A36 Bonanza (QU-22A/B in USAF service). The QU-22B, designed to be pilotless, in fact carried a pilot on operations. With an on-station endurance of some 18 hours, the aircraft automatically relayed information from the sensors to the Infiltration Surveillance Center (**F**).

E. A Lockheed EC-121R worked in conjunction with the QU-22, relaying information.

F. The Infiltration Surveillance Center, far from the operational area, received relayed sensor transmissions and processed them through an IBM 360-65 computer, producing target information for air strikes.

G. Photographic reconnaissance supplemented the sensor effort. Typically a RF-4C Phantom would be used, with three systems: side-looking radar; infra-red detectors; and forward- and side-looking cameras.

H. The Teledyne-Ryan Model 147SC (USAF designation: AQM-34L) Remotely Piloted Vehicle (RPV) carried a 2,000-exposure camera and a TV system which transmitted real-time reconnaissance pictures to an airborne receiving station (**J**) at ranges up to 150 miles (240km). Photographic runs over the target were made at 1,500ft (450m); the RPV climbed to above 50,000ft (15,250m) for the flight home. Control was by pre-programmed on-board navigational system or by remote control from an airborne or ground control station.

Battlefield surveillance

(Right) Many battlefield surveillance aids in use about 1970 are illustrated in this diagram of a US Fire Support Base (FSB) in open country, near jungle and a village.

K. Information from these ADSIDs was fed to the FSB through EC-121R aircraft and the Infiltration Surveillance Center.

L. Laid on a track and at a junction would be unattended seismic detectors which passed their information direct to the FSB Command Post through buried cables (**M**).

N. Two trip-flares of different colors could be used at each site so the enemy's direction of travel could be determined. Weapons were constantly laid on such sites so fire could be brought down immediately.

P (diagram and above). The AN/PPS-5 radar gave long-range night detection up to 11,100yds (10,000m) against vehicles and 5,550yds (5,000m) against personnel. A skilled operator could indicate a target to an accuracy of ± 20 yds in direction and bearing.

Q. (diagram and above). Largest visual detector was the AN/TVS-4 Night Observation Device (NOD). On the ground or tripod-mounted

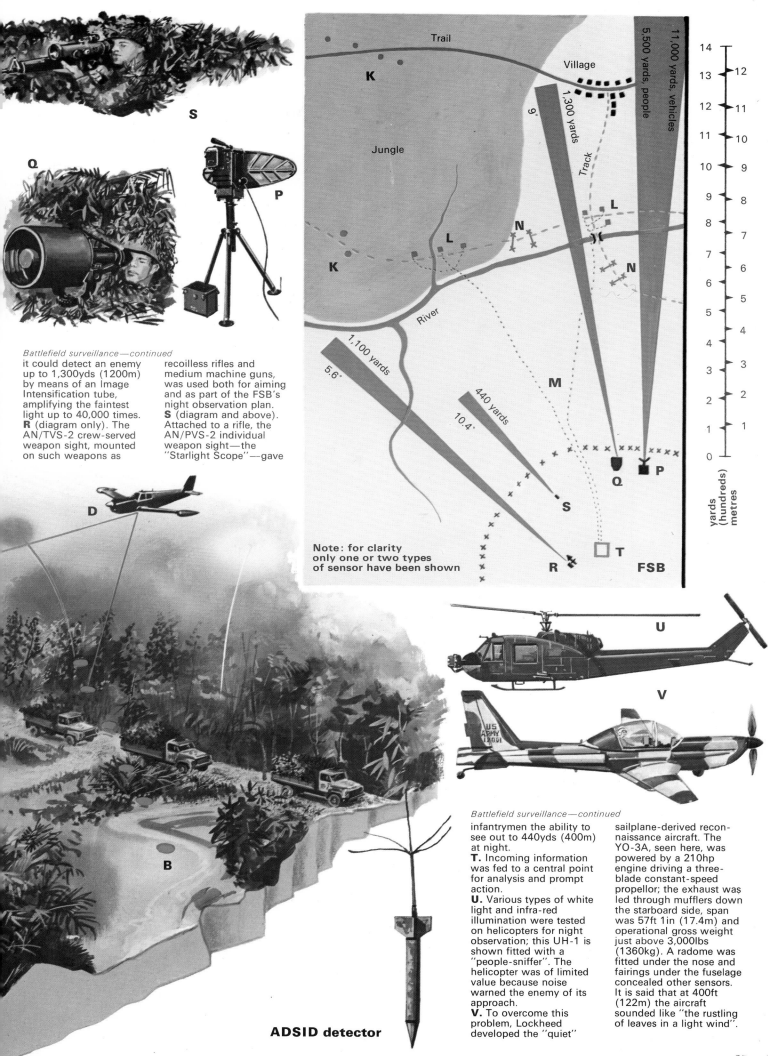

S

Q

P

K

Trail

Village

11,000 yards, vehicles

5,500 yards, people

9°

1,300 yards

Track

Jungle

L

N

K

L

N

River

1,100 yards

5.6°

440 yards

10.4°

M

S

Q

P

R

T

FSB

14
13
12
11
10
9
8
7
6
5
4
3
2
1
0

12
11
10
9
8
7
6
5
4
3
2
1

yards (hundreds) metres

Note: for clarity only one or two types of sensor have been shown

Battlefield surveillance—continued

it could detect an enemy up to 1,300yds (1200m) by means of an Image Intensification tube, amplifying the faintest light up to 40,000 times. **R** (diagram only). The AN/TVS-2 crew-served weapon sight, mounted on such weapons as

recoilless rifles and medium machine guns, was used both for aiming and as part of the FSB's night observation plan. **S** (diagram and above). Attached to a rifle, the AN/PVS-2 individual weapon sight—the "Starlight Scope"—gave

D

B

U

V

US ARMY 1X001

ADSID detector

Battlefield surveillance—continued

infantrymen the ability to see out to 440yds (400m) at night.
T. Incoming information was fed to a central point for analysis and prompt action.
U. Various types of white light and infra-red illumination were tested on helicopters for night observation; this UH-1 is shown fitted with a "people-sniffer". The helicopter was of limited value because noise warned the enemy of its approach.
V. To overcome this problem, Lockheed developed the "quiet"

sailplane-derived reconnaissance aircraft. The YO-3A, seen here, was powered by a 210hp engine driving a three-blade constant-speed propellor; the exhaust was led through mufflers down the starboard side, span was 57ft 1in (17.4m) and operational gross weight just above 3,000lbs (1360kg). A radome was fitted under the nose and fairings under the fuselage concealed other sensors. It is said that at 400ft (122m) the aircraft sounded like "the rustling of leaves in a light wind".

US Fire Support Base

An important American innovation in Vietnam was the Fire Support Base (FSB) which was established as a self-contained and self-defended artillery base from which infantry operations—usually "search and destroy" missions—could be supported. Because it was within range of the supported force, the support from the FSB was responsive, always available, and totally reliable, being able to function in conditions that precluded air support. In addition, since the North Vietnamese Army and and the Viet Cong regarded such field artillery bases as attractive and vulnerable targets, FSBs were sometimes deliberately disposed to invite retaliatory action, tempting the Communists to concentrate attacking forces where they could be engaged and destroyed. A typical Fire Support Base could be expected to deploy a battery of six M102 105mm field howitzers; an infantry company for local defense; four 81mm mortars from an infantry battalion; and communications, medical and administrative personnel. The FSB was never isolated from support from other units; supporting fire from other FSBs could always be called upon, together with helicopter gunships and tactical air support.

Construction and layout of a Fire Support Base

There was a standard drill for construction of a Fire Support Base. After reconnaissance and site selection, a stake was positioned at the center of the chosen site and a 131ft (40m) rope was used to mark the bunker line. This line was marked by stakes at 15ft intervals to indicate the infantry bunker positions. A circle of 246ft (75m) radius marked the line of the perimeter wire. At each bunker stake helicopters dropped a standard pack of one shaped demolition charge, two sheets of pierced-steel planking, and empty sandbags, which were used to construct a 9ft (2.7m) bunker. Bulldozers excavated ground for the command post and fire support coordination center, and pits for the guns and mortars. A prefabricated 20ft (6m) observation tower was flown in by a CH-47 Chinook helicopter. Time of construction varied—but it was essential that the outer defenses and infantry positions were completed by last light on the first day of occupation of the FSB site.

The FSB shown here is well established, and comprises:
A. Two triple M102 105mm howitzer emplacements.
B. Two twin 81mm mortar positions (to fire HE or provide close-in illumination during enemy night attacks).

C. Command Post.
D. Observation Tower.
E. Fire Support Coordination Center.
F. Communications Center.
G. Administration, cookhouse, and stores.
H. Ground surveillance and anti-personnel radar emplacements.
J. Night observation devices: searchlights for visible or infra-red illumination.
K. Bunkers for an infantry company with rifles, grenade launchers, machine guns, and recoilless rifles. (The perfect circle seen here, at 131ft/40m radius, was the ideal configuration, seldom achieved because of variations in terrain.)
L. Helicopter landing area.
M. A CH-54 Tarhe helicopter, capable of lifting a 155mm howitzer as a single load, delivers up to 18,000lbs (6714kg) of cargo by sling.
N. Camouflaged claymore mines and trip flares between infantry bunkers and perimeter wire all round the base.
P. Triple-dannert barbed wire (ie, three coils in pyramid structure) all round.
Q. Guarded exit/entry point for aggressive and continuous infantry patrols around FSB.
R. Aerial rocket artillery support from a "Huey" helicopter carrying between 48 (UH-1B/-1C) and 76 (AH-1G) 2.75in rockets.

Howitzer emplacement

Semi-permanent emplacement in a Fire Support Base for a 105mm self-propelled howitzer:
1. Sandbag wall and cover.
2. Section equipment and tool room.
3. Ammunition racks, with HE, ICM (fragmentation), smoke, illumination, chemical, and propaganda rounds in segregation.
4. Standing for howitzer: pierced-steel planking, gravel, or cement.
5. Powder pit.
6. Crew ready room.
7. Crew quarters.
8. Fire barrels.

Mutual support

(Below) Mutual support between Fire Support Base was always available. The FSB in foreground has come under a major enemy attack (**A**), and a diversionary attack (**B**), so it calls in supporting fire from two other FSBs, as well as air support from helicopter gunships.

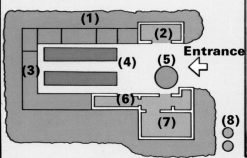

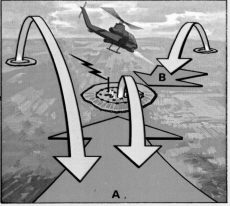

The infantry in battle

In Vietnam, as in all conventional warfare up to the present day, the heaviest combat burden was borne by the infantry. The illustrations here show some of the combat activities of the US and ARVN infantryman in Vietnam, with (far right) a detailed plan of a classic infantry battle at battalion level. In spite of massive air support, the implementation of the airmobility concept in such a way as to give new meaning to the term "war of movement", and the development and deployment on a huge scale of sophisticated hardware, the US/ARVN infantryman in Vietnam faced a daunting task. It was a war without front lines where the doctrines of earlier wars meant little. It was fought against an enemy who was, in the case of the Viet Cong guerrillas, often indistinguishable from the civilian population and who tended to avoid open combat in favor of ambush and terror. As well as meeting the enemy in battle, every infantryman also had to fight the campaign to win the hearts and minds of the people of Southeast Asia from Communism. Thus, the waging of conventional warfare was only one part of the task of the men on the ground.

The Claymore mine

The Claymore mine (below) was first tested in combat in Vietnam. Invaluable in ambushes, it was fired remotely, and was often sited so that lethal areas overlapped (right); the mine fired horizontally, covering an area some 6ft (1.8m) high out to 54yds (50m), and could be precisely aimed.

A classic infantry battle in South Vietnam

The battle setting
The action illustrated on the right took place near Phong Cao in the highlands of Phu Yen province on 6–11 November 1966. Steeply sloping hills made movement difficult and thick jungle imposed poor visibility and navigational problems.

Opening situation
The 5th Battalion, 95th Infantry Regiment, North Vietnamese Army (5/95 NVA), only 214 strong, awaits reinforcements. It must re-train, while engaging small enemy patrols but withdrawing if faced by superior forces. Its base camps are in the saddle between Hills 450 and 350. The 2nd Battalion (Airborne), US 502nd Infantry Regiment (2/502 USA) knows there is an enemy camp on Hill 450. Realizing the enemy will avoid a superior force, the US C.O. plans to land troops by helicopter west of Hill 450, lead off in the wrong direction, and then swing eastward toward the objective.

Phase I, 6–8 November
The helicopter fly-in is successful and Companies A, B, and C (**Cy A, B, C**), and the Reconnaissance/Commando (Recondo) Platoon, 50 strong, move out in a direction that will not alarm 5/95 NVA. After a few contacts—5 enemy killed on 6 November; brief encounters on 7 November (red flashes)—the whole battalion swings eastward at noon on 8 November. By dusk, Recondo scouts can observe enemy on Hill 450 without themselves being seen.

The US battle plan
The C.O. plans for 2/502 USA to surround and eliminate the enemy on Hill 450: Company A will move by helicopter to a blocking position in the northeast sector; Company B will provide one force to attack from the west and another to block in the south; Company C will make a forced march to take up the southeast sector; Recondo Platoon (**R**) will block in the north.

Phase 2, 9 November
At 1000 hours on 9 November, Section A, Recondo Platoon, bumps an enemy platoon on the western slope of Hill 450 and reports its position. 2 Platoon, Company B, quickly joins the fight. 3 Platoon, Company B, is moving north to the supposed position of the fight when the commander realizes the firing is behind him; he reaches the action around noon. The C.O. carries out a noon helicopter reconnaissance to resolve the confusion, finding that the fighting is not on Hill 450 but on Hill 350. He calls in an airstrike, but bomb fragments fall among his own platoons, so he calls in helicopter gunships, followed by an artillery bombardment. When this ends, 2 and 3 Platoons, Company B, charge up the hill, clear the remaining enemy, and dig in.

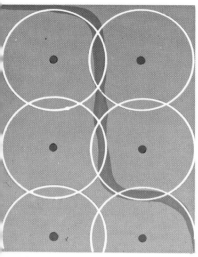

The battle setting

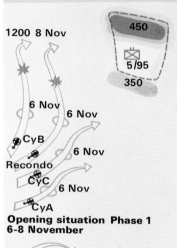

Opening situation Phase 1 6-8 November

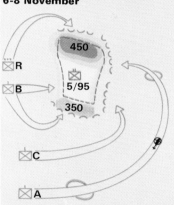

The US battle plan

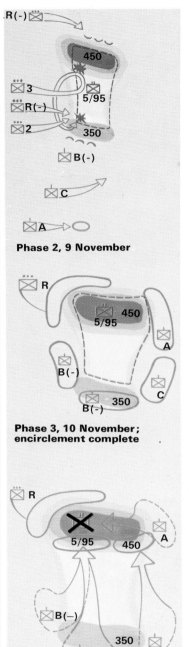

Phase 2, 9 November

Phase 3, 10 November; encirclement complete

Phase 4, 11 November; the enemy eliminated

Phase 3, 10 November
The rest of 2/502 USA is in position by last light and encirclement of 5/95 NVA is completed during the night with illumination provided first by mortar flares and later by a C-47 flare-ship. Throughout 10 November, 5/95 NVA probes the circle, losing 12 men killed. In the afternoon the Americans use loudspeakers without apparent effect. By nightfall the circle has closed to some 600 yards in diameter.

Phase 4, 11 November
During the night five NVA probes are easily repulsed. In the morning Companies B and C move up the southern slope of Hill 450 with a loudspeaker team. An NVA soldier surrenders and uses the loudspeaker to appeal to his comrades to join him; a number quickly do so. When Companies B and C reach the top of Hill 450, Company A sweeps across from east to west and eliminates the last elements of the enemy.

The tally
36 NVA soldiers are captured and 39 bodies found, for US losses of 5 killed and 15 wounded. Five mortars, 11 machine guns, and 44 rifles are captured, as well as much equipment and ammunition. Some enemy escape, but many more are killed or wounded: 5th Battalion, 95th Infantry Regiment, North Vietnamese Army, has ceased to exist.

The helicopter and airmobility

The helicopter was used in assault operations in Korea, at Suez, and in Algeria, but the concept of helicopter-borne airmobility was not fully realized until the US involvement in Southeast Asia. It was a bold and imaginative development which enabled security forces to place a large force at the required location rapidly and at short notice. But the fact that airmobile units tended to operate from a fixed base, emerging by air to deal with specific incidents and then returning by air to base, limited the contact of the force with the indigenous population. Thus the concept was of limited value in the "hearts and minds" campaign fundamental to counter-revolutionary war.

The assault force lands

Bell UH-1Ds with a maximum capacity of 14 men and a range of up to 327 miles (526km) were normally the first to land (**A**). Next, also in the first wave were wide-bodied Boeing-Vertol CH-47 Chinooks (**B**), each carrying up to 44 troops and having a normal mission radius of 115 miles (185km) with a 10,366lb (4729kg) pay-load. In the second wave were more CH-47s (**C**), with loads slung beneath them on strops. Here, the leader carries a 155mm wheeled gun with an ammunition pallet suspended from it; the second has ammunition in a cargo sling. Overhead, Cessna A-37 Dragonfly ground attack aircraft (**D**) stood by to give offensive air support.

LZ control party

The members of the Landing Zone Control Party (left) deployed from the first UH-1D to land and exerted ground control over landing operations. They were in radio contact with the air-mobile force commander, in his airborne CP (see opposite, above), and with the helicopters of the "Pink Team" (see right) which carried out low-level reconnaissance operations near the landing zone.

"Pink Team"

"Pink Team" reconnaissance mission included a Hughes OH-6 Cayuse (left) carrying out a low-level search, following trails, flying fast and low over suspected enemy positions, and examining clearings. The Bell AH-1G Huey Cobra gunship guarded the OH-6, providing suppressive fire and relaying information when its partner's radio was "screened" by trees or hills.

The force commander

The airmobile force commander (right) controlled operations from a Bell UH-1D fitted as an airborne Command Post (CP). In addition to its normal radio rig it carried an AN/ASC-15 console which provided three secure UHF/FM speech links. A typical command team consisted of the force commander, a staff officer, the air liaison officer (controlling offensive air support), and the artillery support liaison officer (responsible for calling up fire from fire support bases within range).

Recovery and observation

The CH-54 Tarhe "Sky Crane" (lower right) can carry a payload of 15,400lbs or an external load of 20,760lbs. Its use in airmobile operations included the transportation and positioning of heavy artillery and the recovery of downed aircraft.
The Bell OH-58A Kiowa (bottom right) carries up to four passengers and was typically used for visual observation and target acquisition.

The force commander

Recovery and observation

Casualty evacuation from the battlefield

The helicopter made a very significant contribution to casualty evacuation in Southeast Asia. Nearly all US and ARVN battlefield casualties were helilifted to rear areas. Transport aircraft of the US Air Force were used for the evacuation of patients needing major medical facilities in Southeast Asia or in the United States; the USAF's Military Airlift Command evacuated a total of 406,022 patients, including 168,832 battle casualties, between 1965 and 1973.

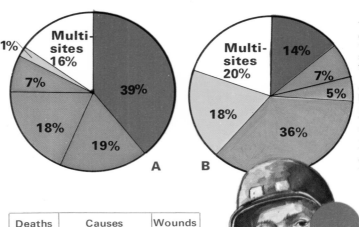

A B

Location of wounds

The two segmented circles, color-keyed to the figure of the soldier, shows the location of fatal (**A**, far left) and non-fatal wounds (**B**) in casualties reaching hospitals. A high proportion of fatalities were due to head and neck wounds; this was attributed by medical staff to the reluctance of troops engaged in violent activity to wear helmets.

Causes of casualties

The proportion of deaths from small arms in Southeast Asia (see table, right) showed a marked increase over World War II (32 per cent) and Korea (33 per cent) and was mainly due to the advent of the lightweight, high-velocity rounds fired by the Soviet AK–47 (and captured American M16s). These bullets caused large entry and exit wounds, left severe tissue damage, and affected blood vessels out of the direct path of the missile. These weapons' rapid-fire capability increased the proportion of multiple wounds. Wounds caused by mines and booby-traps were often very large and dirty, because the victim was usually close to the device when it exploded. The figures here are averaged over the years 1965–70; actual proportions varied year to year.

Deaths	Causes	Wounds
51%	small arms	16%
36%	fragments from artillery	65%
11%	booby traps, mines	15%
—	punji stakes	2%
2%	others	2%

Serious casualties, Allied forces, 1966-1971

The numbers of serious casualties sustained during the years 1966–1971 by US (red), South Vietnamese (green), and Allied (orange) troops are shown below. The death ratio for those who reached US hospitals was 2.6 per cent, a very significant improvement on the 4.5 per cent death rate of World War II. The ratio would have been even more favorable had it not been for the helicopter, which delivered to hospital a proportion of mortally-wounded soldiers who would have died on the battlefield in previous conflicts. Of the wounded who survived, a massive 83 per cent were able to return to military duty either in South Vietnam or in the United States.

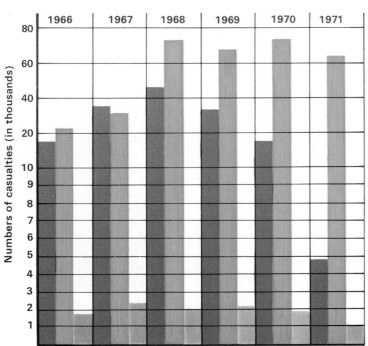

Helicopter ambulances

Any helicopter was, of course, capable of carrying wounded from battlefields in South Vietnam, but specialized units were also formed; at the peak of US involvement there were 116 Bell UH-1 helicopter ambulances in service, fitted to carry six litter patients. Each US division had a medical battalion and most of these had helicopter ambulances whose task, in theory, was to evacuate casualties from the battlefield to a medical clearing station. From there—again in theory—non-divisional helicopters collected the patient and took him to a field hospital. But in practice helicopter resources were used according to the situation; the main criterion was that the patient should reach a suitable medical facility in the shortest possible time.

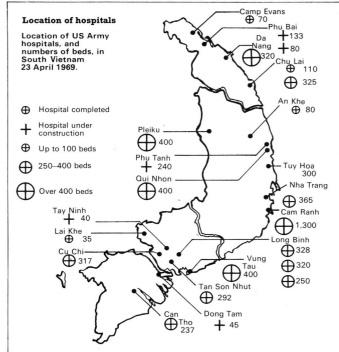

Location of hospitals

Location of US Army hospitals, and numbers of beds, in South Vietnam 23 April 1969.

⊕ Hospital completed

✛ Hospital under construction

⊕ Up to 100 beds

⊕ 250–400 beds

⊕ Over 400 beds

Camp Evans ⊕ 70
Phu Bai ✛ 133
Da Nang ✛ 80
⊕ 320
Chu Lai ⊕ 110
⊕ 325
An Khe ⊕ 80
Pleiku ⊕ 400
Phu Tanh ✛ 240
Qui Nhon ⊕ 400
Tuy Hoa ✛ 300
Nha Trang
⊕ 365
Cam Ranh ⊕ 1,300
Tay Ninh ✛ 40
Lai Khe ⊕ 35
Long Binh ⊕ 328
Cu Chi ⊕ 317
⊕ 320
Vung Tau ⊕ 400
⊕ 250
Tan Son Nhut ⊕ 292
Can Tho ⊕ 237
Dong Tam ✛ 45

Helicopter hoist

Unable to land, the helicopter lowered a hoist, using a spring-loaded "forest penetrator" to avoid entanglement with trees. While in the hover the helicopter was an easy target for enemy fire (35 were hit in 1968; 39 in 1969), but many thousands of men were rescued who would otherwise have had to be carried to a site where a landing could be made, with a consequent delay in medical care.

Emergency landing area

"Dust-Off" Bell UH-1Hs—named from the radio call-sign of Major Charles Kelly, a famed pilot killed in action in 1964—landed in emergency clearings made by explosives and chain-saws. Many obstacles remained that could have pierced the vulnerable underside of the helicopter's fuselage, and enemy were often in the vicinity. The helicopters were crewed by two pilots, a flight crewman, and a medical aidman to give emergency treatment in the air. In earlier conflicts, casualties in such a remote area would have had an agonising journey on a stretcher in which the chances of death from wounds or shock would have been far greater. Between 1965 and 1969, 372,947 casualties were evacuated by helicopter (this figure includes US personnel, ARVN and Free World troops, and civilians).

North Vietnamese air defense systems

Launching sites for Soviet-built SA-2 Guideline surface-to-air missiles first appeared in North Vietnam in July 1965; numbers built up rapidly, until by 1972 there were some 300 sites throughout the country, and even inside and south of the Demilitarized Zone. The US Air Force countered the SA-2 by destroying missile sites, by violent evasive action, by avoiding tight formations, by varying tactics, and by electronic countermeasures (ECM).

Surface-to-air missile site
(Right) Six SA-2 missiles (**A**)—of which four are seen here—are on their launchers, equally spaced at about 55yds (50m) from the central Command Post (**B**). Roadways to each launcher give access for workshop and reloading vehicles (**C**); bamboo mats (**D**) cover cable ducts and reinforce road surfaces in bad weather. The Spoon Rest A radar (**E**) gives early warning. Missile guidance depends on the Fan Song radar (**F**), which acquires the target and feeds data to a computer. Commands from the computer are transmitted to the missile over a UHF link, vectoring it into the radar beam to intercept.

Twin 37mm AA gun M38/39
(Left) This Soviet-designed 37mm twin AA gun is mounted on a 4-wheeled trailer. Used only with optical sights, it fires a 1.58lb (725gm) shell to an effective AA range of 1,640yds (1500m). Its rate of fire is 180 rounds per minute, and its elevation is from —5° to +85°.

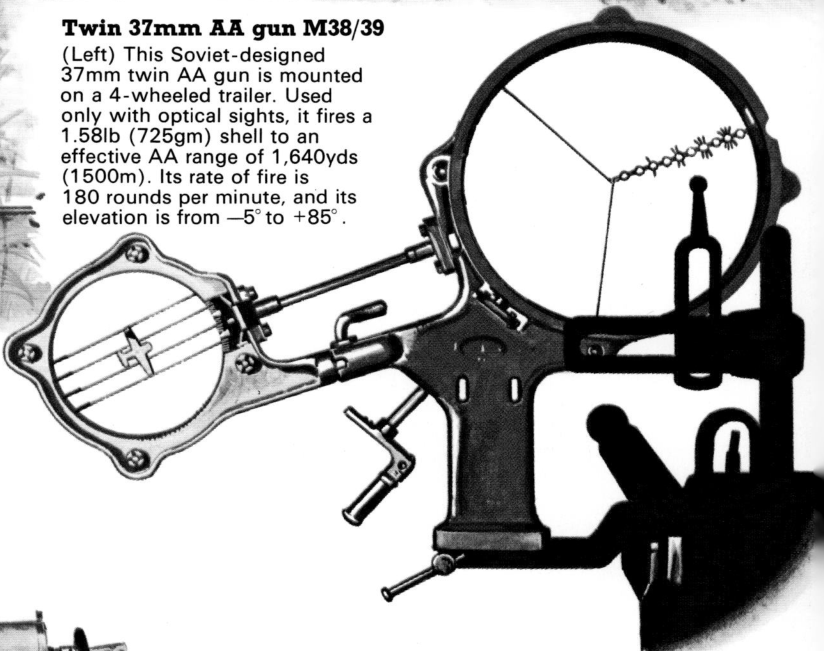

Optical anti-aircraft sights
(Right) These rather basic optical sights were fitted to a Chinese-supplied machine gun captured from the Viet Cong in Long An province, South Vietnam, in November 1963. To the surprise of experts, small arms and machine gun fire accounted for so many US aircraft that, late in 1964, pilots striking at North Vietnamese targets abandoned low-altitude, high-speed tactics in favor of dive-bombing attacks from 15,000–20,000ft (4570–6095m).

Chinese Type 24 7.92mm heavy machine gun
(Left) The first line of North Vietnam's air defenses consisted of normal infantry weapons, of which the heavy machine gun was the most effective. Seen here is a Chinese-supplied Type 24 7.92mm MG, a copy of the German 08 Maxim of World War I vintage.

Length: 55in (1398mm)
Weight: 39lb (17.7kg)
Barrel: 24in (610mm)
Rifling: 4 groove r/hand
Operation: recoil
Feed: 250-round belt
Cooling: water
Cyclic rate: 400 rpm
Muzzle velocity: 2,900ft (885m) per second.

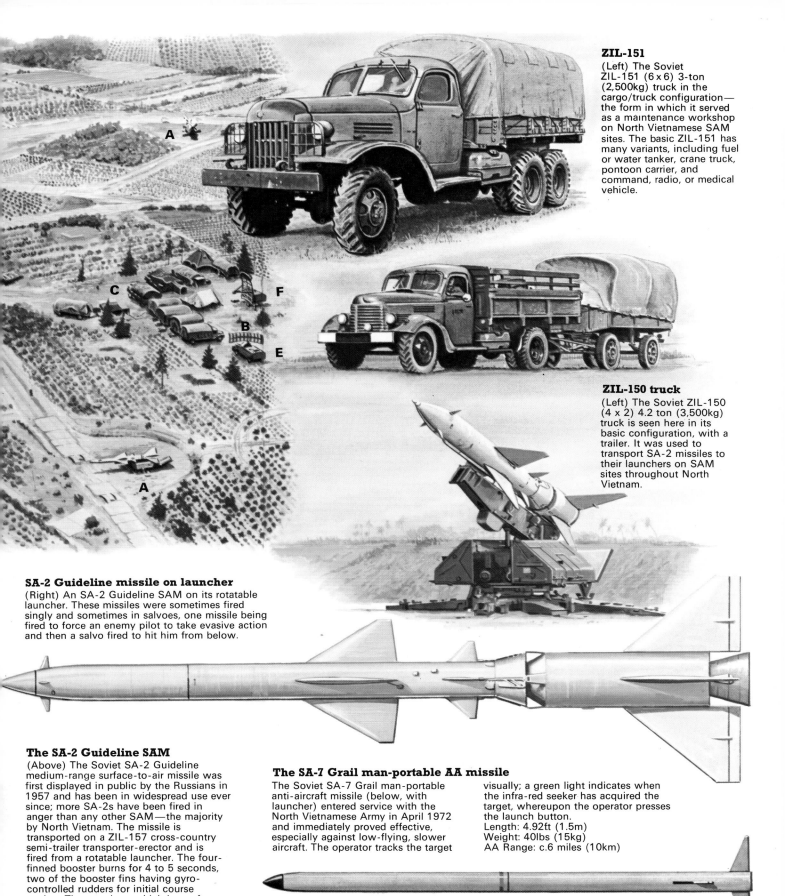

ZIL-151

(Left) The Soviet ZIL-151 (6 x 6) 3-ton (2,500kg) truck in the cargo/truck configuration—the form in which it served as a maintenance workshop on North Vietnamese SAM sites. The basic ZIL-151 has many variants, including fuel or water tanker, crane truck, pontoon carrier, and command, radio, or medical vehicle.

ZIL-150 truck

(Left) The Soviet ZIL-150 (4 x 2) 4.2 ton (3,500kg) truck is seen here in its basic configuration, with a trailer. It was used to transport SA-2 missiles to their launchers on SAM sites throughout North Vietnam.

SA-2 Guideline missile on launcher

(Right) An SA-2 Guideline SAM on its rotatable launcher. These missiles were sometimes fired singly and sometimes in salvoes, one missile being fired to force an enemy pilot to take evasive action and then a salvo fired to hit him from below.

The SA-2 Guideline SAM

(Above) The Soviet SA-2 Guideline medium-range surface-to-air missile was first displayed in public by the Russians in 1957 and has been in widespread use ever since; more SA-2s have been fired in anger than any other SAM—the majority by North Vietnam. The missile is transported on a ZIL-157 cross-country semi-trailer transporter-erector and is fired from a rotatable launcher. The four-finned booster burns for 4 to 5 seconds, two of the booster fins having gyro-controlled rudders for initial course setting. The sustainer, which burns for some 22 seconds, is fueled by nitric acid and a liquid hydrocarbon (probably kerosene). The missile has cruciform delta wings and steerable fins. Four small canard surfaces are mounted just aft of the tail-cone.

Guidance: radio command
Propulsion: solid-propellant booster
   liquid-propellant sustainer
Warhead: 348.5lb (130kg) HE
Fusing: contact, proximity, command
Missile length: 35ft (10.7m)
Slant range: 25–31 miles (40–50km)
Ceiling: 59,060ft (18,000m)

The SA-7 Grail man-portable AA missile

The Soviet SA-7 Grail man-portable anti-aircraft missile (below, with launcher) entered service with the North Vietnamese Army in April 1972 and immediately proved effective, especially against low-flying, slower aircraft. The operator tracks the target visually; a green light indicates when the infra-red seeker has acquired the target, whereupon the operator presses the launch button.
Length: 4.92ft (1.5m)
Weight: 40lbs (15kg)
AA Range: c.6 miles (10km)

The electronic war in the air

The electronic battle was a long and bloody struggle in which the combat elements on both sides looked to their scientists and technicians for new measures and counter-measures and each advance by one side brought a counter from the other. Nowhere was this more clearly demonstrated than in the battle between US aircraft and surface-to-air missiles over North Vietnam.

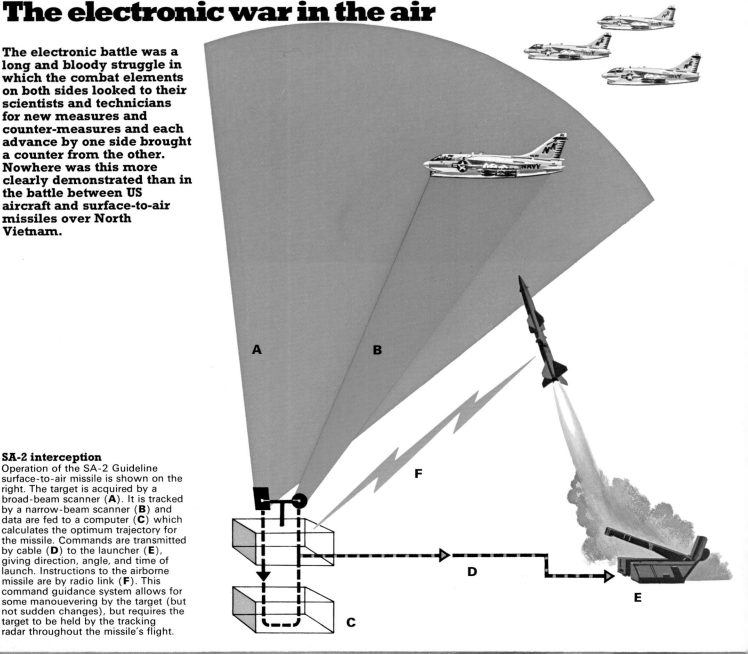

SA-2 interception
Operation of the SA-2 Guideline surface-to-air missile is shown on the right. The target is acquired by a broad-beam scanner (**A**). It is tracked by a narrow-beam scanner (**B**) and data are fed to a computer (**C**) which calculates the optimum trajectory for the missile. Commands are transmitted by cable (**D**) to the launcher (**E**), giving direction, angle, and time of launch. Instructions to the airborne missile are by radio link (**F**). This command guidance system allows for some manouevering by the target (but not sudden changes), but requires the target to be held by the tracking radar throughout the missile's flight.

Low-level attack
One of the earliest US counters to the SAM was an approach to the target at very low level (above right), using two prominent ground features to locate the target. At the "initial point" (**A**, at island) the pilot changed course on to a planned bearing which brought him, after a known time, to the "pitch-up point" (**B**, at pagoda), where he made a wing-level pull-up, climbed in a carefully planned manouever to a set height (**C**), and then dived on the target (**D**). (The red line indicates the ground track taken by the attacking aircraft.) The fault of this tactic was that it brought the aircraft within range of anti-aircraft and small arms fire on the

long, low-level approach. This caused an unacceptable loss rate. Further, the "pop-up" manouever, however carefully planned, gave the pilot very little time to make a positive indentification of the target, thus contributing to inaccuracy. New measures to counter the surface-to-air missile threat had to be sought.

"Chaff" corridor
Another counter to SAMs was to lay a "chaff" corridor of millions of pieces of silver foil cut to the right lengths to interfere with enemy radar frequencies. If the chaff was correctly sown, strike aircraft could fly through the corridor with no threat from SAMs. But F-4s or A-7s sowing chaff

from underwing dispensers had to fly in formation (**A**) at reduced speed, straight and level, and were vulnerable to SAM and MiG attack (**B**). They carried electronic countermeasures pods which jammed the SAM radars so that these could not determine range and bearing, but to counter the MiGs, the chaff-sowing planes had to have their own MIGCAP (combat air patrol) cover (**C**).

Shrike anti-radar missile

One counter to the SAM was the AGM-45A Shrike anti-radar missile with a range of 2.6nm (5km), whose operation is shown on the right. The pilot detected the transmissions of the missile's target acquisition radar (**A**) and when within range launched the Shrike, which flew straight down the radar beam (**B**) guided by an on-board detector.

(Far Right) After the Shrike's early successes, the North Vietnamese countered it by ceasing to use the SA-2's target acquisition radar and gathering information on US aircraft positions on remote EW/GCI radars (**C**). The tracking radar at the missile site was kept on "dummy load" (warmed up but not transmitting) and switched to "operate" only when the US aircraft was within range. The missile was launched almost immediately, guided, and the radar was then switched back to "dummy load".

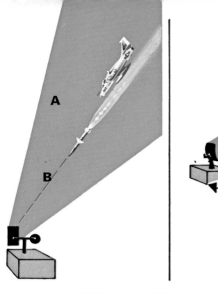

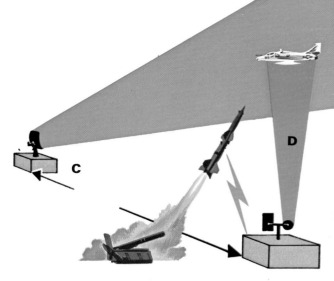

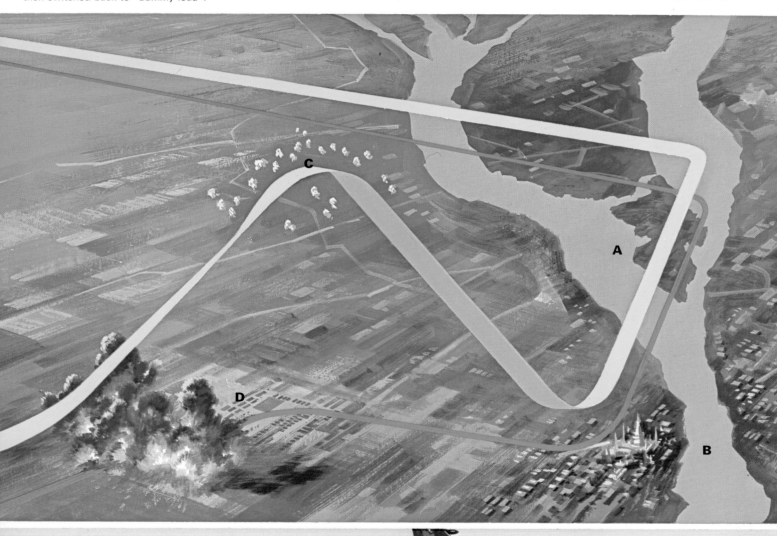

Rescue of downed aircrew

The Americans made prodigious efforts to rescue downed aircrew, both in South and North Vietnam, and this was naturally a considerable morale booster for the crews themselves. The helicopter, with its unique ability either to land in a restricted area or to hover and winch up the survivors, played a major part. The agencies involved in such an operation were numerous, even in a straightforward operation in the South, and the hazards to the rescuers were such that it could become very costly. Illustrated here are the various elements involved in a typical rescue mission in the northern part of South Vietnam, in 1972.

Forward air control
Rockwell International OV-10 Bronco aircraft, acting as Forward Air Controllers, keep radio contact with the survivors from the downed aircraft, with support and rescue aircraft, and with the US Navy vessel offshore.

Enemy countermeasures
An SA-2 Guideline surface-to-air missile is fired at the rescue aircraft from a North Vietnamese missile installation. The Soviet-supplied SA-2 has a slant range of some 25 miles (40km).

Radar picket

The Lockheed EC-121 Warning Star acting as radar picket monitors the missile launch. The EC-121 passes information on enemy aerial countermeasures to the US Navy "Red Crown" vessel for evaluation and relay to the rescue force.

G: The rescue force

A typical rescue mission

A. The survivors from a shot-down US aircraft (seen burning in the jungle) have parachuted safely and are sheltering in a thicket on the edge of a jungle clearing some distance from the nearest friendly ground troops (**E**).

B. Overhead are two Rockwell OV-10 Bronco aircraft acting as Forward Air Controllers (FACs). The USAF OV-10, a twin-engined, twin-boomed reconnaissance aircraft, is fitted with the "Pave Nail" system, which includes night sights, a target illuminator, and special electronics. The OV-10s seen here are in radio contact with the survivors, with fire support and rescue forces (black dotted lines), and with the US Navy vessel offshore (blue dotted line).

C. Enemy activity in the area includes infantry eager to capture the downed aircrew, AAA up to 100mm caliber, and SA-2 Guideline surface-to-air missiles.

D. Attack aircraft are called in by the FACs to strike at any enemy forces who threaten the rescue effort. Two Cessna A-37s are seen here; originally built as trainers, a number of these were converted into very useful close-support aircraft, carrying various combinations of stores, including six 500lb (226kg) bombs.

E. The FACs call in artillery support from a conveniently-situated Fire Support Base.

F. Some distance away from the action flies an EC-121 radar picket aircraft, a modified Lockheed Super Constellation, watching for MiG take-offs and SAM launches, which might threaten the rescue force and supporting forces. Here, the EC-121 passes real-time information on the missile launch (blue dotted line) to a specially-equipped US Navy warship —code-named "Red Crown"—patrolling in the Gulf of Tonkin. "Red Crown" analyses all information from the airborne pickets and rapidly relays the necessary instructions to the threatened aircraft.

G. The rescue force is brought in. It comprises:

H. Two Sikorsky HH-53C transport helicopters. The HH-53C is a developed version of the "Jolly Green Giant", fitted with an in-flight refueling probe, two jettisonable 450 gallon US (1703 liter) fuel tanks, and a special rescue hoist with 250ft (76m) of cable.

J. The helicopters are refueled before beginning the run-in. The refueling aircraft is a Lockheed HC-130P Hercules, one of twenty HC-130Hs converted for the in-flight refueling of helicopters. In a typical mission the HC-130P carries 73,601lb (33,385kg) of fuel; it meets up with the helicopters some 575 miles (925km) from base, passes over 48,500lb (22,000kg) of fuel, and then returns to base.

K. Escorting the helicopters are six Douglas A-1 Skyraiders; piston-engined aircraft, code-named "Sandy". Although the slow speed of the A-1 makes it more vulnerable to ground fire than jet aircraft, it is much better suited to operations in marginal weather conditions, especially during the monsoon seasons, when low ceilings and poor visibility are often encountered.

During one rescue mission, the navigator of a downed EB-66 spent 12 days in the jungle just south of the Demilitarized Zone (DMZ). In attempts to extricate him, three helicopters were shot down by AAA fire and an OV-10 was destroyed by a direct hit from an SA-2. Seven aircrew were killed, one was captured, and one was himself rescued after ten days on the ground.

Air attack on North Vietnam

A bombing operation against North Vietnam was a complex undertaking, involving many aspects of US air power. Illustrated here are the various air components of a mission during the "Linebacker I" bombing campaign of May-October 1972. The central plan view shows the strike group and supporting aircraft; other support groups are shown upper left and right. The lower illustration shows a raid with "Smart" bomb bombs on the Thanh Hoa bridge, also during "Linebacker I". As can be seen, escort and supporting aircraft might outnumber the strike force, but despite this back-up strength the US Air Force did not achieve total air supremacy in "Linebacker I", during which 44 US aircraft were lost: 27 were shot down by MiG interceptors; 12 fell to surface-to-air missiles (SAMs); and 5 were lost to anti-aircraft artillery fire.

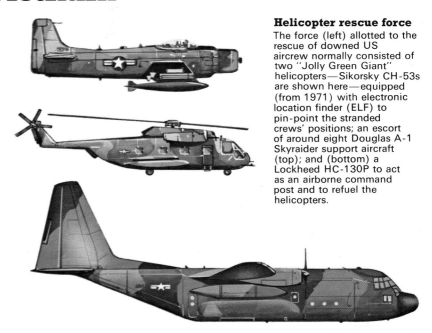

Helicopter rescue force
The force (left) allotted to the rescue of downed US aircrew normally consisted of two "Jolly Green Giant" helicopters—Sikorsky CH-53s are shown here—equipped (from 1971) with electronic location finder (ELF) to pin-point the stranded crews' positions; an escort of around eight Douglas A-1 Skyraider support aircraft (top); and (bottom) a Lockheed HC-130P to act as an airborne command post and to refuel the helicopters.

Strike group and escort
(Right) The heart of the raiding force is the Strike Group (**A**) comprising 32 McDonnell Douglas F-4E Phantom IIs carrying a mix of "iron (conventional) bombs" and "Smart" laser guided bombs. The Strike Group is preceded by "Iron Hand" flights and "chaff" bombers (see extreme right) and receives close-in protection from F-4E Phantoms configured for air-to-air combat (**B**). The outer defense against enemy fighters is provided by roving flights of Phantoms on MiG Combat Air Patrols/MIGCAP (**C**). Finally, some distance behind the Strike Group, come two McDonnell Douglas RF-4C reconnaissance aircraft (**D**), responsible for photographing the target after the raid so that accurate assessments of the damage may be made.

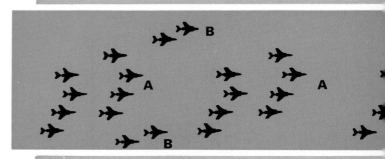

Attack on the Thanh Hoa Bridge
The Thanh Hoa rail and highway bridge, some 70 miles south of Hanoi, was a key link in North Vietnam's transportation system and was listed as a vital target for destruction from April 1964. During "Operation Rolling Thunder", from 2 March 1965 to 31 October 1968, some 700 sorties (in which eight US aircraft were lost) were flown against the bridge—which remained open. It was badly damaged on 27 April 1972 by USAF F-4 Phantoms with 2,000lb "Smart" laser guided bombs and was closed for several months after a similar raid by Phantoms armed with 2,000lb and 3,000lb laser guided bombs during "Linebacker I" operations on 13 May 1972.

Supporting aircraft

(Right) Supporting the Strike Group are the Douglas EB-66 "Brown Cradle" electronic countermeasures (ECM) aircraft (top) to jam/suppress AAA and SAM radars (although US fighters carried their own ECM pods from 1967–68, EB-66s remained in service); the Lockheed EC-121D "Big Eye" (center), exerting airborne command and control and equipped with search radar and radio relay transmitters to determine the range and altitude of enemy interceptors and issue warnings to friendly aircraft; and the Boeing KC-135 Stratotanker (bottom), the "gas station in the sky", with more than 30,000 gallons of fuel for pre- and post-strike aerial refueling of bombers, fighters, and supporting aircraft.

The "Chaff" bombers

(Right) The "chaff" bombers—eight A-7 Corsair IIs (**F**)—followed about 2–3 minutes behind the "Iron Hand" flights. They laid a "chaff" carpet, through which the strike force flew, to mask enemy radars and help frustrate SAM attacks. Heavily laden and flying straight and level in precise formation, they were very vulnerable and, in addition to their own ECM equipment, needed the protection of a close escort of two flights of F-4E Phantoms (**G**), flying some two miles behind on either flank, to guard against MiG interceptors.

"Iron Hand" flights

(Above) Leading the raiding force would be two "Iron Hand" flights (**E**), each of two F-4E Phantoms with Sparrow AAMs and cluster bombs and two Republic F-105G Thunderchief "Wild Weasels" with anti-radiation missiles to locate and destroy SAM sites and their radars.

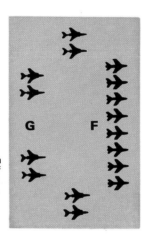

"Smart" bomb

The "Smart" laser guided bomb used against the Thanh Hoa bridge (left) comprises a laser sensor attached to a 2,000lb (746kg) or 3,000lb (1119kg) bomb. A pod under the aircraft contains an optical viewer and a laser. The Weapons Systems Officer acquires the target with the optical system and illuminates it with the laser. The LGBs are launched and ride down the laser "basket" to impact on the point illuminated. Because the target must be continuously illuminated until impact, the system is sensitive to clouds and rain.
(Right) The Weapons System Officer of an F-4E Phantom checks out a 2,000lb LGB loaded on his aircraft before taking off for a strike mission.

Air-to-air combat

From 1950 onward US aviation personnel of all services were sent to Southeast Asia as advisers, maintenance and supply experts, and combat crews, first in support of the the French colonial regime and then to strengthen the resistance of the democracies of South Vietnam, Laos, and Cambodia to Communist aggression. US aircraft flew reconnaissance and defoliation missions from 1961; interception missions over South Vietnam were flown from March 1962 onward. The first air-to-air combat between US and North Vietnamese aircraft took place on 4 April 1965, when two US Air Force F-105D Thunderchief fighter-bombers were shot down by MiG-17 interceptors. Shown here are the aerial tactics that evolved during the course of the air war over North Vietnam.

"The Wagon Wheel" the MiGs' defensive maneuver

The North Vietnamese devised the defensive tactic known as the "Wagon Wheel" (right) in 1967. When under attack the MiG-17s entered a low-level circular orbit to give mutual defense and six-o'clock cover of the preceding aircraft. Under attack the MiGs could tighten the circle, or the MiG on the far side could turn inward and cut across the chord at full speed to engage the attacker. Because of low altitude the US aircraft had to contend with radar "clutter" from ground echoes, and missile "lock-on" was hard to achieve. This tactic made good use of the MiG's ability to turn inside the heavier US aircraft, and although purely defensive was a reasonable development in view of the MiG pilots' limited experience in 1967.

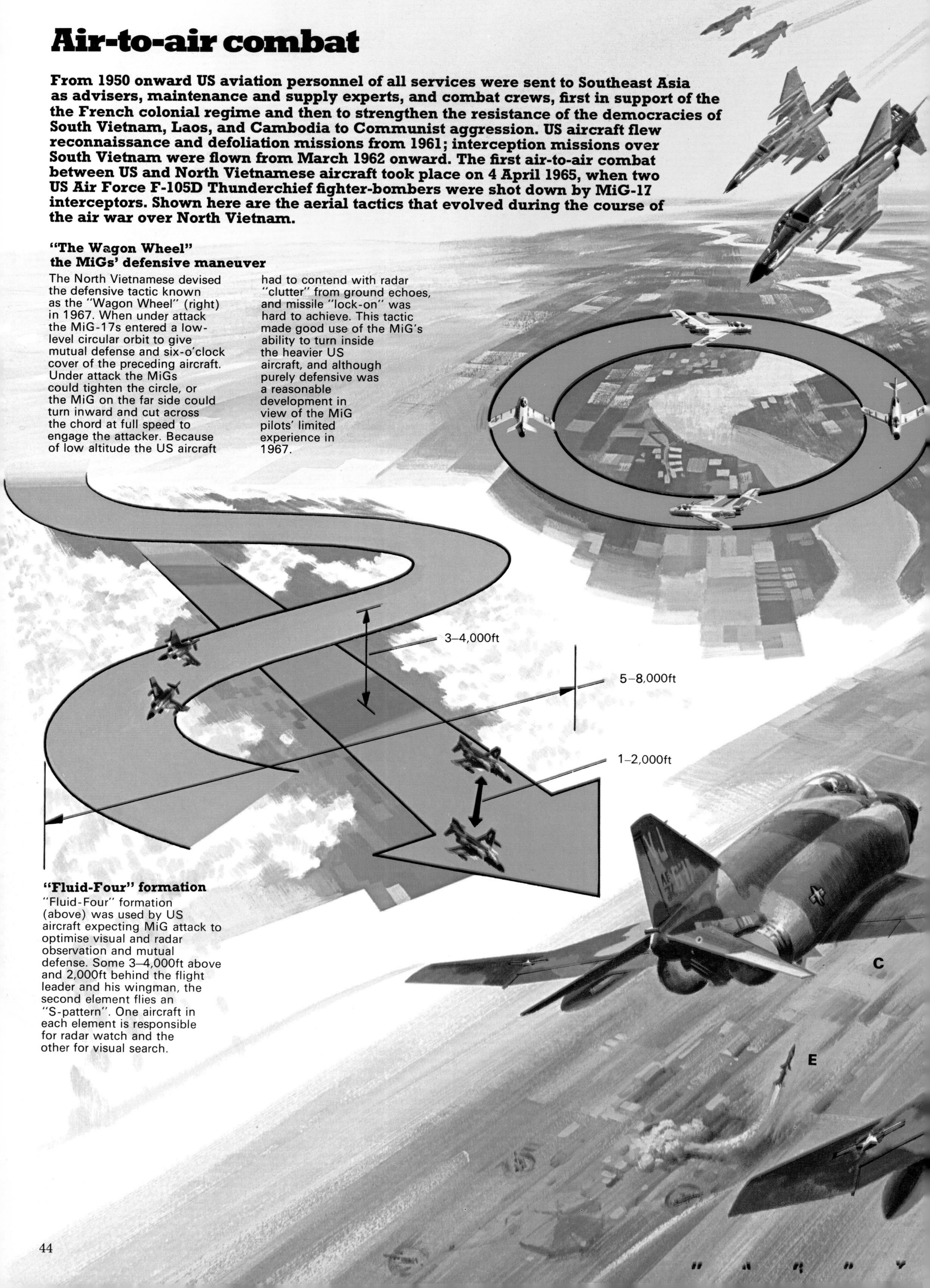

3–4,000ft

5–8,000ft

1–2,000ft

"Fluid-Four" formation

"Fluid-Four" formation (above) was used by US aircraft expecting MiG attack to optimise visual and radar observation and mutual defense. Some 3–4,000ft above and 2,000ft behind the flight leader and his wingman, the second element flies an "S-pattern". One aircraft in each element is responsible for radar watch and the other for visual search.

C

E

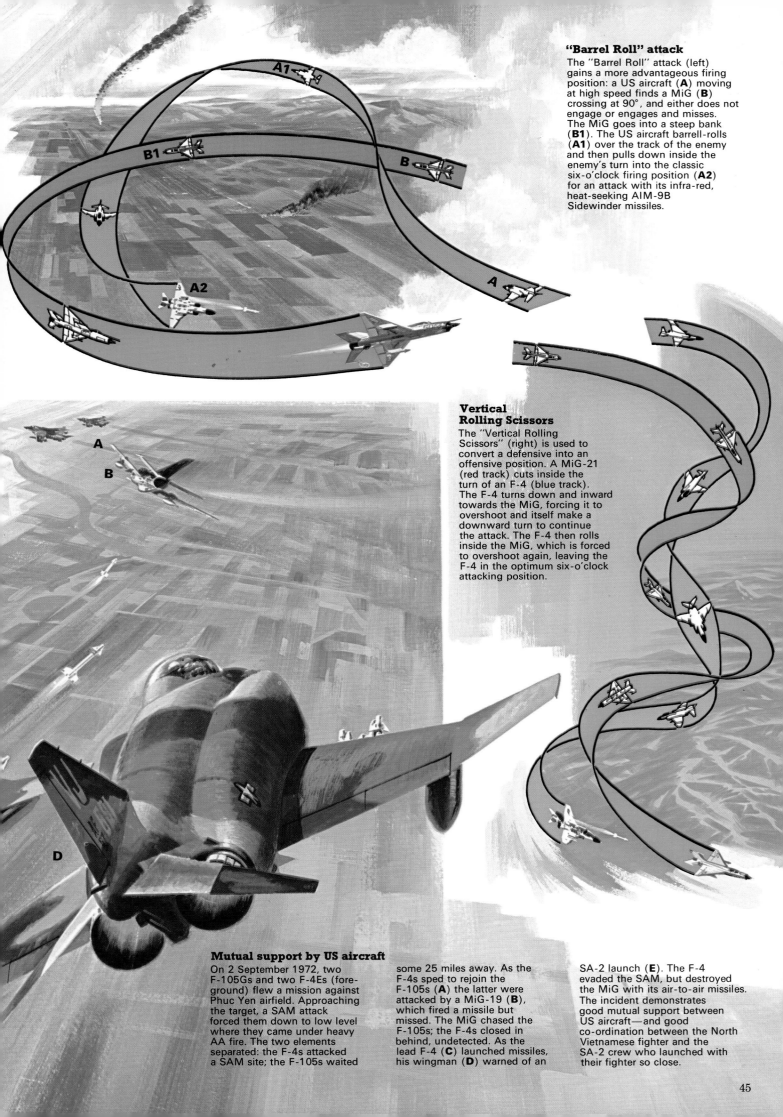

"Barrel Roll" attack

The "Barrel Roll" attack (left) gains a more advantageous firing position: a US aircraft (**A**) moving at high speed finds a MiG (**B**) crossing at 90°, and either does not engage or engages and misses. The MiG goes into a steep bank (**B1**). The US aircraft barrell-rolls (**A1**) over the track of the enemy and then pulls down inside the enemy's turn into the classic six-o'clock firing position (**A2**) for an attack with its infra-red, heat-seeking AIM-9B Sidewinder missiles.

Vertical Rolling Scissors

The "Vertical Rolling Scissors" (right) is used to convert a defensive into an offensive position. A MiG-21 (red track) cuts inside the turn of an F-4 (blue track). The F-4 turns down and inward towards the MiG, forcing it to overshoot and itself make a downward turn to continue the attack. The F-4 then rolls inside the MiG, which is forced to overshoot again, leaving the F-4 in the optimum six-o'clock attacking position.

Mutual support by US aircraft

On 2 September 1972, two F-105Gs and two F-4Es (foreground) flew a mission against Phuc Yen airfield. Approaching the target, a SAM attack forced them down to low level where they came under heavy AA fire. The two elements separated: the F-4s attacked a SAM site; the F-105s waited some 25 miles away. As the F-4s sped to rejoin the F-105s (**A**) the latter were attacked by a MiG-19 (**B**), which fired a missile but missed. The MiG chased the F-105s; the F-4s closed in behind, undetected. As the lead F-4 (**C**) launched missiles, his wingman (**D**) warned of an SA-2 launch (**E**). The F-4 evaded the SAM, but destroyed the MiG with its air-to-air missiles. The incident demonstrates good mutual support between US aircraft—and good co-ordination between the North Vietnamese fighter and the SA-2 crew who launched with their fighter so close.

The end of French rule in Indochina

Dr. George M. Watson, Jr., and Richard O'Neill

Vietnam, bounded by China to the north, Laos to the west and northwest, and Cambodia to the southwest, is an S-shaped country occupying the eastern coast of the Indochinese Peninsula. Its coastline of some 1,500 miles (2,415km) lies on the Gulf of Tonkin in the northeast, the South China Sea to the east and south, and the Gulf of Siam to the southwest. The bulk of the population is Annamese, originally thought to be a Mongolian people pushed south to the Red River Delta of North Vietnam around the 4th century B.C., but now more often considered to be of predominantly Indonesian-Mongoloid-Chinese stock and indigenous to the Delta area. Their establishment as a people dates from around the 3rd century B.C. Their traditional culture is predominantly Chinese; their dominant religions are ancestor-worship and Mahayana Buddhism with a strong Taoist influence. The major ethnic minorities are the highland tribes of the Moi, Muong, Man, and Miao.

The recorded history of Vietnam began in 207 B.C., when the renegade Chinese warlord Trieu Da (Chao T'o) established the kingdom of Nam Viet, extending from modern Da Nang into South China and ruled from the Canton area. In 111 B.C., Trieu Da's non-Chinese kingdom was overthrown by the Chinese under the Han emperor Wu Ti, and Vietnam began more than one thousand years under Chinese rule. But although the Chinese held the north, the kingdoms of Champa, on the east coast, extending from north of the Mekong Delta to around the 18th Parallel, and Funan, occupying the Mekong Delta and what is now Cambodia, were Hindu states where the influence of India was dominant. Funan was conquered by the Mon-Khmer peoples of the Cambodian Empire in the 6th century A.D., but Champa, often at war with Vietnam, retained its individuality until overrun by the Vietnamese in the 16th century.

Vietnam's first period of independence began in the 10th century, when the decline and fall of the T'ang dynasty triggered off a series of risings by the Vietnamese, culminating in the defeat of the Chinese by Ngo Quyen in 939. A period of civil strife and external conflict with the Chinese and with Champa was followed by a time of stabilization under the Ly dynasty (1009–1225), who ruled the kingdom of Dai Viet from Dong Kinh (modern Hanoi). A Chinese invasion was beaten off in 1057–1061, as were repeated incursions by Champa and Cambodia. The most serious threat was averted by Tran Hung Dao, the great general of the Tran dynasty (1225–1400): between 1257 and 1287, three massive invasions by the Mongol armies of Kublai Khan were repulsed.

The Tran dynasty fell after a bloody war with Champa lasting for most of the 14th

---

War was no stranger to Vietnam. For some 2000 years the nation struggled towards unity and independence in the face of civil strife, Chinese incursions and European imperialism. In the 1950s the nationalist and Communist Viet Minh forces led by Ho Chi Minh and Vo Nguyen Giap destroyed French power in Indochina. However, their successes brought no peace but resulted in the partition of the Vietnam nation in 1954

---

century. In 1400, the throne was usurped by Ho Qui Ly. The ousted Tran rulers asked for help from the Ming dynasty of China: in 1407, the Chinese successfully invaded Vietnam—but instead of restoring the Tran attempted to set up a puppet state. Repression provoked resistance; after a campaign lasting from 1418 to 1427, the Vietnamese under Le Loi (who eventually took the throne as Le Thai To) administered a resounding defeat to the Chinese at Hanoi. Under the Le dynasty—nominally in power until 1787, although from around 1600 the real rulers were the rival Nguyen and Trinh families—Champa was conquered by 1471, the Mekong Delta area and Saigon were taken from Cambodia in 1700–1760, and Vietnam achieved the greater part of its present size.

The Trinh, in the north, and the Nguyen, in the south, engaged in a struggle for overall power until the late 18th century. Then, in the revolt led by the Tay Son brothers, who took Hanoi in 1786 and beat back a Chinese invasion two years later, the country achieved unification. The Tay Son were not long in power: Nguyen Anh, a survivor of the Nguyen family, occupied the Mekong Delta and Saigon and, after a 14-year campaign, took Hue and Hanoi in 1802, becoming Emperor Gia Long of a united Vietnam. His victory was achieved only with French military aid.

European penetration of Vietnam was begun by Portuguese explorer-traders and missionaries from 1516 onward. Spanish and French traders and priests followed, notably the French Monsignor Alexandre de Rhodes, who came to the mission established near modern Da Nang in 1615. De Rhodes prepared the way for Western cultural influence by creating the *quoc-ngu*, a Latinized alphabet of the Vietnam-

ese language—and also lost no opportunity to encourage a trade relationship with France. Although the first French trading center, established at Hanoi in 1680, failed—as earlier Dutch and British ventures had done—the decline of Portugal encouraged the French to continued efforts.

The need of Nguyen Anh for support in his struggle against the Tay Son was France's opportunity: the future emperor relied heavily on the French mercenaries raised by Bishop Pigneau de Behaine—after French government aid had been refused. The influence of French advisers was thus strong at the court of Gia Long, but his successors, even more suspicious of Christianity than Gia Long himself, pursued a policy of persecution. The expulsion of missionaries and the execution or imprisonment of their converts, from 1820 onward, provoked French retaliation—Da Nang harbor was bombarded in 1847—and the accession of the imperially-minded Napoleon III in 1852 signaled a French policy of colonial conquest.

French take control of provinces

In 1857, after Emperor Tu Duc had refused to guarantee religious liberty and, more important, had failed to give preferential treatment to French commercial ventures, the French naval commander in the Far East, Admiral Rigault de Genouilly, was ordered to take Da Nang (called Tourane by the French), not far from the imperial capital of Hue. Da Nang fell to the French on 2 September 1858; Saigon on 17 February 1859. However, the campaign (in which the Spanish cooperated until 1862) at first made little headway: Genouilly lacked equipment for riverine operations, his men suffered severely from tropical diseases, and Vietnamese Catholics failed to rally to his support. Not until 1861, when the Saigon garrison was relieved and French reinforcements brought in from China, was Saigon itself and the three adjacent provinces brought under French control.

A treaty forced upon Tu Duc and ratified in April 1863 recognized French control of the Saigon area and opened major ports to French trade; in 1867, faced by civil unrest and needing military support, Tu Duc was constrained to recognize French rule over the greater part of southern Vietnam, then called Cochin China (Nam Bo or Nam Ky to the Vietnamese; central and highland Vietnam was called Annam by the French, who also referred to the entire country by this name, and Trung Bo or Trung Ky by the Vietnamese; north Vietnam was Tonkin to the French, Bac Bo or Bac Ky to the Vietnamese). The French had already

1. Ho Chi Minh addresses the Socialist (ie, Communist) Congress at Tours, France, in 1920; the 30-year-old delegate from Indochina condemned the "abominable crimes" of French colonialism. 2. The Russian Bolsheviks quickly established links with Asian Communism: Ho (circled) is seen with delegates from Indonesia, India, and Japan at the Moscow Comintern Congress, 1922. 3. Vo Nguyen Giap, seen swearing in recruits to the Vietnam Liberation Armed Propaganda Group in 1944, later the People's Army, was the military genius of Vietnamese Communism. 4. Indochinese nationalist/Communists operating against the Japanese during World War II were supplied with American arms.

in 1863, established a protectorate in Cambodia.

French policy in Indochina was rarely consistent, and the situation in metropolitan France—notably the defeat in the Franco-Prussian War of 1870–1871—meant that the Vietnamese possessions were, until around 1880, ruled in effect by French naval officers. By the 1880s, however, France was economically and militarily able to take a stronger line: in August 1883, French ships bombarded Hue and a strong ground force moved on Hanoi. Emperor Tu Duc had recently died, no successor had been enthroned, and the court mandarins feared to oppose the French. A treaty of 25 August 1883 recognized Annam and Tonkin as French protectorates, paving the way for direct French rule. Laos was removed from Thai control to become a French protectorate in 1893, joining Vietname and Cambodia in the Indochinese Union established in 1887. Henceforth, the Vietnamese would have little voice in the running of their own country: although the colonial regime was both inconsistent and often inept, a fixed policy of excluding native Vietnamese from positions of power was always maintained.

French rule benefits only landowners

French rule in Vietnam cannot be said to have benefited France any more than it did the indigenous inhabitants. The equitable distribution of land, a recurrent problem throughout Vietnam's history, was never attempted; industrial investment and development was neglected in favor of quick profits made by exporting raw materials; public health and education were neglected—in 1939 it was estimated that some 80 percent of the population was illiterate. French merchants, and the Vietnamese landowner class (no more than 7,000 strong) which was their only eager collaborator, were the only beneficiaries of a system which created a climate in which nationalist and revolutionary movements were bound to have an ever-increasing appeal to the mass of the people. As in Algeria, the French *colons* lived a life completely divorced from that of the colonized, seldom attempting to arrive at any rapport with the Vietnamese.

Resistance to French rule, at first headed by disaffected members of the former mandarin administrative class, began as soon as it was established. The early revolutionaries aimed at restoring imperial power: Phan Boi Chau sought Japanese help in putting Prince Cuong De in power. Failing, he proclaimed a republican government in exile in China in 1912. Chau's League for the Restoration of Vietnam succeeded in raising nationalist sentiment against the French before and during World War I, but in 1925 he was abducted by French agents and imprisoned until his death in 1940. A revolt proclaimed by the young Emperor Duy Tan in 1916 failed ignominiously, as did a military insurrection at Thai Nguyen the following year.

Of much greater significance was the foundation in Vietnam in the 1920s of such clandestine, militant organizations as the Vietnamese Nationalist Party (Viet Nam Quoc Dan Dang) of Nguyen Thai Hoc, executed after the failure of a revolt centering on Yen Bay in February 1930, and the Revolutionary League of the Youth of Vietnam (Thanh Nien) in 1926 by Nguyen Ai Quoc—who was later to be known as Ho Chi Minh. A leader of great charisma and infinite cunning, Ho was at various times known as Nguyen That Thanh, Ly Thuy, Song Man Tcho, Nguyen O Phap, and Nguyen Sinh Chin. He had almost as many political stances as pseudonyms, presenting himself as a Nationalist, Communist, pro- and anti-French, Chinese, or Japanese, as the situation demanded. It has been claimed that it was he who betrayed Phan Boi Chau to the French.

Ho Chi Minh, to use the name by which he is best known, used the Thanh Nien as the nucleus of the Indochinese Communist Party, which he formed in Hong Kong from an amalgamation of rival Communist groups in 1930. Communist-inspired uprisings in Vietnam in 1930–1931 were savagely repressed by the French—but this had the effect of strengthening the Communist Party by removing many of its rivals and uniting dissident groups under its leadership. Repression again worked to Communist advantage at the beginning of World War II, when the political concessions made to indigenous Vietnamese movements by the French Popular Front government were withdrawn. The Communist Party, better organized and disciplined that its Trotskyite or religious-nationalist rivals like the Cao Dai and Hoa Hao sects, was then able to present itself as the most viable national liberation movement.

Ho Chi Minh enlists international aid

Japan, with it own colonial ambitions in Southeast Asia, took advantage of the fall of metropolitan France to move into Indochina: in September 1940, the Vichy authorities in Vietnam were constrained to allow Japan to use the country as a base and staging point. Ho Chi Minh was at this time in southern China, where the Japanese invasion of 1937 had forced the Nationalist leader Chiang Kai-shek into an uneasy alliance with the Communists. In 1941, at Liu Chou and at Bac Bo in Vietnam, Ho succeeded in uniting several Communist and Vietnamese Nationalist groups into the League for the Independence of Vietnam (Doc Lap Dong Minh Hoi, subsequently abbreviated to Viet Minh). But in 1942 Ho was imprisoned by the Chinese Nationalists, who had set up the Vietnam Revolutionary League (Dong Minh Hoi) as an anti-Communist counter to his movement. The Dong Minh Hoi's leaders proved ineffectual; Ho was able to convince the Chinese Nationalists that he himself was a Nationalist first and a Communist second, his efforts aimed at China's enemy, the Japanese, as much as against the French. Ho was set at liberty and given command of the Dong Minh Hoi. Returning to Vietnam, where the Viet Minh under Vo Nguyen Giap had won Allied confidence by their operations against the Japanese, Ho was able to advance the Viet Minh cause with help from Chinese Communists, Nationalists, Americans, and British.

During the war the French had pursued their policy of repression unchanged,

1

3

4

2

1. Faced with the task of maintaining order in Vietnam south of the 16th Parallel after the Japanese defeat, the British Major General Douglas D. Gracey made use of former enemies: a Japanese soldier posts the British declaration of martial law in Saigon, September 1945. 2. Disarmed then rearmed for police work: a Japanese guard greets HMS *Waveney* at Saigon, 4 October 1945. 3. General Gracey (center) welcomes General Leclerc, commander of the French Expeditionary Corps, to Saigon on 5 October 1945; by December, 21,500 French troops had arrived in southern Vietnam. 4. Field Marshal Count Terauchi, commander of the Japanese Army of the South, surrenders his sword to Admiral Lord Louis Mountbatten, commanding Allied Southeast Asia Command, at a formal ceremony in Saigon, 30 November 1945. 5. General Gracey commanded some 26,000 troops, comprising his own 20th Indian Division, two squadrons of the Royal Air Force, a Royal Navy port party, and the armored cars of the 16th (Indian) Light Cavalry, seen here on an Armistice Day parade on the Rue Catinat, Saigon, in November 1945.

5

refusing the offers of the Viet Minh to aid them in resisting the Japanese. The Japanese, while making token gestures to Vietnamese aspirations towards independence, had not won the confidence of the people. In March 1945, a Japanese *putsch* removed the Vichy authorities. Seeing the Viet Minh as now the main anti-Japanese force, the American Office of Strategic Services (OSS) began an increased supply of arms and instructors to Ho and Giap. When the Japanese surrendered in August 1945, Ho was strong enough to order a general uprising, seize Hanoi, and declare an independent Democratic Republic of Vietnam on 2 September. Emperor Bao Dai abdicated to become chief counsellor to the Hanoi government. In Saigon, the Communist-dominated Provisional Executive Committee of South Vietnam, led by Tran Van Giau, recognized the authority of Ho's northern government.

The conference of Allied leaders at Potsdam had decided that the responsibility for disarming the Japanese north of the 16th Parallel should lie with Chiang Kai-shek's Chinese Nationalists, while the British would do the same in the south. The Chinese, with no sympathy for French colonial aspirations, carried out their task without interfering with the Hanoi regime. The British — who, in spite of the anti-colonialist sympathies of their American ally, favored the restoration of French rule — were less impartial. Major General Douglas D. Gracey's 20th Indian Division, seasoned jungle fighters with artillery and air support, some 26,000 men in all, allowed Japanese units to keep their arms—as well as arming released French prisoners—and used them in police actions against supporters of the Provisional Executive Committee, which had been behaving with moderation in the hope of attracting Allied support.

On 23 September 1945, two days after General Gracey had proclaimed what amounted to a state of martial law in Saigon, a mixed force of French Gaullist and released Vichy troops, with armed *colons*, stormed the Viet Minh headquarters at Saigon town hall, arrested members of the Committee (most escaped), and hoisted the tricolor. The colonial reconquest of Vietnam, and the first Indochina War of 1946–1954, had begun.

At first, however, it seemed that the French and the Viet Minh might reach a compromise. Ho had admitted a fair proportion of non-Communist Nationalists to his government as the price of Chinese Nationalist support, and in November 1945 had made the token gesture of dissolving the Indochinese Communist Party. In March 1946, following Sino-French agreement on the replacement of Chinese troops in the north by French, Ho agreed to the presence of 25,000 French and French-officered Vietnamese troops in the north's major urban areas. France agreed to recognize the Democratic Republic of Vietnam as a free state—part of an Indochinese Federation within the French Union, although the real meaning of these terms was not clearly defined. French troops were to be withdrawn in five annual instalments, ending in 1952 when, subject to a referendum, the provinces of Cochin China would again be part of an independent Vietnam. When the non-Communist Nationalists denounced the agreements and began anti-French agitation, the Viet Minh helped the French to suppress them. But in spite of this show of solidarity, subsequent events showed that neither the French nor the Viet Minh had much intention of adhering to the agreements.

Disregarding the referendum provision, the French High Commissioner for Indochina, Admiral d'Argenlieu, proclaimed Cochin China an autonomous republic—in fact, a French puppet state—on 1 June 1946. The political powers promised to the Democratic Republic of Vietnam were vested in the "Indochinese Federation", an organization under direct French control. Conferences in Vietnam and France in April and July 1946 collapsed without result; both sides were maneuvering for position in the forthcoming conflict. On 15 October 1946, French forces moved to take over the customs houses in Haiphong in order to reassert France's political authority in the north and to prevent military supplies from reaching the Viet Minh. A French naval bombardment of the port's Vietnamese quarter on 23 November resulted in the deaths of some 6,000 Vietnamese civilians. On 19–20 December, the Viet Minh (now openly a Communist rather than a Nationalist movement) countered with a revolt in Haiphong. The rising failed because of superior French firepower, but Vo Nguyen Giap was encouraged by the fact that it took the French some seven days to rid the city of his ill-equipped forces.

Viet Minh follow the teachings of Chairman Mao

After this abortive rising the Viet Minh pursued a policy of quiet consolidation. Giap avoided all-out confrontations and thus conformed to one of Mao Tse-tung's key principles of warfare—retaining the initiative. Giap believed that in keeping the French bogged down he had entered what Mao termed the second phase of protracted warfare (the first being the French occupation of cities, towns, and communications routes; the second the stalemate; and the third the general counter-offensive). For the Viet Minh, self-preservation was essential. Even when confronted by inferior numbers of French troops, the guerrillas dispersed. Thus Mao's principle prevailed: "In every battle concentrate absolutely superior forces—double, treble, quadruple, and sometimes five or six times those of the enemy." When this maxim was adhered to, the Viet Minh's temporary strategy succeeded; when it was ignored, the insurgents suffered severely.

Besides taking military action against the Communists, the French were active politically. In April 1948, they induced the former Emperor Bao Dai to come to Indochina to form and head a Vietnamese government. Although the French promised to provide economic support and independence at a later date, hidden clauses insured French control over foreign and military affairs. Militarily, the French were barely holding their own. Although they increased their strength to almost 150,000 men in mid-1949, much effort was expended in such purely defensive measures as conducting searches and

1

3

5

2

1. Arriving in Paris on 22 June 1946, following France's recognition of the Republic of Vietnam as a free state within the French Union and Indochinese Federation, Ho Chi Minh is greeted by Marius Moutet (right), Minister for Overseas Territories. **2.** On 21 December 1946 Ho repudiated the agreement with France and war followed; even with sacrifices like this "suicide soldier" with an explosive lance, the Viet Minh could not hold the cities. **3.** The Chinese Communists supported the Viet Minh: Ho, whose portrait shares the wall with Mao Tse-tung's, is flanked by Vo Nguyen Giap (right) and a Chinese technical adviser. **4.** Ho with his soldiers in 1950, when Giap launched an offensive against French outposts near the Chinese border. **5.** French Legionnaires keep the tri-color flying in northern Vietnam.

4

patrols and escorting convoys. While the French were being harassed and tied down by an elusive enemy, the Viet Minh were gaining military strength and experience.

Perhaps the most significant boost to the Viet Minh was the Communist victory in China. With the defeat of the Nationalist Chinese, arms could flow freely across friendly borders. Giap, now confident of Viet Minh success, announced in February 1950 that the time of guerrilla warfare had passed and that the counter-offensive had begun.

During the campaign season of 1949–1950, the French adhered to their *laissez faire*—or "leave things as they are"—policy. Leon Pignon, the French High Commissioner, tended to be overmuch concerned with military rather than civil matters, and influenced his military commanders to undertake policies which were not always the wisest. He failed to reinforce the Red River Delta—the Hanoi-Haiphong area—and made no effort to pacify its agricultural areas. The French also tended to underestimate enemy strength, even when it was realized that the Viet Minh were receiving supplies from China. A "wait-and-see" attitude prevailed, buttressed by the hope that the United States would supply much-needed modern military equipment and that the French National Assembly would sanction the use of conscripts.

French estimates of the time it would take Giap to arm his forces sufficiently proved erroneous. Indeed, early in 1950 Giap had two infantry divisions whose equipment included heavy mortars and anti-aircraft guns; and by the end of that year another, similarly armed, division was ready.

On 16 September 1950, confident of success, Giap attacked Dong Khe, a French outpost on the ridge forming the northeast border with China. The post was manned by two companies of the French Foreign Legion, some 260 men, who resisted valiantly. After an accurate barrage of mortar fire, wave upon wave of infantry began the assault. Bitter hand-to-hand fighting followed and then, after enduring another shelling, the French defenders who were outnumbered eight-to-one managed an escape through the encircling troops.

After the fall of Dong Khe, Giap attacked a force retreating from Cao Bang (another post on the ridge) and a relief column headed there. On 9 October, he caught the reinforcements on the move and in the open, forcing a disorganized retreat and inflicting a costly defeat upon the French.

By the end of October, Giap had driven the French out of northern North Vietnam. The Viet Minh success was mainly due to superior numbers and greater mobility. Giap's excellent communications system enabled him to concentrate his troops at key times and places. Weather also favored the Viet Minh: a ground mist, to be expected after the rainy season, prevented effective action by the French Air Force.

The defeat was one of the worst in French colonial history. Out of some 10,000 troops stationed along the border, about 6,000 became casualties or prisoners. Loss of equipment was enormous, including more than 900 machine guns, 125 mortars, and some 13 heavier guns, as well as 1,200 automatic rifles, around 8,000 rifles, and some 450 trucks. French military morale was at a low ebb. Politicians blamed soldiers and vice versa. The troops were despondent because they believed that they had been beaten by an ill-trained and ill-equipped guerrilla force.

The French recover and Giap retreats

Into this scene entered one of France's most famous soldiers: General Jean de Lattre de Tassigny was appointed High Commissioner and Commander in Chief of Indochina in December 1950. Unlike his predecessors, he had freedom of action and thus did not have to consult Paris before undertaking an operation.

Under de Lattre's leadership the French Air Force began to play a much more significant role. American-built aircraft—including Grumman F8F Bearcats and Douglas B-26 Invaders—hampered Viet Minh deployment, forcing them to move by night. Napalm, the jellied petroleum bomb which bursts into a widely-distributed carpet of flame on contact with the ground, was used in Vietnam for the first time on 22 December 1950, against a Viet Minh concentration at Tien Yen.

Giap rose to the challenge posed by the appearance of a soldier as able as de Lattre and sought an immediate showdown. Vinh Yen, a small post 35 miles (56km) northwest of Hanoi, was selected for this purpose, and on 14–15 January 1951 two Viet Minh divisions were massed for attack. General de Lattre reacted by taking personal command of the battle. The Viet Minh threw wave after wave of soldiers at about 8,000 French troops. De Lattre countered with every available aircraft, employing napalm, bombs, and guns, but the Viet Minh pressed the attack though hundreds burned to death in the billowing napalm. But the French held—and, on the afternoon of 17 January, Giap gave the order to retreat.

This victory proved a morale builder for the French. It was estimated that between 6,000 and 9,000 of the enemy had been killed and some 7,000 to 8,000 wounded, while around 600 were taken prisoner. Giap had made several errors, among the most critical being his inability to foresee the effectiveness of the French Air Force. Napalm had been dropped in huge quantities, taking the Viet Minh by surprise.

Even so, as the French realized, the victory had been close and had made apparent a serious weakness—their inability to pursue the retreating enemy. The French were road-bound. This lack of mobility was further stressed when, to prevent future Communist invasions from the north, the Commander in Chief ordered the construction of a series of defensive positions which became known as the "de Lattre line". It protected both Hanoi and Haiphong with encircling outposts, extending from the sea to the vicinity of Vinh Yen, and then southeast to the sea again. General de Lattre also formed guerrilla groups comprised of both French and Indochinese, the latter recruited from captured Viet Minh. But this innovation was short-lived; French officers simply disliked "irregular" warfare.

Giap was not content to remain idle after the Vinh Yen defeat, for he desired to penetrate the Red River Delta. He attempted twice more to confront the French in full-scale battle in the Delta area, at Mao Khe in March and along the Day River in June 1951. The French were victorious at Mao Khe because of superior artillery and superb defense. At the Day River confrontation the French succeeded because they were able to cut the Viet Minh supply line and had the support of a local population unsympathetic to the Communists. At the Day River, Giap over-extended his forces, leaving himself without reserves and thus causing some to question his expertise as a commander.

These victories of 1951 led to a restoration of morale among the French. Equally, the defeats had repercussions among the Viet Minh leadership. A scapegoat was found in the person of Nguyen Binh, leader of Viet Minh affairs in southern Indochina. He was unjustly blamed for suggesting the Red River Delta action and for not providing sufficient support for the Viet Minh in his area. After the disgraced Nguyen Binh died in a skirmish with a French patrol, Ho Chi Minh and Vo Nguyen Giap continued to lead the movement.

Giap reverts to former tactics

The summer of 1951 was a time of preparation for both sides. Giap reorganized his command structure and attempted to tighten his control over various functions such as the War Bureau, Central Political Office, and the Supply Service. General de Lattre sought to use the respite of the rainy season to build up his forces, in both men and modern equipment. He hoped to utilize a recently organized Vietnamese National Army more effectively by letting Vietnamese take over the defensive sectors, thereby freeing French troops for operations. Of prime importance for the General was to strengthen the de Lattre line.

Giap, eager for some type of victory, decided to attack the border forts again, this time at Nghia Lo. For four days in early October 1951 he ordered wave after wave of his 312th Division against the French position with little success. Each time, the French repulsed the attackers with small-arms fire. French paratroops were dropped initially as reinforcements and then to seek out and scatter the retreating Vietnamese forces. This success gave the French a feeling of false security. While they believed in the importance of reinforcement by air, they saw no reason why they should not continue to hold their line of outposts along the ridge.

General de Lattre de Tassigny was not satisfied with defensive victories. He realized that a big offensive success was needed to silence critical French politicians and to persuade the government to provide more funds and reinforcements. The General also believed that such a victory would sway the skeptical Americans towards the provision of additional materiel and monetary aid. (Of the $23.5 million in economic aid allotted by the United States to Vietnam, Cambodia, and Laos, up to July 1951, by far the greater part went to Vietnam.)

For his offensive, de Lattre decided upon

Communist Chinese Aid to the Viet Minh January to November 1953	
105mm guns	24
Recoilless cannon	412
Machine-guns	416
Sub machine-guns	1,050
Automatic pistols	5,050
Mortars (60, 81 and 120mm)	339
Artillery, mortars, rockets	170,000
Small arms (rounds)	6,000,000
12.7mm	2,000,000
Mines	40,000
Explosives (tonnes)	246
Detonators	850,000
Fuse (metres)	170,000
Vehicles	260
Petrol (gallons)	855,800
Combat uniforms	310,000
Combat boots (pairs)	362,000
Mosquito nets	153,000
Metal plates	25,000
Communications (tonnes)	200
Surgical equipment and medicine (tonnes)	45

2

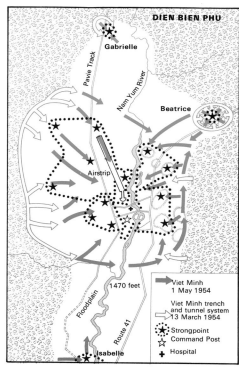

5

the town of Hoa Binh, a Viet Minh staging area about 50 miles (80km) west of Hanoi and 25 miles (40km) from the de Lattre line. On 14 November 1951 three French paratroop battalions successfully occupied the town while other French troops began opening up two land routes to it. By setting up additional posts along these routes the French over-extended themselves—and Giap took advantage of this. He ordered his regional troops to harass French road opening efforts, and on 9 December ordered a key French outpost at Lang Tu Vu attacked. The assault proved a success, but because it was Giap's intent to cause enemy casualties rather than to retain territory, he vacated his newly-won position and allowed the French to retake it. Giap's strategy was successful; he inflicted heavy casualties and threatened to take Hoa Binh, which the French were openly committed to hold at all costs.

Having claimed a victory in the Hoa Binh operation, the French did not wish to "lose face" by effecting an orderly withdrawal, which would have saved many lives. A further blow was the departure of General de Lattre de Tassigny, who died of cancer in January 1952. General Raoul Salan, his successor as Commander of the French Expeditionary Force, inherited an almost desperate situation. He ordered the attempts to open the road to Hoa Binh halted, a withdrawal from French posts along the Black River between Hoa Binh and Viet Tri, and finally the abandonment of Hoa Binh. Giap was quick to pursue his aim of inflicting casualties. By laying ambush after ambush, he was able to hamper the retreat and destroy many elements of the French rearguard.

1. US military and economic aid to the anti-Communist regimes of Southeast Asia began in 1950; here, French and Vietnamese soldiers man US-built M8 light armored cars. 2. Marcel Bigeard (center), now a four-star general, served in Indochina from 1945 onward and commanded the 6th Colonial Parachute Battalion's drop at Dien Bien Phu on 20 November 1953. 3. Franco-Vietnamese infantry advance inland during "Operation Camargue" in August 1953; the Viet Minh were generally successful in evading such sweeps and seeking battle on their own terms. 4. Ho and other members of the Political Bureau of the Vietnam Workers' Party Central Committee listen while Vo Nguyen Giap (standing) explains his plan for confronting the French at Dien Bien Phu. 5. Map: Indochina in 1953–54, showing zones of French and Viet Minh influence. 6. Not all Vietnamese supported the Viet Minh: in a village near Hanoi, citizen militia organized by the Catholic priest man their combat post with ex-British arms, including a Bren light machine gun.

With the French retreat both sides settled down to re-group; for the most part, activity during the summer of 1952 was restricted to guerrilla encounters. The Viet Minh brought their divisions up to full strength and concentrated on training with new weapons received from China.

On the other side General Salan prepared for an all-out fall offensive. He received some American supplies: small arms, artillery, trucks, amphibious vehicles, M26 tanks, and Douglas C-47 Skytrain aircraft. His hope of partial "Vietnamization" of the war proved a disappointment, however. The Vietnamese National Army suffered from a shortage of officers and from desertions among troops serving outside their home regions. General Salan now found himself without sufficient French troops to conduct his planned offensive.

For more than a year Giap had hoped to clear the French from the ridge line overlooking the French outpost at Nghia Lo, which would give him control of the important watershed area between the Red and Black Rivers. With this target in mind he ordered his troops to advance toward the Delta, fight a withdrawal action, and then make an all-out attack on Nghia Lo. The assault began on 17 October 1952: after several attacks the position fell, followed by other nearby posts.

After advancing westward for a month the Viet Minh over-extended their supply lines and were forced to halt their offensive. Nevertheless, it was a Viet Minh victory. The French blamed poor weather, leading to ineffective air support, as well

as Viet Minh numerical superiority, for the defeat.

While the Viet Minh were pressing forward into the rugged country around Nghia Lo, General Salan planned an offensive that would take his forces deep into Viet Minh territory. "Operation Lorraine", which began on 29 October 1952, involved a French force of nearly 30,000 which spread out from the Delta region in two groups. The operation met with some success, capturing the important supply center of Doan Hung (Phu Doan), but the road-bound French forces were vulnerable to ambush. Further, a force of such magnitude created a logistical problem for the French C-47 transport aircraft. The operation had to be curtailed and a retreat ordered. Thus Lorraine failed to achieve its initial objective of forcing the Viet Minh divisions into a full-scale battle.

Between December 1952 and March 1953 there were no full-scale encounters, but lesser activities caused mounting casualties on both sides. French hopes that the Viet Minh planned no more full offensives until after the summer rains were shattered in April 1953, when it became clear that the enemy was massing for an invasion of Laos. For a month Giap deployed his divisions with the skill of a chess master. He fought a war of movement—very little encounter but constant maneuver — thereby thoroughly confusing the French.

Giap was able to force the French into two centers of defense, then, realizing that his primitive supply system could no longer sustain a full offensive, he withdrew. Although loss of life was minimal on both sides, the Viet Minh had clearly won a strategic battle. The Communists now had freedom of movement through a large part of northern Laos and could dominate the territory west of the Black River. Giap had proved that despite his lack of air support he could control the countryside while keeping the French tied down. The French, in order to retain their defense centers some 300 miles (480km) from Hanoi utilized their entire fleet of C-47s, leaving no reserve for action elsewhere.

Navarre pleas for reinforcements

In May 1953 General Henri Navarre succeeded Salan as Commander in Chief. Assessing the situation, Navarre realized that his forces were over-extended and tied to their defensive positions. To counter this condition he planned to avoid decisive battles over the next campaigning season, in order to gain time to create a large mobile force. But in order to accomplish this task he needed American materiel. Like his predecessors, Navarre hoped to build up the Vietnamese National Army for defensive purposes. The new commander believed that with reinforcements, as well as American arms, he could at best hold the Delta and Cochin China for two years and then resume the offensive in 1955.

Navarre went to France to plead his case but returned disappointed with only ten battalions. A factor that impaired his plans was the unpopularity of the conflict in metropolitan France. As casualties mounted, support for the war waned, and the French Communist Party, committed to the support of the Viet Minh, did everything it could to foster anti-war sentiment.

Nevertheless, General Navarre sought to carry out operations which would improve the French position. During the rainy season he attempted to seek out the enemy and destroy their caches of equipment. He met with some success; but when he tried to clear the Viet Minh from the northern strip of Cochin China, between Quang Tri and Hue, he failed to score a major victory because the Viet Minh managed to slip away into the swamps. In general, the French made the mistake of failing to comprehend the improvement in both training and equipment that the Viet Minh had accomplished during a single year.

A pressing problem for General Navarre was the presence of Communist divisions in Tongkin, to the north of Laos. The General decided to block the main route into Laos instead of penetrating the Viet Minh's long established mountain stronghold of Viet Bac. Navarre hoped that Giap would be forced to divert several divisions to the blocking area and, to be in a position to stop such a move, he ordered the village of Dien Bien Phu to be taken and held. Three paratroop battalions, dropped from C-47s in November 1953, reoccupied the area and began preparations for the establishment of a fortified camp.

Meanwhile, in the south, General Navarre launched "Operation Atlante" in January 1954. Designed to clear the coastal areas of Viet Minh, the operation ended in March; its failure demonstrated the poor quality of the Vietnamese National Army and reinforced the views of those who believed the French cause hopeless. The disappointing performance of the Vietnamese discouraged the French who had been forced to replace indigenous units with troops from the mobile reserve force which Navarre was trying desperately to build. But generally the campaigning season from October 1953 to March 1954 was marked by indecisive action. As before, both sides sought to avoid major confrontations. It was a war of movement in which Giap again proved superior despite his lack of air mobility.

The village of Dien Bien Phu, 170 miles (275km) west of Hanoi, had little strategic significance, although it lay only 10 miles (16km) from the Laotian border at the junction of three main roads. It was situated in a basin about 12 miles (19km) long and 10 miles (16km) wide, encompassed by wooded hills. The troops who parachuted into the valley late in 1953 built two airstrips to link the base with the French forces around Hanoi.

Three main bastions surrounded the larger airstrip: Huguette, to the west; Claudine, to the south; and Dominique, to the north-east. Four smaller outposts—Gabrielle, Beatrice, Isabelle, and Ann Marie—formed the outer defense, while the stronghold named Elaine included the village itself. The auxiliary airfield lay just north of Isabelle, southernmost of the outposts. Against this "land-air base", so the French hoped, Giap would hurl his army to destruction.

By March 1954, Navarre had a dozen battalions dug in around Dien Bien Phu. He had almost emptied his arsenal to provide them with artillery—two groups of 75mm guns, two of 105mm, and four

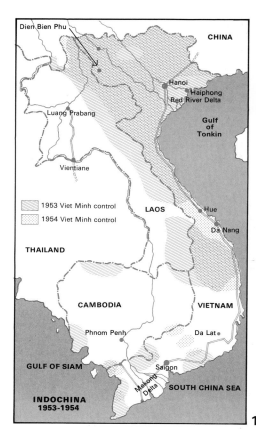

1953-1954
Dien Bien Phu
CHINA
Hanoi
Haiphong
Red River Delta
Gulf of Tonkin
Luang Prabang
Vientiane
LAOS
Hue
Da Nang
THAILAND
CAMBODIA
VIETNAM
Phnom Penh
Da Lat
GULF OF SIAM
Saigon
Mekong Delta
SOUTH CHINA SEA
INDOCHINA 1953-1954

1953 Viet Minh control
1954 Viet Minh control

1

Battle of Dien Bien Phu

Date
13 March–8 May 1954

Objective
To draw the Viet Minh into a set battle where French firepower would inflict a decisive defeat.

Forces
French: c.16,000 men, 28 × 105mm guns, 10 light tanks
Viet Minh: c.50,000 men (+ c.54,000 in support), c.48 × 105mm guns, c.150 lighter artillery pieces

Result
After taking heavy losses, Communist troops overran the French garrison
French losses: 2,293 killed, 5,134 wounded, c.11,000 captured (including wounded), 62 aircraft destroyed, 167 aircraft damaged
Viet Minh losses: c.8,000 killed, c.15,000 wounded

4

1. Map: Dien Bien Phu. 2. In "Operation Castor" on 20 November 1953, three battalions of French, Vietnamese, and Senegalese paratroopers dropped from 64 C-47 transports to reinforce Dien Bien Phu.
3. Giap launched his final offensive on 1 May 1954; Dien Bien Phu fell one week later after a 55-day siege. Here, Viet Minh troops, whose losses amounted to some 8,000 killed and 15,000 wounded, swarm over French positions in the last hours of the battle. 4. Although outgunned at Dien Bien Phu, where the Viet Minh deployed some 48 105mm guns and many more smaller pieces, the French were generally better equipped than the guerrillas; here, a French soldier brings to bear a Châtellerault Model 1924 M29 light machine gun while a comrade with a slung M1949 MAT49 submachine gun directs his fire.
5. French prisoners begin the march into captivity from Dien Bien Phu. Many died on the journey or during "re-education" in prison: of the garrison's original 16,000 men, only about 3,000 survived both the battle and subsequent captivity.

2

3

5

155mm weapons, plus a number of mortars. Colonel Charles Piroth, the garrison's artillery officer, boasted that his guns would easily destroy any artillery pieces that the enemy might manhandle into firing position. Transports flew in ten M24 Chaffee light tanks, which were assembled at the base. Six Grumman Bearcat fighters, armed with napalm, remained on alert at the larger airstrip.

To Colonel Piroth's astonishment, Giap's men dragged artillery through the northern highlands, battered the airfields on 10 March, and then advanced behind heavy barrages against the weaker outposts. Bursting shells uprooted defensive positions, few of which were reinforced with heavy timbers, and infantry closed for the kill. By 18 March, the enemy occupied Beatrice, Gabrielle, and Ann Marie, and Colonel Piroth was dead, having committed suicide on 15 March.

Although the Viet Minh had already lost an estimated 2,500 killed, the French were in a desperate plight. Enemy artillery hammered them unceasingly, and from newly-captured Gabrielle and Ann Marie anti-aircraft guns dominated the valley. Neither the Fairchild C-119s, some of which were flown by American civilians, nor the smaller C-47s could fly low enough to parachute supplies or reinforcements with any accuracy.

Sobered by the losses his troops had suffered, Giap attempted to strangle the surviving strongholds, moving forward every night and then digging in. A shortage of artillery ammunition prevented the French from so much as harassing the enemy: the defenders had to husband their shells for the final Viet Minh assault.

This siege warfare ended on 30 March, when Giap ordered another mass attack which lasted until 5 April. Fierce hand-to-hand fighting characterized the battle. The Viet Minh penetrated some of the French perimeters and destroyed French bunkers, but Giap failed to crush French resistance. The defenders clung to a portion of strongpoint Huguette, almost all of Elaine and Claudine, and Isabelle, the latter the only one of the distant outposts not yet overrun.

Severe losses and signs of mutiny forced Giap to pause. He built up his army to a strength of 50,000 against some 16,000 French and then, on 1 May, resumed the offensive. The attackers overran one position after another; on 7 May, the Viet Minh 308th Division broke through the French defenses on Elaine. By evening the battle was over, as some 11,000 French survivors laid down their arms.

The courage of the French and the hideous suffering of their wounded and captured, many of whom died on the long march to Viet Minh prison camps, were to no purpose. The distance from supply depots to the battlefield was too far, the number of transport planes too few, the artillery support inadequate. Despite Giap's previous success, Navarre and his colleagues had gravely underestimated the Viet Minh and had paid a high price for their folly. The fall of Dien Bien Phu deprived France of bargaining strength at Geneva, where diplomats were attempting to work out a settlement for Southeast Asia. The War, unpopular in France and grudgingly supported, drew to a close.

Rival ideologies in a divided nation

Bernard C. Nalty

The Geneva Agreements of 1954 deprived France of its Southeast Asian colonies. Even as the diplomatic negotiations progressed, Viet Minh forces overwhelmed Dien Bien Phu, dashing French hopes of maintaining a foothold in this region. For a time, the United States had considered intervening at Dien Bien Phu with B-29 Superfortress bomber strikes. Secretary of State John Foster Dulles, backed by the Navy and Air Force, advocated this course, but the Army opposed it. General Matthew B. Ridgway had already sent a mission to Indochina and received a report on the difficulties American ground forces would encounter in fighting there. After sounding out Congressional leaders and seeking British participation, which was not forthcoming, President Dwight D. Eisenhower ruled against American involvement.

The end of the Indochina War left Vietnam divided by a Demilitarized Zone (DMZ) that generally followed the 17th Parallel. An International Control Commission with representatives from Canada, Poland, and India—a balance of western, Communist, and neutral nations—had the duty of supervising compliance with the Geneva Agreements on both sides of the demarcation line. Although the agreements called for free elections within two years, resulting, it was hoped, in the unification of Vietnam, none took place and two separate states evolved. The Viet Minh regrouped in the Communist-dominated North Vietnam, and the United States inevitably allied itself with South Vietnam.

Collective security in Southeast Asia

Although the United States had neither intervened at Dien Bien Phu nor signed the Geneva Agreements, Secretary Dulles hoped to extend the principle of collective security to Southeast Asia. In September 1954, he played a leading part in the creation of the Southeast Asia Treaty Organization (SEATO) to protect Laos, Cambodia, and South Vietnam from Communist aggression. The Geneva Agreements, however, excluded these nations from membership, forcing him to look elsewhere for partners. The original SEATO members were the United States, the United Kingdom, France, Australia, New Zealand, the Philippines, Thailand, and Pakistan (which withdrew from the Organization in 1972). Dulles hoped for an organization resembling NATO, but he realized that the widely scattered SEATO nations lacked the shared interests and cultural and political homogeneity that held the Atlantic alliance together.

On 9 October 1954 the last French troops left Hanoi, which became the capital of

While Ho built a nation in North Vietnam American fears for the security of Southeast Asia led to increasing US support for the authoritarian regime of Ngo Dinh Diem in the South. Lacking popular support, Diem could neither solve South*a* Vietnam's internal problems nor make an adequate response to the terrorist threat posed by the Communist guerrillas known as the Viet Cong.

North Vietnam. With the departing French were a few Americans, members of the Saigon Military Mission, headed by Colonel Edward G. Lansdale, a US Air Force officer seconded to the Central Intelligence Agency (CIA), who specialized in unconventional operations. Lansdale's men had gone to Hanoi to harass the Viet Minh and gather intelligence. All that the group accomplished in the way of sabotage was to contaminate the fuel supply for Hanoi's bus line, a mere pinprick to the conquerors.

Although these saboteurs and those who followed failed to do much damage Lansdale's propagandists proved to be masters of their trade. Taking advantage of the period of regroupment agreed upon at Geneva, they spread the stories of Viet Minh terrorism and the slogans—such as "The Virgin Mary has gone South"—that helped persuade as many as 900,000 civilians, most of them Catholics, to flee North Vietnam. This exodus generated sympathy for South Vietnam, their place of refuge, and its new premier, Ngo Dinh Diem.

While the flood of refugees moved southward, around 100,000 Viet Minh troops and sympathizers left South Vietnam for the Communist North. The recall of these troops, required by the Geneva Agreements, represented a setback for Ho Chi Minh and Vo Nguyen Giap. They believed the Viet Minh could have seized all Vietnam if the Soviet Union and China had not pressured them into compromise at Geneva. In defiance of the agreement, approximately 1,000 of Giap's soldiers remained in the South as a cadre for future action.

In fact the break in hostilities proved to Ho Chi Minh's advantage, for converting a revolutionary movement into a stable

government proved difficult. While the French had been entrenched at Hanoi, the Viet Minh had controlled the countryside, collecting taxes, maintaining order, and dispensing justice. The new regime encountered problems in applying the techniques of local administration over an area of 62,000 square miles (160,000 sq km). Inefficiency and outright embezzlement cost the government heavily, as did the lack of trained men to replace the technicians and supervisors who had operated the power plants, mines, and textile mills that made up the North's industry. Many of these trained individuals were French or Vietnamese Catholics who had left the country or fled south.

The Soviet Union, China, and the East European Communist states provided advice and training that helped compensate for the loss of skilled men. Included in the aid program was the Russian-built Thai Nguyen steel mill, the symbol of the new Socialist order. But Ho Chi Minh treated this assistance as a temporary expedient and put together a spartan industrial base that could survive without outside help. His ultimate aim was for North Vietnam to build its own factories and train Vietnamese technicians and managers to run them.

Although a propaganda triumph for the Americans, the departure of 900,000 refugees from North Vietnam created a reservoir of land and other property for the Communists to distribute among the populace. Even so, the same party functionaries who had rallied the peasantry against French landlords mismanaged land reform and harmed the very people they were trying to help. In carrying out a scheme for classifying population in terms of land ownership, they established categories so narrow that a mere quarter-acre might mean the difference between agricultural worker and landlord, with members of the latter class bound over for trial and possible confiscation of property, or even death.

"Uncle Ho", the shrewd propagandist

As many as 50,000 of these "landlords" may have perished before August 1956, when Ho realized his error and promised justice to those persons wrongly classified, who had escaped execution. This pronouncement came too late—or perhaps the administrative machinery responded too slowly — for in November a rebellion erupted. Giap's army swiftly restored order, killing or relocating some 6,000 dissidents.

The disastrous scheme of land reform, with its attendant injustices and resultant uprising, failed to undermine the popularity of Ho Chi Minh. He shunned

1

The Geneva Conference, 1954

Participants: USA, USSR, UK, France, People's Republic of China, Laos, Cambodia, Vietnam (Viet Minh and anti-Communist delegates).

Agreements

1 Cease-fire line established along 17th Parallel (later DMZ), with 300-day "free movement" across line for Vietnamese pro- and anti-Communist forces. This resulted in the partition of Vietnam and the creation of:

	North Vietnam	South Vietnam
Area	63,344 sq.miles	66,281 sq.miles
Population (1970)	c.22,000,000	19,300,000
Capital	Hanoi	Saigon

2 Free elections to reunite the country in 1956.
3 Viet Minh guerrillas to evacuate Laos and Cambodia.
4 An International Supervisory Commission to enforce ceasefire; members: Canada, India, Poland.

1. The Geneva Agreements of July 1954 provided for a 300-day period of "free movement" across the 17th parallel to allow pro- and anti-Communists to relocate. Here soldiers of the former French-officered National Army and their families leave their trucks to board ships that will carry them south. As many as 900,000 civilians joined the exodus from North Vietnam. **2.** Map: the partition of Vietnam in 1954. **3.** Members of the Viet Minh were among those who changed their allegiance after partition: a former Secretary General of the Viet Minh in Quang Nam rips a Soviet flag to shreds as he pledges loyalty to Ngo Dinh Diem, Premier of South Vietnam.

THE PARTITION OF VIETNAM, 21 July, 1954

Demilitarised Zone
10 km (6¼ miles) wide

DEMOCRATIC REPUBLIC OF VIETNAM

LAOS

Ben Hai River

SOUTH CHINA SEA

Gio Linh

Con Thien

Cua Viet River

Cam Lo River

Cam Lo

Dong Ha

Thon Son Lam

Quang Tri
Route 1

Rao Quan River

SOUTH VIETNAM

Ca Lu

Quang Tri River

Route 9

Lang Vei

Khe Sanh

2

3

the trappings of office, wore black peasant garb, and lived the image he had chosen for himself—that of venerable "Uncle Ho". He was a self-created propaganda masterpiece, but he was also a shrewd and pragmatic leader, willing to abandon any program that did not work, no matter how ideologically sound, and to attempt to correct its failings.

Nor did Ho appeal only to a narrow segment of the populace. He gained the support of North Vietnam's ethnic minorities, especially the mountain tribes. During the war against the French he recruited some of his best regiments from among these groups, and after partition he granted them representation in party councils. He created three autonomous administrative zones for the mountain peoples but, ever a pragmatist, abolished one of them when its ethnic composition proved too diverse for effective government.

Despite temporary setbacks, Ho Chi Minh guided North Vietnam along the path he had chosen. Administration improved, industry grew, and agriculture recovered. The nation evolved into a Socialist state, drab to western eyes, but proud of its accomplishments.

Ngo Dinh Diem chosen as "strong" premier

In June 1954, while the Geneva Conference was in session, France recognized the existence of an independent Vietnam ruled by the one-time emperor (1925–45) Bao Dai who, after collaboration with the Japanese and a brief period as "Citizen Prince" under Ho Chi Minh, had fled the country in 1946 only to return as a French-backed puppet premier in 1949. When he took charge of the territory south of the demarcation line, Bao Dai faced a dilemma: he needed a strong premier to form a cabinet, but he did not want someone strong enough to unseat him.

His choice was Ngo Dinh Diem, a fiercely independent man who had collaborated with neither the Japanese nor the Viet Minh, and only briefly with the French. During his short-lived career as a provincial administrator under the French, and as Bao Dai's Minister of the Interior in the 1930s, he had earned a reputation for industry and honesty. Before World War II, convinced that France would not grant Vietnam self-government, he left the service of the colonial regime. After the war, he was offered high administrative posts by both Ho Chi Minh and Bao Dai, but refused to commit himself to either party and went into voluntary exile. During this time, he spent two years in the United States, where he met a number of influential fellow Catholics and others committed to the cause of a non-Communist Vietnam.

When Bao Dai again approached him in 1954, Diem insisted upon full authority over both the Army and the civil administration. Aware of the danger that he was creating a rival, Bao Dai nevertheless agreed, after receiving from Diem an oath of personal loyalty. The new premier soon learned that exercising power was even more difficult than gaining it.

Unlike North Vietnam, where Vo Nguyen Giap had forged a single army,

the South was cursed with private military forces. Besides the regular South Vietnam National Army (SVN), organized by the French and nominally loyal to Diem, and the Viet Minh cadremen, loyal to Ho and Giap, there existed three independent forces. Two of them represented religious sects; the third fought on behalf of organized crime.

The older of the religious groups was the Cao Dai, which dated from the early 1920s. Membership totaled 1.5 to 2 million persons, most of them peasants living northwest of Saigon, South Vietnam's capital. This sect combined aspects of Asian religions with Christian beliefs, venerating a variety of gods and demigods that included St. Joan of Arc and Sun Yat-sen, and maintaining a hierarchy modeled on that of the Roman Catholic church. Although they had cooperated with the Viet Minh, they broke with the Communists and accepted French arms which they used against their former allies. The Cao Dai "army" consisted of some 30,000 men.

The other sect, the Hoa Hao, was a schismatic Buddhist group, slightly smaller than the Cao Dai, with its membership concentrated in the Mekong Delta. The Viet Minh attempted to recruit the Hoa Hao as allies, failed, and waged war against them. The Communists, however, merely succeeded in driving the sect, with its army of 10,000 to 15,000 men, into an uneasy alliance with the French.

The third group, the Binh Xuyen, controlled gambling, opium distribution, and prostitution—along with several more or less legitimate businesses—in the Saigon-Cholon area. The Viet Minh had incurred the hatred of this nationalistic secret society, and Bao Dai permitted Le Van Vinh (or Van Le Vien), the group's leader, to buy control not only of Saigon's underworld but also of the city police. With 2,500 soldiers and possibly three times that number of police and thugs, Le Van Vinh prevented the Viet Minh from operating in the capital city.

Colonel (later General) Edward Lansdale, who had remained at Saigon, persuaded Diem to eliminate these rivals and provided American funds to help him. Diem was able to combine bribery with force to prevent the three groups from joining forces against him. He invited the two religious sects to nominate officers for his cabinet, then used American money to replace the subsidy the French had given them. An estimated $12 million found its way into the Hoa Hao and Cao Dai treasuries.

Victory over sects bodes ill for future

The Binh Xuyen made such immense profits from its legal and underworld endeavors that it could not be bought. Diem had to use force. In January 1955, Diem canceled the "arrangement" that Bao Dai had made with this group. Furious, Bao Dai ordered his prime minister to leave the country, but Diem refused. Fighting between Diem's SVN Army and the Binh Xuyen erupted during the following month. Assisted by French junior officers who, among other things, operated Diem's communications center, the Army

1

3

4

1. By late 1957 Communist guerrillas had begun campaigning in the south; the villagers of Moc Hoa welcome troops of the Army of the Republic of Vietnam (ARVN) who engaged the guerrillas west of Saigon. 2. Men of the 30,000-strong private army of the pantheistic Cao Dai sect parade in Saigon in 1955 before integration with the ARVN.
3. Swayed by bribes from Premier Diem out of US-supplied funds, General Trinh Minh, Cao Dai commander, led his men into the ARVN and became a brigadier general. 4. US Vice President President Lyndon B. Johnson with Ngo Dinh Diem during his visit to South Vietnam in May 1961. 5. Guerrillas of the National Liberation Front of South Vietnam—the Viet Cong—patrol in South Vietnam, where some 1,000 Communist cadres remaining after partition were joined by about 2,000 North Vietnamese infiltrators to form the nucleus of the Viet Cong in 1960. 6. Potential officers of the Viet Cong receive instruction at a clandestine school in a jungle area of South Vietnam.

drove the Binh Xuyen forces into the Rung Sat, a swamp east of Saigon. Le Van Vinh found a comfortable refuge in Paris.

Diem now turned upon the two religious sects. The bribes given the Cao Dai persuaded them to stand aside as the Hoa Hao came under attack. Once again Diem's army prevailed, thanks in no small measure to secret aid from the French Navy, which ferried troops and supplies throughout the Mekong Delta. The Hoa Hoa forces were scattered and the Cao Dai isolated.

These victories, though decisive in terms of Diem's survival, proved far from complete. Numerous Hoa Hao survivors, infuriated by the execution of their captured leader, became potential allies of the Viet Minh cadres that remained in the South. The existence of smaller groups of Binh Xuyen stragglers and embittered Cao Dai also boded ill for the future of South Vietnam.

The autocratic rule of Premier Diem

Securely in command, at least for the moment, the premier turned his attention to Bao Dai. While in exile in the United States, Diem had acquired influential friends who now rallied behind the hardworking premier in his efforts to depose the weak-willed, self-seeking ruler. They included Senators Mike Mansfield and Hubert Humphrey, a Minnesota Democrat, who told his colleagues that Diem was "the best hope that we have in South Vietnam", declaring that, if prince and prime minister were to clash, "it is Bao Dai who must go. . . ."

In April 1955, as the campaign against the private armies approached a successful conclusion, Diem convened an extralegal assembly that, obedient to his wishes, called for the dismissal of Bao Dai, the creation of a new government headed by Diem, and the prompt departure of those French officers permitted to remain in the South by the Geneva Agreements. The final part of Diem's plan was a brazenly rigged referendum, held in October 1955, which endorsed the new republic. In one area, 450,000 voters cast 600,000 ballots; 98 percent of the electorate were deemed to have spurned Bao Dai in favour of Diem.

Although a few French officers had aided Diem during the 1955 fighting, their government now favored Ho Chi Minh as potential ruler of a united Vietnam. The North Vietnamese leader, it was thought, might evolve into an Asian Tito, independent of Moscow and Peking and willing to deal with France. Diem understandably detested Vietnam's former colonial masters, who now refused to support him, and once he had toppled Bao Dai he uprooted the remaining French influence. Confident of American aid, he turned his back on French economic assistance and demanded that France cease its overtures to Hanoi and follow the policies that Diem dictated.

Like Ho Chi Minh in the North, Diem faced the problems of satisfying land-hungry peasants and winning the loyalty of ethnic minorities, especially in the Central Highlands. The arrival of some 900,000 refugees, already noted, further complicated the difficult task of land reform. Diem gave precedence to these

newcomers as he tried to provide plots in uninhabited areas, usually in the Highlands, or on tracts purchased from landholders. In either case, the new tenant was required to pay for the land he received, so that the peasant seldom saw much improvement in his lot—he would continue to make payments, though perhaps smaller than before, far into the future. Under Diem, although the number of individual landowners increased, some 45 percent of the land ended up in the hands of two percent of the landholders, with many of the larger tracts belonging to refugees from the North. Thus, Diem failed to create a loyal peasantry by his agricultural reforms.

Nor did the South Vietnamese government succeed in winning the support of the mountain tribes. Lowland Vietnamese looked upon these tribesmen as savages and treated them with contempt. Later, when Diem began gathering villagers into *agrovilles* to protect them from Communist guerrillas, his agents ignored the traditions of the mountain peoples. Discontent caused by this resettlement effort, with other instances of Lowland Vietnamese insensitivity, created sympathy for Communist insurgents instead of loyalty to the government.

In 1956 South Vietnam adopted a new constitution, a document that contained the seeds of genuine democracy. The North Vietnamese constitution, adopted four years later, appeared to establish a model Communist state. In practice, however, the constitution of South Vietnam became the vehicle through which Diem and his family—especially his brother Ngo Dinh Nhu—autocratically ruled the country, while the constitution of North Vietnam legitimized the equally despotic reign of Ho Chi Minh and the Communists.

The similarity between North and South extended into domestic politics. Ngo Dinh Nhu created the Can Lao Kan Vi (Revolutionary Labor Party) to perpetuate his brother's rule. Made up of disciplined cells like the Communist party, upon which it was modeled, the Can Lao, sometimes called "the invisible government", infiltrated government agencies, rival political organizations, and army units, rewarding Diem's supporters and punishing his enemies. Ngo Dinh Nhu's wife, whose father became Ambassador to the United States, performed a similar task in organizing women and youth. Of Diem's other brothers, one became political boss of central South Vietnam; another Archbishop of Hue; and a third Ambassador to Great Britain. (The dictator's elder brother had been executed by Viet Minh forces in 1945.)

The Viet Cong begin guerrilla warfare

American military advisers believed that Diem was growing stronger as the regular Army of the Republic of Vietnam (ARVN), with a strength in excess of 135,000, completed training. Backbone of the force was the 10,000-man infantry division, armed with standard US weapons such as the M1 semi-automatic rifle, the 105mm howitzer, and the 107mm (formerly designated 4.2in) M30 mortar. Had the enemy chosen to attack across the De-

1

2

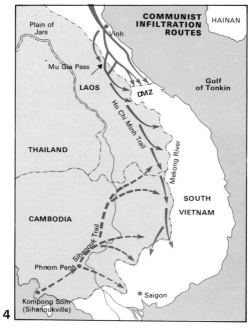

4

militarized Zone, these divisions might have proved effective, but they could not defeat the guerrillas of the National Liberation Front of South Vietnam, popularly known as the Viet Cong.

For almost three years after the Geneva settlement, Ho Chi Minh had devoted all his energy to consolidating control over North Vietnam. From the South, Le Duan, the senior Viet Minh leader remaining there after partition, constantly urged that Diem be overthrown. In 1957 he visited Hanoi, and by the year's end guerrilla warfare against Diem had begun.

Strength of the Viet Cong insurgents

During 1957, the Viet Minh cadremen who had remained in South Vietnam since the Geneva settlement began preparing for action. They retrieved weapons hidden away for three years, arming themselves with a variety of rifles and automatic weapons manufactured in the United States, Russia, Japan, and Western Europe. The most prized weapons were American-made M1 rifles and M2 carbines, some of them captured by Chinese Communist troops on the mainland or in Korea and shipped to Southeast Asia. Their principal attraction was not only effectiveness but the availability of ammunition, which could be captured from government forces.

Joined by fewer than 2,000 North Vietnamese troops who infiltrated the South before 1960, these Viet Minh veterans formed the nucleus of the Viet Cong. They recruited followers from among the surviving Binh Xuyen and Hoa Hao and from Cao Dai dissidents. The mountain tribes, thoroughly alienated by Diem's policies, proved a valuable source of support.

Besides enlisting, arming, and training guerrillas, the Viet Cong conducted acts of

1. Alienated minorities in the South —stragglers from the Cao Dai and other suppressed sects and tribesmen traditionally scorned by lowland Vietnamese—swelled the ranks of the Viet Cong: here, Mekong Delta villagers are seen in the "black pajamas" of the guerrilla with Soviet-designed weapons. **2.** Although North Vietnam suffered from the exodus of French-trained and Catholic technicians in 1954, Chinese and Russian aid allowed the construction of such major industrial facilities as the Thai Nguyen steel mill. **3.** At a jungle school in South Vietnam, Communist cadremen study the works of Mao Tse-tung, whose philosophy of warfare informed their strategy from 1946 onward. **4.** Map: the Demilitarized Zone, 21 July 1954. **5.** The Viet Cong carried Soviet, Chinese, East European, and captured US and French arms: this guerrilla has a Russian 7.62mm SKS (Simonov) carbine of World War II.

terrorism, set up bases, and created an intelligence network. This web of agents, added to the inherent mobility of Viet Cong units, enabled the insurgents to ambush the slower-moving government forces or to assassinate local officials and vanish into the shadows before soldiers or police could react.

The tempo of the fighting gradually increased. Individual acts of terrorism—kidnapping, bombing, and murder—escalated to raids and ambuscades. South Vietnamese patrols discovered tracks leading into their country from Laos, links to the rapidly developing supply and infiltration route that came to be called the Ho Chi Minh Trail. During 1958, organized Viet Cong units attacked a government prison, releasing 50 persons arrested in a round-up of suspected Communists, and defeated a company of South Vietnamese regulars in an attack on a rubber plantation. By the year's end, around 2,000 Viet Cong had formed military organizations varying in size from 50 to 200 men.

In spite of Viet Cong successes in irregular warfare, Lieutenant General Samuel Williams, who late in 1955 had replaced General J. W. O'Daniel as Chief of the US Military Assistance Advisory Group (MAAG) established early in 1953, insisted that Diem's army concentrate on conventional warfare, leaving the police and irregular forces to deal with the insurrection. When the regular army did attack Viet Cong entrenched in War Zone D, some 19 miles (30km) northwest of Saigon, the defenders fought back until scattered by artillery. Meanwhile, as terrorism increased in the South, Ho Chi Minh called a Party Congress at Hanoi in September 1960, where it was vowed to "liberate" South Vietnam. In December of that year, Ho announced the formation of a National Front for the Liberation of South Vietnam. Although presented as a coalition of Diem's enemies, the organization remained under Communist control and was to become known as the Viet Cong.

The internal problems facing Diem

Ngo Dinh Diem did not lack enemies. His suppression of the religious sects and his apparent program of fighting Communism by arresting anyone who opposed him alienated many anti-Communists. He ruled with a puritanical zeal and could be as ruthless as Ho Chi Minh—but without the North Vietnamese leader's charisma. "Uncle Ho" mingled with the people and always preserved the illusion that he was carrying out their desires. Diem remained isolated from the masses, surrounded himself with openly self-seeking family members, and ruled by decree. Even his clothing betrayed him; while Ho dressed like a peasant, Diem wore the white, western-style suits favored by French colonial administrators.

Diem, moreover, could not entirely trust the regular troops of what was now the Army of the Republic of Vietnam (ARVN). In November 1960, three airborne battalions laid siege to the presidential palace, extracting promises that Diem would broaden the government dominated by the Can Lao party and members of his family. Even as he made these pledges,

Diem summoned loyal troops who surrounded and disarmed the rebels. Once the threat had passed, Diem failed to implement the promised reforms.

After six years as virtually unchallenged chief of state, Diem remained insecure. His popular support was waning, his army could not fight the kind of war the Viet Cong had begun, and his nation's economy depended almost exclusively upon American aid. Yet, compared to Laos and Cambodia, the other states depending upon the Geneva Agreements, South Vietnam seemed the best place to resist Communism.

Communist intervention in Cambodia and Laos

Besides signaling the end of French rule in a divided Vietnam, the Geneva Agreements of 1954 had conferred independence on the kingdoms of Cambodia and Laos. In Cambodia, which had, in fact, refused to sign the Agreements, Prince Norodom Sihanouk walked a tightrope of neutrality. As King (1941–55), political leader (1955–60), and head of state (1960–70), he succeeded, even though he had to allow the Communists to move supplies through his country, permit American bombing, and ignore ground probes that crossed the border from South Vietnam.

In Laos, Prince Souvanna Phouma tried to carry out the Geneva Agreements by fashioning a neutral coalition, balancing the Communist Pathet Lao under his half-brother Prince Souphanouvong against Prince Boun Oum's American-supported faction. Boun Oum enjoyed the support of a 25,000-man Royal Army, commanded by General Phoumi Nosavan and paid for by the United States. While the Royal Army recruited and trained the lowland peoples, Souphanouvong's Pathet Lao enlisted members of the more warlike mountain tribes such as the Meo. Eventually the Americans followed the example of the Pathet Lao, creating their own Meo contingent under Colonel Vang Pao.

After Souphanouvong polled the greatest number of votes in the 1958 election, the United States pressured Souvanna into resigning. His successor, the American-backed Phoui Sananikone, tried to continue the policy of neutrality, but early in 1959, when Souphanouvong was arrested, one of the Pathet Lao battalions scheduled for integration with the Royal Army fled northward and began a guerrilla campaign along the North Vietnamese border. About a year later, in May 1960, Souphanouvong himself escaped to the north to rejoin the Pathet Lao.

Skirmishing between the Royal Army and Pathet Lao continued during the summer, with Captain Kong Le's parachute battalion emerging as the best government unit. On 5 August 1960, however, Kong Le's 600 paratroopers seized Vientiane, the administrative capital of Laos. Kong Le accused the United States of colonialism and demanded the forma-of a truly neutral government under Souvanna Phouma, Phoui Sananikone having been deposed in December 1959 by a rightist army faction led by Phoumi Nosavan. The General Assembly promptly directed the prince to form a new cabinet.

Souvanna Phouma's new regime, although receiving support from Britain,

1. In Laos the neutralist regime received US support against the Communist Pathet Lao: an American military adviser demonstrates a Browning .50-caliber M2 machine gun to barefoot Brigadier General Kouprasith of the Royal Laotian Army in 1961. **2.** As well as bringing men and materiel through Laos, the Viet Cong were supplied by sea; a South Vietnamese junk patrol attempts to interdict the coastal routes. **3.** North Vietnam also supplied the Pathet Lao: these North Vietnamese regulars were captured by Royal Laotian troops while guarding a cache of Chinese-manufactured materiel near Thakhek, in the Laotian panhandle near the Thai border. **4.** This cave in north-central Laos was a supply dump for the Vietnamese Communists.

France, and the Soviet Union, was strongly opposed by Phoumi Nosavan and Boun Oum, supported by the United States and Thailand. The Soviet Union reacted to the crisis by using Ilyushin Il-14 transports to fly materiel from Hanoi to Vientiane to help Kong Le repel the Royal Army, now advancing to depose the neutralist regime. The two forces engaged in a long-range artillery duel, destroying much of Vientiane and killing or wounding some 1,600 persons, almost all noncombatants. Kong Le had to retreat to the Plain of Jars in north-central Laos, but Phoumi Nosavan did not press his advantage and Kong Le was able to link up with the Pathet Lao.

The Soviet Union now sent additional aid, including trucks and anti-aircraft guns, to the Pathet Lao-neutralist coalition. Meanwhile, the United States increased its aid to Phoumi Nosavan, providing six North American AT-6 Texan (Harvard) single-engine trainers of World War II vintage. These aircraft served as fighter-bombers in support of the Royal Army's sluggish advance toward the Plain of Jars. US Army Special Forces training teams tried to improve the skills of Phoumi's men, but the North Vietnamese matched this effort by assigning Viet Cong cadres to Pathet Lao units.

The North Vietnamese attack Laos

America's lack of strategic reserve, West European opposition to armed intervention, and the poor quality of the Royal Army of Laos, persuaded newly-elected President John F. Kennedy to settle for a neutral Laos. Nikita A. Khrushchev, the Soviet premier, also felt that Laos was not worth a war. North Vietnam's main concern was safeguarding the Ho Chi Minh Trail; the Pathet Lao felt that victory was a matter of time; China thought primarily of border security. As a result, these powers agreed to another bargaining session at Geneva in May 1961, devoted to creating a neutral Laos.

Giving the lie to Communist charges that he was an American puppet, Phoumi Nosavan almost singlehandedly disrupted President Kennedy's plans for Laos. Confident that he had the backing of the United States military, he refused to cooperate in forming a coalition cabinet, as agreed at Geneva in mid-1962, and rashly massed his troops in the Muang Luong–Nam Tha area, near China's sensitive border. On 6 May 1962, after three months of probing, North Vietnamese forces attacked. The 5,000 defenders retreated in panic, some of them fleeing to Thailand. Phoumi Nosavan's humiliation enabled the factions to agree on a coalition government including both Pathet Lao and rightist elements, headed by Souvanna Phouma, which took office later that summer.

The struggle, however, continued throughout the 1960s. North Vietnam used the Pathet Lao to protect the Ho Chi Minh Trail; the United States jabbed at the enemy with Vang Pao's Meo guerrillas. The Kingdom of Laos remained a pawn in a larger struggle; just four years after he had rebelled against a US-dominated regime, Kong Le denounced the Soviet Union for trying to make Laos its colony.

US intervention and the fall of Diem

Dr. William Michael Hammond

President John F. Kennedy confronted a deteriorating situation in Southeast Asia almost from the moment he took office in January 1961. In Laos, a pro-American faction led by Phoumi Nosavan was losing ground to a pro-Communist group supported by the Soviet Union. In South Vietnam, President Ngo Dinh Diem was fighting a losing battle with Communist insurgents.

Kennedy was at first more concerned with Laos than with South Vietnam, but his policies toward the one came to affect his relationship with the other. Deciding, in May 1961, not to send US troops to Laos, Kennedy attempted to dampen down the situation there by agreeing to a cease-fire and by supporting a coalition government headed by the neutralist Prince Souvanna Phouma. Yet in doing so he recognized that other Southeast Asian leaders would view his action as a sign of American weakness and would begin to doubt America's commitment to their mutual defense. Already politically embarrassed by the recent Bay of Pigs fiasco in Cuba, Kennedy could ill afford another defeat. Thus, he decided to demonstrate American resolve by standing firm against further Communist aggression in South Vietnam.

Kennedy's decision came at a difficult time in South Vietnam, where Communist insurgents were waging large-scale guerrilla warfare, instigating more than 600 incidents each month and exercising varying degrees of control over some 58 per cent of the countryside. Meanwhile, Eldridge Durbrow, American Ambassador to South Vietnam, was reporting widespread popular dissatisfaction throughout the country, both with Diem's failure to cope with the Viet Cong and with his autocratic methods of government. For months Durbrow had been urging Diem to implement reforms to put the country on a strong wartime footing and to win the allegiance of the people to the government. But Diem—mistrusting foreigners and intent upon preserving his own power—procrastinated by issuing token decrees that changed nothing.

America presses Diem to make reforms

Nevertheless, Kennedy felt compelled to show his support for South Vietnam and decided on a new approach that he hoped would gain Diem's cooperation and stabilize the situation. Sending Vice President Lyndon Baines Johnson to Saigon on 12 May 1961, Kennedy told him to proclaim American solidarity with the South Vietnamese. With Johnson travelled Frederick E. Nolting, Jr., the new American Ambassador to South Vietnam, with instructions to abandon Ambassador Durbrow's forthright approach and to "get on Diem's

---

While rioting Buddhists and students tore apart South Vietnam's cities Communist terror squads murdered Diem's officials and US military advisers died in battles half-heartedly fought by the South Vietnamese Army against the Viet Cong. In November 1963, with the tacit support of American officials, Diem's generals launched a coup against the dictator, who died at the hand of an unknown assassin

---

wave-length''. If hammering at Diem for reforms had failed, Kennedy and his advisers reasoned, perhaps coaxing would work.

Although he established a friendly relationship with Diem, Nolting had little more success than his predecessor: Diem remained unwilling to make the changes the United States desired. Nolting, for example, advised that control of counter-guerrilla operations should be completely in the hands of military officers, as opposed to Diem's practice of forcing military commanders to work in concert with provincial leaders who were primarily politicians. But Diem, fearing the *coup* potential of his generals, preferred to leave control of local military units (the bulk of South Vietnam's fighting forces) in the hands of men personally loyal to him. The result was a needlessly complex chain of command leading to military operations that accomplished little. Nolting also advised Diem to break up the large land-holdings of South Vietnam's upper classes and to distribute the acreage among the country's landless peasantry—in one step stealing a major program from the Viet Cong and cementing the peasants' interests firmly to those of the government. Diem, who owed much of his power to the landowners and upper classes, was unwilling to trade their support for the possibility that the common people might rally to his side. Himself a product of the "mandarin" class—the Confucian ideology predominant in Vietnam from the 11th to the 19th centuries had never been truly eradicated—Diem believed that, like the former Emperors of China, he possessed a "mandate from heaven", and expected the people to follow him as a leader by "divine right".

The worsening situation in South Vietnam reached a new low in September 1961,

when the Viet Cong captured a provincial capital, Phuoc Vinh, only some 55 miles (89km) north of Saigon, and publicly "tried" and decapitated the provincial chief. ARVN forces recaptured the town next day; 75 ARVN personnel and civilians were killed, with an estimated 100 Viet Cong dead. By November, the terrorist organization had grown from the few thousand men of the late 1950s to an estimated strength of 17,000; Communist infiltrators were entering the country from North Vietnam by way of Laos; and the Viet Cong were threatening the approaches to Saigon.

When Vice President Johnson visited South Vietnam in May, he mentioned the possibility either of sending US combat troops into the country or of negotiating a security treaty. Diem had then refused both suggestions, preferring to preserve his government's complete autonomy; but with his increasing difficulties in September, he decided to ask the United States for a bilateral defense treaty. The low morale of his people and Army, he told President Kennedy, was caused by their fear that America might abandon them as it had Laos—although most American officials put the blame on Diem's failure to deal effectively with the Viet Cong.

Increased US aid to South Vietnam

On 11 October, President Kennedy dispatched General Maxwell D. Taylor, his personal military adviser, and Dr. Walt W. Rostow, one of his aides, to South Vietnam to study the alternatives open to the United States. The two envoys concluded that the situation was indeed serious, but that an anti-Communist victory was still possible if the United States acted promptly to shore up South Vietnamese morale. What the President should do, they asserted in their final report, was commit American combat troops to South Vietnam to resolve the doubts caused by the Laotian settlement. Further, generous American aid in both money and manpower to all levels of the South Vietnamese government and Army might well result in the reformation of the Diem regime and give South Vietnam the will to win.

Kennedy and his advisers at first considered sending a token combat force, but for the time being dropped this idea on the grounds that victory must be accomplished by the South Vietnamese themselves. Instead, they settled upon a program of increased American aid. Ambassador Nolting was told that if Diem would agree to a series of political, military, and economic reforms, the United States would deploy helicopters, aircraft, intelligence and air reconnaissance groups,

1. Among the arms used by the Viet Cong were American weapons captured in Korea and handed on by China; the guerrilla in the bow of the boat carries a US-made Browning Automatic Rifle. **2.** Vice President Lyndon B. Johnson greets South Vietnamese during an Asian fact-finding tour. **3.** Men of the South Vietnamese Junk Force search a fishing boat suspected of carrying arms and supplies for the Viet Cong. **4.** ARVN troops after a victory over the Viet Cong; the Army's counter-guerrilla campaign was hampered by President Diem's distrust of his generals and his consequent insistence on subordinating military commanders to civilian officials.

and other men and equipment to improve the ARVN's training and logistical capabilities.

Diem readily agreed to the arrangement, and on 11 December two US helicopter companies—33 H-21C Shawnee helicopters (later designated CH-21) and 400 men to fly and maintain them—arrived in South Vietnam. In the months to come, more Americans appeared: pilots, ostensibly to train the South Vietnamese Air Force but actually to fly combat missions under the guise of training; US Army Special Forces officers, to advise South Vietnamese Army units in the field and often also to take command themselves; and a wide range of political, economic, and military experts. Early in February 1962, the Kennedy administration established an umbrella agency, the Military Assistance Command, Vietnam (MACV), to coordinate US military policy, assistance, and operations in South Vietnam. General Paul D. Harkins was appointed its commander.

The Americans immediately began centralizing the South Vietnamese Army's logistical functions, improving its intelligence capabilities, and restructuring its system of training. By September 1962, all the country's major military units were linked by telephone and all radio frequencies were standardized, so that the total force available to a local combat commander could be coordinated, if necessary, against a single point.

As early as June 1962, Australia became the first Free World country to share the burden with the United States, when 30 jungle-warfare specialists of the Australian Army arrived to serve as training advisers alongside US personnel. They were the forerunners of the Australian Army Training Team, an élite force whose members would, among other accomplishments, win four Victoria Crosses—their country's highest award for valor—before they were the last Australian contingent to be withdrawn from Vietnam in December 1972.

Two views on the Fortified Hamlets system

By early July 1962, Secretary of Defense Robert S. McNamara could tell the American public that he believed US aid to South Vietnam had begun to tip the balance against the Communists, while two months later Roger Hilsman, one of McNamara's assistants, asserted in a widely-publicized newspaper interview that American assistance had given the South Vietnamese "new confidence". More than 2,000 fortified hamlets had come into being in recent months, Hilsman stated, and they were becoming increasingly identified with the Diem government, which gained credit from the medical, economic, and educational programs the United States provided. Meanwhile, the Viet Cong defection rate was rising and the number of enemy recruits had fallen off.

American newspapermen in South Vietnam at first shared McNamara and Hilsman's optimism. While a few, Homer Bigart of the New York *Times* and François Sully of *Newsweek Magazine* among them, remained skeptical, most were impressed by the progress US officials cited. David Halberstam of the New York *Times* (who

was later to be disillusioned) wrote glowingly of a South Vietnamese victory in the Plain of Reeds, a well-established Communist stronghold in the Mekong Delta near the Cambodian border, that had cost the Viet Cong about 150 lives; Halberstam asserted in a number of his reports that the government of South Vietnam was keeping the enemy on the defensive and that the Viet Cong remained overawed by the helicopters.

Yet while massive American aid had indeed thrown the enemy off balance militarily, the political war for the minds of the South Vietnamese people remained undecided. Ambassador Nolting and General Harkins believed that victory in battle would necessarily ensure the loyalty of the people to the government, but Americans working at lower level, in direct contact with the Vietnamese, had few illusions of that sort. McNamara believed that the population was turning to Diem; field officers recognized that Diem's failure to reform his administration and his maintenance of corrupt officials in office so long as they remained loyal to him had created dangerous political apathy among large segments of the population. Hilsman might speak of progress in the fortified hamlet program, but most Americans concerned with day-to-day operations knew that many of the hamlets' occupants had been rounded up and resettled forcibly, and that the walls protecting the villages were designed as much to keep the residents in as the enemy out.

The same was true of the military position. American advisers had indeed improved the organization of the South Vietnamese Army, but Diem remained fearful of his generals. Rather than have a hero arise from among them to capture the imagination of the people and challenge his authority, he tended to punish military success rather than reward it. Lieutenant Colonel John Paul Vann, US adviser to the South Vietnamese Army's IV Corps (who later retired in order to "tell the American public the truth"), cited the case of a Vietnamese colonel who had won a notable victory against the enemy at the cost of several of his own men. Diem immediately summoned the officer, a brigadier general designate, to Saigon and threatened to stop his promotion if he incurred any more casualties. The intimidated colonel returned to his unit and from that day onward attempted to avoid combat, refusing to send his men forward if the enemy attacked and calling instead upon air strikes and artillery. He received his promotion. When Colonel Vann reported the behavior of the officer, and others like him, to General Harkins, his protest was ignored.

Other junior members of the US advisory team attempted to convince their superiors that the war was going poorly and that the South Vietnamese people had yet to side with Diem, but to no avail. Ordered to maintain the best possible relationship with Diem, and sincerely believing that the South Vietnamese needed optimism rather than criticism, Nolting and Harkins put their trust in statistics: "kill ratios"; estimates of the population "pacified"; and tallies of enemy-initiated incidents. In reality, these told very little about the condition of the war, because they were

4

5

6

1. An Australian Army Training Team adviser instructs a man of the 3rd Battalion, 3rd Regiment, 1st Vietnamese Division, in the use of the 106mm recoilless rifle.
2. A USAF C-123B flies a defoliation mission over Route 1, east of Saigon, in February 1962.
3. After an unsuccessful coup against

Diem, the Vietnamese Air Force swears loyalty to the President in March 1962. 4. Early air support for South Vietnam: a North American T-28 trainer converted to a light attack aircraft with gun pods and weapon pylons.
5. CH-21 Shawnees of the US Army's 121st Aviation Company embark South Vietnamese Marines at Bac Lieu for

airlift to a Viet Cong-infested area.
6. Vietnamese laborers maintain the airstrip at Da Nang as a Shawnee takes off on a training mission. 7. US equipment for the ARVN: a Vietnamese soldier on a training exercise fires a .50-caliber machine gun mounted on an M113 reconnaissance vehicle of the US Army's 4th AC Squadron.

7

drawn from South Vietnamese reports designed to show progress whatever the facts. Denied a hearing by their superiors, the junior officers began leaking classified information to the press, hoping that at least part of what they saw as the truth would reach Washington.

The news reports that resulted provoked an angry reaction in both Washington and Saigon. Fearful that the leaking of derogatory information to the press would harm the ability of the US Mission to work with Diem, yet also afraid that any attempt to invoke press censorship would anger the American public, US officials attempted privately to restrain their dissenting colleagues and to control adverse press coverage by restricting the news that official spokesmen released to correspondents. The Diem regime viewed every critical report as a sign of the newsmen's sympathy for the Communists and attempted either to silence or to expel the reporters concerned.

The result was the polarization of the American community in Saigon. Nolting, Harkins, and other senior American officials tried to moderate Diem's attempts to muzzle the correspondents, recognizing that adversity would only strengthen the newsmen's convictions; yet they themselves clung stubbornly to their own point of view and refused to entertain any doubts. The correspondents and junior officials were just as stubborn. Temporarily abating their criticisms, they began seeking proof that Diem's earlier successes had been merely the products of chance.

The South Vietnamese defeated at Ap Bac

Events early in January 1963 seemed to provide such proof. South Vietnamese intelligence revealed that an enemy radio station was operating near the village of Ap Bac in the Plain of Reeds and estimated that only a small guerrilla force was guarding it. Expecting an easy victory, South Vietnamese commanders immediately dispatched a multi-battalion force composed of infantry, ranger (commando), helicopter, and armored units, with 51 American military advisers.

Almost everything went wrong in the ensuing battle. Instead of encountering a company of guerrillas, the ARVN arrived at Ap Bac to face the 514th Viet Cong (regular) battalion—a formidable force of 400 men. Five American helicopters supporting the operation were destroyed within a few minutes: two fell to enemy gunfire; one to engine failure; and two because their pilots gallantly flew into the direct fire of the enemy's guns to rescue downed comrades who were, in fact, already safe behind friendly lines. As the battle developed, American advisers suggested that the South Vietnamese, who had considerable superiority in numbers and firepower, should advance, but the ARVN commanders—none above the rank of captain, because field-grade officers considered themselves above field service —were well aware of Diem's attitude toward casualties. Thus they delayed, one of them taking three-and-one-half hours to move his armored personnel carriers 1,500 yards (1,370m) against small-arms fire. When the US advisers called for an

airborne drop east of Ap Bac to close an enemy escape route, the troops dropped to the west, where they could do no good. When the advisers called for a heavy artillery barrage, the gunners delivered only four rounds an hour. The Viet Cong escaped under cover of darkness, but not before a South Vietnamese air strike had accidentally hit a friendly unit causing, according to official reports, an "undetermined" number of casualties. A reliable source states that besides the five helicopters destroyed, eleven were damaged and 65 ARVN personnel and three American advisers were killed.

American reporters knew nothing of the battle when it began, but, arriving shortly after its end, they recorded the US advisers' angry analyses. One correspondent contrived to eavesdrop on a confidential briefing for General Harkins; others were present the next day when mopping-up operations began with South Vietnamese gunners accidentally shelling their own troops. As a result, the correspondents had enough evidence to substantiate their most pessimistic beliefs.

The news reports that followed caused an angry outcry against Diem in the United States. American newspaper commentators charged that the United States had spent $400 million on South Vietnam, and had forfeited the lives of 50 American servicemen, only to have Diem refuse to make the reforms he had pledged in return for American aid. Meanwhile, enemy guerrillas had the run of the countryside and South Vietnamese officers were reluctant to fight even when the advantage was on their side. The only thing the United States could do, many commentators asserted, was to take full control of the war.

American officials in Washington and Saigon attempted to reassure Diem that they supported him despite the adverse press reports, but even now their efforts did nothing to sway him toward reform. In fact, they made matters worse. When State Department spokesmen asserted that the South Vietnamese had fought with "courage and determination" at Ap Bac, and General Harkins and Admiral Harry D. Felt, US Commander in Chief, Pacific, stated that the battle had been a victory for Diem's troops, some American newspapers retorted that the situation in South Vietnam must be bleak indeed if loyalty to policy required American officials to spread "such thin and unconvincing whitewash".

The Ap Bac controversy further divided the American community in South Vietnam. Embarrassed and annoyed by the press reports, high-level officials within the US Embassy limited their contacts with newsmen to formal occasions and determinedly turned an increasingly optimistic face toward the war. The correspondents, for their part, tended more and more to see the war in the worst light and to emphasize, sometimes to the point of exaggeration, everything they judged was wrong.

The South Vietnamese might have silenced the critical newsmen by winning battles or by inaugurating the reforms the United States desired, but Diem would seek neither alternative and instead allowed events to drift.

In May 1963, conditions began to deteriorate rapidly. Early in the month, govern-

2

1. South Vietnamese paratroopers in training. In spite of US-funded and supervised improvements in equipment and training, the ARVN often showed marked unwillingness to engage the Viet Cong during the early 1960s. **2.** A South Vietnamese paratrooper makes a free-fall jump. The lack of aggression of ARVN troops provided ammunition for critics of increasing American commitment. **3.** Silent and impassive, although wreathed in flame from the gasoline drenching his robes, this young Buddhist bonze (priest) set himself ablaze in central Saigon on 5 October 1963; the fifth, and by no means the last, Buddhist to choose death in this spectacular fashion as a protest against President Diem's heavy-handed repression of religion-inspired disturbances.

ment officials in Hue, the old imperial capital of Vietnam, allowed Roman Catholics to fly religious flags in celebration of the birthday of the city's archbishop (Diem's brother), but on 3 June the traditional display of flags to mark the birth of Buddha was banned. Local Buddhists (representing some 80 percent of Hue's population) immediately complained that the decision was discriminatory and, when city officials refused to lose face by admitting they had been in error, took to the streets to protest. The government responded by calling out troops; in the disturbance that followed nine Buddhists perished.

Buddhist riots and burning bonzes

Rioting soon spread from Hue to Saigon, where what had been a purely religious matter became a full political crisis centered on Diem's arbitrary and sometimes repressive rule. Ambassador Nolting, instructed by the State Department, urged Diem to take responsibility for the Hue incident and to make peace with the Buddhists by reaffirming his government's adherence to the principles of religious equality. Diem agreed to begin discussions—but destroyed any chance for compromise by allowing his sister-in-law, Madame Ngo Dinh Nhu, to denounce the religious protestors as traitors and Communist sympathizers. The Buddhists responded on 11 June when, in accordance with an ancient tradition, a monk called Thich Quang Duc publicly burned himself to death in Saigon, perishing in a holocaust of gasoline while his co-religionists prevented fire engines from approaching. There were to be more ritual suicides of this kind.

Associated Press reporter Malcolm Browne, the only American newsman present at the suicide, took a photograph of the burning monk that shocked the world. Diem denounced Browne, a critic of the regime whom he had already attempted to expel, as a Communist sympathizer who had engineered the whole episode by bribery, but to no avail. The next day, Nolting being absent on vacation, US Deputy Chief of Mission William Trueheart informed Diem that if South Vietnam refused to act on the Buddhists' grievances the United States would dissociate itself from the regime. Diem then began negotiations with the Buddhists in earnest, and on 16 June reached ostensible agreement with them.

Diem nevertheless recognized that the United States had little choice but to support his regime, having no alternative, and never carried out his promises. Instead, he allowed his sister-in-law to continue her taunts; Madame Nhu issued a series of provocative statements, calling the Buddhists "murderers" and declaring that her family would "ignore the bonzes (Buddhist priests) so that if they burn 30 women we shall clap our hands".

Madam Nhu's taunts proved literally inflammatory: the Buddhists replied with more suicides. Recognizing that good relations with the American correspondents in Saigon would give them a world audience—and that Diem would never be able totally and brutally to repress them

as long as that audience was watching— the dissident Buddhists did everything they could to win the press to their side. Newsmen were accorded access to the highest Buddhist dignataries and received advance warning of the dates, times, and places of demonstrations. Diem, meanwhile, inadvertently furthered the Buddhists' purposes by alienating the correspondents even more. His police harassed reporters in the streets and his censors removed every offending remark from their dispatches.

The news reports that resulted — smuggled out of Vietnam aboard US Air Force transports by sympathetic flight crews—were often filled with errors. For example, correspondents asserted that 70 percent of South Vietnamese were Buddhists and that the protesters spoke for the majority of the population. In fact, most Vietnamese were ancestor-worshipers and the Buddhists were mainly urban dwellers. Nevertheless, the newsmen contrived to present the religious crisis as a symbol of everything that was wrong in South Vietnam. As David Halberstam, now one of Diem's most avid critics, wrote in the New York *Times* on 16 June:

"The government's reaction to this protest is not an isolated episode but part of a pattern in which (the Diem regime's) strong qualities—true anti-Communism, stubbornness, resilience —are no longer enough. Observers feel that its limitations—suspicion of its major ally, suspicion of its own army, insistence on dictating the aspirations of its people instead of sensing and reacting to them—are now greater than its positive abilities, and that it has virtually neutralized itself at a time when it desperately needs to harness all resources in this country."

The US government was coming close to that opinion itself, but Ambassador Nolting returned to Washington in June to argue that there was no alternative to Diem but chaos. The American military chiefs backed him, asserting that the war was going well despite the complaints of junior officers and that any change of government could only upset that trend. However, President Kennedy decided that a change of personnel in Saigon might have some effect on Diem and, Nolting having submitted his resignation some months before, appointed as Ambassador Henry Cabot Lodge, a politician from one of America's first families.

Disguised troops attack Buddhist pagodas

Nolting, returning to Saigon for one last attempt to reason with Diem, received assurances that the government would remedy Buddhist grievances. Yet on the night of 21 August, only one week after Nolting's departure, Diem's brother Ngo Dinh Nhu attempted to settle the Buddhist problem once and for all by using an Army-ordered declaration of martial law to justify a massive raid on their pagodas. In the resultant violence, Nhu's troops wounded 30 bonzes and arrested more than 1,400.

Realizing that, because of Diem's promises to Nolting, the attacks were in direct defiance of the United States, Nhu attempted to fix blame for the whole affair on the South Vietnamese Army by disguising the élite police and Vietnamese Special Forces units that carried out the pagoda attacks as regular Army troops. The ruse succeeded only in alienating both the South Vietnamese Army and the US government. On 23 August, while students from Saigon University demonstrated for the release of the imprisoned Buddhists, representatives of Diem's generals contacted the US Embassy in Saigon to ascertain the probable reaction of the United States to a *coup*. Following instructions from Washington, Lodge told them that the United States could never support a government controlled by Nhu, but that the retention of power by Diem was a matter for the Vietnamese themselves to decide.

The fall and death of President Diem

The *coup* failed to materialize because the generals had yet to resolve differences among themselves, but rioting by Buddhists and students continued into September, with Diem ordering more mass arrests. For the time being, the Kennedy administration decided it had little choice but to maintain apparent support for Diem and Nhu, but it began seeking ways to coerce them into following American wishes. On 23 September, Secretary of Defense McNamara arrived in Saigon to review the situation. He decided to recommend a cut-back in the American economic aid program for South Vietnam and suspension of support for the special military units that had carried out the pagoda raids.

These decisions were a direct blow at Diem—and one that South Vietnam's generals immediately interpreted as a signal that the United States would welcome a change of government. Contacting Lodge, they told him they were once more preparing a *coup*.

Lodge and General Harkins were in disagreement. Lodge asserted that Diem was unlikely ever to respond to American pressure, as his past record showed; Harkins declared that a group of untried generals could never replace a leader of Diem's stature. In the event, the Kennedy administration sided with Lodge and opted for a policy of benign non-involvement in the *coup*. Lodge told the generals that the United States would support any government that could both attract the allegiance of the people and fight the Communists effectively.

The generals acted accordingly. Moving on the afternoon of 1 November to isolate forces potentially loyal to Diem, they surrounded the Presidential Palace in Saigon and called for Diem and Nhu to surrender. The brothers escaped through a secret passage into the city, only to be captured the next morning. Shortly thereafter, while on their way to the generals' headquarters, they were mysteriously murdered.

Three weeks later, President Kennedy himself died, the victim of an assassin's bullet.

1

4

7

1. Village Civil Defense personnel in South Vietnam conduct firing practice under the eyes of General Paul D. Harkins (center), Commander, US Military Assistance Command, Vietnam, and General George H. Decker (right), Chief of Staff, US Army, in June 1962. **2.** Viet Cong gunners with light anti-aircraft artillery. **3.** The Kennedy administration hoped that the provision of US equipment and advisers would preclude sending a combat force; here, Sergeant William Bowen of the US Military Assistance Command discusses operational tactics with Vietnamese infantrymen. **4.** Showing aggression that they were often accused of lacking, ARVN troops disembark from a US Army helicopter to engage Viet Cong. **5.** In a resettlement camp, an adviser from the US Agency for International Development discusses problems with villagers moved from homes in Communist-threatened areas. **6.** A US Army M113 armored personnel carrier makes a river crossing in South Vietnam. **7.** Viet Cong prisoners captured during airborne operations in the Mekong Delta area of South Vietnam in 1962 are marched to a rear area under guard by soldiers of the ARVN.

Communist aggression provokes US retaliation

Dr. William Michael Hammond

The overthrow of Diem and the establishment of a new military government under a triumvirate formally headed by former Vice President Nguyen Ngoc Tho but dominated by General Duong Van Minh (called "Big Minh") did nothing to arrest the decline of South Vietnam. Shortly after the *coup*, the Viet Cong went on the offensive across the country, overpowering a number of poorly-designed and poorly defended military installations and destroying the weakest of Diem's fortified hamlets. Minh, despite his high-sounding rhetoric promising democracy of efficiency, had no real plan for governing the country; instead of resisting the enemy forcefully, he allowed his subordinates to engage in a destructive struggle for power. Scores of provincial chiefs and minor officials supposedly loyal to Diem were removed, to be replaced by inexperienced administrators loyal to Minh. Such disastrous fumbling drove the country rapidly toward chaos. By January 1964, protesting workers were on strike in Saigon, students were once more demonstrating, and rumors abounded to the effect that Minh himself planned to betray the country to the Communists.

President Johnson steps up financial aid

On 30 January, Major General Nguyen Khanh overthrew Minh in a bloodless *coup*—but little changed. Nevertheless, the United States, convinced that political stability was essential to save South Vietnam from Communism, gave total support to the new government. For a time Khanh reciprocated, attempting to make himself a genuinely popular political figure by visiting the provinces and holding rallies to solicit the people's support. Yet after a period of relative calm, the Buddhists began to agitate for a dominant voice in Khanh's government and, finding Khanh unreceptive, once more took to the streets in Saigon and Hue to protest. Khanh avoided the violent confrontations between police and demonstrators that had brought Diem down and, after a time, made a number of concessions that proved conciliatory. Yet, in the interim, more than 40 percent of South Vietnam came under Communist control. American advisers in the provinces soon began reporting that support for the government was waning among the people because of the administrative chaos caused by Khanh's new round of purges aimed at replacing Minh's appointees with his own men.

Visiting South Vietnam early in March 1964, Secretary of Defense McNamara recognized that the situation was deteriorating and that another *coup* was possible at any moment. Convinced that if South Vietnam fell the rest of Southeast Asia

As Communist aggression escalated, political stability in South Vietnam appeared to be an impossible goal; it seemed that only an increase in US military commitment could back up political initiatives. When Communist torpedo boats attacked US destroyers in the Gulf of Tonkin in August 1964, American airpower was openly unleashed against North Vietnam for the first time in the conflict

would be driven into the Communist camp, he returned to Washington to recommend that the United States increase its aid to Khanh, who must in turn promise to implement a program of national mobilization. This increased aid would both improve South Vietnam's fighting ability and forestall further disruptive political conspiracies by emphasizing that America supported Khanh.

Khanh and President Lyndon B. Johnson, Kennedy's successor, agreed with McNamara: on 17 March, Johnson ordered an increase in US aid to South Vietnam of $60 million. Promising to exchange South Vietnamese aircraft and armored vehicles for newer equipment, Johnson also told Khan that the United States would finance a 50,000-man increase in the South Vietnamese armed forces and would provide funds for the modernization of the country's system of government and administrative techniques.

At the same time, President Johnson directed the US Joint Chiefs of Staff to begin planning retaliatory air raids against North Vietnam, to be launched at 72 hours' notice. They were also to draw up a program of "graduated overt military pressures" against North Vietnam as a means of increasing the cost to the Hanoi regime of its aggression. Johnson had no mandate from the American Congress or people for such outright attacks on North Vietnam. He sincerely hoped that the South Vietnamese would be able to win the war on their own—but Communist terrorism was increasing and he intended to be prepared to react quickly if necessary.

From its inception, Khanh experienced difficulty in implementing McNamara's program. Lacking a firm political base and hampered by a bureaucracy that clung to a "business-as-usual" attitude even in a

time of crisis, he was unable to generate support for the new policy. As a result, the promised mobilization never came about, and the 50,000-man increase in the armed forces took place so slowly that the enemy never felt its effect.

Khanh himself had little enthusiasm for long-range reforms and wished instead for some spectacular action that would unify the country and win his people's confidence. Arguing that it was wrong to go on incurring casualties "just... to make the agony endure", he approached Ambassador Lodge early in May with a suggestion that any further Communist interference in South Vietnam's affairs be met with "tit-for-tat" bombing raids upon North Vietnam. Such a strong policy, he avowed, accompanied by a suspension of civil liberties in South Vietnam similar to the measures adopted by Abraham Lincoln in the United States during the American Civil War, would spur his people to action.

Although he himself had contingency plans for air raids upon North Vietnam, President Johnson was for the time being unwilling to make such a move. Communist China might make such attacks an excuse to intervene—and there were the coming American elections to consider. Johnson had no wish to inaugurate his re-election campaign by appearing as the advocate for a major war in Southeast Asia—especially when his probable opponent Senator Barry Goldwater, was already arguing for tougher American action in Vietnam. Refusing Khanh's request, Johnson attempted a compromise, shoring up South Vietnamese morale by publicly declaring that the United States had every intention of honoring its commitments, yet simultaneously seeking to reassure

Khanh's call for an attack on the North

both the Communists and the American public that the United States had no aggressive intentions concerning North Vietnam and sought no escalation of hostilities.

Thus the matter stood until mid-July 1964, when Khanh recommenced his urgings for a more aggressive policy. Shortly after Maxwell D. Taylor succeeded Lodge as American Ambassador and General William C. Westmoreland replaced Harkins as Chief of the Military Assistance Command, Khanh told an American reporter—and later declared at a Saigon rally—that North Vietnam was engaged upon a full-scale invasion of his country and that the South Vietnamese people demanded a "march north" in retaliation. Possibly led on by "cheer-leaders" acting on Khanh's instructions, the crowd took up Khanh's call and began to shout, "To the north! To the north!"

1. "National Shame Day", 19 July 1964: demonstrators parade in front of the US Information Service building in Saigon to mark the 10th anniversary of the partition of Vietnam by the Geneva Agreements. 2. A demonstration of another kind: a member of the US 1st Special Forces Group conducts a grenade practice class for Vietnamese volunteers. 3. General Duong Van Minh's accession to power in South Vietnam late in 1963 was met by the Viet Cong with a country-wide offensive, deploying weapons like the rocket launcher seen here.

General Nguyen Cao Ky, commander of South Vietnam's Air Force, joined Khanh's campaign the next day by openly declaring at a news conference that his country was prepared to retaliate against Communist aggression and that his pilots were already training for such attacks. In an apparent effort to embarrass the United States, he then revealed that with American assistance the South Vietnamese armed forces had for the past three years been sending sabotage teams into North Vietnam. State-controlled newspapers immediately praised Ky for his candor and condemned the United States for its apparent duplicity.

Having no evidence that North Vietnamese troops were fighting as units in South Vietnam, the American Mission in Saigon attempted to refute Khanh's allegation. Ambassador Taylor himself reacted calmly to the furor. Arguing that Khanh's political problems demanded that he advocate dramatic action, but adding that South Vietnam might secretly negotiate with the Communists to end the war on a basis unfavorable to American interests if the United States refused to become more involved, Taylor suggested that joint US–South Vietnamese contingency planning for bombing raids on North Vietnam might calm Khanh. President Johnson agreed, and the agitation died down just as Taylor had predicted.

US destroyers attacked in the Tonkin Gulf

The United States had, in fact, been moving against North Vietnam for some time. In addition to the operations "exposed" by Ky, President Johnson, shortly after taking office, had authorized "OPLAN 34A"—a program of clandestine operations against North Vietnam. These included commando raids upon coastal installations; the kidnapping of civilians who, indoctrinated with anti-Communist ideas, might return home and sow dissent; and destroyer patrols (code-named "DESOTO") along the coast to gather intelligence. Since May 1964, in response to a Communist offensive on the Plain of Jars in Laos, the US had also conducted aerial reconnaissance missions over Laos, with pilots instructed to fire if fired upon.

In case the North Vietnamese failed to take these activities seriously, American officials also publicly acknowledged US contingency stockpiling in support of the possible introduction of American troops into Southeast Asia; for example, great publicity attended the dedication of a newly-constructed airbase at Da Nang in South Vietnam. Meanwhile, American resolve to resist aggression in Southeast Asia was communicated directly to the Communists through Ambassador Blair Seaborn, Canadian member of the International Control Commission in Hanoi. Stressing that American ambitions were limited and "essentially peaceful", Seaborn nevertheless told his Communist contacts that American patience had limits.

Despite these pressures, the North Vietnamese continued the flow of men and materiel into South Vietnam. By July 1964, the Viet Cong were planting bombs at will on Saigon's streets and making conditions so difficult for Americans living in the city

that General Westmoreland ordered his officers to go out in pairs when in uniform. So bold did the enemy become that American intelligence analysts began to speculate that the Communists were preparing a decisive push against South Vietnam's demoralized Army and unstable Government.

Although President Johnson's advisers were deeply concerned and, during July 1964, began to draft a Congressional Resolution sanctioning American attacks on North Vietnam as a means of stemming the Communist tide, the President refused to be hurried. Adopting a posture of self-restraint, while Senator Goldwater argued for a more militant American stance in Southeast Asia, Johnson could hardly give the appearance of taking the advice of his political rival.

The North Vietnamese took the initiative, attacking the American destroyer *Maddox* outside North Vietnam's 12-mile limit on the afternoon of 2 August. The ship was steaming across the Gulf of Tonkin after making an intelligence-gathering sweep along the coast of North Vietnam when three torpedo boats were seen closing at high speed. Warning shots failed to deter the boats, so the destroyer brought its 5in (127mm) guns to bear and quickly disabled one of the attackers and damaged another. The Communists fired two torpedos that missed *Maddox* by 200 yards, breaking contact shortly after aircraft from the carrier *Ticonderoga* arrived on the scene. There were no US casualties.

The attack may have been provoked by recent South Vietnamese commando raids into North Vietnam under the protection of American Seventh Fleet ships such as the *Maddox*, or it may have been designed to embarrass Johnson on the eve of his Presidential campaign. Whatever the enemy's reasoning, Johnson held to his policy of restraint and responded calmly that, "The United States Government expects that North Vietnam will be under no misapprehension as to the grave consequences which would inevitably result from any further unprovoked military action against United States forces."

North Vietnamese aggression, or American imagination?

In accordance with Presidential instructions, the Tonkin Gulf patrol was reinforced the next day by a second destroyer, the *C. Turner Joy*. On the evening of 4 August, the two ships were steaming on an easterly course at 20 knots when a *Maddox* radarman reported what he judged to be five torpedo boats making toward the ships from a distance of 36 nautical miles (67km). In the maneuvering that followed, the skippers of both the *Maddox* and *C. Turner Joy*, convinced that they were under attack, called for air support and directed their gunners to open fire. It was reported that two North Vietnamese boats were sunk and two damaged.

Some critics, including US intelligence officers whose words were printed in the *Pentagon Papers*, later asserted that the "enemy vessels" had in reality been radar "blips" caused by the wake of the *C. Turner Joy*, which *Maddox*'s inexperienced radarman had misinterpreted. However, assured by field commanders that an attack had

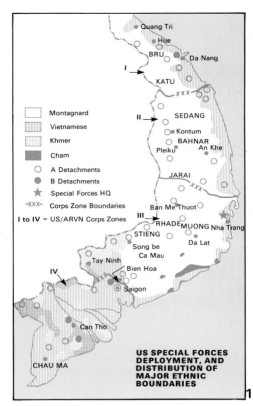

US SPECIAL FORCES DEPLOYMENT, AND DISTRIBUTION OF MAJOR ETHNIC BOUNDARIES

1

3

US Economic Aid for Vietnam, 1953–1967	
US Fiscal Year	Amount ($ millions)
1953–1957	823.3
1958	188.8
1959	207.1
1960	180.5
1961	144.6
1962	143.2
1963	197.5
1964	230.3
1965	268.9
1966	620.6
1967	648.1
Total:	**3,652.9**

1. Map: Major ethnic groups in South Vietnam; US Special Forces deployment in June 1963. 2. When General Khanh resisted Buddhist demands new religious riots swept South Vietnam, persisting even after Khanh's resignation; here, Catholic youths challenge Buddhists to attempt to recover the body of a Buddhist killed in an attack on a Catholic high school in Saigon in August 1964. 3. Patrol boats—possibly Chinese-built *Shanghai* class craft—of the North Vietnamese Navy.
4. General Khanh and members of the International Control Commission inspect a photomap showing the site of a Communist arms cache. 5. On 2 August 1964 three North Vietnamese torpedo boats attacked the destroyer USS *Maddox* as she patrolled the Gulf of Tonkin; this photograph taken from aboard *Maddox* shows one of the attackers. 6. Another photograph from *Maddox* shows a North Vietnamese torpedo boat approaching the destroyer at high speed. 7. USS *Maddox* was involved in the only attempts made by the North Vietnamese Navy to engage anti-Communist forces at sea, August 1964.

taken place and believing that the North Vietnamese would equate further restraint with weakness, President Johnson decided to retaliate. Ordering air strikes on the bases from which the attackers operated, he moved swiftly to present his aides' draft resolution to Congress for approval.

On 5 August, while Johnson announced that he was making a measured response to North Vietnamese aggression but had no intention of seeking a wider war, fighter-bombers from the carriers *Ticonderoga* and *Constellation* struck four naval bases and an oil storage depot in North Vietnam. An estimated 25 torpedo boats were destroyed and 90 percent of the oil storage facilities at Vinh went up in flames. Two American aircraft fell to anti-aircraft fire and two were damaged. No North Vietnamese aircraft were encountered.

Opinion polls taken in the United States shortly after the attacks revealed strong public support for Johnson's actions. On 7 August, Congress did the same, declaring approval of the President's determination to "take all necessary measures to repel any armed attack against the forces of the United States and . . . to take all necessary steps including the use of armed force to assist any member or protocol state" of the Southeast Asia Treaty Organisation.

On 11 August, President Johnson signed the Southeast Asia (Gulf of Tonkin) Resolution. Although this fell short of declaring outright war against North Vietnam, it nevertheless gave the President power to take any action he deemed necessary. Thus, Johnson avoided the possibility that China or the Soviet Union might react to an American declaration of war by themselves declaring war upon the United States. He also secured the kind of political and popular support he felt he needed. As Johnson himself later avowed: "The President is not about to commit forces and undertake actions to deter aggression in South Vietnam to prevent this Communist conspiracy, unless and until the American people through their Congress sign on to go in."

Internal opposition to Khanh's dictatorship

The Gulf of Tonkin Resolution and the raid on the North's naval bases boosted morale in South Vietnam, but Ambassador Taylor warned the State Department that the effect would be only temporary and that Khanh had at best only an even chance of retaining power. On 16 August, Khanh, still aware of his shaky political base, took advantage of the temporary euphoria in Saigon to proclaim himself President and to promulgate a new constitution giving him dictatorial powers.

Although a newly-established Military Revolutionary Council of senior generals rubber-stamped the move, Khanh's action immediately alienated the Buddhists, who saw in it a threat to their political aspirations. Encouraged by Viet Cong sympathizers and aided by dissident students, they began more riots. As urban discontent overflowed into rural areas, popular feeling turned so strongly against Khanh that he resigned the Presidency, annulled his constitution, and withdrew to Dalat, a resort town north of Saigon.

Since no new effective government

emerged and civil disturbances became more violent, Westmoreland and Taylor prevailed upon Khanh to return to Saigon. Even so, political stability was not attained: dissident generals almost immediately staged a *coup* that only aborted because General Ky and other young officers rallied to Khanh and threatened to bomb the positions of the rebellious troops.

Hardly had that threat subsided when a new one emerged. On the night of 19 September, Montagnard tribesmen in South Vietnam's Central Highlands attempted to secede in order to create an autonomous state free from the racial discrimination practiced against them by their lowland neighbors. Disarming their American Special Forces advisers, many of whom probably sympathized with them, and seizing the town of Dak Mil, the Montagnards executed over 70 government soldiers and took 60 civilians hostage before nearby government units could react. A battle was averted only by the intervention of US advisers and the timely arrival of a special emissary from the US Mission in Saigon with word that the tribesmen would receive no more American subsidies until they submitted to government authority. That ended the rebellion, but sporadic trouble continued for several weeks.

The continuing upheavals in Saigon, combined with intelligence reports indicating that the Communists were stepping up their infiltration of South Vietnam, induced an increasingly pessimistic attitude among American officials in the United States. When Ambassador Taylor visited Washington early in September, he found that some officials believed that the present policy of support for the South Vietnamese was ineffective and that the United States would have to take unilateral action—if only to improve the American image before pulling out. Taylor himself, with no intention of abandoning the South Vietnamese, told Secretary of State Rusk that he believed the Johnson administration would have to change radically its relationship with Khanh. In the past, the United States had used the possibility of joint US–South Vietnamese attacks on North Vietnam as a lever to keep Khanh in line; in future, the United States must make such attacks unilaterally in the hope that they would maintain South Vietnam's will to combat Communism.

Recognizing that without American initiative the situation in South Vietnam would deteriorate further, the Joint Chiefs of Staff agreed with Taylor—and suggested that the United States deliberately provoke a North Vietnamese attack upon American forces similar to that in the Gulf of Tonkin. This would provide the United States with a reason for beginning a bombing campaign against North Vietnam—a continuous campaign of increasing or decreasing severity according to the enemy's response. The Communists, the Joint Chiefs asserted, would quickly recognize that their own actions determined the amount of destruction visited upon them.

President Johnson approved a number of limited measures to put more pressure upon North Vietnam and agreed to respond to future North Vietnamese attacks on American units with "tit-for-tat" air raids. But he rejected the idea of a concerted air

1. Major General Duong Van Duc, commanding IV Corps, ARVN, describes the failure of his attempted coup against President Khanh to newsmen in September 1964. **2.** Men like this member of the US 1st Special Forces Group, seen atop a bunker on Nui Ba Den Mountain, helped keep the South Vietnamese flag flying in the early days of US involvement. **3.** President Johnson resisted pressure to unleash an aerial bombardment on North Vietnam in 1964—but Communist anti-aircraft gunners stood ready.

2

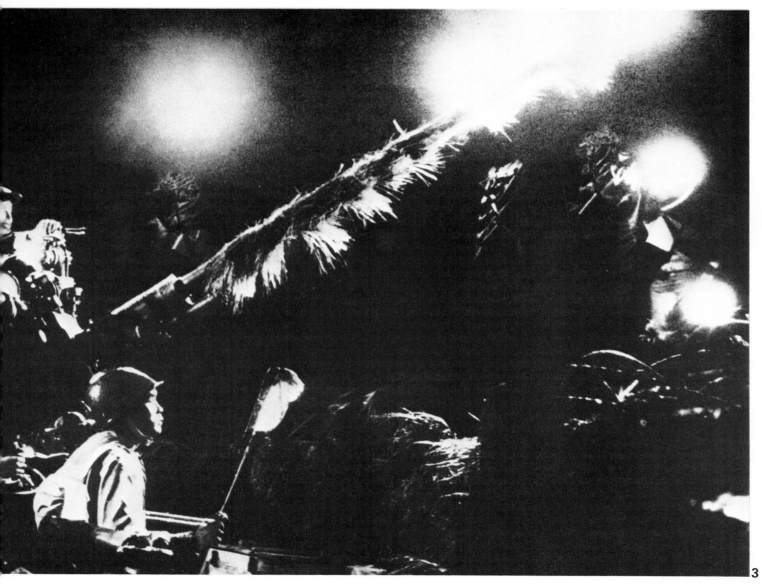

3

campaign against the North. Although he was willing to resume the DESOTO patrols (suspended since the Gulf of Tonkin incidents), he believed the South Vietnamese were still too weak for an aggressive policy to work. If the enemy responded with all-out attacks in the South, the Khanh regime might collapse.

Despite Johnson's caution, the resumption of naval patrols and clandestine operations along the coast of North Vietnam almost immediately caused renewed trouble. On the night of 18 September, the destroyers *Morton* and *Parsons* were steaming in the Gulf of Tonkin when their radar operators reported sighting what appeared to be torpedo boats. After maneuvering for 40 minutes and failing to elude their pursuers, the two ships opened fire and apparently scored hits, the images of the supposed enemy craft disappearing from the radar screens. Twice more that night, more images appeared on the ships' radar and disappeared after being fired upon. In all the *Morton* and *Parsons* fired over 200 5in (127mm) and 100 3in (76.2mm) shells.

Since neither ship had made visual contact with its targets, and since no torpedoes or gunfire originated from the radar contacts, President Johnson considered the attack questionable and refused to bomb North Vietnam in retaliation. Deciding the situation in the Gulf of Tonkin had become too sensitive, he again suspended the DESOTO patrols and postponed the resumption of South Vietnamese maritime operations in North Vietnamese waters. On 4 October, he authorized continuation of clandestine, but tightly controlled, operations against North Vietnam.

The American public question the war plans

Throughout October, Ambassador Taylor continued to recommend air strikes against North Vietnam, but time and again encountered the President's unwillingness to begin military adventures on the eve of the election and at a time when South Vietnam remained unstable. On 2 November, the Viet Cong made a surprise attack against the American air base at Bien Hoa near Saigon, killing five Americans, wounding 76, and destroying six Martin B-57 Canberra bombers. Taylor again recommended retaliatory raids upon North Vietnam, only to have his request once more rejected.

Johnson's restraint apparently paid off politically two days later, when the President defeated Goldwater by gaining an unprecedented 61 percent of the vote. Yet the victory had a dark side. For although the American public gave Johnson a strong mandate, no more than 42 percent of the individuals questioned by pollster Louis Harris on voting day gave the President high marks for his handling of the war. By early December, that figure had fallen to 38 percent. Whether the public wanted Johnson to move decisively to win the war or to withdraw from Vietnam was not clear, but it obviously wanted to see unequivocal leadership. If President Johnson did not take vigorous action of one kind or another in Vietnam, he would risk losing the popular support demonstrated by his victory in the election.

1

2

4

3.

1. A mother weeps over the body of her son, killed when a Viet Cong mine blew up the truck in which they were riding, August 1964. 2. Aircraft from USS *Constellation* (foreground) took part in retaliatory strikes on North Vietnamese naval bases on 5 August 1964, following the Tonkin Gulf incidents; other elements of Task Force 77 seen here are (left to right) the destroyer *George F. Mackenzie*, carrier *Oriskany*, destroyer *Rogers*, and ammunition ship *Mount Katmai*. 3. US Navy river patrol boats intercepted many small craft of this kind during "visit and search" operations. 4. US Navy men. with an interpreter, question a Vietnamese villager during a counterguerrilla sweep. 5. The urgency of these Vietnamese troops and US advisers shows why resupply missions to ground troops like the one made by this helicopter of US Marine Air Group 16 were called "touch and go" operations.

5.

The US commitment becomes irrevocable

Dr. William Michael Hammond

On the eve of his re-election in the first week of November 1964, President Johnson appointed an inter-agency working group in Washington to examine all alternatives open to him in Vietnam. He was reluctant to widen the war but recognized that something new was needed to encourage the South Vietnamese. Their government was still riven by factional strife and their Army had made little headway against the enemy. Meanwhile, intelligence from MACV indicated that the Communists were pouring men and materiel into South Vietnam at an unprecedented rate.

The American people shared Johnson's sense of urgency. By mid-November 1964, Gallup polls revealed that the US public now put Vietnam near the top of the list of problems it wanted solved. "President Johnson's first order of business, now that the election is over," *Life Magazine* asserted at the time, "is to come to grips with the badly deteriorating situation in South Vietnam. Last month, more Americans were killed there than in any month since the war began." The United States appeared to have few options, the *National Observer* added: "We either have to get out or take some action to help the Vietnamese. They won't help themselves."

US leaders bargain for South Vietnamese reform

Speculation concerning the future of Southeast Asia rose mightily on 27 November, when Ambassador Taylor returned to Washington for consultations. Although the State Department played down the visit as merely a routine review of the Vietnam situation, most newspaper commentators recognized that change was in the offing and speculated that Taylor would suggest some degree of escalation. Many thought this foolhardy, on the grounds that the United States could never rely upon the South Vietnamese in an emergency; yet few envisaged that the Johnson administration might consider withdrawal.

Ambassador Taylor indeed recommended escalation, if only to boost South Vietnamese morale; but he found the President convinced that political stability in South Vietnam was basic to any course the United States might adopt. Taylor therefore decided to propose a compromise. The President's working group had recommended a series of plans incorporating gradually intensifying air attacks against the Communists, beginning with strikes on enemy infiltration routes in Laos and culminating in limited but progressively more severe attacks upon North Vietnam itself. This program, Taylor remarked, resembled that advocated by Khanh in his "march North" campaign, and thus might

---

As one unstable government followed another in South Vietnam, while the Communists seemed ready to move from guerrilla warfare to a large-scale conventional campaign President Johnson reluctantly decided to take tougher action. In March 1965, the US launched a sustained aerial bombing offensive against North Vietnam and the 9th Marine Expeditionary Brigade landed at Da Nang

---

provide a useful lever. The United States could tell Khanh and his generals that it was considering direct pressure upon North Vietnam and, when the excited Vietnamese leaders began to urge immediate strikes, could offer a *quid pro quo*: air attacks on North Vietnam in exchange for reforms in the South. The program, said Taylor, would thus serve two purposes: it would create the stability and unity the United States had long sought in South Vietnam, and it would convince the Communists that continued aggression would prove ultimately self-destructive.

President Johnson accepted Taylor's proposal, but cautiously authorized no more than the first stages of the program. Although the United States would intensify its strikes against enemy infiltration routes in Laos and would approve clandestine South Vietnamese naval operations (in which ships of the US Navy would be involved) along the coast of North Vietnam, it would go no further. Taylor might inform Khanh of the possibility of joint US–South Vietnamese air strikes against the North as reprisals for enemy depredations in the South, but he must also stress that such attacks would not begin until the United States had evidence that the South Vietnamese government was capable of withstanding the probable enemy response.

The moves approved by President Johnson were implemented almost as soon as Taylor returned to Saigon, but neither the naval operations nor the air attacks in Laos unduly troubled the Communists. The naval program had hardly begun before the monsoon season set in, bringing heavy seas and precluding commando operations. The expansion of the air war over Laos began on 14 December with the inauguration of "Operation Barrel Roll";

but that, too, was ineffective because President Johnson had authorized only two weekly missions of four aircraft each. So feeble were the resulting strikes that the North Vietnamese never realized a new program had begun and considered that the attacks were merely a part of the armed reconnaissance flights the United States was already conducting.

In the same way, although Khanh readily agreed to Taylor's *quid pro quo*, the situation in South Vietnam failed to improve. The problem centered on the High National Council, a body created shortly after the August 1964 governmental crisis to draft a constitution and establish a civilian government. Composed of elderly civilians representing a broad cross-section of South Vietnamese society, the Council pleased no one and soon antagonized Khanh, who had no intention of allowing a civilian government to function as anything but a front for the military.

Controversy dogged the Council almost from its inception. Nicknamed the "High National Museum" because of the age of its members, the Council appointed an elderly agricultural engineer, Phan Khac Suu, as Chief of State. Suu appointed a former schoolteacher and mayor of Saigon, Tran Van Huong, as Premier. Huong, in turn, chose technicians rather than politicians for his cabinet, thus alienating the Buddhist and Catholic factions, both of which wanted a measure of political power. Soon, both religious groups were rioting in the streets.

Disenchanted army officers plot against Khanh

Backed by Khanh's promise of military support, Huong declared martial law and managed to suppress the rioters—but his difficulties were only beginning. Khanh's assurances lacked substance: the general was himself in political trouble. A group of young officers who called themselves the "Young Turks" (a reference to the organization of young officers that dominated Turkish politics from 1908 to 1918) had emerged as his main supporters, but the group was growing disenchanted. The deteriorating situation in the countryside, General Ky told Westmoreland at the time, together with Khanh's compromises with the Buddhists and his continuing vacillation, had so disturbed these officers that they had decided a change of command was needed.

Soon after Ky's conversation with Westmoreland, senior officers from the South Vietnamese armed forces formed an Armed Forces Council to "assist" Khanh in military matters. Recognizing that a clash was imminent, Westmoreland and Taylor immediately called the opposing factions together and, at an informal

1. Men of the 1st Battalion, 31st Infantry, ARVN, after an ambush by the Viet Cong in the south of the Mekong Delta; a US adviser calls a halt while a wounded man is brought in by boat. **2.** Viet Cong tactics late in 1964 suggested a move towards large-unit actions in which North Vietnamese regulars, like the gunners seen here, would play an increasing role. **3.** Members of a US Air Force combat control team watch paratroopers of the ARVN Airborne Division drop into a zone the team has marked out after jumping first into a Viet Cong-infiltrated area. **4.** Terror in South Vietnam: these children were killed by Viet Cong guerrillas during a raid on a village 10 miles north of the capital, Saigon.

meeting, pointed out that further disorder would seriously disrupt South Vietnam's relationship with the United States. Political stability, they reiterated, was "crucial" to any increase in American aid.

The generals' promise to work together in harmony proved to be a polite fiction. Their true sentiments surfaced on 19 December, when the Young Turks asked Khanh to eliminate the senior officers standing in the way of their promotions by having the High National Council retire all generals who had served for more than 25 years. Khanh complied—and when the Council refused, dismissed it summarily.

A series of angry confrontations involving Taylor, Khanh, and the Young Turks ensued. Recognizing that Khanh's action constituted a *coup d'etat* and that there was no longer any hope for the *quid pro quo* policy, Taylor summoned Ky and other leaders of the Young Turks to his office and delivered a stinging reprimand. The irresponsible actions of the officer corps, he asserted, had frustrated all the military plans dependent upon South Vietnamese stability: "We cannot carry you for ever if you do things like this." The generals riposted that they had merely attempted to reinvigorate the armed forces and, offended by Taylor's rebuke, left the meeting complaining that the Ambassador had treated them like "puppets" and "schoolboys".

Next day, at a meeting with Khanh, Taylor intimated that the general might have outlived his usefulness and suggested that he consider retirement and exile. Khanh responded on 22 December with an obvious attempt to unify the officer corps behind him by invoking national honor. In an "Order of the Day" he declared that it was "better to live poor but proud as free citizens of an independent country than in ease and shame as slaves of the foreigners and Communists". He soon compounded this insult to the American Ambassador by inviting a New York *Herald Tribune* correspondent to his office and accusing Taylor of activities "beyond imagination as far as an ambassador is concerned".

Viet Cong bombing outrages strike Saigon

When Khanh's charges appeared in print, the US State Department backed its ambassador and confirmed that Taylor had acted throughout with the full support of the US government. At a news conference, Secretary of State Rusk himself began the process of bringing the Vietnamese generals back into line by stating that the United States would shortly curtail some of its assistance programs for South Vietnam. Khanh's government, Rusk avowed, was obviously incapable of using that aid properly.

If Khanh and his generals needed proof that Rusk meant what he said, they soon received it. On the afternoon of 24 December, while many Americans in Saigon were preparing to celebrate Christmas Eve, the Viet Cong bombed the Brink Hotel, a US officers' billet situated near the city's business district. The strike was one of the most spectacular acts of Viet Cong terrorism and, with two Americans dead

1

2

1. These Viet Cong are "elite" troops, wearing uniforms like those of North Vietnamese regulars and armed with Soviet AK 47 assault rifles. 2. The aftermath of a Viet Cong terrorist bombing incident in Saigon. 3. The interdiction of Viet Cong movement on inland waterways: a South Vietnamese Landing Craft, Vehicle and Personnel (LCVP) on patrol. The vessel is some 55ft long, mounts 20mm and 30mm cannon, and has an operating speed of 8 to 10 knots. 4. These Viet Cong, captured by South Vietnamese troops, are held prisoner in a jungle fort.

and 51 Americans and South Vietnamese injured, a perfect justification to inaugurate the joint US-South Vietnamese reprisals Taylor's *quid pro quo* agreement had sought. Yet, although Taylor argued forcefully for immediate retaliation, President Johnson refused to authorize the strikes on North Vietnam. Without indisputable evidence of the Viet Cong's responsibility for the bombing, he feared that the American public might see the attack as a deliberate provocation engineered by Khanh. There seemed also some hope that the young generals might attribute the lack of retaliation to their own recent conduct and decide to drop their internecine disputes in favor of a united stand against Communism.

Johnson's stratagem apparently worked. Over the next ten days, the US Mission, Khanh, and the generals arrived at a compromise which, although failing to restore the High National Council, at least returned Huong and a civilian government to office. Unfortunately, the settlement did little to restore order to South Vietnam. The Buddhists were already sworn to oppose any regime headed by Huong and, when he returned to power, immediately began seeking a pretext to bring him down.

Riots in the cities, fighting in the countryside

They found one on 17 January 1965, when Huong issued a decree enlarging the Army's draft calls. Within hours, Buddhist agitators were on the streets preaching rebellion. Civil disturbances quickly spread from city to city, culminating in the destruction of the 8,000-volume US Information Agency Library in Hue and in the self-immolation of a 17-year-old girl —the first Buddhist to commit suicide by fire since the riots against Diem more than a year before. On 27 January, the generals decided they must act. Instigating yet another *coup*, they declared Huong incapable of maintaining order and called upon Khanh to form a new government.

While government succeeded government in Saigon, heavy fighting continued in the countryside around the capital, with the Viet Cong gradually gaining the upper hand. During the last week of December 1964, for example, shortly after Khanh had dismissed the High National Council, Communist troops occupied the village of Binh Gia, an anti-Communist community of 6,000 people, on the coast near Saigon. Armed with modern weapons recently brought in from North Vietnam, the Communists held the town for four days and virtually annihilated several government battalions sent to dislodge them. Having killed 6 American and 177 South Vietnamese soldiers, they finally abandoned their positions voluntarily.

The event appeared to have grave implications. Westmoreland believed that the enemy was experimenting with new tactics, perhaps in anticipation of moving from a guerrilla and small-unit war to a more conventional conflict in which large units attacked and then stood their ground. Ambassador Taylor saw the event in the context of Vietnam as a whole. "We are faced here," he told President Johnson, "with a seriously deteriorating situation characterized by continuing political turmoil, irresponsibility and division within the armed forces, lethargy . . . growing anti-US feeling, signs of mounting terrorism by Viet Cong directed at US personnel, and deepening discouragement and loss of morale throughout South Vietnam." Some innovation must be made to remedy the situation, Taylor concluded—something that would help to unite the various factions in South Vietnam in support of its government. This could only be a bombing campaign against North Vietnam.

Retaliatory bombing raids on North Vietnam

Assistant Secretary of State William P. Bundy agreed, asserting that the defeat at Binh Gia was a sign that South Vietnamese morale had fallen to a new low. "The blunt fact," he told Secretary Rusk, "is that we have appeared to the Vietnamese (and to wide circles in Asia and even in Europe) to be insisting on a more perfect government than can reasonably be expected before we consider any additional action (against North Vietnam)." There was only one thing to do, Bundy concluded: conduct reprisals against the North just as soon as the enemy provided a justification for doing so. Although attacks on the North might not save South Vietnam, if the country did fall, "we would still have appeared to Asians to have done a lot more about it".

President Johnson, remaining unconvinced that bombing the North would have the desired effect, still refused to authorize reprisal attacks. However, in late January he went so far as to authorize joint US-South Vietnamese planning for reprisals. At Taylor's suggestion he also sent a personal representative, his National Security Adviser, McGeorge Bundy, on an observation mission to Saigon.

McGeorge Bundy and a team of experts arrived on 3 February and rapidly concluded that the situation was as bad as had been feared. Any optimistic feeling that remained vanished on the morning of 7 February, shortly before the team was scheduled to leave, when the Viet Cong attacked the US advisory compound and airstrip at Camp Holloway, near Pleiku in the Central Highlands, killing nine Americans and wounding more than 100. The attack, immediately following the "Tet Truce", a virtual cease-fire by the Viet Cong from 1 to 6 February to mark the Vietnamese New Year, seemed to be a deliberate provocation aggravated by the fact that Soviet Premier Alexei Kosygin was at that time visiting Hanoi.

Believing the provocation too blatant to be ignored, Bundy immediately telephoned the White House to recommend a retaliatory raid. The President agreed, and that same day 49 US Navy fighter-bombers struck an enemy barracks at Dong Hoi just above the Demilitarized Zone, a target far enough away from Hanoi to be of no threat to Kosygin. Delayed by inclement weather, the South Vietnamese element of the attack hit another barracks at Vinh, in the same area, the next day, with General Ky flying the lead plane. "We have no choice now but to clear the decks," President Johnson told the American

1

2

Communist weapons captured in South Vietnam, 1962–1964

Chinese Communist origin

75mm recoilless rifles	3
57mm recoilless guns	3
75mm shells	120
57mm shells	155
80mm mortar	1
60mm mortars	3
60mm mortar shells	183
fuses for 60mm shells	150
90mm bazooka	1
27mm rocket launchers	2
7.92mm model 08 Maxim machine-guns	6
7.92mm cartridges	100,000
MP-82 rockets	142
TNT charges	577

Soviet origin

Mossin Nagant carbines	15
rifles	46
rifle cartridges	160,000
automatic pistol	1
grenades	5
submachine-guns	2

Czech origin

7.65mm automatic pistol	1
K-50 submachine-guns	40
rifles	26
machine-gun cartridges	14,000
grenade launcher	1
3.5in anti-tank bazooka	1

3

4

1. Incidents like this gave support to those who pressed for stern retaliation, by aerial bombardment, against North Vietnam: the ruins of the Victoria Hotel, Saigon, a US officers' billet destroyed by a truck-load of Viet Cong explosives, with three Americans and three Vietnamese killed and close on 100 injured. 2. US Air Force C-123 transports drop Vietnamese paratroops into a Viet Cong-infiltrated area in South Vietnam. 3. Aboard a patrol craft of the South Vietnamese River Force—manned by Vietnamese with US Navy advisers—Vietnamese sailors fire an 81mm mortar. Based in strategic positions throughout the southernmost part of Vietnam, the main task of the River Assault Groups (RAGS) was to transport troops in assault missions against the Viet Cong. 4. A South Vietnamese fighter-bomber pilot flies over suspected Viet Cong territory. Nguyen Cao Ky, commander of the SVN Air Force, was a leading advocate of bombing reprisals against North Vietnam; on 8 February 1975, Ky himself led a strike by Vietnamese fighter-bombers on a barracks area at Vinh, North Vietnam, just above the Demilitarized Zone.

5. The supply carrier USS *Core* arrives in Saigon harbor with more than 70 replacement aircraft aboard, including Douglas A-1 Skyraiders seen on deck.

5

public, "and make absolutely clear our continued determination to back South Vietnam in its fight to maintain its independence."

Shortly after the raids, Ambassador Taylor urged President Johnson to begin "a measured, controlled sequence of actions" against North Vietnam. Back in Washington by that time, McGeorge Bundy advocated the same move, calling it a policy of "sustained reprisal".

The Viet Cong struck another severe blow on 10 February, destroying a hotel in Qui Nhon that was being used as an American enlisted men's billet. Twenty-three soldiers died in the collapse of the building and as many more were trapped and injured in the rubble. Deciding that the Communists could no longer be allowed to threaten American lives with impunity, President Johnson immediately approved a second series of reprisals: two days later he announced his decision to begin "Operation Rolling Thunder", a program of "measured and limited air action" against military targets in North Vietnam south of the 19th Parallel.

Johnson scheduled the first strike for 20 February but another attempted *coup* in Saigon, ending in the final downfall of Khanh and the installation of a civilian, Phan Huy Quat, as nominal premier (the military in effect retaining power), forced the cancellation of that attack and of several others. The program at last began on 2 March, when US and South Vietnamese fighter-bombers destroyed an ammunition depot and a naval base in North Vietnam. On 24 February, the first official admission that American airmen were flying combat missions against the Viet Cong had been made.

Westmoreland warns of mounting US casualties

Conceived as a gradual tightening of the screw, "Rolling Thunder" had little apparent impact upon the enemy and may actually have strengthened North Vietnamese resolve. President Johnson at first allowed only two to four raids each week by a few dozen planes at a time: hardly enough to do much damage but sufficient to inject what Westmoreland saw as a "considerable and growing risk" into the situation. The North Vietnamese responded by building a comprehensive air defense system under centralized control; one that Westmoreland believed would "result in mounting casualties as the war goes on—perhaps more than we will be willing or even able to sustain."

Meanwhile, the military situation in South Vietnam continued to deteriorate. Early in March, MACV forecast that if the current trends persisted, South Vietnamese strength would soon be confined to district and provincial capitals only—and these would be clogged with large numbers of refugees. Within a year, it predicted, the country might well be completely in Communist hands.

The only hope early in 1965 was American air power and its ability to strike both at North Vietnam and at the Viet Cong's infiltration routes through Laos. But Westmoreland, reflecting upon the Pleiku and Qui Nhon incidents, had little confidence in the South Vietnamese Army's ability to defend American airfields. MACV estimated, for example, that there were some 12 enemy battalions totalling 6,000 men within easy striking distance of the airbase at Da Nang, yet the installation and its large stockpiles of expensive equipment was defended by a poorly-trained and motivated South Vietnamese force that did no more patrolling than it had to. Added to Da Nang's importance as a center for many of the US air strikes against North Vietnam, this made the base an almost irresistible target for the Viet Cong.

US Marines hit the beaches at Da Nang

Early in February, the United States took the first step toward improving Da Nang's defenses by assigning a US Marine Corps Hawk surface-to-air (SAM) missile battalion to the base. The Hawk (Homing All-the-Way Killer), effective against aircraft flying at heights between treetop level and about 38,000 ft (11,600m), has a speed of Mach 2.5 and a range of about 22 miles (35 km). A Hawk unit normally consists of some 50-plus launchers. The next step came later in the month, when Westmoreland's deputy, General John Throckmorton, returned from an inspection of Da Nang to report that the situation there was so precarious that a full Marine Expeditionary Brigade—three infantry battalions with artillery and logistical support—was needed. Cutting Throckmorton's requirement from three battalions to two in order to keep the number of US ground troops in South Vietnam to a minimum, Westmoreland immediately passed the request on to Washington.

Although Ambassador Taylor believed that sending American units to Vietnam would lead to ever-increasing troop commitments, which might lead the South Vietnamese to relinquish as much as possible of the fighting to their allies, he shared Westmoreland's concern and backed his request. So did Admiral Ulysses S. Grant Sharp, Commander in Chief, Pacific, who told the Joint Chiefs of Staff that committing Marines to Da Nang was "an act of prudence which we should take before and not after another tragedy occurs".

On 26 February, President Johnson approved the deployment, and on 8 March the 9th Marine Expeditionary Brigade, commanded by Brigadier General Frederick J. Karch, came ashore at Da Nang. They were welcomed by a contingent of South Vietnamese and by a number of young girls who distributed *leis* (floral garlands). To one side stood a group of US Army advisers to the South Vietnamese—old hands at fighting the Viet Cong—with a large sign reading, "Welcome to the gallant Marines."

The humor seemed appropriate at the time. But although they were not the first Marines active in Vietnam—US Marine Corps advisers had served with the Vietnamese Marines since 1954, and the Marine Corps' "Shu-Fly" helicopter task unit had been operational at Da Nang since 1962—the arrival of the 9th Marine Expeditionary Brigade marked a most significant step in the course of American military commitment in Vietnam.

1. Napalm from a US Air Force A-1 Skyraider blasts a Viet Cong position in a jungle area of South Vietnam in 1965. **2.** A McDonnell Douglas A-4E Skyhawk of the US Navy fires a salvo of 3in rockets against a Viet Cong concentration, 1965. **3.** Military aid from the Free World: men of the Royal Australian Regiment—with supporting artillery, armor, and aircraft—served in Vietnam from early 1965. **4.** US Marines dig in while on a sweep against the Viet Cong late in 1965; the 9th Marine Expeditionary Brigade (MEB) came ashore at Da Nang on 8 March 1965, one Battalion Landing Team disembarking from a Special Landing Force of the Seventh Fleet, another airlifted from Okinawa in KC-130 transports. **5.** Tough terrain and a heavy load: US Marines in all-too-typical jungle conditions in South Vietnam. The Marine in the foreground carries a 7.62mm M60 general purpose machine gun. **6.** A Hawk missile battery of 9th MEB moves to the top of Hill 327, Da Nang, during the relocation of part of the airfield defenses in March 1965. The Hawk (Homing All-the-Way Killer) surface-to-air missile, deployed at Da Nang from February 1965, is effective against aircraft flying at a height of up to about 38,000ft (11,600m), over a range of some 22 miles (35km).

The air war against North Vietnam

Bernard C. Nalty

In considering the policy of bombing North Vietnam to save the South, President Johnson's administration had three major options: purely retaliatory strikes, like that following the Bien Hoa attack; a "fast/full squeeze", a swift and heavy offensive against targets of military significance; or a "slow squeeze", an escalating campaign designed to demonstrate to the enemy that punishment was directly geared to his own aggression. As mentioned previously, President Johnson had approved the retaliatory policy suggested by William P. Bundy, although internecine political struggles between South Vietnam's generals and politicians had forced postponement of the onslaught. The first significant retaliatory air strikes were those of "Flaming Dart I", following the Pleiku incident of 7 February 1965, and "Flaming Dart II", provoked by the attack on Qui Nhon on 10 February. Following these raids, "Rolling Thunder"—the "slow squeeze" policy—was launched on 2 March. President Johnson's decision to implement a policy of "persuasion" through air power was accompanied by Secretary of Defense McNamara's suggestion that bombing North Vietnam might also serve as a warning to China against possible involvement.

North Vietnam's network of air defenses

A key target during the early "Rolling Thunder" attacks was the strategically important Thanh Hoa bridge which carried a highway and a rail line across the Song Ma (Ma River), which flows into the Gulf of Tonkin. On 4 April, as US Air Force Republic F-105D Thunderchief fighter-bombers were approaching this objective, four North Vietnamese MiG-17s, under radar control from the ground, intercepted a four-plane American flight. The escort of USAF North American F-100 Super Sabres, concentrating on protecting the Thunderchiefs during the actual bomb run, failed to see the MiGs homing on their target. Although one of the Thunderchiefs recognized the danger and radioed a warning, the enemy interceptors scored two kills.

MiG-17s, joined later by MiG-21s and a few MiG-19s, formed one component of North Vietnam's air defenses. Another was the radar-directed surface-to-air missile (SAM). The SAM was especially dangerous when launched through a layer of cloud, but a pilot who saw the weapon had an excellent chance of outmaneuvering it.

Throughout the spring of 1965, American intelligence officers had received aerial photographs, taken by Navy and Air Force planes, showing SAM sites in North Vietnam. Committed to a policy of gradual

From March 1965 to October 1968, the "Rolling Thunder" bombing offensive pitted sophisticated US weaponry and electronic countermeasures against the formidable network of missiles, anti-aircraft batteries and interceptors guarding military targets in North Vietnam. Because political considerations would not permit an all-out offensive, "Rolling Thunder" failed to restrain increased aggression by the Communists

escalation, the United States refrained from hitting the launchers until it could be proved beyond doubt that the weapons were operational. A USAF Douglas EB-66C Destroyer electronic warfare aircraft obtained the necessary evidence by intercepting radar signals from one of the sites. Proof positive was forthcoming on 24 July 1965, when a SAM launched west of Hanoi destroyed a USAF F-4C Phantom.

Anti-aircraft guns formed the third element in the North Vietnamese air defense network. Controlled by radar and ranging in size from 37mm to 100mm, these weapons were responsible for most of the American planes shot down over the North. Anti-aircraft batteries protected SAM sites, which were vulnerable to low altitude attack, and defended most other targets. Early in the war, a favorite North Vietnamese trick was to set up a dummy SAM battery, surround it with camouflaged anti-aircraft guns, and wait for a US attack.

The measures employed against MiGs differed from those used against missiles and anti-aircraft guns. Of particular value against interceptors was the airborne radar in the USAF EC-121D. Operators on board this military version of the Lockheed Super Constellation filled a gap in American radar coverage over North Vietnam. As the war progressed, radars in EC-121s, on the ground, and in ships off the coast maintained surveillance of the North, at first issuing warning of MiG attacks and later directing F-4 Phantoms into position to shoot down the interceptors.

Electronics enabled the American bombing forces to counter the SAMs. At the outset, the Air Force's EB-66C Destroyer or the Navy's almost identical EA-3 Skywarrior provided warning that SAM guidance radars were transmitting. When installed in the individual fighter-bomber, warning and homing gear alerted the crew

to SAM launchings. In addition, the Navy's Lockheed EC-121Ms could detect SAMs as well as MiG formations.

On 17 October 1965, radar detection equipment figured in the first successful attack on a North Vietnamese SAM site. A flight of four McDonnell Douglas A-4 Skyhawk carrier bombers, led by one of the Grumman A-6 Intruders acquired by the Navy as all-weather attack aircraft, struck a site near Kep airfield northeast of Hanoi. Lieutenant Commander Pete Garber, who piloted the A-6, reported that radar vans, stored missiles, and nearby buildings were burning as the Navy flight departed.

Detection helped, but the strike forces also needed some means of disrupting the radar that controlled the SAMs. At first, Marine EF-10B Skynights, former night fighters with jamming transmitters instead of armament, joined Navy EA-3s in performing this mission. Later the USAF's EB-66B, with a more powerful jamming signal, took over, but enemy fighter strength forced the Americans to find an alternative.

Electronic countermeasures against SAM activity

An effective means of suppressing SAM activity, and sometimes destroying the sites, was the "Wild Weasel", a two-place USAF F-105F carrying the Navy-developed Shrike (air-to-surface, originally designated "anti-radar") missile and equipped with radar homing and warning gear. Upon detecting radar waves from a missile site, the Wild Weasel turned toward the transmitter and launched a Shrike which followed the radar beam to its source. The threat of Wild Weasel forced the enemy to rely on other types of radar to locate targets, limiting the use of the SAM tracking set to a few seconds only. By limiting transmitting time and shutting down whenever a Shrike was launched, the radar might escape damage—but these restrictions reduced the accuracy of the missiles.

The "countermeasures pod" provided the best electronic protection against the SAM. This device consisted of a transmitter, enclosed in a streamlined underwing housing, that broadcast a signal capable of jamming radar. The pod could be adjusted to jam radars controlling either anti-aircraft guns or SAMs. On 7 October 1966, 10 anti-aircraft and 12 SAM radars tracked an eight-plane strike formation, but jamming from the pods completely frustrated the North Vietnamese missile crews and the gunners. When using the pods, American pilots generally focused on the SAM defenses, flying beyond reach of light anti-aircraft guns, but at altitudes where the missiles would normally have been deadly.

1

1. The policy of retaliation for Communist aggression in the South with air attacks on North Vietnam had its first significant expression in the "Flaming Dart" strikes of February 1965; the "Rolling Thunder" offensive began on 2 March. Here, A-4 Skyhawks from the carrier USS *Oriskany* head for targets in North Vietnam. 2. A weapons mechanic at Da Nang instals fins on one of a trailer-load of Sparrow IIIB air-to-air missiles, to be carried by the US Air Force F-4C Phantoms in the background. 3. B-52 Stratofortresses struck at North Vietnam for the first time in April 1966, bombing the Mu Gia Pass, a vital access route to the Ho Chi Minh Trail network in Laos. 4. North Vietnam's highly-sophisticated air defense system incorporated anti-aircraft batteries and Soviet-built MiG interceptors, as well as radar-directed surface-to-air missiles like the SA-3 Goa battery seen here.

2

3

4

Flying fast, maneuverable, but short-range MiG interceptors, North Vietnamese pilots preferred to make a radar-directed hit-and-run pass, attacking American strike aircraft from astern with heat-seeking missiles or cannon. Although the aircraft thus attacked might escape, the attack sometimes forced them to jettison their bombs in order to get away. When a combat air patrol (CAP) intervened to protect the strike formation, a dogfight might ensue.

The first MiG kills of the war occurred on 17 June 1965, when Lieutenant John Smith, radar operator in a patrolling F-4 Phantom II fighter from the carrier *Midway*, spotted four MiG-17s. The pilot, Commander Louis Page, made a head-on attack: two Navy Phantoms and the four MiGs closed at a speed in excess of 1,000mph (1,600kph). Page singled out one of the Soviet-built interceptors and destroyed it with a radar-guided Sparrow missile. His wingman, Lieutenant Jack Batson, shot down a second MiG with a similar missile.

Three days later, a unique dogfight occurred between piston-engined US Navy Douglas A-1 Skyraiders and MiG-17 jets. Four A-1s, nicknamed "Spads" after the World War I fighter, were covering a rescue mission when two MiGs suddenly attacked. The slower Spads kept turning inside the jets. After five minutes of maneuvering, two of the Navy pilots, Lieutenant Clinton Johnson and Lieutenant (j.g.) Charles Hartman, closed in behind a MiG-17 and shot it down with 20mm cannon fire. The surviving MiG broke off the fight.

Air Force F-4 Phantoms scored their first victories of the war on 10 July 1965. On that day a combat air patrol of four Phantoms trailed the bombing aircraft as a precaution against sudden MiG attacks on the strike force as its escort, low on fuel, was retiring. These tactics worked; the enemy took the bait and attacked the Phantoms. Using afterburner to increase speed, Captain Kenneth Holcome and Captain Arthur Clark, pilot and radarman in one of the F-4s, shook off a MiG, then came up behind it and scored a hit with a heat-seeking Sidewinder missile. After momentarily losing sight of the interceptor that had jumped their F-4, Captain Thomas Roberts and Captain Ronald Anderson came up with it as it was recovering from a tight turn and fired three heat-seeking missiles, one of which exploded deep inside the enemy's fuselage.

Phantoms set a trap for the MiGs

The most spectacular air battle of the war was "Operation Bolo", planned and led by Colonel Robin Olds of the 8th Tactical Fighter Wing. Because President Johnson had not yet given permission for MiGs to be attacked on the ground, Olds planned to lure the enemy into the air and destroy him. The plan, carried out on 2 January 1967, involved a strike force in which F-4Cs took the place of the usual F-105Ds. The enemy aircraft intercepted what they thought were bomb-laden Thunderchiefs, only to discover that they had engaged the faster Phantoms. In the melee that followed, Olds personally destroyed one MiG-21, launching a heat-seeking missile

that penetrated the victim's tail pipe, exploded, and blew off a wing. This was one of seven MiGs shot down that day.

"Rolling Thunder" continued, with pauses and frequent adjustments of the target area, from 2 March 1965 until 31 October 1968. At first, Secretary McNamara stressed the importance of overawing the enemy with a show of American determination. Both McNamara and President Johnson kept a tight rein on American air power, authorizing attacks only upon military barracks, depots, or similar targets and occasionally suspending operations to give the enemy an opportunity to back down. When the North Vietnamese showed no sign of abandoning their campaign to conquer the South, McNamara approved gradually intensified attacks against enemy supply lines. It was claimed that armed reconnaissance missions over the North had, during 1965, resulted in the destruction or damaging of 1,500 boats and barges, 650 railroad cars and locomotives, and 800 trucks.

In early 1966, after a long bombing pause over Christmas and Tet, Rolling Thunder aircraft again launched strikes upon military targets, concentrating upon oil storage depots throughout the North. Bridges and other transportation elements came under attack, and Air Force and Navy aircraft also hit the comparatively primitive industries of North Vietnam, such as cement factories and power-generating plants. Secretary McNamara refused to unleash total air power, however, forbidding attacks on Hanoi and designating buffer zones to prevent strikes from violating the Chinese border or endangering ships unloading at Haiphong.

North Vietnam forced to disperse fuel stocks

The 1966 raids on oil storage depots appeared to be spectacularly successful. The huge tanks at Haiphong erupted in columns of greasy smoke, cutting storage capacity thereby an estimated 90 percent. The enemy countered, however, by dispersing their fuel stocks in small storage sites throughout the North.

During 1967, the use of air power moved even farther from the original goal of persuading North Vietnam to suspend operations in the South. American aircraft attempted to disrupt the movement of supplies from China by bombing bridges, severing rail lines, shooting up rolling stock, and conducting armed reconnaissance of roads and waterways. A similar air campaign sought to isolate Haiphong and to prevent military aid from passing through that port. At one time an estimated 200,000 short tons (178,000 tons; 180,000 tonnes) of supplies were clogging Haiphong docks, but the cordon could not be maintained. By year's end, American aircraft had bombed all but one of North Vietnam's MiG bases, and air-laid mines were being planted in the country's inland waterways.

Industrial sites near Hanoi, including the Thai Nguyen steel plant, came under attack during 1967. In March, while attacking this target, Captain Merlyn H. Dethlefsen, USAF, earned the Medal of Honor, America's highest award for valor. He received the decoration not for shooting down enemy aircraft but for courage

1

3

6

90

1. A North Vietnamese pilot climbs into a Soviet-built MiG-21 Fishbed interceptor. 2. The bombs of an A-4C Skyhawk from the carrier USS *Ranger* fall earthward during a strike on a highway bridge in North Vietnam in July 1966. 3. A US Air Force reconnaissance aircraft obtained this picture of MiG-17 Fresco interceptors in their protective shelter at Phuc Yen airfield, 20 miles northeast of Hanoi, in October 1966. 4. An RA-5C Vigilante reconnaissance attack aircraft of the carrier USS *Constellation* comes in for an arrested landing. 5. Shot down over North Vietnam, Captain M. N. Jones, USAF, is paraded in a truck by his captors. 6. Its bombs gone, a USAF A-1E Skyraider rolls down through light cloud to make a strafing pass at its ground target. 7. A Republic F-105F, nicknamed "the Thud", makes a level bombing run; this aircraft carries underwing AGM-45A Shrike anti-radiation missiles, normally carried only by "Wild Weasel" F-105G ECM aircraft.

and persistence in attacking the SAM defenses. Flying an F-105F Wild Weasel, Dethlefsen and his electronic warfare officer, Captain Mike Gilroy, arrived over the target about 30 minutes in advance of the strike force and began searching for SAM sites. Gilroy picked up radar signals, but as Dethlefsen was preparing to launch a Shrike missile, two MiGs swept down in a tail attack. In order to escape, Dethlefsen had to dive into the concentrated fire of the 57mm installations protecting the steel mill. Climbing again, he encountered another pair of MiGs and again dived into the flak, taking a hit in the fuselage from a 57mm shell and sustaining superficial wing-damage from shell fragments. By now the US fighter-bombers were departing, but Dethlefsen remained behind to help suppress radar-controlled fire during the withdrawal. Despite dust and smoke, he located the missile site that Gilroy had detected earlier and destroyed it, first launching a Shrike and then attacking with bombs and gunfire. Captain Gilroy received the Air Force Cross for his skill in pinpointing the source of the radar signals—and for his courage.

Bombs against the North Vietnam bridges

Some four months after the first raids on the Thai Nguyen steel plant, USAF fighter-bombers attacked the Paul Doumer bridge, which carried both rail and road traffic over the Red River at Hanoi. On 11 August 1967, a total of 26 F-105D Thunderchiefs, each aircraft carrying one 3,000-pound (1,360kg) bomb, attacked the bridge in three waves. Each wave had four F-4s as overhead cover against MiGs, four more F-4s to attack anti-aircraft batteries, and four Wild Weasels for SAM suppression. While anti-personnel bombs burst among the anti-aircraft crews, the strike force climbed from tree-top height to 13,000 feet (3,965m), dived at a 45-degree angle toward the bridge, dropped their bombs, lowered their air brakes, and pulled out. The second Thunderchief to attack released its bomb after diving to 7,000 feet (2,135m), scoring a direct hit that dropped one span of the bridge into the water. By the time the last F-105D turned towards its base in Thailand, one railroad and two highway spans had been destroyed. The bridge remained out of service for seven weeks.

The Paul Doumer bridge again carried traffic until late October, when F-105Ds knocked it out once more. North Vietnamese repair crews swarmed over the structure and had trains and trucks moving before the end of November. The fighter-bombers returned twice in December, blasting several gaps in both highway and railroad spans. The enemy then gave up repairing the bridge and built a pontoon replacement some distance away to carry rail traffic.

To lighten the traffic on the Paul Doumer bridge and its replacement, the North Vietnamese ferried freight cars across the Red River. One night in October 1967, the US Navy carrier *Constellation* launched a lone Grumman A-6A Intruder, carrying 18 500-pound (227kg) bombs, with orders to destroy the loading slip for the railroad ferry. While Lieutenant Lyle Bull interpreted radar echoes to pick out

landmarks and avoid dangerous ridges, Lieutenant Commander Charles Hunter guided the plane at low level through the darkness. Just 18 miles (29km) from the target, a SAM, clearly distinguishable by its trail of burning propellant, rose toward the US aircraft. In all, the defenders launched 16 missiles, one of which missed the Intruder by only 200 feet (61m). Diving to rooftop height, too low for the missile batteries to track and destroy them, the Navy fliers found the ferry slip and dropped their bombs directly on it.

The most difficult target faced by American pilots was the Thanh Hoa bridge, on the Ma River some 80 miles (130km) south of Hanoi. This target was attacked repeatedly throughout the course of Rolling Thunder. Navy, Air Force, and Marine airmen flew 700 sorties at the cost of eight aircraft, but the bridge defied destruction. The Navy used its newly-developed "Walleye" glide bomb (operational in 1966) against the Thanh Hoa bridge. A television camera in the nose of the 1,100-pound (499kg) missile relayed a picture to a monitor screen in the cockpit, enabling the pilot to make sure the television had locked on to the target before launch. This bomb scored hits on the span but failed to bring it down.

Not until 1972, when the US Air Force employed "Smart" laser guided bombs, was the Thanh Hoa bridge destroyed. The 2,000-pound (907kg) or 3,000-pound (1,365kg) "Smart" bomb homed on a laser beam directed at the target, usually achieving remarkable accuracy. The destruction of the Thanh Hoa bridge disproved a legend, circulated during Rolling Thunder, that the world was composed of two spring-loaded hemispheres, hinged somewhere under the Atlantic and held together by the Thanh Hoa bridge; if the bridge was severed, the world would fly apart!

USAF missions to rescue downed pilots

Throughout the war, every attempt was made to rescue downed airmen when recovery seemed at all possible. Until the arrival of the Sikorsky HH-53, the best aircraft for this mission was the turbine-powered Sikorsky HH-3 helicopter, called "Jolly Green Giant" by the USAF rescue units flying out of Thailand. If other aircraft in the downed crewmen's formation picked up the radio signal that indicated a good ejection—and if the defenses in the area were not so powerful as to make the mission suicidal—one or more helicopters, sometimes assisted by a modified Lockheed C-130 Hercules transport doubling as a flying tanker and aerial command post, searched for the fliers, alert for either a message over the portable radio that crewmen carried or for improvised signals from the ground. Because enemy troops might be nearby, A-1 Skyraiders stood by to saturate North Vietnamese or Viet Cong forces with 20mm cannon fire.

As the US Navy's carriers steamed toward Tonkin Gulf to take part in Rolling Thunder, crewmen modified the Sikorsky SH-3 Sea King anti-submarine helicopter, increasing fuel capacity and mounting remote-controlled 7.62mm Miniguns in the rear of each sponson, to make it the

1. USAF F-4 Phantom IIs carrying "Smart" laser-guided bombs like those used to knock out the Thanh Hoa bridge, North Vietnam, in 1972. **2.** A-6A Intruders from USS *Constellation* unload; the Intruder carried a maximum bomb load of 15,000lb. **3.** A Forward Air Controller flies a Cessna O-1E Bird Dog at low altitude to locate ground targets, guide in air strikes, and coordinate air and ground action. **4.** Aboard USS *Constellation*, Lieutenant Randall Cunningham, first air ace of the Vietnam war, describes how he downed three MiG-17s during a single mission. **5.** Map: Tactical Airfields in the Republic of Vietnam, 1968.

DMZ

△ Da Nang

△ Chu Lai

△ Jet operational airfields

● Tactical airstrips

- XXX - Corps Zone boundaries

I – IV US/ARVN Corps Zones

△ Phu Cat

Tuy Hoa △

● Cam Ranh Bay

△ Phan Rang

● Bien Hoa

Tan Son Nhut

TACTICAL AIRFIELDS IN S. VIETNAM, 1968

5

Aircraft and weapons combinations used in MiG victories

USAF Aircraft	Weapons/Tactics	MiG-17	MiG-19	MiG-21	Total
F-4C	AIM-7 Sparrow	4	0	10	14
	AIM-9 Sidewinder	12	0	10	22
	20mm gunfire	3	0	1	4
	Maneuvering tactics	2	0	0	2
	Total	*21*	*0*	*21*	*42*
F-4D	AIM-4 Falcon	4	0	1	5
	AIM-7 Sparrow	4	2	20	26
	AIM-9 Sidewinder	0	2	3	5
	20mm gunfire	4	0	2	6
	Maneuvering tactics	0	0	2	2
	Total	*12*	*4*	*28*	*44*
F-4E	AIM-7 Sparrow	0	2	8	10
	AIM-9 Sidewinder	0	0	4	4
	AIM-9 + 20mm gunfire	0	0	1	1
	20mm gunfire	0	1	4	5
	Maneuvering tactics (2 F-4Es)	0	1	0	1
	Total	*0*	*4*	*17*	*21*
F-4D/F-105F	20mm gunfire	1	0	0	1
F-105D	20mm gunfire	22	0	0	22
	AIM-9 Sidewinder	2	0	0	2
	AIM-9 + 20mm gunfire	1	0	0	1
	Total	*25*	*0*	*0*	*25*
F-105F	20mm gunfire	2	0	0	2
B-52D	50 caliber gunfire	0	0	2	2
Grand Total		**61**	**8**	**68**	**137**

naval equivalent of the Jolly Green Giant. On 6 November 1965, these rescue aircraft were put to the test when an F-105D went down not far from Hanoi.

Two USAF A-1s appeared on the scene almost immediately, but as one of them approached the area where the Thunderchief had gone down, enemy gunners set the Skyraider on fire. The pilot managed to bail out safely and soon made contact with the surviving A-1. A Jolly Green Giant arrived in mid-afternoon to make the rescue, only to be shot down near the wrecked Thunderchief and Skyraider.

Meanwhile, two modified Sea Kings from the carrier *Independence* were standing by. Another pair of Air Force A-1s arrived, re-established contact with the downed Skyraider pilot, and summoned a helicopter. Lieutenant Commander Vern Frank responded, but darkness by now hid the rugged, heavily-forested area from which the signal came. A Navy A-1 escorting Lieutenant Commander Frank's helicopter flew over the point of origin of the radio message and flashed its lights, but the rescue crew could not determine where to lower the hoist. Finally, the downed aviator was asked to show a light; luckily, he had a lighter, which he flicked on to mark his position for the rescuers.

When the rescue effort resumed next morning, a different crew was flying Frank's helicopter. After dropping beneath a cloud layer to evade MiGs, the rescue craft came under fire from the ground. The crew managed to extinguish a blaze in the cabin, and the pilot attempted to nurse his crippled helicopter over the hills that barred his way to the coast and safety. He had to crash-land far short of his goal. A small (three-man) Kaman UH-2 Seasprite naval helicopter responded to the distress call, located the wreckage, but had the capacity to lift out only one crew member. A Jolly Green Giant from Thailand completed the rescue. But meanwhile the radio signals from the area where the F-105D pilot and the four-man crew of the downed Jolly Green Giant waited had ceased. The five men became prisoners of the North Vietnamese.

Sometimes a crippled aircraft reached Tonkin Gulf before the pilot ejected. If he were lucky, a Navy helicopter might pick him up almost at once—but North Vietnamese junks might arrive first and take him prisoner. Grumman HU-16 Albatross amphibians, flown by USAF crews, made many sea rescues until replaced by helicopters which, being able to hover over the ditched airmen and lower a hoist, did not have to risk damage by landing and taking off.

Aerial tankers and reconnaissance planes were essential to the air war against the North. All the services flew tankers: the Marines used the Lockheed KC-130 Hercules; the Navy operated Douglas KA-3B Skywarriors; and the Air Force had Boeing KC-135 Stratotankers. Aerial refueling not only increased range and endurance but also enabled strike aircraft to carry heavier bomb loads. In the hot, humid climate of Southeast Asia, where fighter-bombers and other aircraft required a longer takeoff run than normal, mission planners got the craft safely airborne by reducing the amount of fuel on board (while retaining a full bomb load) and having the pilots top up their fuel supply from waiting tankers.

Reconnaissance planes select targets, assess damage

Aerial reconnaissance was carried out both to select targets and to assess the damage caused by air strikes. Navy aircraft like the Ling-Temco-Vought RF-8, the photo-reconnaissance version of the Crusader fighter, kept the carrier task force informed of the construction of SAM sites early in 1965. More complex than the RF-8 was the North American RA-5C Vigilante, a huge (maximum gross weight: 79,588lb/36,100kg) twin-jet aircraft, unarmed but laden with cameras and other sensors. Automatic flight controls and an inertial navigation system kept the aircraft on course as it thundered low over North Vietnam at supersonic speed. To facilitate interpretation, film from the Vigilante's cameras incorporated an imprint of the latitude and longitude.

For low altitude photo-reconnaissance missions, the US Air Force used the McDonnell RF-101 Voodoo, designed originally as a long-range fighter, and the McDonnell Douglas RF-4C Phantom, carrying cameras and electronic gear instead of armament. A converted target drone collected information on enemy defenses in areas judged too dangerous for manned aircraft. Launched from a DC-130A mother-ship, the pilotless craft made its programmed flight and then headed toward a rendezvous with a CH-3 recovery helicopter. As the two converged, the drone's jet engine shut down and a para-

chute opened; the recovery crew snagged the shroud lines and carried the craft back to intelligence technicians at the base.

On the night of 31 March 1968, confronted by growing public opposition to the war, President Johnson suspended bombing north of the 20th Parallel (some 250 miles/400km north of the DMZ), announcing at the same time that he would not seek another term of office. Six months later, on 31 October, the eve of the presidential election, he halted all bombing of North Vietnam—although aerial reconnaissance continued and American aircraft were allowed to make an occasional retaliatory strike.

"Rolling Thunder" fails to deter the North

Rolling Thunder failed on two counts. Those who advocated persuasion by bombardment had both underestimated North Vietnam's determination and overestimated its vulnerability. No worthwhile strategic targets existed in the nation; there was nothing comparable to the synthetic fuel plants upon which Germany had depended during World War II. The North Vietnamese were able to survive the loss of thermal power plants and even of their only steel mill—an object of great national pride. They were prepared to make such sacrifices for their cause.

Nor did Rolling Thunder halt the flow of materiel from foreign suppliers, through North Vietnam, to the forces fighting in the South. Secretary McNamara became convinced that the cost of Rolling Thunder in lives and aircraft was out of proportion to the results. The movement of supplies could not be disrupted unless Haiphong and the other ports were sealed, the rail link with China severed, and steady pressure maintained against enemy ground forces in South Vietnam.

When the air war against North Vietnam began again after the Viet Cong's all-out offensive against the South in March 1972, President Richard M. Nixon approved a strategy that showed the effect of many of the lessons learned from the failure of Rolling Thunder. Minefields closed North Vietnamese ports; the rail line to China came under attack; and South Vietnamese troops, given massive air support, eventually fought the enemy to a standstill.

In a purely tactical sense, the Americans profited in 1972 from improved weapons, such as laser-guided bombs, and new techniques that had not been available for Rolling Thunder. "Chaff" — aluminum strips acting as radar reflectors and released in clouds to saturate an area— supplemented other forms of jamming (although this was by no means an innovation; the technique was pioneered by Britain's Royal Air Force in World War II).

Wild Weasel and countermeasures pods were available from the outset. Boeing B-52 Stratofortresses (whose operations are described in detail in a separate chapter) attacked the North, greatly increasing the tonnage of bombs aimed at the most important targets, and these bombers, with the Navy's A-6 Intruder and the Air Force's General Dynamics F-111 all-weather tactical fighter-bomber, enabled the United States to conduct heavy bombing around the clock.

5

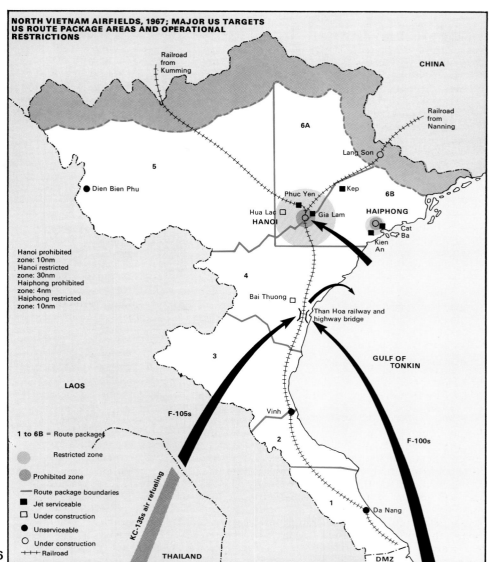

NORTH VIETNAM AIRFIELDS, 1967; MAJOR US TARGETS US ROUTE PACKAGE AREAS AND OPERATIONAL RESTRICTIONS

Railroad from Kumming

CHINA

Railroad from Nanning

6A

Lang Son

5

Dien Bien Phu

Phuc Yen

Kep

6B

Hua Lac

Gia Lam

HAIPHONG

HANOI

Cat Ba

Kien An

Hanoi prohibited
zone: 10nm
Hanoi restricted
zone: 30nm
Haiphong prohibited
zone: 4nm
Haiphong restricted
zone: 10nm

4

Bai Thuong

Than Hoa railway and highway bridge

GULF OF TONKIN

3

LAOS

F-105s

Vinh

2

F-100s

1 to 6B = Route packages

Restricted zone

Prohibited zone

Route package boundaries

■ Jet serviceable
□ Under construction
● Unserviceable
○ Under construction
+++ Railroad

1

Da Nang

KC-135s air refueling

THAILAND

DMZ

1. A US Navy F-4B Phantom makes a bombing run over jungle terrain. **2.** Two 500lb "Snakeye" bombs —used for low-altitude missions, with retarding gear to slow the rate of fall—being wheeled across the flight deck of USS *Constellation*. **3.** A crew chief of the 20th Helicopter Squadron, USAF, looks down on an ARVN helicopter which has crashed in a rice paddy; with the help of Vietnamese troops, the US helicopter crew recovered the wrecked aircraft. **4.** The reconnaissance version of the F-4 Phantom was generally used for low-level missions. **5.** Two HH-53E helicopters of Detachment 7, 38th Air Rescue and Recovery Squadron, USAF, fly over Da Nang harbor en route to an airstrip south of the Demilitarized Zone, where they will stand ready for the call to retrieve downed aviators. **6.** Map: US bombing route packages and major targets in North Vietnam; North Vietnamese air bases. **7.** A B-52 Stratofortress refuels from a Boeing KC-135 Stratotanker before striking targets in North Vietnam.

6

7

A US strategy to stem the Communist tide

Charles B. MacDonald

As the 9th Marine Expeditionary Brigade (soon redesignated III Marine Amphibious Force), the first significant contingent of American combat troops committed to South Vietnam, began arriving in March 1965, General William C. Westmoreland, commanding the MACV, viewed the South Vietnamese military situation as increasingly critical. If the current trend continued, he believed, within six months the South Vietnamese would hold only "a series of islands of strength clustered around district and province capitals", while the government would be riven by various groups advocating some agreement with the Communists. Underlying Westmoreland's concern was his knowledge that a division of the North Vietnamese Army (VPA — Vietnamese People's Army; a term embracing all North Vietnamese forces) had infiltrated the mountains and jungles of the Central Highlands. Although he did not then know how large a force the North Vietnamese intended to commit, the division was, in fact, the vanguard of sizable forces designed to implement a decision made by the North Vietnamese Politburo (cabinet) in 1964. The Communists planned to force a decision in South Vietnam before the Americans could intervene in force. Even with the limited knowledge he possessed early in 1965, the North Vietnamese presence in the Central Highlands seemed to Westmoreland to presage a shift from an internal war of insurgency in the South, supported by North Vietnam, to a conventional war directly involving major North Vietnamese forces.

It would require about one year, Westmoreland reckoned, to bring the South Vietnamese Army (ARVN; often spoken as "ARVIN") up to a strength sufficient to cope with the increasing activity of the Viet Cong insurgents — without the added peril inherent in the presence of North Vietnamese regulars. Even if American bombing of North Vietnam caused the North Vietnamese to back down, which Westmoreland doubted, it would take at least six months' bombing to accomplish this. By that time, the South Vietnamese might well have collapsed.

Westmoreland calls for an international commitment

The ideal solution, as Westmoreland saw it, was to create an international force of about five divisions, to be deployed from the China Sea along the DMZ and across the Laotian panhandle (that part of Laos lying west and south of Vietnam above and below the DMZ, through which ran the Ho Chi Minh Trail). The creation of such a force might also invoke world opinion as an instrument to deter North Vietnamese aggression. But even if Presi-

Even when a military government headed by General Nguyen Van Thieu and the dynamic air force commander Nguyen Cao Ky took power, US commander General Westmoreland questioned South Vietnam's capability to withstand an all-out assault. But his appeals for more American troops and for Free World aid were grudgingly answered, forcing him to implement an unsatisfactory strategy of attrition

dent Johnson approved such a force (in fact, he did not), it would take several months to create and deploy it. Westmoreland saw no other solution than to bring in more American combat troops to hold the line until the ARVN could be strengthened.

The presence of a North Vietnamese division in the Central Highlands seemed to indicate an enemy plan to cut South Vietnam in two and then conquer the northern provinces. Therefore Westmoreland wished to commit an American division to the area. He also wanted two more battalions of US Marines to guard the vital air bases in the northern provinces; their security was essential to the bombing campaign against North Vietnam.

When Ambassador Taylor went to Washington in late March he presented these proposals to the President, only to find that Johnson was still hesitating over increased American commitment. The President would approve only the two Marine battalions for air base protection.

Taylor nevertheless persuaded the President to adopt what became known as an "enclave strategy" — with which Westmoreland disagreed. It involved creating defensive enclaves about air bases and ports, thereby limiting troop commitment while at the same time demonstrating America's will to stand by the South. President Johnson also agreed that American troops might abandon a strictly defensive stance and patrol to a depth of up to 50 miles (80km) outside the enclaves in order to forestall an enemy concentrating with aggressive intent.

Although the President would not then commit large numbers of American troops, he manifested obvious indecision. That was fully apparent when he ordered a conference in Honolulu between Taylor,

Westmoreland, and senior Washington officials, including Secretary of Defense McNamara and General Earle G. Wheeler, Chairman of the Joint Chiefs of Staff. When the Conference convened on 20 April, no one expressed any hope of decisive outcome from the bombing campaign without some improvement in the military situation on the ground. The only way to achieve that, it was agreed, was to send in more American troops (9 battalions, making a total of 13 committed) and to solicit help from other concerned powers: notably Australia, New Zealand, and the Republic of Korea (South Korea).

The decision to seek aid from other nations, sometimes called the "More Flags" policy, dated back to 1961, when Walt Rostow and other advisers had suggested the deployment of 25,000 men from the SEATO nations — the USA, UK, Australia, France, New Zealand, the Philippines, Thailand, and (until 1972) Pakistan — either on the border between Laos and South Vietnam or in the Central Highlands. Of these nations, the UK, France, and Pakistan were to respond with varying degrees of unhelpfulness, while the first to undertake a share of America's stand against Communism was Australia: 30 Australian experts in jungle warfare arrived in South Vietnam, to reinforce the US advisory teams in the northern provinces, in August 1962. By 1969, more than 7,000 Australians would be serving in Vietnam, along with some 550 New Zealanders: constituting a maximum commitment of three combat battalions, three air transport squadrons, a bomber squadron, and a helicopter squadron. The Royal Australian Navy's guided missile destroyer *Perth*, later relieved by her sister-ship *Hobart*, served with elements of the US Navy.

The command structure of the Free World forces

Eventually five other nations contributed troops — Australia, New Zealand, Thailand, South Korea, and the Philippines (with tiny contingents of no more than 30 men from the Republic of China (Taiwan) and Spain), amounting to a peak strength, in 1969, of 68,900 — while 34 others provided non-combat support. The impending arrival of troops from other nations raised the question of unity of command. The American public could not be expected to sanction American troops under South Vietnamese command, yet the South Vietnamese, too, had their pride. Westmoreland was thus reluctant to press for command of Vietnamese troops: he wished neither to further the image of "puppet forces" that Communist propagandists had long sought to project, nor to contribute to a South Vietnamese failure

1. Early in 1965, when a request for more troops to counter the presence of a North Vietnamese division in the Central Highlands of South Vietnam was denied, General Westmoreland was forced to adopt an "enclave strategy": defensive zones incorporating weapons like this 105mm M101 were created around vital bases. **2.** To clear enemy forces from the southern Demilitarized Zone, US Marines launched "Operation Hickory" early in 1967; Marines in a supporting action are seen with an M48 tank. **3.** The North Vietnamese made every effort to penetrate the Demilitarized Zone, in spite of US retaliation with bombing raids on the North. This anti-aircraft battery in the Hanoi area, Communist propaganda claimed, shot down 12 American aircraft in the battle against "US air pirates". **4.** A Viet Cong column in South Vietnam; the Communists stepped up infiltration in 1964—65, hoping to force a decision before the US could intervene in strength.

to develop the military skills and self-reliance essential if they were eventually to prosecute the war by themselves. He settled for a dual command system augmented by close coordination at all levels; the forces of other nations, maintaining their separate identities, also accepted close coordination. It was a loose system, making possible internal rivalries like those that had plagued Allied armies in both World Wars, but in Vietnam it worked with little apparent friction.

The position of Westmoreland's headquarters in the American chain of command was the same as it had been since the creation of MACV in February 1962. It was a joint command (i.e., including representatives of all four military services, but with a preponderance from the US Army) subordinate to the Commander in Chief, Pacific, Admiral U. S. Grant Sharp, who from his headquarters in Hawaii was responsible for activities throughout the Pacific region. While Westmoreland controlled all operations within South Vietnam and tactical air strikes in Laos and a portion of North Vietnam just beyond the DMZ, Sharp was responsible for air operations over most of North Vietnam. The US Navy's Seventh Fleet was also under Sharp's authority, but Westmoreland was able to call for tactical air strikes by carrier-based planes within South Vietnam. The B-52 bombers that subsequently operated over Vietnam were under the Commander in Chief, Strategic Air Command, in Washington, but Westmoreland's headquarters was responsible for designating targets, subject to approval from Washington. The practice gradually developed that Westmoreland's communications with Sharp went at the same time to the Joint Chiefs of Staff, and vice versa.

Excessive caution creates a credibility gap

As American commitment grew, Westmoreland established subordinate commands for the three major American services (the Marine Corps was technically under the US Navy): the United States Army, Vietnam (essentially a logistical and administrative command); the Seventh Air Force; and Naval Force, Vietnam. In three of the four "corps tactical zones" into which the South Vietnamese had divided their country, Westmoreland established parallel American commands that resembled a corps headquarters. In the I Corps zone, embracing the northern provinces, the headquarters was known as the III Marine Amphibious Force; in the central provinces of the II Corps zone, the I Field Force; and in the provinces around Saigon of the III Corps zone, the II Field Force. In the provinces of the Mekong Delta, where no major US forces were to be committed, control of the limited American contingent was exercised by the senior adviser to the South Vietnamese IV Corps commander. The role of senior adviser in the other corps zones would be filled by the commanders of the two field force headquarters and the III Marine Amphibious Force.

As the nine battalions approved by President Johnson began to move into South Vietnam in May and June 1965, the President in effect abandoned the enclave

strategy by authorizing General Westmoreland to engage in "counter-insurgency combat operations". Yet Johnson and other Washington officials, concerned lest the American public react adversely to widening of the American role, did not state publicly that Westmoreland's authority had been broadened. Although American newsmen in South Vietnam could see for themselves that US troops were not simply waiting in entrenched positions for the enemy to come to them, the White House insisted that there had been no change in the "defensive" mission. This marked the beginning of a credibility gap between the Johnson administration and the press (and thus between the administration and the public) that was to have a serious effect on the conduct of the war.

Viet Cong activity provokes a tough response

The American units moved slowly into South Vietnam; it would be a long time before they could make their presence felt. Meanwhile, the Viet Cong gathered more recruits and stepped up their attacks. Operating in regimental strength, the insurgents overran several district capitals, ambushed and destroyed a battalion of the South Vietnamese Army, and laid siege to an outpost in the Central Highlands. Those events in themselves pointed to impending crisis, but the North Vietnamese division in the Central Highlands reacted sluggishly.

President Johnson sent a number of US Coast Guard ships to help the embryonic South Vietnamese Navy prevent infiltration of enemy replacements by sea. He authorized the US Seventh Fleet to provide air and naval gunfire support for American Marines in the northern provinces. He also approved a request from General Westmoreland to use B-52 bombers, at first based on Guam but later in Thailand, to attack the enemy's base camps in remote jungles and mountainous regions. So well entrenched were the enemy bases that tactical aircraft had little effect on them; but the B-52s, flying so high (with a service ceiling of about 55,000ft/16,750m) they were beyond sight and sound from the ground, could devastate the bases with hundreds of tons of high explosive. The B-52s were to become the weapon the enemy feared most.

Even so, these were stop-gap measures for a military situation growing increasingly critical and made the more so by another upheaval in the South Vietnamese government. Following a feeble attempt by dissidents at a *coup d'etat* in May, Premier Quat attempted to reshuffle his cabinet. Failing, he resigned and turned over the government to the military, already the *de facto* rulers. The South Vietnamese generals formed a ten-member Committee for the Direction of the State, with the Air Force General Nguyen Cao Ky as premier and General Nguyen Van Thieu as chief of state. This would bring a measure of stability to Saigon politics—although Ambassador Taylor and General Westmoreland could not know that at the time.

Faced with this political upheaval and with a worsening military situation (the enemy was destroying South Vietnamese

1

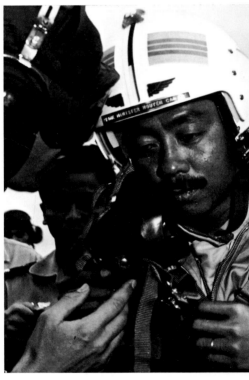

2

3

4

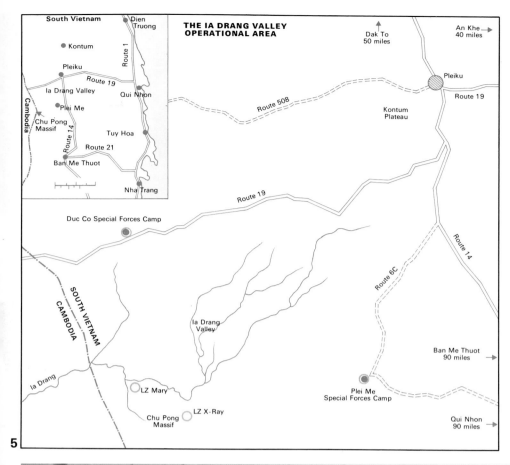

THE IA DRANG VALLEY OPERATIONAL AREA

1. Australian advisers arrived in Vietnam from 1962 onward, and more than 7,000 Australians and New Zealanders were committed by 1969. Here, Private Joe P. Delaney of A Company, 8th Royal Australian Regiment, sets up a claymore mine at a night ambush position in the Xuyen Moc area, east of Saigon.
2. A warrant officer of the Australian advisory team at Duc My Training Center, central South Vietnam, instructs Vietnamese recruits with the aid of a target representing a Viet Cong guerrilla.
3. Soon after his appointment as Prime Minister in mid-1965, South Vietnamese Air Force commander Nguyen Cao Ky is fitted with a helmet and oxygen mask aboard USS *Independence*. 4. The Landing Ship Medium (Rocket) USS *St Francis River* fires a salvo during a bombardment mission. 5. Map: action in the Ia Drang Valley, November 1965; in the first engagement between US troops and North Vietnamese regulars, the 1st Cavalry Division (Airmobile) claimed 1,300 enemy killed for the loss of 300 Americans. 6. The heavy cruiser USS *St Paul* gives fire support to troops ashore with her 8in rifles.

battalions faster than new ones could be organized), General Westmoreland decided that without substantial numbers of American combat troops, South Vietnam would soon collapse. The enemy's major units, he noted, were drawing ARVN troops away from populated regions, leaving the people prey to local Communist guerrillas and political cadremen. The United States, he decided, must commit enough American troops to take over the fight against the VPA's big units, thus leaving the ARVN free to protect the people. Westmoreland asked Washington for a total of 34 American battalions and 10 from other countries: not a force big enough to win the war, but an interim force to stave off South Vietnamese defeat.

While Westmoreland's proposal was sharply debated in Washington, the President authorized the General to use American troops in any situation in which he deemed it necessary "to strengthen the relative position" of the South Vietnamese as compared with the enemy. Although some saw the wording as ambiguous, Westmoreland accepted it as sufficient authority to justify the first large American operation of the war—a raid into a long-established enemy sanctuary known as War Zone D, northwest of Saigon, near the American air base at Bien Hoa.

With the US 173rd Airborne Brigade as a nucleus, an eight-battalion American-Australian-New Zealand (ANZ)-South Vietnamese force struck into the sanctuary on 27 June. Although several sharp engagements ensued, the operation, like most raids, was inconclusive. It may have served to keep the enemy temporarily off balance and thus forestall attacks on Bien Hoa. The Australian troops engaged, men of the 1st Battalion, Royal Australian Regiment, formed part of a 1,400-strong Australian contingent that had only recently arrived in Vietnam. Although at first limited by their government to "local security operations" within about 22 miles (35km) of Bien Hoa (the restriction was lifted in August 1965), the Australians were conducting "search and destroy" patrols in conjunction with the Americans within days of their arrival. A New Zealand artillery unit, arriving at the same time as the main Australian force, was equally quickly committed.

A landmark decision: the President's commitment

President Johnson, still considering Westmoreland's recommendation for more American troops, sent to Saigon a "fact-finding team" (a device soon to become a staple of the war) headed by Secretary of Defense McNamara and Ambassador Henry Cabot Lodge, who was soon to replace Ambassador Taylor for a second tour in Saigon. To McNamara, Westmoreland indicated that simply to stabilize the situation he needed about 175,000 American troops, to be followed by another 100,000. With those numbers, he hoped "to halt the losing trend" by the end of 1965; to undertake an offensive of indefinite duration in 1966; and, whenever that offensive produced decisive results, to round up remaining enemy forces over a period of a year to 18 months.

There was still strong opposition in

Washington to American commitment on such a scale from officials who could see no end to American involvement, but its endorsement by McNamara and by the Joint Chiefs of Staff was enough to sway the President. On 28 July, he announced on national television:

"I have today ordered to Vietnam the Airmobile Division (the 1st Cavalry Division (Airmobile), only recently constituted) and certain other forces which will raise our fighting strength from 75,000 to 125,000 men almost immediately. Additional forces will be needed later, and they will be sent as requested."

That announcement reflected a landmark decision in the war. The United States was now committed to an arduous and frustrating struggle from which it was to extricate itself only after tens of thousands of casualties and seven long years of warfare.

A three-phase strategy to conquer Communism

General Westmoreland's picture of the situation was that of termites (the political subversives and guerrillas) eating away at the underpinnings of a building (the South Vietnamese people and government). In the mountains and jungles, waiting for the moment when the building had been sufficiently undermined to be toppled, were other destructive forces (the enemy's major units). Only by eliminating the major units, or at least so harrying them as to keep them away from the building, Westmoreland theorized, could the "termites" be systematically eliminated and the building shored up sufficiently to withstand outside forces.

From the first, Westmoreland intended to use American troops primarily to combat the enemy's major units; leaving the ARVN to protect the people and eliminate guerrillas and subversives, and giving the task of improving the lot of the people to South Vietnamese civilian ministries assisted by American civilian agencies. Within that broad strategic concept, he contemplated three phases. In the first, American troops would protect developing logistical bases, an essential step in view of the undeveloped nature of South Vietnam and its lack of such vital military facilities as airfields, ports, storage facilities, and roads. Yet even at that stage, if the enemy's big units posed immediate threats, some units might have to be used on occasion as "fire fighters". In a second phase, he intended to push into the hinterlands to penetrate and eliminate the enemy's base camps and sanctuaries, in the process bringing the enemy to battle and inflicting heavy casualties. In a final phase, he intended to mount sustained operations against the big units in order to eliminate them or so to decrease their numbers that a strengthened South Vietnamese Army could control them with minimum American help.

Westmoreland relied on American troops to fight the enemy's major units because they had greater firepower and mobility than South Vietnamese troops; because that firepower could be brought to bear in

1. Australian troops first engaged the Viet Cong near Bien Hoa in mid-1965; a 105mm howitzer of the Australian 1st Field Regiment in action. 2. Men of the US 173d Airborne Brigade man a 105mm howitzer. 3. Map: "Operation Starlite", 18–24 August 1965, the first regimental-sized US battle since the Korean War; some 4,000 US Marines swept the Van Tuong Peninsula on the north-central coast, killing about 700 Viet Cong for the loss of 50 Americans.
4. B-52 Stratofortresses were first used in direct tactical support of ground operations on 14–19 November 1965, in the la Drang Valley.

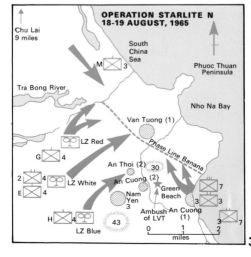

OPERATION STARLITE N
18-19 AUGUST, 1965

Chu Lai 9 miles

South China Sea

Phuoc Thuan Peninsula

Tra Bong River

Nho Na Bay

Van Tuong (1)

Phase Line Banana

LZ Red

An Thoi (2)   30

An Cuong (2)

LZ White   Green Beach

Nam Yen

Ambush of LVT   An Cuong (1)

LZ Blue   43

0   1   2
miles

3

1

2

4

remote regions, thus causing less damage to densely populated regions; and because South Vietnamese troops could be expected to act more efficiently when dealing with their own people. Nevertheless, he intended that American troops not otherwise engaged should be used in populated regions where the enemy was particularly strong. Further, all US combat operations would be allied to civic action programs to improve the lot of the people and encourage their allegiance to the government. It was foreseen that the enemy might deliberately operate in remote regions to keep American troops away from protecting the people, but Westmoreland considered his mobility sufficient to obviate long campaigns in the hinterlands. Furthermore, if the people were to be protected, the major enemy units simply had to be kept at a distance.

The MACV commander was well aware of the long-standing problem of trying to secure South Vietnam's land frontiers, which extended for more than 900 miles. To seal the borders with the troops available was impossible; he must rely instead on patrols, air reconnaissance and bombardment, mobility of combat troops, and isolated outposts manned by the ethnic minorities inhabiting the border regions, helped by advisers from the US Army Special Forces. Westmoreland still hoped to deploy an international force along the DMZ. Although he planned eventually to cut and block the Ho Chi Minh Trail through Laos, he failed at first to press Washington for authority to enter Laos because he considered his forces insufficient for this task in addition to handling the situation within South Vietnam. (By 1968, when Westmoreland did have what he believed to be sufficient forces, President Johnson was opposed to any broadening of the ground war beyond the boundaries of South Vietnam.)

Thus America was committed to what may be described as a strategy of attrition — a strategy which, since the bloody battles of World War I, had been in disrepute. Because political restrictions prohibited ground operations outside South Vietnam, and because he could never hope for enough troops to occupy all the country in strength, Westmoreland saw no alternative. He recognized that it would be a long struggle. Eventually, however, he hoped to establish the South Vietnamese government's control over the population to the point where the Viet Cong would be starved for recruits. This would leave the fight entirely to the North Vietnamese, who might be worn down to the point where they would be compelled to withdraw or sufficiently weakened for the South Vietnamese forces to handle them alone.

The overall military plan was for American brigades and divisions to operate from semi-permanent base camps. The region in the vicinity of a unit's base camp constituted its tactical area of responsibility, although the entire unit or parts of it might be pulled away from time to time to engage major enemy concentrations. When moving far from the base camp, the unit would leave behind a small security force. In the field it would built a temporary base camp with, beyond it, fire support bases equipped for all-round defense and serving as artillery firing positions and patrol bases. Companies, battalions, or several battalions, depending upon the strength of the enemy would, in response to intelligence reports, sweep the area in the vicinity of the fire support bases and bring the enemy to battle. That process Westmoreland called "search and destroy". Misleading press comments were to cause this to be considered by many as less a tactical plan than a strategy leading to long and often fruitless forays in the jungle and wanton destruction of villages.

Even though American firepower would be focused on remote regions, some damage to villages was inevitable. There would be times when the enemy was so deeply entrenched within villages and among the civilian populace that the people would have to be relocated and the villages destroyed, to create "free fire zones" from which the enemy might be eliminated and to which the people eventually might return. The alternatives were to fight among the people or to leave the enemy alone. Neither was acceptable—because of the likelihood of civilian casualties and because the enemy, left alone, would be able to extend his area of control.

Actions against guerrillas and Northern regulars

The first major combat involving American troops occurred in August 1965, when US Marines protecting an airfield on the north-central coast at Chu Lai located a Viet Cong regiment on the Van Tuong Peninsula. Since the Viet Cong force, only some 15 miles (24km) away, constituted a threat to Chu Lai, the commander of the III Marine Amphibious Force, Major General Lewis W. Walt, activated "Operation Starlite", sending in some 4,000 Marines by sea and air to sweep the peninsula. Some 700 Viet Cong were killed, for the loss of 50 Marines killed and 150 wounded, while others fled inland to the mountains. Yet, as was to be the pattern in many an operation to follow, the Marines had insufficient strength to garrison the peninsula: in the months and years to come, the enemy would return and the operation would from time to time have to be repeated.

Meanwhile, the threat that the North Vietnamese (VPA) division in the Central Highlands would drive to the sea and split the country in two had been slowly developing. In October 1965, some 6,000 North Vietnamese troops began to concentrate against a South Vietnamese outpost near the border at Plei Me, as the first step in eliminating three outposts in the region, taking the provincial capital of Pleiku, and pushing on along Highway 19 to the sea.

When the US 1st Cavalry Division (Airmobile) arrived on Highway 19 at An Khe, where they constructed a base camp, Westmoreland planned to commit at least part of the division against the North

Vietnamese build-up. Although the South Vietnamese themselves, with US air support, broke the enemy's encirclement of the outpost at Plei Me, a VPA concentration was reported to be still in the area—in the dense jungle of the Ia Drang Valley. Westmoreland committed a brigade of the 1st Cavalry with an extremely large complement of helicopters to find and fix the enemy—then pulled out that brigade and sent in another. This was the first engagement between US troops and North Vietnamese regulars. Electing to fight, the North Vietnamese launched one attack after another from 14 to 19 November, without denting the American position. Throughout the course of the fighting, B-52s struck at areas where the enemy was reputedly concentrating—the first time the big bombers were used in direct tactical support of ground operations.

When the North Vietnamese at last fell back, they left behind an estimated 1,800 dead against 240 Americans killed, a ratio that was destined to persist or to be substantially lowered in favor of the Americans for the rest of the war. Yet the North Vietnamese division, retreating across the border into Cambodia where, because of restrictions imposed by Washington, American troops were forbidden to follow, was soon reconstituted as a viable fighting force.

The problem of the enemy taking refuge in Cambodia and Laos, rebuilding, then returning to fight again was to trouble Westmoreland for a long time. Although Washington had approved ground patrols to locate the enemy just inside Laos and call in tactical air strikes against him, the US commanders in the field had no authority to pursue the enemy into Laos or to make any move against enemy sanctuaries in Cambodia. State Department officials turned down every request from MACV to patrol, bomb, or shell North Vietnamese extra-territorial camps. Although it was obvious that the Cambodian head of state, Prince Norodom Sihanouk, was tacitly allowing the Viet Cong and North Vietnamese presence in his country, the State Department thought it better to tolerate that policy than to risk driving Sihanouk into open collaboration with the enemy.

Offshore and riverine interdiction operations

More could be done to counter the enemy's infiltration of men and supplies along South Vietnam's extended coast line. From the spring of 1965, US ships and South Vietnamese junks and patrol boats covered the coast in a program code-named "Market Time". By the end of 1966, close on 100 fast patrol boats, more than 30 US Coast Guard cutters, and hundreds of South Vietnamese junks were operating close in-shore, searching any junk or barge deemed to be suspicious. Farther offshore, American destroyers and minesweepers constituted an outer screen. In a related program, more than 100 river patrol boats searched more than 2,000 junks and sampans each day, thus interfering with Viet Cong use of the country's extensive system of inland waterways both for transport and for "tax collection" and general subjugation of the people. But although ocean and riverine infiltration was reduced

1. Search and destroy: men of the 2d Brigade, US 1st Cavalry Division (Airmobile) move through a rice paddy. 2. Close support strikes by B-52s caused the bomb crater through which paratroopers of the US 173d Airborne Brigade scramble during a sweep. 3. From the first, US troops in the field received maximum helicopter support and were often resupplied while under fire; here, a CH-47A Chinook lifts in a water trailer to men of the 12th Infantry Regiment in the Central Highlands. 4. Important part of US armor in Vietnam—an M42 twin 40mm self-propelled AA gun. 5. In "Market Time" operations, South Vietnamese and American warships—like the US Coast Guard cutter *Point Clear*, seen here—patrolled inshore waters to counter Communist infiltration of men and supplies by sea.

to an acceptable minimum, these programs increased North Vietnamese reliance on routes through Laos and Cambodia—including shipping supplies into the Cambodian port of Sihanoukville which, like the rest of Cambodia, was off limits to American reprisal—and eventually to blatant violation of the DMZ.

As additional American combat units arrived, General Westmoreland committed them to the protection of existing or developing logistical support facilities. By the end of 1965, American strength in South Vietnam totalled 181,000, including combat forces of three divisions—one infantry, one airmobile, one Marine—three US Army brigades and a Marine regiment, and three tactical fighter wings. There were, in addition, an Australian battalion and a South Korean division and Marine brigade, the latter country's forces totalling some 20,000 men. As well as some 120 New Zealanders, small numbers of troops had already arrived from Thailand, the Philippines, and the Republic of China (Taiwan). The Thai contingent was to increase to a total of around 11,600 (six battalions) by 1970.

The US logistics system: a major accomplishment

In electing to bring in combat troops before building an adequate logistical base, General Westmoreland took a gamble, forced by what he saw as a critical situation. It succeeded, both because the incoming troops displayed the ability to live on a shoestring until logistical facilities could be developed, and because US Army Engineers, US Navy Construction Battalions ("Seabees"), and US civilian contractors—a relatively new departure in a war zone—made a Herculean effort.

Within two and a half years of the beginning of the American build-up in mid-1965, the logistics system would support more than 1.3 million men, including close on half a million American troops, the South Vietnamese armed forces, troops of other nations, and a number of US civilian agencies, while at the same time helping to maintain South Vietnam's civilian economy. An average of 850,000 short tons (760,000 tons; 771,000 tonnes) of supplies would arrive each month. Troops would consume 10 million field rations and expend 80,000 short tons (71,000 tons; 73,000 tonnes) of ammunition and 80 million US gallons (67 million Imperial gallons; 303 million liters) of petroleum products per month. There would be new ports or vastly expanded facilities at six sites, including modern installations at Saigon and a new port at Cam Ranh Bay, one of the best natural harbors in Asia. Engineers paved 4 million square yards (33,450 hectares) of airfields and heliports, constructed 20 million square feet (18,000 hectares) of covered and open storage facilities, plus 500,000 cubic feet (14,150 cubic metres) of refrigerated storage, and built 1,700 miles (2,740km) of road, 1,000 feet (4,600m) of bridges, and 15 large fortified base camps.

The accomplishment was all the more remarkable in that it was achieved with men and supplies transported halfway around the world.

5

1. On patrol in jungle near Bien Hoa: a paratrooper of the US 173d Airborne Brigade with an M60 machine gun. **2.** Men of the 3d Marines move over "Punji Stake Hill"—named from the bamboo stakes used as booby-traps by the Viet Cong—in an early search and clear mission around Da Nang. **3.** In training, members of the North Vietnamese militia lack the automatic weapons supplied by China and the USSR to the Viet Cong and Northern regulars. **4.** One of the Herculean tasks performed by "Seabees"—US Navy Construction Battalions: a 10,000-barrel storage tank at the Naval Support Activity, Da Nang. **5.** This trawler carrying arms and ammunition for the Viet Cong—seen here being offloaded by crewmen of a US warship—was run aground and set on fire after interception by a "Market Time" patrol. **6.** A Seabee lays aluminium matting on an airstrip damaged by enemy mortar fire. **7.** A trailer loaded with cargo containers moves towards the rear of a US Air Force C-141 Starlifter at Cam Ranh Bay, the major US logistical center, on the east-central coast of South Vietnam, south of Nha Trang.

6

7

A battle for the people's hearts and minds

Richard A. Hunt

In the context of Vietnam, "pacification" was a catch-all description of the American-supported efforts of successive South Vietnamese governments to counter the appeal and pre-empt the political strength of its internal enemy—the Communists generally called Viet Cong (VC). In its efforts to keep the loyalty of the rural population, mainly by protecting them and improving their living conditions, the Saigon government initiated various programs, sent out several kinds of cadres, and deployed an array of military and para-military forces. The battle for the allegiance of the people of South Vietnam was the keystone of the struggle between the VC and the government: success in "pacification" was vital for South Vietnam's survival.

Pacification activities fell into separate programs, some designed to improve security and others to foster economic development and political loyalty. To safeguard the population from VC terrorism and infiltration, the South Vietnamese government deployed specially-trained police and para-military forces in areas its armed forces had cleared of VC. Regional Force companies were assigned to provinces and District and Popular Force platoons to villages. Police units maintained law and order in villages and hamlets.

Operations against the Communist infrastructure

The government sought security in other programs aimed at weakening the VC. Intelligence operations such as the much-criticized "Phoenix program", described below were directed at the Communist network of subversion; "Chieu Hoi" ("open arms") operations tried, through the promise of amnesty, to induce VC rank and file to leave their units. Because of their racial affinities with the Vietnamese peoples, Thai and South Korean troops were able to make an especially noteworthy contribution to the Chieu Hoi program, which aimed at extracting the maximum information — by persuasion rather than force—from VC deserters. By 1969–70, some 49,000 South Korean and 12,000 Thai troops were deployed in Vietnam. The Revolutionary Development cadre, with other cadres from Saigon ministries, had the double aim of organizing support for the government in rural communities and providing technical assistance to the people. Other programs sought to resettle refugees or to stimulate the rural economy by building or improving bridges, roads, and canals. Still more programs were launched to promote the democratic election of local government officials in the villages. The common aim of all programs was—in words that would

> **Continuing efforts by the Americans to improve internal security and eradicate popular support for the Communist cause in South Vietnam met with considerable success later in the war, but only by implementing much-needed political and social reforms could the South Vietnamese government truly "win the hearts and minds" of the people —and this was never fully accomplished**

become a cliché—to "win the hearts and minds" of the people.

Despite the importance both American and South Vietnamese officials attached to pacification in their public pronouncements throughout the war, the program received fluctuating degrees of support. The US government provided funds, advice, training, and equipment for Vietnamese personnel, as well as financing economic development projects. With the deterioration of security following Diem's fall in 1963, and the commitment of increasing numbers of American troops, pacification as a strategy and as a program took second place to military operations against North Vietnamese and VC units.

Before the fall of the Diem regime, its apparent ability to survive and even grow stronger encouraged the American government to regard Diem as the most important anti-Communist leader in Southeast Asia. Meanwhile, the Communists in South Vietnam, expecting Diem's government to collapse because of its internecine weaknesses, waited for the general elections called for under the Geneva Agreements to bring them to power—if Diem lasted that long.

When Diem survived and, in addition, refused to hold the elections, his opponents, Communist and non-Communist alike, began to undermine his regime in earnest. At first, most of those taking up arms against the government were isolated groups of South Vietnamese engaged in the sporadic assassination or abduction of government representatives in rural areas. North Vietnam's part in such early acts of insurgency was at first ill-defined. However, in December 1960, the North Vietnamese government in Hanoi announced the formation of the National Front for the Liberation of South Vietnam

(NLF; its members were generally called the Viet Cong) and increased its support for the southern insurgents. Hanoi saw the NLF as an organization to consolidate the wide-spread discontent in the South— largely occasioned by the policies and behavior of Diem's officials. By openly favoring the wealthy and powerful, by harsh repression of political opponents, and by its aversion to necessary reforms, Diem's government alienated potential supporters among the mass of the population.

Diem's attempts at repression, or pacification, did little to halt insurgency or win popular support. In fact, some of Diem's measures to strengthen his position had the opposite effect. In 1956, Diem abolished local elections for village councils and instead imposed upon them officials he considered loyal to himself. His intention was to prevent the election of VC to local office: in practice, the VC continued to form their own "shadow" councils, while otherwise uncommitted villagers were antagonized by the presence of Saigon's place-men. Resettlement schemes dictated by military considerations, under which landless peasants were moved into strategic enclaves in traditional Montagnard tribal areas in the Central Highlands, to form a barrier against infiltrating VC, were resented by peasants and mountain peoples alike.

Among other measures against the VC, Diem moved his army into Communist-held areas to shield his civic action cadres, theoretically the cutting-edge of a government-sponsored social revolution. The cadres were intended to rally the community's support by carrying out public works projects, forming local militia and para-military units, and publicizing the government's agrarian reform. In fact, the ARVN's conduct towards the rural population was often so insensitive as to reinforce the effects of Communist propaganda. Thus, the cadres failed as instruments of a social revolution, becoming instead political action units in Diem's poorly-planned anti-Communist crusade.

The high price of Diem's anti-Communism

Besides politicizing the cadres, Diem began to go to extremes in demanding outward expressions of anti-Communism. Political re-education centers were established, where suspected Communists— or almost anyone the government considered a danger to the state — were detained. Diem set up military tribunals to try suspects, and abolished freedom of the press on the grounds of both anti-Communism and anti-Fascism — categories wide enough to encompass Diem's opposition on the left (the insurgents)

1. Pacification—but no peace: a crewman of a US Navy River Patrol Boat engaged in Chieu Hoi ("Open Arms") operations—persuading guerrillas to rally to the Saigon government—mans an M60 machine gun as Viet Cong fire on his craft. **2.** Viet Cong defectors are re-educated at an "Open Arms" center in a pacified area. **3.** The dark side of pacification: a Vietnamese intelligence agent (right) persuaded this village chief (center), who collaborated with the guerrillas, to talk by pouring water on to a cloth over his nose and mouth until he was almost drowned.

as well as on the right (followers of the deposed Emperor Bao Dai and anti-Diem nationalists). Thus, instead of uniting his politically and socially divided country, Diem alienated potential supporters, even driving some into the camp of the most dangerous of his enemies—the Viet Cong.

Other measures had a similar effect. The *agrovilles* (fortified villages) and "Strategic Hamlet" programs, which involved moving peasants from their ancestral holdings to defended locations chosen by the government, where security forces could protect and cadres indoctrinate them, were Diem's major attempt to improve rural security. The peasants resented not only the forced relocation, but also the fact that they were compelled to labor unpaid to build the defensive works. The government might forcibly move people and exact their labor—but it seemed incapable of carrying out its promised reforms. It failed to protect its citizens from VC cadres, who easily slipped into the fortified settlements where they attempted to subvert government forces and spread propaganda among peasants alienated by Diem's policies. Nor did the barbed wire and armed outposts of the strategic hamlets check the steadily increasing number of killings and abductions of government officials.

Land reform was another of Diem's ill-fated attempts to win popular support. Forced to respond to Communist-initiated reform that distributed land directly to the agricultural workers, Diem decreed in 1956 that no individual might own more than 0.386 square miles (1 sq km, or 100 hectares) of land. But loopholes in the law allowed owners of large estates to retain far greater amounts of land by dedicating some of it to ancestor worship or by deeding it to a relative. Even if the government had fully implemented the law, fairly distributing all the expropriated land, the reform would not have alleviated the plight of tenants plagued by high rents and exorbitant interest rates, and working plots of land barely large enough to provide both rent in kind and a subsistence living.

While the government failed to win over the people, the VC continued to gain rural support. Their acts of terrorism increased and they organized larger combat units. The ARVN was increasingly perturbed by Diem's failure to recognize the deterioration of rural security and by his interference in military affairs. When the armed forces overthrew Diem in November 1963, not a single general came to his defense.

Political instability slows the pacification program

Between the fall of Diem and the emergence in mid-1965 of General Nguyen Van Thieu and Air Force commander Nguyen Cao Ky as political leaders, South Vietnam's war effort was greatly hampered by political instability. Although the military establishment dominated politics, it was unable to prevent the succession of six hastily-formed governments, each seemingly with less popular support than its predecessor.

This period of some 18 months saw the stagnation of the pacification programs and the continued deterioration of rural security as the VC took advantage of the

lack of direction in Saigon. Saigon did initiate new pacification programs—"New Life Hamlets", in effect those "Strategic Hamlets" that had not already been abandoned (some 55 percent of the original number), "officially" replaced "Strategic Hamlets" early in 1964—and the American government increased the number of its advisers in the field, thereby obtaining a clearer picture of the widespread insecurity. But the instability in Saigon was mirrored in the provinces and districts of South Vietnam. It was difficult under the best of circumstances to carry through rural pacification programs; it became virtually impossible with the constant changing of local officials, intrigued between political factions, VC incursions and monetary levies, and increased enemy infiltration and recruitment. By 1965 the situation was so grave that American and South Vietnamese officials concluded that all efforts to date—including pacification plans, counterinsurgency operations, and the reorganized ARVN—were insufficient to stave off defeat at the hands of the Communists.

Poor coordination limits American effectiveness

In 1965, the large-scale commitment of American forces, together with the appearance of North Vietnamese regular army units in South Vietnam, enlarged the purely military aspect of the war and diverted attention and resources from pacification. But even after American firepower stabilized the military situation in 1966, the Saigon government's efforts at weakening the political and military position of the VC, and expanding its own control, were disappointing. Not only had the conventional war diverted resources from pacification; American advice and support for the Vietnamese pacification effort was poorly organized. Because pacification presented the South Vietnamese government with the dual task of developing the countryside politically and economically while protecting the rural population from the Viet Cong, American support for pacification was provided by US civilian as well as military agencies. Yet the State Department and the US Agency for International Development (a body specifically charged with co-ordinating and helping to finance US aid to South Vietnam) had neither the authority nor the ability to assist the Vietnamese in combating terrorism. Nor had the US Army a mandate to foster political development or economic growth.

President Johnson repeatedly stressed that American non-military activities in Vietnam were essential to US aims. During the troop build-up of 1965, fearing that pacification might be neglected, he urged the American Mission in Saigon to emphasize non-military programs and to give them increasing priority. Johnson believed that progress in pacification was as essential as military progress and, at the Honolulu Conference of February 1966, stressed his desire for an improved pacification program. In March 1966, Johnson appointed Robert W. Komer as his special assistant in Washington to direct, co-ordinate, and supervise non-military programs—further evidence of the priority

5

1. In the "battle for the hearts and minds" of the Vietnamese people, US personnel undertook many projects for the benefit of civilians. Here, a US Navy doctor accompanying US Marines on amphibious search and clear operations treats an old man for an eye infection during a regular civilian sick call.
2. The crew of a South Vietnamese River Patrol Boat watch as one of their shipmates distributes psychological warfare material to villagers.
3. This USAF C-47 of the 5th Air Commando Squadron, operating from Nha Trang, is equipped with huge, high-altitude loudspeakers which are turned down in flight to deliver a barrage of tape-recorded "psywar" messages to the Viet Cong. **4.** Villagers built this well in a "New Life" hamlet for Vietnamese relocated from guerrilla-infested areas. **5.** Pacification must be backed up by firepower—like that of these US 105mm howitzers. **6.** And pacified areas must be defended: women of a village Civil Defense Guard drill with their menfolk.

6

which the President gave to pacification.

Komer became the most articulate and influential advocate of pacification, the prime mover of the reorganization of American advice and support for the program. After research, including several trips to South Vietnam in 1966, Komer reported that pacification was at a virtual impasse and recommended to the President a number of measures that might produce better results. The main task of improving security, weakening the Viet Cong, and winning the support of the people could, he believed, be furthered by consolidating American assistance under a single manager empowered to eliminate overlapping programs and disentangle competition for resources.

A firmer foundation for pacification

Poor results and unsuccessful interim organizational shake-ups finally induced President Johnson completely to reorganize American support for the pacification program. In May 1967, taking into account both Komer's recommendations and the apparent military success in Vietnam against the enemy's main forces, Johnson gave General Westmoreland responsibility for both the civil and military aspects of pacification. He appointed Komer as Westmoreland's deputy for pacification, heading a new pacification support organization designated Civil Operations and Rural Development Support (CORDS). CORDS integrated the duties and personnel of military and civilian agencies at all levels, so neither was dominant: for example, Komer, although subordinate to Westmoreland, had a general officer as his deputy.

Australian and New Zealand teams, both civilian and military, took part in programs aimed at winning the confidence of the Vietnamese people. Both countries sent surgical teams and civilian experts in agriculture, water supplies, hygiene, and road-building. Textbooks were provided for rural schools, equipment for high schools and universities, and more than 200 students were awarded study places in Australia and New Zealand. In Phuoc Tuy province, the area of responsibility of the 1st Australian Task Force, a civic action program went into effect from July 1966. The activities of the ANZAC civil affairs teams ranged from the provision of medical and dental treatment and the construction of schools and markets to the resettlement of villagers from areas threatened by the Viet Cong. The total cost of Australia's participation in the war from 1966 onward was put at around $240 million; non-military aid from New Zealand was provided at an average rate of $347,500 per year.

In the first six months of CORDS' existence, the Americans also won South Vietnamese acceptance of a more reliable and objective system of evaluating the pacification program's results. The Hamlet Evaluation System (HES), initiated early in 1967, involved a computerized monthly report on the security and development status of the hamlets of South Vietnam. The magnitude of this undertaking may be judged from the fact that it covered around 12,750 hamlets, more than 2,000 villages, and 244 districts throughout South Vietnam's 44 provinces. MACV claimed that during 1967 the number of "secure" hamlets rose from 4,702 to 5,340 and that "secure areas" were increased by 5 percent (to a total of 67 percent). To obtain reliable information as a basis for allocation of resources and to monitor progress, American advisers in each district regularly filled out standard questionnaires and forwarded them to headquarters.

South Vietnamese acceptance of HES meant not only more efficient evaluation, but also an increase in American influence; US advisers were, in effect, keeping score on the Vietnamese and making it more difficult for false optimism to creep into reports. The South Vietnamese Revolutionary Development cadres, para-military teams some 50 strong operating at village level, were widely successful. Other political improvements in 1967 were the promulgation of a new constitution in April and the inauguration of General Nguyen Van Thieu as President in September, both bringing increased political stability.

However, as soon as a firmer foundation for pacification had been established, the VC and VPA set the program back by launching a nationwide offensive in January-February 1968—the Tet offensive —against the cities of South Vietnam. With targets ranging from the American embassy in Saigon to the citadel at Hue, the VC bombarded or assaulted 36 of the 44 South Vietnamese provincial capitals and five of the six autonomous cities. Creating new refugee problems and forcing the redeployment of security forces, the offensive forced funds and personnel to be diverted from pacification to rebuilding efforts in urban areas. There was a drop in rural security when ARVN battalions supporting pacification and technical cadres had to be withdrawn from the countryside.

Exploiting Communist losses in the Tet offensive

When Komer and his staff learned of the serious losses that the VC and VPA had sustained in the Tet offensive—the South Vietnamese claimed that some 7,000 Communists were captured and close on 39,000 killed—they saw an opportunity of quickly reversing the setback to pacification, depending on the speedy return of South Vietnamese forces and cadres to the villages and hamlets before the weakened enemy could regroup and attempt to reclaim the countryside. Komer saw other reasons for timely action: he felt that a new, dramatic success might stem growing public disenchantment in the United States and might also improve Saigon's position in the case of a political settlement of the war.

But however apparent the need and opportunity to exploit VC losses by a vigorous pacification counter-offensive, renewed VC attacks, the post-Tet recovery effort, and South Vietnamese caution prevented the implementation of Komer's plans until the fall of 1968. Urged on by American military and civilian officials, headed by Komer, President Thieu agreed to embark on a short-term counter-

1

2

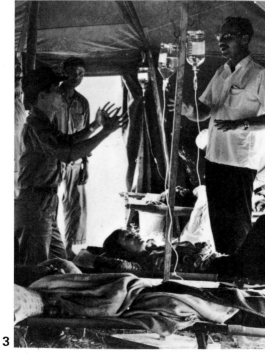

3

1. News media often featured pictures of troops burning "hooches"—but this member of a civil affairs team from 1st Australian Task Force is spraying insecticide around a rural dwelling in Hoa Long village, Phuoc Tuy province, during a campaign to cut down the civilian malaria rate.
2. Men of a South Vietnamese Popular Force unit are carried to a night ambush position aboard a US Navy River Patrol Boat; by this time (1969) modern US arms like the M16 Armalite rifles seen here were available to the para-military units. 3. The US Agency for International Development provided the equipment and drugs used by this Vietnamese doctor and US medical technician to treat cholera victims. 4. Members of a Malaria Eradication Team *en route* to a remote area of South Vietnam. 5. Men of the 716th Military Police Battalion guard the US Embassy, Saigon, on 31 January 1968—the day on which it was attacked by Viet Cong suicide sappers at the beginning of the Tet offensive.

offensive designated the Accelerated Pacification Campaign (APC). The APC, an intensive three-month effort begun in November 1968, set specific goals for each element of pacification — including the Phoenix program, directed against the VC infrastructure; the resettlement of refugees; and the Chieu Hoi operation to induce Communist guerrillas to change sides. It employed Regional and Popular Forces, and police, as well as American and South Vietnamese combat units, integrating military operations and non-military aid programs in a plan aimed at improving internal security and expanding Saigon's control into previously contested areas.

Increased security for the rural population

The Accelerated Pacification Campaign was a turning point in the history of pacification. It marked the beginning of the steady increase in the Saigon government's control of the countryside that had eluded earlier pacification efforts. The most publicized goal of the campaign, raising the security status of 1,000 contested hamlets to a level classified by HES evaluation as relative security, was achieved, as were objectives. When the APC ended, national aggregate HES scores reflected complete recovery from the Tet offensive, rising to the highest levels yet recorded.

Success was in part due to the lack of VC reaction. South Vietnamese and American forces were surprised by the relative ease with which they moved into territory once contested. The lack of concerted opposition to the APC seemed to confirm that the Tet offensive had seriously weakened the military potential of the VC and had left open gaps in the rural areas that the ARVN, Regional and Popular Forces, and pacification cadres might fill.

From 1969 to 1971 the pacification program steadily gained ground. As Sir Robert Thompson noted in his book *Peace Is Not at Hand*, during that period — although HES criteria for secure hamlets were raised — by March 1972, 70 percent of hamlets fell into the highest security categories, and that figure embraced more than 80 percent of the population of South Vietnam. Contemporary figures showed that the VC controlled only 2 percent of the hamlets and 1 percent of the people. In contrast to the earlier pacification schemes which relocated people to already secure areas, the gains of 1969–1971 were achieved by encouraging people to return to villages recently wrested from the VC.

There were other signs of VC weakness and growing South Vietnamese strength. The number of rank and file VC defectors to Saigon reached a peak, in 1969, of 4,000 a month. The Phoenix program — a subject of controversy and unfavorable press comment in the US — was a procedure for collecting intelligence and identifying members of the VC underground, or infrastructure, in order to facilitate their apprehension and detention under South Vietnamese law. While never as successful as its adherents wished, nor as harsh as its critics complained, by 1969 the Phoenix program was making some headway against clandestine VC activities. At the

same time, the South Vietnamese armed forces, financially backed by America, increased in size and received modern arms. For example, the American government provided M16 rifles to replace the World-War-II vintage MIs used by Vietnamese forces from ARVN divisions down to the Popular Force platoons defending their own villages. The American and South Vietnamese governments also paid greater attention to strengthening the local police forces charged with providing internal security and law and order.

With improved security came a better chance to improve the standard of living. As fighting slackened, roads, bridges, and canals were reopened, with a consequent increase in rice production and the area of land under cultivation. In 1970, President Thieu promulgated a sweeping land reform program called "Land to the Tiller": by September 1973, titles of ownership of more than 3,500 square miles (9,000 sq km) of land were distributed among more than 600,000 owners. This program, swiftly carried out, gave the land-hungry peasantry holdings of their own without charge. The government reimbursed the former owners of the land. Allied to relatively free access to markets, the changes in land ownership transformed the rural economy from a subsistence and barter system to a market economy.

Political reforms accompanied economic change. From 1969, the Thieu government encouraged villages under its control to elect their own local officials, and authorized councils thus elected to decide local issues and allocate funds for public works. Saigon also overcame its reluctance to arm the part-time village militia; it now saw the distribution and bearing of arms as evidence of widespread commitment to the anti-Communist cause.

Doubts about the South's determination

And yet, as the rapid collapse of South Vietnam in 1975 demonstrated, the foundations of the political and military gains of 1969–1971 were weak. The size of South Vietnam's armed forces was not a reliable measure of its political stature or the quality of its leadership. In combat, South Vietnamese units too often panicked and showed little fighting spirit. However, to blame South Vietnamese soldiers who failed in the face of well-planned offensives undertaken by well-armed North Vietnamese divisions would be to ignore a combat record of more than 20 years of heavy casualties.

Yet it is axiomatic that the military of any country reflects the society it guards. Were South Vietnamese civilians and military both truly committed to their cause? Did statistical indices of progress really indicate a coherent national community? The true point at issue was not the number of local elections the Saigon government sponsored, nor the number of hamlets it could count as secure, nor the amount of land it distributed to the landless — but whether the people of South Vietnam truly espoused their government's cause.

Despite the success of the pacification program in improving security and material conditions in the countryside, it

1. In the bow of an offshore patrol boat, a South Vietnamese sailor fires a warning burst from a Browning .30-caliber machine gun towards a junk suspected of carrying materiel for the Viet Cong. **2.** Somewhere in guerrilla territory in South Vietnam, a Viet Cong unit plans an assault on a triangular jungle fort of the type built in the French colonial period. **3.** The surrender of this guerrilla to an ARVN patrol near Nha Trang was the result of psychological warfare leaflets in the form of safe conduct passes, dropped by the US 5th Air Commando Squadron. **4.** The "secure hamlet" program eventually protected 80 percent of the people of South Vietnam; here, villagers at Hoai My work on their defenses.

would appear that it failed in its larger, long-term objective—national solidarity. The Saigon government failed in this respect partly because it remained, to the end, a westernized, élite body, buttressed by American military and financial aid. Its internal support came mainly from a minority of the population: Catholics, the military, and the upper classes. Even if pacification succeeded in denying popular support to the Viet Cong, it failed to win completely the support of the masses.

The Communists have no need for caution

Perhaps more time, with continued American aid might have preserved South Vietnam's independence, but the Americans and North Vietnamese denied the country that chance. Steadily decreasing American aid forced the South Vietnamese to retrench—to act always on the defensive—with corrosive effect on morale. Pacification did succeed in making insurgency a doubtful proposition; thus, Hanoi chose to end the struggle for South Vietnam through conventional military operations. By the end of 1973, sensing South Vietnam's internal weakness—and the improbability of further intervention by American combat units—the Communists no longer had any reason to wait.

2

4

The military build-up in north and south

Charles B. MacDonald

An unusual aspect of the war in Vietnam was the observance of cease-fires for major holidays such as Christmas, New Year, Buddha's birthday, and the lunar new year known as Tet. American officials never liked the practice—the Viet Cong and North Vietnamese never truly observed a cease-fire—yet to refuse to comply would have given the enemy a point for propaganda. Besides, however imperfectly the enemy observed them, the cease-fires usually provided some respite from large-scale attacks, so South Vietnamese officials were inclined to welcome them. As anxious as the Americans not to appear callous and unfeeling, South Vietnamese officials, in spite of minor disagreements, usually pursued a liberal leave policy for their troops. Particularly at Tet, a holiday closely associated with ancestor worship, South Vietnamese soldiers yearned to be with their families.

Another unusual aspect of the war were the bombing pauses. These were predicated on the theory that a halt in the bombing of North Vietnam would afford its leaders time to reflect and prompt them to establish contact with the United States as a step toward peace negotiations. In fact, neither President Johnson nor his military advisers believed the bombing pauses would produce results: the President was forced to explore the possibility from time to time as a result of pressure from Communist propagandists and sympathizers, certain foreign capitals, senior US civilian officials anxious to grasp at any chance for peace, and "doves" among middle-level officials and certain elements of Congress and the press.

Bombing pauses: the bait is refused

President Johnson called for the first bombing pause on 10 May 1965. He asked the Soviet Union to act as intermediary, but was refused. Two messages intended for the North Vietnamese—one to their embassy in Moscow, another through another government—were summarily returned without comment. After eight days, the President ordered the bombing renewed.

His critics claimed that the pause was too short: had the United States held off a little longer, they asserted, it might have produced a positive response. Several Communist governments expressed the same opinion; Hungary (and later Russia, Romania, and Poland) professed to be in direct contact with Hanoi and to be convinced that if the United States would halt the bombing, the North Vietnamese would negotiate. Communist leaders made certain that the American press learned of their assertions, so that pressure on the Johnson administration became intense.

Neither the threat of increased bombing of the North nor the inducement of truces and bombing pauses could persuade the Communists to negotiate for peace in earnest. Thus, in 1965–66, US and ARVN forces launched massive "search and destroy" operations to drive the Viet Cong from their strongholds in the South, and fought large scale actions with North Vietnamese regulars who pushed south across the Demilitarized Zone

---

At Christmas 1965, when even Secretary of Defense McNamara supported a pause, President Johnson, although fearing that another halt would merely be interpreted by the North Vietnamese as a faltering of American will, sanctioned an extension of a bombing pause already approved as part of a Christmas cease-fire. The President also mounted a world-wide diplomatic offensive, sending emissaries to various capitals to make sure that all knew of the United States' readiness to negotiate.

Although the bombing pause lasted 37 days, it was all in vain. After the war, a defecting Hungarian diplomat stated that never at any time during eight bombing halts from 1965 to 1968—despite such conciliatory gestures from President Johnson as pledging post-war aid to all of Indochina, *including* North Vietnam—did the North Vietnamese show any interest in negotiations. Their supporters in other Communist (and non-Communist) countries may have been sincere, or they may simply have been seeking to give the North Vietnamese a respite from bombing, but in no instance did they have the ear of the North Vietnamese leaders. The North Vietnamese had one goal: to subjugate South Vietnam and reunite the country under Communist rule. So long as South Vietnam and the United States were pledged to deny that goal, there were no grounds for negotiation.

Early in 1966, General Westmoreland prepared to fly to Honolulu to present to the Commander in Chief, Pacific, Admiral Sharp, his requirements for additional troops. To proceed with the logistical build-up and move into the second phase of operations—in which he would seek out the enemy's major units in their sanctuaries—he considered that he required a total of 429,000 American troops and

approximately 10,000 more from Asian countries. These must include not only combat troops, but also essential logistical support units such as signal and engineer battalions, aviation and aviation support units, and port battalions.

At the last minute, President Johnson decided to fly to Honolulu himself to meet not only with Westmoreland and Ambassador Lodge but also with the South Vietnamese leaders, Chief of State Thieu and Premier Ky. The President brought with him, in addition to Secretary of Defense McNamara and Secretary of State Dean Rusk, his secretaries of agriculture, health, education, and welfare. This indicated his wish to stress the civilian side of the struggle in South Vietnam—notably the pacification process aimed at providing security for the people and producing social, political, and economic reforms designed to inspire them to cooperate with the government, thus eliminating support for the insurgents.

In the course of the conference, which began on 6 February, Thieu and Ky committed themselves not only to defeating the Communists on the battlefield but also to such broad principles as eradicating social injustice and formulating a constitution, to be followed by elections by secret ballot. They were thus committed to what President Johnson called "the other war" —pacification—on which the President wanted new emphasis by Americans and South Vietnamese alike.

No true measure of military progress

So far as military matters were concerned, an important discussion centered on how military progress should be measured. In a war without conventional front lines whose movements determined which side was winning, there had to be other criteria. What percentage of the population was under government control? How many miles of roads and waterways were open to traffic? How many insurgents were being brought over to the government side? How many enemy weapons were being captured? How many enemy had been killed?

These were at best imprecise measurements of progress. With the possible exception of counts of enemy dead and weapons captured, all involved subjective judgement: all the measurements were subject to question—particularly the number of enemy killed. That figure was determined by actually counting the fallen on the battlefield, a process known as "body count". The press frequently queried the figures, asserting that they were inflated or that civilian dead were included. General Westmoreland, however, having commissioned a comprehensive study of the

1. During the bombing pauses the ground war went on: Australian troops engage the enemy. **2.** President Johnson stresses the need for political and social reform to Premier Nguyan Cao Ky during the Honolulu conference, February 1966. **3.** B-52 Stratofortresses: although US officials had little hope that bombing pauses would further peace, international and domestic pressure made the halts desirable. **4.** Transport and engineer personnel of the Korean Military Assistance Group arrive in Saigon.

Major Truces/Bombing Pauses

1965 *1–6 February:* Tet Truce. *13–18 May:* Bombing pause.
1966 *24 December 1965–31 January:* Bombing pause. *23 December:* Bombing of Hanoi area restricted. *24–26 December:* Christmas Truce.
1967 *8–12 February:* Tet Truce.
1968 *15 January–10 February:* Bombing of Haiphong area suspended. *18 January:* Bombing of Hanoi area suspended. *31 March:* US ends bombing of North Vietnam, except near DMZ. *31 October:* US ends all bombing of North Vietnam.
1972 *6 April:* Bombing of North Vietnam recommences.
1973 *15 January:* US ends all bombing of North Vietnam. *27 January:* Peace Agreement signed in Paris. *28 January:* Ceasefire effective.

process, was convinced that if the statistics erred, they erred on the side of caution, for enemy killed by long-range artillery or air strikes were seldom included in the totals.

For all General Westmoreland's attempts to limit fighting in populated areas, most operations, well into 1966, took place in or near population centers. This was because Viet Cong forces had entrenched themselves there, while incoming North Vietnamese units were still assembling along the Laotian and Cambodian frontiers. The US 1st Cavalry Division (Airmobile), for example, operated for much of the year in the central coastal province of Binh Dinh, long a Communist stronghold, and by early autumn had broken the hold of a Viet Cong regiment on the region. Korean troops operated in a similar fashion in provinces just south of Binh Dinh.

Although Westmoreland counted on the South Vietnamese Army for close-in defense of the capital, he positioned American troops on approaches to Saigon leading from the enemy's long-established base areas and from Cambodia—just 30 miles (48km) from the capital at the closest point. The 1st Infantry Division, the 173d Airborne Brigade, and an Australian battalion swept a big rubber plantation, once owned by the Michelin Tire Company, 20 to 25 miles (32–40km) northwest of Saigon, then probed for enemy command posts and supply bases in two large forested regions, the Boi Loi Forest and Ho Bo Wood. Two brigades of the US 25th Infantry Division operated in Tay Ninh province northwest of Saigon along the Cambodian border, while another brigade of the division beat the bushes in the Central Highlands in search of North Vietnamese units. When firm contacts were made in the Highlands, Westmoreland moved in a brigade of the 101st Airborne Division, later reinforced by the entire 1st Cavalry Division, to probe the jungle-covered mountains and prevent the North Vietnamese from massing for attacks on provincial capitals in the region.

The Viet Cong find refuge in Cambodia

When the 199th Light Infantry Brigade arrived in late summer of 1966, Westmoreland deployed the unit on the fringes of a big enemy base area in Tay Ninh province known as War Zone C. When the enemy appeared ready to make a fight of it in War Zone C, the II Field Force commander, Lieutenant General Jonathan Seaman, was reinforced by the 173d Airborne Brigade, the 1st Infantry Division, contingents of a South Vietnamese division, and a brigade each of the US 4th and 25th Infantry Divisions. The fight that ensued, known as "Operation Attleboro", involved some 22,000 Americans and South Vietnamese, the largest operation of the war up to that time. After more than six weeks of hit-and-run fighting, the Viet Cong fell back to sanctuary in Cambodia.

In the country's northern provinces, the I Corps zone, two US Marine divisions operated in three of the provinces; except for one Marine battalion defending a radio relay station, Westmoreland relied on South Vietnamese divisions to hold the two northernmost provinces. There was always a possibility that the North Vietnamese would change their policy of infiltrating only through Laos and Cambodia and instead push southward across the DMZ—and in February 1966, intelligence reports indicated that this was happening. Judging from the enemy's usual "timetable" for infiltration, it would take several months for the North Vietnamese to concentrate for an attack. In the meantime, Westmoreland ordered two airfields constructed close to the DMZ, together with a port capable of handling tank landing ships (LSTs) at the former imperial capital city of Hue. He had to be ready to reinforce the northern provinces with American troops.

Guerrilla or peasant? Identification problems

No matter how conventional a narrative of either side's moves may seem, it must be emphasized that throughout South Vietnam it was a most unconventional war. The enemy could be anywhere and everywhere. In the case of the Viet Cong, attired in the black "pajamas" of the Vietnamese peasant, he was indistinguishable—unless he openly carried a weapon—from the local people. He could be "nowhere", hiding out among the people, in the jungles, along the overgrown banks of canals and river, or in labyrinthian underground tunnels. He would fight only when cornered or when he sensed an advantage. He might lie in ambush along a trail, road, or waterway, surprise a unit on foot or in convoy, inflict heavy casualties in the opening moments of the engagement, and then fade into the jungle, rubber plantation, village, or hamlet.

It was, for Americans and South Vietnamese, a checkerboard war. Responding to intelligence reports from agents or informers, captured documents, air or ground patrol reconnaissance, or radio intercepts, a unit might be snatched up by helicopter and swiftly set down miles away. Excellent radio communications, troop-carrying helicopters, and armed helicopters called "gunships" were essential to the operation. C-130 Hercules aircraft and Canadian-built de Havilland C-7A Caribous helped transport large loads of men and equipment. Australian Caribou aircraft, first committed in 1964, made a notable contribution to the supply of South Vietnamese ground units, consistently outlifting their US counterparts. In May 1966, General Westmoreland asked for a squadron of 12 Australian Caribous to serve with the US 7th Air Force, but the request was not granted for "political" reasons. Fighter-bombers were on constant call, and B-52s carried out one massive raid after another.

Both sides had first-class individual and crew-served weapons. The Americans had an excellent light automatic rifle, the 5.56mm M16, although because of production delays in the United States, their South Vietnamese allies had to make do until well into 1968 with World War II's semi-automatic Garand M1. The Viet Cong and the North Vietnamese also had excellent automatic rifles—AK-47s, most of them Chinese-manufactured copies of the original Russian weapon. The Ameri-

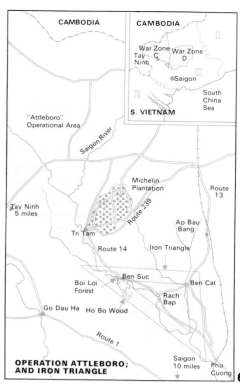

5

6

1. Men of the US 4th Marine Regiment storm a hill held by North Vietnamese regulars, two miles south of the Demilitarized Zone, during "Operation Hastings", July–August 1966. Some 8,000 Marines and 3,000 ARVN engaged the North Vietnamese 324B Division in north Quang Tri province, killing 824 enemy and capturing 214 weapons.
2. Australian troops took part in the sweeps of 1966; here, the crews of RAAF C-7A Caribou transports are briefed by a USAF officer during a terrain familiarization flight. **3.** A US Army M102 105mm howitzer fires on a Viet

Cong position, mid-1966. **4.** Unrest in South Vietnam erupted in riots early in 1966—but not all demonstrations were against the war: in Saigon, in June, more than 100,000 Vietnamese Catholics rallied in support of the anti-Communist allies. **5.** Search and destroy: men of the US 173d Airborne Brigade await transport helicopters to carry them into action against the Viet Cong along the Saigon River.
6. Map: major operations in the Saigon area, 1966. Beginning in January, US, Australian, and South Vietnamese troops launched a major sweep into Viet Cong

base areas near Saigon—the Michelin Plantation, and the Boi Loi Forest and Ho Bo Wood in the "Iron Triangle", a notorious Communist sanctuary. In "Operation Attleboro", 14 September to 24 November, more than 22,000 troops with massive air support were deployed in War Zone C, in the largest operation of the war to date, killing 2,130 guerrillas. Inset: operational areas in relation to Saigon. **7.** After a 37-day bombing pause from Christmas 1975, US aircraft—like the F-4Cs and EB-66 seen here—were once again unleashed against North Vietnam.

7

cans had powerful artillery, including some self-propelled 175mm guns, but the South Vietnamese were less well-equipped in artillery. The North Vietnamese employed artillery only in the northern provinces, along the DMZ, but throughout the country they and the Viet Cong used rockets up to 140mm caliber. With the arrival in early autumn 1966 of the 11th Armored Cavalry Regiment, the Americans added to their arsenal the M48A2 tank with its 90mm gun.

The Americans also employed highly complex electronic fire control and infrared surveillance devices, along with electronic sensors that could be planted on remote trails to send signals whenever bodies of troops passed by. A bulldozer variant called a "Rome plow" cleared vegetation along roads and waterways to forestall ambushes, or leveled great stretches of jungle to deny the enemy hiding places. Chemical defoliants sprayed from aircraft also opened wide areas of jungle to air surveillance. In contrast to such sophisticated equipment, barbed wire and the sandbag were widely used.

The military situation was showing favorable trends when, in the spring of 1966, a new political crisis broke, threatening to waste in political turmoil all that had been accomplished.

Internal unrest threatens national security

Unrest had been endemic in the northern provinces since the overthrow of President Diem. There, remote from Saigon, university students and Buddhists considered that the Thieu-Ky regime had failed to give them a role in the new government commensurate with the part they had played in ousting Diem. When Thieu and Ky relieved a popular I Corps commander, General Nguyen chanh Chi (sometimes spelt "Thi"), for supposedly failing to crack down on Buddhist dissidents, students and Buddhists found the pretext they needed for demonstrations designed to overthrow the government.

Mobs took to the streets in Da Nang and the demonstrations swiftly spread to Hue. Buddhist agitators began to seek sympathizers among South Vietnamese troops, many of them Buddhists themselves; on 3 April, 3,000 soldiers of the 1st ARVN Division marched in uniform behind their band through the streets of Hue, shouting for the resignation of Thieu and Ky. Momentarily, there was a perilous confrontation between US Marines defending the air base at Da Nang and the dissident ARVN troops who planned to occupy the base. As the threat of civil war hung over the northern provinces, demonstrations spread to other cities, including Saigon.

Thieu and Ky had at first attempted to disregard the disturbances, but when South Vietnamese troops became involved, they decided they could delay no longer. Rushing three battalions of South Vietnamese Marines to Da Nang on 4 April, they hoped a show of force would bring the demonstrations under control. An uneasy quiet ensued; delicate negotiations by a US Army officer, Colonel Arch Hamblen, persuaded the leaders of dissident army units to hold their fire and stopped South Vietnamese Marines from full-scale

118

1. At Da Nang, center of anti-government activity by civilians and disaffected South Vietnamese troops in April–May 1966, a Buddhist monk registers his protest by sitting in the path of an ARVN tank. 2. The disturbances quickly spread: in Saigon, a riot policeman seeks to restore order in a debris-strewn street. 3. Alienated by the domestic policies of President Thieu, whom they thought to be biased in favor of Catholic Vietnamese, Buddhist clergy played a leading part in the demonstrations. 4. Dissident ARVN soldiers briefly confronted US Marines at Da Nang Air Base—site of this MIM-23 Hawk missile battery—on 9 April 1966.

Combat Losses: Selected Periods		
1 January 1961–31 December 1965		
US forces	1,484 killed	
	7,337 wounded	
SVN forces	30,427 killed	
	63,009 wounded	
NVN/VC	104,500 killed	
	250,000 wounded	
1966		
US forces	5,047 killed	
NVN/VC	55,000 killed	
	20,000 defected to anti-Communist forces	
1968		
US and Free World forces	9,300 killed or wounded	
SVN forces	10,997 killed or wounded	
NVN/VC	38,794 killed	
	6,991 captured	

attacks on pagodas where armed Buddhists held out. The arrival of four more battalions sent by Ky, on 15 May, triggered off a week of civil strife before calm was at last restored to Da Nang. Demonstrations continued in Hue until mid-June, when a task force of South Vietnamese airborne troops moved into the city and, with considerable restraint, established control. Although no one could have known it at the time, this crisis in the northern provinces was destined to be the last of the violent political upheavals.

Viet Cong attempt to interfere with elections

As part of the effort to quell unrest in the north, Thieu and Ky promised to initiate the drafting of a constitution, to be followed by elections—and they kept their word. Viet Cong attempts to interfere through terrorism and intimidation were generally unsuccessful: in elections for a Constituent Assembly, about two-thirds of the eligible electorate registered and close on 81 percent of those voted. The elections were to be followed in the spring of 1967 by hamlet and village elections in September

119

1967 by senate and presidential elections (when Thieu was elected President and Ky Vice President); and in October 1967 by elections for a lower house.

Domestic violence in the northern provinces was quelled, but almost immediately the level of North Vietnamese infiltration across the DMZ prompted General Westmoreland to order US Marines to the northernmost province, Quang Tri. The III Marine Amphibious Force commander, newly-promoted Lieutenant General Walt, at first sent only one battalion as a reconnaissance force; when that battalion encountered sizeable North Vietnamese forces (the 324th VPA Division), Walt committed six more. In fighting that lasted until the end of September, about 8,000 Marines aided by 3,000 South Vietnamese troops claimed to have killed close on 2,000 of the enemy; the North Vietnamese retreated to sanctuary in the DMZ (which US aircraft "officially" bombed for the first time on 30 July).

Although the Marines had apparently caught the North Vietnamese before they were fully concentrated, General Westmoreland's concern for the northern provinces continued. He was particularly anxious about an outpost in the northwestern extremity of Quang Tri province, at the village of Khe Sanh, which served as a base for ground patrols operating into Laos and provided an air strip for the small reconnaissance aircraft that spotted targets in Laos for the fighter-bombers. To Westmoreland, Khe Sanh was important not only for those operations, but also because he intended to use it as a jumping-off point if ever he received authority for major operations inside Laos. He also saw Khe Sanh as the western "anchor" for a chain of defenses just south of the DMZ.

The only certain way of stopping North Vietnamese infiltration across the DMZ would be to create a conventional defensive line from the Laotian border to the sea. Even then, the enemy could still infiltrate around the line, through Laos—and in any case the thousands of troops required for such a line were simply not available. Westmoreland opted instead for a "strongpoint obstacle system", a series of fire-support and patrol bases intended to channel enemy movement into well-defined corridors where the Marines might bring mobile reserves, artillery, and airpower to bear. Construction of the strongpoints began in late 1966: four—including Khe Sanh—would be sited forward, and three to the rear.

The "McNamara Line": an impractical measure

Work on the strongpoints had begun when Secretary McNamara, in Washington, told a press conference that the United States intended to erect a barrier-line below the DMZ incorporating electronic sensors, mines, barbed wire, and fortified combat bases. Scientists had apparently convinced McNamara that such a barrier could stem infiltration. But General Westmoreland saw a serious flaw: the "McNamara Line" would require thousands of troops to man conventional defenses—or the enemy would simply remove the obstacles. Although Westmoreland told McNamara that he welcomed scientific

devices, he did not want the linear defense the scientists apparently envisaged. He required a defense in depth to help canalize enemy movement between the strongpoints already under construction. McNamara agreed but—whether or not because of his public announcement—the North Vietnamese began moving long-range artillery into the DMZ, making the construction even of Westmoreland's original strongpoints hazardous and costly. Little more was heard of the "McNamara Line".

President Johnson, meanwhile, called another conference at Manila in late October 1966, to review with Thieu and Ky the progress made since the February conference in Honolulu. At Manila the President made another overture to the North Vietnamese, promising to withdraw American troops from South Vietnam within six months of a North Vietnamese withdrawal and the cessation of infiltration. This was a remarkable concession: it implied that if the North Vietnamese withdrew, the South Vietnamese alone could handle the Viet Cong insurgents. Nor did the President demand a guarantee that, once American troops departed, the North Vietnamese would not return. Even so, it elicited no response from North Vietnam.

Reinforcements to counter Northern infiltration

As 1966 came to an end, the United States had some 385,000 men in South Vietnam: five infantry divisions; two Marine divisions; four separate brigades; and an armored cavalry regiment—the equivalent of nearly three conventional army corps. The South Vietnamese Army now numbered 329,000 men, with another 300,000 in the militia known as the Regional and Popular Forces. Among the Free World forces were 4,525 Australians, who had already built a good combat reputation in the Iron Triangle and at the Binh Ba rubber plantation. In a four-hour fire-fight at Binh Ba (Long Tan) on 18 August 1966, 108 men of D Company, 6th Battalion, Royal Australian Regiment, re-supplied by UH-1B helicopters of No 9 Squadron, RAAF, held off a force estimated at 1,500 NVA and VC, killing 245 of the enemy, until relieved by Australian APCs and Allied artillery. Serving at company strength in RAR/NZ (ANZAC) battalions by the end of 1966 were 155 New Zealanders.

But also during 1966, some 60,000 North Vietnamese—the equivalent of five divisions—had entered South Vietnam, raising enemy combat strength to an estimated 300,000 men. Westmoreland asked for a further 100,000-plus US troops and urged that the US should maintain a three-division reserve for commitment if necessary. He would get the troops; but the Defense Department had too many worldwide commitments to maintain a large reserve force unless President Johnson would agree to call up civilian reserves. That the President showed no inclination to do—and the growing volume of anti-war protests, especially from academics and students (the latter class, of course, containing many potential draftees), made it unlikely that he would change his mind.

1. Iroquois helicopters of No 9 Squadron, RAAF, flew support for Australian Special Air Service (SAS) patrols. Four, like the helicopter seen here, were converted to gunships.
2. A US Marine Corps M50 Ontos—designed as a tank destroyer, mounting six 106mm recoilless rifles, but widely used for fire support in Vietnam—en route from Da Nang to Chu Lai in late 1966. 3. US aircraft first "officially" bombed the Demilitarized Zone on 30 July 1966; Communist air defenses included 37mm guns like the one seen here. 4. An Australian Army M113A1 apc and reconnaissance vehicle in South Vietnamese jungle; the M113 family included variants mounting an 81mm or 107mm mortar, a flamethrower, or the TOW anti-tank guided weapon system.
5. Small aircraft like the USAF Cessna O-1E Bird Dogs seen here on forward air control (FAC) duty flew hazardous reconnaissance and coordination missions. 6. An FAC team on the ground maintains radio contact with an airborne FAC in an O-1 Bird Dog. 7. The only possible way into impossible terrain: US troops dismount from a Huey in mountainous jungle.
8. US Marines with an M60 machine gun, engage North Vietnamese regulars near the Demilitarized Zone, September 1966. 9. Off North Vietnam in October 1966, the destroyer USS *Mansfield* answers Communist shore batteries.

The development of the Communist armies

Major David Miller

The Vietnamese Communists performed a feat unparalleled in military history by creating an army which, during its first 30 years of existence, fought almost without a break, humbled the French, and twice created the military conditions in which political victory became possible.

During the 1930s and early 1940s, the Vietnamese Communists sporadically fought first the French and then the Japanese, but it was not until 22 December 1944 that the Vietnamese People's Liberation Army (VPLA) was officially formed. On that day, 34 men paraded in a jungle clearing; some held rifles and one man grasped a flag-pole. Before them stood a 32-year-old history teacher wearing a black Homburg hat, a city suit, and a revolver in a cowboy-style holster. The men were members of the first regular unit of the VPLA, and the man swearing them in was their commander-in-chief—General Vo Nguyen Giap. Under his inspired leadership, that army was to go on to defeat the French within ten years.

The VPLA was a true "people's army" in that the masses were directly involved. It was organised on a three-tier basis:

The *Popular Troops* were raised in every village under Viet Minh control, as well as in many under nominal French control. Members pursued their normal civilian occupation until called out, when they would undertake local offensive or defensive operations, or provide men for portering.
The *Regional Troops* were full-time soldiers with the task of protecting bases and villages and supporting the Main Force whenever it operated in their area. There was normally one battalion per province and one company per district.
The *Regular Troops* were professional soldiers, formed into the battalions, regiments, and divisions of the elite Main Force, known as the *Chu Luc*.

The *Chu Luc* was the force which was intended to defeat the French Expeditionary Corps in battle. It was an invaluable body of men which Giap normally husbanded very carefully, although when he did unleash it he seemed prepared to accept staggering losses. The *Chu Luc* eventually comprised six infantry divisions of about 10,000 men each, some 20 independent infantry regiments, and a similar number of battalions. These independent units could either be given their own missions—for example, operating behind the French "de Lattre Line"—or attached to a "Front" force. In addition, at the suggestion of Soviet and Chinese advisers, a "heavy division" was formed, modeled on the successful Soviet World War II practice. The *Chu Luc* infantry were described by

The Viet Minh and Viet Cong were not ill-armed irregulars living on "a handful of rice a day". The Communist guerrillas in Vietnam were, in fact, tightly organized under rigid political control, well equipped with arms from Soviet Russia and China, and sustained in their campaigns of terror by a massive supply network. Even so, the Communist victory depended finally on the regular troops of the North Vietnamese Army

a French general in 1954 as being the finest in the world: they were tough, brave, and capable of astonishing feats of endurance. With few exceptions, they responded to every call made upon them. Each battalion had a "Death Volunteer Platoon" which undertook suicidal missions to demonstrate their loyalty to "the cause", in the Vietnamese tradition of *nham nho*. At Dien Bien Phu, for example, some of these men staggered into French positions one night shrouded in parachutes—explosives were strapped to their bodies and their intention was to get to a command post and then blow up both their captors and themselves.

The VPLA appreciated from the first the value of fire support, and strenuous efforts were made to obtain weapons and ammunition in sufficient quantities. Initially there was a mixture of old Japanese and French equipment, but this was eventually replaced by modern Chinese and American weapons, together with some Soviet anti-aircraft guns and rockets. The American equipment came from stocks captured in Korea and transferred by the Chinese to the Viet Minh. By 1953, this had resulted in the VPLA having more modern American equipment than the French, whose aid came from old World War II stocks. Weapons used included 75mm and 105mm howitzers, 82mm and 120mm mortars, Soviet 37mm towed M-1939 anti-aircraft guns, and Katyusha rockets. A significant criterion was that no shell, bomb, or rocket could exceed a one-man load; this effectively limited guns to 105mm and mortars to 120mm.

There was a heavy-weapon company in every infantry battalion and regiment, and each division had a heavy-weapons battalion. Major artillery weapons were centralized in 351 Heavy Division, which

had four artillery regiments, an anti-aircraft regiment, and an engineer regiment. The VPLA artillery reached an extremely high degree of effectiveness due to a very good training system and, of course, to constant practice. The engineers had none of the sophisticated equipment found in Western armies; their main mission was to direct unskilled labor in such tasks as road and bridge building, rafting, and laying minefields. During the march to Dien Bien Phu, the engineers ferried 308, 312 and 351 Heavy Divisions across the Red River at a rate of 6,000 men per night.

An organization known as the *Quan Bao*, which controlled the intelligence elements, was unusual by Western standards. Every man was a Communist Party member and had to undergo a rigorous three-month introductory course. Under the control of the *Quan Bao* were the *Trinh Sat* units, which carried out the field work. This included route reconnaissance, selection of ambush sites, security, camouflage, discipline, and the collection of prisoners and weapons after an engagement.

For communications the VPLA depended mainly on High Frequency (HF) radio, field cable systems, and runners. The most commonly used radios were American and were identical with those used by the French; the two opponents regularly picked up each other's transmissions and were also able, on a number of occasions, to communicate with each other.

Trucks and porters supply the Chu Luc

The *Chu Luc* was of no value if it could not be supplied and fed when operating away from its bases. Most supplies came from Communist China and some 600 trucks were used in the rear areas; American GMCs were used in difficult terrain and the less rugged Soviet Molotovas on the better roads. But these could not follow the fighting troops through the jungles and over the mountains, so this requirement was met by hundreds of thousands of porters, assisted by a relatively small number of mules and buffaloes. A porter carried a 55lb (25kg) load and marched 15 miles (24km) per day in flat country, or 9 miles (14km) a day in the mountains. The load was increased to 150lb (68kg) by using bicycles specially strengthened and otherwise modified.

To many people, logistics is a dull and unrewarding subject, but it has never been so to General Giap: "On the Dien Bien Phu front the supply of food and munitions was a factor as important as the problem of tactics. . . . Day and night hundreds of thousands of porters and young volunteers

1. Vietnamese officials inspect a Soviet-built SA-3 Goa surface-to-air missile (SAM) on its rotatable launcher. Combined with AAA, MiG interceptors, and an excellent defense radar complex, the SAMs gave North Vietnam one of the most efficient air defense systems ever devised. **2.** A Soviet-built T-54/55 main battle tank of the Vietnamese People's Liberation Army during training. When North Vietnam committed these 35.9-ton tanks on a large scale during the 1972 invasion of the South, they proved very vulnerable to the US 66mm M72 Light Anti-tank Weapon (LAW). **3.** The only occasions on which North Vietnamese warships like the patrol and attack craft seen here attempted to engage the US Navy at sea were the Tonkin Gulf incidents of August–September 1964.

crossed the passes and forded the rivers in spite of enemy planes and delayed-action bombs. Indeed, a strong rear is always the decisive factor for victory in a revolutionary war." At the five-day battle of Vinh Yen in 1951, for example, 22,000 combat troops required 5,000 tons of supplies which were carried by 180,000 porters. At Hoa Binh, also in 1951, 70,000 troops were supported by 150,000 porters. This suggests that the Western idea that the Asian guerrilla lives on a "handful of rice a day" is a myth. ›

The principal base area for the VPLA was in the northern highlands of the Viet Bac, and it was difficult for foreign aid to reach them until the armies of Mao Tse-tung overran southern China in 1949. Thereafter, aid poured in from China, the Soviet Union, and the "fraternal" countries of Eastern Europe. There were also foreign advisers with the Viet Minh throughout the war, although it is doubtful whether their influence on the way the intensely independent Vietnamese conducted the war was very great. There were some 300 Soviet advisers and a similar number of Chinese. There were also between 20,000 and 30,000 Chinese fighting in the VPLA, but as individual volunteers and not as separate fighting units, although it was reported that there were some Chinese medical units.

The Viet Minh was supposed to be a broad-based, multi-party nationalist movement, but the Communist Party held the VPLA in a grip of iron. There were political commissars at every level of command, responsible for political training, running the innumerable committees, security, education, and — most importantly — morale. The Party's influence exerted itself in every section, and was based on cells of three to five men each. By no means all the soldiers were Party members. One division had a strength of 8,400 men in 1953, of which only 2,050 (24 percent) were registered members of the Communist Party. To doubly ensure Party control, it was laid down in a Presidential decree that where there was disagreement between a commander and his political commissar the latter would always have the power of final decision.

Mao's doctrine is put to work in Vietnam

Between December 1944 and May 1954, the Viet Minh built a massive, capable, and efficient army which was eventually able to take on the French in one of the world's major and most decisive battles— at Dien Bien Phu—and win. The three-tier system (devised originally by Mao Tse-tung) worked brilliantly. At the grass-roots, the Village Militia encouraged (and frequently forced) commitment to the cause. The Regional Troops provided a network of efficient and reliable units throughout the country, which could be used for either independent tasks or to support the *Chu Luc* in major operations. At the top level, the *Chu Luc* gave Giap a mobile army which combined heavy fire-power with the ability to move rapidly over even the most difficult terrain.

Secondly, the rigid control and discipline imposed by the Communist Party ensured that the VPLA always responded to the politicians' wishes and policies; not once did non-Communist officers try to over-ride them.

Thirdly, the high command of the VPLA was prepared to learn from its mistakes and was very flexible in its approach. In particular, there were costly and almost disastrous errors during the "drive on Hanoi" in 1951, but these were analyzed in great detail and never repeated.

Finally, the VPLA made one correct assessment which helped as much as any strategic or tactical decision to achieve victory—the vital importance of logistic support. This realization, coupled with meticulous planning and the efforts of hundreds of thousands of porters, enabled the *Chu Luc* to travel many miles from its bases and then fight, well-armed, with plenty of ammunition, and normally with just enough food to survive. In this first war, the army of "little men in black pajamas" took on a tough, professional, and experienced European army and was successful; the VPLA fully lived up to its motto: "Quyet Chien-Quyet Thang" (To Fight and To Win).

Hanoi retains control of the Southern units

The Geneva Agreements of July 1954 included provisions for the regrouping of forces; those of the Viet Minh were to withdraw northwards into the newly-created Democratic Republic of Vietnam (DRVN) by May 1955. A considerable number of organized military units were, however, deliberately left behind, most of them located in the Vietnam/Cambodia border area or deep in the Mekong Delta. In 1957 these were estimated to comprise 17 major units, each between 50 and 200 strong and fully equipped with normal infantry weapons. There were also numerous arms dumps scattered around the countryside.

During the war against the French, the controlling political body had been in the extreme southern tip of the country, but in 1955 this was moved to Tay Ninh, only a few miles from Saigon. Known as the Trung Uong Cuc Mien Nam—commonly translated as Central Office for South Vietnam (COSVN)—this body was supposedly autonomous and under the control of southerners. This was a propaganda fiction, however, and both the COSVN and the war in general were always firmly controlled from Hanoi.

In the years 1954 to 1956, the government of President Ngo Dinh Diem made serious inroads on the Communist Party infrastructure in the South and appeared to be gaining control. By 1957, the Party cadres in the South were feeling very frustrated and began, on their own initiative, a campaign of small-scale attacks and the assassination of low-level government officials. Such actions escalated through 1958 and early 1959, when armed bands were formed throughout the country. By 1959, the Central Committee in Hanoi began to be concerned about events in the South; they thought that their grip on the South was slipping and decided to reassert control. Accordingly, in May, they resolved that: ". . . the struggle for reunification will now have to be carried out by all means other than peaceful." The assassination campaign reached a new peak in the

1. The mobility of the Communist armies depended to a great extent on human porters; gunners pack the component parts of their weapon through jungle. 2. The heavy rocket fired from a portable launcher, like those seen here, was one of the Communists' most effective weapons. 3. A North Vietnamese Transport Brigade's Soviet-built trucks roll down the Ho Chi Minh Trail. 4. Although well-supplied by Communist allies, North Vietnam also produced small arms and shells in widely-dispersed workshops. 5. Light and medium anti-aircraft guns captured from the Viet Cong; AAA was supplied by China, Czechoslovakia, and the USSR. 6. A Soviet-built MiG-17 "Fresco" of the North Vietnamese Air Force. 7. The MiG-21 "Fishbed" interceptor, seen here, appeared in increasing numbers over North Vietnam from 1966 onward.

6

7

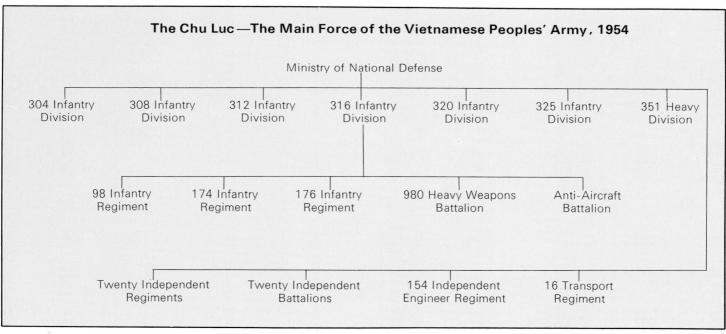

The Chu Luc—The Main Force of the Vietnamese Peoples' Army, 1954

Ministry of National Defense

304 Infantry Division	308 Infantry Division	312 Infantry Division	316 Infantry Division	320 Infantry Division	325 Infantry Division	351 Heavy Division

98 Infantry Regiment	174 Infantry Regiment	176 Infantry Regiment	980 Heavy Weapons Battalion	Anti-Aircraft Battalion

Twenty Independent Regiments	Twenty Independent Battalions	154 Independent Engineer Regiment	16 Transport Regiment

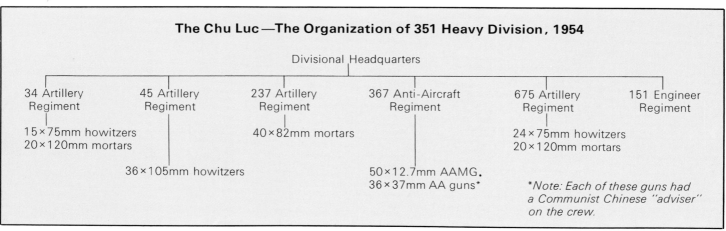

The Chu Luc—The Organization of 351 Heavy Division, 1954

Divisional Headquarters

34 Artillery Regiment	45 Artillery Regiment	237 Artillery Regiment	367 Anti-Aircraft Regiment	675 Artillery Regiment	151 Engineer Regiment
15×75mm howitzers 20×120mm mortars		40×82mm mortars		24×75mm howitzers 20×120mm mortars	
	36×105mm howitzers		50×12.7mm AAMG. 36×37mm AA guns*		

*Note: Each of these guns had a Communist Chinese "adviser" on the crew.

week of Tet (18–25 January) 1960, when many men were killed. (It is a traditional belief in Vietnam that the events in Tet set the pattern for the following year; it is, therefore, scarcely surprising that the Communists always tried to ensure that Tet was bloody and disastrous for their enemies.) Then, on the last day of Tet, a new phase of major military attacks was signaled by an assault on the headquarters of 32d Regiment of the Army of the Republib of Vietnam (ARVN) at Trang Sap.

Also in 1959, the famous Ho Chi Minh Trail was opened. This land infiltration route started in the DRVN and then ran south through Laotian and Cambodian territory, with spurs leading off at intervals into South Vietnam. Early travelers down the Trail were southerners returning from training in the DRVN, but the Hanoi government quickly appreciated that the Trail would become vital for moving North Vietnamese Army (NVA) men and equipment. The confused Laotian wars of 1960–1962 resulted in an international agreement to withdraw all foreign troops and "neutralize" the country. The DRVN was a party to this agreement, but since there were no arrangements for supervision the North Vietnamese were able to ignore it and expand the facilities on the Ho Chi Minh Trail, thus gaining a secure route from the rear base in the North to the operational area in the South. For many years there was also a maritime infiltration route, but this was much reduced in effectiveness after the Americans entered the war.

Viet Cong weapons and terror tactics

In the early 1960s, the DRVN began to reinforce the Viet Cong units in the South with both individuals and units from the NVA. The position for the remainder of the war was that the forces in the South comprised:

The Viet Cong Village Militias, recruited locally as before.
Viet Cong Regional Troops, mostly southerners, but frequently reinforced by individuals and groups from the DRVN.
Viet Cong Main Force units, normally of battalion or regimental size, but sometimes designated "divisions", although nothing like as strong and effective as the NVA divisions.
North Vietnamese Army Main Force units, comprising divisions and independent regiments and battalions.

These units were organized and equipped on similar lines to their equivalents in the earlier war, although the weaponry was obviously updated as and when possible. Primary suppliers were China and the Soviet Union, with the latter playing an increasingly important role. Among the most significant weapons was the AK-47, a light, simple, and robust assault rifle, which was reportedly occasionally used by American and ARVN soldiers in preference to their own. Machine-guns and mortars came from both the Soviet Union and China, but the anti-aircraft equipment was virtually all from the USSR. A particularly important weapon in the ground war was

the 130mm M-1954/M-46 field gun, which the NVA used to destroy American and ARVN fire-bases. The 130mm was sited in isolated individual gun positions, which made it a very difficult target for aircraft— and as it outranged the US 105mm gun/ howitzer by a very considerable margin, it was relatively immune to counter-battery fire.

A new weapon introduced in Vietnam was the individual heavy rocket, fired from a light, easily portable launching stand. The 122mm rocket weighed 112lb (51kg)— of which the warhead accounted for a remarkable 42lb (19kg)—and had a range of 10 miles (16km), but this was superseded in 1968 by a 107mm rocket which was equally lethal but much lighter. Another new weapon unveiled in Vietnam was the Soviet-made RPG-7, which could penetrate 10 inches (254mm) of armor plate at ranges up to 550 yards (503m), besides dealing easily with bunkers and buildings. Finally, the Soviet Union supplied increasingly large quantities of heavier conventional weapons, such as PT-76 and T-54 tanks, which were essential to the invasions of 1972 and 1974.

The strategy of the Communists underwent a number of changes during the war. In the early 1960s, the main thrust was aimed at divorcing the government of South Vietnam from its people, with attacks on the ARVN and a constant campaign of assassination and abduction. The unremitting nature of this campaign of terror among the population should not be underestimated; unfortunately, it became so routine a part of South Vietnamese life that it seldom merited mention in the news reports from Vietnam. In the early days of the second Vietnam War, the campaign really got into its stride in 1960; one of its particular aims was to discredit the Saigon government, and the main method of achieving this was to demonstrate that minor officials could not be protected by the government they served. As these officials were murdered, those that were left had to take measures to protect their lives and those of their families which almost invariably resulted in cutting themselves off from the population, thus furthering the Communist aims. In 1964, for example, 436 government officials were murdered nation-wide, 161 wounded and 1,131 abducted.

Throughout the period of the American military campaigns, there was no let-up in this process. The Viet Cong took their campaign of terrorism to its ultimate conclusion when, among many other horrific incidents in Hue in February–March 1963:

"... a squad with a death order entered the house of a prominent community leader and shot him, his wife, his married son and daughter-in-law, his young unmarried daughter, a male and female servant and their baby. The family cat was strangled, the family dog was clubbed to death, and the goldfish scooped out of the fishbowl and tossed onto the floor. When the Communists left no life remained in the house—a 'family unit' had been eliminated."

In 1963 the Communists swept into what was intended to be the final stage of the

War, and the fragile fabric of South Vietnam began to disintegrate. Infiltration by the NVA suddenly increased, obviously with the intention of ensuring that the Viet Cong did not win on their own.

The arrival of United States ground troops in 1965–1966 undoubtedly saved South Vietnam from defeat and also caused a reappraisal of strategy in Hanoi. In 1965–1968, efforts were concentrated on maintaining a high level of casualties among American forces; the Communists also lost many men, but the difference was that, in the long term, the Communists could afford such losses while the Americans could not. Indeed, by early 1968, despite many deaths, casualties, and defections, the NVA and Viet Cong forces were numerically stronger than in 1966.

The Communist gamble on a major offensive

In 1967 the North Vietnamese decided, after a major row in the Central Committee, to try to short-circuit the normally slow (but sure) process of revolutionary war by staking everything on a major offensive at Tet 1968. The Chinese, and General Giap, argued against this plan, which represented a major aberration of orthodox theory, but the Russians—who have never understood revolutionary warfare—were for it. The aims, as stated in the official operation order, were:

To promote a popular uprising.
To cause the collapse of the South Vietnamese armed forces.
To destroy the United States' political and military position.

Thus, as American self-doubt and criticism were gathering strength, the Tet offensive was suddenly unleashed on 31 January 1968. Viet Cong sappers reached the United States Embassy in Saigon and General Westmoreland's headquarters at

1. The Vietnamese soldier in the foreground fires a Chinese-designed Type 69 40mm anti-tank grenade launcher—a copy of the Soviet RPG-7, with a permanent bipod and no rear pistol grip.
2. A US Air Force reconnaissance picture of an anti-aircraft site in North Vietnam. **3.** AAA in action near Hanoi; the optically-sighted Soviet M38/39 37mm gun and the radar-controlled 57mm S-60 were among the guns deployed.
4. Sophisticated defense: an SA-2 Guideline SAM site. Intensive electronic countermeasures and the relative weakness of the SA-2's own guidance system limited US aircraft losses. **5.** Primitive aggression: a US Marine examines a booby trap of "punji stakes"—sharpened bamboo, often coated with filth to cause blood-poisoning—placed by the Viet Cong in a rice paddy.

5

THE UNREMITTING WAR OF TERROR

By 1962/63 the military actions gained the world's attention and the campaign of terrorism was relegated to the background. Yet, as these figures show it was a fact of life from which the South Vietnamese could not escape.

Viet Cong Killings and Abductions in South Vietnam, 1964

		Jan	Feb	Mar	Apr	May	Jun	Jul	Aug	Sep	Oct	Nov	Dec	Total	Grand total
Killed	**Govt. Officials**	47	34	49	30	25	31	45	36	46	48	21	24	436	1795
	Others	111	110	138	115	105	110	181	103	132	100	66	88	1359	
Abducted	**Govt. Officials**	93	113	91	67	74	132	93	103	144	69	52	100	1131	9554
	Others	694	590	1531	647	727	483	964	834	778	477	200	498	8423	

Viet Cong Killings and Abductions in South Vietnam, 1966–71

	1966	1967	1968*	1969	1970	1971	Totals*
Killed	1732	3706	5389	6202	5947	3391	26,367
Abducted	3810	5369	8759	6289	6931	4788	35,946

These statistics, published by the Comptroller, Office of the Secretary of Defense (US), do not include the figures for February 1968 (Tet), as the number of civil casualties was never fully established.

Viet Cong Terrorism, Sabotage, Forced Propaganda Sessions, and Armed Attacks, 1964

	Jan.	Feb.	Mar.	Apr.	May	June	July	Aug.	Sept.	Oct.	Nov.	Dec.	Total
Attacks	223	217	203	220	175	140	184	113	118	83	60	96	1,832
Terrorism	1,244	1,389	1,632	1,738	1,418	1,390	2,123	1,775	1,938	1,790	1,391	1,719	19,547
Sabotage	129	201	158	169	217	176	286	315	482	480	247	318	3,205
Propaganda	174	271	167	157	140	162	224	173	178	197	109	128	2,080

Tan Son Nhut airbase. Farther north, the Viet Cong occupied the old imperial city of Hue and had to be blasted out in a house-by-house battle reminiscent of World War II. More than 100,000 civilians were made homeless and the Viet Cong carried out a vicious campaign of executions: more than 1,000 bodies were found in mass graves around Hue alone.

Communist defeat and a change in strategy

The Tet offensive was, however, an overall disaster for the Viet Cong; their best units had led the attack and had been decimated: 38,794 dead and 6,991 captured. The great effort to spark off a popular uprising had failed completely, and after some initial faltering the people rallied to the Saigon government. Nor did the much-maligned ARVN collapse — indeed, it fought back splendidly, and both the Army and the Police gained much confidence from the episode. One of the most noticeable features of the offensive was that the NVA units held back and suffered virtually no losses—for the remainder of the war, the predominance of the NVA military forces over the Viet Cong was absolute. Nevertheless, the Communist influence in South Vietnam was drastically reduced as a result of the enormous losses. In spite of the beginning of the American withdrawal, the Saigon government was able to extend its influence over many areas which had been under Viet Cong control for years.

While the Viet Cong was attacking in the south, the NVA was conducting a campaign of its own just below the DMZ, where a major assault was being planned on a United States Marine Corps outpost at Khe Sanh. There can be no doubt that General Giap was trying to recreate the conditions and success of Dien Bien Phu, and the surrender of the garrison would have been a fatal blow to the Americans. The NVA used two divisions in the preparatory attacks with a third in reserve; it was significant that the division designated for the final assault—the 304th—had fought with great distinction at Dien Bien Phu. In this major confrontation, the NVA was defeated by the resolve of the garrison and by the devastating and awesome firepower available to the United States forces.

After these major reverses, a change in strategy was obviously required; it was decided to expand the conventional capability of the NVA. The Russians provided massive aid to achieve this. The result was seen on 30 March 1972, when 54,000 NVA troops drove into South Vietnam in a three-pronged attack, with the aim of freeing two-thirds of the country by the end of the year. Five NVA divisions took part, each with its own artillery, tank, anti-aircraft, and missile units, with Viet Cong regional units attacking ARVN rear areas. The NVA captured one provincial capital—Quang Tri—only to lose it later, and the offensive was another set-back for the North. The NVA also did badly at a tactical level. At An Loc, for example, the attack was opened by a heavy artillery barrage on the town, which reduced much of the place to rubble and gave ideal cover to the defenders. Then, as the Soviet-built T-54

tanks went in, they were canalized by the rubble and then picked off one by one by the defenders using LAW (light anti-tank weapon) missiles. Meanwhile, the main body of the NVA infantry formed up outside the town where it was devastated by B-52 and fighter-bomber strikes.

By the autumn, there was stalemate: the NVA had gained a small amount of territory but could expand no farther, while the ARVN had stopped the invasion but could not expel the Communists from the ground they had taken. In November, therefore, both sides moved towards a political settlement and—following the renewed bombing of the North from 18 to 30 December 1972—the Paris Agreements were signed on 27 January 1973. These resulted in the complete withdrawal of United States and other "foreign" forces from South Vietnam—but not of the NVA, which expanded apace, especially as the cessation of the bombing cut the time needed to traverse the Ho Chi Minh Trail by 75 percent.

As South Vietnam's last remaining friends deserted her, the NVA stepped up the pressure. A general offensive started in 1974, involving 13 divisions (160,000 men) and 600 or more tanks. Once again they learned from their mistakes; the errors of the 1972 offensive were avoided. Steady progress was made; in January 1975 the first complete province was overrun (Phuoc Long) and President Thieu began to abandon other provinces. The steam-roller quickly gathered momentum and the NVA soon took to bypassing even quite major resistance in its drive for the golden prize—Saigon. As the world's attention concentrated first on the evacuation of orphans and then on the final, undignified withdrawal of United States nationals, the tanks of the NVA swung into Saigon. At 1215 hours on 30 April 1975, the Communist flag was hoisted over the city—just one week short of the twenty-first anniversary of the victory at Dien Bien Phu.

The Viet Cong were not victorious

In the second Vietnam War, the general picture propagated in the West was one of unremitting pressure by a well-organized, co-ordinated, and popular armed force. This was simply not correct; the Communists suffered many setbacks, some of them severe. First, from 1954 to 1956 and from 1958 to 1960, Diem's government was clearly winning the battle for the people's hearts and minds; there can be no doubt that left on their own the indigenous southern movement—the Viet Cong—would have been totally defeated. It was only the presence of the NVA which kept the war going. Even the battle-hardened NVA suffered defeats, and its 1972 campaign—following its rapid expansion—was fumbling and amateurish in both concept and execution. Finally, it was a straight, conventional, old-fashioned invasion which drove the abandoned ARVN into defeat. Perhaps one of the most characteristic traits of the VPLA, and its successor the NVA, had been the ability to make startling errors, but then to examine them quite objectively, learn from the mistakes, and try not to repeat them.

1. Framed by their Soviet-type 120mm mortars, Vietnamese soldiers relax with a newspaper. 2. On the way to Saigon, 1975; the Communist soldier in the foreground carries a Soviet RPG-7 anti-tank grenade launcher. 3–4. Vietnamese tankers like this soldier (3) manned Soviet- and Chinese-built armor like the T-54/55 main battle tank seen here (4) en route to Saigon in 1975. 5. Vietnamese gunners with Soviet-type towed howitzers. 6. A US aircraft falls over Hanoi during the "Linebacker" raids of 1972; the US won total air supremacy when North Vietnam exhausted its stock of SAMs. 7. Vietnamese anti-aircraft gunners in training.

US Navy and Marine Corps operations in Vietnam

Lt. Col. Lane Rogers, USMC

In 1964 the US Navy was conducting routine patrols in international waters off Southeast Asia, collecting electronic and hydrographic data and, specifically, observing naval and commercial traffic off the North Vietnamese coast. On the afternoon of 2 August 1964, the patrolling destroyer USS *Maddox*, 28 miles (52km) off the North Vietnamese coast, picked up three contacts on her radar. The contacts materialized as North Vietnamese torpedo boats—closing fast. At a range of 10,000 yards (9,150m), *Maddox* fired a warning salvo. The North Vietnamese craft continued to close. At 9,000 yards (8,200m), *Maddox* opened fire. The naval war against North Vietnam had begun.

At this time the North Vietnamese Navy (NVN) deployed a number of Soviet- or Chinese-built patrol boats of between 70 and 120 tons displacement. The craft concerned in this first attack have been tentatively identified as torpedo boats of the Soviet P6 type, mounting two 21in (533mm) torpedo tubes and four 25mm anti-aircraft guns. One of these boats fired two torpedoes, but *Maddox* evaded them and turned toward the attackers. Four F-8E Crusader fighters from the carrier USS *Ticonderoga*, 160 miles (300km) away, streaked in and fired all their 20mm shells and underwing missiles, leaving one torpedo boat dead in the water and burning. Within minutes, the surface war in Vietnam also became the Navy's air war.

Maddox, ordered to break off action, resumed patrol. The next day, President Johnson warned: "North Vietnam will be under no misapprehension as to the grave consequences which will inevitably result from further unprovoked military action against United States forces." The destroyer *C. Turner Joy* reinforced *Maddox*; on 3 August they re-entered the Gulf of Tonkin.

Retaliatory air strikes on North Vietnam

During the night of 4 August, both destroyers' radars picked up suspicious surface contacts. The contacts maneuvered to take up what appeared to be attack positions; *Joy* and *Maddox* cleared for action, and at 6,000 yards (5,500m) both opened fire. Results were inconclusive. Again, enemy torpedoes were reported in the water, but by midnight, radar contact was lost. As has already been mentioned, critics of US involvement were to claim that the "suspicious contacts" fired upon were, in fact, non-existent. In any case, the incidents of August 1964 represented the NVN's only attempts to engage anti-Communist forces at sea.

On 4 August, the US Joint Chiefs of Staff instructed the Seventh Fleet to plan retaliatory air strikes. Next day, 64 air-

---

Carrier aircraft of the US Navy initiated the bombing of North Vietnam in August 1964 and thereafter played a major part in "Rolling Thunder". USN ships and small craft guarded the coasts and inland waterways, interdicting Viet Cong movement. The US Marine Corps' many operations by air, land, and sea in 1965–71 included "Dewey Canyon", perhaps the most successful regimental-size action of the war

---

craft from the carriers *Ticonderoga* and *Constellation* struck North Vietnamese naval facilities, claiming hits on 29 ships. Smoke from petroleum stores burning at Vinh reached 14,000 feet. Two US Navy planes were shot down. One pilot was killed and the other, Lieutenant (jg) Everett Alvarez, was captured; surviving more than eight years' captivity, Alvarez was to be the North's longest-held prisoner.

On the night of 18 September, the destroyers *Morton* and *Parsons* fired at four radar contacts in Tonkin Gulf. Again, results were inconclusive. On the ground, such incidents as the Viet Cong attack on the US air base at Bien Hoa on 1 November and the bombing of the Brink Bachelor Officers Quarters in Saigon on 24 December, marked an increase in Communist activity. Therefore, the US Navy ordered a third carrier to "Yankee Station", a rendezvous in the Tonkin Gulf, 75 miles (140km) off the North Vietnamese coast.

The Joint Chiefs of Staff now initiated planning for "Operation Flaming Dart" —retaliatory air strikes to be executed at the discretion of higher authority. The 125 ships and 64,000 men of the Seventh Fleet waited: Task Force 77 (TF 77), comprising the attack carriers *Coral Sea*, *Hancock*, and *Ranger*, was at readiness on Yankee Station.

Because no Communist aggression was expected during Soviet Premier Kosygin's state visit to Hanoi early in February, *Hancock* and *Coral Sea* were ordered to stand down, leaving *Ranger* on station. As the two carriers steamed away, the Viet Cong attacked the American billets at Pleiku. *Coral Sea* and *Hancock* rejoined *Ranger*, and on 7 February 1965 "Flaming Dart One" was launched. Forty-five aircraft from *Hancock* and *Coral Sea* hammered Dong Hoi barracks, but weather

---

aborted *Ranger*'s strike against Vit Thu Lu, near the DMZ. The next day, US Navy and South Vietnamese Air Force (VNAF) planes hit Chap Le barracks, 15 miles (28km) north of the DMZ. On 10 February, the Communists retaliated by blowing up the American enlisted men's barracks at Qui Nhon. The US Navy's response was "Flaming Dart Two": USN aircraft attacked Chanh Hoa barracks, 35 miles (65km) north of the DMZ, while the VNAF struck at Vit Thu Lu.

Meanwhile, US planners proposed "Operation Rolling Thunder", a joint air campaign against North Vietnam by both American and South Vietnamese air arms. Rolling Thunder strikes were to "roll" northward from the DMZ toward Hanoi; it was anticipated that the North Vietnamese would seek peace terms when the destruction of Hanoi seemed imminent. To ensure positive control, coverage responsibility, and target analysis for Rolling Thunder, North Vietnam was divided into seven "Route Packages". Coverage was divided between the Seventh Fleet's aircraft, Task Force 77, and the US Seventh Air Force.

Restrictions on the bombing campaign

Rules of engagement dictated by political considerations pervaded US military efforts in Vietnam—and many of the constraints thus imposed were stifling. Tactical commanders were bound by directives from Washington—and Rolling Thunder was no exception. Each strike date, mission, and target was specified by the Pentagon. Pre-strike reconnaissance was not permitted, nor were more than two alternate targets allocated. Once aircraft had attacked, they could not re-arm and attack again. Post-strike bombing was conducted at medium altitude only, by unescorted aircraft. Unexpended ordnance must be jettisoned into the sea. Enemy aircraft had to be positively identified before engaging. But in spite of these restrictions, US military spokesmen asserted that Rolling Thunder achieved impressive results.

While Rolling Thunder was being planned, another incident confirmed Communist intentions to escalate the conflict. On 16 February 1965, A-1H Skyraiders of the VNAF strafed a Communist ship which beached in Vung Ro Bay, about 50 miles (90km) north of Cam Ranh Bay. Its cargo was found to consist of more than 100 tons of munitions, convincing Allied authorities that a tight offshore patrol was needed. Coastal surveillance centers were established at Da Nang, Qui Nhon, Nha Trang, Vung Tau, and An Thoi, and Seventh Fleet's Task Force 71, the Vietnamese Patrol Force, was established to

1

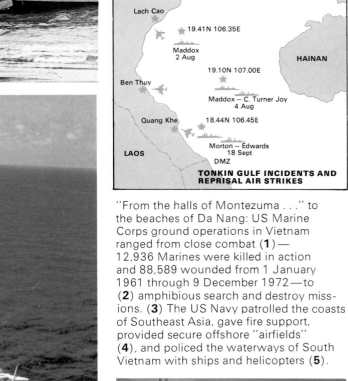

2

NORTH VIETNAM

CHINA

Hongay

Port Wallut

Lach Cao

19.41N 106.35E

Maddox
2 Aug

HAINAN

19.10N 107.00E

Ben Thuy

Maddox — C. Turner Joy
4 Aug

Quang Khe

18.44N 106.45E

Morton — Edwards
18 Sept

LAOS

DMZ

**TONKIN GULF INCIDENTS AND
REPRISAL AIR STRIKES**

3

"From the halls of Montezuma . . ." to
the beaches of Da Nang: US Marine
Corps ground operations in Vietnam
ranged from close combat (**1**)—
12,936 Marines were killed in action
and 88,589 wounded from 1 January
1961 through 9 December 1972—to
(**2**) amphibious search and destroy missions. (**3**) The US Navy patrolled the coasts
of Southeast Asia, gave fire support,
provided secure offshore "airfields"
(**4**), and policed the waterways of South
Vietnam with ships and helicopters (**5**).

4

5

conduct "Operation Market Time" to counter infiltration.

Task Force 77 was not the only active naval force in Vietnamese waters during 1965. Since January, US Marines of the 9th Marine Expeditionary Brigade (9th MEB), in Task Force 76 shipping, had been steaming off South Vietnam, ready to land. At the end of February, President Johnson decided to land the two-battalion brigade to protect Da Nang air base, and at 0903 on 8 March the first Marines of Battalion Landing Team 3/9 (BLT 3/9) stepped ashore. That afternoon, the second battalion of the brigade began landing at the air base, flying in from Okinawa. By 12 March, the 9th MEB, consisting of BLTs 3/9 and 1/3, reinforced, was in position at Da Nang.

The first Rolling Thunder strikes were made on 2 March; by mid-month, Task Force 77 carriers were heavily engaged. On 15 March, Navy planes seriously damaged the North Vietnamese ammunition depot at Phu Qui. On 18 March, Phu Van and Vin Son depots were hit. A 70-plane strike concentrated on radar sites on 26 March, and three days later the Communist's Bach Long Vi radar and communications center was devastated. Sixty *Coral Sea* and *Hancock* planes struck the radar station at Mui Ron Point on 31 March; on 3 April, US Navy pilots wrecked the Dong Phuong Thong bridge, only 70 miles (130km) south of Hanoi.

Surface-to-air missile sites in the North

From April 1965 onward, with the increase in Allied air activity, North Vietnamese unit movements were made in small groups; trucks moved at night, stopping in villages during daylight. And "the rules" forbade US attacks on villages. On 5 April an ominous Communist development was revealed. A *Coral Sea* Crusader photographed surface-to-air missile (SAM) site construction, 15 miles (28km) southeast of Hanoi. By July, a ring of SAM sites surrounded Hanoi and part of Haiphong.

A third US Marine battalion, BLT 2/3, landed at Da Nang on 10 April, and two companies were immediately heli-lifted to Phu Bai, 42 miles (78km) northwest of Da Nang, to defend the airfield there. The first Marine fixed-wing squadron, Marine Fighter Attack Squadron 531 (VMFA-531), flying F-4B Phantoms, had arrived at Da Nang on 11 April. On 14 April, BLT 3/4 arrived and replaced BLT 2/3's companies at Phu Bai. Two Marine enclaves were thus established, and by the end of April 8,878 Marines had landed.

Aircraft from *Coral Sea* and *Midway* and Marine Fighter Squadron 212 flying from *Oriskany* struck Viet Cong positions in April, in conjunction with other Allied planes. General Westmoreland was so impressed by the efficacy of carrier participation that he requested permanent assignment of a carrier to support ground forces in South Vietnam. On 16 May, one of the four Yankee Station carriers was detached to "Dixie Station", 100 miles (185km) southeast of Cam Ranh Bay. Increased demands on Yankee Station carriers resulted in the allocation of a fifth carrier to TF 77 on 5 June.

In a period of three days, 3 to 6 May, 9th MEB became III Marine Amphibious

Force (III MAF), as it was reinforced by the landing of three more battalions at Chu Lai, the site of a projected airfield, 55 miles (102km) south of Da Nang. By mid-May, III MAF consisted of seven infantry battalions, the greater part of an artillery regiment, and the advance echelon of the 1st Marine Aircraft Wing, commanded first by Major General Paul J. Fontana and then, from 5 June, by Brigadier General Keith B. McCutcheon.

As a peace overture, Rolling Thunder was suspended on 12 May, but with no Communist response. Bombing was therefore renewed on 18 May. To the south, on 14 May, naval gunfire was authorized for support in South Vietnam.

Six days before the bombing halt, Da Nang-based Marine VMFA-531 Phantoms flew their first mission over North Vietnam. Marine air participation increased; by mid-1965, four Marine Aircraft Groups (MAGs), two helicopter and two fixed-wing, were in South Vietnam. On 1 June, four A-4 Skyhawks from VMFA-225 landed **1** at Chu Lai. The airfield, a novel Marine Corps development — designated Short Airfield for Tactical Support (SATS) — was in effect an "aircraft carrier" on land, complete with catapult and arresting wires (although the catapult was not installed until 1967, jet-assisted take off being used in the interim). Built by laying some 4,000 feet (1,220m) of aluminum matting runways on highly unstable, sandy soil, Chu Lai was constructed by almost superhuman effort in only 24 days.

On 17 June, Phantoms of *Midway*'s VF-21 shot down two MiG-17s; on 20 June, A-1 Skyraiders ("Spads") of *Midway*'s **2** VA-125 shot down another MiG. Carrier operations were not without serious risk. A fire in one of *Ranger*'s machinery spaces knocked her "off the line" and sent her back to the American west coast for repair.

The US Coast Guard in "Market Time"

On 1 August, Market Time responsibility was shifted from Seventh Fleet to Rear Admiral Norvell G. Ward, Commander, TF 115, Coastal Surveillance Force, and also the Chief of the Naval Advisory Group. Market Time's effectiveness was increased by the arrival of Coast Guard Squadron One with its excellent "Swift" class patrol boats. These 50-foot (15.2m) diesel-engined craft, radar-directed and given fire support by frigates, proved more suited to close inshore patrolling than the US Navy's 225-ton (229-tonnes), 164-foot (50.1m), combined diesel or gas turbine (CODOG) propelled "Asheville" class patrol gunboats. A brief experiment was also made with the Boeing-built hydrofoil *Tucumcari* (64 tons; 65 tonnes) for inshore work. By December 1965, Market Time included Lockheed P-3A Orion turbo-prop patrol planes covering the coast from Vung Tau to the 17th Parallel, and Martin P-5 Marlin seaplanes, operating from tenders, patrolling from Vung Tau to Phu Quoc Island off the southern coast of Cambodia. Lockheed P2V Neptunes, operating from Tan Son Nhut, Saigon, and later from Cam Ranh Bay, augmented and eventually replaced the Marlins.

As the Marine enclaves at Phu Bai, Da Nang, and Chu Lai expanded, the 1st

1. A US Navy helicopter approaches a US destroyer while on a search and rescue mission, primarily for the recovery of downed US aviators, in the Gulf of Tonkin. 2. "Market Time" surveillance: a US Navy Lockheed SP-2H Neptune maritime patrol aircraft checks out a junk south of the Mouths of the Mekong. 3. A typical Riverine Operation and Mobile Riverine Base defense system. The barracks and supply ships of the Mobile Afloat Force (MAF), anchored in the Mobile Riverine Base (MRB), are protected afloat by patrolling US Navy assault support patrol boats (ASPBs) and monitors, and ashore by US Army security forces reinforced by artillery. The MAF normally conducts operations at ranges up to 30 miles (50km) from its base. In the operational area (left of diagram) ASPBs provide all-round security and interdict enemy withdrawal by water, while tactical aircraft and armed helicopters provide air cover. From the Fire Support Base, artillery provides continuous fire support. One element of the Assault Force is landed from armored troop carriers (ATCs) while another is heli-lifted to set up a Blocking Force interdicting enemy withdrawal by land. ASPBs and monitors protect the ATCs and provide close-in fire support. A group of ATCs, including a floating aid station, constitutes a Ready Reaction Force. A battalion-strength MAF can conduct an operation over an area of some 15 square miles (40km²) over a period of four to six days, before being met and withdrawn by boats or helicopters. 4. An F-4 Phantom II of USS *Enterprise* circles above the aircraft carrier.

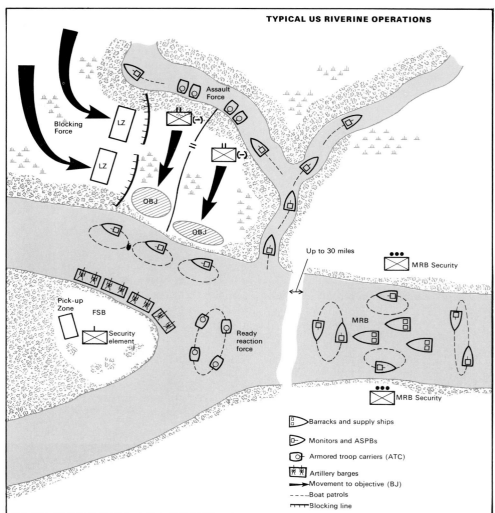

TYPICAL US RIVERINE OPERATIONS

Blocking Force
LZ
LZ
Assault Force
OBJ
OBJ
Up to 30 miles
MRB Security
Pick-up Zone
FSB
Security element
Ready reaction force
MRB
MRB Security

Barracks and supply ships
Monitors and ASPBs
Armored troop carriers (ATC)
Artillery barges
Movement to objective (BJ)
Boat patrols
Blocking line

3

4

Viet Cong Regiment was reported to be concentrating on the Van Tuong peninsula, some 15 miles (28km) south of Chu Lai. On 6 August, III MAF commander Lieutenant General Lewis W. Walt received permission to take offensive action. General Westmoreland authorized "Operation Satelite", but a clerk's error caused by a lighting failure resulted in "Starlite" being typed instead of "Satelite" throughout the order. Too late to change the name, "Starlite" jumped-off on 18 August. The 1st VC Regiment was badly mauled in the next six days as it fought to break through the encircling 7th Marines. The first regimental-size Marine operation of the war resulted in 614 dead Viet Cong; 45 MarineM were killed.

"Iron Hand" strikes at the SAM sites

Losses of aircraft over North Vietnam to SAMs resulted in the implementation, on 12 August, of a plan codenamed "Iron Hand"—with the SAM sites as its objective. The night before, one *Midway* A-4 had been shot down by a SAM, and another damaged. Finding the sites was tedious, and it was not until 17 October that US Navy aircraft armed with anti-radiation missiles scored their first Iron Hand victory, smashing a SAM complex near Kep airfield. Iron Hand tactics paralleled those of the US Air Force's "Wild Weasel", described earlier.

The Viet Cong struck back on the night of 27–28 October, when Communist sappers covered by mortars blew up 24 helicopters and damaged 23 more at Marble Mountain Marine helicopter base south of Da Nang, losing 46 men in the attack, while another VC raiding party destroyed two Marine Skyhawks and damaged six at Chu Lai.

On 18 December, Task Force 116, the River Patrol Force known as "Game Warden", was established under the command of Chief, Naval Advisory Group, Vietnam. Game Warden craft patrolled the Mekong Delta and the Rung Sat, the swampy area between Saigon and the sea. The River Patrol Force operated specially-built 32-foot (9.8m), 8-ton (8-tonnes) fiberglass river patrol boats, drawing only 1 foot (0.305m) and capable of 25 knots (28.75mph; 46.25kph), as well as converted landing craft and purpose-built welded-steel assault patrol boats. Some 50 feet (15.2m) long and capable of 14 knots (16.1 mph; 25.9kph), the latter mounted a formidable armament, including 81mm mortars, 20mm cannon, and flamethrowers.

Another naval highlight of December 1965 was the arrival of the 75,700-ton USS *Enterprise*, with a capacity of 80 to 100 aircraft; the first combat deployment of a nuclear-powered carrier. By the end of 1965, US Navy pilots had logged 56,888 sorties over Vietnam.

On 6 December, Marine pilots joined "Steel Tiger", an operation aimed at the interdiction of VC supply routes in Laos. Pilots from Da Nang and Chu Lai flew 140 strikes against Laotian targets during the month.

In January 1966, the Marines' Combined Action Program (CAP), originated in the Phu Bai area, was extended to the Da Nang region. The CAP tactical unit, the Combined Action Company, consisted of a squad of Marine volunteers serving in each of the five platoons of local Popular Forces (PF) companies. Pacification at the "grass roots" level was one of the most successful Marine ventures of the war, blending Marine know-how with PF local knowledge and skills.

During January, the four battalions of Marine Task Force Delta joined the US Army's 1st Air Cavalry Division in "Operation Double Eagle", aimed at the 325A NVA Division which had concentrated in the area of South Vietnam's I and II Corps boundary. In mid-February the Marines moved back into the Que Son valley to combat the 36th NVA Regiment and the reconstituted 1st VC Regiment. Allied units killed 2,389 Communists in follow-up operations.

A 37-day bombing halt was proclaimed at Christmas 1965, and Rolling Thunder did not resume until 31 January. Hanoi took advantage of this "peaceful" gesture to set up 20 radar installations, more SAM sites, and some 400 anti-aircraft gun positions. In February, the US Navy began an air-dropped mining campaign against North Vietnam. The increase in air activity caused shortages: at sea, TF 77 was running low on munitions, while aircraft losses were increasing. In March, 11 US aircraft were lost over North Vietnam; 21 more went down in April.

Rear Admiral Ward, the Chief, Naval Advisory Group, became Commander, Naval Forces, Vietnam (ComNavForV) on 1 April 1966, commanding both Market Time and Game Warden. The latter operation was expanding rapidly; the first personnel arrived in February, as did the first Navy, Sea, Air, Land (SEAL) platoon, consisting of counter-insurgency specialists. In May, two Bell SK-5 air-cushion vehicles (ACVs) joined to add flexibility, as well as to test hovercraft-types in combat.

Victory at An Hoa: mutiny at Da Nang

In March, the combined US Marine and ARVN operations codenamed "Utah/Lien Ket 26", northwest of Quang Ngai city, and "Texas/Lien Ket 28", in relief of the besieged ARVN outpost at An Hoa, killed 1,029 Communists, but these victories were overshadowed by internal disorders in South Vietnam. In the spring, as has already been described, Saigon, Da Nang, and Hue were torn by open rebellion as Buddhist factions challenged the government. At Da Nang, the internecine struggle was put down by Vietnamese Marines, but not before US Marines had forced rebel ARVN troops to back down at the Thanh Quit bridge, south of Da Nang, on 9 April. Later, on 18 May, General Walt was forced to take action against another dissident leader who threatened to blow up the Da Nang River bridge. The troubles were over by late May.

In March, two-thirds of the 1st Marine Division, commanded by Major General Lewis J. Fields at Chu Lai, was assigned to operate in Quang Tin and Quang Ngai provinces, while the 3d Marine Division, commanded by Major General Wood B. Kyle, covered the Da Nang-Phu Bai region. Meanwhile, the North Vietnamese 324B Division crossed the DMZ into northern Quang Tri province, the concentration

1

Vietnam 1964–1973: The War at Sea

1964
2 August: "Tonkin Gulf Incident": USS *Maddox* attacked by North Vietnamese torpedo boats
4 August: USS *C. Turner Joy* similarly attacked
5 August: Aircraft from USS *Ticonderoga* and *Constellation* attack North Vietnamese naval bases and other military targets in retaliation

1965
7 February: Carrier aircraft of US Seventh Fleet make their first large-scale strikes against ground targets in North Vietnam

1966
c. June: US Navy's Task Force 115 ("Market Time") begins patrolling coastal areas to prevent resupply of Viet Cong and North Vietnamese forces by sea

1968
30 September: USS *New Jersey*, the world's last active battleship, begins bombardment of Communist positions in and near the DMZ, firing 3,000+ rounds of 16in (406mm) and c.7,000 rounds of 5in (127mm) in October–November

1969
April–May: New Jersey returns to the United States; decommissioned in August

1970
21–22 November: Aircraft from USS *Ranger* and *Hancock* make first carrier strikes on North Vietnam since October 1968

1972
3 April: USS *Kitty Hawk* is first of four additional carriers to join the two operational off Vietnam; by October, Seventh Fleet is operating *Midway*, *America*, *Kitty Hawk*, *Saratoga*, *Oriskany*, and *Enterprise* simultaneously
15 April: US carrier aircraft strike Haiphong, damaging Soviet freighters
11 May: Following announcement by President Nixon on 8 May, Seventh Fleet establishes close blockade of North Vietnam, whose harbors are mined

1973
Following the ceasefire agreement of January, the last US troops leave Vietnam.

1. A USMC 105mm howitzer provides artillery support for a Mobile Afloat Force search and destroy operation southeast of Saigon. **2.** A US Navy Patrol Air Cushion Vehicle (PACV) in the Mekong Delta; two Bell SK-5 ACVs were sent to Vietnam in May 1966. **3.** "Operation Game Warden": a USAF

Kaman HH-43 Huskie rescue helicopter hovers above a River Patrol Boat, Mk II, of Task Force 116 on the Bassac River. **4.** A Vought F-8 Crusader of Marine Fighter Squadron, All-Weather, 312 prepares to strike at a Viet Cong mortar position, in support of Marine ground troops.

becoming known in July. At this stage, the III MAF's ground war became two distinct campaigns: the 3d Marine Division's tactical war in the relatively unpopulated northern I Corps area, and the 1st Marine Division's pacification operation south from Da Nang.

On 18 April 1966, two A-6A Intruders from the carrier *Kitty Hawk* made a spectacular night raid on the Uongbi power plant near Haiphong. All 26 of the 1,000-pound (455kg) bombs dropped hit the target; one-third of North Vietnam's electric power production was knocked out. The Rolling Thunder route packages were now redesignated as six areas; the coastal regions were permanently assigned to the US Navy, while the Air Force covered the interior. On 29 June, destruction of the Communists' petroleum supply capacity began. US naval aircraft raiding Haiphong fuel storage installations on 29 June and 7 July caused fires which sent smoke up to 20,000 feet.

On 15 July, "Operation Hastings" launched seven US Marine and five ARVN battalions against the 324B NVA Division in Quang Tri province. US Marines occupied the "Rockpile", a 700-foot (215m) pinnacle which afforded excellent observation of west-central Quang Tri province. Operation Hastings precipitated sharp actions against North Vietnamese regulars. When the operation ended, on 3 August, three US Marine battalions remained in the area to continue to seek out and engage NVA regulars. This operation, codenamed "Prairie", was not completed until 31 May 1967.

Paralleling Rolling Thunder, the US Navy initiated "Operation Sea Dragon"— surface operations against North Vietnamese coastal traffic—on 25 October 1966. Sea Dragon was limited to below 17° 30' North, and the "rules" prohibited engaging vessels involved in non-military activities. Shore bombardment was authorized only in self-defense. On 11

November, the limit was moved up to 18° North, but the enemy responded by concentrating coastal artillery in the Sea Dragon zone. Seventh Fleet reacted by moving the limit up to 20° North on 27 February 1967.

In October, the "Seawolves", detachments of US Navy Helicopter Support Squadron One, joined Game Warden. The Seawolves, flying Bell UH-1 Iroquois helicopters (often called "Hueys") in two unit fire teams, added a new and deadly dimension to the patrol. By December, 40 Game Warden river patrol boats were operating in Rung Sat waterways; 80 more patrolled the Mekong Delta.

In March 1967 the guided missile destroyer (DDG) HMAS *Hobart* was the first RAN warship to be deployed with the US Seventh Fleet. Up to September 1971, *Hobart* and her sistership *Perth* both served three six-month tours; the DDG *Brisbane* served two tours and the destroyer (DD) *Vendetta* one. Also in 1967, RAN clearance divers began operations with USN underwater teams and eight ASW-trained RAN helicopter pilots joined an integrated RAN-US Army unit.

In 1967, Admiral Ulysses S. Grant Sharp, Commander in Chief, Pacific, recommended that six basic targets in North Vietnam (electric power; war support industry; transportation support; military complexes; petroleum storage; and air defense) should be approved as target packages. His appeal resulted in some lifting of target restrictions, but Washington continued the practice of piecemeal target approval.

Meanwhile, the US Marines in I Corps area were killing Communists. "Operation Prairie I", around Con Thien and Gio Linh, ended on 31 January; 1,397 dead NVA were reported. In the follow-on, "Prairie II", the 3d Marine Division claimed another 639 NVA victims. The first battle of Khe Sanh ended on 12–13 May and the Marines moved into the offensive. To the south, the 1st Marine Division's "Operations Union I and II" claimed 2,250 Communist dead.

In February 1967, both Market Time and Game Warden became separate, individual commands under ComNavForV. Another force was added on 28 February: the Riverine Assault Force, TF 117, was activated to carry the ground war into the Delta and Rung Sat marshes.

In the air, the Navy launched its first "Walleye" bomb attack against Sam Son barracks, North Vietnam, on 11 March. The television-guided Walleye scored a perfect hit, entering a window of the building.

Lieutenant General Robert E. Cushman, Jr., relieved General Walt as III MAF commander on 1 June. Within a month, fierce fighting broke out around Con Thien, where the enemy made base defense more difficult by introducing 122mm and 140mm rockets. An attack on 2–3 July cost the Americans 51 dead, 34 missing, and 170 wounded, in spite of support from the air and from naval gunfire; VC dead were estimated at 65 or more, with a further 150 claimed killed in another attack on 6 July. The 3d Marine Division's "Operation Buffalo", near the DMZ in July, claimed another 1,281 NVA; "Kingfisher", which lasted through October, reported 1,117 NVA killed.

Aircraft from *Kitty Hawk* and *Bonne Homme Richard* badly damaged the Hanoi thermal power plant on 19 May, shooting down four MiGs during the raid. Again, on 21 July, "Bonnie Dick" pilots raiding the Ta Xa petroleum storage area shot down three MiGs and claimed a "probable" fourth in seven minutes.

On 29 July tragedy struck US forces again: the carrier *Forrestal* was crippled by fire after a rocket was accidentally fired on the flight deck. Twenty-one planes were destroyed, 134 crewmen died, and *Forrestal* required seven months for repair. In the same month, an estimated 233 SAMs were launched by the Communists—but of the 19 Navy planes lost, most fell to anti-aircraft guns. In August, 249 SAMs were fired, including a record 80 on the 24th, bringing down six Navy aircraft; anti-aircraft batteries claimed 10 more.

Khe Sanh and the Tet offensive

The siege of Con Thien, called "Little Dien Bien Phu" by pressmen, lifted as Marine operations "Scotland" and "Kentucky" began in the Khe Sanh/Con Thien regions on 1 November. The first Marine general died in Vietnam on 14 November, when the 3d Marine Division commander, Major General Bruno A. Hochmuth, was killed when his UH-1E helicopter exploded. The command passed to Major General Rathvon McC. Tompkins. Around this time, US Navy Game Warden units moved to I Corps area to set up "Operation Clearwater", for the protection and coordination of traffic on the Perfume and Cua Viet Rivers, essential supply routes to Dong Ha and Hue.

For a brief period in September, Haiphong could deploy no SAMs and had no anti-aircraft ammunition, but bad weather covered North Vietnamese resupply operations. As adverse weather continued into October, US Navy aircraft were next given the task of attacking boat-building yards and rail-roads in November. Hanoi had by now established the heaviest anti-aircraft defenses in history: 15 operational SAM complexes and 560 guns, with MiG interceptors deployed nearby. It has been estimated that more than 670 US aircraft had been lost to all causes over North Vietnam by the end of 1967.

A 36-hour stand-down took place on New Year's Day 1968, but another scheduled for Tet, 27 January to 3 February 1968, was canceled—by Communist aggression. The second battle of Khe Sanh began on 20 January, and on the 29th the Communists launched the nation-wide Tet offensive in South Vietnam.

While US Navy pilots operated in foul weather over Vietnam, US Marines on the ground were fighting to retake Hue, block by block. By 2 March, three US Marine and 13 South Vietnamese Army and Marine battalions had regained the ruined city, almost completely wiping out an estimated eight to eleven NVA battalions in the process; 5,113 Communists were claimed killed.

Near the DMZ, US Navy pilots flew 1,500 sorties in support of the Marines at Khe Sanh during February, and another 1,600 in March. On 31 March 1968, President

United States Marine Corps Losses in Vietnam
Personnel (1962–1972)
12,936 killed, 88,594 wounded, 26 captured
Aircraft (to October 1970)
252 helicopters lost in combat, 173 fixed-wing aircraft lost in combat, 172 helicopters lost during operations, 81 fixed-wing aircraft lost

1. To fulfil its varied missions, the US Navy used the most sophisticated weapons—and the most primitive: Lieutenant Commander Donald D. Sheppard, commanding River Division 51, aims a flaming arrow at a bamboo hut concealing a fortified Viet Cong bunker on the Bassac River, 2. An accident triggers fires and explosions on the flight deck of USS *Forrestal* on 29 July 1967: crewmen fight to control a conflagration that lasted 18 hours, destroyed 21 aircraft, and killed 134 men. 3. Twin .30-caliber machine guns aboard a USN Bell UH-1B Iroquois helicopter fire on Viet Cong positions in the Mekong Delta. 4. The US Navy's SEAL (sea-air-land) teams specialized in unconventional and para-military operations; here, SEALS descend from a hovering "Huey" to set up a jungle ambush. 5. By late 1967, Hanoi was guarded by the heaviest anti-aircraft defenses in history: a battery of AAA in the North Vietnamese capital. 6. Craft of USN River Assault Flotilla I are led by a monitor—an armored gun-boat mounting 20mm and 40mm guns and 81mm direct fire mortars. 7. On patrol in the Tonkin Gulf in December 1967, the guided missile destroyer USS *Lynde McCormick* comes under fire from North Vietnamese shore batteries.

Johnson announced the halt of bombing north of the 20th Parallel; in October, he ordered the cessation of all attacks on North Vietnam. The naval air war against North Vietnam was over for the time being—although it would begin later in the form of retaliatory strikes.

Khe Sanh was relieved by "Operation Pegasus—a joint US Marine/US Army/ARVN effort—on 12 April. Pegasus was followed in the same area by "Scotland II", which did not end until February 1969, by which time the Marines claimed to have killed 3,921 of the enemy. The 320th NVA Division attacked units of the 3d Marine Division at Dong Ha on 29 April and heavy fighting continued through May. In the course of 1968, such major Marine operations as "Lancaster II", "Jeb Stuart", "Napoleon/Saline", "Pegasus", "Allen Brook", and "Mameluke Thrust", resulted in the deaths of an estimated 13,353 VC and NVA.

Final US operations in Southeast Asia

On 30 September 1968, the battleship *New Jersey*—the last ship of her type to see action—arrived, opening fire with her 16-inch (406mm) guns at targets northwest of Con Thien. In November, the Marines began their Accelerated Pacification Program, "Operation Meade River", to win back territory lost during the Tet offensive. **1** When Meade River ended on 9 December, 1,210 enemy had been flushed out and killed.

The US Navy turned over 7.7 million dollars' worth of riverine assault craft to the South Vietnamese Navy on 1 February 1969. A year later, there were virtually no US Navy combat craft in South Vietnamese waters; 242 Game Warden and Market Time patrol craft had been relinquished to the South Vietnamese.

During the period 22 January to 19 March 1969, III MAF Marines executed perhaps the most successful regimental-size action of the war, "Operation Dewey Canyon", in the Da Krong valley, Quang Tri province. The last of the major Marine operations, Dewey Canyon killed 1,617 NVA and resulted in the capture of large quantities of arms and ammunition.

On 8 June 1969, President Nixon announced the first US troop withdrawal, and "the newsreel started running backward". **2** The 9th Marines left Vietnam in July, the 3d Marines in October, and the 3d Marine Division was gone by 30 November. The phase-down continued as the war was "Vietnamized".

On 1 April 1971, the last US Navy combat force in Vietnam, Light Attack Squadron Four—equipped with the first purpose-designed counter-insurgency light armed reconnaissance aircraft, the North American Rockwell OV-10 Bronco, acquired from the Marine Corps in 1968—left the country. Thirteen days later, the headquarters of III MAF, 1st Marine Division, and 1st Marine Aircraft Wing left Da Nang. All that remained was the 3d Marine Amphibious Brigade. Ground and air operations ceased on 7 May, and by 26 July 1971, 3d MAB was gone too. Only a handful of US Marines remained in Vietnam, as artillery observers, advisers, and embassy guards. **3**

5

6

1. US Marines are carried up the Saigon River by US Navy River Patrol Boats. 2. Two F-4B Phantoms of 1st Marine Aircraft Wing *en route* from Da Nang in January 1969 to support Marines on the ground in northern I Corps zone, where the 16-month "Operation Kentucky", around Con Thien, ended on 28 February. 3. Ammunition dumps were vulnerable to terrorist attack—and accident; here, III Marine Amphibious Force's dump blows up in March 1969. 4. USMC Bell UH-1E Hueys touch down with their loads at a fire support base (FSB) of the 9th Marines; a typical FSB comprised a battery of 105mm and 155mm howitzers and 4.2in mortars, an infantry battalion command post, a logistic support area, and an aid station. 5. A Vought A-7A Corsair II attack bomber prepares to launch from the carrier USS *Constellation*. 6. Men of the 1st Marine Division cool off in a stream. 7. USS *New Jersey*, last battleship of the US Navy to see action, fires her huge 16in (406mm) guns in May 1968; *New Jersey* fired 3,615 16in shells and nearly 11,000 5in in bombardment missions off North Vietnam from September 1968 to March 1969.

7

The in-country enemy: battle with the Viet Cong

Charles B. MacDonald

At the beginning of 1967, the North Vietnamese still continued to increase their strength in the DMZ, bringing in more and more artillery. Because the DMZ, created by the Geneva Agreements of 1954, had so far been held more or less inviolable by both sides, the US State Department was reluctant to grant approval for American and South Vietnamese operations there, despite clear evidence of North Vietnamese violations. That reluctance was based on the long-held concern that any broadening of the conflict might bring Chinese Communist intervention.

General Westmoreland at first could obtain approval only to return artillery fire when fired upon. Not until February 1967, when enemy shelling had reached serious proportions, did the State Department sanction pre-emptive fire, including air strikes, against North Vietnamese artillery positions in the DMZ. It took even longer for Westmoreland to get approval for American and South Vietnamese ground troops to enter the DMZ. Even then, at first, they could do so only in pursuit of enemy forces encountered south of the Zone. That concession carried the additional restriction that pursuit must stop at the 17th Parallel that divided the Zone, roughly along the course of the Ben Hai River.

As post-war evidence revealed, the State Department's concern over China was probably groundless. Contrary to the American view, North Vietnamese leaders, while pleading for and welcoming military assistance from other Communist countries, consistently refused to follow their benefactors' advice. In Moscow and the Communist East European capitals—if not in Peking—North Vietnamese violation of the DMZ provoked marked concern. It was feared that the United States would react violently to such obvious infringement of an international agreement—perhaps even to the point of employing tactical nuclear weapons. There was, reputedly, immense relief in the Communist camp when American reaction showed restraint.

Communist build-up in the northern provinces

Convinced that major North Vietnamese operations were imminent in the northernmost provinces, General Westmoreland provided the US Marines with powerful fire support from two battalions of US Army 175mm guns, with a range of up to 20 miles (32km). He also ordered construction of a new airfield far to the north near Quang Tri city, capital of Quang Tri province; directed upgrading of the existing air strip at Khe Sanh; and afforded the III Marine Amphibious Force commander,

Striking across the Demilitarized Zone, North Vietnamese units threatened US strongholds in the northern provinces in 1967. The advance was stemmed. Farther south US and ARVN forces attacked the Viet Cong infrastructure in months-long operations, while the Riverine Force interdicted Communist activity in the Mekong Delta. But in America there was mounting criticism of the way the war was being handled

General Walt, priority on strikes by B-52 bombers. As further preparation for battle, he instructed his chief of staff, Major General William B. Rosson, to form a head-quarters known as "Task Force Oregon", which would eventually absorb three separate US Army infantry brigades to form the 23d (Americal) Infantry Division and assume responsibility for the southern provinces of the I Corps area, thus enabling General Walt to move his Marines farther north.

Quang Tri province provided sharp contrasts in terrain: towering forested mountains in the west gradually sloping down to foothills, and to flat, sandy coastal plains. Winding valleys led through the mountains from the Khe Sanh area down to the plain near Quang Tri city and, farther south in Thua Thien province, to the city of Hue. South of Hue, the mountains extended to the South China Sea. Thus, the two northernmost provinces were effectively separated from the rest of South Vietnam, except for the link provided across a high ridge by the Hai Van Pass, through which National Route I crossed the mountains near the sea. Westmoreland believed that the North Vietnamese were intent on overrunning the two northernmost provinces before they would consider any agreement to negotiate.

In late March 1967, the North Vietnamese apparently reached the point in their build-up when they were ready to strike. On 20 March, North Vietnamese artillery fired more than 1,000 rounds against South Vietnamese troops and US Marines manning two of the forward strongpoints below the DMZ, Con Thien and Gio Linh. A few days later the North Vietnamese ambushed a Marine convoy; while patrols centering on various points, including Khe Sanh, triggered sharp

reactions from the North Vietnamese.

On the morning of 24 April, a Marine platoon patrolling some five miles (8km) northwest of Khe Sanh had a sharp engagement with a large NVA force. That set off what became known as the "hill fights", centering on three peaks designated, from their height in meters, Hills 861, 881 South, and 881 North. Contingents of a North Vietnamese division had occupied the hills, apparently as a preliminary to attacking the combat base at Khe Sanh. Supported by US Marine Corps fighter-bombers and by 175mm fire, the Marines gradually fought their way up the steep slopes and, in some of the fiercest fighting of the war, eventually secured the three peaks and there established outposts protecting Khe Sanh.

For the moment, that action brought relative calm to Khe Sanh; but the fighting shifted elsewhere, in particular to the forward base at Con Thien. There occurred one of the few instances in Vietnam when American troops were subjected to artillery fire comparable to that experienced during World War II and the Korean War. Although the North Vietnamese clearly intended an assault on Con Thien, pre-emptive air strikes, artillery fire, and forays from the base by Marines companies and battalions, hampered the enemy's troop concentration.

The strategic value of Con Thien

American newsmen unsympathetic to the war began to describe Con Thien as "an American Dien Bien Phu", implying that there was little point in holding on to that miserably small piece of ground at the possible risk of heavy losses. Yet to Generals Walt (who relinquished command of III MAF to Lieutenant General Robert E. Cushman, Jr., on 1 June) and Westmoreland there seemed little likelihood, in view of American firepower, that Con Thien would prove a debacle. Further, if the Marines fell back from Con Thien and other forward bases, the enemy would simply move forward and attack the next line of outposts—thereby coming closer to the Communists' apparent objective of occupying the two northern provinces.

As the fight continued, the commander of the US Seventh Air Force, General William M. Momyer, developed a system for coordinating heavy firepower for the defense of Con Thien. Creating a forward headquarters, he employed the full spectrum of fire support—tactical aircraft (both US Air Force and US Marine Corps), naval gunfire, and B-52s, in close coordination with artillery and other ground fire—to strike enemy concentrations reported by various intelligence sources. This measure severely limited the ability

1

2

3

1. Tactical air support missions, as seen here, played a vital part in base defense, striking enemy artillery and breaking up troop concentrations.
2. Men of the US 173d Airborne Brigade —who made the only sizable paratroop drop of the war during "Operation Junction City" early in 1967—move into action. **3.** A US Army M107 self-propelled gun in action; the gun throws a 147lb (55kg) HE shell to a maximum range of 35,870yds (32,785m).

of the North Vietnamese to mass for ground attacks at Con Thien; those attacks that did develop were relatively feeble. By mid-autumn 1967, the siege of Con Thien—if such it could be called—was at an end. The North Vietnamese withdrew to rebuild their forces for other attacks—perhaps for another blow at Khe Sanh.

Elsewhere in South Vietnam the influx of American forces began to allow the major operations that Westmoreland had long planned. Some, such as "Operation Fairfax", carried out in the midst of a dense cluster of villages and hamlets in the immediate environs of Saigon and involving an American brigade operating with a South Vietnamese Ranger group, lasted for weeks or months. Fairfax consisted primarily of ambushes and saturation patrolling particularly at night, to interdict Viet Cong movement and prevent the Communists from recruiting among or terrorizing the people. In a similar operation, the 1st Cavalry Division returned to Binh Dinh province where the Viet Cong, earlier driven out, had returned with a North Vietnamese regiment in support. Another extended operation took place in the Rung Sat, an inhospitable expanse of mangrove swamps near the mouth of the Saigon River, almost completely inundated at high tide. Units operating there had to rotate almost every day to allow the men to dry out, lest skin diseases and a malady known as "immersion foot" should incapacitate them.

"Cedar Falls" sweep of the Iron Triangle

Other operations involved multiple units and required the same careful preparation and coordination essential to conventional military operations. One of the first was "Operation Cedar Falls", a sweep by two American divisions, an airborne brigade, an armored cavalry regiment, and a South Vietnamese division, into a region known as the "Iron Triangle". This was a 60-square mile (160 sq km) stretch of jungle, rice paddy, and isolated villages along the Saigon River, some 20 miles (32km) north of Saigon in Binh Duong province, long a Viet Cong stronghold and a base for terrorist operations against the capital. Cedar Falls began with a surprise landing by a battalion of the 1st Infantry Division, lifted by 60 helicopters, in the center of the village of Ben Suc, considered the nexus of enemy defenses in the region. In order to achieve surprise, American commanders had not informed South Vietnamese officials of the landing, lest Viet Cong sympathizers pass the word. As a result, the unexpected refugee problem that was quickly created taxed the facilities of the provincial chief. For several days, until shelter could be prepared and food supplied, the refugees lived under harsh conditions in full view of American newsmen, whose dispatches were sharply critical.

The other American units engaged virtually surrounded the Iron Triangle, although the cordon could be but loosely drawn and the number of Viet Cong killed, some 750, was relatively small. The basic aim was to eliminate the Iron Triangle as a base—and to accomplish that, the people had to be relocated away from their villages, and their houses destroyed. Lacking

the capability to level the jungle entirely, bulldozers cut wide swaths through it, so that Viet Cong movement across these lanes could be detected. Although the Viet Cong later returned to the Iron Triangle, the relocation of population made the area a "free fire zone" into which artillery and air strikes could be directed without concern for civilian casualties. Rome plows subsequently completed the job of leveling the entire region, and the Iron Triangle was never again a secure sanctuary for the VC.

A thrust at Communist headquarters

In "Operation Junction City", lasting from late February into May, 22 American battalions and 4 South Vietnamese battalions, more than 25,000 troops, made another foray into War Zone C, centering in Tay Ninh province near the Cambodian border. Their mission was to destroy Viet Cong bases and, if possible, capture COSVN, the headquarters of the Central Office for South Vietnam and the North Vietnamese Communist Party's instrument for military and political control in South Vietnam. American and South Vietnamese troops formed an immense horseshoe about three sides of War Zone C. As they began to press inward, a battalion of the 173d Airborne Brigade, in the only sizable parachute drop of the war, jumped into the open end of the horseshoe at Katum. Close on 3,000 enemy dead were claimed; but many, along with the COSVN headquarters, escaped into Cambodia.

General Westmoreland meanwhile planned to commit American troops to the provinces of the IV Corps zone in the Mekong Delta. Because that was the country's most populous region, American officials had long been wary of sending US troops there lest their presence exacerbate the traditional xenophobia of the South Vietnamese. However, after an American battalion had operated near Saigon in Long An province, a region similar to the Mekong Delta, without undue reaction among the population, Westmoreland considered such fears unrealistic. The presence of American units in Long An appeared to raise the morale of South Vietnamese troops—while US civic action projects, such as medical and dental clinics, school and market construction, well-digging, and bridge-building, appeared to encourage the people to support the Saigon government.

Thus, plans were made to introduce an American infantry division into IV Corps zone. Two brigades of the division would operate as traditional ground troops; but the third would cooperate with a fleet of US Navy accommodation ships, artillery platform barges, troop transports, patrol boats, minesweepers, and armored gunboats generally known as monitors. Together the sailors and infantrymen of the Riverine Force would seek the enemy along the vast network of rivers and canals in the southern provinces.

One of the remarkable feats of the war was the construction over two years, of a base in the Mekong Delta for the Riverine Force. A basin for the river craft had to be constructed by excavating riverside rice paddies. Soil thus displaced, with mud

1

2

3

4

1. A land-based USMC A-4E Skyhawk prepares to take off on an air support mission. 2. Men of C Company, 4 Royal Australian Regiment/New Zealand (ANZAC) Battalion, during a sweep to flush out VC in the Long Binh area. 3. A patrol of the US 11th Armored Cavalry Regiment halts while the point man checks out possible Viet Cong bunkers during "Junction City". 4. Men of the 1st Engineer Battalion, US 1st Infantry Division, descend from a CH-47 Chinook during "Cedar Falls"; using chain saws and explosives, the engineers cleared a helicopter landing zone. 5. Men of the US 1st Cavalry Division (Airmobile) jump from a UH-1D Huey during "Operation Oregon", a search and destroy mission, April 1967. 6. US Navy River Patrol Boats on an inland waterway.

Operation Cedar Falls
8–26 January 1967

Objectives:
US/ARVN multidivisional search and destroy operation in the Iron Triangle–Thanh Dien Forest area
Strength:
US/ARVN: c.15,000
VC/NVN losses: c.750 killed; 280 prisoners; 540 defectors to anti-Communist forces; 512 suspected VC detained; 5,987 refugees evacuated
VC/NVN materiel damaged/captured: 23 crew-served weapons; 590 individual weapons; 60,000+ rounds of small-arms ammunition; 2,800+ mines, grenades, mortar and artillery rounds; 7,500+ uniforms; 2,000+ bunkers, tunnels, and other military structures destroyed; 3,700 short tons of rice (one year's ration for 13,000 troops); 500,000+ pages of documents.
US losses: 72 killed; 337 wounded; 1 tank destroyed; 3 tanks damaged; 3 APCs destroyed; 9 APCs damaged; 2 helicopters damaged.
ARVN losses: 11 killed; 8 wounded.
Result:
Although 4.25sq.m. (11sq.km) of jungle were cleared and the population evacuated, VC were active in the Iron Triangle within a week of the operation's end.

Operation Junction City
22 February–14 May 1967

Objective:
US/ARVN multidivisional search and destroy operation in War Zone C
Strength: US/ARVN: 25,000+.
VC/NVN losses: 2,728 killed; 34 prisoners; 139 defectors to anti-Communist forces (in response to 9,768,000 air-dropped leaflets and 102 hours of aerial loudspeaker appeals); 65 suspected VC detained.
VC/NVN materiel damaged/captured: 100 crew-served weapons; 491 individual weapons; large quantities of ammunition, grenades, mines; 5,000+ bunkers and other military structures destroyed; 810 short tons of rice; c.40 short tons of other foodstuffs; c.500,000 pages of documents
US losses: 282 killed; 1,576 wounded; 3 tanks destroyed; 21 APCs destroyed; 12 trucks destroyed; 4 helicopters destroyed; 5 howitzers destroyed; 2 quad-.50 mgs and carriers destroyed.
NVN claims for US/ARVN losses: 13,500 killed; 993 vehicles destroyed; 119 artillery pieces destroyed.
Result:
The Communist HQ, Central Office of South Vietnam (COSVN), was forced to withdraw into Cambodia and its activities were seriously disrupted; psychological effect on the Viet Cong was judged to be considerable.

sucked up from the river bottom by hydraulic dredges, was used to fill in one square mile (260ha) of flooded paddy. Although attacks by Viet Cong sappers sank one large and two small dredgers, US Navy Seabees and Army Engineers persevered until the huge artificial island was completed. Meanwhile, the Riverine Force searched for enemy enclaves along the banks or in the riverside villages. Like the men operating in the Rung Sat, members of the Riverine Force had to be pulled back from time to time to their accommodation ships to "dry out".

Westmoreland explains the war effort

A justified criticism of almost all US operations was that American troops were never long in one place: the people were afraid to commit themselves to the government lest, when the Americans moved on, the Viet Cong return. Because there were never sufficient American troops to occupy even a major portion of the country, that often happened. The task of defending the people had to be left to the ARVN and to the many Regional and Popular Force platoons and companies that held small, triangular, adobe forts on the outskirts of villages and hamlets. It would require time adequately to train and equip those militia units, but nevertheless they had to be relied upon.

Behind the defensive screen, the pacification process proceeded. Teams from the South Vietnamese government's civilian ministries, assisted and advised by American civilians of the Central Intelligence Agency, the United States Information Service, and the Agency for International Development, moved into urban areas to help establish local government, identify and eliminate Communist cadremen, and finance and assist self-help projects.

Despite apparent progress in South Vietnam, at home President Johnson was beset by a growing anti-war movement. Uncensored newspapers and television reports brought the war into American living rooms—nourishing the civilian's natural abhorrence of the hardships and cruelties that war engenders. Further, despite official reports of progress, there seemed to be no prospect of an end to the conflict: the number of Americans killed soon exceeded the number killed in the Korean War (in which US casualties totalled 33,720 killed and 103,284 wounded). Between 1961 and 1965, American casualties in Vietnam amounted to 1,484 killed and 7,337 wounded; in 1966, when US forces were first committed on a large scale, 5,047 Americans were killed.

At the President's behest, General Westmoreland returned to the United States in April 1967 to make a public report on the war before a dinner held by the Associated Press in New York. "Through a clever combination of psychological and political warfare," Westmoreland remarked, the enemy had gained world-wide public support "which gives him hope that he can win politically that which he cannot accomplish militarily." That, and a remark about demonstrators who burned the American flag, angered anti-war critics—as did press emphasis on Westmoreland's assertion that criticism

of US commitment was encouraging the enemy and costing American lives. The anti-war movement, although a minority, was fast expanding and seemed certain to exert an effect on the future conduct of the war.

A few days later, again at the President's wish, Westmoreland attended a White House conference at which the President, Secretaries McNamara and Rusk, the Chairman of the Joint Chiefs of Staff, General Wheeler, and other officials were present, to discuss the advisability of providing more American troops for Westmoreland's command. Encouraged by the progress achieved with a relatively small force of eight divisions, Westmoreland had furnished the President in advance with two proposals; one involving what he called a "minimum essential force", the other an "optimum force". The first called for a total strength of approximately 550,000 men; the second for a strength of about 670,000. Questioned at the conference, Westmoreland reluctantly estimated that with the minimum force he could end the American role in the war in about five years; with the optimum force, in about three years.

In discussions with Secretary McNamara and other advisers over the next two months, President Johnson agonized over the decision. There seemed no sure way—short of invading North Vietnam, Laos, or Cambodia, and thus risking the involvement of the Chinese Communists—to bring North Vietnam to the negotiating table until after the American presidential election in November 1968. To call up the reserves, a necessary measure if Westmoreland was to have 670,000 troops, would ignite the anti-war movement. It would require gearing the country's economy to a wartime footing, with a subsequent setback to the domestic social programs Johnson had long promoted as the "Great Society". In July, the President told Westmoreland he would have to make do with an increase in the coming year of only about 47,000 men, giving a total of 525,000. This was even less than Westmoreland had calculated as the minimum essential force.

Anti-war "doves" besiege the Pentagon

Even so, the anti-war movement was not appeased. It had become perilous for any government official to appear on a campus, where burning "hawks", including Westmoreland, in effigy had become commonplace. Press and television gave every anti-war demonstration maximum coverage, and such unlikely foreign policy experts as movie stars, a prominent pediatrician, a Harvard economist, and several novelists, emerged as "doves", or anti-war leaders. In October 1967, 35,000 "doves" besieged the Pentagon.

From official reports from Saigon, and from personal conference with Westmoreland and newly-appointed Ambassador Ellsworth Bunker, President Johnson was convinced that there had been real progress in South Vietnam. Seeing his public support shaken by the clamor of the anti-war faction, and conscious that he must maintain that support if he was to carry through a policy of winning a limited war,

1. Troop-carrying Vietnamese Navy boats penetrate a canal in the Rung Sat; a US Navy UH-1E Iroquois flies overhead. 2. Encamped at Andrews Air Force Base, Maryland, the 82nd Airborne Division guards the Pentagon during the "siege" of October 1967. 3. A North Vietnamese postage stamp of 1967 depicts an American POW. 4. US Marshals resist demonstrators on the steps of the Pentagon, October 1967. 5. The war goes on: a reconnaissance patrol of the 173d Airborne Brigade near Dak To, November 1967. 6. The Air Liaison Officer (ALO) camp at Chu Lai, October 1967; an ALO Team consisted of five forward air control pilots and eight radiomen.

the President summoned Bunker and Westmoreland to Washington in November 1967 to make public appearances assuring the American people of progress. Knowing their optimistic views, Johnson had no need to dictate what the Ambassador and the General should say.

Bunker and Westmoreland appeared several times on national television programs—and, on 21 November, Westmoreland made a speech before the National Press Club in Washington that would be long remembered. "We have reached an important point when the end begins to come into view," Westmoreland said. The war, he noted, was soon to enter a phase in which the South Vietnamese Army would be able to assume increasing responsibility for the fighting. In June, he had received a new deputy-commander, General Creighton W. Abrams, to whom he assigned the job of upgrading the South Vietnamese forces. He ventured to say that within two years—by November 1969—or less, token withdrawals at least of American troops might begin.

Border battles in the fall of 1967

While Westmoreland was in Washington he learned of heavy fighting, involving a North Vietnamese division, in Kontum province in the Central Highlands. It centered on Dak To, one of the border outposts manned by Montagnards, troops of the highland tribes, and men of the US Army Special Forces. This was the third of what came to be known as the "border battles" of the fall of 1967, a series of engagements that at first appeared to be a Communist attempt to embarrass the South Vietnamese government on the eve of the inauguration of Thieu and Ky.

The first "border battle" was at the village of Song Be, Phuoc Long province, where a North Vietnamese regiment attacked the command post of a South Vietnamese battalion and was repulsed with heavy losses. The second was at a small rubber-plantation town, Loc Ninh, close to the Cambodian border in the province of Binh Long, where Viet Cong and North Vietnamese regulars attacked an outpost manned by South Vietnamese militia. Reinforcements from a regular ARVN division and from heli-lifted elements of the US 1st Infantry Division helped drive out the enemy, but heavy fighting raged from 29 October, with the Communists launching "human-wave" attacks, until the attackers retired on 2 November, having lost some 900 men, compared to only about 60 Allied dead.

When Westmoreland returned to Saigon and examined accumulating intelligence reports, it began to appear that the border battles might presage more than an attempt to embarrass the South Vietnamese government. Westmoreland was already convinced, as he had stated in Washington, that the American operations sustained through 1967 had hurt the enemy badly (in US offensive operations, the "kill ratio" was running 10 to 1 against the enemy; in enemy attacks, even higher). As early as August 1967, Westmoreland told American newsmen that heavy losses probably would necessitate "a momentous decision" on the part of the Communist leaders—a reassessment of their strategy. Then, just before the Dak To fight, a captured document revealed that the battle was a prelude to a major North Vietnamese offensive in Kontum province—"a concentrated offensive effort in coordination with other units in various battle areas throughout South Vietnam," part of what would be "a prolonged battle".

Sixteen American and South Vietnamese battalions became involved, and the North Vietnamese left behind 1,400 dead; the heaviest fighting in the Highlands since that in the Ia Drang valley in 1966. As the fighting at Dak To ebbed, US Marines patrolling around Khe Sanh combat base detected another North Vietnamese build-up in that area. There were a number of small but vicious attacks throughout the country; the number of enemy coming over to the anti-Communist side dropped sharply; and, as Christmas approached, intelligence reports noted a 200 percent increase in North Vietnamese truck traffic on the Ho Chi Minh Trail in Laos.

Plans for a Communist offensive

In a cable to the Joint Chiefs of Staff shortly before Christmas, Westmoreland remarked that the enemy "has already made a crucial decision concerning the conduct of the war," and that "prolongation of his past policies for conducting the war would lead to his defeat, and that he would have to make a major effort to reverse the downward trend". The enemy, Westmoreland believed, intended "to make a maximum effort on all fronts (politically and military) in order to achieve victory in a short period of time".

As New Year's Day 1968 passed, indications of some major enemy move continued. The North Vietnamese were massing at least two divisions at Khe Sanh: a defecting

lieutenant said that they planned an all-out attack on Khe Sanh during the approaching Tet holiday period. A captured document revealed Communist belief that the time might be ripe for a "general offensive and general uprising" of the South Vietnamese people "to take over towns and cities" and "liberate" Saigon. Another captured document concerned plans for a heavy attack in Pleiku province —to begin "before the Tet holidays".

The current commander of the II Field Force, Lieutenant General Fred C. Weyand, concluded that the enemy in the III Corps zone around Saigon was moving from his border sanctuaries towards the capital. In the central coastal city of Qui Nhon, a house raided by South Vietnamese troops was found to be sheltering 11 Viet Cong, a tape recorder, and two tapes. The captured VC stated that there would be attacks on Qui Nhon and other cities during the Tet period; the tapes were propaganda exhortations to be played once the government radio station was captured. The MACV intelligence officer, Major General Phillip B. Davidson, canceled a planned leave and warned Westmoreland that he expected major country-wide attacks—although he could not specify exact places or dates.

Preparing for the North Vietnamese thrust

On 20 January 1968, ten days before the beginning of Tet, General Westmoreland cabled to the Joint Chiefs of Staff: "The enemy is presently developing a threatening posture in several areas in order to seek victories essential to achieving prestige and bargaining power. He may exercise his initiatives prior to, during, or after Tet." So threatening was the situation that Westmoreland persuaded President Thieu to cancel the planned Tet cease-fire in the northern provinces and to limit it elsewhere to only 24 hours.

Because he could not predict exactly the time or place of the enemy move, Westmoreland made no deliberate effort to alert the press and the American public. He did, however, state in a television interview for the National Broadcasting Company that the enemy planned "a major effort to win a spectacular battlefield success along the eve of Tet". General Weyand, too, issued a warning, telling one reporter that the enemy appeared set to make "critical — perhaps spectacular — moves". In Washington, the Chairman of the Joint Chiefs of Staff, General Wheeler, stated publicly that "there may be a Communist thrust similar to the desperate effort of the Germans in the Battle of the Bulge in World War II". Yet those warnings received little coverage in the news media—and although President Johnson, on a visit to Australia, warned the Australian Cabinet of "dark days ahead", he issued no public alert in the United States.

A warning might, in any case, have been lost on the American public. Had not Westmoreland said at the National Press Club that the war had "reached an important point when the end begins to come into view"? Content with what they interpreted as a reassurance that all was well, few Americans at home suspected an impending crisis.

4

5

1. Although Christmas 1967 brought threats of a Communist thrust, this US Marine on a search and destroy mission north of Con Thien, near the Demilitarized Zone, was determined to make the Yuletide bright. **2.** The Communist buildup to the offensive planned for Tet, 1968: artillery moves down the Ho Chi Minh Trail, where a 200 percent increase in North Vietnamese truck traffic was reported in December 1967. **3.** The interrogation of captives led to information on the forthcoming North Vietnamese offensive: these Viet Cong were captured in a heliborne assault by the US 101st Airborne Division, after their camp near Tuy Hoa had been blasted by USAF A-1E Skyraiders. **4.** Men of the US 4th Infantry Division fire an 81mm mortar. **5.** As a propaganda ploy, Radio Hanoi stated that captured US pilots would be released at Christmas 1967: unsurprisingly, the promise was not kept.

US and North Vietnamese/VC Combat Strengths, 1967

Military strengths given in any war must always be treated with great caution, since widely differing criteria are used in their preparation. In South Vietnam, for example, the figure which really mattered was the number of combat infantrymen available for action.

United States: US strength in South Vietnam in December 1967 was 473,200. From this number was produced 90 combat infantry battalions. Battalion strength at that time was some 700 men, of which some 150 were HQ staff, drivers, clerks, cooks, etc. Actual combat infantry strength was therefore: 90 battalions at 550 = 49,500 men. Thus, of the 473,200 men "in country" only 10.46% were combat infantry. Of the remainder some 12% were artillery and engineers, 2% aviation and the balance—75%—HQ and logistics personnel.

NVA/VC: On the other side the figures must also be treated with great caution and for almost exactly opposite reasons. First, the strength of an NVA/VC battalion was much less than that for a United States battalion and averaged about 320 men. Of these very few were HQ staff or administrative personnel, and so the effective strength was of the order of 280–290 men. NVA/VC strength in South Vietnam was estimated in 1967 to be:

Units	Approximate Strength	Administrative Personnel	Total Men
152 battalions	320	35	43,320
196 companies	100	10	17,640
70 platoons	30	—	2,100
Total			63,060

The NVA/VC also had many tens of thousands of porters and other "non-combat" personnel.

Communist thrust – the Tet Offensive of 1968

Charles B. MacDonald

"There is . . . a very real question," wrote Secretary of Defense McNamara to President Johnson in the fall of 1967, "whether . . . it will be possible to maintain our efforts in South Vietnam for the time necessary to accomplish our objectives there." McNamara feared that neither a big increase in American combat troops nor increased bombing of North Vietnam would achieve victory or force the North Vietnamese to negotiate. How long, he wondered, would the American people continue to accept high casualties and the immense drain on national resources?

The only solution put forward by McNamara was to stop the bombing and announce that the United States would not increase its forces; a demonstration to world opinion that it was not the United States that stood in the way of peace. The United States should concurrently reduce its ground operations to the minimum necessary to maintain security, thus lowering American casualties, and build up South Vietnamese forces so that they could assume increasing responsibility for the war.

Seeking a new Dien Bien Phu

McNamara's memorandum caused sharp clevages within the Johnson administration. The military in the Pentagon sharply objected. There was some disagreement among Johnson's civilian advisers, but most, including such supposed "hawks" as Secretary of State Dean Rusk and Special Assistant for National Security Affairs Walt W. Rostow, were broadly in favor of McNamara's approach. Although after careful consideration President Johnson took no action, it was clear that the seeds of doubt and compromise were deeply rooted within his administration.

Ironically, those seeds began to germinate even while General Westmoreland and Ambassador Bunker assured Johnson and the US public of genuine progress in the war. It was ironic, too, that at the same time the leaders of North Vietnam concluded that a continuation of their present strategy gave them little hope of winning the war: their losses were mounting drastically with no apparent gains. At Dien Bien Phu, skillful coordination of military and diplomatic strategy had broken the will of the French to continue the Indochina War. Now the Communists needed a new Dien Bien Phu to break the will of the greatest power on earth.

Recalling senior North Vietnamese diplomats from around the world for consultation in July 1967, Ho Chi Minh, Vo Nguyen Giap, and the other leaders in Hanoi made, as General Westmoreland

---

Early in 1968 the Communists launched a major offensive to coincide with the traditional Vietnamese New Year celebrations. Suicide sappers struck in Saigon; Hue was temporarily occupied; news media reported immense damage to South Vietnam. But in spite of intimidation and murder the people of South Vietnam refused to rally to the "liberators" and the Communists were bloodily defeated

---

subsequently divined, "a crucial decision concerning the conduct of the war". They decided to launch an all-out military offensive in South Vietnam. To subordinate commanders and their troops, the Communist leaders described the offensive in high-flown terms. As Viet Cong and North Vietnamese troops attacked throughout South Vietnam — primarily against the cities, which had so far been spared all but shelling and terrorist strikes — the Communist underground network in the south would surface and, with the help of southern sympathizers, take over local government, topple the Thieu-Ky regime, and end the war.

How sincere the North Vietnamese leaders were in the belief that they could induce a general uprising by the South Vietnamese people will probably never be determined. But more important than that belief was the effect the big offensive would have on the Americans. The North Vietnamese could hardly have been unaware of growing disenchantment with the war in the United States. A catastrophic military defeat in an American election year, an immense increase in American and South Vietnamese casualties, a demonstration that the South Vietnamese were incapable of shouldering the burden of the war: all these together might prove the equivalent of a Dien Bien Phu. The US might decide that there was no way to victory except at a cost the American people were unwilling to pay. Then, the North Vietnamese might well answer a call to the negotiating table, knowing that the Americans would make almost any concession in order to end the conflict.

If the big offensive was to succeed, it must achieve total surprise. There were various means to that end. The Viet Cong and North Vietnamese were masters of the slow, deliberate, concealed build-up of

men and supplies. They might renew the battles in the remote regions where they had long operated, both to draw US troops away from the cities that were to be attacked and to demonstrate that there would be no change in the nature of Communist operations. They could follow the usual plan of withholding details of the attacks from subordinate commanders and troops until the last minute. There might be a deliberate, open build-up against some objective— such as Khe Sanh—that would distract attention from the real objectives.

Yet the Americans, with their reconnaissance aircraft and other sophisticated intelligence techniques, might still uncover the Communist master plan—unless some spectacular stroke concealed it. Vietnamese history provided a possible answer: in the year 1789, the forces of the Tay Son Montagnard leaders moved against Chinese troops occupying Hanoi, achieving total surprise and victory by launching an attack at the most unexpected time—during the sacred holiday of Tet, the lunar new year.

Few Western nations have a holiday nearly so important to their people as Tet is to the Vietnamese. It is not only a time of revelry—of fireworks and street festivals—but also of worship, at the family altar, of revered ancestors. For several days the entire countryside is on the move as folk visit their ancestral homes, and all business—even the business of war— comes to a halt. The Communists reasoned that few South Vietnamese—and certainly no Americans—would recall the events of 1789. So how better to achieve total surprise than to launch the major offensive at the beginning of the Tet holiday, for which the VC had already decreed a truce lasting from 27 January to 3 February?

The Communists call for peace talks

A further problem for the Communists was to achieve the final build-up without provoking American bombing; ideally, air attacks must cease. So, at a diplomatic reception in Hanoi at the end of 1967, and at diplomatic posts elsewhere, North Vietnamese officials tactfully hinted that if US bombing ceased, North Vietnam "*would* hold talks". That was a change from the usual "*might* hold talks"—and one that could surely not be ignored by Washington.

When Communist Romania, acting as a go-between, sent a representative to Hanoi in mid-January 1968, the US offered to demonstrate its good faith by halting the bombing in the vicinity of Hanoi. That was not the total halt the North Vietnamese wanted, but added to the halt accompanying the usual cease-fire, it would help.

1

1. North Vietnamese rockets burst in Khe Sanh combat base, February 1968: a heavy bombardment of this strongpoint began on 21 January to divert US attention from the imminent nation-wide offensive. 2. Viet Cong in Saigon during Tet; most guerrillas were cleared from the city within six days. 3. The North Vietnamese decision to launch an all-out attack lay mainly with General Vo Nguyen Giap (extreme left) and President Ho Chi Minh (third from right). 4. The first day of Tet—and South Vietnamese Rangers are on the alert in Saigon.

2

4

3

One more strategem was required: the North Vietnamese people should enjoy their own Tet festivities before the offensive precipitated renewed bombing. And that could be achieved simply by decreeing a change in the dates of the holiday. Instead of beginning the lunar new year celebrations in North Vietnam on the "official" date of 30 January, the Hanoi government decreed that it begin one day early. Since celebrations always began on the *eve* of Tet, which would now be 28 January, the North Vietnamese could celebrate for three days before their soldiers attacked in South Vietnam—after the start of the *true* Tet—before daylight on 31 January.

Premature strikes warn of offensive

By the end of 1967, one part of the ruse—the border battles at Song Be, Loc Ninh, and Dak To—had been staged. By mid-January 1968, guns and troops were in position for another key part of the deception: the diversion at Khe Sanh. That began on 21 January, with a heavy bombardment of the American base by mortars, rockets, and artillery, that continued in varying degrees of intensity for some 11 weeks.

In South Vietnam, as the Tet period approached, some of the concern that had gradually built up among General Westmoreland and his commanders spread to a number of South Vietnamese. Although President Thieu could not bring himself to cancel the furloughs granted to his troops for Tet, he agreed, under pressure from Westmoreland, to insure that at least 50 percent of the South Vietnamese troops—now with a total strength of some 732,000—would be on duty. He also agreed to the last-minute cancellation of the cease-fire in the northern provinces and its limitation elsewhere to 24 hours. But Thieu did not forgo his own Tet celebration; he left Saigon to spend the holiday with his wife's relatives in the Mekong Delta town of My Tho.

However, there were some ARVN general officers so concerned about what might happen over Tet that they took it upon themselves to deny leave to their troops. This was the case with two units operating in the environs of Saigon, another in the Central Highlands, and another in the city of Hue, where a divisional commander in the vicinity had his headquarters within the old part of the city, encircled by a thick wall and called the Citadel. He alerted his troops outside the city and put his HQ staff on full alert.

For all Hanoi's careful preparations, a mistake was made in the timing of the Tet offensive. Before daylight on 30 January, as revelers crowded the city streets setting off firecrackers, the Communists attacked eight towns and cities in the Central Highlands and in the central coastal provinces. A ground attack in battalion strength hit the port of Nha Trang; another struck Hoi An, a district capital near the coast. Mortar and rocket fire preceded a ground attack on the Highlands town of Ban Me Thuot. A sapper attack was launched against the HQ of the ARVN's I Corps in Da Nang. Two battalions participated in a ground attack at Qui Nhon,

where the garrison was on full alert following the capture of the propaganda tapes described earlier. Attacks were also made on Pleiku and on a remote district capital.

Why those Communist forces struck 24 hours in advance of the main offensive is not known. Because all the premature attacks occurred within the area of jurisdiction of a single North Vietnamese HQ, it is possible that some communications failure—perhaps concerning the change in celebration dates in North Vietnam—was the cause.

The warning given to the Americans and South Vietnamese by these premature attacks was brief but valuable. "This", remarked Major General Phillip B. Davidson, Westmoreland's chief of intelligence, "is going to happen in the rest of the country tonight or tomorrow morning." After daylight on 30 January, President Thieu canceled the cease-fire throughout the country and alerted all South Vietnamese military units—a step also taken by Westmoreland for American units—but it was too late to call back those South Vietnamese soldiers already on leave. It was too late, also, to comb out the Communist soldiers in civilian dress who had for days been infiltrating towns and cities amid the crowds of holiday travelers.

Controversy over the embassy attack

One of the first attacks and one of the smallest, involving only 15 Viet Cong "suicide" sappers, was destined to have an importance well out of proportion to its size. It struck the American Embassy in Saigon, only a few blocks from the South Vietnamese Presidential Palace and the downtown hotels where American reporters and television cameramen were quartered. The embassy was a new building of reinforced construction surrounded by a sturdy wall—perhaps the only embassy in the world with a helicopter pad on the roof.

Before daylight on 31 January, sappers in civilian clothing blew a hole in the wall. Two military police guards killed the first two VC to enter the grounds of the embassy but were themselves killed in the exchange of gunfire. Two more military policemen in a jeep patrol responding to a call for help also died, as did a US Marine who climbed atop a nearby building to fire into the compound. Another military policeman closed the heavy doors of the chancery so that no Viet Cong were able to enter the building. Under fire from a helicopter and, soon after daylight, from a platoon of American airborne troops heli-lifted to the chancery roof, all the VC were killed within about six hours.

The firing quickly drew the American media reporters to the scene; confused by gunfire and darkness, they concluded that the VC had penetrated the chancery. The erroneous report went swiftly over the wires to make glaring headlines in American newspapers. Even after General Westmoreland toured the building and informed the newsmen that no VC had entered the chancery, the reporters continued to quote "other sources" denying Westmoreland's assertion. The civilian correspondents were convinced the worst had

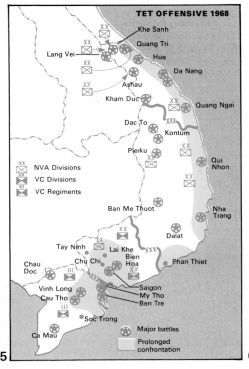

TET OFFENSIVE 1968

Khe Sanh
Quang Tri
Lang Vei
Hue
Da Nang
Ashau
Kham Duc
Quang Ngai
Dac To
Kontum
Pleiku
Qui
Nhon
NVA Divisions
VC Divisions
VC Regiments
Ban Me Thuot
Nha
Trang
Dalat
Tay Ninh
Lai Khe
Bien
Hoa
Chau
Doc
Chu Chi
Phan Thiet
Vinh Long
Saigon
Cau Tho
My Tho
Ben Tre
Soc Trong
Major battles
Ca Mau
Prolonged
confrontation

5

6

1. General Westmoreland in the Saigon embassy after the Viet Cong attack of 31 January 1968. **2.** US Marines duel with North Vietnamese snipers across the Perfume River, Hue, 22 February. **3.** A

USMC observation plane makes a low-level pass over Hue, 23 February.
4. Flares and tracers streak the sky at Tan Son Nhut Air Base as US aircraft strafe attacking Viet Cong, 1 February.

5. Map: Communist deployment on the eve of Tet; major battles of the Tet offensive. **6.** US troops make a house to house search for Viet Cong snipers at Bien Hoa, 2 February.

THE TET OFFENSIVE, 1968

Objective
A determined assault by the North Vietnamese Army and Viet Cong on major urban centers and military installations in South Vietnam, timed to begin during the truce scheduled for the Lunar New Year (Tet) holiday, 29–31 January. The Communists intended to destroy South Vietnam's military potential and rally the civilian population to the National Liberation Front.

Strength
NVA/VC: 80,000+ men

Targets
36 out of 44 provincial capitals
5 out of 6 autonomous cities
23 airfields/bases
numerous district capitals and hamlets
Major assaults on: Saigon, Hue, Quang Tri City, Da Nang, Nha Trang, Qui Nhon, Kontum City, Ban Me Thuot, My Tho, Can Tho, Ben Tre
The VC/NVA achieved temporary control of 10 provincial capitals.

Comparative US artillery expenditure in III Corps Tactical Zone
Daily average, pre-Tet

105mm	2,376 rounds
155mm	925 rounds
8 inch	200 rounds
4.2 inch	1,100 rounds
Total	4,601 rounds

Daily average during Tet

105mm	5,616 rounds
155mm	1,459 rounds
8 inch	235 rounds
4.2 inch	1,570 rounds
Total	8,880 rounds

Three Tet Actions
Hue, 31 January–25 February
NVA/VC strength: 6th NVA Regiment (3 battalions), 4th NVA Regiment (1 battalion), 6 VC battalions,
US/ARVN strength: 4 US Army battalions, 3 USMC battalions, 11 ARVN battalions

US artillery expenditure: 105–203mm field artillery: 52,000 rounds, 5in–8in naval guns: 7,670 rounds, air-delivered ordnance: 600 short tons

US losses: 119 killed, 961 wounded
ARVN losses: 363 killed, 1,242 wounded
NVA/VC losses: c.5,000 killed in Hue City, c.3,000 killed in surrounding area
Civilian losses: 5,800 killed or missing (2,800+ graves found), c.116,000 homeless

Bien Hoa (combat bases)
NVA/VC strength: 2 infantry battalions 1 reinforced infantry company

NVA/VC losses (at base): 139 killed, 25 prisoners; *(in area)* 1,164 killed, 98 prisoners
US losses: 4 USAF personnel killed, 26 USAF personnel wounded, 2 USAF aircraft destroyed, 20 USAF aircraft damaged

Tan Son Nhut (base–Saigon area)
NVA/VC strength: 4 infantry battalions, 1 sapper battalion

NVA/VC losses: 962 killed, 9 prisoners
US losses: 19 US Army personnel killed, 4 USAF personnel killed, 75 US Army personnel wounded, 11 USAF personnel wounded, 13 aircraft damaged
ARVN losses: 32 killed, 79 wounded

Results
The Communist offensive failed, largely because the attacks on primary objectives were badly coordinated, communications were poor, and the South Vietnamese people generally failed to rally to the invaders. The Communists were driven away from most of their objectives within 2 to 3 days, and their overall losses exceeded those of US forces in the entire Korean War. The Tet Offensive showed that the ARVN's effectiveness had greatly increased and, in its effect on US public opinion, accelerated the "Vietnamization" of the war. President Johnson, whose decision not to seek reelection was seen (wrongly) as a result of the Tet Offensive, ordered a bombing halt above the 19th parallel on 31 March, hoping to further peace negotiations: thus, the Communists gained a moral success to compensate for their material losses.

Overall Losses

US/Free World MAF: killed	1,536
wounded	7,764
missing	11
ARVN: killed	2,788
wounded	8,299
missing	587
NVA/VC: killed	c.45,000
prisoners	6,991
crew-served weapons	c.1,300
individual weapons	7,000+
Civilian: killed	14,000
wounded	24,000
homeless	c.630,000

happened and were determined that Westmoreland should not deny them a great news "break".

From a strictly military viewpoint, it mattered little whether or not the VC sappers had entered the chancery; from a psychological angle, it was of profound importance. To many newsmen, and thus to many people in the United States, the attack seemed to confirm that Westmoreland and President Johnson had been disseminating falsehoods. If the United States could not protect its own embassy, how could the war have reached a point "when the end begins to come into view"? The facts that no solid line of manned trenches encircled any South Vietnamese city—hardly a viable measure—and that even a weakened enemy could launch small, suicidal attacks on almost any installation, were disregarded in sensational press and television reportage. A long-smoldering antagonism between newsmen and officials had flared up.

Elsewhere in Saigon, there were five similar attacks by small sapper groups—including one by VC in ARVN uniforms against the Presidential Palace, which was driven off. Forces of battalion size occupied a cemetery and a race-track and had to be driven out by South Vietnamese troops. More serious attacks developed at Tan Son Nhut airport and at the ARVN Joint General Staff HQ on the outskirts of the capital, but these too were eventually suppressed. President Thieu decreed a state of martial law on 31 January, but by 5 February Saigon was free of all but small, isolated enemy units.

As information came in from other parts of South Vietnam, it became clear that the Communists had launched a major country-wide offensive involving some 84,000 men, mainly Viet Cong, except in the northern provinces where North Vietnamese regulars predominated. The Communists made ground attacks or mortar and rocket strikes on 36 of the country's 44 provincial capitals, five of six autonomous cities, 64 of 242 district capitals, and 50 hamlets. In 13 towns and cities they penetrated in some strength, but were largely driven out in two or three days. Fighting was protracted only in Saigon and Hue. Except for the ARVN's 3d Division HQ inside the Citadel and a compound housing US Army advisers, Viet Cong and North Vietnamese regulars occupied all Hue. The Allies were reluctant, at first, to employ artillery fire and air strikes likely to damage historic buildings, and an ARVN division assisted by three US Marine Corps battalions required 25 days to clear Hue. At Khe Sanh, the North Vietnamese launched no ground attack, but shelling continued.

A defeat for the Communist forces

In the first fortnight of attacks, the Communists lost some 32,000 killed and 5,800 captured, close on half the troops actively committed, against about 2,800 ARVN and some 1,000 US troops killed. Only at Hue did the attackers hold any objective for an appreciable length of time; this may explain why the North Vietnamese failed to commit troops held in reserve to exploit success. Although under-strength at many places because of the holiday furloughs, the South Vietnamese militia and regulars—who bore the brunt of the fighting—performed efficiently and courageously. Nowhere did anything remotely resembling an uprising of the people against the Saigon government occur. To American officials, it all added up to a severe defeat for the Communists.

But this was not the impression given by the copy and television film footage of American newsmen. As one of their number, Peter Braestrup, then reporting for the *Washington Post*, was to note in a carefully-documented study nine years later: "Rarely has contemporary crisis-journalism turned out, in retrospect, to have veered so widely from reality."

Misinformation in the Western media

Aside from the pressure of deadlines, which almost inevitably tends to journalistic error, there was another reason. Having forgotten or disregarded the few official warnings that a major enemy strike might be in preparation, newsmen instead recalled the optimistic assessments of the President's fall campaign. Had not Westmoreland even predicted American withdrawals beginning in 1969? This seemed rank folly to newsmen who saw South Vietnam a shambles under the enemy blows—although, as it turned out, withdrawals *did* begin in 1969. Few reporters and television commentators had had combat experience and few had studied military history. To them, the Tet offensive was an incredible shock, an unmitigated disaster, a clear American and South Vietnamese defeat. None of them thought to draw parallels with other wars in which a losing side had staged a grand surprise assault—as Germany had in 1918 and in late 1944. Confirmed in their long-held skepticism, they were determined to expose the subterfuge and chicanery they saw behind the Johnson administration's claims of progress. There was no conspiracy among them, merely a group reaction based on shared biases and imperceptions; but the effect was much the same.

Damage in the cities, light by the standards of World Wars I and II or Korea, was to most newsmen appalling. Television cameras focusing on one badly damaged block could give the impression of an entire city in ruins. One newsman quoted an unidentified US Army major in the town of Ben Tre, of which some 25 percent was severely damaged, as saying that "it became necessary to destroy the town to save it". That became a kind of theme—and the culprits who wrought such devastation were never the Communists, who had brought the war into the cities, but the Americans and South Vietnamese with their artillery and airpower. The civilian casualties (some 7,000) and refugees (close to 700,000) generated by the fighting made the headlines—not the 5,000 or more civilians systematically tortured and executed by the Communists in Hue and elsewhere. More sympathy for the plight of starving, homeless civilians was shown by the government of the Republic of China (Taiwan), which sent immediate material aid in addition to its small military

1. The US Headquarters Area Command Reaction Force guards US Bachelor Officers Quarters, Saigon—a guerrilla target on 31 January 1968. **2.** US Marines investigating a guerrilla-occupied building set up a CS tear gas pod launcher. **3.** US Marines in Hue haul 3.5in rocket rounds to the University roof; to minimize civilian casualties and damage, fire support for clearing operations was largely limited to direct fire weapons such as rocket launchers, recoilless rifles, and tank guns. **4.** In a bunker in the canal district of Hue, US Marines watch for North Vietnamese snipers. **5.** Exodus from a strategic hamlet "liberated" by the Viet Cong during the Tet offensive. **6.** Map: the battle for Hue, 31 January–2 March 1968. **7.** An airstrike on retreating North Vietnamese troops, February 1968.

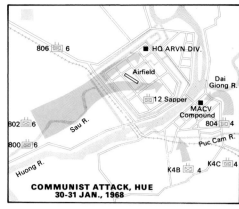

COMMUNIST ATTACK, HUE
30-31 JAN., 1968

6

7

5

2

4

commitment (a maximum of 31 advisers), as did the governments of two nations uncommitted to the war, Canada and Norway.

Reporters claimed that the imperial palace in Hue was totally destroyed: damage was, in fact, superficial. Saigon, most of which suffered only light damage, was shown to American television audiences as a smoldering ruin. A world-wide furore was created by the publication of photographs taken by Eddie Adams of Associated Press, showing a civilian-clothed Viet Cong prisoner being executed —with a pistol, at point-blank range—by Brigadier Nguyen Ngoc Loan, Chief of the Saigon Police Force.

Negative reporting but positive response

At Khe Sanh, newsmen created a "Dien Bien Phu syndrome", and continually predicted a terrible fate for the garrison of US Marines and South Vietnamese Rangers, indicting the American command for choosing to stand and fight there. In fact, 6,000 US and South Vietnamese troops at Khe Sanh—only one-sixtieth of Westmoreland's total combat troops—were holding at bay 20,000 North Vietnamese. But newsmen persistently stated that the enemy had succeeded in tying down sizable American forces, failing to remark that those 20,000 North Vietnamese might have been aiding the Commu-

nist cause more profitably in the cities.

Newsmen countered official claims of a Communist defeat by saying that even if it were true (which they refused to accept, as they did the official account of enemy losses), the Communists had achieved a psychological victory. Unable to speak the language of the South Vietnamese people, reporters nevertheless buttressed their case by "psychoanalyzing" the people and uncovering their alleged disenchantment with a government unable to protect them. And although they were not in a position to assess what effect the Tet offensive had had on the pacification program in the countryside, newsmen pronounced that pacification was "torn to shreds", "beyond retrieval", or with remarkable redundancy, "killed dead".

Even so, as public opinion polls subsequently revealed, such negative reporting, far from turning the bulk of the American people against the war, rallied them to President Johnson's support. Only when the President failed to take strong retaliatory action against the Communists did large numbers of the American people turn against him.

Bias in the media was primarily effective on the Congress and on middle-level, civilian bureaucrats and presidential advisers in Washington. Congressional "hawks" fell silent, while "doves" coo-ed ever more loudly. Many civilian officials reacted like the presidential special assistant who noted that whenever he read the official cables from Saigon, he found them "almost hallucinatory" in view of what he had seen on television the night before. There the story, told in gruesome pictures and doleful words, was presented so convincingly that he believed the reporters rather than the officials.

US reaction to the Tet Offensive

Not even military men were immune. The Chairman of the Joint Chiefs of Staff, General Wheeler, after a visit to Saigon (where his quarters were subjected to enemy shelling) was markedly concerned. And although Westmoreland himself had been optimistic about the outcome of the Tet offensive, he estimated that the enemy was capable of other strikes. There were serious headaches for Wheeler and his Pentagon colleagues elsewhere: the North Koreans had recently seized the US communications ship *Pueblo*; trouble in Berlin or the Middle East might flare up again at any time. The US Army's strategic reserve had fallen to one division—and the war in Vietnam had had marked ill-effects on the morale of American forces everywhere.

General Wheeler, anxious both to rebuild the strategic reserve and to be prepared for further enemy moves in South Vietnam, urged Westmoreland to press for sizable American reinforcements. Eager to take advantage of the situation, Westmoreland saw this as an opportunity to acquire forces that might be used, should the President permit, for invading Laos and Cambodia, and launching an amphibious attack to trap North Vietnamese forces within the DMZ. Westmoreland felt, moreover, that calling up the reserves would impress on the North Vietnamese that the United States would settle for nothing short of victory.

President Johnson was in two minds as to the request for a further 206,000 troops —half for South Vietnam, half for the strategic reserve. He called for two intensive studies of what the reinforcements might achieve: one by a committee chaired by the new Secretary of Defense, Clark M. Clifford; one by a panel of senior ex-military men, including prominent World War II commanders. Perhaps unduly impressed by what they had read in the newspapers and seen on television, both groups recommended against reinforcement.

The President accepted that advice; but before any public announcement, the *New York Times* published the fact that the administration was considering 206,000 more troops "for Vietnam". Press and television reacted in the critical style by then common to almost anything connected with the war. The media attributed the President's relatively poor showing in a Democratic presidential primary in New Hampshire a few days later to an "anti-war" protest by the voters. In fact, as time would show, the vote was more a protest against Johnson's failure to take a firmer stand following the Tet offensive.

Events in South Vietnam over the next few months proved that the enemy had, as Westmoreland claimed, been badly hurt in the Tet offensive. The Communists attempted two follow-up strikes—one in May and another in August—but these were little more than short-lived attacks by rocket and mortar. The pacification program, prematurely buried by the press, picked up momentum. Government control was swiftly restored to that part of the countryside relinquished during the offensive and was even considerably expanded. Far from being demoralized, the ARVN displayed heightened ability and morale: recruiting flourished, and the Americans stepped up the program to provide new and better weapons and equipment for both regulars and militia. As for the people, for the first time they appeared to rally in genuine support of the Saigon government, which was soon able to arm thousands of them to form a nationwide self-defense force. Surely, no government that feared its people would provide them with weapons that might be turned against it?

President Johnson had now decided that after four and a half years in South Vietnam, General Westmoreland should be promoted to fill the position of US Army Chief of Staff, and that his deputy in Saigon, General Creighton W. Abrams, should be the new American field commander. Although Johnson had made that decision in mid-January, before the Tet offensive, its delayed announcement enabled Westmoreland's critics to maintain that the President had become disenchanted with the General because of the Tet offensive and had "kicked him upstairs".

President Johnson "hounded out of office"

The news media's negative handling of the Tet offensive caused the President to yield to increased pressure from anti-war critics, and from civilian officials in his administration, and proclaim another bombing halt—with yet another invitation to the North Vietnamese to negotiate. To add weight to his initiative, Johnson also announced that he would not be a candidate for the presidency in the fall of 1968. Although he had informed Westmoreland of that decision, based largely on failing health and the wishes of his family, late in 1967, the anti-war lobby quickly claimed that they had hounded him out of office. (Perhaps there was some truth in this claim. Since his death in January 1973 at the age of 64—within one week of the agreement "ending" the war—those who were close to Johnson have spoken of his "heart-broken" reaction to the anti-war demonstrators' mindless chant: *"Hey, Hey, L.B.J.—How many kids did you kill today?"* A brave, sincere man, Lyndon Johnson deserved better of his countrymen.)

To President Johnson's surprise, the North Vietnamese agreed to talk. Over the next four years they would agree to little more than the shape of the conference table in Paris. However, in accepting Johnson's offer, they effectively chained the United States to the negotiating table until they had launched a conventional invasion of South Vietnam, and until the American people had become so war-weary that a new president would make concessions that, while taking the United States out of the war, assured eventual North Vietnamese victory. However much a Communist defeat, the Tet offensive of 1968 prepared the way for their eventual victory.

5

1. Communist losses during Tet were reflected in their weak follow-up strikes—although these Tan Son Nhut Defense Force and ARVN Airborne personnel are temporarily pinned down by sniper fire in the French National Cemetery during the attack on the air base in May 1968. 2. South Vietnamese Marines remove weapons and ammunition from a Viet Cong killed in Saigon in May 1968. 3. Following Tet, the North Vietnamese agreed to peace discussions in Paris; the US Delegation in May 1968 is headed by W. Averell Harriman (third from left), with Cyrus R. Vance and Philip C. Habib to his left.
4. ARVN Medics carry a casualty from the French National Cemetery, Tan Son Nhut.
5. Summary justice that shocked world opinion: Police Chief Nguyen Ngoc Loan executes a Viet Cong officer captured in Saigon during the Tet offensive.
6. This boy's home in Saigon was destroyed by 122mm rockets during the Viet Cong attack on the South Vietnamese capital in May 1968.

6

Seventy-seven days: the siege of Khe Sanh

Bernard C. Nalty

The Khe Sanh combat base, located in northwestern South Vietnam some six miles (10km) from the border with Laos and about 14 miles (23km) south of the DMZ, posed a threat to the Ho Chi Minh Trail linking North Vietnamese supply depots with Communist forces deployed in South Vietnam. As early as 1962, when there were already more than 10,000 US advisers in Vietnam, a handful of US Army Special Forces, the "Green Berets", had set up a camp at Khe Sanh from which patrols probed the maze of roads and trails nearby. The enemy put up with these activities for more than four years, before shelling the camp in January 1966.

Communist pressure on Khe Sanh increased during that year, and in January 1967 the US Marines arrived: Colonel John Lanigan's 3d Marines took over from the Green Berets, who moved their camp westward to the Montagnard village of Lang Vei. A Seabee battalion built a 1,500-foot (460m) runway of pierced steel planking. In mid-May, after Lanigan's men had cleared the enemy from the nearby hills, Colonel John Padley's 26th Marines replaced them.

Paradropping supplies to the Khe Sanh base

Khe Sanh's new garrison immediately began improving the defenses, while Air Force C-130 Hercules transports flew in supplies. The pounding from the transport planes—each weighing a maximum 135,000 lbs (61,240kg)—caused the rain-soaked clay beneath the planking to shift; the airstrip had to be closed to the C-130s until the Seabees could make repairs. The smaller de Havilland C-7A Caribou transports that replaced the C-130s could not handle the heavy equipment and bulky materials needed for the job. The Hercules transports para-dropped some items to the Seabees, but they could not drop the aluminum matting needed to replace the pierced steel runway surface.

"Parachute extraction" was the only way to deliver the matting. Riggers lashed the strips of aluminum to metal pallets and loaded them into the transports. The hatch at the rear of the cargo compartment was opened as the C-130 flew low over the outpost. At a signal from the pilot, the crew released the bonds holding the pallet and a parachute, filled by the force of the plane's slipstream, snatched out the load, which fell a few feet to the ground.

But although the Seabees extended the rebuilt runway to 3,900 feet (1,190m), Khe Sanh was difficult to defend. A chain of hills overlooked the plateau from the north and northwest. Drinking water came from a river that passed through enemy-controlled territory. During the early months of the year, fog shrouded the base on most

For 77 days, some 5,000 Americans and South Vietnamese at Khe Sanh were besieged by more than 15,000 Communists. The conflict embraced sophisticated electronics, a massive air-lift of materiel, tactical air support on a scale that made the Khe Sanh area the most-bombed target in military history—and savage hand-to-hand combat with knives. But was this immense combined effort superfluous?

mornings, complicating air operations and limiting visibility from defensive positions.

In December 1967, General Westmoreland's staff detected two North Vietnamese divisions, each with about 10,000 men, massing around Khe Sanh. Patrols from the base clashed with North Vietnamese regulars dug in among the hills. On 20 January 1968, an enemy officer who surrendered to a group of Marines told of an impending offensive designed to overwhelm Khe Sanh and the other American strongpoints along Route 9, the highway leading from the coast at Dong Ha into Laos.

In Washington, President Johnson traced each development on a terrain model set up in the White House basement. He sought reassurance from his military leaders, who told him that Khe Sanh could and should be defended. General Westmoreland believed that the Communists intended to make Khe Sanh "an American Dien Bien Phu"—but he was confident the attempt would end in disaster for the enemy.

The battle began early on 21 January 1968, with an unsuccessful assault on a Marine outpost across the river from the base. As this action drew to a close, North Vietnamese artillery and mortars began hammering the plateau, blasting holes in the aluminum runway, setting fire to the main ammunition dump with the loss of some 1,500 short tons (1,340 tons; 1,360 tonnes) of munitions, destroying a helicopter, killing 18 US troops and wounding 40. The 26th Marines, some 3,500 strong, retired within their prepared defenses; the civilian population was air-lifted to Da Nang.

The Seabees immediately went to work, but could not repair enough of the runway for C-130s to land. As a result, Brigadier General Burl McLaughlin, USAF, responsible for aerial supply, ordered smaller Fairchild C-123 Providers to fly in ammunition to the Marines. Although the C-123K had undergone modernization, with a pod-mounted jet engine under each wing providing STOL capability, the capacity of this veteran twin-engine transport was no more than 16,000 lbs (7,260kg), less than half the payload of the Hercules.

The last explosions had scarcely died away when McLaughlin began diverting C-123s to Da Nang to take on ammunition for Khe Sanh. The first Providers unloaded 8,000 lbs (3,630kg) of ammunition at the combat base during the afternoon of 22 January. The previous day's shelling had knocked out the landing lights, so flares illuminated the runway during darkness. By the following evening, the C-123s had landed 130 short tons (116 tons; 118 tonnes) of ammunition, enough for the Marines to weather the initial crisis.

Lieutenant General Robert E. Cushman, Jr., commanding III MAF, authorized Major General Rathvon C. Tompkins, commanding 3d Marine Division, to reinforce Khe Sanh with the 1st Battalion, 9th Marines. Colonel David Lownds, Padley's successor at Khe Sanh, now commanded one artillery and four infantry battalions. The 37th ARVN Ranger Battalion increased his garrison to some 6,000 men by 26 January. Because his forces were spread thin, Cushman decided against an immediate attack to re-open Route 9. For the time being, the base would have to be supplied by and partly defended from the air.

Electronic sensors surround the base

A surprise awaited the estimated 18,000 North Vietnamese regulars who now surrounded Khe Sanh. (The actual number of North Vietnamese troops committed to the siege of Khe Sanh at any one time is a matter for dispute between various authorities. General Westmoreland often spoke of the Communist strength as "two divisions", perhaps some 15,000 men. Other sources put the number as high as 50,000, for short periods, or as low as "a few thousand" second-rate troops for whom General Giap had no other use at the time.) Before the siege began, Air Force and Navy aircraft had planted electronic sensors along roads in southern Laos. These devices picked up either sound or seismic vibration and transmitted a signal to a surveillance centre at Nakhon Phanom, Thailand (more fully described in the following chapter) where analysts determined the route and speed of Communist supply convoys. Air Force Brigadier General William McBride, in com-

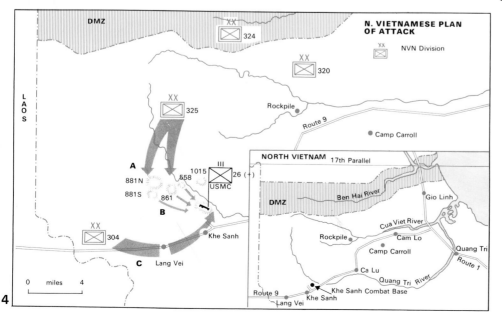

N. VIETNAMESE PLAN OF ATTACK

NVN Division

DMZ

LAOS

324

320

325

Rockpile

Route 9

Camp Carroll

A

881N

881S

558

861

1015

III

26 (+)

USMC

B

304

Khe Sanh

Lang Vei

C

0   miles   4

NORTH VIETNAM 17th Parallel

DMZ

Ben Hai River

Gio Linh

Cua Viet River

Rockpile

Cam Lo

Camp Carroll

Ca Lu

Quang Tri River

Route 9

Khe Sanh

Lang Vei

Khe Sanh Combat Base

Quang Tri

Route 1

1. Smoke rises from a fuel dump at Khe Sanh combat base, northern Quang Tri province, after a Communist mortar barrage in March 1968. **2.** The long-threatened North Vietnamese offensive against Khe Sanh combat base began with an unsuccessful assault on a US Marine outpost on 21 January 1968; this Marine was wounded in the first attack. **3.** Communist artillery and mortar teams like the one seen here hammered Khe Sanh in pre-assault bombardments. **4.** Map: the North Vietnamese plan of attack at Khe Sanh, January 1968—(A) North Vietnam-ese 325 Division takes the hills overlooking Khe Sanh combat base; (B) Hills 881S and 861 are used as fire bases; diversionary attacks are made on the northern perimeter; (C) 304 Division takes Lang Vei and Khe Sanh village and then rolls up the combat base from the southeast.

mand of sensor operations, had been preparing to test the devices against infiltrating troops when the fight began at Khe Sanh.

McBride and his director of intelligence, Colonel William Walker, USAF, flew to Dong Ha to confer with Major General Tompkins. Walker told the Marine general that he could lay a field of 250 sensors around Khe Sanh in a week or ten days: Tompkins could give him only four days.

Planting the sensors proved difficult. Intelligence analysts, working mainly from aerial photographs, had to determine which routes most needed covering. Then the electronic devices had to be placed with accuracy enough to enable the specialists at the surveillance center to track the hostile columns. Infantry patrols aided by maps and current aerial photos could guarantee accurate placing—but they could not penetrate far enough into enemy territory to cover the most likely routes. Helicopters provided a solution, hovering over the precise spot while a crewman tossed out the appropriate sensor. Acoustic sensors were dropped into trees or brush, where they hung suspended and picked up the sounds of motors or human voices. Seismic sensors, designed to react to earth vibrations, had spiked noses which dug into the ground.

Walker met his deadline, and the sensors were functioning in time to warn the Marines of enemy activity on the approaches to one of the hills overlooking Khe Sanh. At the base fire support coordination center, Captain Mirza Baig collated sensor information with other intelligence and concluded that the North Vietnamese would storm the Marine outpost on Hill 881 South before first light on 5 February. Massed Marine and Army artillery began pounding the slopes of this hill at 0320 hours, and the Communist attack never materialized.

Hand-to-hand combat on Hill 861A

Unfortunately, Marines manning the outpost on Hill 861A received no warning of an almost simultaneous thrust against them. At one point, the enemy advancing upon Hill 881 South had passed through an area not covered by sensors, and it was there that the attackers divided—one force to storm Hill 861A, while the other marched into the waiting US barrage, which was supported by air strikes.

The attack took the defenders of Hill 861A by surprise, forcing them back to a new position. Lieutenant Donald Shanley rallied his men, however, and launched a counter-attack. For about 30 minutes, the Marines fought back with grenades, automatic rifles, knives, and fists. So close was the fighting that a Marine and a North Vietnamese struggling for a knife were caught in the same burst of gunfire. The Marine, wearing an armored vest, survived; the Communist soldier died instantly. Shortly after dawn the assault force fell back, regrouped, and advanced into a wall of fire from mortars and artillery. The Marines remained in control of Hill 861A.

Meanwhile, the Tet offensive had erupted throughout South Vietnam. But the enemy, instead of slackening pressure

in the Khe Sanh area, attacked the Lang Vei Special Forces camp. Before first light on 7 February, about 10 Soviet-built PT-76 light amphibious tanks spearheaded an assault on the perimeter held by 24 Green Berets and around 900 Montagnard irregulars and Laotian troops (the latter refugees from a Communist attack some days earlier). The 14-ton vehicles rolled over the defenders' bunkers. The Special Forces fought back with grenades, 106mm M40AI recoilless rifles (Bats), and rocket launchers, knocking out at least three tanks and damaging others. Forward air controllers directed strikes in support of the Lang Vei defenders, despite darkness, cloud and smoke, and the danger of mid-air collisions with artillery shells fired from Khe Sanh. One controller used rockets to mark a target for an Air Force Martin B-57 Canberra bomber whose bomb-load triggered 15 secondary explosions and possibly damaged three more tanks.

The Communists take the Lang Vei camp

Captain Frank C. Willoughby, the Army officer in command at Lang Vei, radioed Khe Sanh for help. Although a rescue force was ready to move, Generals Tompkins and Cushman agreed that it should not be dispatched: to advance in darkness invited almost certain ambush, and the enemy now held all the helicopter night-landing zones near Lang Vei. Two Green Berets rallied some of the surviving irregulars and attempted to fight their way to Khe Sanh, failing in spite of support from Navy A-I Skyraiders. Taking advantage of the confusion caused by subsequent air strikes, Captain Willoughby, 13 of his Green Berets, and some 60 Montagnards managed to reach Khe Sanh.

From Lang Vei, the action shifted back to Khe Sanh. Before dawn on 8 February, the North Vietnamese attacked the position held by the 1st Battalion, 9th Marines, just west of the combat base. While mortar and artillery fire pinned down the Marines at the main battalion position, the enemy stormed a company outpost, blasting holes in the barbed-wire barrier or crossing it over heavy mats carried into the assault. Sappers blasted Marine bunkers with satchel-charges and grenades. The attackers overran some 50 percent of their objective. A remarkable escape was that of Lance Corporal Robert Wiley, temporarily paralyzed by the explosion of a satchel charge, conscious while enemy soldiers searched him and took the photographs and documents he carried, and left for dead. He was one of those rescued by a relief force led by Captain Henry Radcliffe, advancing behind air strikes and fire from M48 Patton tanks. The North Vietnamese retired, leaving around 150 dead.

In spite of air attacks (it was estimated that 60,000 short tons (53,600 tons; 54,500 tonnes) of napalm alone were dropped in the Khe Sanh area in the four-week period ending in mid-February) and shelling, the Communists were able to move anti-aircraft guns into position to fire at US transport planes. On 11 February, one scored a hit on a Marine KC-130 Hercules carrying helicopter fuel. Trailing a plume of leaking fuel, the plane touched down safely, only to burst into flame and swerve

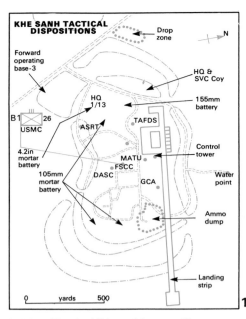

1. Map: Tactical Dispositions at Khe Sanh combat base. Key: ASRT = Air Support Radar Team; DASC = Direct Air Support Center; FSCC = Fire Support Coordination Center; GCA = Ground Controlled Approach; MATU = Marine Air Traffic Control Unit; TAFDS = Tactical Airfield Fuel Dispensing System; B/1/26 = Company B, 1st Battalion, 26th Regiment; USMC = United States Marine Corps. 2. "Operation Pegasus"—the relief of Khe Sanh by some 30,000 US and ARVN troops— began on 1 April 1968; here, a CH-47 Chinook helicopter is unloaded by men of the US 1st Cavalry Division (Airmobile) at Khe Sanh on 6 April, when the first elements of "Pegasus" were airlifted into the base. 3. US Marines await attack in sand bag bunkers on the Khe Sanh perimeter during the siege. 4. In spite of Communist anti-aircraft batteries like that seen here, air supply delivered more than 12,000 tons of cargo to Khe Sanh during the 77-day siege: six fixed-wing aircraft and 17 helicopters were lost. 5. Khe Sanh's defenses included three batteries of 105mm howitzers like those seen in action here, in April 1968.

2

3

5

KHE SANH, 21 January–14 April 1968

Objective

As a part of the Tet Offensive effort, elements of two North Vietnamese Army divisions attempted to reduce the US Marine Corps outposts on the hills dominating Khe Sanh and take the base itself. Khe Sanh was a combat base for units operating in the DMZ and against Communist supply routes.

Strengths

Garrison: 9th Marine Regiment (1bn)
26th Marine Regiment (3 bns)
ARVN 37th Ranger Battalion
Total: c.6,000 men
3 batteries 105mm howitzers
1 battery 155mm howitzers
1 battery 4.2in mortars
7 batteries (18 guns) 175mm guns
Total: 46 artillery pieces
10×106mm recoilless rifles
6×90mm tank guns
2×M-42 (duel 40mm)
2×M-55 (quad .50 cal)
US artillery fired 158,981 rounds during siege

NVA: 304 Division
325C Division
Total: c.20,000 men (peak strength)
152mm and 130mm artillery rockets and mortars
Communist artillery fired c.150 rounds per day during siege
Peak artillery effort: 1,307 rounds on 23 February

Air Support

Daily Average:
tac air sorties/carrier a/c sorties   300+
B-52 "Arc Light" sorties   45
short tons of ordnance dropped   1,800
Operational Total (70 days):
tactical sorties   24,000+
B-52 sorties ("Operation Niagara")   2,700
short tons of ordnance dropped 110,000
Air Supply (to 8 April):
496 drops by C-130s, 105 drops by C-123s, 57 parachute extractions by C-130s, 273 landings by C-130s, 179 landings by C-123s, 8 landings by C-7s, 12,400 short tons of cargo delivered
Losses:
3 C-123s destroyed, 1 USMC KC-130 destroyed, 1 A-4 destroyed, 1 F-4 destroyed, 17 USMC helicopters destroyed, c.35 USMC helicopters damaged

Result

After a siege of 66 days, sustained by the defenders largely because of tactical and logistical air support, Khe Sanh was relieved by "Operation Pegasus/Lam Son 207"; the attackers withdrew. The effect of the Khe Sanh operation on the Communist thrust remains, like the losses sustained by either side, problematical.
NVA Material Losses:
2 antiaircraft guns, 207 crew-served weapons, 557 individual weapons, 17 vehicles (incl. PT-76 tanks)

from the runway. Eight of its crew survived; six burned to death.

Aircraft that succeeded in running the gauntlet of anti-aircraft fire faced danger from mortars and rockets while taxiing to the unloading zone. To speed unloading, the C-130s and C-123s had rollers built into the cargo compartment floor. When the aircraft halted, crewmen released the pallets to which the cargo had been secured. Then the pilot opened his throttles, the plane surged forward, and the pallets rolled out of the open hatch, down a metal ramp, and on to the taxiway. Within 30 seconds, the transport was unloaded and moving into position for takeoff.

But even this could not guarantee safety. The week before the Marine KC-130 burned, enemy fire ignited the ammunition carried by an Air Force C-130E. The pilot, Lieutenant Colonel Howard Dallman, taxied off the runway and joined Sergeants Charles Brault and Wade Green in putting out the blaze. The crew made emergency repairs and flew back to Da Nang.

Another Air Force Hercules sustained damage while on the ground when shell fragments cut a hydraulic line and the fluid caught fire. The crew, assisted by members of the Air Force cargo handling detachment, extinguished the flames. Although replacement parts failed to arrive, a mechanic flown in from Da Nang patched the severed line. Aware that hydraulic failure meant certain death, Captain Edwin Jenks coaxed his aircraft back to Da Nang, where mechanics counted 242 holes in the transport. This incident persuaded General William Momyer, commanding Seventh Air Force, to withdraw the $2.5-million Hercules transports from the Khe Sanh supply effort—a ban only rarely lifted.

Thus, the smaller, less costly C-123K Provider became the workhorse of Khe Sanh. This aircraft could land and lose enough momentum in 1,400 feet (430m) to turn into the unloading area. In contrast, the Hercules had to cover about 2,000 feet (610m) before slowing down enough to turn sharply, raising the danger that it might roll past both unloading bays and have to double back under fire.

Ironically, although the C-123K need spend less time on the ground than the C-130, the only transports destroyed on the ground at Khe Sanh were Providers. On 1 March, a C-123K was gathering speed for takeoff when a mortar shell burst alongside, knocking out an engine. The plane veered from the runway and caught fire, but the crew escaped. Enemy fire damaged an accompanying Provider so severely that it could not take off. Before spare parts arrived, a direct hit from a mortar destroyed the aircraft.

Another Provider lost at Khe Sanh fell to anti-aircraft fire on 6 March. As he was making his final descent, the pilot radioed that his port jet engine had been hit. The plane crashed in the hills east of the runway, killing all 48 on board. This disaster led to the increased use of helicopters for supply duties.

Deliveries to the combat base formed only part of the supply effort. The hilltop outposts around the plateau had to be sustained and the wounded had to be carried to safety. Marine helicopters did this

essential job, flying in formation and escorted by Marine A-4M Skyhawks. The Boeing Vertol CH-46 Sea Knight helicopters each carried up to 4,000lbs (1,800kg) of cargo in nets slung beneath the fuselage, simply cutting the nets loose when they reached their destination. As soon as an outpost had accumulated several nets, the defenders bundled them together for a helicopter to retrieve. On one occasion, a Marine responsible for this task became entangled in the cargo slings and had a wild ride to Da Nang.

The hazards of air supply under fire

The C-123K Providers alone could not sustain Khe Sanh. Their cargo capacity was small and bad weather hampered their operation. Further, the Tet offensive created a nationwide demand for the cargo handlers and unloading equipment that might have improved efficiency at Khe Sanh. The obvious solution was to para-drop supplies into the base.

Late in January, C-130s flew five test missions and para-dropped 134,000lbs (60,800kg) of rations, ammunition, and fuel. At that time, the Hercules transports were still landing at the base, and the parachute method was not yet essential. The January experiments proved, however, that accuracy was impossible when dropping through clouds. Moreover, aircrews dare not para-drop a 2,000-lb (907kg) supply pallet directly on to the base, for fear of causing casualties or damaging the runway. Instead, they had to aim at a small dropping zone between the main perimeter and the position held by 1st Battalion, 9th Marines.

To hit this zone in adverse weather, radar control was essential. A ground radar operator guided the incoming transport to a point 400 feet (120m) above the runway's end. While the pilot maintained a fixed speed and altitude, the navigator gave windage corrections and counted off the seconds until the plane reached a point that would put the cargo on to the drop zone. The loadmaster released the pallet locks, the pilot suddenly increased airspeed, and the cargo rolled from the open hatch. A small parachute opened in the slipstream and dragged out the main canopy.

Parachute delivery had two disadvantages. It was not suitable for bulky items, and it brought Marines under enemy fire when retrieving loads from the drop zone. As a result, the Air Force fell back on cargo extraction — at first implementing the techniques (described above) used to supply the Seabees in 1967. From 16 February, C-130s began delivering cargo, including heavy timbers for bunkers, by the parachute extraction system. But the heavily laden pallets soon began to tear the aluminum matting of the runway. Besides, low-level parachute extraction endangered both aircrews and Marines because, at the moment of releasing the cargo, the C-130s had to fly dangerously close to a wrecked C-123K. The slightest miscalculation could send 2,000lbs (907kg) of cargo into Marine positions, as happened on 2 March, when a container crashed into a bunker and killed one man.

The Air Force therefore adopted a modi-

1. Combat controllers of the USAF 8th Aerial Port Squadron stand by during the first para-drop of supplies to Khe Sanh in March 1968; more than 600 para-drops were made by Lockheed C-130 Hercules and Fairchild C-123 Provider aircraft during the siege. 2. The Ground Proximity Extraction System: a parachute (out of picture) filled by the aircraft's slipstream snatches a supply pallet from the cargo compartment of a C-130. 3. A C-123 over the mountainous Central Highlands of South Vietnam; C-123s made 179 landings and 105 para-drops at Khe Sanh. 4. One of the 496 para-drops made by C-130s at Khe Sanh. 5. Pallets sometimes overshot the Khe Sanh drop zone; here, US Marines recover ammunition pallets from a rice paddy.

2

3

5

fied extraction system. As before, the C-130 skimmed the runway—but now a hook was extended from the cargo hatch to engage a cable strung across the runway. Thus the cargo was pulled out and the transport flew on. Pallets no longer skidded wildly across the runway. Further, the cables could be installed where runway damage would have the least effect on landings.

Marines contend with boredom—and sudden danger

While many media reporters were predicting a grim fate for the Khe Sanh garrison, the Marines endured long hours of boredom, interrupted by fierce barrages— sometimes more than 1,000 rounds per day —and sudden ground attacks on the base and its outposts. Although the enemy relied largely on artillery, the threat of an all-out assault persisted: Colonel Lownds had to keep his men alert. That meant keeping them meaningfully occupied, so Lownds spread the word that the North Vietnamese might be tunneling beneath the plateau to emerge suddenly in the midst of the base. He organized teams of "tunnel ferrets" to drive metal stakes into the earth and press stethoscopes against them. These improvised sensors were to detect the vibrations of underground digging.

In fact, as Lownds realized, the deep ravines scoring the sides of the plateau were the best defense against tunnels. The enemy could not dig deep enough to burrow beneath these gullies and reach the base. The only tunnel dug by the Communists was detected and destroyed near Hill 861A.

Trenches rather than tunnels represented the gravest threat to the base. The enemy dug a network of entrenchments around Khe Sanh, often excavating close on 1,000 feet (300m) in a single night. Delayed action bombs proved the best defense against such traditional siege tactics.

Colonel Lownds sent out frequent patrols to keep the enemy off balance and to collect intelligence. One of these, letting aggression override caution, fell into an ambush. Another Marine patrol went to the rescue, but the North Vietnamese anticipated the move and sprang a second ambush. After four hours' fighting, the patrols extricated themselves at the cost of 25 lives.

North Vietnamese fall to US sharpshooters

Along with the spectacular artillery and air bombardments, Marine snipers played an important role in defending Khe Sanh. Carrying bolt-action sporting rifles with telescopic sights, these sharpshooters waited patiently until an unwary North Vietnamese showed himself. Although comparatively few enemy were killed by sniper fire, the effect of seeing men shot down by an unsuspected, invisible enemy, cannot have helped North Vietnamese morale. In fact, realizing the effect of sniper fire on morale, the Communists retaliated in kind, usually against Marines manning the outposts. One enemy marksman wounded ten men before the sun reflecting from his 'scope betrayed his position to the crew of a 106mm recoilless rifle.

The North Vietnamese launched a large-scale final attack on the night of 29 February. Alerted by the electronic sensors, the defenders called upon mortars, artillery, tactical aircraft, and B-52 heavy bombers to create a barrier of high explosive across the approaches to the eastern end of the main perimeter. The attack petered out before reaching the barbed wire of the South Vietnamese Rangers' position. Two weeks later, American intelligence reported that the enemy had begun withdrawing troops from Khe Sanh.

Air support—a massive effort

The defense of Khe Sanh called for co-operation between Air Force, Navy, and Marine Corps pilots, as well as airborne and ground controllers. Although the terminology used by one service might momentarily confuse the members of another, clarification had to be prompt. Typical of the spirit of cooperation was the Marine private whose radio requests called up 200 air strikes. Sometimes aircraft of different services responded directly to instructions from the ground; at other times, a forward air controller either relayed the request or himself located the target.

The Marine and Air Force forward air controllers faced difficult problems as they flew low over Khe Sanh. Often, they had to make immediate decisions, based solely on their observations from the cabin of a light aircraft, as to whether a specific target should be attacked. For example, early in February, Air Force Captain Charles Rushforth saw a body of people moving westward from Khe Sanh in the opposite direction from that followed by most refugees. Suspicious, he was on the point of calling up artillery fire when a final, low altitude, pass convinced him that they were genuine refugees, probably hoping to salvage their belongings from the ruins of Lang Vei. There were many such unfortunate stragglers: some 6,000 refugees had to be excluded from the Khe Sanh perimeter after the fall of Lang Vei. Attempts to air-lift them from the combat zone proved largely ineffectual.

Weather was both a help and a hindrance so far as tactical air support for the besieged was concerned. Cloud over North Vietnam meant that aircraft directed there could be diverted to Khe Sanh. But when low cloud hung over the base, the forward air controllers' task was formidable. They must grope through the cloud cover, locate the target, and then climb again above the overcast before directing the waiting fighter-bombers to the attack.

Radar and computers guide US combat aircraft

Radar was invaluable in guiding tactical fighters and heavy bombers, as well as in bringing transports to Khe Sanh through foul weather. Especially important was "Combat Skyspot", a technique combining radar and computer, which enabled a ground operator to give a pilot the exact moment to drop his bombs in order to hit a selected target. The Marines had their own radar, controlling both air strikes and supply drops.

Utilizing data from sensors, the fire support coordination center at Khe Sanh could cover likely avenues of attack with combined tactical air, mortar, and artillery barrages that could devastate an area up to 125 acres (50 hectares). Even more impressive were the strikes by B-52 Strato-fortresses, when three aircraft flying at 25,000 feet might drop some 150,000lbs (68,000kg) of explosives. When the battle was over, General Westmoreland declared that the air supply of the base was the "premier air logistical feat of the war".

Planning for the relief of Khe Sanh began on 25 January, only four days after the battle opened—but the Tet offensive forced postponement. Finally, on 1 April, Major General John J. Tolson, USA, launched "Operation Pegasus", spear-headed by his 1st Air Cavalry Division (Airmobile) and an ARVN airborne battalion.

As Tolson's command advanced towards Khe Sanh, the 1st Battalion, 9th Marines, attacked an enemy-held hill that dominated Route 9, the highway for Pegasus. The Marines seized the crest against unco-ordinated opposition; an enemy counter-attack the following morning, 5 April, was thrown back. The first element of Pegasus, a South Vietnamese airborne company, reached Khe Sanh on 6 April. Two days later, the Air Cavalry joined up with the Marines.

Relief of the combat base

Route 9 was cleared for supply traffic by 12 April, and the skirmishing around Khe Sanh itself ended on 14 April—Easter Sunday—when Colonel Bruce Meyers, who had replaced Colonel Lownds, sent out two battalions to clear the area northwest of the base. Advancing behind a massive barrage, the Marines routed the enemy.

During the advance of General Tolson's column, which continued beyond Khe Sanh, the North Vietnamese seemed to melt away and the body count and number of weapons captured was disappointingly small. The enemy's failure to storm Khe Sanh, added to his comparatively feeble resistance during Operation Pegasus, raised doubts concerning Communists strategy. Did the North Vietnamese ever intend to seize the base—or were they creating a diversion to pin down troops and aircraft needed elsewhere in the aftermath of the Tet offensive?

President Johnson was convinced that the siege was the unsuccessful prelude to what was planned as an all-out attack along Route 9. However, it is more probable that the Tet offensive constituted the main Communist effort. Khe Sanh was a desirable objective which the enemy would have stormed if the defense had seemed "soft"—but it is unlikely that the North Vietnamese ever envisaged the base as a second Dien Bien Phu. It is difficult to sustain General Walt's claim that Khe Sanh was "the most important battle of the war". It has, however, been stated that during the 77-day siege, American aircraft dropped more than 100,000 short tons of bombs on the area around Khe Sanh—making it the most heavily-bombed target in the history of warfare.

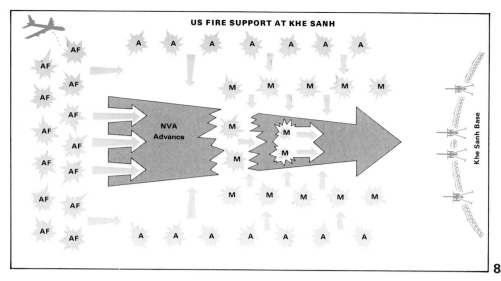

US FIRE SUPPORT AT KHE SANH

1. A-4 Skyhawks on the flight deck of USS *Hancock*; USN aircraft helped give air support to the defenders of Khe Sanh. **2.** Air strikes drove Communist soldiers from their trenches to give targets to this Marine machine gunner. **3.** Forward Air Controllers directed air strikes and artillery; here, a USAF FAC's OV-10A Bronco fires smoke rockets to mark an enemy position. **4.** Marines occupying the hills north of Khe Sanh were supplied by helicopter; these are USMC CH-46 Sea Knights. **5.** US Marines inserted by helicopter scramble for positions near the Rockpile, northeast of Khe Sanh. **6.** Marine gunners fire on enemy positions around Khe Sanh. **7.** Between 22 January–31 March, tactical support aircraft—like these USAF F-105 Thunderchiefs on a "Combat Skyspot" mission—expended 35,000 tons of bombs and rockets at Khe Sanh. **8.** How fire support destroyed enemy attacks on Khe Sanh: A NVA column is allowed to advance until its head approaches the US perimeter. Fire is then opened. Three 105mm batteries within the base fire fixed concentrations (M) forming three sides of a box, with the open end towards the base. A fourth battery fires a walking barrage which moves up and down within the box. Infantry deal with any enemy emerging from the box's open end. Two batteries of 175mm guns from the Rockpile and Camp Carroll fire fixed linear concentrations (A) about 550 yards outside the inner box, while fighter-bombers and B-52s under radar control drop a rolling barrage of ordnance (AF) to smother the enemy's reserves.

The air war on the Laotian supply routes

Bernard C. Nalty

Among the first of President Johnson's advisers to question the effectiveness of "Rolling Thunder", the "slow squeeze" air offensive on North Vietnam initiated in March 1965, was Secretary of Defense McNamara. Attacks in 1966 upon oil storage depots throughout North Vietnam, which McNamara had approved, resulted in claims that some 70 percent of the North's storage capacity had been destroyed—but did not impair the effectiveness of the enemy's military operations in South Vietnam. The North Vietnamese continued to import oil, which they now dispersed among many small, well-hidden depots.

Thus, Secretary McNamara sought a substitute for the bombing, an effort in which the resources now committed to Rolling Thunder might be deployed with fewer risks and a greater return. Some American scientists and strategists not in government employment were already considering how best to employ advanced technology against North Vietnamese infiltration. As early as January 1966, well before the bombing of North Vietnam's oil storage depots, Professor Roger Fisher of the Harvard Law School suggested to John McNaughton, one of McNamara's assistants, a possible alternative to Rolling Thunder.

The ground-air barrier concept

As submitted by McNaughton, Fisher's plan advocated the creation of a land barrier along Route 9, the highway running from the coastal plain of South Vietnam, past Khe Sanh, and beyond Tchepone in Laos. This "interdiction and verification zone" would consist of minefields, bunkers, ditches, and barbed-wire barriers. Air-dropped defoliants would strip away natural cover all along the barrier. McNaughton suggested that the bombing of North Vietnam could be ended if the enemy accepted this zone and stopped infiltrating men and materiel into the South.

The Fisher proposal surfaced again in Mid-1966, when civilian scientists from Harvard University and the Massachusetts Institute of Technology proposed that an independent group should study the potential role of advanced technology in Vietnam. Secretary McNamara approved and arranged that the Institute for Defense Analysis, an organization under contract to his department, sponsor the meeting. In July, 47 scientists and technicians—among them Dr. Carl Kaysen, Dr. George Kistiakowsky, and Dr. Jerome Wiesner — met at Wellesley, Massachusetts. One topic scheduled for discussion was the viability of a barrier like that suggested by Professor Fisher.

> **Throughout the Vietnam War trucks and porters flooded through Laos, along the Ho Chi Minh Trail, with materiel for the Communists in South Vietnam. The network of sensors and strongpoints planned as the "McNamara Line" could not stem the flow; nor could intensive fighter-bomber activity and the awesome fire power of US "gunships". The vital task of closing the Communists' major supply route was never fully accomplished**

The committee's evaluation of Rolling Thunder concluded that the air offensive thus far "had no measurable direct effect on Hanoi's ability to mount and support military operations in the South at the current level". The North Vietnamese had ample manpower to restore bombed communications and supply routes; the Soviet Union and China supplied oil, weapons, and other necessary war materiel. The scientists did not believe that an intensified Rolling Thunder, including the mining of harbors, would pose insoluble difficulties to North Vietnam and its suppliers.

The bombing, stated the study group, had not altered the Communists' aim to conquer the South. American leadership had failed "to appreciate the fact, well documented in historical and social scientific literature, that a direct, frontal attack on a society tends to strengthen the social fabric . . . to increase popular support of the existing government, to improve the determination of both the leadership and the populace to fight back . . . and to develop an increased capacity for quick repair and restoration of essential functions".

To replace the bombing campaign, the scientists endorsed an anti-infiltration barrier extending from the South Vietnamese coast to Tchepone in Laos. They proposed an "air-supported barrier" which would stop ground infiltration and halt truck traffic down the Ho Chi Minh Trail. The barrier would vary in complexity from a series of conventional strongpoints, protected by barbed wire and defending a defoliated area several miles deep, to an electronically-prepared combat zone guarded by patrolling aircraft responding to signals from sensors.

To stop foot traffic, the scientists pro-

posed scattering miniature anti-personnel mines. Acoustic sensors would report such detonations to a central headquarters where an electronic display, showing the location of all sensors, would indicate which had been activated. Aircraft would then bomb the trails where movement had been detected. In the case of motor vehicles, engine noise or the explosion of anti-vehicular mines would trigger the sensors, to the same purpose. The scientists estimated the cost of such a barrier at about $800 million per year.

By October 1966, McNamara was committed to a version of the Fisher Plan, proposing that the US spend approximately $1,000,000,000 to establish an "interdiction system" that would "comprise to the east a ground barrier of fences, wire, sensors, artillery, aircraft, and mobile troops; and to the west—mainly in Laos—an interdiction zone covered by air-laid mines and bombing attacks pinpointed by air-laid acoustic sensors". McNamara further suggested that the bombing of North Vietnam either be abandoned, or that Rolling Thunder should be limited to the panhandle region, well south of Hanoi and Haiphong. The aircraft thus freed could attack the Communists' infiltration and supply routes.

The latter measure was of considerable importance: large-scale infiltration of North Vietnamese troops had begun in 1965 and the increase in Communist troop strength within South Vietnam created a growing need for supplies. Most cargoes entered North Vietnam by rail from China, or by sea through the port of Haiphong, and then were routed to the Dong Hoi vicinity, where the supply line divided. Until US and South Vietnamese naval patrols intervened—sinking some 1,400 junks and barges in 1967 alone—large quantities of materiel traveled south by sea. Combat units and some supplies penetrated the DMZ, while the Ho Chi Minh Trail provided a secure supply and reinforcement route.

Maintenance of the Ho Chi Minh Trail

The Ho Chi Minh Trail had once been little more than a footpath used by guerrillas and porters, each estimated to be capable of transporting some 60lbs (27kg) with the aid of a bicycle, but by the end of 1967 it had become a complex network of trails and roads, carefully camouflaged, defended by infantry and anti-aircraft units, and continuously maintained or improved by engineers. Supply dumps, rest areas, truck parks, and maintenance depots were hidden beneath the jungle canopy. Radio and telephone linked the various sections of the trail; trucks shuttled back and forth between cargo trans-

1. "Igloo White"—the USAF's anti-infiltration campaign: an airman prepares to drop a Phase I Air Delivered Seismic Detection Sensor (ADSID), which will penetrate the ground and simulate a plant, from the door of a helicopter in flight.
2. Communist sappers repair a section of the Ho Chi Minh Trail after US bombing attacks. 3. C-123 Providers of the USAF 12th Air Commando Squadron spraying defoliant.

shipment points; and men marched from one bivouac area to another. Interdicting movement along the Ho Chi Minh Trail was no easy task.

Rival concepts for a defensive line

Work on both parts of the interdiction system began in 1967. The eastern portion, nicknamed the "McNamara Line", did not take the form the Secretary of Defense had intended. The enemy, observing Seabees moving into position with bulldozers, mines, and barbed wire, deployed 152mm guns to shell the construction units. General Westmoreland, who doubted the viability of a continuous defense line, canceled construction of the eastern part of the barrier, and established instead a series of strongpoints sited so as to force infiltrators into "corridors" where American planes, artillery, and infantry could locate and destroy them. The strongpoints served a double purpose: they attracted the attention of enemy troop concentrations which could then be subjected to swift and savage attack.

Con Thien, one of the northern strongholds, underwent heavy bombardment from July 1967 onward, with as many as 1,000 rounds falling around the US Marine defenses of the 520-foot (158m) hill during a single day. Aggressive ground patrols and aerial bombing kept the enemy from storming Con Thien: especially effective were pin-point B-52 attacks, delivered within 110 yards (100m) of US positions. General William Momyer, commander of the Seventh Air Force, described his airmen's tactics by the acronym SLAM: Search, Locate, Annihilate, Monitor.

The Defense Communications Planning Group headed by Lieutenant General Alfred Starbird, USA, was responsible for developing equipment for the air-supported barrier. Created by McNamara in the autumn of 1966, Starbird's group set up an electronic surveillance network within about a year. By the time of the dry season in southern Laos, in October 1967, when North Vietnamese trucks were again on the move, the computer radio center at Nakhon Phanom, Thailand, was picking up, interpreting, and displaying data reported by sensors and relayed by transmitters in Lockheed "Bat Cat" electronic warfare aircraft.

Pin-point detection by electronic means

From the outset, the system successfully detected trucks and furnished information on volume of traffic, convoy speed, and hours of operation. It has been claimed that a tactical analysis officer at Nakhon Phanom, picking up an unusual sound which the computer identified as a tank engine, was able correctly to anticipate the attack by Soviet-built light tanks on the Lang Vei Special Forces Camp in February 1968—although his report was not believed at the time.

Despite such accuracy, the anti-truck campaign suffered because the Tet offensive forced the Americans to re-deploy the aircraft that could have attacked the Communist supply routes in southern Laos. "Task Force Alpha", which operated

the surveillance center, had to abandon plans to fix and attack infiltrating troops when sensors intended for this purpose were instead committed to the defense of Khe Sanh.

Sensor equipment proved so important at Khe Sanh, as mentioned earlier, that simplified systems featuring portable monitoring equipment soon entered service with Army, Marine Corps, and Navy units throughout South Vietnam. Task Force Alpha, however, concentrated on stopping the flow of supplies rather than the movement of troops, in a series of operations called "Commando Hunt".

During the dry season (usually from November to March) truck traffic in Laos reached its peak, and US aircraft destroyed vehicles and bombed truck parks, storage areas, and similar facilities that the sensors located. The coming of the monsoon rains caused traffic to decline; and truck "kills" dwindled accordingly. When President Johnson restricted Rolling Thunder to the panhandle of North Vietnam, from 1 April 1968, and then halted the operation altogether in November of the same year, additional aircraft became available for Commando Hunt.

1

Sensors: tools for the truck war

Battery-powered sensors were at the heart of Commando Hunt operations and must now be destribed in more detail than has been given in the earlier account of their role at Khe Sanh. The acoustic type, based on a Navy submarine detection buoy, was air-dropped. A device intended to hang from the treetops where its parachute became entangled was called an "Acoubuoy"; a sensor mounted on a metal probe that plunged into the earth was called a "Spikebuoy". The "Acoubuoy" was 3ft (0.9m) long and weighed 26lbs (11.8kg). The "Spikebuoy" was 5.5ft (1.68m) long and weighed 40lbs (18.1kg). The "Adsid"—air-delivered seismic intrusion detector—was widely sown along the roads of southern Laos. F-4 Phantoms or slower aircraft could deliver the 25lb (11.3kg) "Adsid", which buried itself about 30ins (76cm) deep so that only its long antenna remained visible. Ground vibration also triggered the "Acousid"—acoustic and seismic intrusion detector—which buried most of its 48in (122cm) length in the ground. At the base of its antenna was a microphone that could be switched on by remote control to monitor more closely activity that the seismic device had reported. The "Acousid" weighed 37lbs.

From the exterior, the infiltration surveillance center at Nakhon Phanom resembled a hastily-built warehouse. Beside it stood several steel towers similar to those used to support batteries of lights at a railroad marshaling yard. Atop these pylons were the antennae that maintained contact with the sensors. The shape of the largest antenna inspired the nickname "Dutch Mill", for the entire complex.

The nerve center of Dutch Mill was a computer which automatically categorized and stored all data reported from the sensors via the Lockheed Warning Star aircraft, and provided the center's analysts with a print-out showing sensor activations classified by time and location. From

4

5

6

2

3

7

1. Although road surfaces were cratered and many trucks were destroyed by US bombing, porters bearing loads of up to 150lb (56kg) on specially-modified bicycles were still able to travel along the Ho Chi Minh Trail. **2.** This US Navy Lockheed OP-2E Neptune flying over Laos from Nakhon Phanom, Thailand, carries a load of "Spikebuoy" and "Adsid" sensors for sowing along Communist supply routes.

3. An Adsid (air-delivered seismic intrusion detector) falls from a US Navy OP-2E over Laos. **4.** Strongpoints defended by aggressive ground patrols—like that seen here by men of the US 4th Marines at Con Thien in February 1968— were ultimately favored instead of the "MacNamara barrier". **5.** US Air Force personnel load "Acoubuoy" sensors into an SUU-42/A rear-firing dispenser. **6.** A

US Air Force helicopter drops an Adsid sensor over Laos. **7.** These Communist trucks were hit on their home ground: a US Air Force reconnaissance aircraft obtained this picture of a truck parking area in North Vietnam after a strike by US fighter-bombers in July 1966. **8.** On impact, the 25lb (11.3kg) Adsid sensor buries most of its length in the ground, leaving only the antenna visible.

8

this information, the analysts established traffic patterns. The trucks were off the roads before daylight, but examination of traffic patterns indicated the possible location of their parks or trans-shipment points. Additional sensor drops could confirm the locations of these installations, which were vulnerable to air attacks, especially by B-52s. Sensor data also helped Air Force intelligence estimate how many of the cargo-laden trucks that entered Laos actually reached South Vietnam.

Anti-personnel bomblets on the Trail

The war against trucks involved munitions ranging from pebble-sized XM27 "Gravel" mines to 2,000lb (907kg) laser-guided bombs. Among the more common types of ordnance dropped on the Ho Chi Minh Trail were orange-sized bomblets, either explosive or incendiary, packed inside a canister that burst open after release from the aircraft and seeded a large area. An anti-personnel bomblet thus distributed proved deadly against anti-aircraft gunners and, when showered upon truck convoys, pierced tires, punctured radiators, and killed or wounded drivers.

Backbone of the interdiction force

In describing Commando Hunt operations to a Senate subcommittee, the US Air Force Director of Operations, Major General Maurice Talbott, declared that the McDonnell Douglas F-4 Phantom II fighter-bomber was the "backbone of our interdiction force". The daytime threat from F-4s and other aircraft forced the enemy to run their supply convoys at night. Phantoms also patrolled after dark, either attacking anti-aircraft positions to protect other aircraft or bombing the truck routes.

When attacking the night convoys, some specially-equipped Phantoms operated under radio guidance from the infiltration surveillance centre. Strings of sensors planted along carefully-plotted stretches of road alerted the analysts at Nakhon Phanom to the location and general size of a convoy. A display panel at Dutch Mill showed a plot of the road net and the location of active sensors. The computer continuously revised this display, specifying exactly where the Phantom should bomb to hit the moving target. Other aircraft, such as the Air Force B-57G Canberra and the Navy A-6 Intruder, employed airborne radar or other sensors to home in on truck convoys. Airborne detection equipment carried by various aircraft included low-light-level television; infra-red scanners to detect the heat from truck motors or camp-fires; and devices capable of picking up the electromagnetic signal from a truck's ignition system. Ground radar directed B-52s into position to drop their heavy bomb-loads on suspected truck parks, maintenance facilities, or supply depots. The plan initiated by Secretary McNamara and his scientific advisers thus marshaled a complex and expensive technology in an effort to defeat the truck.

Especially deadly against trucks were the Air Force gunships, converted trans-

port aircraft fitted with low-light-level television, infra-red sensors, ignition detectors, night observation scopes, and other electronic detection devices. Their usual weapons were multi-barrel, rapid-fire cannon sighted so that the aircraft could circle a target and destroy it with explosive shells. Although comparatively slow, gunships could remain on station throughout the night, when road traffic was heaviest. For protection against anti-aircraft guns, they had a flak-suppression escort—usually F-4s carrying napalm or anti-personnel bombs.

The gunship concept had peaceful origins. About a decade earlier, Nate Saint, an American missionary who flew a Piper light plane while serving in Ecuador, found that he could circle one wing low, over a village, and lower food and medicine on the end of a 1,000ft (305m) rope. The technique of this continuous "pylon turn" had obvious military value against guerrillas like the Viet Cong, who had no fighter cover and little in the way of anti-aircraft weapons. Using an aiming point etched on his port-side window, a pilot could circle a target—such as a hostile encampment—and keep it under steady fire from a fixed gun protruding from the side of the cabin.

During 1964, Captain Ronald Terry of the Aeronautical Systems Division at Wright-Patterson Air Force Base, Ohio, mounted three .50-caliber machine guns in a Convair C-131 Samaritan transport and tested the theory. Over firing ranges at Eglin Air Force Base, Florida, technicians learned the ballistic characteristics of weapons fired during left-hand pylon turns. In effect, they discovered how to make the aiming point and the center of impact coincide.

Gunships strike the guerrillas by night

Meanwhile, US Air Force units in Vietnam were learning that the night belonged to the Viet Cong. During the day, light observation planes could detect enemy movement and call in air strikes or artillery—but after sundown the insurgents moved almost at will, attacking South Vietnamese military outposts and defended villages. The supersonic F-100D Super Sabres that responded to daylight strike calls flew too fast to locate targets in the darkness. The gunship seemed an excellent night-time substitute for the fighter-bomber.

The first gunship to see action in Southeast Asia was the Douglas AC-47, the veteran transport, operational since 1935, variously known as the "Skytrain", the R4D (US Navy), the "Dakota" (British usage), and the "Gooney Bird". For service as a gunship in Vietnam, the AC-47 was armed with three multi-barrel 7.62mm M133 (gas-driven) or M134 (electric-driven) "Miniguns", machine guns with a rate of fire of 6,000 rounds per minute. Aircraft thus equipped were nicknamed "Spooky" or (from a pop-song of the 1960s) "Puff-the-Magic-Dragon". The pilot used a sight at his left shoulder to adjust the angle of bank and relied on his experience to compensate for the effect of the aircraft's forward motion on the trajectory of the shells. Because accuracy depended

1

2

3

4

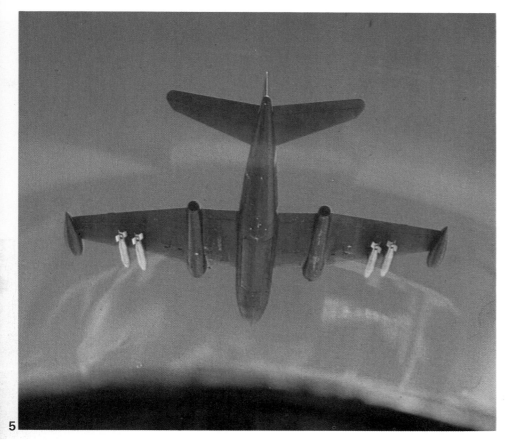

1. A USAF Fairchild AC-119G Shadow gunship: its four Miniguns are complemented by an electronic array including night illumination systems, image intensifiers, and computer fire-control. **2.** These multi-barrel 7.62mm Miniguns aboard an AC-119 have a rate of fire of 6,000 rounds per minute. **3.** F-4 Phantom II: "the backbone of the interdiction force". **4.** A Canberra bomber of No 2 Squadron, RAAF, drops its six 750-pound (340kg) bombs on a VC strongpoint in the Delta area.

5. The veteran Martin B-57 served in Vietnam as the B-57G Night Intruder, equipped with low-light TV, infra-red detection gear, and laser ranging devices. **6.** Round-the-clock interdiction aircraft: a Grumman A-6A Intruder from USS *Constellation*. **7.** USAF Phantom revetments at Ubon Airfield, Thailand; the infiltration surveillance center at Nakhon Phanom guided Phantoms in night attacks on Communist truck convoys along the Ho Chi Minh Trail.

so heavily upon the pilot's judgment, he himself fired the weapons via a button on the control column. The "gunners" in the converted cargo compartment reloaded and cleared stoppages.

On night missions, the AC-47 carried a flare dispenser operated by an airman who bore the nickname "flare kicker". On an AC-47 mission over South Vietnam in February 1969, an enemy shell burst inside the plane, knocking a "live" flare to the cabin floor. Airman 1st Class John Levitow, although badly wounded by shell fragments, threw himself on the smoldering flare, crawled with it to an open hatch, and pushed it out just as it ignited. Levitow survived his injuries to receive the Medal of Honor.

Electronic aids for anti-truck missions

With its lack of speed (a maximum of about 230mph (370kph)), comparatively light defensive armament, and crude aiming system, the AC-47 was not effective against trucks. The task of interdicting the movement of vehicles along the Ho Chi Minh Trail fell to the more complex AC-119 Stinger and the AC-130 Spectre. The different variants of these aircraft had one feature in common—a fire-control computer installed for night attacks on road convoys. Target data came from the gunship's electronics — radar, infra-red scanners, ignition detectors, night optical equipment, television—and the computer automatically established a line of aim with corrections to compensate for airspeed, wind, and the ballistic traits of the aircraft's armament. The computer passed instructions to the pilot by way of the instrument landing display on the control panel and the port-side gunsight; electronics, rather than experience, told him what kind of turn to make.

The AC-119G Shadow was a modification of the twin-piston engine, twin-boom Fairchild Flying Boxcar, mounting four 7.62mm Miniguns like those carried by the AC-47. The AC-119K Stinger had greater firepower, mounting two multi-barrel 20mm cannon as well as four Miniguns. Two underwing, pod-mounted jet engines gave the added thrust that enabled the Stinger to carry the extra armament, make a shorter take-off, and survive the loss of one engine.

The deadliest gunships were reckoned to be the AC-130s, variants of the Lockheed Hercules transport, which had three basic forms. The crew manning the prototype of the series reported six trucks set afire in

only 15 minutes during the plane's first mission. The AC-130A had slightly heavier armament than the Fairchild gunships: four 7.62mm guns and four 20mm cannon. Some AC-130As and the AC-130Es mounted laser target designators to fix targets for fighter-bombers carrying laser-guided bombs. AC-130As thus equipped mounted two 7.62mm Miniguns, two 20mm, and two 40mm cannon, while in the AC-130E and AC-130H a 105mm howitzer in a movable mount replaced one of the 40mm weapons.

The AC-130's 14-man crew consisted of pilot, co-pilot, navigator, flight engineer, three sensor operators (one doubling as electronic warfare officer), fire control officer, five gunners, and an illuminator operator—the "flare kicker", who now operated a searchlight as well as a flare dispenser. He had the additional duty of watching from the open cargo hatch for antiaircraft fire and had to wear a safety harness to keep from being thrown out of the plane during sudden maneuvers.

On a typical mission, an AC-130 Spectre with a laser target designator and the armament specified above took off into the gathering darkness, checked out its various sensors, and adjusted its fire control computer, usually by firing a dozen 40mm rounds at a flare on the ground. While escorting F-4s circled high above, the gunship's crew searched the road net with its sensors. If anti-aircraft fire was encountered, the escorting Phantoms attacked with anti-personnel bombs, napalm, or laser-guided weapons. As well as hunting blacked-out trucks and watching for anti-aircraft fire, the men on board the Spectre had to be on the alert for other gunships, forward air controllers, or fighter-bombers, looming suddenly out of the night.

Many supply traffic kills are claimed

From about 5,000 truck "kills" claimed in the first Commando Hunt operation, the number of transport vehicles claimed destroyed or damaged increased dramatically. When the monsoons returned to southern Laos in May 1971, US Air Force spokesmen claimed 25,000 trucks destroyed since November of the previous year—with as many as 3,000 knocked out by air attack during one week in March. Gunships, especially the AC-130A Spectre, received credit for most of the destruction, although the handful of B-57Gs serving in Southeast Asia also scored impressively. Fitted with much the same electronic devices as the gunships, the B-57G light bomber—a much-modified version of the British-designed Canberra, built in the 1950s by Martin and General Dynamics—could employ laser-guided ordnance instead of side-firing guns.

Some military intelligence specialists concluded that the 1970–1971 Commando Hunt operation had cut deeply into North Vietnam's truck fleet. Although an estimated 8,000 vehicles were in storage in the North after the 1971 monsoons, and some 12,000 arrived during the seasonal interdiction campaign, these did not make up for the estimated losses on the Ho Chi Minh Trail.

The effects of the truck kills, analysts believed, were compounded by the wide variety of vehicles available to the North Vietnamese. Chinese copies of Russian trucks required different spare parts from those for the Soviet-built originals; the Soviet Union provided six different types of truck; Czech, Polish, and East German vehicles needed unique replacement parts.

The real result of the "truck war"

Reported truck kills and the Communists' apparent logistical problems inspired optimism about the ultimate result of Commando Hunt. Early in 1971, some journalists suggested that the "truck war" was straining the industrial resources of North Vietnam's major suppliers. It seemed possible that those nations might decide that the cost of manufacture and delivery outweighed the ultimate contribution to world Communism.

Yet questions persisted about the anti-truck campaign. If so many vehicles loaded with supplies had perished in Laos, how had the enemy retained the initiative in South Vietnam? Did a hit from a 20mm or 40mm round *ensure* that both truck and cargo were destroyed? Might not the vehicles be repaired or the salvaged supplies transferred to another truck, to pack animals, or to the shoulders or bicycles of porters? Finally, where were the tens of thousands of burned-out wrecks that should have littered the roads of southern Laos? (To answer this last question, irreverent junior officers invented the "Great Laotian Truck Eater", a monster which arose before dawn to devour the vehicles killed during the night!)

The war against trucks did *not* prevent—although it may have delayed—the build-up of Communist forces in South Vietnam prior to the March 1972 invasion. In assessing the effects of Commando Hunt operations, those who claimed victory disregarded problems other than the difficulty of destroying a loaded truck. Interdiction on the Ho Chi Minh Trail could not, by itself, fatally wound the enemy in South Vietnam—for as long as he retained the initiative, he could vary his operations according to the resources to hand. To make the truck war really effective, South Vietnamese forces should have supplemented US air operations by maintaining unremitting pressure, compelling the enemy to expend lives and materiel, throughout the year. This they did not do. The North Vietnamese could, therefore, wage war despite their comparatively meager flow of supplies and reinforcements. Nor were bombing operations able to prevent the enemy from expanding and improving his supply routes: each year, US intelligence detected more miles of better-constructed roadway.

In planning the campaign against infiltration, Secretary McNamara and his scientists demanded too much of technology. The "barrier" concept finally proved no more effective than Rolling Thunder, the bombing campaign it was designed to replace. Neither operation inflicted unacceptable losses on the North Vietnamese—and their cost to the Soviet Union and North Vietnam's other suppliers was insignificant compared to what the United States expended in continuing the war.

1

2

3

4

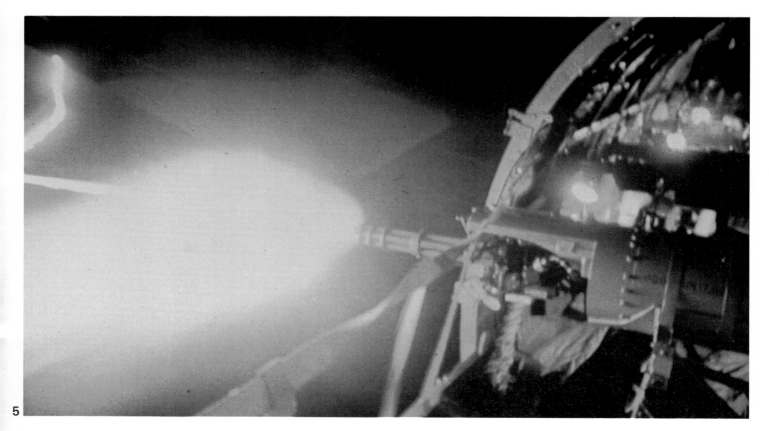

1. Most powerful gunship—the Lockheed AC-130; the AC-130H's armory comprised a 105mm howitzer, a 40mm cannon, two 20mm cannon, and two 7.62mm Miniguns, with optional grenade dispenser, bombs, rockets, and missiles. 2. This view of an AC-130 gunship clearly shows its 20mm and 40mm mountings; in the gun ship role this aircraft carried a 14-man crew—pilot and co-pilot, navigator, flight engineer, three sensor operators, fire control officer, five gunners, and "flare kicker". 3. The navigator of a USAF AC-47 gunship; AC-47s based at Tan Son Nhut in November 1965 were the first to serve in this role. 4. A downed USAF C-123 Provider is lifted by a US Army CH-54 Tarhe helicopter; Providers with night sensors and cannon served as AC-123K gunships. 5. "Puff the Magic Dragon": night action for a 7.62mm Minigun of an AC-47 gunship. 6. This enlargement from an aerial photograph, taken by a USAF RF-4C Phantom in late 1967, shows the high quality reproduction of the reconnaissance camera then on test. 7. An aerial reconnaissance photograph shows the destruction caused in a supply and staging area on the Ho Chi Minh Trail in a raid by USAF, USN, and USMC aircraft.

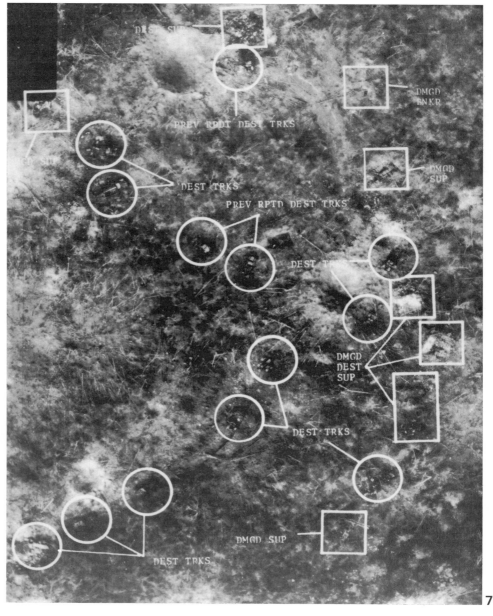

Vietnamization: the south must save itself

Dr. Jeffrey J. Clarke

Although Presidents Kennedy and Johnson had characterized the war in Vietnam as a struggle that only the South Vietnamese themselves could win or lose, the military forces of the Saigon regime had played only a minor role on the battlefield since 1965. American tactical units, with their tremendous firepower, mobility, and logistical support, were best suited to operations against large conventional Communist combat units; South Vietnamese forces, largely infantry, seemed best employed in local security operations directed against small, locally-recruited Viet Cong guerrilla groups. But this division of tasks began slowly to change in 1967, when restrictions on the number of American troops committed, dictated by Washington, forced General Westmoreland to reconsider the role of the ARVN and selectively to increase their part in conventional combat operations. The process was accelerated in 1968—when some kind of peace settlement after a mutual withdrawal of American and North Vietnamese troops seemed possible—and after the Tet offensive, when a series of US programs to enlarge and modernize the South Vietnamese Army was initiated. At the end of 1968, however, there was still no basic change in military roles and missions; American forces still played the major part in the war effort.

Nixon implements his withdrawal plans

Following his inauguration in January 1969, President Richard M. Nixon quickly moved to change this situation. His policy was that the United States should provide arms and logistical support to Allied nations-engaged in internal counter-insurgency operations, but no combat forces, especially ground troops. Allied armies, such as the ARVN, must do their own fighting. The new administration put this policy into effect almost immediately. In April, the US Secretary of Defense ordered the American military chiefs to prepare a withdrawal plan for US troops in South Vietnam. On 8 June, at a conference held at Midway Island between Presidents Nixon and Thieu, the administration announced that an initial 25,000 American troops would be withdrawn from South Vietnam almost immediately. Subsequent announcements, on 16 September and 15 December, stipulated the withdrawal of 35,000 and 50,000 troops respectively.

There was never any comprehensive withdrawal plan or schedule: the 1969 measures and subsequent withdrawals were decided on a "cut and try" process—largely dictated by American public opinion, the current level of Viet Cong activity, and the apparent improvements

Revelation of the My Lai massacre fueled anti-war feeling in the USA in 1969. President Nixon had come to power with a promise to reduce US commitment, but the rate of withdrawal had to depend on the capacity of the South Vietnamese to take over the major role. Modern American equipment and training could be provided —but deep-seated political and social problems hampered the process of Vietnamization

in South Vietnamese military capabilities. By the end of 1969, there was no question that US ground involvement in the Vietnam war was being terminated—and it was highly unlikely that, once started, this policy could ever be reversed.

ANZAC strength in Vietnam had now risen to above 8,000 men. An Australian armored unit of up to 26 Centurion tanks was operational from 1968; the RAAF's C-7 Caribou supply aircraft, deployed as early as 1963, had been joined in 1967 by the Canberra bombers of No 2 Squadron, RAAF, based at Phan Rang.

Between 1965 and 1968, ARVN strength rose from 250,000 to 427,000 troops. The territorial security forces — Regional Forces and Popular Forces — increased from 264,000 to 393,000. The four original corps headquarters, one for each tactical zone, were retained, and the number of infantry divisions remained at ten, each with three regiments of four rifle battalions. Most expansion took place in the combat support forces. By 1968, divisional mortar battalions had disappeared; each division had two 105mm howitzer battalions, an armored cavalry squadron of light tanks and armored personnel carriers; and expanded engineer, signal, logistic, and other combat service support units. The four corps headquarters controlled several 155mm artillery battalions, 20 "Ranger" light infantry battalions, signal and engineer groups, and special area logistical commands with their own ordnance, quartermaster, transportation, and depot units. The reserve forces, controlled directly by the Joint General Staff, the South Vietnamese high command, consisted of airborne and marine units which had been raised from brigade to division strength.

In contrast, the territorial forces were still divided primarily into Regional Force rifle companies and Popular Force rifle platoons, controlled by the 44 provincial chiefs and their subordinate districts. Vietnamese efforts to weld these forces into larger units were successfully resisted by American advisers.

In the aftermath of the Tet offensive, the Thieu regime finally announced general mobilization and the United States began intensive efforts to modernize South Vietnam's armed forces. Initial modernization programs replaced World War II-vintage weapons with modern American materiel: M16 automatic rifles, M60 machine guns, and M79 grenade launchers. Subsequent programs replaced outdated radios, generators, vehicles, and other mechanical equipment of all types. Much of the equipment thus replaced had been inherited from the French or sent to South Vietnam in the 1950s, and was worn out rather than obsolete.

Modernization programs in 1968 and 1969 affected troop strength and organization. While the number of basic rifle units in the ARVN—infantry, ranger, airborne, and marine units—remained the same, supporting units and territorial security forces were greatly expanded. Such US-inspired expansion constituted one of the basic tenets of Vietnamization, and was tied to general strategy or policy in two ways.

First, it was expected that more powerful Regional and Popular Forces would free regular ARVN rifle battalions for offensive operations. In 1968–1972, the strength of the territorials rose steadily to the half a million mark and beyond. For similar reasons, the National Police were also greatly expanded. By 1972 the Saigon government had a police force 116,000 strong and a territorial security army of 550,000 troops in about 1,679 Regional Force companies and 8,356 Popular Force platoons.

Encouraging the build-up of indigenous strength

The second hope of American planners was that the expansion of the South Vietnamese combat support forces would greatly increase the offensive power of the rifle battalions, while a similar expansion in the size of the logistical supporting force would give these units better endurance in the field. Thus, the United States approved an increase in the number of armored cavalry squadrons from ten to twenty; allocated four artillery battalions for each division and more for the corps headquarters; and created 18 helicopter squadrons with over 500 machines. Similar increases in numerical strength took place in engineer, signal, ordnance, mili-

1. The first South Vietnamese Ranger units were formed in the early 1960s by President Diem—against US advice— for counter-guerrilla operations; here, a Ranger in Cholon tosses a grenade into a Viet Cong-held building, June 1968. **2.** South Vietnamese Marines prepare to set out on an operation to cut an enemy supply route in the Rach Gia area, Mekong Delta, November 1968. **3.** At a Fire Support Base in Phuoc Tuy province, area of responsibility of the 1st Australian Task Force, a New Zealand infantryman checks the M16 rifles of an ARVN squad.

tary police, transportation, medical, naval, and air units over the same period.

In 1970, the US Secretary of Defense approved the Consolidated Improvement and Modernization Program (nicknamed "Crimp"). This attempted to outline the establishment of South Vietnamese armed forces after all American units had departed. Along with selected increases in support units and territorial forces, Crimp took into account such factors as the employment of civilian contractors to operate the extremely complex long-range communications system in South Vietnam, and to perform certain maintenance tasks temporarily beyond the capabilities of the South Vietnamese. Under the auspices of Crimp—which US planners reviewed and modified almost continuously—the United States later turned over anti-aircraft weapons, anti-tank missiles, 175mm self-propelled guns, and M48 main battle tanks to the ARVN.

A residual support force is envisaged

Crimp, like the early modernization programs, was guided by several factors. First, American military planners expected to retain a large "residual support force" in Vietnam, or, should the North Vietnamese decide to withdraw all their regular units, a large advisory contingent. Second, they expected that the United States would continue to support the South Vietnamese armed forces logistically with supplies, munitions, equipment, and, for certain complex types of equipment, maintenance. Combat support from fighter-bombers and B-52 heavy bombers was also expected to be available for an indefinite period. Any peace agreement which might reduce this support would, it was hoped, be matched by similar reductions on the Communist side.

It was planned that once American withdrawal was completed, all of the ground fighting would be done by revitalized and modernized South Vietnamese armed forces. The territorials and police would accomplish all area security tasks; the ARVN would engage the enemy in remote jungle and western border areas. Although the Saigon forces lacked the huge US air transportation network, mobility would be achieved through the new system of modern paved highways built in the last five years by American, South Vietnamese, and contractor engineers, and maintained by the ARVN's expanded engineer force. Finally, the Civilian Irregular Defense Groups (CIDGs)—the Montagnard border force created by the US Army Special Forces—would constitute special Ranger battalions, reinforced with their own 105mm artillery platoons, to blunt any major Communist thrust over the border. Although never detailed in any one document or plan, this was the operational strategy of General Abrams, Westmoreland's successor, and his South Vietnamese counterparts.

But it was questionable whether new equipment and reorganization could turn the South Vietnamese military into an effective fighting force. In February 1969, a survey of key American field commanders in South Vietnam revealed their conviction that Saigon's forces might be able to

deal with a residual or indigenous Viet Cong threat, but that they could not be expected to cope with North Vietnamese regulars unless the South Vietnamese military and political systems were completely overhauled. The US field commanders' response emphasized that the various modernization and improvement plans never truly tackled the basic problems of the South Vietnamese military establishment. These problems were well known to American military and political leaders—but finding solutions which did not threaten the stability of the Saigon government seemed impossible. The most serious difficulties stemmed from the organizational and administrative structure of the military system, involving the appointment of officers, promotions, pay, and assignments. A second problem centered on South Vietnamese military and civilian morale, and the failure of the Thieu regime to gain popular support. A final weakness was the regime's reliance on American-dictated military planning that left the strategic initiative entirely with the enemy.

Since the fall of Diem in 1963, the military and political leadership of South Vietnam had been inseparable, and no strong civilian leadership had emerged. Despite American advice, the Vietnamese generals had never opened up the officer corps to the lower economic classes: the corps had remained a relatively uniform group, recruited primarily from the urban middle class. Potential leaders of peasant origin normally could not meet the educational requirements for officer candidates and thus were ignored. As a result, the average South Vietnamese officer was comparatively sophisticated and wealthy, and often found it difficult to relate to enlisted men who almost all came from rural areas.

Social factors affect military strength

Another problem stemmed from Vietnamese social tradition and the political orientation of the army. Traditionally, family ties and personal loyalty were much more highly valued than experience or ability. Promotions and assignments were often based on such bonds, rather than merit; ambitious officers often shunned combat commands for more prestigious staff posts where they might find the favor of some important benefactor. Equally, general officers filling major command posts were often chosen for their loyalty to the government rather than for their ability. The same factors, combined with low pay, also made lucrative civilian posts at provincial and district headquarters more desirable: as early as 1965 most of these posts were filled by military appointees. Thus, corruption and favoritism were accepted as a normal part of military life. The result was a severe deficiency in combat leadership which could not be solved by special leadership courses based on American textbooks, or even by more training and better weapons. But it seemed impossible to disentangle the military from the political system of the country without having the government fall apart.

The organization of the ARVN also posed problems. With the exception of the airborne and marine divisions, and the

1. General Creighton W. Abrams, USA—seen with men of the US 1st Cavalry Division (Airmobile) near the Cambodian border—took over as Commander, MACV, in mid-1968. 2. It was planned that after the US withdrawal ethnic minority troops like these would form special Ranger battalions to guard border areas. 3. A Biet Hai tribesman with an M16 rifle makes radio contact with his headquarters. 4. President Nixon came to office with a promise of disengagement in Southeast Asia; here, he greets US troops while visiting South Vietnam in July 1969. 5. Under the "Crimp" program initiated in 1970, large stocks of US weapons were given to the South Vietnamese; this Marine manning the Citadel at Quang Tri in 1972 is armed with an M79 grenade launcher.

small units resembling the US Special Forces, all ARVN units were territorial in the worst sense of the term. Each unit maintained its own recruiting force and supplemented government draftees with its own acquisitions; in either case, its members were normally drawn from the population near the unit's home base. These local ties were further reinforced by the traditional close social and economic relationship, common in Asian countries, between the soldier and his extended family. Paternalistic unit commanders often considered the security and well-being of their soldiers' dependents a personal responsibility; the soldiers themselves often depended on their families for extra income and for the performance of domestic chores of all kinds. Under American sponsorship, some improvements were made in the weak South Vietnamese Post-Exchange/Commissary system, but unit messes remained rare and housing for dependents marginal. Most bases were surrounded by ramshackle settlements of military dependents. Until the invasion of Cambodia in 1970, South Vietnamese units rarely operated very far from their home bases, and families would often visit, and sometimes even live with, soldiers in the field.

Such factors made it almost impossible for the ARVN to achieve anything approaching the mobility of North Vietnamese military units. Each ARVN infantry division was normally confined to a fixed Division Tactical Area in one of the four corps zones. Its subordinate regiments and battalions were also assigned fixed operational zones. Regional Force, Popular Force, Police, and military support units were, if anything, even more firmly rooted to specific areas, while the border camps of the Montagnard soldiers were usually situated near their own tribal areas. Moving such forces from their home areas often triggered mass desertions. Indeed, many volunteer soldiers had secretly paid substantial sums of money in order to join units as close to their homes and families as possible. The system had the advantage of making military service more attractive, thus greatly aiding recruitment. In view of the large size of the armed forces in relation to the total male population, US military advisers generally approved of the system, feeling the local recruitment led to better military-civilian relationships — and also denied recruits to the Viet Cong. But the resulting military force tended to be overly locally-oriented, defensive-minded, and lacking in mobility.

Association program to raise ARVN skills

In an effort to improve South Vietnamese military capabilities, General Abrams sponsored a country-wide program associating Vietnamese units with similar American formations. He hoped that American skills, techniques, and aggressive qualities would somehow "rub off" on to the participating South Vietnamese forces; at the same time, they would be gradually eased into their new responsibilities as the US units departed. The idea was not a new one: since 1965, the US Marine Corps had pursued a program

mating special Marine rifle platoons with Popular Force units of the same size guarding hamlets and villages. General Westmoreland had done the same on a larger scale in 1966, in an effort to animate the three "coup" divisions (i.e., those most closely concerned with governmental stability) near Saigon. The program had culminated in 1967 with "Operation Fairfax", an integrated effort by the US 199th Light Infantry Brigade and a South Vietnamese Ranger group on the outskirts of the capital.

The main faults of the program included its decentralized implementation, lack of follow-up, and vague objectives. Once the American units left, usually to take part in some conventional combat operation, the South Vietnamese units lost most of their newly acquired aggressiveness — partly because they lacked the vast amount of artillery, armor, air, signal, and logistical  strength available to the Americans, and thus could not operate successfully in the same manner. Also, South Vietnamese commanders, with no fixed tour of duty and no system of assignment rotation, tended to become war-weary and found it difficult to duplicate the enthusiasm of their American counterparts.

A notable exception was the South Vietnamese 1st Infantry Division, based at Hue to the north, whose performance often rivaled that of the nearby élite US airmobile and Marine units. Credit for the division's superior performance was due  mainly to its commander, General Ngoc Quang Truong, one of the best ARVN officers. Truong, however, was an exception: most South Vietnamese units stumbled along with adequate but hardly inspiring commanders.

South Vietnam's lack of training facilities

The association program launched by Abrams in 1969 was more extensive than previous efforts—but in other aspects  there was little difference. Almost all US military units took some part in the effort, from the support forces of the 1st Logistical Command to the land-clearing plow companies of the engineers. But there was still no centralized direction to ensure operational uniformity; no master plan to coordinate association programs with troop withdrawals. Implementation of the program was left to individual commanders.

The most successful association programs were those closely coordinated with the activation and training of new South Vietnamese units. An excellent example of what could be done was the extensive on-the-job training of Vietnamese helicopter pilots with US Army aviation units in 1970 and 1971, both before and during the formation of the new South Vietnamese helicopter units. US military planners carefully monitored the entire transition — but even so the problem of providing highly-trained repair and maintenance crews was not solved satisfactorily.

The US Navy, for its part, virtually dumped hundreds of vessels and much sophisticated equipment on the unprepared South Vietnamese Navy. Similarly, the abrupt withdrawal of US Army combat units often left South Vietnamese ground

5

6

1. Watched by an American instructor, a South Vietnamese trainee assembles an M16 rifle at the US Navy's Small Boat School, Saigon, December 1969. **2.** The US Navy's Intermediate Support Base at Thuan An, near Hue, is turned over to the Vietnamese Navy in October 1971; the USN was criticized for "dumping" sophisticated equipment on an unprepared ally. **3.** Only in the United States were top-class training facilities available: South Vietnamese Navy recruits at the US Naval Training Center, San Diego, California, in December 1968. **4.** South Vietnamese Marines parade as 80 US Navy river patrol boats are transferred to the Vietnamese Navy, October 1969. **5.** Learning to use newly-acquired equipment: a US Navy gunner's mate and a Vietnamese trainee aboard a patrol boat on the Vinh Te Canal. **6.** A USMC mortarman instructs ARVN troops on the 60mm mortar. **7.** Vietnamese Marines wait to board UH-1 Iroquois helicopters during joint US/ARVN operations in the Mekong Delta.

forces to defend vast stretches of territory with no opportunity gradually to appreciate and assume their new responsibilities. Their lack of firepower and mobility on the American scale only made the transition more difficult. US commanders who tried to ease the transition were often hampered by lack of guidance from their superiors—or by the need for secrecy and by the reluctance of some ARVN general officers to play a combat role. Thus, despite its scope, Abrams' association effort had, at best, limited and local benefits: it may have made the existing South Vietnamese leadership more secure, but without achieving the desired improvements.

Training remained another weak point of the ARVN. Many US officers felt that there was not enough time to provide the South Vietnamese with the supply and maintenance capability needed to sustain an enlarged and modernized army. To fill highly-skilled jobs, suitable personnel needed to be selected, given extensive English-language training, schooled for long periods at American training centers, and then returned to Vietnam for several years' on-the-job instruction, before they achieved true proficiency. Attempts to speed up this process could only be unsatisfactory: a shortage of properly-trained personnel reduced the efficiency of Saigon's expanded air, naval, and communications units.

The domestic training system of the South Vietnamese armed forces was open to even more serious criticism. Outwardly, Vietnamese training camps and military schools resembled those of the US Army, with five national camps for basic and unit training and several specialized camps for rangers, special forces, airborne, and marine forces, as well as divisional and territorial training centers serving specific units and geographical areas. The elaborate officer-training system involved a Military Academy at Dalat, modeled on West Point; a National War College and a

7

Staff College also on the American model; and various service schools for infantry, armor, transportation, engineers, intelligence, and other specialist branches of the armed forces. One innovation, a school for political warfare officers, was based on a similar system established in the Republic of China (Taiwan). Most of these special facilities had a small detachment of American advisers and were comparatively well-endowed with classrooms, administrative facilities, training aids, and US training manuals in translation.

The quality of the instructors was the major deficiency of Vietnamese training establishments. ARVN commanders never put a high value on training and tended to use training centers as a dumping ground for their worst officers. Because there was no centralized officer rotation system, such instructors, often with no combat experience, tended to fill their positions indefinitely. It was not uncommon for ARVN officers dismissed from combat operations for incompetence or corruption to be given senior positions at such establishments as the Infantry School at Thu Duc, the Staff College or the Military Academy at Dalat, or even the Training Directorate of the Joint General Staff—where, presumably, they would find it impossible to get into more trouble. Officers were rarely cashiered except in cases of gross insubordination or disloyalty, which were often punished by imprisonment or exile. Seldom was an officer dismissed for incompetence.

The American commanders were aware of their ally's leadership problems, but feared that any abrupt or far-reaching reform of the officer corps might threaten the stability of a government dependent, for the forseeable future, on military support. The traumatic "*coup* period" of 1963–1965 was always in the minds of US advisers. American military leaders nevertheless tried to insure that South Vietnamese combat commanders down to battalion level were the best available, and that unsatisfactory officers were posted elsewhere. This policy, while never clearly articulated, was followed between 1965 and 1973, proving successful in its limited objective of providing the ARVN with at least a veneer of competent leadership. A major drawback was that good officers thus identified and placed in responsible positions were often overworked, while officers holding staff positions, commanding support units, or supervising training programs were often less than satisfactory and contributed little to the war effort.

One aim of Vietnamization: cutting US casualties

One important objective of the Vietnamization program was the reduction of American combat casualties in order to make the continuation of the war more acceptable to the American public. Fewer casualties meant less anti-war feeling and correspondingly greater freedom for the US administration in such matters as the bombing campaign, South Vietnamese military expansion, a slower withdrawal schedule, and greater activity in Thailand, Laos, and, perhaps, Cambodia. In 1969, however, the administration suffered two major setbacks in efforts to make the

Vietnam commitment acceptable to the American public: the "Hamburger Hill" assault in May, and, even more damaging, the revelation of the My Lai massacre.

The first incident was just one episode in what had become a thoroughly frustrating war for the US commanders. After the Tet offensive, the character of the war had slowly changed. By 1969, wary of American firepower—and anticipating the withdrawal of US troops from South Vietnam—the Communist leaders sought to avoid combat and conserve their military strength. Most large Viet Cong and North Vietnamese regular units took refuge beyond the Cambodian and Laotian borders. Communist units remaining in South Vietnam broke down into platoons and squads of ten to thirty men and lay low in remote jungle base areas and strongholds.

The unnecessary assault on "Hamburger Hill"

In response, American and some South Vietnamese units also redeployed in small groups. The ensuing operations were characterized by constant patrolling, small ambushes, and occasional skirmishes lasting only a few minutes. The year saw three Viet Cong successes in well-coordinated but extremely minor hit-and-run operations. For example, on 11 August, small Viet Cong detachments attacked 179 widely-scattered bases with artillery fire—mainly mortars or long-range rockets fired in small salvos—and simultaneously launched a number of ground attacks. Damage was minimal, but the Viet Cong had demonstrated their continued ability to conduct larger operations if they chose to do so.

Earlier in the year, to halt such harassing attacks, US commanders had launched many sweeps through suspected enemy base areas and artillery sites—including the Michelin Rubber Plantation north of Saigon; the coast of Quang Nam province south of Da Nang; and, on 10 May, in the A Shau Valley along South Vietnam's northern border with Laos. Here, on 14 May, ARVN units and American troops of the 101st Airborne Division assaulted Hill 937—Ap Bia Mountain, or "Hamburger Hill"—about one mile from the Laos frontier. The initial attacks were repulsed by entrenched Viet Cong and the action became a battle of attrition between opposing infantry forces. Finally, after nine assaults over six days of heavy fighting in which severe losses were incurred US and ARVN forces took the hill—only to abandon the virtually worthless objective several days later. The battle had occurred only because the Viet Cong had elected to stand and fight where the terrain was to their advantage; once the US committed large forces, the VC withdrew across the Laos border. The American infantry assault was a tactical blunder; observers commented that more use should have been made of artillery or B-52 strikes.

To the American public, the rapid abandonment of such hard-won territory seemed to typify the purposelessness of the war. As one of the few major actions of 1969, Hamburger Hill received more than its warranted share of press coverage and consequent domestic attention. Other

1. A South Vietnamese Air Force (VNAF) Northrop F-5 Freedom Fighter is overhauled at the VNAF's Air Logistics Command Facility, Bien Hoa, April 1971; the F-5 was operational with the VNAF from June 1967. 2. Newly-commissioned ARVN reserve officers from the Thu Duc School parade in Saigon. 3. The Michelin Rubber Plantation was subjected to periodic sweeps; here, US medics move from tanks of the 34th Armored Regiment to aid infantrymen wounded by a mine during one such mission. 4. The Viet Cong waged hit-and-run warfare through 1969: this USAF North American F-100 Super Sabre, parked in an incomplete wonder shelter at Bien Hoa, was destroyed by a 107mm rocket. 5. A VNAF Cessna A-37 Dragonfly light strike aircraft near Da Nang September 1971; between March and July 1969, three VNAF squadrons with 54 A-37Bs delivered from the US became operational. 6. A Vietnamese Scout (extreme left, with M16 rifle) with men of a Long Range Patrol Team of the US 151st (Ranger) Infantry, as they engage the enemy, September 1969.

press reports concentrated on the Special Forces camps which were besieged from time to time: the exploits of the "Green Berets", though highly dramatized in both fact and fiction, were of little importance to the overall war effort at the time.

Revelation of the My Lai massacre

Journalists played a key role in a far more tragic episode. In April 1969, a young Vietnam veteran called Ronald L. Ridenhour wrote a number of open letters to President Nixon and important government officials, giving a hearsay account of a major atrocity allegedly committed by troops of C Company, 1st Battalion, 20th Infantry, US Americal Division, in South Vietnam during the preceding year. In September, a formal investigation began, and eventually a junior officer, Lieutenant William L. Calley, Jr., was charged with the murder of more than 100 Vietnamese civilians. Little information about the incident reached the American public until November, when a series of newspaper articles disclosed the extent of the affair.

On 16 March 1968, a company of US soldiers had landed by helicopter near My Lai, a hamlet in the "Free Fire Zone" established near the provincial capital of Quang Ngai. The Americans, mostly young and inexperienced soldiers, had taken casualties from snipers and booby-traps and were thoroughly upset and demoralized. Expecting to trap Viet Cong at My Lai, they instead found only women, children, and old men. During the hours that followed, these civilians were murdered and their homes razed. There was no justification for an act that, according to the final US investigation, took the lives of 347 innocent non-combatants.

Shortly after the public disclosures, the Army established a panel under Lieutenant General William Peers to investigate the atrocity and to determine why inquiries in 1968 had failed to expose the killings. Between November 1969 and March 1970, the panel – with mixed military and civilian membership—interviewed more than 400 witnesses. It finally recommended that charges be brought against 15 officers, including the former divisional commander, Major General Samuel Koster, who had since become Superintendent of the US Military Academy at West Point. The results stunned both the military and the American public, many of whom had discounted the story as a piece of sensational journalism. Even more disturbing to critics of the military establishment was the Army's later decision to dismiss without a court-martial charges against senior defendants. To many, it seemed that the Army was unjustly protecting career officers and making scapegoats of younger soldiers like Lieutenant Calley, who was sentenced to life imprisonment (later reduced to 20 years and made subject to further review) on 29 March 1971.

When the findings of the Peers' Panel were made public early in 1971, the shock of the incident had worn off. Yet the testimony given suggested several unpleasant conclusions about the Vietnam War. First, the massacre at My Lai was not an isolated event: the investigation revealed that a similar episode—said to have involved some 50 civilian casualties—had occurred the same day in another hamlet nearby. Second, examination of the operational procedure of the Americal Division showed that most of the field-grade officers concerned had little knowledge of what was going on in the field. Third, the testimony clearly revealed that the US military and civilian chain of command instinctively tended both to minimize any adverse or embarrassing information and to pass on favorable reports with little, if any, confirmation. Thus, instead of a massacre, a battle at My Lai in which 128 Viet Cong were killed and three weapons captured had been reported to General Westmoreland's HQ in Saigon. The fact that such reports— noting high "body counts" but few weapons captured—were common seemed to imply that incidents like the My Lai massacre were far from unique. Public horror over My Lai, whipped up by antiwar organizations and by a large section of the press (the reporter who "broke" the story was awarded a Pulitzer Prize), tended to overshadow many far worse atrocities committed before and since by the Communists. For example, in April 1968 it was established that during the brief occupation of Hue by the insurgents, during the Tet offensive, more than 1,000 civilians had been murdered—often after torture— by the Viet Cong.

Combat activity falls —infiltration goes on

Despite such grim events, there was some cause for optimism at the end of 1969. The tempo of war at last seemed to be slowing down sufficiently for thought to be turned to a new struggle at the conference table. By US reckoning, American losses for 1969 totalled 9,249 dead, 69,043 wounded, and 112 missing—compared to more than 132,000 Communists claimed killed. During the last months of the year, combat activity had fallen to its lowest level since 1964, and Vietnamization was now proceeding apace. In Saigon, President Thieu had consolidated his power by replacing the civilian Premier Tran Van Huong with his military friend and mentor, General Tran Thien Khiem, and had even brought back from exile the difficult yet efficient soldier Do Cao Tri to put new life into the three weak divisions around Saigon.

Although the venerated North Vietnamese leader Ho Chi Minh had died in September, the Viet Cong and NVA could also view 1969 with some satisfaction. They had infiltrated an estimated 115,000 soldiers into the South during the year, and still maintained an army of about 250,000 men—100,000 North Vietnamese regulars; 50,000 Viet Cong main force troops; and some 100,000 regional force and militia soldiers. Most of the larger units were patiently waiting beyond South Vietnam's borders for the withdrawal of US troops. For the Communists inside South Vietnam, however, life was still hazardous: most Viet Cong "local" units were now composed almost entirely of northern-born recruits, a result of the great losses of indigenous troops during the 1968 Tet offensive.

5

1. Lieutenant William L. Calley, Jr, USA—charged with the murder of 102 South Vietnamese civilians in the My Lai massacre of March 1968—with his attorney, November 1970. **2.** Victims of war: Vietnamese civilian dead. **3.** The Viet Cong murder campaign: South Vietnamese civilians whose bodies were discovered by US Marines in April 1966 had been chained together before death. **4.** This young Vietnamese was held prisoner for two years at Duc Pho, a Viet Cong camp some 300 miles north of Saigon, before liberation by US troops in July 1967. **5.** Long-term confinement in the stocks was one of the milder punishments at Duc Pho. **6.** Men of the ARVN 5th Cavalry carry a wounded comrade during a Communist attack on Bien Hoa, February 1969.

4

6

Striking the Communist sanctuaries in Cambodia

Dr. Jeffrey J. Clarke

Within South Vietnam, the major trends of 1969 persisted during 1970. The war was characterized by small-scale patrols and ambushes by American and South Vietnamese units; "stand-off" rocket and mortar attacks by isolated Viet Cong detachments; a continuation of the Vietnamization program and the withdrawal of US troops; and the steady expansion of the South Vietnamese military forces—especially the territorial, militia, and police strength—to improve local security throughout the country. Fighting inside South Vietnam was largely confined to the border regions of the four northern provinces, in areas like the A Shau Valley. In keeping with the low level of Viet Cong activity, only about 60,000 Communist troops infiltrated from the North during 1970. By this time, the difference between Viet Cong and North Vietnamese regular formations had become almost negligible because of the paucity of South Vietnamese recruits to the Communist cause.

One of the heaviest Viet Cong attacks was made against the US Army Special Forces camp at Dak Seang, on 1 April. Located in the remote corner of northern Kontum province, near the junction of the Cambodian and Laotian borders, Dak Seang was defended by some 400 Montagnard irregulars and a small Special Forces detachment. The attackers, some 3,000 strong, also had to contend with US airpower and a South Vietnamese relief force of similar size. American ground participation was minimal: US observers considered the battle a test of the Vietnamization effort. A South Vietnamese rifle battalion finally reached the camp on 10 April, and the Viet Cong were slowly beaten back, although fighting continued there, and at Dak Pek, another camp 17 miles (27km) to the south, for several weeks.

Commando raid on a prison camp

Elsewhere in Indochina, the air war escalated. Although the United States had halted the bombing of North Vietnam in 1968, extensive air reconnaissance of the North continued. Early in 1970, a series of engagements between US reconnaissance aircraft and North Vietnamese interceptors and SAMs led to major American retaliation strikes. One of the largest "protective reaction" operations took place on 2 May, when about 400 US jets attacked military targets—mostly missile sites and support installations—inside North Vietnam. On 21 November 1970, a different kind of air operation was launched when a specially-trained unit of American volunteers was heli-lifted to raid Son Tay, some 23 miles (37km) west of Hanoi. US military analysts had identified

Nourished by the "Sihanouk Trail" in spite of clandestine B-52 strikes, North Vietnamese and Viet Cong border sanctuaries dominated eastern Cambodia by 1970. When indigenous Communists rose against the government, American and South Vietnamese forces crossed the border in strength —but the damage inflicted would not avert the Communists' ultimate triumph in Cambodia

Son Tay as an active prisoner-of-war camp —but all that the would-be rescuers found was an almost empty base that had obviously been abandoned for several weeks. The endeavor only cast doubt on the efficiency of US intelligence.

The most significant events of 1970 occurred not in Vietnam but in its hitherto quiet neighbor, Cambodia. Under Prince Norodom Sihanouk, Cambodia had clung to neutrality and had avoided the rigors of war. But Sihanouk had been forced to pay for his country's relative peace and quiet by making substantial concessions to both North and South Vietnam. Nevertheless, Cambodia had remained an island of tranquility in Indochina, and had even prospered from the war.

In the early 1960s, the Viet Cong gradually supplemented the long Ho Chi Minh Trail through Laos with a similar system running north and east from the Cambodian port of Kompong Som (formerly Sihanoukville) to southern South Vietnam. The "Sihanouk Trail", a network of roads, bicycle trails, footpaths, and waterways, was operated and guarded by the Viet Cong. The system was later expanded to include regular military training camps, rest and staging areas, and supply dumps close to the South Vietnamese border. These border bases, called "sanctuaries" by American officials, were greatly expanded in 1969. By 1970, the mixed North Vietnamese/Viet Cong forces in Cambodia included some 5,000 combat and 40,000 support troops, together with thousands of transient soldiers and units awaiting the US troop withdrawals from South Vietnam. This military presence gave the Viet Cong control over the bulk of eastern and northeastern Cambodia.

Although both the National Liberation Front and the government of North Viet-

nam maintained diplomatic representatives at Phnom Penh, the capital of Cambodia, their relationships with the Sihanouk regime fluctuated. Sihanouk tacitly allowed the Viet Cong to occupy sparsely inhabited parts of Cambodia and clashes between Cambodian and VC troops were rare. Only about 1,000 Cambodian soldiers were killed or wounded in such skirmishes between 1963 and 1970, and not until 1966 did Sihanouk publicly admit that the NLF had base areas along the Cambodian frontier. However, so long as the VC kept to the remote jungles and border regions, peopled for the most part by Montagnards or ethnic Vietnamese, there seemed little cause for concern in the anti-Communist camp.

Reliable information concerning the VC's Cambodian sanctuaries was difficult to obtain; much American intelligence relied unduly on rumor and speculation. Most known VC base areas were located just inside the Cambodian border, an extremely irregular frontier that was often unmarked and at best poorly defined. Between the cities of Phnom Penh and Saigon, the major border feature was the "Parrot's Beak", a 25 by 15 mile (40 by 24km) bulge of Cambodian territory into South Vietnam, a fertile plain with dirt roads and a few widely-scattered towns. Route 1, a major highway, bisects the area and links Phnom Penh and Saigon. North of the Parrot's Beak, the border runs through heavy jungle, resuming its northeastern trend at a configuration nicknamed the "Dog's Face" near the town of Krek; makes a smaller loop back into South Vietnam called the "Fish Hook"; and then runs northeast again. South of the Parrot's Beak, the border extends west, past the Mekong River linking Phnom Penh with the Vietnamese Delta, and then turns southwest to the sea. Major VC sanctuaries were located in the border region around the Mekong River, in the Parrot's Beak, and in the Fish Hook, with smaller jungle base areas at intervals to the northeast, just inside the Cambodian and Laotian borders. Here lay the bulk of the Communist guerrilla forces and supplies— temporarily secure but a tempting target.

Sihanouk grants US right of pursuit

In December 1967, perhaps to balance the growing Communist presence, Sihanouk announced that the VC enclaves on Cambodian territory were not officially sanctioned by Phnom Penh, and indicated that he had no objection to American troops entering the Cambodian border regions in "hot pursuit" of the guerrillas. With the apparent approval of Sihanouk, the right of pursuit was later extended to US air strikes on VC base areas: the US

1. Following the disestablishment of the US Mobile Riverine Force in August 1969, inland waterways were policed by the US Navy/Vietnam Marines SEA LORDS (Southeast Asia Lake Ocean River Delta Strategy); here, in June 1970, a US Navy strike assault boat patrols the Mekong River near the canal linking Ha Tien on the Gulf of Siam to Chau Doc, upper Mekong—a major Communist supply route through Cambodia. 2. A USAF air reconnaissance photograph of Son Tay, the prison camp near Hanoi, North Vietnam, raided on 21 November 1970; although US POWs had been held at the camp, the heli-lifted raiders found it deserted. 3. President Nixon briefs Congressional committeemen on his decision to commit US ground troops in the attacks on Communist military sanctuaries in Cambodia; the White House, Washington, DC, 5 May 1970.

Department of Defense later revealed that, prior to March 1970, the US Air Force had secretly conducted 3,630 B-52 strikes in Cambodia. The steady build-up of NLF troops along the Cambodian border, and the escalation of combat on the frontier, finally drove Sihanouk to Moscow on 13 March 1970, in an effort to reduce Vietnamese pressure on his country.

Sihanouk's long effort to keep Cambodia out of the war ended on 18 March 1970, when the absent prince was deposed by the head of the Cambodian Army, General Lon Nol. Lon Nol quickly made known his support for the United States and the Thieu regime: one of his first actions was to close Cambodian seaports to the Viet Cong. Unfortunately for his country, the general proved an inept administrator; Cambodia was soon riven by civil war. By early April, full-scale warfare had broken out between the Viet Cong and military forces loyal to Lon Nol, with other armed factions and paramilitary groups joining in as they saw fit. Atrocities by Cambodian troops and civilian mobs against Vietnamese living in the country exacerbated the situation. At first, only Thailand and South Vietnam sent arms to aid the new Phnom Penh regime; the United States remained aloof, seeing no need for hasty action. By the end of April, however, it was evident that the 38,000-man Cambodian Army was no match for the battle-hardened VC who, with some help from Cambodian Communists, had taken over most of rural Cambodia north and east of Phnom Penh. By May, Lon Nol's troops had been forced back into the larger cities and towns. Phnom Penh, cut off from the sea, was virtually isolated.

In mid-April, therefore, the US government abandoned its policy of non-interference in Cambodia and launched a program of direct aid to the Lon Nol regime. At the same time, MACV began planning a series of cross-border operations, or "incursions", into Cambodia to eliminate the VC sanctuaries and take pressure off the embattled Cambodians. South Vietnamese forces had already entered Cambodia, on 14 April, to sweep an area called the "Angel's Wing".

South Vietnamese advance into Cambodia

On 29 April, the Saigon regime launched a full-scale invasion, with 12,000 South Vietnamese troops and American advisers, of the Parrot's Beak area along Route 1. On 1 May, this force was joined by an even larger American and South Vietnamese force pushing into the Fish Hook near the towns of Snoul and Mimot. Three days later, far to the north opposite Pleiku, a smaller combined task-force crossed the border into the Se Sam Valley. On 6 May, cross-border operations began in three more areas: the Dog's Face, just north of the Parrot's Beak; northeast of the Fish Hook, above the town of Loc Ninh; and north of the provincial capital of Phuoc Binh. Finally, on 8 May, South Vietnamese units pushed into Cambodia along the Mekong River, entering the Parrot's Beak area from the south. The incursions into the Parrot's Beak and the Fish Hook were the largest and most important. Possession of these areas would make more secure the heavily-populated Third and Fourth Corps

Tactical Zones of South Vietnam, as well as Saigon itself.

The invasion of the Parrot's Beak was conducted by Lieutenant General Do Cao Tri, one of the few South Vietnamese commanders who was both efficient and popular with his troops. As head of Third Corps, General Tri bypassed his three subordinate, heavily politicized, divisional commands and organized his own attacking force. As his main strike units, he employed three armored cavalry squadrons equipped with M113 armored personnel carriers and M41 light tanks; two infantry regiments, each with two rifle battalions on line; and a Ranger Group headquarters with two Ranger battalions. These units were formed into three mobile task-forces, each with two rifle battalions and an armored cavalry squadron controlled by one of the three regimental-level headquarters. Small South Vietnamese and US artillery units were also attached. After several days in the field, Tri began to replace his tired battalions with fresh ones so that each task-force remained up to strength. Later, other infantry regiments and Ranger Group headquarters replaced those in the field, and they, in turn, brought new battalions into the operation. The same procedures were followed in other cross-border operations, with battalions rotated every week or so. The practice also ensured that the greatest number of rifle battalions participated and gained combat experience in what proved a fairly successful campaign.

American support for the ARVN thrust

General Tri sent a picked staff up to Tay Ninh, a provincial capital between the Parrot's Beak and the Fish Hook, to form a small operational command post from which, and from field locations in Cambodia, he directed the operation personally. His forces, with infantry riding on the fast armored vehicles, swept through the area in about three days and then conducted extensive search and sweep operations on both sides of Route 1. Opposition was almost non-existent: the VC had learned of the impending assault and had withdrawn most of their units deeper into Cambodia. Nevertheless, the South Vietnamese captured tons of supplies and military equipment with only minimal casualties. In the few skirmishes that took place, Tri's forces performed well; the mere act of moving out of their own territory and taking the battle to the Viet Cong sanctuaries—and away from their own homes and families—led to a considerable improvement in South Vietnamese morale and aggression.

But the operations also revealed many weaknesses in the ARVN. The delay in launching the main assault, especially considering the warning given by the earlier sweep through the Angel's Wing, meant that surprise was lost—allowing most VC troops to avoid battle. At the time, South Vietnam's four helicopter squadrons were employed elsewhere, and Tri's divisional and corps artillery units were still fragmented and engaged in area security missions. Therefore, the bulk of ARVN fire support had to be provided by US

1. Cambodian Communist guerrillas booby-trap a trail with poisoned bamboo stakes. 2. ARVN M41 tanks move to the Cambodian border, May 1970.
3. Supporting ARVN attacks on Communist bases, heavily-loaded US infantry patrol near the Cambodian border.
4. Intelligence of Communist deployment was gathered by reconnaissance aircraft like this unarmed McDonnell Douglas RF-101 Voodoo, based at Udorn Royal Thai Air Force Base, Thailand.
5. A patrol of the Cambodian Communist Party's guerrilla army. 6. This 60mm mortar round was supplied to Communist forces in Cambodia by the People's Republic of China. 7. US-supplied armor spearheaded the ARVN thrust into Cambodia: South Vietnamese troops with M48 tanks and M113 armored personnel carriers.

heavy artillery firing from inside the Vietnamese border, and by US fighter-bombers. American helicopters provided air transportation, liaison, medical evacuation, and close fire support for General Tri. American advisers also noted that South Vietnamese commanders tended to rely heavily on fire support from helicopter gunships and fighter-bombers, even when artillery support was more quickly available and more effective: too many ARVN officers lacked confidence in their ability to adjust howitzer fire by radio and preferred to pull their units back and mark targets with smoke for the airmen. On the credit side, Tri's staff proved able to handle logistical requirements without the usual American assistance, and, instead of costly airlifts, the attackers depended on trucks carrying supplies north from the Saigon depots along the recently-constructed system of asphalt roads linking the capital with the interior.

US troops committed across the border

The second major offensive into Cambodia involved both South Vietnamese and American troops. On 29 April 1970, the US 1st Cavalry Division began preparing a coordinated attack into the Fish Hook with South Vietnamese Airborne Division. The two units had been conducting "buddy" operations for several months near the border and had already developed considerable rapport. Their task, however, was ambitious: it involved assaulting a dense jungle area where air superiority would be less decisive than in the Parrot's Beak. One objective was the destruction of the Central Office for South Vietnam (COSVAN), the regional military headquarters for all Viet Cong forces in southern Indochina.

Brigadier General Robert M. Shoemaker, the 1st Cavalry Division's Assistant Division Commander for Maneuver, commanded the effort. "Task Force Shoemaker" consisted of the division's 3d Brigade, reinforced with tanks and mechanized infantry; the US 11th Armored Cavalry Regiment; and the South Vietnamese 3d Airborne Brigade. The American forces would move into the Fish Hook from the west, south, and east, while the three airborne battalions of the 3d Brigade, ferried by helicopters into landing zones north of the objective area, would seal off VC escape routes and move south. Artillery positioned in Vietnam would be supplemented by howitzers airlifted into the airborne landing zones, once these were secured. The success of the operation depended on surprise and speed.

The attack began early on 1 May, with waves of B-52 strikes and an intensive artillery bombardment. During the initial preparation, 94 artillery pieces, including 44 155mm, four 8-inch, and six 175mm howitzers, fired 2,436 rounds. Total fire support on the first day included 185 tactical air strikes, 36 B-52 missions, and 5,460 artillery rounds. Landing zones for the ARVN airborne units were cleared by dropping 15,000lb (6,800kg) bombs fused to detonate about 7 feet (2.1m) above the ground.

The first combat action occurred at 0740 hours, when US helicopter gunships destroyed a North Vietnamese Army truck. Opposition was light, none of the airmobile assaults was opposed, and surprise appeared to be complete. The Viet Cong sought to avoid engagement, break down into small groups, and filter to the east to escape the converging forces. Most action occurred when gunships attacked retreating VC driven into the open by the advancing armor and infantry. The ARVN airborne units, pushing through dense jungle on unfamiliar terrain, took severe casualties at first; they were often harassed by short-range mortar fire which proved difficult to locate and destroy.

On 3 May, American forces entered Mimot; on 5 May, Snoul was occupied. Two days later, US troops discovered a vast bunker complex—nicknamed "the City"—in nearby jungle. Intelligence analysts later determined that the complex was the supply depot for the 7th North Vietnamese Division. It contained some 182 large storage bunkers—most of them full of clothing, food, medical supplies, weapons, and ammunition—as well as 18 mess halls, barracks, training and classroom facilities, and a small farm. Items captured included 1,282 individual and 202 crew-served weapons; more than 1.5 million rounds of small arms ammunition; 58,000lbs (26,300kg) of plastic explosive; 22 cases of anti-personnel mines; 30 short tons (26.8 tons; 27.2 tonnes) of rice; and 16,000lbs (7,260kg) of corn. This was only part of the materiel uncovered in the sweep: many smaller supply dumps were later found elsewhere, some reserved for such equipment as automotive parts and communications gear. The searchers located more than 300 vehicles—mostly trucks, but including a Porsche sports-car and a Mercedes-Benz sedan. But no trace was found of COSVAN, the VC headquarters reputed to consist of 2,400 personnel, and most of the VC were able to escape west through the jungle into more remote Cambodian sanctuaries.

Supply losses not a major blow to VC

By mid-May, the remaining two brigades of the 1st Cavalry Division and the 9th Regiment of the ARVN were conducting similar cross-border forays northeast of the Fish Hook. As before, the VC avoided battle and the main activity of the attackers was the location of enemy supply dumps. On 8 May, the US 1st Cavalry's 2d Brigade found another large base—"Rock Island East"—containing 329 short tons (293.75 tons; 298.4 tonnes) of munitions. But American commanders estimated that about half the Viet Cong supply bases remained hidden and that to find them would take many months of careful searching. Although the captured bases yielded far more supplies than those previously found in South Vietnam, the Viet Cong would in time replace all their captured stores. At best, the Cambodian incursion only gave the South Vietnamese a respite from the final battle.

Equally serious was public reaction, in America and elsewhere, to the Cambodian incursions. For a time, criticism of US policy in Vietnam had been muted by the increase in troop withdrawals, with the consequent reduction in casualties; the announcement, on April 20, that 15,000

1. Communist traffic along the Ho Chi Minh and Sihanouk Trails was monitored by aircraft like this Douglas EC-47 multi-spectral sensing and electronic reconnaissance plane of the USAF 360th Tactical Electronic Warfare Squadron.
2. A US mortar team at an outpost near the Cambodian border; in the early stages of the Cambodian incursion, US operations were limited to air and artillery support, but from 1 May 1970 US ground forces were committed to cross-border operations. 3. South Vietnamese troops in the "Parrot's Beak" area of Cambodia captured this Communist supply dump, containing 120mm mortar rounds, machine gun and rifle ammunition, and ammunition canisters and crates. 4. Heli-borne operations and fire support from helicopter gunships played a major part in the Cambodian incursion; here, in March 1970, a US Army CH-47 delivers equipment to Republic of Korea troops serving in a support capacity. 5. Map: objectives of the Cambodian incursion and Communist supply routes.

4

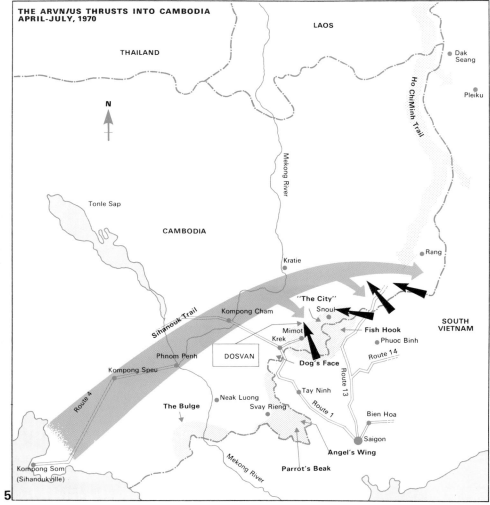

THE ARVN/US THRUSTS INTO CAMBODIA
APRIL-JULY, 1970

LAOS

THAILAND

Dak Seang

Pleiku

Ho Chi Minh Trail

Mekong River

Tonle Sap

CAMBODIA

Kratie

Rang

"The City"

Kompong Cham

Snoul

Sihanouk Trail

Mimot

Fish Hook

Krek

Phuoc Binh

SOUTH VIETNAM

Phnom Penh

DOSVAN

Dog's Face

Route 14

Kompong Speu

Route 13

Route 4

Neak Luong

Tay Ninh

The Bulge

Svay Rieng

Bien Hoa

Route 1

Saigon

Kompong Som
(Sihanoukville)

Mekong River

Angel's Wing

Parrot's Beak

5

more troops would leave by the spring of 1971; and such factors as the New Year and Tet truces. Even the details of the My Lai massacre had gradually faded from the consciousness of the general public.

Now the attacks across the Cambodian border brought down a new torrent of abuse on the Nixon administration. The American anti-war movement, temporarily dormant, gained new life. In protest against the apparent widening of the war effort, anti-war leaders, especially student groups, sponsored a series of demonstrations and strikes across the country. Most were peaceful—but tragic violence erupted at Kent State University, Ohio, where National Guard troops killed four students. The event provided a focus for the entire protest movement. Opposition to the war also increased in the US Congress, which repealed the Gulf of Tonkin Resolution and forced the President to withdraw all US combat troops from Cambodia by 30 June. President Nixon's contention that the Cambodian incursion was undertaken to protect American troop withdrawals from South Vietnam failed to satisfy his critics. The war remained unpopular in the United States and neither the announcement of more troop withdrawals nor the President's decision, in December, to ban the use of dangerous defoliants in South Vietnam improved matters.

Communist demands stall peace negotiations

While war engulfed Cambodia, the search for a lasting settlement of the conflict through diplomacy proceeded haltingly. Peace talks in Paris during 1969 were stalemated by Communist demands that all "foreign" troops should be withdrawn from South Vietnam prior to a settlement, and by disagreement on what constituted an "acceptable" South Vietnamese government. The chief American negotiator, Henry Cabot Lodge, insisted that the Thieu government must be involved in any final agreement; the North Vietnamese and National Liberation Front delegations pressed for the creation of some kind of coalition regime in Saigon. On 10 June 1969, the NLF sponsored the establishment of a new Provisional Revolutionary Government (PRG), at an unspecified location in South Vietnam, as a rival to the Saigon administration. A PRG delegation replaced that of the NLF at Paris two days later. The PRG supposedly represented a broader spectrum of South Vietnamese society, including democrats, ethnic minorities, and religious groups. Saigon spokesmen denounced the move; American officials accepted it—but all parties remained deadlocked.

In July, President Thieu proposed that free elections be held in the South with the participation of the NLF. The suggestion was quickly rejected by the Communists, who felt that the Saigon regime would manipulate any such contest to its own advantage. Nguyen Cao Ky, Thieu's Vice President and former faithful supporter, also objected; later Ky warned that the Army would not sanction any coalition government that included Communists. Ky was the spokesman of those American and South Vietnamese officials who felt that the best way to end the war lay on the battlefield.

The departure of Lodge from Paris, in November, left Philip Habib as the acting US delegation chief until the arrival of David K. E. Bruce in August 1970. The American position, however, remained virtually unchanged: US and South Vietnamese representatives continued to oppose any coalition government other than one resulting from free elections sponsored by the Thieu regime. During the second half of 1970, the negotiators put forward various peace plans based on different aspects of the coalition question. In September, the Viet Cong offered to release all prisoners-of-war in exchange for a deadline for the withdrawal of American troops and elections supervised by a provisional coalition government. President Nixon countered, in October, with a five-point plan including provisions for a cease-fire based on the present military position, a general release of prisoners, and a negotiated US troop withdrawal.

In the following months, each side made minor concessions in an effort to stimulate the interest of the other. The Viet Cong agreed to international supervision of elections — but objected to President Nixon's cease-fire proposal because the Saigon government maintained that it controlled more than 99 percent of the population. Bruce intimated that a US troop withdrawal timetable might be forthcoming—*if* North Vietnam would produce a similar schedule for its forces. All these proposals came to nothing; neutral observers wondered if the negotiators were not merely putting on a show to influence world opinion in favor of their respective causes.

Military aid for Lon Nol's regime

Meanwhile, during the first half of 1970, US intervention in Cambodia continued. The anti-Communist forces were pursuing a second objective: the preservation of the Lon Nol regime by both direct and indirect measures.

On 25 April 1970, the Nixon administration initiated a program of direct military assistance to the Lon Nol government, later agreeing to the Cambodian request for $7.5 million in arms and supplies. Most of this aid consisted of 20,000 World War II-vintage small arms, some .30-caliber machine guns, and ammunition, and was in no way comparable to the assistance given to South Vietnam. The Saigon regime, for its part, turned over thousands of AK-47 automatic rifles captured from the Viet Cong to Phnom Penh, and even sent its own contingent of advisers there. But material assistance could do little: Lon Nol's main need was for efficient military leaders and well-trained and motivated troops.

On 1 May, ethnic Cambodian troops trained by US Army Special Forces tried unsuccessfully to open the river route from Phnom Penh to South Vietnam. On 8 May, a large American and South Vietnamese gunboat flotilla sailed up the Mekong River with more success. To reinforce this thrust, on 14 May, one of General Tri's mechanized infantry columns drove west from the Parrot's Beak to the Mekong along Route 1, establishing a road link to the Cambodian capital.

Operations in support of Cambodia were further widened on 9 May by the initiation of a combined American and South Vietnamese naval blockade of about 100 miles (160km) of the Cambodian coastline. Its purpose was to halt VC attempts to reinstate their former supply line through the port of Kompong Som or to bring in materiel over the beaches. The United States also provided direct air support to the Cambodian Army—although American officials claimed that such strikes were part of the normal air interdiction campaign and did not constitute special aid to the Phnom Penh regime.

The Communists gain control in Cambodia

Inside Cambodia, Lon Nol's troops slowly retreated from the rural areas to the larger urban centers. Here, with considerable material and military aid from the United States, including the cross-border operations which tied down sizable VC forces, they were able to hold out and achieve a temporary stalemate. They could not, however, launch a viable offensive. Very rapidly, Lon Nol expanded his army first to 100,000 men and then to 200,000—but the Cambodians showed little enthusiasm for the war, and the ill-trained, hastily-formed units, much better in defense than attack, tended to disintegrate in combat. The arrival of several thousand Cambodian mercenaries trained in South Vietnam by the US Special Forces failed to tip the balance. But for some time the Viet Cong and North Vietnamese leaders failed to press their advantage. It is possible that they feared the struggle might degenerate into a racial war between the traditionally hostile Cambodians and Vietnamese—or that the collapse of the Lon Nol regime might cause a slow-down in US troop withdrawals from South Vietnam. Instead, the Vietnamese Communists expended much effort in building up the military potential of Cambodian Communists.

South Vietnamese troops continued to operate extensively in Cambodia long after American troops had been withdrawn. Major objectives were keeping open Route 1 and the Mekong River between Phnom Penh and South Vietnam, and preventing the Viet Cong from returning to their former border sanctuaries. A second objective, in 1970, was clearing Route 4, which linked Phnom Penh to the port of Kompong Som, the commercial and logistical center of Cambodia. The key to control of Route 4 appeared to be the provincial capital of Kompong Speu, midway between the two cities. The Viet Cong captured Kompong Speu on 13 June, but South Vietnamese and Cambodian troops reoccupied it three days later after a fierce battle. Communist troops renewed their assaults on the town on 24 to 26 June without success. This fighting, some 50 miles (80km) inside the border of Cambodia, marked the deepest penetration of South Vietnamese troops into the country. But despite their repulse at Kompong Speu, the VC kept Route 4 closed at other locations, and later efforts

1

2

Equipment Captured at "The City" Bunker Complex, 5–13 May 1970
202 crew-served weapons
1,282 individual weapons
1,559,000 rounds of AK-47 ammunition
400,000 rounds of .30-caliber ammunition
319,000 rounds 12.7mm ammunition
25,200 rounds 14.5mm AA mg ammunition
16,920 propelling charges for 120mm mortar
2,110 grenades
58,000lbs (26,310kg) plastic explosives
22 cases of antipersonnel mines
30 short tons (26,8 tons; 27.2. tonnes) of rice
16,000lbs (7,260kg) of corn
1,100lbs (500kg) of salt

to clear the entire road failed. On 17 June, Cambodia's link to neighboring Thailand, a railway between Phnom Penh and the Thai border, was severed; only the southern routes to South Vietnam remained open.

In 1971, South Vietnamese and Cambodian troops suffered a series of defeats at the hands of revitalized North Vietnamese forces. While Lon Nol's forces were slowly forced back to Phnom Penh, the South Vietnamese retired across their own border—this time for good. Between 1972 and 1975, increasingly strong Cambodian Communist forces slowly overran the remainder of Cambodia, isolating and occupying the lesser towns and cities one by one, and confining Lon Nol's troops to the capital. After a long siege, and in spite of a dramatic US airlift of supplies and the provision of extensive combat air support, Phnom Penh finally fell to the Communists on 17 April 1975, only two weeks before the fall of Saigon.

1. "Brown water navy" riverine craft are seen over the twin .50-caliber guns of a South Vietnamese river patrol boat; US and Vietnamese craft opened riverine routes into Cambodia in May 1970 while allied warships blockaded the coast. 2. A USN strike assault boat makes a high-speed patrol near the Cambodian border, June 1970. 3. Cambodian Communists with locally-made twin-barreled guns. 4. A Cambodian businessman heading an anti-Communist delegation to the US in July 1970 displays pictures of North Vietnamese and Viet Cong depredations in Cambodia. 5. Khmer Rouge guerrillas in action in Cambodia. 6. An armored unit of the Khmer Rouge with a Chinese-built tank, learning flag drill since they apparently have no radios!

Southern defeat on the Ho Chi Minh Trail

Ronald H. Cole

From 1963 to 1971, both North Vietnam and the United States sought to control Laos as an invaluable adjunct to success in South Vietnam. The Ho Chi Minh Trail in the Laotian panhandle provided the North Vietnamese with a major reinforcement and supply route to the Communist forces within South Vietnam. The United States hoped not only to shut down that route, but also to deny Laos itself to the Communists. The Americans felt that a Communist takeover in Laos would not only endanger the independence of South Vietnam but also that of Thailand, another anti-Communist ally.

North Vietnam secretly maintained up to 100,000 troops in Laos from 1963 to 1971 to help (and also to control) the indigenous Communists known as the Pathet Lao. Both Communist factions sought to overthrow the royalist-neutralist government. To frustrate them, the United States openly provided the Laos government forces with advisers, financial aid, and airpower. The US Central Intelligence Agency covertly supported and helped to lead a 30,000-man guerrilla army dominated by the Meo tribesmen and their commander, Major General Vang Pao.

The war in Laos followed an annual pattern. During the dry season—from November to the end of April—the North Vietnamese and Pathet Lao emerged from their jungle sanctuaries in eastern Laos and struck westward: into the Plain of Jars in the north; the panhandle in the center; and the Bolovens Plateau in the south. With the arrival of the southwest monsoon rains in April and May, the royalists, neutralists, and the Meo guerrilla forces under the umbrella of US airpower, recaptured most of the positions lost during the preceding six months.

Communist deployment to protect supply routes

In March 1970, the fall of the Cambodian government interrupted this pattern. Prince Norodom Sihanouk, attempting to placate the Communists, had allowed North Vietnam to use the seaport of Kompong Som (Sihanoukville) and routes and bases in eastern Cambodia to supply Communist forces in South Vietnam. With US assistance, the new Cambodian government of Lon Nol began a campaign to expel the North Vietnamese intruders. Already denied free use of the DMZ and the South Vietnamese coast, the North Vietnamese turned toward Laos as their last corridor into South Vietnam. In late 1970, Hanoi decided to expand and improve the Ho Chi Minh Trail; considerable progress was made before Washington and Saigon decided to take stern countermeasures.

By October 1970, the North Vietnamese

Temporarily repulsed in Cambodia, the Communists stepped up traffic on the Ho Chi Minh Trail, provoking a South Vietnamese incursion into Laos early in 1971. In operation "Lam Son 719/Dewey Canyon", some 16,000 ARVN troops aided by US air support and massive heli-lifts, struck across the border. Both Saigon and Hanoi claimed victory in this first major test of the Vietnamization program

---

Army deployed in the central panhandle of Laos the equivalent of three divisions (estimated at 18,000 men), equipped with tanks, artillery, and anti-aircraft batteries. With hard-won experience of the strikepower of American fighter-bombers, B-52s, and helicopter gun-ships, the North Vietnamese positioned overlapping fire rings of anti-aircraft weapons near every site where airpower might be used to cover the landing of heli-lifted US or South Vietnamese troops. From September 1970 to February 1971, the North Vietnamese brought 26,000 short tons (23,200 tons; 23,600 tonnes) of supplies into the panhandle, compared with an overall total of 20,000 short tons (17,860 tons; 18,140 tonnes) for the previous five years.

The North Vietnamese build-up in the panhandle, and the activation in 1970 of the North Vietnamese 70B Corps, indicated a Communist dry-season offensive against Cambodia or the northern provinces of South Vietnam. The 70B Corps coordinated the bulk of North Vietnamese units in the border area of Laos and the two Vietnams: the 304th, 320th, and 308th Infantry Divisions, two artillery regiments, and one armored regiment. In December 1970, the US Commander in Chief, Pacific, Admiral John S. McCain, Jr., was ordered by President Nixon to ask General Abrams, Commander of MACV, to submit a plan for a pre-emptive strike into Laos by South Vietnamese ground forces. Because Congressional restrictions enacted after the Cambodian incursion prohibited the use of US ground troops in Cambodia or Laos, Abrams was instructed to limit the American military role to that of air and logistical support: President Nixon and his chief national security adviser, Dr. Henry Kissinger, had previously emphasized to the US Joint Chiefs of Staff the

---

need to step up Vietnamization.

By January 1971, the South Vietnamese leader Nguyen Van Thieu had agreed to invade the Laotian panhandle. Thieu selected the commander of the ARVN's I Corps, Lieutenant General Hoang Xuan Lam, to direct invasion planning, authorizing him to utilize the nation's general reserve—the élite Airborne Division and Marine Brigade. From I Corps, General Lam selected the 1st Infantry Division, the 1st Armored Brigade, and a Ranger Group of three battalions.

As the final objective for Lam's operation, Thieu designated the town of Tchepone, about 22 miles (35km) inside Laos, where Highway 9 intersected the Ho Chi Minh Trail. Thieu believed that the seizure of Tchepone would cut the Ho Chi Minh Trail and thus disrupt the enemy's wetseason offensive. General Lam planned to advance toward Tchepone along three axes: the 1st Armored Brigade was to move westward on Highway 9; the Airborne and Ranger battalions were to move by helicopter along the hilltops north of Highway 9; the 1st Infantry Division was to be heli-lifted along the escarpment—some 1,000ft (300m) high—south of the Xe Pon, a river flowing parallel to the south side of Highway 9. The Marines would form a reserve force.

Preparation for a joint US/ARVN operation

Named after a Vietnamese victory over the Chinese in 1427, "Operation Lam Son 719" (the American part of the operation was designated "Dewey Canyon II") comprised four phases. Beginning on 30 January, ARVN and US forces would clear Communist ambush sites and mines on Highway 9, from central Quang Tri province to the Laotian border, so that South Vietnamese ground forces could concentrate near the former combat base of Khe Sanh in northwest Quang Tri province. In Phase II, beginning on 8 February, 16,000 South Vietnamese would advance in tanks, armored personnel carriers, trucks, and helicopters to Tchepone. For the next two days — the consolidation phase — Lam's men would consolidate against counterattack and destroy all enemy supply dumps in the Tchepone area. The withdrawal phase would begin on 10 March or later, depending on the strength of enemy resistance.

During the planning of Lam Son 719, Lieutenant General James W. Sutherland, commanding XXIV Corps—the largest US military formation in the South Vietnamese I Corps tactical area—was ordered by General Abrams to assist General Lam. Sutherland committed several units to the operation: XXIV Corps Headquarters contributed an artillery group, an engineer

1

2

1. Men of the ARVN 1st Infantry Division wait for US Army UH-1D "Huey" helicopters at Khe Sanh, 5 March 1971. On 6 March, in "Operation Lam Son 719", two ARVN battalions were lifted over 40 miles by 120 Hueys to a landing zone neat Tchepone, Laos; although they encountered air defense estimated to be the most hostile of the entire war, only one Huey was damaged. **2.** Target of the Laotian operation: Communist supply trucks roll down the Ho Chi Minh Trail in the Laotian panhandle. **3.** Communist engineers hasten to repair a section of the Ho Chi Minh Trail after a raid by US aircraft.

3

group, a combat aviation battalion, and a military police battalion; the 101st Airborne Division (Airmobile) provided two brigades of airborne infantry, three battalions of divisional artillery, and a combat aviation group; the 1st Brigade of the 5th US Infantry Division (Mechanized) and the 11th Brigade of the 23d US Infantry Division (Americal) also participated. The total American force numbered 10,000 men, 2,000 fixed-wing aircraft, and 600 helicopters—but only the aircraft were to cross the border in close support of the South Vietnamese.

Tough opposition from the North Vietnamese

The Lam Son operational area extended for some 22 miles (35km) from east to west, and about 19 miles (30km) from north to south. Much of the terrain was mountainous and heavily forested, and even in good weather the area offered few suitable landing sites for large-scale helicopter operations. During the northeast monsoon period, rain, fog, haze, and low cloud cover prevailed, forcing pilots providing air support to ground missions to fly very low. Anticipating this, the North Vietnamese had sited anti-aircraft batteries in those valleys where such aircraft were most likely to be operational.

One minute after midnight on 30 January 1971, the 1st Brigade of the 5th US Infantry (Mechanized) spearheaded the South Vietnamese advance to Khe Sanh. Phase I had begun. Despite a six-day news blackout imposed by General Abrams, the logistical build-up in northwest I Corps area and the movement towards Khe Sanh had alerted the enemy. On 1 February, even before Lam's men crossed the border, Hanoi, Peking and Moscow denounced the US for extending its "imperial war of aggression" into Laos. Within a week, the anti-war lobby in Washington headed by Senator Mansfield, the Secretary-General of the United Nations, and the government of Laos itself had expressed strong disapproval of the Lam Son/Dewey Canyon operation.

Phase II began at 1000 on 8 February, when tanks and armored personnel carriers of the ARVN's 1st Armored Brigade crossed the frontier into Laos. North of Highway 9, the South Vietnamese Airborne Division and Ranger Group each established two hilltop firebases. South of the Xe Pon River, the ARVN's 1st Infantry Division constructed two firebases atop the escarpment. By 9 February, General Lam's armored column had reached the Laotian village of Aloui, about halfway to Tchepone.

After determining that the ARVN's advance was not merely a diversion for an invasion of North Vietnam or Cambodia, the commander of the North Vietnamese 70B Corps committed the Communist troops to battle. Elements of three North Vietnamese divisions attacked from the north, hitting the ARVN's Airborne and Ranger bases with artillery, sapper assaults and infantry attacks. In the mornings and in the afternoons, thick haze mingled with the smoke from artillery shells hindered US helicopter support and reduced the amount of close air support given to the ARVN troops. By 22 February, the North

Vietnamese had surrounded Ranger Base South; their anti-aircraft fire prevented aerial resupply of Ranger Base North. Under great pressure, the South Vietnamese Rangers withdrew. Their casualties were 298 killed and wounded, and they claimed to have killed 639 of their enemy.

On 25 February, some 7 miles (12km) northwest of Aloui, a force of 20 Soviet-built PT-76 light tanks and about 2,000 Communist infantry tried to storm Airborne Objective 31. Supported by air strikes, the 500 paratroopers repulsed two waves of North Vietnamese and killed up to 1,000 enemy soldiers. After holding out for three days, the surviving ARVN paratroopers abandoned their position and fought their way south. The Communists captured 120 South Vietnamese, including the battalion commander.

By 1 March, the loss of two firebases, and the isolation of two more on the ARVN force's northern flank, prompted General Lam to change his tactical plan. With three Communist divisions pressing hard from the north towards Highway 9, Lam realized that he could not push forward his armored brigade from Aloui to Tchepone. He deployed the armored, airborne, and Ranger battalions defensively, and ordered his 1st Infantry Division to make a series of helicopter landings along the escarpment from Route 9, south of Aloui, to Tchepone. Aided by helicopters from an American combat aviation battalion, the 1st Infantry division established three landing zones by 5 March.

North Vietnamese propaganda characterized the combat helicopter assaults as "leapfrogging"—tactics intended to give the illusion of a rapid and victorious thrust to the west when, in fact, no South Vietnamese battalion stayed in any landing zone long enough to hold it against counter-attack. Hanoi further charged that by naming the three landing zones after western movie stars—"Lolo" for Gina Lollobrigida; "Liz" for Elizabeth Taylor; and "Sophie" for Sophia Loren—American planners had inadvertently betrayed the "myth" of Vietnamization.

An aerial armada of "Huey Slicks"

On 6 March, a bright clear day, USAF B-52s bombed the Tchepone area in preparation for the climax of Lam Son 719—the arrival of an enormous helicopter armada. On that day, 120 "Huey Slicks" (Bell UH-IH Iroquois helicopters) left Khe Sanh, carrying two ARVN infantry battalions a distance of up to 48 miles (77km)—the largest, longest-ranging combat helicopter assault of the Vietnam War. To the front, flanks, and rear of the helicopters, gunships from an American air cavalry squadron poured heavy fire on the landing zone and anti-aircraft batteries in the vicinity. The two battalions lost only one helicopter to anti-aircraft fire during the approach, and encountered little resistance on the ground.

Two days after the landing at Tchepone, General Sutherland at Da Nang and General Abrams at Saigon pronounced Lam Son 719 an unqualified success. Abrams stated that General Lam's forces had seized enough rice to feed 159 battalions for 30 days: enough rifles and other

3

1

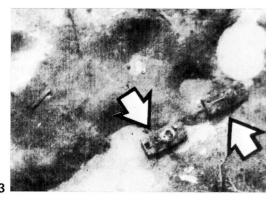
2

4

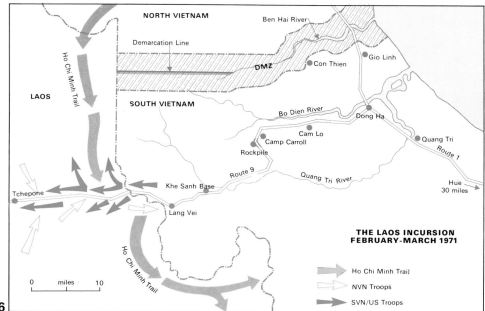

THE LAOS INCURSION
FEBRUARY-MARCH 1971

→ Ho Chi Minh Trail
⇨ NVN Troops
→ SVN/US Troops

1. Close support from a "Huey" gunship for ground forces in "Lam Son 719"; some 108 helicopters were lost and around 600 damaged in Laotian operations between 8 February–9 April 1971. **2.** ARVN forces encountered Soviet-built armor during the thrust into Laos; this aerial reconniassance photograph shows Soviet-made T-54/55 tanks destroyed by US air strikes in the Laotian panhandle in March 1972. **3.** Soviet-built PT-76 light amphibious tanks of the kind encountered in 1971; these were destroyed by US fighter-bombers northeast of Tchepone in March 1972. **4.** This PT-76 captured by the ARVN in Laos in 1971 was repaired and returned to action against the Communists. **5.** US Marine Corps CH-46 Sea Knight helicopters take off for an air-ground support mission. **6.** Map: Operation Lam Son 719. **7.** ARVN infantry move through thick tropical vegetation while searching for enemy supply depots and bunkers along the Ho Chi Minh Trail.

small arms to equip eight North Vietnamese infantry battalions; enough machine guns, mortars, and artillery pieces to equip nine infantry battalions; and 800 short tons (714 tons; 726 tonnes) of ammunition. Moreover, General Lam's forces claimed to have killed some 7,100 North Vietnamese up to 8 March.

Laotian withdrawal: both sides claim victory

On 10 March, however, anticipating the heavy rains of April and a massive counter-offensive by the reinforced units of the Communist 70B Corps, General Lam ordered his troops to begin withdrawal from all bases—although the South Vietnamese were still heavily engaged with strong enemy forces. For the next five days, North Vietnamese mortar, sapper, infantry, and anti-aircraft battalions repeatedly struck at Lam's troops as they were helilifted back to Quang Tri province. To minimize the time spent by US helicopters over "hot" landing zones, the Assistant Commander of the 101st US Airborne Division, Brigadier General Sidney B. Berry, Jr., ordered his pilots to pack in as many South Vietnamese as possible. Seeing helicopters filled to the point of overflowing and afraid of being abandoned, some ARVN personnel panicked and climbed onto the helicopters' skids for a most perilous flight.

On the escarpment, about 10 miles (16km) southeast of Aloui, North Vietnamese forces on 22 March attacked the ARVN 147th Marine Battalion, defending Fire Base Delta. After four hours' fighting, the North Vietnamese forced the Marines to evacuate the hill by helicopter. Commenting on this last battle of Lam Son 719, the North Vietnamese propaganda machine said:

"Typical of that total debacle was the sight of Saigon soldiers trying to cling to the choppers' skids, and being kicked down by American airmen.... The Americans ended by plastering grease on the skids... a fine picture of Vietnamization!"

After the 101st US Airborne Combat Aviation Group had removed the last South Vietnamese soldiers from the Laotian panhandle on 25 March, Hanoi and Saigon both published impressive casualty figures. Calling the battle "a complete victory", Hanoi claimed to have killed, wounded, or captured 16,400 men, including 200 Americans. Saigon, however, alleged that General Lam's troops had killed 13,636 North Vietnamese at a cost of a little more than 6,000 killed and wounded. American experts estimated that the South Vietnamese had actually suffered approximately 50 percent casualties— nearly 10,000 killed, wounded, or missing.

Was Lam Son 719 an impressive South Vietnamese victory, a stalemate, or a devastating defeat? In answer, it must be determined whether General Lam's invasion attained its two fundamental objectives: first, to foil enemy preparations for a spring offensive; second, to show that the South Vietnamese could fight virtually on their own—the measure of the Vietnamization program.

Lam Son 719 succeeded in disrupting many North Vietnamese offensive preparations in the Laotian panhandle. General Lam's forces inflicted enormous losses upon the Communists: General Sutherland's staff officers estimated that the South Vietnamese had killed 10,505 enemy, and that US air support and artillery had accounted for a further 8,900. Sutherland predicted that these losses would compel 70B Corps to postpone a general offensive in the South for up to six months; in fact, he under-estimated by six months the time the North Vietnamese would need before launching another major offensive. However, whether Hanoi waited twelve months because of the losses sustained during Lam Son 719—or whether the North Vietnamese were instead awaiting the withdrawal of American troops before renewing their assault—cannot be determined from the intelligence available.

Along the Ho Chi Minh Trail, Lam Son 719 had disrupted Communist logistical activity only briefly. Within a week of the battle at Fire Base Delta, US pilots reported that North Vietnamese vehicles again moved freely down the Trail. In May, intelligence sources reported that the North Vietnamese had rebuilt Tchepone. Only permanent deployment of large ARVN ground forces along Highway 9, from South Vietnam to Thailand, could have substantially interdicted the Ho Chi Minh Trail.

Limitations in the ARVN command are revealed

As a test of Vietnamization, Lam Son 719 revealed both strengths and weaknesses in ARVN leadership and training. Early in the operation, a comparative lack of opposition had made the South Vietnamese overconfident. But when the ARVN's advance bogged down near Aloui, that overconfidence was quickly replaced by undue reliance on US air support, helicopters, and artillery.

General Lam's staff had made a major planning error in placing the Ranger and Airborne battalions on the most vulnerable northern flank. Trained and equipped as light infantry and inexperienced in operations at divisional level, the Ranger and Airborne troops lacked the skill, armor, and firepower to withstand armored assault and North Vietnamese artillery bombardment. The ARVN 1st Infantry Division, with its armor, artillery, and extensive experience in large operations, would have been better able to hold off the North Vietnamese and keep Highway 9 open. The inflexibility of I Corps' staff prevented it from recognizing and rectifying the error until early March.

The North Vietnamese had displayed fairly efficient conventional tactical skill against a strong South Vietnamese task force. Adverse weather and rugged terrain, compelling US pilots to fly low along predictable routes, enabled Communist anti-aircraft gunners to put up effective barrages over every hilltop occupied by the ARVN. The North Vietnamese also exploited the ARVN's failure to throw out patrols beyond fire base perimeters to prevent the enemy from establishing avenues of approach to South Vietnamese positions. Whenever US aircraft threat-

Operation Lam Son 719, 8 February–9 April 1971

Objective
Disruption of Communist supply and reinforcement operations in the Laotian panhandle by ARVN forces with US air support

Strengths
Laotian forces (estimates, 1971)
pro-Government:

Royal Laotian forces	c.60,000
Meo tribesmen	c.12,000
Other irregulars	c.8,000
Thai troops in Laos	c.5,000
US advisers	c.2,000

Anti-Government:

Pathet Lao	c.30,000
Irregulars	c.3,000
NVN in Laos	c.70,000

Lam Son 719 forces:

ARVN (maximum)	c.17,000
US (in support)	c.10,000
Viet Cong combat troops	c.13,000
support troops	c.9,000

US air support operations
1st Marine Air Wing:

Sorties by CH-53 helicopters	3,025
Short tons of cargo lifted	5,927
Troops lifted	2,524
Sorties by fixed-wing aircraft	945
Short tons of ordnance dropped	2,630

US Air Force:

Tactical air strikes	c.8,000
Sorties by B-52s	1,358
Short tons of ordnance dropped by B-52s	c.20,000

US aircraft losses:

US Air Force aircraft lost	6
US Navy aircraft lost	1
USMC helicopter lost	1
US Army helicopters lost	c.107
US Army helicopters damaged	c.600

Ground forces losses
US: 176 killed, 1,942 wounded, 42 missing
ARVN (Govt. figures): 1,483 killed, 5,420 wounded, 691 missing

Tanks destroyed or captured	75
Crew-served weapons destroyed or captured	198
Individual weapons destroyed or captured	c.3,000

Communist:

Killed (c.4,800 by air strikes)	13,636
captured	69
Artillery pieces	76
Tanks	106
Trucks	405
Crew-served weapons	1,934
Individual weapons	5,066
Short tons of rice	12,000

(Figures for Communist equipment destroyed or damaged relate only to equipment lost to ground forces)

1. A downed USAF pilot is lifted from Laotian jungle by a helicopter of the USAF's 40th Aerospace Rescue and Recovery Squadron, 22 April 1971. Because the North Vietnamese often used downed aircraft as bait to draw rescue personnel into ambushes, many aircraft had to be abandoned.
2. Pathet Lao troops with a Soviet-built apc in the Plain of Jars, their stronghold in northern Laos.

ened Communist troops besieging an ARVN-held hilltop, the enemy easily advanced to the defense perimeter and "hugged" it so closely that American pilots often held their fire for fear of hitting friendly troops.

The heavy losses incurred by the ARVN's three best divisions in Lam Son 719 probably discouraged South Vietnam's military leaders very greatly. Thieu had deployed his general reserve divisions alongside General Lam's 1st Infantry Division—a unit often praised by US Army officers as a model for Vietnamization. But despite support from Sutherland's XXIV Corps and from nearly half the US air power available in Indochina, the élite ARVN formations left the Laotian panhandle under great pressure and with considerable losses. Without substantial American air support, it is doubtful whether the South Vietnamese could have stayed so long in Laos—or have withdrawn with a casualty rate of *only* 50 percent.

During Lam Son 719, Communist aggression in other areas of central and southern Laos slackened when North Vietnamese reinforcements were rushed toward Highway 9. The war in northern Laos, however, continued briskly: the Communists closed in on the Royal Laotian capital of Luang Prabang and the major Meo stronghold at Long Tieng.

Communist offensive in northern Laos

The North Vietnamese and Pathet Lao began their push to take Luang Prabang on 2 February, with the seizure of Muong Soui, just west of the Plain of Jars. By 20 March, six Communist battalions (some 3,000 men) had moved close enough to hit Luang Prabang with 150 rocket and mortar rounds. In five days' fighting, 250 government troops were killed or wounded. On 24 March, three battalions from Vientiane reinforced government troops at Luang Prabang, holding the North Vietnamese west of the Plain of Jars for the remainder of the dry season.

South of the Plain of Jars, on 12–14 February, North Vietnamese and Pathet Lao besieged General Vang Pao's headquarters at Long Tieng. Although the Communists inflicted up to 700 casualties on the CIA-sponsored Meo guerrilla force during February, they failed to dislodge it. On 6 March, the Laotian defense ministry dispatched to Long Tieng a relief force made up of three battalions of Laotians and four battalions of Thai volunteers. While the Communists waited on the hills and ridges overlooking Long Tieng, Vang Pao readied his troops for their annual wet season counter-offensive.

Washington, disillusioned by the indecisive nature of the seasonal offensives and counter-offensives, decided to cut US military assistance to Laos. General Abrams reflected this political decision when, in the spring of 1971, he planned to halve the number of sorties flown in Laos after 1 July 1971. Allocating a total of 11,750 sorties per month to Laos, Abrams directed 70 percent of them to the panhandle and southern Laos, believing that after Lam Son 719 the North Vietnamese would work desperately to rebuild the Ho Chi Minh Trail in both areas. The re-

maining fighter-bomber, B-52, and helicopter sorties were directed to northern Laos. This meant that the Royal Laotian Army at Luang Prabang and Vang Pao's guerrillas at Long Tieng could expect to benefit from only 32 sorties daily, instead of the former 60.

General Vang Pao's CIA advisers warned him of the imminent cutback in US air support. He therefore decided to begin the wet season offensive early, to get the maximum benefit from American air support before 1 July. The Meo commander planned his fiercest attack of the campaign, aimed at disrupting Communist preparations for a 1972 offensive in northern Laos. But before Vang Pao could strike deeply into the Communist base areas in the Plain of Jars, he had to drive out 3,000 or more North Vietnamese entrenched on the hilltops north of Long Tieng.

A Communist victory is foreshadowed

Vang Pao began his 1971 campaign on 15 April, with a victorious sweep of "Skyline Ridge", about 4 miles (6km) north of Long Tieng. From 23 April until the end of May, Vang Pao drove the enemy from Hill 1662, Hill 1798, and the Phou Phaxai Ridge with a series of feints and frontal assaults. On 3 June, 700 Meo guerrillas were airlifted over the North Vietnamese positions to Phou Seu on the Plain of Jars. By threatening the Communist rear area, Vang Pao hoped to draw off the 3,000 troops menacing Long Tieng. But not until 29 June did the Communists react as the Laotian general hoped and withdrew to protect their logistical base areas.

When the US air sorties over Laos were cut down on 1 July, Vang Pao's push into the Plain of Jars had just begun. In an attempt to reach important Communist supply dumps, the Meo leader swiftly advanced three task forces towards the Plain. The Communists decided to delay their dry season offensive no longer and counter-attacked immediately. On 7 to 13 July, two North Vietnamese regiments supported by PT-76 light tanks partially drove back the Meos. A month later, Communist forces repulsed Vang Pao's column on Highway 4, east of the Plain of Jars.

In December, some 15,000 North Vietnamese with strong tank and heavy artillery support drove the greatly outmatched Meo guerrillas from the Plain of Jars. By 27 December, the Communists had recaptured Phou Phaxai, Skyline Ridge, and all the northern approaches to Long Tieng. The evacuation of 30,000 Meo women and children began while the Communists shelled Vang Pao's stronghold.

The shelling of Long Tieng signalled that the seasonal nature of the war in Laos had been restored. Once again, North Vietnamese and Pathet Lao troops dominated the highlands, the plateaus, and the panhandle of eastern Laos, while the government forces clung to the western lowlands. The withdrawal of South Vietnamese troops from the Tchepone area, and the cutback in US air support, had destroyed the near-equality of both sides in Laos. Early in 1972, many expert observers concluded that time was running out for the anti-Communist forces in Laos.

1. A USAF air reconnaissance picture shows trucks destroyed by air strikes on the Ho Chi Minh Trail, February 1971. 2. ARVN troops hold a section of the Ho Chi Minh Trail during the thrust into Laos; behind the soldiers is the entrance to a storage cave. 3. Men of the ARVN rearguard are heli-lifted from Laos at the close of ''Lam Son 719''. 4. ARVN troops in action; in spite of the heavy casualties they inflicted on the North Vietnamese, Communist supply traffic was only briefly halted. 5. North Vietnamese AAA put up the toughest air defense of the war during ''Lam Son 719''.

B-52s: strategic bombers in a tactical role

John T. Greenwood

The war in Southeast Asia turned many things upside down. For more than seven years, the Boeing B-52 Stratofortress strategic jet bombers of the US Strategic Air Command (SAC) hauled and dropped millions of "iron bombs" (i.e., non-nuclear ordnance) in an essentially tactical role, while tactical fighter-bombers attempted to conduct a quasi-strategic air war against North Vietnam. Throughout these years, the B-52s flew routine missions to support ground forces, attack hostile base areas, blunt enemy offensives, and interdict infiltration routes in South Vietnam, Laos, and Cambodia. Then, during eleven days in December 1972, the big bombers played their most spectacular, costly, and successful role—in the "Linebacker II" bombing campaign against targets in the Hanoi-Haiphong area of North Vietnam. Their attacks helped to urge the North Vietnamese back to the Paris peace talks that eventually produced a settlement in January 1973. This "Eleven-Day-War" was the only time in some eight years of bombing that the B-52s were employed in a nearly strategic role, and it brought the air war against North Vietnam to a close.

When the Kennedy administration adopted the "flexible response" strategy, stressing conventional warfare, Strategic Air Command closely examined the tactical potential of its strategic bombers. The B-52 was chosen for operations over Vietnam because it was much better suited for such activity than the smaller B-47 or B-58. Although originally designed for both nuclear and conventional roles, the B-52s were, by the early 1960s, dedicated solely to strategic deterrence.

Stratofortresses deployed for "Arc Light" strikes

Early in 1964, Secretary of Defense McNamara asked SAC to improve its capabilities for limited war. The command conducted tests with "iron bombs" to determine the best weapons, loads, and release intervals to obtain concentrated impact patterns for the 27 bombs a B-52 could carry. Multiple ejector racks for 12 bombs were attached to the two underwing pylons normally used for "Hound Dog" air-to-ground missiles. The bomb load of the B-52Fs selected for conventional operations was thus nearly doubled, from 27 to 51, and SAC ordered racks for the 2d and 320th Bomb Wings assigned to Far East contingency plans.

As the situation in South Vietnam worsened, the Joint Chiefs deployed the modified B-52Fs to Andersen Air Force Base, Guam, in February 1965. Under the operational designation "Arc Light", the B-52s stood by to strike targets in North Vietnam in reprisal for terrorist actions against US personnel in the South.

In "Arc Light" strikes against the Viet Cong in South Vietnam and Cambodia, in "Commando Hunt" operations against Communist supply routes in Laos, in "Linebacker" raids on military targets in North Vietnam, and in close-support missions thought at first to be suitable only for fighter-bombers, the B-52 Stratofortresses of the USAF delivered massive blows with their destructive "iron bombs"

General Westmoreland wished to employ the idle B-52s on Guam in support of his ground forces, but he found no support for the proposal. An operation by American and South Vietnamese tactical aircraft on 15 April 1965, near Black Virgin Mountain, changed matters. Ineffectual bombing, in spite of the large number of fighter-bombers involved, led Westmoreland to press even more strongly for the B-52s: their large loads could provide the well-planned bombing pattern over a wide area needed to root out dispersed Viet Cong base camps. After meeting Westmoreland in Honolulu on 19–20 April, McNamara decided to use the strategic bombers for tactical operations in South Vietnam. Accordingly, the JCS ordered SAC and its Third Air Division on Guam to prepare the B-52s for conventional bombing operations—Arc Light.

Westmoreland wanted Arc Light strikes primarily for saturation bombing of Viet Cong base areas. A great bonus was that the B-52s would free tactical aircraft for more time-sensitive battlefield targets. In addition, the bombers could attack regardless of time of day or weather. This was especially valuable during the consistently bad flying weather of the northeast monsoon season (November to April) that restricted tactical air strikes. Thus, SAC's intercontinental strategic bombers became a huge reserve of flying artillery, able to reach targets beyond the range of Westmoreland's heaviest guns.

After some weeks of sifting intelligence data, MACV finally settled on the Ben Cat Special Zone, in Binh Duong province northwest of Saigon, for the first strike. SAC's Third Air Division executed "Arc Light I" on 18 June 1965: 30 B-52Fs flew the 12-hour, 5,500-mile (8,850km) round-trip from Guam to South Vietnam, refueled by

KC-135s from Kadena Air Base, Okinawa. The force was divided into the three-aircraft cells that became the standard formation for all Arc Light operations. Tragedy struck the first mission when two aircraft, their pilots unused to formation flying, collided during air refueling and crashed into the South China Sea, killing eight of twelve crew members. Only 26 B-52s released over target, and post-strike reconnaissance revealed little damage to the Viet Cong. But Westmoreland considered the results significant enough to warrant further operations.

Throughout the summer and fall, missions of up to 30 Arc Light B-52s attacked enemy bases and troop concentrations, indirectly aiding South Vietnamese and American ground operations. In November, B-52s supported US ground forces for the first time, when the 1st Cavalry Division encountered North Vietnamese units in the Ia Drang Valley near the Cambodian border. Eighteen B-52s struck enemy troop concentrations on 15 November, and additional strikes took place on subsequent days. In all, 96 sorties were flown and 1,795 short tons (1,603 tons; 1,628 tonnes) of bombs were dropped. By the end of 1965, when the large formations of 18 to 30 aircraft had been dropped in favor of smaller missions, the B-52s were averaging 300 sorties per month.

Structural modifications increase the bomb load

Even as the B-52Fs shuttled off to South Vietnam on their missions, SAC was planning to replace them. The prospect of a long commitment to Arc Light prompted SAC to employ the more numerous B-52Ds and to give them greater conventional striking power. The "Big Belly" program of 1965 modified 82 B-52Ds to carry 42 750-pound (340kg) bombs—or as many as 84 500-pounders (227kg)—inside the plane, with 24 750-pounders or 500-pounders suspended from simple "stub" pylons beneath the wings. These changes increased the B-52s' maximum "iron-bomb" load from 51 bombs totaling 27,000 pounds (12,247kg) to 108 bombs totaling 60,000 pounds (27,216kg). Also developed were "C-racks" that could be loaded with 28 500-pounders and "clipped" into the bomb bays. Between December 1965 and September 1967, the entire B-52D fleet was modified.

Studies made by Boeing of the heavier weight carried by the Arc Light B-52s resulted in a structural strengthening program to extend aircraft service life. While undergoing "Big Belly" and structural modifications, all B-52Ds received new radar transponders for ground-directed bombing and coats of camouflage paint. After tests to find upper-surface

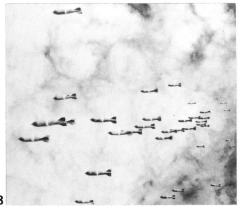

1. Strategic bombers in a tactical role in Southeast Asia: a flight of B-52s seen from the cockpit of another Stratofortress. The big bombers flew their first mission in Vietnam— against a Viet Cong base northwest of Saigon—on 18 June 1965. **2.** For their missions in Southeast Asia the B-52s carried non-nuclear ordnance—''iron bombs''. Under the ''Big Belly'' program of 1965, a B-52 could carry 42 of the 750lb bombs, seen here, internally and 24 more on underwing pylons. **3.** Bombs fall from a B-52 over North Vietnam, which was first struck by Stratofortresses on 11 April 1966.

camouflage schemes that would hamper visual detection of low-flying B-52s by enemy interceptors, SAC chose a mottled pattern of tan and two shades of green. A black under-surface and tail fin were chosen for searchlight suppression in the case of strikes on North Vietnam, where optically-guided anti-aircraft guns constituted a major defense element. The B-52Fs based on Guam received temporary coats of black over their white nuclear-blast-reflection paint; only the B-52Ds received coats of camouflage and black.

From June 1965 to March 1966, the B-52Fs of the 7th, 320th, and 484th Wings conducted Arc Light operations, spending alternating 90-day rotations at Andersen Air Force Base, Guam. On 1 April, however, the 28th and 454th Wings, with "Big Belly" B-52Ds, assumed responsibility for Arc Light.

"Combat Skyspot" aids bombing accuracy

Because improved intelligence had resulted in a three-fold increase in targets for B-52 strikes, early in 1966 Westmoreland requested a sortie increase from 300 to 450 per month, then to 600, and later to 800. McNamara approved the 800 sortie level for August, but munitions shortages and construction work at Guam delayed achievement of even 600 sorties per month until November 1966. But although the desired 800 sorties could not be flown, the added hitting power of the "Big Belly" B-52Ds pleased Westmoreland.

The arrival of ground-directed bombing equipment in 1966 solved many problems associated with B-52 employment. The movement to South Vietnam and Thailand of SAC Radar Bomb Scoring teams, which normally trained radar bombardiers, provided the flexibility and accuracy required to use Arc Light bombers in direct support of ground forces. Operating with aircraft carrying the new radar transponders, the radars of the bomb-scoring detachments could direct bombers and tactical aircraft to targets up to 100 international nautical miles (185km) away with good accuracy. The first of seven radar sites was established at Bien Hoa air base in March 1966, and a modification increased the radars' range to 200 international nautical miles (370km). These units, later named "Combat Skyspot", made the B-52s more responsive to growing ground force demands.

The presence of Combat Skyspot allowed Third Air Division, on 1 July 1966, to place six B-52s on 10-hour alert as a "Quick Reaction Force", to respond to strike requests by field commanders. This was a marked improvement over the 24 hours previously required to hit a planned target 1,100 by 2,200 yards (1 by 2km) in area. Combat Skyspot also permitted controllers to divert aircraft to targets that appeared while the bombers were in flight. But despite these improvements, Arc Light missions could not strike within 3,300 yards (3km) of friendly forces.

In 1966, B-52s struck North Vietnam for the first time. On 11 and 27 April the bombers attacked the Mu Gia Pass, leading into the Ho Chi Minh Trail network in Laos, but slowed infiltration and supply movement only briefly. After the initial Arc Light sorties hit Laos in December 1965, B-52s

routinely bombed roads and trans-shipment points in the panhandle area. As the war dragged on, SLAM (Seek, Locate, Annihilate, Monitor) zones and special areas were set up in Laos as "free fire zones" for B-52s and tactical aircraft. However, the B-52s did not strike northern Laos until 1970.

MACV incessantly requested more Arc Light sorties to allow wider latitude for the use of airpower in different bombing campaigns. Additional B-52 sorties would permit ground support and strikes against Viet Cong territory and base camps, as well as continued bombing of infiltration routes and supply bases along the trails in Laos and South Vietnam. MACV prevailed: the sortie rate was raised to 800 per month in February 1967, thus requiring more B-52Ds at Andersen. This, however, was the saturation point for Guam. In order to increase the sortie rate and relieve basing problems, it was necessary to base the bombers closer to their targets. U-Tapao airfield at Sattahip, Thailand, was chosen and Thai approval gained for its use by B-52s. By 10 July 1967, B-52s from U-Tapao, based just a few hours from their targets, were flying more than half the Arc Light sorties without aerial refueling.

Sortie rates were never far from the minds of American planners during 1966 and 1967. Any increase over 800 promised serious repercussions in the Western Pacific because it would require additional aircraft, crews, and bases — notably Kadena, Okinawa. In November 1967, despite SAC's reservations concerning the impact on the strategic alert forces and crews, McNamara approved a sortie rate of 1,200 from 1 February 1968.

Stratofortresses give close-in support

Arc Light operations in the last half of 1967 were mainly concentrated near the DMZ, where North Vietnamese gunners were shelling US Marine Corps fire support bases at Con Thien, Camp Carroll, and Dong Ha. In "Operation Neutralize" (11 September–31 October), the concentrated firepower of artillery, tactical aircraft, naval gunfire, and B-52s was used in an around-the-clock SLAM operation to destroy enemy positions and guns threatening the bases. Two Arc Light missions were flown each day; 910 sorties hit targets in the DMZ alone. This hammering appeared to blunt the enemy drive, for shelling declined sharply after October.

As the rainy season began, enemy pressure shifted away from the DMZ to the Central Highlands. Arc Light sorties in the northern provinces decreased considerably from September to November. One of the November sorties, however, was to prove as significant for the later defense of Khe Sanh as Operation Neutralize. During a mission, a B-52 accidentally breached the 3,300-yard (3km) limit by bombing within 1,500 yards (1.4km) of the Marine lines at Con Thien. The strike set off a series of secondary explosions, indicating that the enemy were "hugging" the Marine positions to exploit the safety zone. This led to a reappraisal of earlier proposals for using the B-52s for "close-in" support.

In late 1967 and early 1968, clear indica-

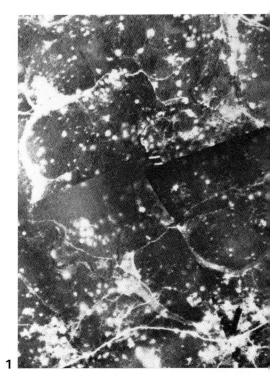

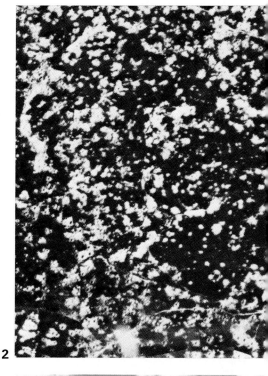

4

US Air Force Losses in Southeast Asia, January 1962–August 1973	
Aircraft lost—combat and operational/causes	2,257
USAF personnel killed	2,118
USAF personnel wounded	3,460
USAF personnel missing/captured	586
Cost of USAF operations: $3,129,900,000	

1. An aerial reconnaissance photograph of an area of the Demilitarized Zone prior to intensive air strikes.
2. Extensive cratering in the same area after B-52 bomber and tactical air strikes. When an enemy buildup in the DMZ threatened the US Marine base at Con Thien in September 1967, intensive B-52 action contributed to a "Dien Bien Phu in reverse"—about 10 per cent of the North Vietnamese force concentrated in the DMZ was killed or wounded. **3.** A B-52 drops 750lb and 1,000lb bombs on a target near Bien Hoa, December 1966. **4.** B-52s striking into Southeast Asia from Guam required 12 hours flying time and aerial refueling; from the base at U-Tapao, Thailand, seen here, targets could be reached in two to five hours.
5. Loading the internal bomb-racks of a Stratofortress.

5

tions of an impending enemy offensive around the Marine base at Khe Sanh prompted MACV to plan "Operation Niagara", a sustained SLAM air effort to disrupt the enemy's preparations and help hold Allied positions. A large part of the Arc Light effort was already devoted to interdiction strikes in the general area, and preliminaries to Niagara were underway when the North Vietnamese struck Khe Sanh on 21 January 1968. Westmoreland ordered Operation Niagara to be fully implemented next day.

Khe Sanh: breaking the enemy's back

Between initiation of the attack on Khe Sanh and the opening of the Tet offensive on 30 January, President Johnson responded to the North Korean seizure of the USS *Pueblo* by sending 26 more B-52s to the Pacific—15 to Kadena and 11 to Guam. The force needed to support the approved 1,200 sorties was already present, so the new B-52s formed a handy reserve to combat the Tet offensive in South Vietnam. While air operations at Khe Sanh continued unabated into February, the sortie rate was soon pushed to 1,800 monthly to meet the enemy threat. To achieve this, the Kadena-based B-52s joined the flight.

New tactics enhanced the B-52s' effectiveness in defending Khe Sanh. Three Stratofortresses were now over their targets every 90 minutes; this was later changed to six aircraft every three hours. Khe Sanh was receiving 48 of the 60 daily sorties, and the introduction of close-in missions made the strikes even more deadly. Based on the Con Thien experience, close-in support against targets within 1,094 yards (1,000m) of Marine positions proved feasible when two Combat Skyspot sites were used to direct the aircraft. During Operation Niagara, 101 close-in missions with 556 sorties were flown. One mission "Yankee 37", struck some 1,400 yards (1,300m) from Marine lines and touched off secondary explosions lasting more than two hours. In the Khe Sanh fighting, B-52s completed 2,548 sorties and dropped 59,542 short tons (53,162 tons; 54,006 tonnes) of bombs. The precise effect of the strikes will never be known, but Westmoreland told Third Air Division personnel at Andersen on 13 June 1968 that "the thing that broke their backs was basically the B-52s".

After President Johnson halted Rolling Thunder operations against North Vietnam on 1 November 1968, much greater target emphasis was placed on the Laotian trail network and its entry points from North Vietnam. B-52s played an essential role in Seventh Air Force's "Commando Hunt" operations to interdict the southward flow of men, supplies, equipment, and fuel during the Laotian dry season. In the first Commando Hunt, B-52 sorties were directed mainly against transshipment points and truck parks.

B-52s effectively engaged in three rainy-season Commando Hunt campaigns from 1969–70 to 1971–72. Cambodia became a target for Arc Light in 1969. Stratofortresses also supported the Cambodian incursion, in May 1970, and "Lam Son 719", the following year's unsuccessful South Vietnamese attempt to block the Communist trails in Laos by seizing Tchepone.

After Richard M. Nixon's election, the costs of the war, domestic unrest, and the administration's policy of "Vietnamization" began to influence the air war. Secretary of Defense Melvin R. Laird cut the Arc Light sortie rate to 1,600 on 15 July 1969 and to 1,400 early in October. Fiscal constraints and the continuing US withdrawal from the ground fighting reduced Arc Light sorties to 1,000 monthly from 1 June 1971. When that rate went into effect, the Eighth Air Force—as the Third Air Division had been redesignated in April 1970—could fly all sorties from U-Tapao. For the first time in five years, only 42 B-52s supported Arc Light. Many aircraft and crews returned to the United States to resume strategic alert duties.

Early in 1972, an enemy build-up in the Laotian trail network and on various fronts in the South indicated an imminent offensive. General Abrams and Admiral John S. McCain, Jr., Commander in Chief, Pacific, requested additional Arc Light support to forestall this threat. On 8 February, the Joint Chiefs of Staff authorized 1,200 sorties monthly and ordered 29 more B-52Ds to Guam. B-52 strength now allowed a further increase, to 1,500 sorties, at Abram's request. Meanwhile, the extra B-52s were operational against the Laotian trails, supply caches, and truck parks, to augment "Commando Hunt VII".

The bombers strike North once more

On Good Friday, 30 March, the enemy offensive struck South Vietnamese positions in Quang Tri province and quickly spread to the tri-border area at Kontum-Pleiku and Binh Long province (Loc Ninh and An Loc). The JCS immediately ordered more B-52s to Guam and raised the sortie rate to 1,800. Two more deployments in April sent all available B-52Ds to the theater and provided the reserves needed to mount more than 1,800 sorties per month. Once again, 105 Stratofortresses were in the Arc Light force. The steadily worsening situation on all three fronts led the JCS to send 28 B-52Gs to Guam. Although limited to 27 internal weapons, the newer B-52Gs could complete the round-trip to South Vietnam without refueling. However, they were not as well equipped as the B-52Ds—their electronic countermeasures gear incorporated older and less powerful transmitters. But with the addition of the B-52Gs, the Arc Light force of 133 aircraft was capable of 75 sorties daily and 2,250 monthly.

Because of the invasion, the President and JCS soon lifted the ban on bombing North Vietnam and allowed tactical aircraft and B-52s to attack progressively farther north as the enemy offensive continued. The bombers were ordered north in April 1972, for the first time since July 1968. In five missions, the B-52s struck Vinh, Bai Thuong airfield, Haiphong Petroleum Products storage area, and finally Hamn Rong trans-shipment point and Thanh Hoa on 21 and 23 April. The strike against Haiphong was the first time that B-52s had ventured into the heavily defended Hanoi-Haiphong area; they came away unscathed by surface-to-air missiles or anti-aircraft fire.

1

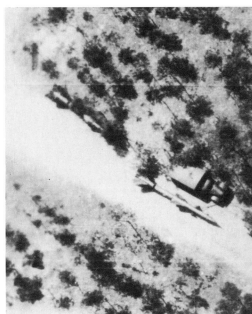

2

3

1. Safe from bombing, in an area prohibited to US aircraft, more than 100 military trucks and light tanks are parked in the streets of central Haiphong, North Vietnam. Dumps of fuel drums and other supplies can also be seen in this USAF reconnaissance photograph of March 1968. 2. The B-52s were not alone in striking North Vietnam; here, a Grumman A-6A Intruder, capable of carrying up to 15,000lbs of ordnance, from USS *Enterprise*, heads for a target in the North. 3. An aerial reconnaissance photograph shows SA-2 missiles, the major Communist counter-measure to the B-52s, near Thanh Hoa, North Vietnam, in May 1972. 4. Post-strike reconnaissance shows supply-packed railroad trucks destroyed at Kinh No, just north of Hanoi, during "Linebacker" strikes in December 1972. 5. Loading bombs on a B-52's underwing pylons. 6. A briefing for North Vietnamese pilots; Soviet-built MiG-21 interceptors are seen in the background.

4

5

6

More deployments in May sent 70 B-52Gs to Guam. Fifty B-52Ds at U-Tapao, together with 52 B-52Ds and 98 B-52Gs at Andersen, were flying 105 sorties daily (3,150 monthly) by late June. Between February and June, SAC had increased Eighth Air Force strength from 50 to 200 bombers, and had raised the sortie rate from 1,000 to 3,150.

Countering the Spring Invasion of 1972

The Arc Light bombing effort expanded quickly during April and May 1972, to support the hard-pressed South Vietnamese in Quang Tri province, at Kontum, and at An Loc, northwest of Saigon. Shifting from Laos and Cambodia, B-52s flew 6,000 sorties in April–June 1972. Their accurately-delivered bomb loads helped blunt and then turn back the enemy onslaught. During the enemy's final major thrust, at An Loc in mid-May, B-52s struck 91 targets with 56 sorties hitting between 660 and 875 yards (600–800m) from friendly lines. Here, as at Kontum and in Quang Tri, the planes frequently caught massed North Vietnamese troops, killing hundreds at a time and destroying entire units in a single strike.

In Quang Tri in April, two Arc Light cells demonstrated their ability to break up ground attacks when a forward air controller spotted enemy tanks boldly moving down Highway 1 toward Dong Ha. The area lay in a planned target box, so the controller called in B-52s. Thirty minutes later, six bombers attacked, knocking out 35 tanks and one divisional command bunker.

Blunting the Spring Invasion of 1972 had required the massive, coordinated employment of airborne controllers, USAF gunships, tactical aircraft, US Army helicopter gunships, transports, and B-52s. Brigadier General John R. McGiffert of the Third Regional Assistance Command later said that the B-52 "has become the most effective weapon we have been able to muster . . .". General John Vogt, Commander of Seventh Air Force, commented that the B-52 was "absolutely central to the successful defense efforts against the invading forces. Its massive fire power has made *the* difference in such key areas as An Loc and Kontum."

By mid-June the Communist offensive stalled, and the South Vietnamese began to regain some of the ground lost. B-52s now began regularly to range farther north than ever before, striking southern North Vietnam during "Linebacker" operations. In cooperation with tactical aircraft, the Stratofortresses blasted a variety of targets until late October, when President Nixon halted the bombing north of the 20th Parallel in anticipation of a truce. No progress was made in the Paris negotiations, however, and the North Vietnamese used the respite to rebuild their strength. The President therefore ordered the Joint Chiefs to plan the resumption of strikes against North Vietnam if necessary—this time concentrating on the Hanoi–Haiphong area.

On 13 December 1972, the North Vietnamese walked out of the Paris peace talks. Two days later, President Nixon ordered execution of "Linebacker II"—a three-day maximum effort by B-52s against the Hanoi–Haiphong area. The targets were storage and supply complexes, railroad yards, trans-shipment points and repair facilities along the major northwest and northeast rail lines, communications stations, and some MiG airfields. The primary aim was to strangle the North Vietnamese war effort by shutting off the flow of equipment and supplies.

To maintain pressure, three waves of B-52s were to strike each night, with F-111s and A-6s following up during the day. The B-52s operated at night to minimize visual tracking by anti-aircraft gunners and MiG pilots. Heavy anti-aircraft concentrations meant that the bombers must fly above 30,000 feet (3,050m), where the SAMs were deadliest. However, judging by the experience of the five strikes of the previous April, escort aircraft and mutual electronic jamming by each three-aircraft cell seemed adequate protection. Although planners called for pre-strike raids against MiG airfields, they did not have enough support aircraft to attack SAM sites as each of the three bomber waves approached. The same lack of support aircraft meant that only limited "chaff support" could be provided to confuse the enemy radars.

"Linebacker": the crowded air above Hanoi

This factor limited the approach and exit routes available to the B-52 waves. To take advantage of the expected strong winds from the northwest, ingress routes  for major targets in the Hanoi area were invariably from the northwest. Immediately after bomb release, the aircraft were to make extremely large post-target turns to get out of SAM range as quickly as possible. Only minor altitude and heading variations were planned for the cells composing the bomber "streams". Cells were "compressed" within the streams to reduce exposure to SAMs, to enhance electronic countermeasures protection within and among cells, and to stay within the chaff coverage. Because SAC crews  seldom flew in large formations at night, and because the airspace over Hanoi would be crowded, crews were told to avoid collision by maneuvering as little as possible.

Less than 30 minutes before the first of 129 scheduled B-52s arrived over target on the evening of 18 December, F-111s struck four MiG airfields. F-4s sowed two chaff corridors to cover strikes against the Kinh No and Yen Vien complexes just north of Hanoi. That night, as on the two following, the prevailing northwest winds of over 100 knots that hastened the B-52s down the Red River Valley also blew the chaff out of the corridors before the Stratofortresses arrived.

The first B-52s hit Hoa Lac, Kep, and Phuc Yen airfields, with one plane downing a MiG for the first confirmed B-52 aerial victory of Linebacker II and of the war. Kinh No and Yen Vien were then hit. Aircraft "Charcoal 1", leading nine Guam-based B-52Gs against the Yen Vien/Ai Mo warehouse area, was struck by two SAMs prior to bomb release and crashed north-west of Hanoi—the first B-52 lost to hostile

CONFIRMED 122MM CD GUNS ON D

1. To minimize the effects of US bombing, North Vietnam's armaments industry was dispersed in underground workshops like that seen here.
2. B-52s, F-4 Phantoms and the more recently deployed General Dynamics F-111s delivered the punch of "Linebacker" raids in December 1972; here, a USAF F-111 takes off from its base in Thailand. **3.** A USAF air reconnaissance photograph shows two 122mm guns deployed as coastal artillery on a dike near Thai Binh, south of Haiphong, in July 1972. **4.** A black, bomb-laden B-52D BUFF (Big Fat Ugly Fella) thunders aloft from the switchback runway at Guam, bound for distant North Vietnam. Because targets were seldom seen, most of the B-52's iron bombs were rained down without precision aiming. The B-52D to F models carried up to 70,000lb (31,750kg) of iron bombs.
5. A B-52 heads for a ground support mission in South Vietnam: of the 126,615 combat sorties flown by Stratofortresses between June 1965 and August 1973, 55 percent were flown against targets in South Vietnam, 27 percent in Laos, 12 percent in Cambodia, and 6 percent against North Vietnam.

Linebacker II, 19–30 December, 1972	
Tactical aircraft sorties	1,000+
B-52 sorties	c.740
SAMs fired	c.1,000
MiGs destroyed	8
Tactical aircraft lost	11
B-52s lost	15
B-52 aircrew killed	4
B-52 aircrew captured	33
B-52 aircrew missing	29
B-52 aircrew recovered	26

fire in the operation and the second of the war. At midnight, 30 planes from Guam hit Hanoi again. Another B-52 was heavily damaged by a SAM during its post-target turn and crashed in Thailand after the crew bailed out. Five hours later, the third wave came in, losing one aircraft. On Day 1, 121 of 129 planned sorties were flown against Kinh No and Yen Vien complexes, three MiG airfields, the Hanoi railroad repair shops at Gia Lam, and Hanoi radio station. The defenders fired more than 200 SAMs and thousands of rounds of anti-aircraft ammunition, downing three B-52s and damaging two others. Gunners on the Stratofortresses destroyed at least one of the MiGs that tried ineffectively to intervene.

But Day 1 operations also revealed serious weaknesses in planning and execution that would become tragically evident in succeeding days. Tactics adopted from Arc Light bombing in the South were inappropriate to the heavily defended Hanoi area. The five missions flown in April, especially the Haiphong strike, misled American planners. Hanoi's defenses were not soft—that was obvious from earlier Linebacker operations—but they were evidently taken too lightly. The lack of more chaff corridors per wave prevented the bombers from using the high tailwinds to best advantage. Three waves nightly hindered more chaff support or SAM suppression, while allowing the enemy's defenses time to recover and prepare for another assault. The high winds aided the bombers to their targets—but also blew away the chaff so that the B-52s had to rely for radar protection on their own jamming gear alone. Further, the steeply-banked post-target turns put the B-52s head on into the 100-knot winds, considerably slowing their retreat, and diverting their countermeasures patterns, enabling nearby SAM radars to penetrate weak spots in the jamming barrage. Moreover, the long bomber streams and the imposition of a single point for post-target turns allowed the defenders to zero in on the turning-point after the first cells had passed.

A savage greeting from the SAMs

For Day 2, only minor variations were made in tactics: three losses from a force of 121 aircraft was considered acceptable. B-52s again hit Kinh No, Yen Vien, and Hanoi radio station, and also attacked Bac Giang trans-shipment point and Thai Nguyen thermal power plant north of Hanoi. Waves again were spaced four and five hours apart. No aircraft were lost, although the enemy fired nearly 200 SAMs.

The strikes on 19 December created a false sense of confidence, and few changes were made for Day 3. The first planes of the first wave on 20 December found the going easy—but many SAMs challenged the following aircraft. SAMs hit two B-52Gs that were belly-up to their attackers in post-target turns, and both crashed in Hanoi. One B-52D, hit before bomb release, limped back to Thailand before crashing. The last wave began its attack in the early morning hours—and the B-52s striking at Hanoi were greeted as savagely as their predecessors in the first wave. A SAM

heavily damaged a B-52D that crashed in Laos, and two B-52Gs attacking the city were also brought down by missiles. More than 220 SAMs were fired on the night of 20 December, and six B-52s were lost in nine hours. Two significant factors distinguished the aircraft lost to date—five were in their post-target turns, and five of the B-52Gs were not modified to carry the more powerful jamming transmitters.

However, except for the losses on 20 December, the first three days of attacks were judged successful. Most of the major targets suffered severe damage. Over 300 sorties were flown, and nine aircraft lost—slightly under 3 percent. Losses like those taken on Day 3, however, could soon bring an end to the bombing.

Even before the three-day maximum effort ended, the JCS ordered the extension of the bombing campaign, but at reduced levels. Crews blamed poor planning and tactics for the losses and argued for changes. A tactics panel at U-Tapao heard these grievances: crewmen complained in particular about the large post-target turns that disrupted jamming coverage and made them so vulnerable to SAMs. They wanted to make shallow turns and get out of the area fast, exiting "feet wet" over the Gulf of Tonkin. In addition, they sought more freedom to use evasive maneuvers, crossing tracks, shorter bomber streams, approaches from varying directions, random altitudes and spacing, and random changes of altitude to confuse enemy defenses.

New tactics introduced to minimize losses

SAC accepted these ideas and made other changes, some of which were incorporated in planning for Day 4. All sorties against Linebacker II targets on 21 December were flown from U-Tapao, while Guam-based bombers resumed Arc Light operations. On 22 December, Day 5, the B-52Ds moved east to strike Haiphong's rail yards and petroleum storage area. The attacking aircraft employed the revised tactics and escaped damage, despite near-misses. Christmas Eve, Day 7, completed the first week of Linebacker II. Much had been learned and significant damage done—but at the cost of 11 B-52s and many crewmen.

After a 36-hour bombing pause over Christmas, B-52 operations resumed on 26 December with a meticulously-planned and coordinated attack by 120 aircraft. Blankets of chaff covered Hanoi and Haiphong as seven separate waves of bombers battered ten different targets within some 15 minutes. This large force required more than 100 support aircraft: F-111s struck airfields while US Navy A-6s suppressed SAM batteries in the Haiphong area. Two compact bomber streams approached Hanoi from the northwest and southwest via Laos, departing by way of the Gulf of Tonkin. Two other streams flew a reverse course, coming from the northeast and southeast over the Gulf and exiting through Laos. Planes attacking Haiphong came in from northeast and southeast. The more vulnerable B-52Gs were assigned to Thai Nguyen and Haiphong.

The new tactics worked perfectly. The

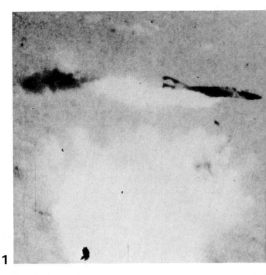

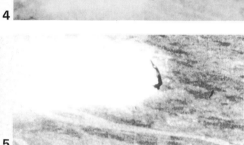

1 to **5.** A US Air Force Phantom RF-4C multi-sensor reconnaissance aircraft is destroyed by a North Vietnamese SA-2 Guideline missile fired from a site near the Red River area of Hanoi, 12 August 1967: (**1**) the surface-to-air missile explodes beneath the aircraft, from the underside of which a thin stream of fire begins to trail; (**2**) following the explosion, the aircraft is in flames; (**3** to **5**) the burning aircraft makes an upward turn. The two crewmen of the RF-4C successfully ejected and were captured and interned; one died in captivity. **6.** A total of 586 USAF personnel were listed as captured or missing in Southeast Asia in 1962–1973; here, captured "US air pirates" are paraded in Hanoi—both to humiliate them in the eyes of the population and, the Communists hope, break their morale and render them more receptive to indoctrination.
7. A North Vietnamese propaganda photograph—almost certainly posed—shows a downed US aviator "surrendering" to a typical rural civilian.
8. In another staged propaganda picture, a captured US pilot is guarded by Communist militamen.

defenses were saturated, confused, and degraded—although SAMs downed one plane at Hanoi. A second aircraft crashed short of U-Tapao's runway while trying to land with extremely heavy battle damage. In just over 15 minutes, 113 B-52s struck their targets in the most concentrated bomber attack in history. Indeed, it was a tactical masterpiece, demonstrating how well the lessons of the preceding raids had been learned.

Measuring the results of B-52 operations

Sixty Stratofortresses struck on Day 9. One B-52D from Guam was lost. A B-52D from U-Tapao was severely damaged attacking a SAM site, but Captain John D. Mize nursed his crippled plane toward Nakhon Phanom, Thailand, where the crew bailed out. Mize was the first SAC pilot to win the Air Force Cross for action in Southeast Asia. Two other planes were damaged on 27 December, but these were the last. Sixty aircraft struck with impunity on Days 10 and 11, with SAM firings declining significantly because the combination of blockade and bombing had cut off the supply of missiles.

At midnight on 29 December 1972, operations north of the 20th Parallel ceased. In the 11 days of Linebacker II operations, B-52s flew 729 sorties—340 from U-Tapao and 389 from Guam. SAM's accounted for all 15 B-52s lost—nine B-52Ds and six B-52Gs—and nine others were damaged. Twenty-nine crewmen were killed in action or crashes, 33 were captured and later returned, and 26 were rescued in post-strike operations. Stratofortresses hit 34 targets, expending nearly 49,000 bombs totaling over 15,000 short tons (13,395 tons; 13,605 tonnes). The bombing was extremely accurate in view of the strong defensive reactions and the number of aircraft involved. The North Vietnamese claimed to have sustained between 1,300 and 1,600 civilian casualties—surprisingly few considering the tonnage dropped and aircraft shot down in Hanoi. The bombing, a naval blockade, and the stalemate on the battlefield, all combined to force the North Vietnamese to negotiate in Paris. The extensive damage caused by Linebacker II required immediate repair and may have delayed the North Vietnamese invasion of the South that took place in 1975.

One more B-52 was lost before the cease-fire ended bombing operations in Vietnam on 27 January 1973. Bombing continued in Laos until mid-April, and then the B-52s shifted to Cambodia until 15 August, when Congress cut off funds for the air war. In eight years and two months, a total of 124,532 sorties successfully bombed their assigned targets, expending over 2,949,000 short tons (2,633,035 tons; 2,674,745 tonnes) of conventional ordnance. Eighteen B-52s were lost to enemy action, and 13 more were lost in mid-air collisions or accidents.

Aside from Linebacker II, Khe Sanh, Tet, and the 1972 Spring Invasion, the effectiveness of Arc Light was a matter of deep concern and frequent controversy from the first. General Westmoreland and MACV believed the bombing prevented enemy forces from massing for offensives,

harassed them, destroyed their bases, supplies and lines of communications, and placed troops under severe psychological strain by forcing constant movement and imposing the fear of sudden, devastating attacks. Ground commanders often thought more in terms of what did *not* happen—of the potential enemy operations disrupted—but US Air Force leaders were more concerned with damage done and enemy killed. However, effectiveness soon came to be expressed in terms of tons of bombs dropped in desired target boxes, release efficiency, and sorties completing missions—quantitative measures adopted because of the lack of hard facts from in-total of 124,532 sorties successfully bombed their assigned targets, expending over 2,949,000 short tons (2,633,035 tons; frequent ground follow-ups, the difficulty of post-strike photographic reconnaissance, and dubious POW accounts. SAC especially wanted to see a bigger return on its investment than large areas of jungle torn up and innumerable snakes, monkeys, and insects killed. It was footing the bill in terms of aircraft, crews, fuel, flying hours, and—by 1969—a severe moral problem throughout the B-52D crew force and their families. Above all, the operational requirements of Vietnam affected Strategic Air Command's primary mission of strategic deterrence.

Since the B-52 strikes occurred in remote jungles, far from friendly forces, where US observers were unable to observe their effect, Arc Light's impact was frequently questioned. However, when the enemy appeared in mass—as at Khe Sanh, during the Tet offensive, or at An Loc—the B-52s' achievements were readily visible. These were ideal targets for the bombers' massive killing power—and in these operations the B-52s made the North Vietnamese and Viet Cong pay a huge price. Perhaps Westmoreland correctly estimated Arc Light's role in the war, and its ultimate effectiveness, when he wrote in 1968 that: "The use of this weapon has won many battles and made it unnecessary to fight many more."

208

4

1. A B-52 takes off from Andersen AFB, Guam—from which the bombers made their first "Arc Light" strike into South Vietnam on 18 June 1965. 2. The US Navy flew bombing and reconnaissance missions alongside the USAF; here, aircraft of Attack Carrier Air Wing

Nine are seen on the after flight deck of USS *Constellation,* May 1972.
3. North Vietnamese air defense: Communist troops race to man their SA-2 site. All 15 of the B-52s lost in "Linebacker II" strikes, 18–29 December 1972, were downed by SAMs.

4. Bombs away: during "Linebacker II", B-52s expended more than 15,000 short tons of bombs in 729 sorties. 5. Damaged in the Spring Invasion of 1972, when 200 of the bombers were deployed in Southeast Asia, this B-52 was forced to land at Da Nang.

5

Disengagement abroad — disenchantment at home

Jacob Neufeld

The year 1971 marked the beginning of the second decade of the Vietnam War; the longest conflict in American history—and, next to the War between the States, probably the most divisive. By 1971, many Americans were tired of what they saw as an interminable and senseless conflict contributing no apparent benefit to the nation's security. President Nixon had begun to implement his strategy of disengagement, withdrawing American troops while strengthening South Vietnam's government and armed forces. This "Vietnamization" program envisaged that with the help of US air power and a residual force of between 40,000 and 50,000 American troops, the South Vietnamese could hold their own.

Vietnamization won popular support because it meant, primarily, that American servicemen were coming home at last. It was also a positive indication that the United States intended to terminate the war. On the other hand, Vietnamization was also used by the Nixon administration to justify even the most extreme military measures in Southeast Asia by claiming that they contributed to policy of disengagement. Thus, on 18 January 1971, the Pentagon confirmed that US aircraft were fully committed to the fighting in Cambodia.

Winding down the US combat role

Naturally, the North Vietnamese took advantage of the Vietnamization program to step up their infiltration into the South. To counter the Communist build-up, US bombers attacked enemy supply dumps and routes in southern Laos and in the northwest corner of South Vietnam, as a prelude to the large-scale offensive into Laos known as "Lam Son 719/Dewey Canyon II". This operation, described in more detail in an earlier chapter, began on 8 February 1971 and lasted for 44 days. Whatever the results of this controversial operation, it did not greatly increase confidence in the fighting ability of the South Vietnamese Army—or in the promise of Vietnamization, for the sake of which the Nixon administration was obliged to react strongly to every Communist threat. In fact, during the latter part of the Laotian operation, on 18 to 23 April, the US launched its heaviest bombing raids on North Vietnam since the November 1968 moratorium.

But even as fierce fighting raged in Indochina, President Nixon announced that the withdrawal of American personnel was proceeding ahead of schedule. On 26 April, there were 281,000 US servicemen in South Vietnam—2,600 fewer than the President's target for 1 May, and the lowest total since July 1966. The administration

It seemed that the rate of withdrawal of US troops from Vietnam could never match the growth rate of the anti-war movement at home, where politicians, students, and veterans marched together in the ranks of protestors. The publication of the "Pentagon Papers" contributed to the downfall of a President —and to a polarization of attitudes that continues to trouble the Free World

predicted that there would be only 184,000 Americans in South Vietnam by 1 December. However, this announcement also incorporated a severe warning to North Vietnam to speed settlement of the question of prisoners-of-war—or face continued bombing.

In mid-1971 the scale of fighting seemed to have diminished considerably. On 18 August, the premiers of Australia and New Zealand announced plans to withdraw their combat forces from South Vietnam by the end of 1971. (At the end of 1970, there were 6,763 Australian military personnel in Vietnam—providing three combat battalions—and 441 New Zealanders.)

In late September, President Nixon ordered heavy strikes by some 250 aircraft against a Communist concentration north of the DMZ, in order to forestall a Communist push through that buffer area. Even so, there seemed many signs that the war was on the wane. Combat activity involving US forces dropped sharply; on 9 October, the Defense Department announced that during the preceding week there had been only eight American combat fatalities—the lowest number of deaths since 28 August 1965. The next week only five Americans died, while the number of US troops committed fell to 196,000. Encouraged by these developments, President Nixon declared that America's offensive combat role in Vietnam had ended. He also announced further reductions amounting to 45,000 troops by 1 February 1972, by which time only 139,000 US servicemen would remain in South Vietnam. The President pointed out that there had been 544,000 US troops deployed when withdrawals began on 15 June 1969. During 1970, the rate of withdrawal was 12,500 troops per month,

increasing to 14,300 per month during the second half of 1971.

Stressing that American forces were now deployed in a strictly defensive posture, President Nixon emphasized that continued withdrawals depended on enemy activity, on the success of Vietnamization, and upon progress in freeing American prisoners held by the Communists. The Pentagon favored speedier withdrawal because of the increased vulnerability of the declining number of American troops. On 1 December, there were 177,000 US servicemen in South Vietnam—7,000 fewer than predicted in the President's announcement earlier in 1971.

War commentators, however, noted that there were some 13,000 US Navy personnel aboard Seventh Fleet vessels in the China Sea and 32,000 airmen based in Thailand—all directly involved in the war, but not included on the "in country" roll. They also noted that, unlike past withdrawal announcements which specified seven or eight-month periods, the latest announcement concerned a two-month period. This they interpreted as Nixon's warning to the Norrh Vietnamese that the rate of withdrawal depended on their response.

In December 1971, the military situation became critical in Laos and Cambodia: Communist forces advanced with alarming rapidity against government forces. Unwilling to risk the wreck of his Vietnamization policy by the collapse of Laos and Cambodia, President Nixon played a trump card. On 26 December, he ordered "Operation Proud Deep Alpha"—heavy raids by US fighter-bombers on enemy logistical facilities, anti-aircraft batteries, and airfields. The raids lasted for five days and marked the sharpest escalation of the war since November 1968. The raids were officially designated as retaliation for the enemy's failure to honor agreements related to the bombing halt, violations of the DMZ, the shelling of Saigon, and unprovoked attacks on US reconnaissance aircraft. The US government's critics, however, saw the bombings as a preemptive move against a Communist attack on the South Vietnamese Highlands and, as such, an exposure of the futility of the Vietnamization strategy.

The President fails to please the "doves"

President Nixon claimed to be winding-down the war in Indochina—but peace movement leaders in the United States accused the administration of duplicity. They asserted that fighting had actually increased; the only change being that most of the casualties were now Asian instead of American. The peace movement, which

1.

2.

1. Back from Vietnam, the 1st Marine Division honors its colors at Camp Pendleton, California. **2.** The Laotian incursion of 1971 provoked a new wave of anti-war protest: peaceful demonstrators picket the Naval Air Station, Moffett Field, California. **3.** US withdrawal operations in April 1971: a plastic-protected "Huey" is lowered on to the deck of the amphibious cargo ship USS *Durham*.

3.

had suffered from splits between outright pacifists and those who opposed only the Vietnam War—and from internal divisions in either camp—attained a new unity in the spring of 1971. A significant indication of growing opposition to involvement in Indochina was the diversity of organizations and individuals who flocked openly to oppose the Vietnam War. They represented a wide cross-section of American society, including students, war veterans, political leaders, businessmen, and labor unions.

Falling morale and rising drug abuse

The involvement of Vietnam veterans in the protest movement emphasized the grave morale problems faced by the American military authorities. Correspondents in Vietnam made sweeping allegations of corruption among supply personnel (in Saigon, especially, a black market in US military supplies flourished); of "fragging", the assassination by their own men of over-keèn officers and noncoms in the combat zones; of brutality towards civilians; and of widespread drug abuse. The last charge was certainly not without foundation. As early as September 1966, MACV had made a survey of drug availability: in the year ending June 1966, 100 drug cases (96 involving marihuana) were investigated; by 1967, cases involving opium and morphine had been uncovered, and there were 1,391 investigations involving 1,688 persons, with 427 courts-martial, in that year.

The Army-wide monthly average of drug cases in 1967 was .30 per 1,000 troops; the average in Vietnam was only .25 per 1,000. But by December 1968 the marihuana use rate had risen to 4.5 per 1,000 in Vietnam, with an opium rate of .068 per 1,000. More than 8,000 personnel were arrested on drug charges in 1969, and in 1970 there were 11,058 drug cases, of which 1,146 involved "hard" drugs. In August 1970, a Drug Abuse Task Force was formed: antinarcotic programs involved unit commanders, medical staff, chaplains, and legal personnel in lectures, counselling, amnesties for self-confessed offenders, and the establishment of detoxification centers. But in 1971, heroin and other hard drugs alone accounted for 7,026 cases—and that at a time of decreasing troop strength. Not until 1972, when strength declined to pre-1964 level, did drug abuse cease to be a serious problem.

On 18 April 1971, as a prelude to massive demonstrations for peace, a group called the Vietnam Veterans Against the War staged an "incursion" into the District of Columbia. Called "Dewey Canyon III"—parodying "Dewey Canyon II", the US drive that had been part of the "Lam Son 719" incursion into Cambodia—the veterans' activities in Washington included conventional anti-war demonstrations, "guerrilla theater" (street performances depicting the brutality of the war), and lobbying in the halls of Congress for amnesty for draft dodgers and improved veterans' benefits. John Kerry, a former naval officer and a Vietnam veteran, emerged as the protestors' leading spokesman, gaining considerable public attention with his speeches and forceful testimony before the Senate Foreign Relations Committee. The veterans' protest was dramatically highlighted at a ceremony at the Capitol, where hundreds publicly discarded medals and campaign ribbons won in Vietnam.

The veterans were merely the vanguard of a massive protest staged on 24 April by an estimated 200,000 persons (according to Washington police) or 500,000 (by the count of the protest's sponsors). These sponsors—the National Peace Action Coalition and the People's Coalition for Peace and Justice—organized simultaneous mass protests in Washington and San Francisco. The Washington "March for Peace" was remarkable both for its great size and its orderliness. Demonstrators from all sectors of American society loudly and clearly demanded: *"Get out of the War!"* The San Francisco demonstration—said to have drawn about 150,000 participants — was disrupted by militant Mexican-Americans who charged that the peace movement was a conspiracy aimed at distracting the nation from the coming "revolution".

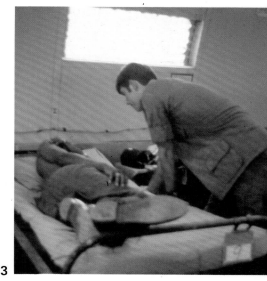

A world-wide storm of protest breaks

The rallies of 1971, unlike those of previous years, were not one-day events but lasted until the end of April. Meanwhile, other factions in the protest movement pursued their own activities; for example, the People's Lobby petitioned Congress for legislation to ameliorate the hardships to ordinary citizens created by the military draft, war taxes, and poverty in the US (not all of which could, of course, be justly blamed on the war effort). In cities throughout the country, tens of thousands paraded to demand an end to the war.

Nor was protest limited to the United States: in Australia and New Zealand crowds demonstrated against their countries' involvement; in the United Kingdom, although no British troops were committed in Vietnam, tens of thousands of demonstrators converged on the American Embassy in Grosvenor Square, London, in the largest of many demonstrations. In many other non-committed countries, notably Japan, left-wing movements used the Southeast Asian conflict as a peg on which to hang wide-ranging demonstrations against their nations' commitment to free-world, American-dominated policies. A special feature of demonstrations in the United States was the involvement of militant black organizations which claimed, with some justice, that the draft laws bore unfairly upon young blacks, who were more likely to be unemployed and less likely to be deferred for educational reasons than their white contemporaries. Some black "nationalists" claimed that their people were being called on to fight a "white man's war" against a colored race.

Although the April demonstrations were generally peaceful, May saw more aggressive tactics from the "doves". A group called the "Mayday Tribe" vowed to launch a para-military operation aimed at disrupting the business of government in Washington, and camped in West Potomac Park to prepare for their demonstrations. But although the Veterans Against the War had been permitted to camp on the

4

1. An ANZAC soldier flies the flag near the DMZ—but the withdrawal of all Australian troops was announced in August 1971. **2.** A US Army photographer providing the official view— many media reporters presented a distorted picture of the war. **3.** A fall in morale among US troops was reflected in rising drug abuse; here, a counselor talks with a distressed addict. **4.** A Negro trooper of the US 173d Airborne Division calls medics to a wounded comrade; many US blacks claimed that the draft laws bore un- fairly on their race. **5.** Former Am- bassador Edmund Gullion acts as spokesman for the Citizens' Committee for Peace with Freedom in Vietnam, May 1970; on the left is General Omar Bradley. **6.** Demonstrators at Sasebo, Japan, clash with police when protest- ing the arrival of the nuclear-powered aircraft carrier USS *Enterprise*, 1968.

5

6

Mall, Washington authorities would not grant similar privileges to the Tribe. Instead, 5,000 city police, backed by about 10,000 troops, raided the demonstrators' camp site on 1 May and dispersed them. However, this action did little to deter the demonstrators, who implemented their plan of disrupting government machinery by blocking roadways, strewing garbage in the streets, and urging federal employees not to work. On 3 May, Washington police cracked down on the demonstrators: 7,000 persons were summarily arrested for acts of civil disobedience. Confrontations between police and demonstrators lasted until 5 May, by which time 12,000 people had been arrested and—because of the lack of detention facilities for so many—confined by the police in an enclosure on a practice football field of the Washington Redskins. The stern police action did little good: most of those arrested were subsequently released for lack of evidence—the result of careless or illegal arrest procedures. Although the arrests helped to end three weeks of demonstrations in Washington, the protestors promised that they would return for a "Fall Offensive".

President Nixon's officials reacted fiercely to the May demonstrators, likening their behavior to the mob rule of Hitler's brown-shirted Nazi hooligans in Germany before World War II. Administration spokesmen also charged that Communist influence was apparent in the organization of the demonstrations. Now pro-administration rallies were staged in Washington, including some by Vietnam veterans who repudiated the views of the Veterans Against the War. On 8 May, the Reverend Carl McIntyre, a right-wing fundamentalist clergyman, led his third annual "Victory March" in support of the war against Communism. Although this demonstration at the Washington Monument grounds was supported by a major ex-servicemen's organization, the Veterans of Foreign Wars, it was attended by only 15,000 to 20,000 people.

Demonstrations fail to "Keep Connie Home"

The spring demonstrations were the high-point of the anti-war effort in 1971: protest leaders met with mixed results when trying to sustain the drive against the administration's policy. One of their more publicized efforts involved an attempt to prevent the aircraft carrier USS *Constellation*, then at San Diego, from returning to Vietnam. The effort to "Keep Connie Home" involved a poll of 45,000 civilian and 7,000 military "voters". Although the vote was five to one against a return to the war, "Connie" left home!

In October, protest leaders David Dellinger, Rennie Davis, and Jerry Gordon revealed extensive preparations for the "Fall Offensive". On 26 October, they launched in Washington a rally initiating a year-long campaign to defeat President Nixon in the 1972 election. They scheduled peace rallies in 16 cities, including Washington, for 6 November. The FBI and the Washington police, however, were now better prepared to deal with the demonstrators: they foiled numerous demonstrations and raids against federal buildings—and

this time took care to implement correct arrest procedures.

The subsequent lowering of the volume of anti-war protest matched the relative quiet in Indochina later in 1971—but the "Proud Deep Alpha" bombings at the end of December again brought demonstrators into the streets.

The "Pentagon Papers" shock the nation

On 13 June 1971, the *New York Times* created a national uproar when it began to publish a series of articles, supported by official documents, based on what came to be known as the "Pentagon Papers". These were drawn from a top-secret study of the governmental policies and actions which had resulted in the US commitment to the Vietnam War. The *Times* printed three instalments of the series before the Justice Department won a temporary court injunction banning publication on the grounds that disclosure of the documents would cause "irreparable injury" to the nation's defense.

On 17 June 1967, Robert S. McNamara, then Secretary of Defense, had commissioned an analysis of America's policy in Indochina since World War II. Begun on a modest scale, the project ultimately involved a total of 36 analysts and lasted 18 months—culminating in a 47-volume *History of the United States Decision-Making Process on Vietnam Policy* which ran to some 3,000 pages of text and included some 4,000 pages of documents. Reportedly, only 15 copies of the top-secret study were produced on its completion in 1968, and these were restricted to the National Archives.

The Pentagon Papers detailed the United States' military role in Vietnam during the Kennedy and Johnson administrations, and the diplomatic proceedings of the Truman and Eisenhower years. The overall revelation of the Pentagon Papers was that, between 1945 and 1968, US policy-makers had consistently underestimated the strength and the resourcefulness of the enemy. The Papers revealed that, while the presidents and their advisers often failed to appreciate the increasing extent of American commitment in Indochina, some governmental officials clearly grasped the implications of their policies and prepared contingency plans accordingly. During the 1960s, the United States had emphasized its image as the free world's bastion against Communism—but at the same time had disregarded its obligation to South Vietnam. Finally, the US government had not dealt honestly with the American people: it had not told them what was being done in their name in Indochina, and it had not truthfully reported to them the way the war was progressing.

The Nixon administration, priding itself on its "New Vietnam Policy", attempted to disassociate itself from its predecessors' handling of the Vietnam war. Nonetheless, the government denounced this "clear violation of national security", and filed a civil suit permanently to enjoin the *Times* from any further publication. The *Times* was muted—but now, on 18 June, the *Washington Post* began publishing its own Pentagon Papers series. The *Post*, too, was

1. North Vietnamese propaganda: "well-treated" US POWs in a prison library beneath a peace slogan. 2. President Nixon designates 21–27 March 1971 as a "National Week of Concern" for Americans captured or missing in Vietnam. 3. An American women's delegation lobbies the US Ambassador to the UN on the plight of POWs. 4. Grave faults in US planning were revealed by the "Pentagon Papers", originally published by *The New York Times* in June 1971. 5. An exhibition in the Capitol Building, Washington, seeks to evoke concern for the fate of US POWs, summer 1971.

"All the News That's Fit to Print"

The New York Times

LATE CITY EDITION
Weather: Partly sunny, cool today; cloudy and cool tonight, tomorrow. Temp. range: today 58-72; Monday 62-74. Temp.-Hum. Index yesterday 69. Full U.S. report on Page 85.

VOL. CXX...No. 41,415

© 1971 The New York Times Company

NEW YORK, TUESDAY, JUNE 15, 1971

15 CENTS

MAYOR'S BUDGET OF $8.8-BILLIONS AVOIDS LAYOFFS

ATTRITION ON JOBS

Losses Put at 14,320 And 5,013 Vacancies Due to Go Unfilled

By MARTIN TOLCHIN

Mayor Lindsay reduced his proposed expense budget by $37-million yesterday — mostly by postponing payments rather than reducing services — and presented an $8.8-billion budget that called for no layoffs of city employes.

"Right now, right at the hairline we feel it is possible for us to avoid layoffs," Edward K. Hamilton, the city's Budget Director, said at a City Hall briefing.

Mayor Lindsay said that the proposed budget "would allow New York City to maintain at minimally adequate levels the essential services which our citizens rely upon." The Mayor had described his previously submitted $9.5-billion budget as a "survival" budget.

[... for Employes]
[...million of the ...]
[for the f...]

The New York Times
Thomas J. Cuite, City Council majority leader, with new budget papers.

JERSEY APPROVES LINK

COURT SAYS CITIES MAY CLOSE POOLS TO BAR RACIAL MIX

5-4 Ruling Backs Shutdown of Recreational Facilities to Blacks and Whites

By FRED P. GRAHAM
Special to The New York Times

WASHINGTON, June 14—The Supreme Court ruled 5 to 4 today that communities may close their publicly owned recreational facilities rather than comply with court orders to desegregate them.

The dissenters protested that such closings expressed an official policy that "Negroes are unfit to associate with whites," but the majority held that Jackson, Miss., acted constitutionally when it closed its swimming pools rather than operate them on an integrated basis.

Because the city closed all pools to whites and blacks alike, its action did not deny Negroes the equal protection of the laws, the Court held.

Warning by Black

Justice Hugo L. Black, who wrote the majority opinion, went beyond the written decision in his statement from the bench to declare that the ruling was not an invitation to Southern communities to avoid school integration by closing schools.

"Any subterfuge used or utilized" to avoid school desegregation "will not be allowed," he said. He promised that "we will look through" any schemes by which public schools are closed and publicly supported segregated schools take their place.

The Court majority was composed of Justice Black plus Nixon's two nomi[...]

FACTORY OUTPUT CLIMBED IN MAY

MITCHELL SEEKS TO HALT SERIES ON VIETNAM BUT TIMES REFUSES

Vietnam Archive: Study Tells How Johnson Secretly Opened Way to Ground Combat

By NEIL SHEEHAN

President Johnson decided on April 1, 1965, to use American ground troops for offensive action in South Vietnam because the Administration had discovered that its long-planned bombing of North Vietnam—which had just begun—was not going to stave off collapse in the South, the Pentagon's study of the Vietnam war discloses. He ordered that the decision be kept secret.

"The fact that this departure from a long-held policy had momentous implications was well recognized by the Administration leadership," the Pentagon analyst writes, alluding to the policy axiom since the Korean conflict that another land war in Asia should be avoided.

Although the President's decision was a "pivotal" change, the study declares, "Mr. Johnson was greatly concerned that the step be given as little prominence as possible."

The decision was embodied in National Security Action Memorandum 328, on April 6, which included the following paragraphs:

"5. The President approved an 18-20,000 man increase in U.S. military support forces to fill out existing units and supply needed logistic personnel.

"6. The President approved the deployment of two additional Marine Battalions and one Marine Air Squadron and associated headquarters and support elements.

"7. The President approved a change of mission for all Marine Battalions deployed to Vietnam to permit their more active use under conditions to be established and approved by the Secretary of Defense in consultation with the Secretary of State."

The paragraph stating the President's concern about publicity gave stringent orders in writing to members of the National Security Council:

"11. The President desires that with respect to the actions in paragraphs 5 through 7, premature publicity be avoided by all possible precautions. The actions themselves should be taken as rapidly as practicable, but in ways that should minimize any appearance of sudden changes in policy, and official statements on these troop movements will be made only with the direct approval of the Secretary of Defense, in consultation with the Secretary of State. The President's desire is that these movements and changes should be understood as being gradual and wholly consistent with existing policy." [See text, action memorandum on change of mission, April 6, 1965, Page 21.]

The period of increasing ground-combat involvement is shown in the Pentagon papers to be the third major phase of President Johnson's commitment to South Vietnam. This period forms another section of the presentation of those papers by The New York Times.

The papers, prepared by a large team of authors in 1967-68 as an official study of how the United States went to war in Indochina, consist of 3,000 pages of analysis and 4,000 pages of supporting documents. The study covers nearly three decades of American policy toward Southeast Asia. Thus far The Times's reports on the study, with presentation of key documents, have covered the

> This is the third in a series of articles on a secret study, made in the Pentagon, of American participation in the Vietnam war. The study was obtained from other sources by The New York Times through the investigative reporting of Mr. Sheehan. The series was researched and written over three months by Mr. Sheehan and other staff members. Three pages of documentary material begin on Page 19.

Continued on Page 22, Col. 1

Italian Neo-Fascists Make Gains in Regional Voting

COURT STEP LIKELY

Return of Documents Asked in Telegram To Publisher

By MAX FRANKEL
Special to The New York Times

WASHINGTON, June 14—Attorney General John N. Mitchell asked The New York Times this evening to refrain from further publication of documents drawn from a Pentagon study of the Vietnam war on the ground that such disclosures would cause "irreparable injury to the defense interests of the United States."

If the paper refused, another Justice Department official said, the Government would try to forbid further publication by court action tomorrow. The Times refused to halt publication voluntarily.

The Justice Department's request and intention to seek a court enjoinder were conveyed by Robert C. Mardian, Assistant Attorney General in charge of the internal security division, to Harding F. Bancroft, executive vice president of The Times.

Spoke by Telephone

They spoke by telephone at about 7:30 P.M., which was some two hours before tomorrow's first edition of the paper was scheduled to go to press with the third installment of the articles about the Pentagon study.

A short time later, a telegram [...]

U.S. SUES SUBURB ON HOUSING BIAS

4

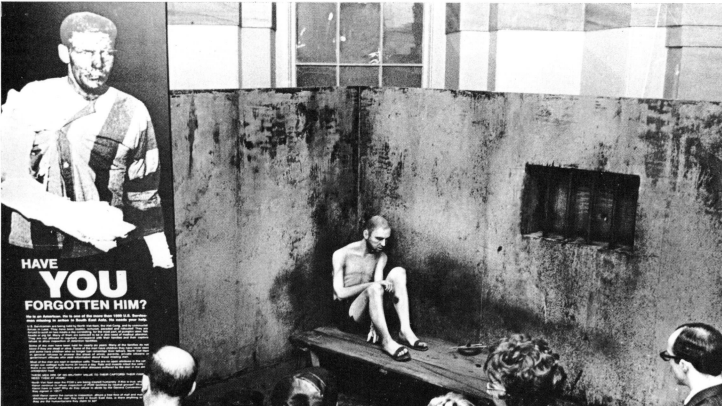

5

legally barred from publication when the Justice Department again filed suit.

Congressional reaction ranged from delight at the administration's embarrassment to shock at the threat to national security. Many congressmen expressed anger at the way in which the American people had apparently been so badly served and deliberately deceived by their own government. Congressmen resented the fact that they themselves had not been informed when crucial decisions to escalate the war were taken. Senate Democratic Leader Mike Mansfield, for long a leading "dove", promised to hold public hearings on the United States' involvement in the war.

Moreover, injunctions against the *New York Times* and *The Washington Post* did *not* prevent publication of the Pentagon Papers; instead they merely shifted the action elsewhere as new "leaks" from the Papers appeared in newspapers all over the United States. By the end of June, the Pentagon Papers had been published by the *Boston Globe*, the *Los Angeles Times*, the *Chicago Sun-Times*, and the *St. Louis Post-Dispatch*. All these were subsequently restrained by court action—but the courts did not stop the wire services from disseminating reports to their subscribers. Nor did legal action prevent hundreds of newspapers, magazines, and radio and television stations from making public a variety of accounts of the contents of the Pentagon Papers. And although the *New York Times* was barred from publishing the documents in its possession, it could not be prevented from reporting accounts published in other newspapers.

Legal battles over the Papers were fought in courtrooms throughout the country until 30 June, when the US Supreme Court settled the issue. By a six to three vote, the high court ruled *against* the government's claim that the disclosure of the Pentagon Papers would cause irreparable harm to the national defense. The Supreme Court's ruling thus meant that "prior restraint" by the administration was illegal.

Watergate: the fall of President Nixon

The source of the Pentagon Papers leak was 40-year-old Daniel Ellsberg, a former Marine officer and, later, an analyst for the State and Defense Departments. In the latter capacity, he had helped to write the study. Ellsberg, in 1971 a Fellow of the Massachusetts Institute of Technology, had become an ardent opponent of the Vietnam War, believing that the United States was responsible for funding and supplying the entire war in Indochina from 1945 onward. He was particularly distressed by what he saw as the total insensitivity of US officials to the tragic effects of the war on the people and the land of Vietnam. Moreover, Ellsberg was convinced that the Nixon administration was preparing to escalate the war and, thereby, compound the mistakes already made.

Soon after the Pentagon Papers filled the front page of the *New York Times*, Daniel Ellsberg became a prime suspect of the FBI and quickly went into hiding. After several days, however, Ellsberg gave himself up to a federal court and admitted that he was the *Times'* source. Indicted on charges of having unauthorized possession of national defense documents, he was released on $50,000 bail bond.

The investigation of Ellsberg led authorities to Representative Paul N. McClosky of California, a prominent critic of the Vietnam War. McClosky admitted that Ellsberg had given him a copy of the Pentagon Papers, but insisted that he could not possibly determine whether that particular copy was the one obtained by the *New York Times*. McClosky refused to discuss his relationship with Daniel Ellsberg any further. The trail led also to Anthony J. Russo, a former colleague of Ellsberg in the employment of the Rand Corporation. Russo refused to testify and was summarily jailed for contempt of court. In December, both Ellsberg and Russo were re-indicted by a Los Angeles grand jury for the grave crimes of theft of government property and conspiracy.

Two years later, in May 1973, all charges against the defendants were dropped—because of "governmental misconduct". Enumerating factors that, he stated, precluded a fair, dispassionate trial, presiding Judge William M. Byrne cited illegal wiretaps, a Watergate-style burglary of Ellsberg's psychiatrist's office—and an attempt to bribe Judge Byrne himself.

The publication of the Pentagon Papers undoubtedly helped to drive President Nixon and his advisers into an intensive and ill-judged campaign to maintain the President in power and, as a contribution to this end, to cover up "irregularities" in the conduct of the Vietnam War—such as the authorization of "secret" bombing in Cambodia which would be one of the House Judiciary Committee's possible grounds for impeachment in 1974. From the intensive drive to secure Nixon's re-election in 1972 stemmed the scandal that destroyed him.

On 17 June 1972, James McCord, security chief of the Committee for the Re-Election of the President, and four more "plumbers", were arrested while attempting to penetrate the Democratic Party's national headquarters in Washington's Watergate development. The trial and conviction of the "Watergate Seven", who included former Presidential aide E. Howard Hunt, Jr., could not prevent President Nixon's landslide victory—with 60.7 percent of the popular vote, carrying every state except Massachusetts and Washington, D.C.—in November 1972, to which his policy of withdrawal from Vietnam greatly contributed. Subsequently, however, continued investigation into the "dirty tricks" of the President's associates refueled the anti-administration, anti-authority mood across the nation engendered by the years of widespread protest against the war. Judicial processes resulted in the disgrace of former Cabinet members and White House officials, and although Nixon maintained that he had no knowledge of the illegal activities of his aides, popular opinion, led by sensational journalism like that of *The Washington Post*, turned strongly against him. Because the President had apparently "conspired" to keep facts about Vietnam hidden—albeit for the national good, as he judged—it was assumed by many that he was equally

1

guilty of political double-dealing.

The President might with dignity have stood on his record as a peacemaker and have weathered the storm—but his own personality betrayed him into unwise measures for self-defense that only served to tarnish his image further. The resignation of Vice-President Spiro Agnew, faced with criminal charges connected with his former service as Governor of Maryland, in October 1973, and the overwhelming evidence of corruption among the President's closest associates—illegal surveillance, perjury, burglary, fraud, extortion, illegal raising and use of campaign funds, and conspiracy to thwart justice were among the charges proven—pointed towards the inevitable downfall of Nixon himself. Any public approval gained by the release of Presidential "tapes" of intimate White House conferences, on 30 April 1974, was nullified by the President's refusal to release the crucial records until compelled to do so by the Supreme Court. On 5 August 1974, fresh releases revealed that Nixon had ordered a Watergate cover-up only six days after the original arrests. On 8 August, facing impeachment, President Nixon announced his resignation; he was succeeded on 9 August by Gerald R. Ford.

An abiding problem for the Free World

The Vietnam War had contributed to the death of President Johnson and, by helping create a climate of opinion that saw all authority as heartlessly corrupt, had helped to destroy President Nixon. The erosion of public faith in the processes of democratic government—which was immeasurably increased by the anti-war protests, the Pentagon Papers, and Watergate—constitutes a problem that still troubles and threatens the free world.

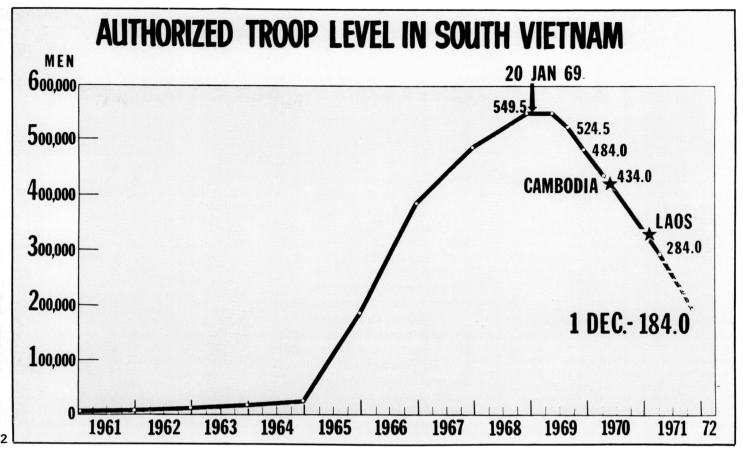

AUTHORIZED TROOP LEVEL IN SOUTH VIETNAM

MEN

600,000

500,000

400,000

300,000

200,000

100,000

20 JAN 69.

549.5
524.5
484.0
434.0
CAMBODIA

LAOS
284.0

1 DEC.- 184.0

1961 1962 1963 1964 1965 1966 1967 1968 1969 1970 1971 72

2

1. Re-elected in 1972, largely due to his policy of "Vietnamization" and US disengagement, President Richard M. Nixon takes the inaugural oath before Supreme Court Chief Justice Warren E. Burger, as Mrs Nixon holds the two Bibles, 20 January 1973. **2.** This is the chart used by President Nixon in a nationwide television broadcast on 7 April 1971. Announcing the withdrawal of an additional 100,000 men from Vietnam by 1 December, bringing the total committed down to 184,000, the President claimed that "The day the South Vietnamese can take over their own defense is in sight". **3.** On this recording equipment, the House Judiciary Committee considering the impeachment of President Nixon in May 1974 heard recordings of the White House "Watergate tapes".

3

Spring 1972: northern invasion repulsed

William L. Allen

Early in 1972, North Vietnamese and Viet Cong units entered South Vietnam in force in their strongest and best coordinated effort to topple the Republic since the Tet offensive of 1968. The invasion came close to spoiling American plans to withdraw from the conflict with integrity unimpaired. Although it was thwarted militarily, the 1972 offensive was a political catalyst much like Tet, for domestic and international opposition to the increased involvement of American air and naval forces drove the US military to the brink of unilateral withdrawal from Vietnam. It aggravated many controversial issues: popular concern over US prisoners of war; the military's doubts about the ability of South Vietnam to maintain its sovereignty; continued presidential insistence that the withdrawal of US forces continue on schedule; and increasing congressional discussion of the financial burden of supporting the South Vietnamese government. The 1972 invasion, and US reactions, also influenced strongly the progress of the long-standing peace talks.

In the years preceding the invasion, increasing responsibility had been given the South Vietnamese under the "Vietnamization" program, which built up the nation's indigenous capability to withstand Communist aggression. As Vietnamization progressed, President Nixon's 1969 plan for gradually phasing out American ground forces was accelerated. By 1 May 1972, there were 68,200 US personnel in South Vietnam—the lowest number in seven years.

Advance warning of a major offensive

The Communist thrust of 1972—sometimes called the Nguyen Hue offensive, the Easter offensive, or the Spring invasion—comprised major drives in three of the four military regions, beginning with a devastating attack south across the DMZ. From mid-December 1971, intelligence had reported increased enemy activity along the Ho Chi Minh Trail and in the DMZ. As this build-up continued, forming a pattern of sorts, South Vietnamese commanders and American advisers prepared to counter a major Communist offensive which they believed to be scheduled for the Tet holidays in mid-February. Enemy movements increased during January 1972, as did the vigilance of the Republic of Vietnam Armed Forces (RVNAF), but Tet passed without incident—and military readiness relaxed. Meanwhile, American leaders viewed the situation with trepidation: the major thrust they expected would be a real test of Vietnamization, perhaps with the preservation of a non-Communist Vietnam at stake.

The enemy's full intentions may never

The Communists talked peace in Paris and plotted invasion in Vietnam. Their Easter Offensive of 1972 aimed at the destruction of the ARVN and the overthrow of the Thieu government. Demoralized at first, the South Vietnamese fought back and expelled the invader. In January 1973, following a renewed US bombing offensive, cease-fire terms were agreed—but the peace was to be only brief

be known, but generally the Communists wanted to defeat ARVN forces, disrupt the Vietnamization program, and take over the government of South Vietnam. Enemy activity took many forms. Aerial photographs showed thousands of trucks in North Vietnamese supply dumps, apparently loaded and waiting for the roads to dry. Fuel pipelines were extended into the DMZ, and road-building efforts were intensified. During March, new SAM missile sites were located in the North. Major enemy units—including the North Vietnamese Army's 324B Division in Military Region 1 (MR-1)—were on the move.

Allied tactical aircraft sorties in February and March, mostly flown by South Vietnamese Air Force pilots, were targeted against these enemy deployments; for example, 24-hour "maximum strike efforts" were made in February against suspected Communist targets near Pleiku and in the DMZ. Country-wide results were impressive, and there continued to be little significant enemy offensive action.

The first thrust of the Easter offensive in MR-1 was made across the DMZ in northern Quany Tri province and was coupled with an easterly drive towards Hue. The initial massive artillery, infantry, and armor attacks began on 30 March 1972. They quickly drove the South Vietnamese from their forward artillery fire support bases (FSBs), installations which were never meant to be used as a defense against full-scale invasion. Besides the weight of three North Vietnamese divisions—some 40,000 troops—the Communists used weapons seldom seen in South Vietnam: Soviet T-54, T-34, and PT-76 tanks; SA-2 and SA-7 missiles; and the formidable 130mm gun. Defending MR-1 were three ARVN divisions, including the untested 3d Division; two brigades of Vietnamese

Marines; and Regional and Popular Forces. The South Vietnamese were numerically inferior to the attackers, and difficulties of command and control compounded the problem. During the first few days, overcasts and low ceilings shielded the Communists from attack by tactical aircraft. Thus, the only aerial assistance available to ground units was radar-controlled bombing—although additional artillery support came from US warships offshore.

By the end of the fourth day, during which enemy artillery barrages and ground attacks were among the most intensive of the war, RVNAF units had consolidated along a line from Dong Ha to Quang Tri combat base. The Communist advance then halted, giving South Vietnamese forces time to regroup and reinforce. By 14 April, ARVN units were able to conduct limited offensive operations.

Combat activity remained light in Quang Tri province until 27 April. Then the North Vietnamese took advantage of a day of bad weather to renew their advance and capture the town of Dong Ha. RVNAF units had to fall back on Quang Tri combat base. The situation deteriorated rapidly: on 30 April the decision was made to evacuate the combat base and set up a strong defense at Quang Tri city. As night fell, RVNAF units regrouped to the south. On 1 May, threatened by another major attack and with the intensity of the artillery barrage—including the feared 130mm fire—increasing, the troops around the city began to panic. Afraid, and in many cases out of control, they headed south once more. One Marine brigade withdrew in generally good order, but most other units abandoned tanks, artillery, and trucks in their haste to flee the enemy. New defensive positions were finally established along the southern bank of the Tach Ma River, where the RVNAF held the line until they were able to begin a counter-offensive in June.

Hue is held and a counter-offensive begins

The second enemy thrust in MR-1 also began on 30 March, when North Vietnamese forces moved from the A Shau Valley to the southwest of Hue, on a line generally parallel to Route 547. Elements of the 1st Division ARVN resisted strongly for some time at fire support bases "Bastogne" and "Checkmate", but these were captured on 29 April. South Vietnamese units then established themselves in the area of fire support base "Birmingham" to hold the enemy at bay.

A so-called defense of Hue began on 1 May. Efforts were made to reform the tactical units in the best way possible under the circumstances, and areas of

1. Spring 1972: North Vietnamese gunners open the way to Quang Tri.
2. Although a massive increase in Communist activity near the DMZ signalled a major offensive from December 1971 on, the ARVN were at first driven back in disorder; a South Vietnamese trooper calls for support on his field radio during the retreat from Quang Tri. 3. The Communists march south: three North Vietnamese divisions attacked across the Demilitarized Zone on 30 March 1972.

responsibility were newly assigned or changed to meet various contingencies. Broadly, the northern and eastern approaches to Hue were assigned to the newly-reinforced Marine Division, and the veteran 1st Division was assigned the southern and western approaches. Especial attention focused on the key avenues of approach from the northwest and southwest. A strong reserve served as a reaction force. Command and control was improved by placing the Regional and Popular Forces, which had fought very well, under the operational control of I Corps commander.

By 9 May, an airborne brigade—weary from intense fighting in the Kontum area, but reinforced with a battalion of artillery—arrived at Hue, where it was placed under control of the Marine Division. Four days later, the division began a brigade-size attack across the Thac Ma River. Other limited offensive actions were also undertaken; on 24 May the Marines made an amphibious assault behind enemy lines. Meanwhile, in the 1st Division area, FSB "Bastogne" was recaptured on 15 May, followed by the reoccupation of FSB "Checkmate".

Thus the RVNAF had been able to stiffen the resistance—with the aid of massive air and naval artillery support, including large numbers of B-52 strikes—and establish firm defensive lines. Once checked, the North Vietnamese were never able to regain the initiative.

On 28 June, the South Vietnamese began a general counter-offensive to recapture lost territory and to help restore public confidence in the military. Well-timed artillery and air attacks inhibited enemy build-ups and prevented large-scale Commust attacks. After a two-month battle, one of the most bitter of the war, Quang Tri city was completely reoccupied by South Vietnamese Marines on 16 September. Afterwards, and continuing until the cease-fire, RVNAF forces in MR-1 slowly retook much of the lost territory.

In Military Region 3 (MR-3), one NVA and two VC divisions were poised in Binh Long province by early April for the phase of the Easter offensive that had Saigon as its ultimate objective. The Communists planned to occupy An Loc, which would then become their new capital in the South, by 20 April.

Intelligence reports during March seemed largely to discount the likelihood of an enemy offensive as large as that in MR-1. Although increased enemy action was deemed probable near Tay Ninh city, intelligence placed great reliance on the ability of Allied operations in Cambodia to keep the NVA and VC divisions busy defending their lines of communication. Unfortunately, no reports were made of the presence of enemy armor in MR-3, and there was no warning that an attack might be mounted against towns and villages along Route 13, the main avenue of approach to Saigon from the north. The overall evaluation was that Communist units would continue to conduct their usual guerrilla, terrorist, and propaganda activities.

An Loc, and ultimately Saigon, were the main Communist objectives—but they were not to be realized. The first significant contact came about on 2 April, when

FSB Lac Long, about 22 miles (35km) northeast of Tay Ninh city, was overrun by a regimental-sized, armor-equipped Communist unit. Soon, another FSB at Thien Ngon fell to the enemy. ARVN forces began to react against the apparent threat to Tay Ninh city.

The Tay Ninh action was a ruse. For several days after the fall of the two FSBs, the Communists confined their movements to reconnaissance forays. On 5 April, however, as a prelude to the long siege of An Loc, the NVA overran the town of Loc Ninh in a little over 24 hours. What happened there is difficult to determine, for there were few survivors. Pitted against the NVA division was an ARVN regiment with cavalry and a Ranger battalion attached. These units were on search missions and were not expecting an attack. On the first day, the South Vietnamese on several occasions forced the enemy back from the barbed wire surrounding the Loc Ninh military base. The defenders were helped by many "close-in" air strikes, but the end came when the Communists committed their armor on 6 April.

Communist artillery hammers at An Loc

During a slack period between 8 and 12 April, the ARVN corps commander, realizing that the main Communist advance would be in Binh Long province rather than Tay Ninh, decided to reinforce An Loc and hold it at all costs to prevent the enemy from advancing against Saigon. Two additional units—the 21st Division ARVN, moving north from MR-4 along Route 13, and an airborne brigade from the general reserve—were initially assigned as reinforcements. A few days before the offensive, a task force assigned to screening operations some 9 miles (15km) north of An Loc was severely mauled by the enemy. This force was also ordered to reinforce the city, but as a result of its encounter with the Communists it was forced to destroy its equipment and move south on foot. However, the bulk of the command eventually contributed to the An Loc defense.

Skirmishing increased around An Loc during the five days before the first battle. Because intelligence reports showed heavy concentration of enemy units, B-52 and tactical air strikes were directed to suspect locations in a prelude to a defense which has been called a "monument to air power".

The first phase of the siege of An Loc began on 13 April; fortunately, B-52 strikes immediately preceding the attack were planned in depth around the threatened city. Just after midnight, Communist infantry and armored units were detected moving up to An Loc in force. The ensuing battle, made even more intense by the early execution of the pre-planned B-52 strikes, raged for three days. ARVN soldiers soon found that the M72 Light Anti-tank Weapon (LAW) would stop enemy armor, and "everybody wanted to see how many tanks they could kill". Helicopter gunships, Allied tactical aircraft, and B-52s tipped the scales in favor of the South Vietnamese, and when the dust of battle cleared on the morning of 16 April only a northern sector of the city and the

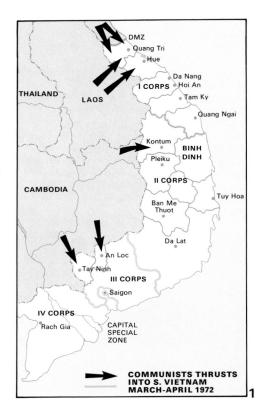

COMMUNISTS THRUSTS INTO S. VIETNAM MARCH-APRIL 1972

1

3

1. Map: the Communist thrusts of March–April 1972. **2.** Quang Tri was retaken by the South Vietnamese in September 1972; ARVN troops hold a captured Viet Cong flag and propaganda publication. **3.** With US air and naval artillery support, South Vietnam stemmed the Communist invasion and launched a counter-offensive in late June 1972; here, captured Communists are seen with their arms. **4.** Although no US combat troops were re-committed in Vietnam during the Spring invasion, materiel support was maintained; here, ARVN soldiers are moving up to the Dong Ha River on an M113 apc.

2

4

ammunition dump were controlled by the Communists. But An Loc lay in siege. Allied efforts failed to recapture lost ground, and on 19 April the enemy renewed the attack. The Communist deadline for the capture of An Loc—20 April—was not met, in spite of determined ground attacks and intense artillery bombardment. From 22 April, the artillery phase of the battle began in earnest. Helicopter entry into the city became almost impossible because of intense anti-aircraft fire. Until 10 May, the situation remained virtually unchanged, with the NVA and VC pouring indirect fire upon the defenders at an average rate of 1,000 rounds a day.

By 10 May, the enemy was ready for the second phase of the siege, redeploying in what was to be a final attempt to capture An Loc. Seven enemy regiments faced 4,000 defenders, of whom nearly one-quarter were wounded, although still able to man their positions. But morale was low, for the siege had lasted for almost a month. Knowing that a renewed attack was imminent, the Allies again pre-planned massive B-52 and tactical aircraft strikes, which were launched as Communist units began coordinated infantry and armor attacks from the west and north-east. The stubborness of the ARVN, effective use of the LAW, and a massive, timely, and accurate air effort brought the onslaught to a halt by 12 May. By nightfall on 15 May, the enemy had all but withdrawn. US advisers believed that one reason for the cessation of the attack was a new threat from the south. The 21st Division ARVN, which had been advancing slowly north along Route 13 from MR-4, was beginning to exert strong pressure on the Communists, as was another reinforcing regiment from MR-4. These two ARVN units successfully engaged the enemy on several occasions.

From mid-May to mid-June, RVNAF forces cleared the remaining pockets of resistance in An Loc; the siege was officially concluded on 18 June. During the remainder of the year, South Vietnamese troops pushed the Communists back from An Loc and brought in fresh soldiers to replace those who had fought for so long in the city's defense.

A new threat in the Central Highlands

An Loc was supplied entirely by air from 7 April to 25 June. During the first week, USAF aircraft were not needed. Only gradually did commanders realize the danger ground fire presented to slow-moving American and South Vietnamese helicopters and Vietnamese C-123 aircraft. Soon the cost became prohibitive: helicopter operations ceased on 12 April. Vietnamese Air Force C-123s continued to deliver supplies for another week, using the "low level paradrop" method, but after a C-123 was downed by anti-aircraft fire, the defenders were entirely dependent on USAF C-130s for resupply. Methods used were daylight low-altitude container drops, and high-altitude, low-opening paradrops. For various reasons, neither method proved satisfactory until aerial resupply experts arrived from the US. From 4 May onward, high-altitude systems began to prove themselves: eventually,

more than 90 percent of the supplies hit the drop zones. Most people on the ground in An Loc, while agreeing that aerial resupply was effective, had no idea of what it took to achieve such success. One US adviser remarked casually: "I always had plenty of rice and tuna, and there were always plenty of bullets lying around. . . ."

The course of the war had seemed to suggest that in the rolling, sparsely populated Central Highlands neither side tried very hard to win. From mid-December 1971, however, intelligence reports began to forewarn of a new urgency in enemy operations. Some sources reported that in Military Region 2 (MR-2) a Communist offensive was to be launched in three phases, scheduled to end on 24 February. Towards the end of January the first sightings of enemy armor were made—but because these observations could not be substantiated by ground reconnaissance, little credence was given the reports, although ARVN units received increased armor reinforcement in February. This move was prompted by additional sightings of enemy tanks and by reports that the Communists were bringing 122mm and 130mm guns into the nearby tri-border area. Other reinforcements were made: in February an airborne brigade was sent to strengthen vital FSBs on Rocket Ridge, west of Kontum city. During the first week in March, Airborne Division HQ and another airborne brigade were sent to defend the city and the southern part of Kontum province.

Tet passed in relative quiet as B-52s disrupted enemy timetables. Tactical air strikes pounded Communist troop concentrations, training areas, and bunker complexes. During March, ARVN units successfully engaged the Communists on several occasions, when the latter began to turn to larger unit tactics. There can be no doubt that air power and ARVN aggressiveness delayed the plans of the two NVA divisions located in the Central Highlands—but by 23 April the Communists were ready to attack.

The first enemy objective was Tan Canh, which dominated Route 14, the northern approach to Kontum city. During April, FSBs "Charlie" and "Delta"—both strategically located on Rocket Ridge, overlooking Route 14 from the west—fell to the enemy, while ARVN forces strengthened the defenses at Tan Canh. By 23 April, NVA artillery was saturating the area, having captured several features that enabled observation of the results of the fire. Early on 24 April, when ARVN M41 tanks came under fire, the Communists began their assault. By noon, their accurate fire had destroyed all five of the defenders' tanks as well as the division command bunker. Even more serious was the psychological effect of the onslaught upon the South Vietnamese troops: they did not react to the assault. Towards nightfall the ammunition dump was destroyed, and in spite of heavy Allied tactical air strikes the ARVN soldiers were driven deep into their bunkers. When enemy tanks appeared in force early next day, 900 undisciplined soldiers fled in fear. The NVA had taken its first objective.

Almost concurrent with the attack on Tan Canh was an assault on another ARVN regimental headquarters and airfield at

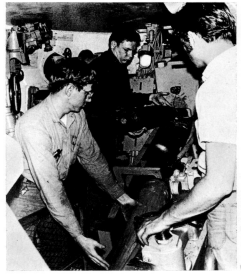

2

3

4

7

nearby Dac To II. Although ARVN troops made an armored counter-attack on 24 April, US advisers believed the compound was in imminent danger of being overrun. Like the regiment at Tan Canh, the ARVN Force at Dak To II was soon out of control and soldiers began to leave their positions. This compound was also lost.

Close support from B-52s at Kontum

Because of these enemy successes, the forces defending Kontum city were reorganized. One result of this was that an ARVN colonel was required to command several officers of equal rank, posing a severe command problem that had to be solved by American advisers. On 4 May, FSB "November", north of the city, fell to the enemy. Attacks-by-fire increased against Ranger camps astride Communist supply routes west of Kontum. Two camps —Ben Het and Polei Kleng—bore the brunt of these attacks. Ben Het held firm, but Polei Kleng was systematically pounded into submission.

The first attack on Kontum city began on 14 May; it came from the north and northwest and was spearheaded by massed T-54 tanks. Tactical air strikes, ARVN soldiers with LAWs, and US Cobra gunships mounting the TOW missile broke this attack by mid-morning. Although the defenses were penetrated in places, front lines were restored by nightfall after fierce hand-to-hand fighting. The Communists renewed the attack at 2000 hours and a new penetration was made, putting the defenders in a desperate situation. In a last, successful, effort to halt the enemy, ARVN units withdrew from their lines which were then bombed in close support by B-52s, killing hundreds of the attackers. After two days of relative quiet, enemy artillery fire increased and persisted. During a Communist attack on 20 May, some ARVN troops were driven from their defensive positions, but the majority held fast. A fifth assault came on 21 May: hand-to-hand fighting and tactical air and B-52 strikes beat it back.

During a four-day respite, the ARVN began limited counter-attacks, but these could not forestall a Communist attack in force on Kontum on 25 May. This time, enemy penetrations were more extensive. Shortly after noon, a "tactical emergency" was declared and all available air and gunship support was dispatched to support the defenders. Enemy artillery attacks increased in tempo, and after dark a new penetration was made in the northern perimeter as enemy tanks and infantry tried to drive a wedge between two ARVN regiments. At first light, the enemy tanks, having no cover in the open terrain north of the city, were taken under fire by TOW-equipped helicopters and, within the city, by LAW-equipped ARVN soldiers. South Vietnamese reinforcements arrived, but for several days the situation remained critical. On 30 May, President Thieu visited the city, talked with the defenders, and promoted the harassed colonel to brigadier general. Thieu ordered Kontum to be held at all costs. Slowly but surely the Communists were driven back, steadily losing tanks and men to the defenders. By 31 May the enemy was withdrawing and was in danger of being encircled by the counter-attacking South Vietnamese. The main battle was over; Kontum had been held.

While the Communists were attempting to capture Kontum, another NVA division, assisted by VC main force units, launched an assault in the coastal regions of Binh Dinh province. One of the aims of the Easter offensive was to cut South Vietnam in half by taking Kontum, Pleiku, and Binh Dinh provinces: the effort in Binh Dinh was a step towards that end. The North Vietnamese captured several district capitals and succeeded in cutting Route 1, but B-52 and tactical air strikes helped ARVN units turn back this phase of the enemy thrust.

Elsewhere in MR-2, the RVNAF began clearing operations to reopen Route 14 between Kontum and Pleiku—severed on 22 April—and to force the enemy out of areas north of Kontum city that had fallen during the first few days of the offensive. From mid-year to the cease-fire in January 1973, several sharp battles were fought following various RVNAF offensives.

Bombing of the North triggers new protests

In 1972 the US began a concerted bombing effort to blunt the Easter offensive and to hasten a cease-fire. Air power, including the B-52, was used in close support of the ground forces and against North Vietnam, the latter effort being intended to influence the desultory peace talks in Paris.

On 12 April, B-52s bombed deep in the North for the first time since November 1967. One especially heavy attack was made on 17 April against targets of military significance in the Hanoi and Haiphong areas. Communist-aligned nations assailed the bombing as an American escalation of the war: it sparked hundreds of anti-war demonstrations across the US, and Democratic presidential aspirants denounced reliance on bombing to stem the offensive and force negotiations. Defending the bombing, Secretary of Defense Melvin R. Laird said on 18 April that the United States had been "very restrained" but had been "answered by an invasion" across the DMZ in a flagrant, massive violation of the 1968 understanding that had ended the previous bombing in the North.

Bombardment of North Vietnam—both aerial and from US naval vessels—continued at varying intervals and intensities until the end of 1972. Primary targets included electrical power plants, factories, supply dumps, and bridges and highways. But the US was accused of killing civilians and destroying non-military targets such as dikes. On 8 May, President Nixon ordered the mining of Haiphong and six other North Vietnamese harbors. Controversy continued to mount in the US, and pressure on the administration from anti-war demonstrators, presidential candidates, and members of the House and Senate increased.

Bombing north of the 20th Parallel was halted on 23 October because a cease-fire seemed certain. On 18 December, however, with peace talks stalemated, the President ordered its resumption. This bombing effort, called "Linebacker II", was the heaviest of the war. Absolute air supremacy was achieved over North Vietnam,

1–2. A North Vietnamese T-54 tank destroyed by a US Army helicopter gunship at An Loc, 15 April 1972. **3.** Loading the TOW anti-tank missile system on a US Army UH-1B helicopter. **4.** In answer to the Communist offensive, B-52s struck deep into the North once more in April 1972. **5.** An ARVN Marine guards a bunker complex near Quang Tri. **6.** A US Navy photographer with expended shells and a burned-out tank on the road to Quang Tri.

3

4

6

but the B-52 attacks were criticized by some USAF pilots, who believed that many of bomber losses could have been avoided had evasive flight tactics been ordered. But President Nixon was determined to continue the bombing until Hanoi was prepared to negotiate in earnest. On 30 December, bombing was again stopped north of the 20th Parallel, just as criticism mounted to fever pitch. A cease-fire once again appeared to be likely.

With the exception of warships, aircraft, and their crews, sent temporarily to Southeast Asia to aid the South Vietnamese during the Easter offensive, the US continued the withdrawal of military personnel from South Vietnam which had begun in 1969. By 31 March 1972, US troop strength was 96,000; by 31 October, it had fallen to 32,000. At the year's end, only 24,000 US military personnel remained in the country. Concurrent with the withdrawal was a step-up in the rate of Vietnamization and the replacement of the vast amount of equipment—especially artillery weapons and armored vehicles—lost by the South Vietnamese during the Easter offensive.

1

Cease-fire is agreed and prisoners freed

Formal peace talks, in progress since 1969, continued haltingly during most of 1972. Private talks between US National Security Adviser Henry A. Kissinger and the chief North Vietnamese negotiator Le Duc Tho took place often during the year. Throughout these negotiations, both sides accused the other of wrongdoing, dishonesty, failure to keep promises, and irresponsible changing of demands. Basically, the US wished to make certain that South Vietnam had a chance of autonomy after a cease-fire, insisting also that prisoners of war be returned as a corollary to any agreed total withdrawal of American personnel. The North Vietnamese wished to impose a new government on the South, and consistently called for the resignation of the Thieu government in favor of a coalition. The extremely complicated and sensitive negotiations—both formal and private—increased in frequency until 26 October 1972, when Kissinger announced that he believed "peace is at hand". The talks then stalled, with charges of insincerity being made by both sides. With the mid-December resumption of bombing in the North came renewed criticism of the US, both from internal anti-war factions—now much strengthened—and from other nations, including former allies. On 30 December it was announced that the bombing would stop and that both secret and public talks would soon begin.

The cease-fire resulting from these new initiatives was initialed by Kissinger and Tho on 23 January 1973, and formally signed on 27 January. Final US withdrawals began, and American and South Vietnamese prisoners were freed. Among the first American prisoners released was Lieutenant Commander Everett Alvarez, Jr., the first to be captured. His words expressed the thoughts of many when he said: "God bless the President and God bless you, Mr. and Mrs. America, you did not forget us."

2

3

4

5

6

1. Henry A. Kissinger for the US and Le Duc Tho (foreground) for North Vietnam initial the cease-fire agreement in Paris on 23 January 1973.
2–4. At the cease-fire, the Vietnamese Communists listed 588 US POWs: these aerial photographs of North Vietnamese prison camps, dating from May 1973, include the notorious "Hanoi Hilton"—called Hoa Lo, "hell hole", in Vietnamese—where 352 POWs were concentrated in late 1970 after the abortive US raid on Son Tay prison. 5. Under guard, US POWs shower in a prison compound. 6. Journey into captivity: a US POW rides to prison on an ox-cart. 7. Operation Homecoming"—exchange of prisoners; North Vietnam agreed to release US POWs simultaneously with US troop withdrawals. 8. US and North Vietnamese representatives carry out difficult negotiations over the release of POWs. 9. A double victory salute from President Nixon, preparing to address more than 500 returned POWs at a ceremony in Washington. 10. War-disabled North Vietnamese soldiers are released from captivity in South Vietnam.

Southeast Asia: The Missing Men

At the time of the Peace Accords in January 1973, the US Department of Defense listed:
Servicemen as POWs in Southeast Asia 591, servicemen missing in action 1,380, servicemen unaccounted for 1,929.

In "Operation Homecoming" in 1973, the Communists released:
Servicemen previously identified as POWs 512, servicemen previously identified as missing in action 53, servicemen previously identified as killed in action 1.

In 1976 the Department of Defense still listed:
Servicemen as POWs 36, servicemen as missing in action 795.

In that year, witnesses before the House Select Committee on Missing Persons, Washington, D.C., alleged that "live sightings" of US servicemen still held captive—and of some of the 21 journalists missing—had occurred in Southeast Asia, and that insufficient effort was being made to check out these reports.

7

8

9

10

Defeat and retaliation: the Communist triumph

Ray L. Bowers

Most Americans regarded the 1973 cease-fire with satisfaction, pleased with the release of prisoners and relieved that the killing was apparently over. Few challenged President Nixon's claim that the settlement meant "peace with honor". But most of the North Vietnamese Army was left on the territory of South Vietnam, still committed to a Communist victory and now untroubled by interdiction attacks from the air. With the forces of South Vietnam too widely spread for effective strategic defense, the country's future seemed to depend on the willingness of the United States to repeat air and naval intervention of the kind which had saved the Republic in 1972. Assurances by Nixon to this effect (given to win Thieu's assent to the Paris peace terms), along with the promise of continued American military and economic aid, appeared to give Saigon a thin hope of long-term survival.

Despite the supposed cease-fire, fighting continued at about the level of the early 1960s. Some 145,000 Communist troops controlled about one third of the land area of the South, mainly in the western regions. These "liberated areas" contained approximately five per cent of the total population of the South. Government forces nibbled at the Communist-controlled territory; the Communists persisted in guerrilla and sapper actions, while bringing in additional troops and equipment from the North. The Communists improved and enlarged their network of roadways and pipelines, and began operating trucks along routes east of the mountains. By early 1975, they had completed a roadway, 25 feet (7.6m) wide, reaching from the former DMZ all the way to Loc Ninh, directly north of Saigon. At Khe Sanh, the North Vietnamese developed an airfield complex, including SA-2 missile installations. The South Vietnamese Air Force, lacking the high-performance aircraft and electronic equipment needed to attack the SAMs, could not counter the build-up. Meanwhile, widespread Communist deployment of the SA-7 (the shoulder-launched, heat-seeking rocket first used in South Vietnam during the 1972 offensive) and other anti-aircraft weaponry in the South meant that in any major campaign the Saigon regime's main strength—its air power—would be effectively neutralized.

The waning of US aid to South Vietnam

American command changes reflected the small remaining US role. Upon the release of the last American prisoners from Hanoi, the former theater headquarters in Saigon (MACV) shifted to Nakhon Phanom in north Thailand, which was designated Headquarters, US Support

---

American troops left South Vietnam and US aid to the nations of Indochina was curtailed. The Communists used the cease-fire period to consolidate their strength and step up infiltration. The final assault came early in 1975: as the last Americans were air-lifted to safety, South Vietnam and Cambodia collapsed swiftly and tragically. By the year's end, Laos had joined them in the Communist camp

---

Activities Group. Remaining in Saigon was a largely civilian-manned Defense Attaché Office, for administering American military aid and giving technical assistance.

More crucial events were taking place in the United States. Those who had opposed America's military commitment now attacked the continued military assistance program. On 8 October 1974, after long consideration, Congress appropriated only $700 million for South Vietnamese defense for the year ending 30 June 1975; the figure was well below the previous year's appropriation, and was less than the billion-dollar authorization used as the basis for expenditure during July, August, and September 1974. Such a sudden cut in funds produced very serious physical and psychological impact: of 66 South Vietnamese Air Force squadrons, for example, eleven were disbanded and many of the others' underwent a severe cutback in flying activity. The Communists were fully aware that, henceforth, Saigon must fight a "poor man's war". Meanwhile, President Nixon's resignation on 8 August 1974, as a result of the Watergate scandal, left uncertain the new administration's commitment to the Saigon regime—and the validity of Nixon's earlier assurances to Thieu.

In Cambodia, the unilateral cease-fire announced on 29 January 1973 by the Phnom Penh regime soon proved meaningless. The Communist Khmer Rouge, controlling most of the countryside and reinforced by several thousand North Vietnamese and Viet Cong, increased pressure on the principal cities and lines of communication. The Phnom Penh government appeared critically dependent on American material and air power. The termination of American air strikes on 15 August 1973—

forced by a Congress increasingly opposed to the residual American military role in Southeast Asia—thus seemed a fatal blow. The regime nevertheless clung to survival, aided by regular deliveries of food and munitions by Mekong River boat convoys and by a growing air transport effort.

The Cambodian crisis began in late January 1975, when Communist fire and minefields closed down all Mekong River traffic. Meanwhile, Communist rocket and artillery fire was brought to bear on Pochentong airfield, the last lifeline to Phnom Penh: during January, February, and March, more than 2,500 shells detonated on Pochentong. Lacking sufficient troops to open the river route and defend the capital city at the same time, the regime faced an impossible situation.

Despite the shelling, the Americans stepped up the airlift, now primarily using C-130s and jet DC-8s, operated by civilian contract aircrews. The high-volume airlift effort attained a daily average of 1,200 short tons (1,071 tons; 1,088 tonnes) during March—mainly munitions, fuel, and rice, hauled from Saigon and U-Tapao airfield in Thailand. The fall of Premier Lon Nol in late March appeared to signal the final collapse. Evacuations of Americans and other key personnel on return flights from Pochentong began soon afterwards. With Communist rocket and mortar crews only a mile from the runway, the delivery of 1,400 short tons (1,250 tons; 1,270 tonnes) on 11 April ended the resupply landings at Pochentong.

Cambodia is abandoned to the Communists:

US Marine helicopters carried out the final evacuation of Americans on 12 April, lifting 276 evacuees from a soccer field near the American Embassy. Ambassador John Gunther Dean boarded carrying a folded American flag. Resistance continued for four or five days more at Phnom Penh and at several outlying enclaves, supported to the end by US C-130 para-drops. The distraught Cambodian Ambassador in Washington meanwhile denounced the United States for first causing the Cambodians to resist and then abandoning them. Reports from Phnom Penh soon revealed the triumphant Communists' severe treatment of a population already destitute from years of conflict.

In South Vietnam, the North Vietnamese Army, with as many as 300,000 men in or adjacent to the country by late 1974, stood ready for the kill. Favored by a strategic interior position (a result of the crescent shape of South Vietnam), the Communists could obtain and exploit local superiority of force at any chosen objective.

Major operations in Phuoc Long pro-

1. The North Vietnamese flag waves over a captured bunker; in January 1975 Phuoc Binh was the first provincial capital overrun by the Communists. 2. President Nixon hailed the Paris cease-fire of January 1973 as "peace with honor"—but the withdrawal of US military support from South Vietnam allowed the Communists to plan a major offensive aimed at the final subjugation of the south. 3. Communist troops assault Ban Me Thuot: its imminent fall triggered an ARVN retreat from the Central Highlands.

vince late in 1974 revealed the South Vietnamese government's military weakness. A focal point was the airstrip at Song Be, fewer than 100 miles (160km) north of Saigon, the region's point-of-entry for reinforcements and supplies. Heavy Communist shelling and the capture of the adjacent 2,000-foot (610m) hill forced closure of the airstrip. With road travel already blocked, government forces thereafter were resupplied solely by helicopters, light aircraft, and parachute. The Saigon government's national reserve, already committed in the northern provinces, was unable to intervene in Phuoc Long. The presence of the North Vietnamese 9th Division directly north of Saigon tied down the capital city's defenders. Phuoc Binh city fell on the morning of 7 January 1975—the first provincial capital lost since 1972. Afterwards, comparing the defeat with the successful defense of An Loc in 1972, Lieutenant General Tran Van Minh, commander of the South Vietnamese Air Force, felt that the main differences lay in the greater strength of the attackers in 1975—and in the absence of American air power.

Communist strategy in the Central Highlands

On the eve of the victory in Phuoc Long, the Political Bureau in Hanoi approved an ambitious two-year strategy calling for widespread major attacks in the South in 1975, to create the conditions for a general offensive and uprising in 1976. The standing body of the Central Military Committee translated this resolution into plans for assaulting Ban Me Thuot—the important population center at the curve of the crescent. General Van Tien Dung was sent to the South Vietnamese Highlands as the representative of the Hanoi high command, establishing his command post in the forests west of Ban Me Thuot. Dung judged that General Pham Van Phu, commanding South Vietnamese forces in the region, would look on Kontum and Pleiku as the most probable Communist targets, for these lay near the Communist tri-border stronghold, offered a direct route to the coast, and had been the scene of heavy fighting in 1972. Dung resolved to strengthen this impression, ordering diversionary movements and attacks but meanwhile covertly deploying his forces to achieve a 5 to 1 manpower advantage for the Ban Me Thuot assault. Armored and infantry units took position west of the objective, while sappers and small units infiltrated the city and its environs. Last-hour attacks blocked the roadway between Pleiku and Ban Me Thuot.

Soon after midnight on 10 March, Communist tanks began their 25-mile (40-km) drive to Ban Me Thuot. Sapper units simultaneously began attacks by fire on the two airfields east of the city. Soon after dawn, tanks penetrated the city's northern command center. With the roadways closed and airfields under attack, the defenders were denied early reinforcement. The velocity of the assault paralyzed the defenders' artillery direction and limited the effects of air strikes. By the morning of 11 March, Dung's officers were able to report that "basically the battle is over". Dung in turn informed Giap that he in-

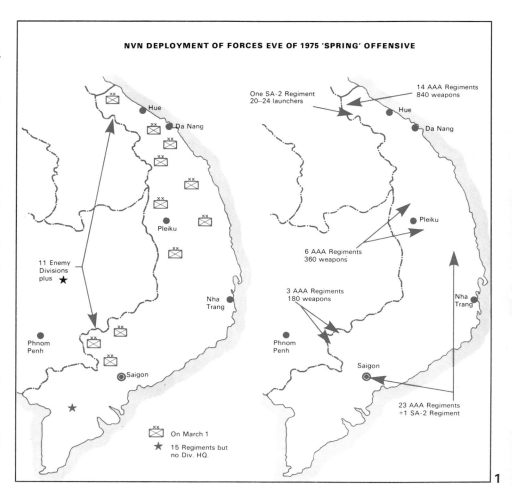

NVN DEPLOYMENT OF FORCES EVE OF 1975 'SPRING' OFFENSIVE

One SA-2 Regiment 20–24 launchers

14 AAA Regiments 840 weapons

6 AAA Regiments 360 weapons

3 AAA Regiments 180 weapons

23 AAA Regiments +1 SA-2 Regiment

11 Enemy Divisions plus ★

XX On March 1

★ 15 Regiments but no Div. HQ.

1

SPRING OFFENSIVE, 1975: COMPARATIVE STRENGTHS

South Vietnam			North Vietnam		
Army	ARVN regulars	180,600	Army	NVN and VC regulars	225,000
	Regional Forces	289,000		Guerrillas	40,000
	Popular Forces	193,000		Administrative	110,000
	Total	662,600		Total	375,000
	Tanks	c.350		Tanks and APCs	c.600
	APCs	c.880	Air Force	Aircraft	342
Air Force	Personnel	63,000		Air Defense (AA regts)	23
	Aircraft	1,673		(SAM regts)	1
Navy	Personnel	40,258	Navy	Personnel	3,000
	Craft	1,507		Craft	39

1. Map: North Vietnamese deployment on the eve of the 1975 offensive. **2.** A US Navy hospital corpsman aboard the amphibious cargo ship USS *Durham* assists a wounded South Vietnamese; the vessel evacuated more than 3,000 refugees from the Phan Rang area south of Cam Ranh Bay, the former logistical base which fell to the Communists on 3 April 1975. **3.** Refugees crowd the decks of the US merchant ship *Pioneer Contender*. **4.** Communist soldiers examine US-made recoilless rifles taken from the ARVN, April 1975. **5.** The price of panic: the feet of an ARVN soldier crushed to death when he tried to steal a ride to safety from Da Nang protrude from the wheel well of a World Airlines Boeing 727, 29 March 1975. **6.** And the cause of panic: North Vietnamese armor rolls through Da Nang. **7.** Hours after the evacuation of US and Vietnamese civilians, Communist troops move into Tan Son Nhut air base, past abandoned ARVN helicopters, on 30 April.

tended to consolidate and expand the victory, possibly extending operations northward. Fighting meanwhile continued east of Ban Me Thuot, government helicopters moving in reinforcements despite heavy losses to North Vietnamese fire.

Meeting with General Phu and other senior ARVN officers at his Cam Ranh Bay White House, President Thieu authorized a withdrawal from Kontum and Pleiku, supposedly to concentrate for a major effort to recover Ban Me Thuot. Returning to Pleiku, Phu conferred briefly with his staff, then ordered a withdrawal to the sea by way of the disused and unrepaired Route 7. Leadership was largely absent during the ensuing exodus from the Highlands; the long column of troops and civilians suffered terribly before reaching Tuy Hoa. Communist forces harassed and tried to annihilate the disintegrating column. Meanwhile, air evacuations from Pleiku quickly became chaotic, with frightened people fighting to board departing transport planes. In retrospect, Thieu's decision to authorize withdrawal from the Highlands was much criticized: the North Vietnamese General Dung termed it a mistake in strategy; Nguyen Cao Ky, former South Vietnamese Air Force chief and head of state, wrote that Thieu should have moved from Pleiku toward Ban Me Thuot, to trap the North Vietnamese there in a vise. But the order to withdraw was probably less disastrous than the chaotic nature of its execution.

During late March 1975, Communist forces in the northern provinces drove southward from Quang Tri and eastward from the hill country, toward Hue. Resistance was short-lived, partly because of an earlier decision to withdraw the ARVN airborne division. South Vietnamese Marines in and to the north of Hue were accordingly ordered to take the place of the paratroops at Da Nang. The result was a disorderly exodus of troops and civilians toward Da Nang, by land, sea, and helicopter. Disorder soon overwhelmed Da Nang and its major air base. Thousands fled by water, while air evacuations produced scenes of panic similar to those at Pleiku. The last flight from Da Nang was by an American contract Boeing 727 transport which took off on 29 March carrying some 300 persons—most of them soldiers who forced their way aboard. The crowds, and Communist fire, made further landings impossible. Hue and Da Nang thus fell after little or no resistance, although supposedly defended by 100,000 troops. As in the Highlands, discipline and military duty in many cases took second place to the safety of individuals and their families.

Preparations for the advance on Saigon

Meanwhile, in the Highlands, the victorious Communists dealt with the administration of the "liberated" provinces and at the same time deployed forces eastward to the coast. One by one, the coastal cities and bases fell: Tuy Hoa, Nha Trang, and (on 3 April) Cam Ranh Bay. Tens of thousands of refugees fled by American and other vessels to the island of Phu Quoc, amid great human suffering. Transport aircraft carried refugees and delivered relief supplies. Rumors of coups or political accommodations with the Communists swept the regions still controlled by Saigon. Thieu responded with declarations of firm purpose—and arrested members of the non-Communist opposition.

Meeting in Hanoi on 24 March, the Political Bureau concluded that the opportunity for quickly ending the war was at hand. Next day, General Dung was ordered to advance on Saigon. Speed was important; it was hoped to take the capital city before the heavy rains expected in two months. Communist planning for the race to Saigon was complex. Units in the Central Highlands had to change direction and make six river crossings on the way south. Through early April, trucks loaded with troops and equipment moved from Ban Me Thuot toward Loc Ninh; others rolled south from the northern provinces along coastal and interior routes, in the wake of the military victories. Each column moved under the protection of an anti-aircraft artillery regiment. Communist ships and boats landed men and supplies at Cam Ranh Bay; transport aircraft landed at Da Nang, Kontum, and elsewhere.

The Communist leaders watched closely for signs that US air units in Thailand might enter the campaign. Whatever President Ford's inclination, however, the Fulbright Amendment of July 1973 denied funds for American combat activities in or over Indochina. Given the nation's climate of opinion, any request by Ford for authority to commit US air power was certain to be rejected. For Ford instead urged the approval of funds originally requested in January: $300 million in additional military aid for Saigon; $222 million for Phnom Penh.

The American public opposes involvement

A Gallup poll released in March concluded that 78 per cent of the American public opposed further assistance to the Southeast Asian nations. Most Congressmen adopted previously-established attitudes on the additional aid request; Congressman Paul McClosky, long an opponent of American war roles, argued that sufficient aid should be provided to protect the people of Cambodia from the violence obviously in store after an insurgent victory. Early in March, the Democratic caucuses of both houses voted against the Ford request. Several senators expressed what appeared to be the national consensus—that further aid would only prolong the killing, and that defeat was inevitable. General Westmoreland, in retirement in South Carolina, raised what seemed a lone voice in favor of resuming American air strikes. The failure of the aid request made clear America's determination to keep out—and added a final blow to the morale and will to resist of the ARVN.

The administration persisted in requesting the additional funds. Henry Kissinger, now Secretary of State, when pressed by the Senate Committee on Appropriations on 15 April, could offer no assurance that such funds could stabilize the military situation. Nevertheless, Kissinger held that a failure to acknowledge a moral obligation would weaken America's

1. Attacks by Communist sappers on the airfields east of Ban Me Thuot, seen here, accompanied the thrust into the city by North Vietnamese General Van Tieng Dung's armor on 10 March 1975.
2. "The Convoy of Tears": a helpless target for Communist gunners, military and refugee transport clogs the poorly-maintained Route 7 west of Tuy Hoa during the retreat from the central Highlands. **3.** The fall of Saigon: immediately following President Duong Van Minh's cease-fire order to South Vietnamese forces, Communist troops advance on the Presidential Palace.
4. During evacuation operations on 28–29 April, so many South Vietnamese Air Force helicopters flew to the amphibious command ship USS *Blue Ridge* that, as seen here, many had to be pushed overboard to make room for new arrivals.
5. Crewmen on USS *Blue Ridge* carry the children of South Vietnamese Air Force personnel to a place of safety.

credibility and honor in the eyes of the world—to the detriment of the United States' ultimate goal of peace and world order. But Congress remained unwilling to vote the funds, engaging in debate over whether to give the President authority to use American troops to safeguard the evacuations. Ford's later action in ordering American military forces to protect the evacuations had to be based only on the "moral rationale".

On 3 April 1975, without authority from either South Vietnamese or American officials, a World Airways DC-8 lifted off from Saigon carrying around 50 orphan children, most of them of mixed blood, destined for homes in the United States. A few hours later President Ford announced his decision to launch what became known as "Operation Babylift"; US military transports fitted with seats and comfort facilities for the enterprise were already on the way to Southeast Asia. There was great emotional reaction to the tragic crash on 4 April of a giant C-5A carrying 257 orphans and adult escorts, many of them American women evacuated from their posts in Saigon. The aircraft was attempting to return to Tan Son Nhut without rudder and elevator control, after loss of a rear door; 155 died in the accident. Operation Babylift nevertheless continued, despite Communist propaganda attacks, bringing nearly 3,000 children from Vietnam and 52 from Cambodia.

Air evacuations of other Vietnamese, Americans, and other nationalities, began in the first week of April, thus "thinning out" the numbers who would require transport in any last-minute exodus. The flow was at first slow, blocked by red tape and by the unwillingness of many Americans to leave Vietnamese dependents and friends. Many transports brought cargo into Tan Son Nhut and departed without passengers. By 19 April, the total evacuated stood at 5,000—far short of the 170,000 Vietnamese refugees forecast by some Americans. At about this time, South Vietnamese authorities relaxed most of the exit formalities, resulting in an increase in the flow. US Air Force C-130s and C-141s joined the large-scale efforts, carrying evacuees to Clark Field in the Philippines for further transport to encampments on Guam and Wake. On 26 and 27 April, 6,000 persons left Saigon on 46 C-130 and 28 C-141 flights. American military personnel administered the processing and loading activities. The United States government received little help from the free world in this humanitarian venture.

Thieu resigns as the Communists approach

Meanwhile, the Communist race to Saigon had reached its final stages. Heavy fighting at Xuan Loc, 30 miles (48km) east of the capital, resulted in the isolation of some of the government's best remaining units. President Thieu announced his resignation on national television on 21 April, tearfully and angrily denouncing the United States for abandoning Vietnam, and making public Nixon's earlier assurances. Thieu was replaced by the elderly and ineffectual vice-president, General Duong Van Minh, while the

charismatic General Nguyen Cao Ky remained on the sidelines, talking of leading a defense of Saigon akin to that at Stalingrad.

Events now moved rapidly. Communist shelling and anti-aircraft fire forced the cessation of C-141 operations after the missions of 27 April. C-130 landings continued, although Bien Hoa was in flames and the situation at Tan Son Nhut was fast deteriorating. Several ex-US Cessna A-37 Dragonfly attack aircraft, flown by North Vietnamese pilots, wreaked further destruction at Tan Son Nhut. Shortly after midnight on 29 April, newly-emplaced North Vietnamese 130mm guns opened up on Tan Son Nhut, destroying several aircraft including a US Air Force C-130. Soon after dawn, the shelling and the practically uncontrollable crowds forced Ambassador Graham Martin to take the painful decision to send away the C-130s waiting overhead and to begin the final evacuation by helicopter.

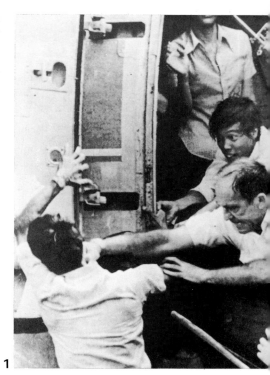
1

Last-minute exodus from the capital

During the 18 hours of "Operation Frequent Wind", a fleet of helicopters—mainly US Marine and US Air Force H-53s and H-46s—carried to vessels offshore a total of 1,373 American evacuees, 6,422 non-Americans, and 989 members of the US Marine force inserted at the outset to protect the loadings. Many evacuees moved in vehicle convoys to the pick-up points at the US Embassy and at Tan Son Nhut, harassed by mobs and armed South Vietnamese troops. Air America UH-1s lifted some individuals from scattered locations in the city. US Navy and US Air Force fighters, including "Wild Weasel" anti-SAM aircraft deployed shortly before to Korat, Thailand, circled overhead. Two F-4s took out an enemy 57mm anti-aircraft site 10 miles (16km) northeast of Saigon in late afternoon. Ambassador Martin held back the flow of Americans in order to bring out as many Vietnamese as possible. Although half the flights were made in darkness, they were without loss or casualty. Frequent Wind **3** ended soon after the departure of Martin, who boarded a helicopter only after insistent White House orders. The last Marines left the roof of the Embassy after dawn on 30 April, when looters were already in possession of the building's lower floors.

Tens of thousands more Vietnamese left their country by sea, undertaking voyages of great hardship. Many transferred at sea to US Navy vessels, and many made it all the way to the Philippines or Thailand. Some escaped crammed into Vietnamese helicopters and fixed-wing transports. Of the 130,000 refugees from Vietnam in spring 1975, most began new lives in the United States, but several thousand settled elsewhere, and at least 1,500, many of them men whose families had been left behind, returned to Vietnam.

After the "night of the helicopters", Saigon remained relatively quiet. At mid-morning on 30 April, General Duong Van Minh, president for only two days, called upon government forces to stop fighting. The Army quickly dissolved—troops threw away their uniforms and **4**

1. As the Communists sweep into Nha Trang, terrified refugees battle for places on the last evacuation aircraft —and an American official is forced to use his fists to stem the tide.
2. No place to land, so a South Vietnamese pilot leaps from the UH-1 "Huey" he is deliberately ditching near a US warship; 29 April 1975. **3.** After flying to safety in a Vietnamese Air Force helicopter, General Nguyen Cao Ky (farthest from camera) is escorted across the flight deck of USS *Midway*. **4.** On 30 April, the day of the South Vietnamese capital's fall, ARVN prisoners are marched through Saigon by a Communist guard. **5.** A ship's boat stands by to pick up the pilot of a South Vietnamese helicopter ditched near USS *Blue Ridge*.
6. Airfield installations burn, but abandoned C-7A Caribou and C-47 Skytrain transports are apparently untouched, as Communist soldiers storm across Tan Son Nhut air base.

many joined the looting. Only sporadic firing met the North Vietnamese tanks which rumbled in at noon. Five hours after the final helicopter departure, the tanks rolled through the gates of the Independence Palace. The fall of Saigon had been mercifully bloodless.

Swift action to rescue SS Mayaguez

The Laotian cease-fire of 22 February 1973 left the Communists in effective control of vast territory, including the panhandle region which gave access to South Vietnam and Cambodia. The rival military forces in Laos remained in unstable confrontation, marked by occasional minor clashes. The United States continued a modest military assistance program, scaling down sharply the contract air transport effort.

Spreading left-wing violence early in 1975 revealed the impotence of the coalition regime nominally under Prince Souvanna Phouma. An American contract C-130 crew reported that, on 31 May, armed Pathet Lao soldiers at Vientiane threatened to seize the aircraft, because it had been "stolen from Vietnam". The Communist take-over in Laos became complete in December 1975, when the coalition was dissolved and the People's Democratic Republic of Laos proclaimed.

The Cambodian seizure of the American merchantman *Mayaguez* on 12 May 1975, while en route to Thailand, recalled the taking of the *Pueblo* by the North Koreans seven years before. Stern and swift American action seemed necessary—both to prevent lengthy and humiliating negotiations like those accompanying the *Pueblo* affair, and to strengthen America's image of authority in world affairs. US military forces quickly prepared for an assault operation, deploying to U-Tapao all available helicopters, US Air Force security policemen from Nakhon Phanom, and a battalion of US Marines flown from Okinawa by the Air Force. Mechanical failure caused the crash of one of the Air Force CH-53 helicopters, killing all 23 crewmen and security policemen aboard. Several naval elements, including the carrier USS *Coral Sea*, set course for the Gulf of Thailand.

Reconnaissance aircraft kept track of the *Mayaguez*, anchored near Koh Tang off the Cambodian coast. American jets remained over the captured vessel at all times, turning back or sinking all boats attempting to reach the mainland—except for one suspected of having *Mayaguez* crewmen on board. US intelligence, however, was uncertain of the whereabouts of the ship's captain and 39 crewmen.

Nor did intelligence reports that 150 to 200 Cambodians defended Koh Tang with heavy weapons reach the Marine planners at U-Tapao. Eight Air Force CH-53s left U-Tapao before dawn on 15 May, intending to assault two designated landing zones on the island. Because the location of the *Mayaguez'* crew was unknown, pre-landing air and naval gunfire strikes were not made. The first helicopter to touch down on Koh Tang came under small arms, rocket, and mortar fire. After discharging his Marines, the pilot managed a single-engine take-off but, unable to

2

1

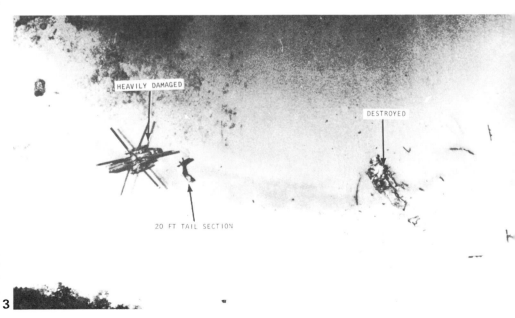

3

1. Soviet-built T-54 tanks of the North Vietnamese Army surround the Presidential Palace, Saigon, on 30 April 1975; most South Vietnamese soldiers turned to looting rather than resistance and the capital's fall was relatively bloodless. 2. US Marines deploy from a US Air Force CH-53 helicopter on Koh Tang Island, on 15 May 1975, following the seizure of the US merchant ship *Mayaguez* by Cambodia. 3. Destroyed and damaged US helicopters lie on the beach at Koh Tang; 18 American lives were lost and five helicopters destroyed or heavily damaged during rescue operations. 4. "Operation Frequent Wind": the fact that this photograph was taken by a North Vietnamese cameraman emphasizes the urgency of the last-minute evacuation of US and Vietnamese personnel from Saigon on 29–30 April, when more than 8,000 persons were airlifted to offshore shipping. 5. When these US Marines from the escort destroyer *Harold E. Holt* stormed aboard the *Mayaguez*, they found the ship abandoned. 6. Watched by victorious Communist soldiers, South Vietnamese Guards officers surrender at the Presidential Palace, Saigon, on 30 April 1975.

remain airborne, the helicopter fell into the sea just offshore. The second helicopter took many hits while attempting to land and barely managed to stagger back to the Thai coast, with its Marines still on board. The third CH-53, attempting a similar escape, lost an engine and came down on the beach. Number four burst into flames while still inbound—13 men died in the wreckage at the water's edge. The fifth helicopter managed to unload at Koh Tang, but returned to U-Tapao too badly damaged to undertake another mission. The last three helicopters waited offshore until, over a period of several hours, each was able to set down its troops on the island.

Meanwhile, three more CH-53s lifted Marines to the destroyer escort USS *Holt*. They formed a boarding party which quickly seized the abandoned *Mayaguez*. At mid-morning, word came that the *Mayaguez'* crew had been picked up in a boat, having been released by their captors on the mainland. The plight of the Marines already ashore on Koh Tang, however, remained serious. Before they could be withdrawn, reinforcement was needed to assure fire superiority. To prevent the Cambodians from sending troops or aircraft to Koh Tang, jets from the USS *Coral Sea* struck Ream airfield and other mainland targets. Meanwhile, with the *Mayaguez'* crew safe, American forward air controllers, gunships, and strike aircraft were free to hit Koh Tang itself. A C-130 dropped a 15,000-pound (6,800kg) bomb, helicopters shuttled in reinforcements and, after further fire exchanges, a heli-lifted evacuation began. The last Marines were brought out by CH-53 after nightfall.

Rescue operation seen as an American warning

The assault of 15 May cost 18 American lives and was of questionable point. The seizure of the *Mayaguez* had been made by local officials, unknown to the new leaders in Phnom Penh. The initial strong US actions—the patrolling aircraft and Washington's stern tone—apparently secured the release of the crewmen. But American intelligence had failed to locate the captured crewmen or to provide accurate information on the Koh Tang defenses.

However, the *Mayaguez* affair may be said to have removed some of the sting of America's sense of failure in Indochina, by showing that, where the lives of American personnel were concerned, the nation would take strong action. So far as the presence of US forces in South Korea and Europe was concerned, that lesson might be of importance in the future.

The continuing conflict in Southeast Asia

by Lt. Col. David Miller

The end of the Vietnam War was so sudden and final that most observers were taken by surprise. Many had expected that a smaller South Vietnam, centered on Saigon, would survive for a few more years—but the most protracted war of modern times ended with the total collapse of the South Vietnamese government, with the abrupt flight of the last Americans from Saigon, and with North Vietnamese troops parading through their enemy's capital city. The victory was complete.

The war affected not only the Indochinese countries directly involved, the United States, and the other countries prepared to commit troops, but also placed enormous strains on political links throughout the world, as well as giving rise to major agitation in countries far removed from the conflict. In the United States there had been considerable unrest, the sight of armed soldiers patrolling the streets had become almost commonplace, and President Johnson had been brought to the point where he felt forced to say, on 31 March 1968:

"With America's sons in the fields far away, with America's future under challenge here at home, with our hopes and the world's hopes for peace in the balance every day, I do not believe that I should devote an hour or a day of my time to any personal partisan causes or to any duties other than the awesome duties of this office, the Presidency of your country. Accordingly, I shall not seek, and I will not accept, the nomination of my Party for another term as your President."

Powerful reasons for Communist persistence

One of the basic facts of the war was that the existence of the Democratic Republic of Vietnam was never threatened. North Vietnam was bombed, shelled, and subjected to intense political pressures, but it was always stated quite explicitly by the government of the United States that these measures had the sole object of stopping Communist aggression against the South. "Our objective in South Vietnam has never been the annihilation of the enemy. It has been to bring about a recognition in Hanoi that its objective, taking over the south by force, could not be achieved," stated President Johnson. This placed the DRVN in a "can win, cannot lose" position. At any stage in the war, the bloodshed in the South and the bombing of the North could have been stopped within hours by a single command from the Central Committee in Hanoi.

The persistence of the Hanoi government is not really surprising, since it was

The ordeal of Southeast Asia did not end with the Communist victory in Vietnam in 1975, or the fall of Kampuchea (Cambodia) and Laos. Subjected to rival Soviet and Chinese influence, troubled by racial and political minorities, and threatened by escalating border conflicts, the area remains one that the Free World—however disillusioned by the US experience in Vietnam—ignores at its peril

normally made quite clear to the North Vietnamese what retaliatory action the United States would take to counter each escalation of the war. This meant that Hanoi was always able to calculate the cost of a projected action *beforehand* and to accept it; this, of course, made most American retributory actions ineffective, even before they had been taken, except insofar as they contributed to the overall cost of the war to Hanoi. Only once did the DRVN seriously miscalculate—in December 1972, when its representatives walked out of the peace talks in Paris. President Nixon unleashed a storm of bombing on the North in which many of the earlier target restrictions were lifted. Although a number of B-52s were shot down, the DRVN quickly ran out of surface-to-air missiles, leaving the United States with total air supremacy. The DRVN did not have any alternative but to return to the negotiating table; it had completely underestimated the scale and determination of Nixon's response, the cost of which was becoming unbearable.

The support given to the DRVN by the Communist countries was another major factor in the war. This concerted campaign was in marked contrast to the other side where, in all but a few cases, the support given to the United States and South Vietnam was lukewarm. Nevertheless, it is noticeable in retrospect that the major Communist countries did little to widen the scope of the conflict. Nor did they commit their own nationals, other than relatively small numbers of "advisers".

The DRVN's cynical disregard for international agreements was very marked and was reinforced not only by the lack of adequate supervision of the various agreements, but also by the failure of the "international community" to criticize even the

most blatant violations. The Laos Agreement of 1962, for example, was intended to ensure that country's neutrality, but the actual effect was to exclude the United States, while leaving the DRVN free to maintain the vital Ho Chi Minh Trail. The Paris Agreements of 1973 were also broken, the most important and conclusive breach being the invasion of the South by the NVA in 1974–1975. In one attempt to bring international pressure to bear on Hanoi, the United States asked the European Community (EEC) to condemn the invasion. At a meeting of EEC Foreign Ministers on 14 April 1975, it was decided to send food and medical supplies to *both* zones in SVN, and not to condemn the DRVN, on the grounds that the EEC was not prepared to apportion blame for the fighting.

One of the most maligned characters of the War was President Ngo Dinh Diem, who headed a ruling clique which eventually attracted such universal condemnation that its brutal elimination in the "Generals' Coup" caused surprisingly little adverse comment. What tends to be forgotten is that when the Geneva Agreements of 1954 partitioned the French colonial territory of Vietnam, there was no such entity as a State of South Vietnam. The Viet Minh had governed the northern provinces briefly from Hanoi in 1946–1947, and throughout the years of the first Indochina War they had controlled most of the population, especially in the north, through a tight-knit and highly effective political and administrative organization. Thus, when the DRVN was established, this organization simply moved into the open and carried on without a pause. There was no equivalent in the south: Ngo Dinh Diem was called back from the United States to try to take control of a state which did not exist and for which no plans had been made.

Diem strives to impose responsible government

In the cities power was split between the withdrawing French, a weak, indigenous, colonially-oriented civil service, and the absent but nevertheless powerful Emperor Bao Dai. The police and army were beginning to appreciate the power of their position and there was, inevitably, jockeying for position as Vietnamese officers jumped many ranks to take over from the departing French. Outside the cities and towns there were gangsters, the religious sects, and the Viet Minh. Diem's primary task was to create a state and a government out of chaos, and this inevitably resulted in autocratic rule. He was at first surprisingly successful, bringing the religio-political sects (Cao Dai, Hoa Hao, and Binh Xuyen) under control, while also preventing the

1. Fleeing from the Communist onslaught, boat-loads of refugees from the Cam Ranh Bay area await evacuation on USS *Durham*. Thousands more have perished in their attempts to escape.
2. A recruit to the Army of the Socialist Republic of Vietnam swears allegiance to the flag, 1977.
3. Road construction in a "new economic zone" of Vietnam; in January 1978 the Saigon government announced that more than one million had been "resettled" in these areas since 1976.
4. Citizens in "liberated" Hue greet the triumphant Communists.

army from becoming too powerful. He also managed to resettle more than 500,000 refugees who fled south in 1954–1956 under the terms of the Geneva Agreements. With massive American aid, Diem established a relatively secure republican regime and was beginning to make an impression in the rural areas when the Viet Cong, worried by this success, first struck. Thereafter the problem in Saigon always centered on the maintenance of stable government and the increase of the democratic process in the face of a campaign by a ruthless enemy, who was determined to prevent by force the successful implementation of any such popular measures.

Administrative corruption obscures military virtue

There can be no doubt that at certain periods the regimes in Saigon were both repressive and corrupt. They sometimes indulged in torture and assassination to achieve political (and even private) ends, while many people at all levels in the government not only condoned, but also were themselves involved in corruption. It is, however, equally true that the South Vietnamese fought from 1957 to 1975 and that, contrary to the publicity given to the American military involvement, the ARVN was always the largest single combat force in the South. Despite many hazards, not the least of which was incessant criticism in the Western press, the ARVN frequently fought well, especially during the Tet offensive of 1968 and the 1972 invasion, although it suffered setbacks. In 1974–1975, however, deprived of the material needs of war, with ammunition running out, with an almost total lack of air support, and knowing that South Vietnam was isolated internationally, the ARVN did not stand a chance. Given such circumstances it is scarcely surprising that, with a few honourable exceptions, "*sauve-qui-peut*" became the order of the day.

For the United States there were three fundamental problems:

1. How could a Western, technically-oriented nation best support an under-developed and politically immature society which was threatened by the techniques and skills of Communist revolutionary warfare?
2. How could a strong armed force, designed and equipped for nuclear and conventional warfare in Europe, participate effectively in a counter-revolutionary campaign in Southeast Asia?
3. How could a democratic society maintain a consensus throughout a protracted war being fought far away, in which its essential national interests were not obviously involved?

Even the most chauvinistic proponents of American involvement could not deny that in the euphoria of 1965–1967 the US forces were vastly overconfident and that they suffered from a widespread belief that technological resources and traditional military might would inevitably lead to a quick conclusion. The very size of American operations and the disproportionate amount of firepower brought to bear against most targets led to the un-

intentional involvement of (usually) innocent civilians, which, in terms of revolutionary warfare, was counter-productive. The NVA and Viet Cong, in fact, deliberately provoked such over-reaction because, in the long-term, the consequences were in their favor. American technological resources could be used effectively only in battles in remote areas, such as Khe Sanh and the A Shau Valley. There, far from population concentrations, the two military machines were able to match their skills and resources without harming innocent by-standers. On the few occasions when such situations arose, United States forces won decisively. It is, however, scarcely surprising that the enemy declined to play the game according to those rules.

It has become conventional wisdom to judge the war of attrition of 1965–1968 as a failed strategy, and to attribute the favorable situation of 1970–1971 to the strategies of "Vietnamization" and pacification, implemented from mid-1968 onward. It was frequently pointed out that, despite US claims of heavy enemy casualties, the enemy seemed always to be increasing in numbers. It would appear, however, that although unpleasant and costly in lives, the "main force" strategy of 1965–1968 played a vital role in depleting the manpower resources of the NVA and Viet Cong, especially in view of the restrictions placed upon US military actions against the DRVN itself. NVA and VC losses between January 1966 and May 1968 amounted to 252,384 deaths and 52,031 surrenders, with an uncounted number of wounded and missing. Although such losses did not bring the DRVN close to military defeat in traditional terms, they nevertheless represented a cumulative loss in a vital resource. This process of attrition was unintentionally, and most unwisely, accelerated by the DRVN itself in the Tet offensive of 1968—in which the VC suffered enormous casualties.

A US defeat with far-reaching effects

Finally, as has been shown repeatedly in this book, the military battle is but half of the war; it is the political decision which is both essential and enduring. In the case of Vietnam, the military forces of SVN and its allies, after much tribulation, eventually created the circumstances in 1970–1971 where defeat of the enemy was possible—but the position in the United States was such that no political advantage could be taken of the favorable military situation. Hanoi did not threaten the existence of the United States, not did the United States intend physically to take over the DRVN; instead, their military forces met head-on in the territory of a third party, South Vietnam, and in the final analysis it was a question of whose political willpower could last the longer.

The greatest single consequence of the North Vietnamese victory was the defeat of the United States, a proud nation with a hitherto unbroken series of military triumphs in its history. Successive governments in Washington had publicly set themselves the aim of preserving a non-Communist, free South Vietnam, and the failure was incontrovertible. However,

1

1. "Operation New Life": on the US-administered island of Guam, refugees from the Communist regime in Vietnam await resettlement in the Free World. By 1979, the US, Great Britain, Australia, Canada, West Germany, and France were among the western nations offering refuge. **2.** Vietnamese on Guam read of the problems imposed on resettlement by the flood of refugees; late in 1977 it was estimated that some 1,500 were leaving Vietnam by sea every month. **3.** Many of the ARVN soldiers who surrendered in 1975 were imprisoned in "political re-education camps", which were estimated to have up to 400,000 inmates in 1975–78. **4.** Pol Pot, Prime Minister, Secretary of the Communist Party, and dictatorial ruler of Kampuchea makes an official visit to the People's Republic of China in 1977.

the process of recovery from this traumatic experience has been fairly rapid and United States leadership in the West has not been subjected to any serious questioning. Indeed, with the Vietnam conflict over, United States concentration upon, and involvement in, the defense of Europe is greater than ever, and the NATO allies have absolute faith in the United States commitment. But it is extremely improbable that the United States will ever again become involved in a war on the Asian mainland.

Communist expansion: the "domino theory"

Throughout the years of the Second Vietnam War there was impassioned argument as to what would happen when the war was over—especially if the Communists were to win. The "domino theory", generally attributed to President Eisenhower, postulated that the Communists would rapidly expand from Indochina and, by a mixture of subversion and direct involvement, take over Southeast Asia, the countries falling one after another like a "train" of dominoes. The active, aggressive Vietnamese would, so the argument ran, quickly dominate the gentler, more insouciant Khmers and Laotians. The existing insurgencies in Thailand, Malaysia, and Burma would be encouraged by injections of materiel, "advisers", and eventually military units as well. Further, the island republics of the Philippines and Indonesia were seen as prime targets for Hanoi-style revolutionary wars, either in parallel with, or in succession to, the conflict on the mainland.

A contrary view was generally held by those who opposed US involvement in the war. Their belief, although less coherently expressed, envisaged a benign Ho Chi Minh presiding over a peaceful Vietnam and living in tranquility with his neighbors. Supporters of this proposition vehemently rejected the domino theory, arguing that Vietnam was a "special case" and that once the country was reunited the Vietnamese would leave their neighbors strictly alone.

An examination of the literature of the period shows that neither side in this debate ever really questioned whether Vietnam would be able to coexist with China, Laos, and Cambodia, since the Communist ties and commonality of purpose were assumed to be so close. The reality of events since the fall of Saigon had differed from all expectations.

It was very unlikely that, after 40 years of almost continuous conflict, the states of Indochina would return to normality straight away; nor was it likely that all the anti-Communist inhabitants would accept defeat easily. Many wealthy Vietnamese managed to make their own way abroad as soon as the collapse of South Vietnam appeared irreversible, and a relatively small number managed to escape with the Americans in the final, desperate, undignified scramble. After the Communist takeover in Vietnam, however, the extraordinary saga of the "boat people" astonished the world: many thousands of refugees undertook epic voyages across the seas of Southeast Asia. Some simply sailed across the gulf to Thailand or north-

241

east Malaysia, but others voyaged direct to Brunei, Indonesia, and even Australia. A brave but sad postscript to the war, they have proved embarrassing to their hosts.

Dissident elements still hold out in Vietnam itself; reports intermittently reach the West of the Vietnamese Army carrying out operations against these groups. Similar groups abandoned by the French in the north in 1954 were gradually eliminated by the Communist regime, but since 1975 a renewed threat to Hanoi and Vientiane has come from the minority tribes in northwest Vietnam and Laos. Many of these tribes have a long history of resistance to domination by the lowland people, and they supported first the French and then the Americans against the Communists. The Vietnamese and Laotians knew for some time that the Chinese supported these tribes, especially the Meos, but they were surprised to learn in August 1978, that the legendary General Vang Pao had left his refuge in the United States to travel to Peking. General Pao was the leader of the CIA-backed Meo army: it would be ironic if he returned to fight his old enemies, but with Peking rather than Washington as the paymaster.

One of the most unexpected developments was post-war behavior in Kampuchea (formerly Cambodia). The Khmer people have long been considered a tolerant, kind, and artistic race, devout Buddhists, and normally peaceful and gentle. The brutality and inhumanity of events after the fall of the Lon Nol regime are staggering. The need to move virtually all inhabitants and refugees from the desperately overcrowded capital of Phnom Penh to the villages was the starting point of a horrifying and bloody campaign to eliminate every vestige of opposition to the *Angkar* ("Organization"), the central body responsible for the revolution. Murder by soldiers of the regime became commonplace, two of the most common methods being simple cudgeling, and suffocation in an airtight plastic bag—apparently to conserve ammunition.

Escalating conflict: Vietnam and Kampuchea

There were several attempts to overthrow the government by disaffected elements of the Khmer Rouge, notably in September 1976 and early in 1977, and there were also reports of a third group in the country: the *Khmer Serai Kha* (Free Khmer Movement). In mid-1978 there was an insurrection in the eastern part of Kampuchea, and in retrospect it is clear that this was a sign of what was to come in December.

Any beliefs that the neighboring Communist countries would coexist in peace and amity were rudely shattered at a very early stage. In 1975–1976, the victorious Vietnamese talked of "Indochinese solidarity"—which would inevitably take the form of Vietnamese domination. The Kampucheans, in particular, had good reason to doubt their neighbor's goodwill.
1. At Geneva in 1954, the Viet Minh obtained their own Communist state (with the prospect of the south as well in 1956–1957), but tacitly agreed that the Khmer Rouge should disband and accede to Prince Sihanouk's control.

2. During most of the Second Vietnam War, DRVN forces used the Ho Chi Minh and Sihanouk Trails through Cambodia and set up large depots near the border with South Vietnam, but did nothing to help the Khmer Rouge who were being actively harassed by Sihanouk. Only when Lon Nol took over and turned on the North Vietnamese did the latter decide to help their fellow Communists.
3. At the Paris conference in 1973–1974, the DRVN obtained a cease-fire with the United States, but made no attempt to prevent the resources released, particularly B-52 bombers, being redeployed to operations in Cambodia. The Khmer Rouge felt, and not without reason, that the DRVN had failed to protect their fellow Communists' interests.

These events reinforced the traditional and mutual mistrust of the Kampucheans and Vietnamese. The first clashes between the two Communist states occurred in 1974 and there was further fighting over the islands of Phu Quoc and Tho Chu within days of the fall of Saigon in 1975. These conflicts gradually increased in scale and frequency until 30 April 1977, when the Kampucheans utilized a classic Vietnamese technique and attacked on the second anniversary of the fall of Saigon, a public holiday with many Vietnamese military units stood-down for the celebrations. Following heavy artillery and mortar fire, the Kampucheans pushed some six miles (10km) into Vietnamese territory near the town of Chau Doc (which had to be evacuated) and then withdrew.

Communist rivals in border campaigns

The next attack was on 24 September 1977 (also a public holiday), at a time when Kampuchea's premier Pol Pot was on an official visit to Peking. This much larger operation involved an advance on several lines spread over a 93-mile (150km) front in Tay Ninh province. With Vietnamese units again taken by surprise, the Kampucheans were able to penetrate deep into enemy territory. Many local residents fled, but an official Hanoi communique alleged that the Kampucheans had massacred some 2,000 civilians. The Kampucheans again withdrew, but stopped short of the border and took up positions just inside Vietnamese territory. A few weeks later, following Pol Pot's return to Phnom Penh, there was a third raid which was supported by armored vehicles (probably ex-US M113 armored personnel carriers) and aircraft. In the ensuing air actions, some Vietnamese aircraft were shot down by Chinese-manned anti-aircraft guns, an ironic blow in view of the many years in which Chinese "advisers" had served with anti-aircraft units of the North Vietnamese Army. By the end of October 1977, Vietnamese patience had run out: they began a military offensive under Lieutenant General Tran Van Tra, who had commanded the NVA in the Parrot's Beak area in the Second Vietnam War, and thus knew the area well.

In 1978 the forces of Vietnam were far stronger than those of Kampuchea but, as both sides realized, military might is not the sole criterion in such circumstances and the Vietnamese kept hostilities at a

1. Kampuchean POWs in Vietnam; conflict between the rival Communist states began in 1974 and escalated into major border campaigns before the Soviet-backed Vietnamese and guerrillas over-ran Kampuchea in 1979. **2.** Vietnamese Army recruits in training; the strength of this force—estimated at 615,000 regulars and 1,600,000 paramilitary troops in December 1977, with excellent arms of largely Soviet origin—makes it a vital factor in Asia today. **3.** Communist ground crew with a Northrop F-5 Freedom Fighter, supplied to South Vietnam by the US and captured in 1975.

fairly low level. Some reports stated that the Ho Chi Minh Trail through Laos had been reactivated to bring supplies down to the troops fighting in northeast Kampuchea.

In June 1978 the Vietnamese struck again. They had moved battle-hardened professional units down from Tonkin and, following strikes by Northrop F-5 aircraft of the former South Vietnam Air Force, and supported by tanks and artillery, the infantry penetrated to within 10 miles (16km) of Kompong Cham. The few reporters allowed to witness these operations recorded a distinct feeling of *deja vu*: the setting, the equipment, and even the tactics were the same as in 1968 or 1971; only the faces of some of the participants were different.

These operations drew attention to an important factor in contemporary Asia: the size, standard of equipment and training, and the battle experience of the Vietnamese Army, which comprises 25 infantry divisions, supported by 45 field artillery regiments, 60 air defense regiments, and some 25 to 30 tank battalions. The navy and air force are substantial compared to others in Southeast Asia. The weaponry is mostly of Soviet design, although many of the lighter weapons were manufactured in Vietnam itself. Much equipment was captured from the South Vietnamese forces in 1974–75, which was almost exlusively of American manufacture. This war booty is estimated to have included: 550 medium and light tanks; 1,200 armored personnel carriers; 1,300 artillery pieces; 80 small ships and landing craft; and 1,000 aircraft, including about 200 fighter and ground-attack aircraft, 100 transports, and 500 helicopters. Spare parts and ammunition will, however, soon become a problem for many of the aircraft and tanks.

For the Soviet Union, the War and its aftermath have been most satisfactory. Two of its major foreign policy goals are to diminish the power and influence of the United States, and to contain China. There can be no doubt that the Indochina Wars seriously affected the United States' international reputation, while the Soviet Union's consistent support for Hanoi led to the Vietnamese becoming part of the Soviet "camp". The Soviet Union has often seemed unable to adopt correct attitudes in dealing with client states, which has led to the loss of considerable investments: Egypt and Somalia, for example. Recently, the Soviets have adopted a new approach of binding the client state economically through membership of COMECON. Vietnamese entry to this organization was formalised at a meeting in Bucharest, despite the reluctance of the non-Soviet members.

The Soviet Union clearly wishes to make Vietnam a major strategic distraction on China's southern flank, while also obtaining permanent bases in the area: it is now operating two air bases in Laos (at Phong Savan and Seno) and the Soviet Navy has facilities at the former USN base at Cam Ranh Bay.

Soviet ambitions seem to parallel those of the Vietnamese leaders: General Giap is reported to have stated that the narrow waist of central Vietnam is strategically indefensible unless Laos is held. The identity of the potential enemy remains obscure, but the Vietnamese have tightened their grip on Laos, where they have been operating continuously since 1950. In early 1979 there were some 50,000 Vietnamese troops in Laos, including one of their best infantry divisions near Vientiane. Further, every unit of the Laotian army has at least one Vietnamese "adviser".

It is possible that the Soviet Union may bide its time and then "call-in" its debts by requesting the Vietnamese to follow Cuba's example and send troops to participate in other wars in Asia, Africa, or even South America. Vietnamese credentials are impeccable: they are authentic revolutionaries, with a brilliant reputation for military organization and bravery, and a wealth of experience. However, the USSR may have been making another of its strategic miscalculations. The Vietnamese have proved quite conclusively that they are not prepared to be anyone's pawn; they resisted Chinese occupation for a thousand years and never totally accepted French colonial rule, even in the early 20th Century heyday of imperialism. It seems probable that the Vietnamese will follow the Moscow line for precisely as long as it suits them, but if the Soviets become too over-bearing, or if they try to push Vietnam too hard in a particular direction, then they would be told to leave.

There has been an ethnic Chinese minority, the *Hoa Chiao,* in Vietnam for several centuries. Most of these Chinese residents operated small businesses; many of them supported both the Viet Minh and then the Viet Cong in their revolutionary campaigns. But in 1978 a wide gulf opened up between the government and the Hoa Chiao, which quickly involved Peking and led to serious border incidents. Many of the Hoa Chiao took fright and an exodus began.

The whole affair landed Peking with a delicate problem, for there are Chinese minorities in almost every country in Southeast Asia, whose governments watch very closely to see whether too much interest is being taken in their affairs by the mainland authorities. Despite this, the situation reached such a state that the Chinese sent ships to take those who wished to leave.

By late 1978, China was involved in border problems with the Soviet Union in the north and with Vietnam in the south. Vietnam, supported by the USSR, was confronting China and was also involved in a relatively "hot" war with Kampuchea in the south-west.

This situation looked as if it would continue for some time, but in late 1978 events, as so often before in Indochina, suddenly gathered momentum. On 3 December the existence of the Kampuchea National United Front for National Salvation (KNUFNS) was announced, led by Heng Samrin, a 44-year old former commissar in the Khmer Rouge, and Chea Sim (46) who had held a number of political posts; both men had broken with Pol Pot in May 1978.

On 25 December 1978 Vietnamese and KNUFNS troops suddenly swept into Kampuchea. Progress was rapid; the whole strategy was conventional, with 12 divisions of the Vietnamese Army taking part, supported by tanks, artillery and ground-attack aircraft. Pol Pot's regime collapsed quickly, but then an unexpected little figure bounced into the headlines as Prince Sihanouk, one of the world's great survivors, was released from palace-arrest and despatched to the United Nations to plead Kampuchea's case. Few nations outside the Soviet bloc supported the Vietnamese invasion, but nobody regretted the demise of the barbarous Pol Pot regime either. By 15 January 1979 the invaders had closed up to the Thai border and their victory was virtually complete, although pockets of resistance remained.

China's "punitive" invasion of Vietnam

China had every intention of reacting, but was forced to move slowly because of the need to make diplomatic preparations (especially during Teng Hsiao-ping's visit to the USA), and also because the PLA divisions for the punitive action had to be moved from their positions facing Taiwan and Hongkong, and such journeys take time in China. Overall command was given to General Hsu Shih-yu (73), while the "front" commander was Yang Teh-chih (69), both veterans of the famous "Long March". Their initial goals were five towns whose names brought back memories of the war against the French—Lai Chau, Lao Cai, Ha Giang, Cao Bang and Lang Son—and after the very obvious preparations they crossed the border on 17 February 1979. They moved slowly, partly restrained by the pace of the foot-soldiers, and partly by the natural caution of elderly commanders and young soldiers untried in battle.

As it would have been had their roles been reversed, the first line of resistance was the village militia, who harrassed the advancing Chinese columns, while the main force units of the VPA were rushed up from Laos and the south. The ensuing propaganda battles made it very difficult to sort out who achieved what and Western Press reporters were kept under careful control by both sides. The Chinese made their point by pushing deep into Vietnamese territory (quite how far is still debatable), although there is no doubt that they suffered very heavy casualties before withdrawing, but still in good order, behind their frontier.

The USSR did little except issue propaganda statements and make some limited troop movements. Her own vital national interests were not directly involved, but the close relationship with Vietnam suggested to most people that some sort of gesture of solidarity would have been appropriate. China made preparations for such an eventuality: troops in the northern military regions were put on alert, but, interestingly, the main reinforcements went to the forces in Sinkiang to face a possible Soviet drive against the key nuclear installations at Lop Nor.

Following the Chinese withdrawal, talks aimed at reaching an "understanding" have been held in Hanoi. These, together with any assessment of casualties, are, however, largely irrelevant, for China has achieved the great strategic

aim of her invasion, which was to demonstrate to the aggressive Vietnamese that they cannot undertake any further military adventures in Southeast Asia against the wishes of the Chinese government, or they will find themselves involved in a war on two fronts. The Chinese invasion may have been slow to mount, ponderous in execution and costly in casualties, but it was completely successful in demonstrating China's belief in "perceived power" and the Vietnamese (and the Soviet Union) would be well advised to heed that lesson.

The continuing problems of Southern Asia

So, the balance of power shifted once again. In late January 1979 it had appeared that Vietnam was the dominant power in Southeast Asia and that its 600,000-strong army was hungry for further conquests. The much criticised "domino theory" had taken on a new relevance with the fall of Kampuchea; Thailand felt herself to be in the front-

1. The skills of guerrilla warfare for which the Viet Cong were famed are turned against Vietnam by these Kampuchean soldiers setting up a bamboo-stake booby trap on a border trail. **2.** Kampuchean warships, supplied by China. On 16 January 1979 Thai Navy sources reported a fierce naval battle in the Gulf of Thailand between Vietnamese-led forces and Kampuchean units loyal to former leader Pol Pot. At least 22 boats were said to have been involved in a struggle for control of Koh Kong island. **3.** Khmer Rouge troops man a 105mm gun captured from Cambodian government forces during the insurrection of 1970–1975. **4.** Vietnamese paramilitary troops defend a "liberated area" on the border with Kampuchea; although the Vietnamese called for a border cease-fire and the establishment of a demilitarized zone in 1978, they were actually planning a major offensive during which they over-ran Kampuchea early in 1979. **5.** Map: the continuing conflicts in Southeast Asia.

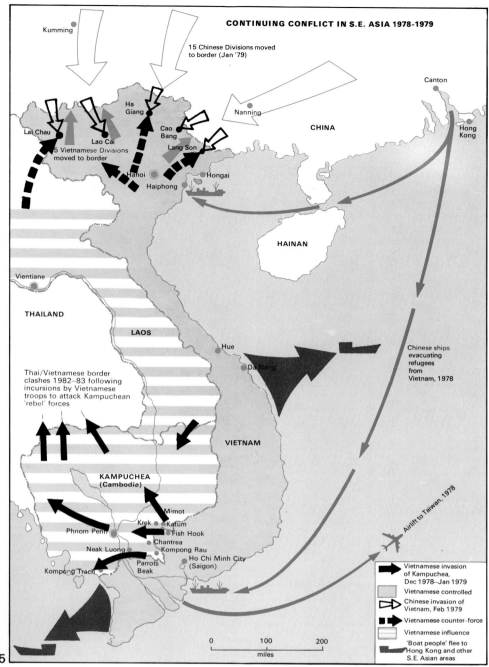

CONTINUING CONFLICT IN S.E. ASIA 1978-1979

line, and the governments of Burma, Malaysia, Singapore and Indonesia were very worried indeed. The mighty army that had defeated the French, the United States, South Vietnam and now Kampuchea appeared to be unstoppable, and nobody seemed to be prepared to do more than just make threatening noises against any further Vietnamese expansion. Further, the Vietnamese had apparently achieved their long planned purpose of forming an Indochinese confederation of their own country, Laos and Kampuchea, with a population base of some 60 million people.

The Chinese invasion in February has reversed all that—for the time being—and the Vietnamese may, indeed, find their newly expanded territories hard to control. Laotians and Khmers have hated the Vietnamese for centuries, while there are many groups in Vietnam itself which are by no means reconciled to rule from Hanoi. Nevertheless the Vietnamese People's Army is a power which has to be reckoned with in any consideration of the future of Southeast Asia.

A number of outside interests are in-

extricably involved in the area. The USSR clearly sees Southeast Asia as ripe for the expansion of its influence, with Vietnam acting as its agent. China cannot ignore events in the area and has clearly demonstrated that she will place limits on any further expansion of Vietnamese territory, by force if necessary. The USA is quite obviously determined to avoid any further direct involvement in the area—having learnt a terrible and costly lesson in the years 1956–75—but as a world power cannot remain totally aloof. Although the USA was only an observer of the invasions of Kampuchea and Vietnam in 1978/79 she could by no means remain a disinterested one because any escalation, particularly between China and the USSR, must involve her. Japan, too, must be affected by such events since the vital oil routes from the Arabian Gulf pass through the South China Sea, but such involvement must inevitably remain an indirect one.

Western Europe has shown an increasing interest in China in the past two to three years, both because of the trading opportunities and because of the possi-

bility that the Chinese might provide a strategic threat to the Soviet Union which would divert that country's attention away from the NATO powers in Europe. But, generally, Western attention turned away from Southeast Asia with the ending of the Second Indochina War and the final disengagement of the European colonial powers from the area.

As Vietnam established control over Laos and Kampuchea, the United States, concentrating like the other Western nations upon relations with China, relied upon diplomacy and military assistance in an attempt to influence the future of Southeast Asia. A small diplomatic mission at Vientiane tried to fan any lingering spark of Lao nationalism and offset Vietnamese influence. Factors that might help in this American effort were the close ethnic and commercial ties between the people of Laos and Thailand.

Kampuchea posed a greater challenge, for the United States opposed both the deposed faction headed by Pol Pot, a mass murderer, and the Vietnamese puppet regime of Heng Samrin. Backing the efforts of the Association of South East

Asian Nations (ASEAN)—consisting of the Philippines, Malaya, Singapore, Thailand, and Indonesia—to obtain the withdrawal of Vietnamese forces and self-determination for the Khmer people, American diplomats sought to encourage a coalition that excluded Pol Pot and his fanatics. Representatives of factions opposed to Vietnamese domination met at Singapore in September 1981. The potential leaders included Khieu Samphan of the Khmer Rouge, Prince Sihanouk, whom the United States had alternately supported and opposed over a quarter century, and Son Sann, a member of Sihanouk's recent Cambodian Government.

Kampuchean refugees create pressure in Thailand

Pol Pot's crimes against his people, followed by the turmoil of war, destroyed the agricultural basis of the Kampuchean economy, and starvation ensued. By mid-June 1980, 150,000 Khmer refugees had found a haven in camps just beyond the Thai border, as twenty-nine nations contributed more than $113 million to feed, shelter, and clothe them. The displaced persons, unfortunately, posed a potential danger to Thailand's sovereignty.

This threat materialized on 23 July 1970, when Vietnamese troops crossed the border, entered the camps, and attacked members of Khmer factions opposed to Heng Samrin. Thai troops fought back, killing 86 of the intruders at the cost of 22 soldiers killed or wounded in a two-day battle that killed a hundred refugees, wounded many more, and drove thousands into the jungle. The incident caused President Jimmy Carter to accelerate the delivery of weapons and ammunition to Thailand.

Soviet influence in SE Asia

In November 1982, Secretary of Defense Caspar Weinberger visited the associated nations of Southeast Asia to offer assurance that the Reagan administration supported their organization's attempts to bring about by peaceful means an independent and democratic Kampuchea. He warned of the growing Soviet presence in Southeast Asia, citing as an example the use by Russian ships of the American-built base at Camranh Bay, and sought to strengthen the bonds between the United States and Thailand. Besides offering the Thais additional military aid, he reaffirmed the American pledge of aid in the event of communist attack.

As well as promising this help for Thailand, the details of which were not specified, the United States pursued the quest for irrefutable proof that the recent conquerors of Kampuchea had employed outlawed chemical agents. Reports surfaced of a burn-causing "yellow rain" that disabled those upon whom it fell, but the eyewitness testimony aroused little interest.

The West, it seemed, had turned its back upon Southeast Asia, ignoring the possibility that unanticipated realignments among the great powers—such as a rapprochement between China and the Soviet Union—might jeopardize the fragile stability of the region and endanger world peace.

1

2

1. Reacting to the Soviet-backed expansionism of the "Asian Cuba", China moved an estimated 15 divisions across the Vietnamese border in February 1979. Chinese T-59 MBTs head for Lao Cai, which fell on 22 February. **2.** Moving on Lang Son, only 80 miles (130km) NE of Hanoi, Chinese armor crosses the Khi Khong River, 4 March; withdrawal began next day. **3.** One of several factions in arms against Vietnamese domination of Kampuchea: the Khmer Sereika, headed by former premier Son Sann, parades with Chinese Type 56-1 assault rifles. **4.** "Boat people" fleeing Vietnam are taken aboard a US warship. **5.** One of the 2,000-plus Vietnamese refugees taken aboard US Navy and merchant ships between June 1979, when the US 7th Fleet was ordered by President Carter to aid the boat people, and March 1980. **6.** Snatched from an unseaworthy boat by a Navy helicopter, a refugee is lowered in the arms of a medic to the fantail of a US warship.

US veterans and POWs return to their homeland

Bernard C. Nalty

For more than six months, a lone American endured confinement in the vast Hoa Lo prison at Hanoi, North Vietnam. The occasional arrival of a letter or Red Cross package broke the monotony of days divided between the exercise yard, where he paced back and forth under the supervision of a guard, and his cell, where he used a nail to scratch on the masonry wall a record of the passing of time. The prisoner was a naval aviator, Everett Alvarez, Jr., shot down during an air strike made in retaliation for an attack by North Vietnamese torpedo boats on a patrolling American destroyer.

From August 1964 until the spring of 1965, Alvarez lived in a kind of limbo, kept in confinement but not physically abused by his captors. Although no state of war existed between the United States and North Vietnam, a systematic American air campaign against the North began in the spring of 1965, and the number of airmen held captive at Hoa Lo rapidly swelled. By the time Alvarez regained his freedom after some eight-and-a-half years, he was one of almost 600 Americans held in North Vietnam. The Hoa Lo prison, nicknamed the Hanoi Hilton, was just one of several confinement sites; others included the Zoo, Alcatraz, the Plantation, and the Powerplant in Hanoi or its immediate suburbs; the Briarpatch, Camp Hope (at Son Tay); and Camp Faith, somewhat more distant from the capital; and Dogpatch, not far from the border with China.

USAF hero POW interrogated by The Dog

Among those who joined Alvarez at the Hanoi Hilton was Air Force Colonel Robinson Risner, who had participated in the first strikes of the air campaign that came to be called Rolling Thunder. Shot down while attacking a weapons control radar, he had parachuted into the Tonkin Gulf and been rescued by a Grumman SA-16 amphibian. Returning to the United States, he received the Air Force Cross, appeared on the cover of *Time* magazine, and toured the country explaining the Vietnam conflict to the American people. In September 1965 he was back in Southeast Asia, flying an F-105. While searching for a surface-to-air missile battery, automatic weapons fire crippled his plane; this time, however, he could not limp to the friendly water of the Gulf but had to bail out over North Vietnam.

Risner's parachute brought him down beside a dike, where an armed soldier took him prisoner. A civilian seized the airman's revolver and shoved the barrel against Risner's forehead. To the downed flier, civilians whose home had just been bombed presented a greater danger than disciplined soldiers, but in this instance

The last American combat troops left Vietnam on 29 March 1973—but not to any conquering heroes' welcome. It was not until almost a decade had passed that a permanent monument was erected in honor of the 57,939 American men and women killed or missing in action in a war the authorities and general public seemed to want to forget. Efforts are still made, however, to account for the 2,494 MIAs

the captive suffered only minor injury. Luckily for the colonel, North Vietnamese wrath spent itself in a few blows with fists or sticks before Communist authorities regained control of the townspeople and started Risner toward a cell in the Hanoi Hilton.

A North Vietnamese nicknamed "The Dog" referred to the *Time* article when interrogating Risner, claiming that the only way the airman could have become so famous was by murdering innocent North Vietnamese. The interrogator vowed to turn the American over to the people of Than Hoa, where the air strike had occurred, but did not carry out the threat. Being chosen to question Risner became a source of pride to The Dog, who boasted of the assignment to Air Force Maj. George E. Day, after the latter joined the Colonel among the prisoners at Hanoi.

When Risner arrived at the prison, Commander Jeremiah Denton, Jr., already occupied a cell there. He and his bombardier-navigator, Lt. (j.g.) Bill Tschudy, had parachuted on 18 July, when antiaircraft five punctured the hydraulic lines of their Grumman A-6 during a dive bombing attack. An infected leg, injured when he bailed out, almost cost Denton his life, but the guards at last allowed a doctor to treat him.

As the number of prisoners increased, communication networks and command structures had to be established to exchange news, sustain morale, and encourage resistance. The methods of communicating were varied and ingenious. The prisoners used the Morse code, either tapping out the dots and dashes or flashing them by making shadows on the wall. The inmates dug away at the mortar in their cell walls to create openings for conversation or the passing of notes. A few whispered words might serve as an alert

that a tiny scrap of paper bearing a message hung by a thread from a matchstick placed athwart the grate of a shower drain. The most common method of communication was the tap code, in which 25 letters of the alphabet, all but K, were arranged in a five-column grid. The first tap, cough, or sneeze indicated the horizontal row, the second the vertical, so that one-one was A, two-two G, and so forth, with two-six standing for K.

The command structure was simple at first, with the senior officer at each compound taking charge. At the Zoo, as the Cu Loc detention center was called, Commander Denton was in charge until someone senior, Colonel Risner, arrived. The Air Force officer demanded of his captors, and received, a few concessions, such as an electric light in each cell and brooms for cleaning. Late in the war, when the North Vietnamese gathered their prisoners at the Hanoi Hilton, Col. Vernon Ligon organized the men into squadrons, each with a commanding officers. Col. John P. Flynn took over this basic structure and improved the means of communication so that directives could be smuggled from his wing headquarters to the various squadrons.

At the outset, the Hanoi regime treated the prisoners with indifference rather than calculated cruelty, but not long after Risner's capture Ho Chi Minh's government realized that the captives could serve a political purpose. The Geneva Convention, to which North Vietnam had acceded, prescribed minimum humane standards for the treatment of prisoners of war, but the captors circumvented this agreement and achieved their political aim by declaring the Americans criminals, since no state of war existed, and using torture to extract confessions.

Cruel North Vietnamese transgressions of Geneva code

The prisoners had been trained to follow a code of conduct that required them to resist, to attempt to escape, and to make no statement beyond giving name, rank, and serial number. The code assumed, however, that the captors would either observe the Geneva Convention or yield before the abhorrence among civilized nations of the use of torture against helpless prisoners. North Vietnamese cruelty overwhelmed the code and those who sought to uphold it.

"I don't care who you are," a former captive told a journalist, ". . . short of killing you, I can subject you to such pain that in a relatively short time your mind is going to overcome your will, and you are going to give something to get out of this pain, short of dying. Because they will not let you die."

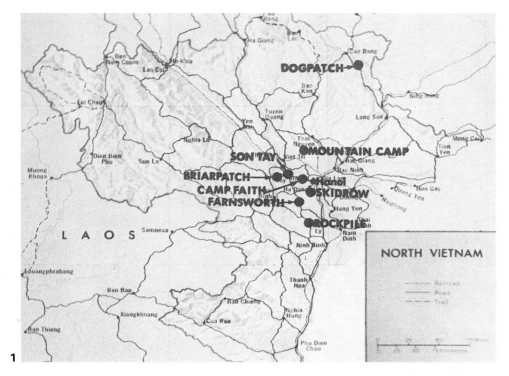

PLANTATION 3

ZOO 2
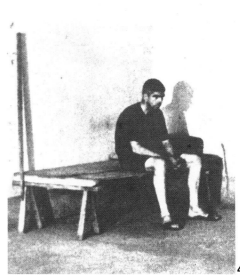

1. US PoWs were held under harsh and primitive conditions at these camps in North Vietnam. 2–3. Following the abortive US raid on Son Tay in November 1970, the North Vietnamese concentrated their prisoners in the Hanoi area, where nicknamed compounds included the Zoo and the Plantation. 4. The mental torment of captivity is memorably expressed in a photograph of Lt-Cdr R. A. Stratton, USN, in isolation in his cell. 5. Some prisoners found themselves literally "in the pen". 6. Senator Jeremiah Denton of Alabama, a former PoW, Troops the Line on PoW/MIA Recognition Day, Pentagon, July 1982. 7. A starkly simple wall on Constitution Avenue, Washington, D.C., bears the names of 57,931 men and eight women killed or missing in action in the Vietnam War.

Magnifying the physical pain was the suspense involved in selecting victims. The sound of footsteps echoed in the corridor, the prayer that the torturers would pass by, and finally the rattle of keys. Equally demoralizing was the inability to resist totally, the helplessness, the feeling of humiliation after yielding, even though further resistance was impossible.

Refusal to respond to a question brought immediate torture. The usual method, simple but painful, consisted of binding the victim's arms behind him, tied at the wrist and elbow, and then forcing the arms upward over the head, repeating the treatment until the subject lost consciousness or gave the desired information. The questions might be pointless—asking an airman how long it would take to train a division of army reservists—or the answer already known—demanding to know what kind of plane a pilot had been flying when the wreckage had already been recovered and examined. But the enemy had to have an answer.

Nor did the North Vietnamese care whether a war crimes confession was believable. Prisoners forced to read statements over the radio were sometimes so weak from torture that their words could scarcely be understood. At other times, the victims distorted their voices or mispronounced words to alert the audience that they were acting under duress. In the course of an interview being taped for television viewing, Commander Denton blinked his eyes to spell out in Morse code the word "torture".

By ignoring the Geneva Convention and civilized usage, the North Vietnamese thus forced the Americans to give information, much of it useless, and to read aloud or sign confessions that obviously were the result of torture.

1

2

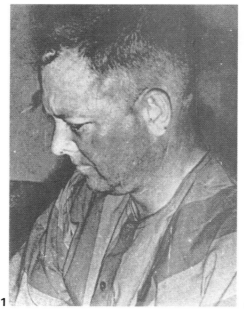

3

4

Tall American escapees could not hide

Another aspect of the code of conduct, the emphasis on escape, also yielded to special circumstances. Towering over the average Vietnamese, with different skin color and facial structure, Americans found it impossible to travel undetected after escaping from confinement. Nor was there an underground organization of dissident Vietnamese to help the escapee; he was alone in a hostile society.

So unfavorable were the odds that both Colonel Risner and Colonel Flynn counseled against escape attempts unless outside aid was available, and just four persons tried. Two of the escapees, Air Force officers Ed Atterbury and John Dramesi, darkened their skin, donned conical straw hats and surgical masks, and fled through a loosened ventilation grate. The two were recaptured after traveling less than five miles and were returned separately to prison. Dramesi survived, but Atterbury disappeared and later was said to have died of disease. The other two who tried to flee, George Coker and George McKnight, also were quickly recaptured, but both survived their imprisonment.

Once a captive entered prison, he had no real hope of escape. The downed airman had to get away immediately, if at all, but injuries sustained in ejecting from his plane might leave him all but crippled. Despite a broken arm and sprained knee, Major Day escaped shortly after being shot down and reached the demilitarized zone before again falling into enemy hands. After evading the enemy for six weeks, Air Force Captain Lance P. Sijan was captured by the North Vietnamese. Although half starved and seriously injured, the captain tried to crawl to freedom, but was recaptured immediately. He died of pneumonia contracted while in prison.

The war crimes campaign launched in 1965 included a march through Hanoi by some fifty of the prisoners, who were subjected to blows and verbal abuse by the crowd that lined the route. The threat of a war crimes trial seemed so real that American political leaders, including men opposed to the war, warned the North Vietnamese that reprisals against the prisoners, whatever the legal pretext, would bring prompt retaliation. This threat may have deterred Hanoi's rulers, or they may have concluded that a trial and possible executions would have brought discredit to their nation. Whatever the reason, in July 1966 Ho Chi Minh assured President Johnson that no trial would take place.

Even though the war crimes crisis had passed, the treatment of the prisoners scarcely improved, and most of the mail sent them was returned by North Vietnamese authorities. To make sure the captured men were not forgotten, their families banded together to marshal public opinion and prod the American Government into acting. Beginning in 1969, the National League of Families of American Prisoners and Missing in Southeast Asia launched a campaign that ultimately persuaded hundreds of thousands of Americans to put on a bracelet bearing the name of one of the prisoners or missing men and to pledge to wear it until the captives regained their freedom. In a country divided over a war that rapidly was becoming Vietnamized, the fate of the prisoners became a rallying point.

The Nixon administration promptly endorsed the actions of the League of Families. Hanoi, after all, had backed down in 1966 on the war crimes issue and might do so again. The President himself denounced North Vietnam's treatment of its prisoners and arranged a press conference at which two recently freed captives, Navy Lieutenant Robert F. Frishman and Seaman Douglas B. Hegdahl, described the treatment they had received. The safe return of the prisoners rapidly became a war aim.

Long before the release of the prisoners evolved into a motive for America's continuing the war, North Vietnam had tried to link repatriation with opposition to the war, from time to time releasing prisoners to American opponents of the conflict. The first to gain their freedom were two Air Force fliers, Maj. Noris M. Overly and Capt. Jon D. Black, and a Navy aviator, Ens. David P. Matheny, released in February 1968 to representatives of the National Mobilization, an anti-war group. In August of the same year, peace activists brought back three Air Force officers—Maj. James F. Low, Maj. Fred N. Thompson, and Capt. Joe V. Carpenter.

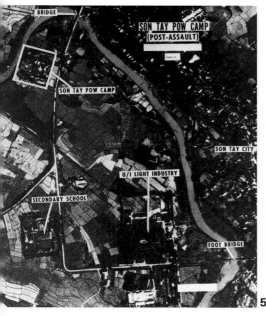

5

7

6

1. Captured in 1967, Capt. Edwin L. Atterbury, USAF, was one of only four men to attempt escape from Hoa Lo ("the Hanoi Hilton"). Quickly recaptured, Atterbury did not figure on later lists of PoWs: it was claimed that he had died of disease. **2.** Lt. Col. John Dramesi, USAF, who escaped and was recaptured with Atterbury, returns in triumph with a home-made flag, 1973. **3.** A returned PoW studies photographs of men listed MIA: some 2,494 servicemen and civilians were unaccounted for after the release of prisoners in 1973. **4.** This flag flew over the White House and Pentagon on National PoW/MIA Recognition Day, 9 July 1982. **5.** Aerial reconnaissance photograph of the deserted Son Tay camp, following the abortive rescue operation of November 1970. **6.** Col. Arthur D. "Bull" Simons, USA, leader of the volunteers heli-lifted into Son Tay, faces the press. **7.** Freedom is at hand—but the expressions of these PoWs awaiting release at Gia Lam airfield, near Hanoi, reflect their grim ordeal.

The releases resumed in July 1969. Next to return were Lieutenant Frishman, who had shattered an elbow in ejecting from his plane, Seaman Hegdahl, a sailor washed overboard from his ship and plucked by the North Vietnamese from the waters of the Tonkin Gulf, and Air Force Capt. Wesley L. Rumble. All of the repatriated prisoners provided information on treatment while in captivity, the location of camps, and the names of prisoners still in enemy hands, but not until the joint press conferences held by Frishman and Hegdahl did the American Government publicize North Vietnam's maltreatment of its prisoners. The Hanoi regime freed no other men until September 1972, when it released two Navy lieutenants, Norris A. Charles and Markham L. Gartley, and Air Force Maj. Edward K. Elias.

Political use of POWs boomerangs on North Vietnamese

The upsurge of public sentiment on behalf of the prisoners frustrated the North Vietnamese attempt to use them as a means of encouraging American opposition to the war. Nor was this support for the captives confined to the United States. Wives of the prisoners visited the leaders of governments friendly to the United States, urging them to exert influence on Hanoi to obtain humane treatment, and even confronted the North Vietnamese delegation to the Paris truce talks.

By the spring of 1970, the prisoner issue had boomeranged upon North Vietnam. Throughout the West, many of those who felt that North Vietnam might well have been the victim of unnecessarily violent force, if not of actual war crimes, now realized that the leaders of that nation had orchestrated a sadistic campaign to break the will of the prisoners. The Hanoi regime had little choice but to improve its treatment of the Americans.

Besides supporting the efforts of the League of Families to rally public opinion throughout the world on behalf of the prisoners and missing men, the United States tried to rescue the men being held at Son Tay, a camp some distance from Hanoi. While strikes by Navy aircraft distracted North Vietnam's air defenses, a rescue force landed in the prison compound, only to discover that the Americans were no longer being held there. An Air Force helicopter was disabled and had to be destroyed and one of the expedition members broke an ankle, but otherwise the force returned unscathed, if empty handed.

The Son Tay raid caused the North Vietnamese to concentrate all the American prisoners in the Hanoi area, but brought little change in the treatment afforded them. During 1972, as the war entered what promised to be its final phase, the enemy again divided the group, sending some to a camp near the Chinese border and keeping the others at the Hanoi Hilton, presumably to deter renewed bombing of the capital. The B-52s attacked nevertheless, raising the morale of the captives and signaling that Hanoi's most recent attempt to overrun the South had failed. North Vietnam agreed to a settlement that ended the fighting, gave the prisoners their freedom, and left the Communists in control of the infiltration routes into South Vietnam.

The Hanoi Government on 12 February 1973 repatriated the first of 588 Americans being held by the North Vietnamese, Pathet Lao, or Viet Cong. In addition, China agreed to set free three US prisoners, one of whom had been held since the Korean War. Also eligible for release were 5,000 South Vietnamese and a handful of persons from other nations, who were prisoners of the Communists, and 26,000 North Vietnamese or Viet Cong jailed in the South. When North Vietnam allowed the exchange to fall behind schedule, Nixon halted the withdrawal of the few American troops remaining in South Vietnam, a gesture, but perhaps an effective one, for on 29 March the last of the prisoners held by the North Vietnamese boarded an Air Force plane at Gia Kam airfield near Hanoi. Still unaccounted for after these 591 persons regained their freedom were some 2,494 servicemen and civilians who had disappeared during the Southeast Asia conflict.

The release of the prisoners prompted an outpouring of joyous affection as crowds gathered to greet the returnees. The family of one ex-prisoner fashioned a hand-lettered sign: "Welcome back to the world." The transition, however, would not be easy.

The ex-prisoners, despite the warmth of their reception, could not simply pick up the severed threads of a life disrupted years before. The children of 1965 had become young men and women; wives

251

had achieved an unexpected, perhaps frightening, independence, a result in part of the initiative they had shown in organizing a campaign to free their husbands. The accepted family relationships of the previous decade no longer seemed valid, and some marriages could not survive the strain.

Nor was the return to the profession of arms easy for an officer who might have spent a quarter of his career in prison. Promotions received during confinement caused the recently freed individual to receive new and demanding assignments. These, in turn, required hard work to make up for experience or professional education denied the prisoners during their captivity.

The veterans' problems back home

Some of the freed prisoners overcame these obstacles to resume successful careers. John P. Flynn rose to the rank of Lieutenant General and served as Air Force Inspector General, while Jeremiah Denton became a Rear Admiral, retired, and was elected to the Senate from Alabama. Nor was Denton the only former prisoner to enter politics. Leo K. Thorsness of the Air Force, for example, ran for the Senate from South Dakota but failed to become elected, while John S. McCain became a Congressman from Arizona.

A source of concern to leaders of the prisoner wing was the behavior of a few of the prisoners, a hard core of about eight men, who had formed an anti-war clique. Air Force Col. Ted Guy preferred charges against the men, one of whom committed suicide, but the authorities decided that the effect of years of confinement, rather than any conscious desire to betray their country, had led them to collaborate.

None of the group was ever prosecuted.

Indeed, the only former prisoner to face a court martial was Marine Pfc. Robert Garwood, who for a time was numbered among those missing Americans for whom the United States Government was searching. Garwood revealed his presence in Hanoi in 1979, almost 14 years after his capture near Da Nang, when he announced that he wished to return to the United States. Two members of Congress, visiting Vietnam in search of information on the fate of missing Americans, arranged the details of his repatriation. Upon returning, however, Garwood had to face charges that he had collaborated with the enemy. Testimony that the marine had lived with the North Vietnamese guards and abused prisoners outweighed his claim that he had been a victim of brainwashing, and led to a conviction for collaborating with the enemy and striking one of the captives.

Visits to Southeast Asia, like that of Representatives Elizabeth Holtzman and Billie Lee Evans, who had accepted Garwood from the Vietnamese, closed the cases on several other missing men. For instance, Representative Sonny Montgomery and a delegation of six other Congressmen obtained the remains of 15 persons. A mortuary center in Hawaii identified 13 of them as missing Americans, but the other two were Asians.

These occasional examples of cooperation barely lifted the shroud of silence that enveloped the missing Americans. Leonard Woodcock, a labor leader and chairman of a commission sent by President Jimmy Carter to negotiate with the Vietnamese and Lao on this subject, advised that the best hope of "obtaining a proper accounting . . . lies in the context of . . . improved relations" between the United States and Communist Vietnam. President Carter then declared that a

satisfactory accounting could lead to normal diplomatic relations between the two countries, but no such enumeration was forthcoming.

In the spring of 1981, the *Washington Post* claimed that American-led Asian mercenaries had investigated a suspected prison site, allegedly located on satellite photographs, but had found no trace of any Americans. The Department of Defense withheld confirmation until early 1983, when an official acknowledged that a retired Special Forces officer, Lt. Col. James "Bo" Gritz, had led just such an incursion. After training in Florida, reportedly at a school for cheer leaders, Gritz led a team of about a dozen men, Americans and Asians, into Laos, where they collided with a security patrol that captured one of the American mercenaries. The Lao, however, accepted a ransom payment and released the captive.

Colonel Gritz later boasted that film actors Clint Eastwood, who had portrayed Dirty Harry on film, and William Shatner, Captain Kirk of television's starship *Enterprise*, had helped finance the venture. The former Green Beret officer also insisted that he had enjoyed the full cooperation of the Federal Bureau of Investigation, the Central Intelligence Agency, and the American embassy at Bangkok, Thailand. If this actually had been policy under President Carter, it no longer prevailed in 1983. Spokesmen for the Reagan administration branded ventures like the Gritz raid as illegal, disruptive of good relations between Thailand and the United States, and counterproductive, endangering any surviving prisoners and preventing the establishment of normal relations with the Communist states.

Although he discouraged freelance operatives like Bo Gritz, President Reagan promised to exhaust all the more conven-

1. Wreckage of a US aircraft in Hanoi, photographed by the delegation of the National League of Families of American Prisoners and Missing in Southeast Asia that visited Vietnam and Laos in September 1982. **2.** Members of the League of Families' delegation examine aircraft wreckage in Laos, hoping that serial numbers may give a clue to the fate of fliers listed MIA. **3.** The Vietnamese erected this monument to commemorate their feat in downing several US aircraft nearby. **4.** President Reagan, who has stated that establishing the fate of those missing in Southeast Asia is a matter of the highest national priority, signs a proclamation to that effect on National Recognition Day, 1982. Among those present are (far left) Ann Mills Griffiths, executive director of the League of Families and (behind the President) Senator Jeremiah Denton, a PoW in North Vietnam for more than seven years. **5.** To honor the dead and missing of a bitter and divisive war that has scarred the Free World, flags are dipped before the memorial wall on Constitution Avenue, Washington, D.C., as veterans from all states of the Union parade at its dedication ceremony, 13 November 1982.

tional means in seeking information on the missing Americans. Instead of dramatic raids, the government would tap the normal intelligence sources in a continuing effort to obtain from Communist authorities in Southeast Asia an accounting called for in the 1973 cease-fire arrangements. Most of the useful information tended to come from Communist radio broadcasts, from refugees, or from approved contacts with Vietnamese or Lao authorities.

Although unable to verify reports that prisoners had been seen, and thus prove that Americans remained captive in Southeast Asia, the administration of President Ronald Reagan based its official policy regarding the 2,494 persons never accounted for on the assumption that some of them survived in captivity a decade after the cease-fire went into effect. The President himself declared that the fate of the missing men was a matter of the highest national priority, and his aides promised to do whatever wes appropriate to investigate reports that Americans had been seen alive in Southeast Asia.

The Reagan administration continued to encourage contacts with the authorities in Vietnam and Laos. For example, representatives of the Vietnam Veterans of America returned from a visit to Hanoi with the remains of two airmen and information that three others had died when their planes were shot down. The National League of Families of American Prisoners and Missing in Southeast Asia also sent a delegation that visited Laos and Vietnam. A Soviet-built helicopter rented from the government of Laos flew the group to Sam Neua Province, site of a cave used as a wartime prison, and to Pakse, where an AC-130 carrying the husband of one of the delegation members had been shot down. In Hanoi, the Americans visited the so-called War Crimes Museum, copying down

serial numbers from the aircraft wreckage displayed there in the hope of obtaining information on the men who had flown the planes.

In this fashion, the United States kept open communication with the Communist leadership on the subject of the missing Americans. Concern focused upon some 20 known to have been alive and in enemy hands, either seen by eyewitnesses or identified on photographs released by the enemy. Shot down in 1965, Col. David Hrdlicka had, for example, been photographed and a radio broadcast attributed to him, but he was not among those prisoners repatriated in 1973. Welles Hangen, a television reporter, survived for at least three days after falling into the hands of the Khmer Rouge in 1974; reports that his captors later executed him have never been verified.

While the attempt to account for individuals like Colonel Hrdlicka and Mr. Hangen went on, the average veteran of the Southeast Asia conflict faced problems of varying severity in adjusting to a society that seemed determined to forget the war and those who had served in it. Some men who had seen combat complained that they were looked upon as victims, at best, or paid killers, at worst, while the heroes seemed to be those who had opposed the war or avoided military service by fleeing the country.

Especially galling was the reluctance of the Veterans Administration to authorize the treatment of disabilities attributable to a herbicide, Agent Orange, widely used in Southeast Asia. Gradually, however, the indifference or outright hostility toward the Vietnam veterans faded away, and the values of service and sacrifice again came to be appreciated.

A wounded veteran of the conflict, Jan C. Scruggs of Columbia, Maryland, became obsessed with the vision of a monu-

ment to the American servicemen killed in Southeast Asia. He organized the Vietnam Veterans' Memorial Fund, which raised all the money required to carry out the project. The only Government grant took the form of a plot of land on Constitution Avenue in Washington, D.C.

An architectural competition won by Maya Lin Ying produced a simple but powerful design, a chevron-like wall that enshrined in glossy black granite the names of 57,931 men and eight women killed in the war, including the names of the 2,494 persons whose fate has never been documented. On 13 November 1982, veterans from all 50 states, General Westmoreland among them, marched to the Constitution Avenue site for a formal dedication, as Jan Scruggs' dream became reality while a crowd of 150,000 watched.

On hand to greet the tens of thousands of veterans who had come to Washington to receive this long-delayed tribute was the deputy administrator of the Veterans Administration, Everett Alvarez, who had spent more than eight years in North Vietnamese prisons. The American people had at last acknowledged the sacrifices of those who had served in Southeast Asia—of the living like Alvarez and of the dead, including those like David Hrdlicka, whose fate has never been documented. The nation thus faced a truth it had tried for years to ignore.

Typically of the Vietnam conflict, this outpouring of appreciation was tinged with controversy. For some, the monument was too stark, too modern, and for them a more conventional piece, a statue of three infantrymen, has been designed by Frederick Hart to complement the original shrine. Perhaps controversy was inevitable, for, as one man has said of his fellow veterans: "They all relate to that patch of ground, but they all relate differently."

Missing in Action

Name – Self Explanatory. Last name, first name, middle name or initial.
Status – Describes the current status of an individual, in two characters:

AA	AWOL Deserter
BB	"KIA" Body not recovered
BR	Body Recovered
CC	Detainee (Civilian Detainee-Released)
EE	Escapee
KK	Died in captivity
KR	Died in captivity, negotiated remains returned
MM	Missing in action
NR	Negotiated remains returned
PP	PW
RR	Returnee
XX	Presumptive finding of death
ZM	Post 75 yacht related detainee
ZR	Post 75 yacht person released
–	Status not recorded

I-Date – Contains the date the individual was lost written in year-month-day order.
Service – An abbreviation for the individual's parent service (US unless otherwise stated):

A	Army
F	Airforce
M	Marine
N	Navy
P	Coast Guard
V	Civilian
W	Foreign National
W(A)	Australian Military Personnel

A

Name	Status	I-date	Service
Abbott, John	KR	660420	N
Abbott, Joseph S Jr	RR	670430	F
Abbott, Robert Archie	RR	670430	F
Abbott, Wilfred Kesse	RR	660905	F
Abrams, Lewis Herbert	XX	671125	M
Acalotto, Robert Joseph	XX	710220	A
Ackley, James H	MM	730307	V
Acosta, Hector Michael	RR	721209	F
Acosta-Rosario, Humberto	XX	680822	A
Adachi, Thomas Yuji	XX	700422	F
Adair, Samuel Young Jr	BR	720512	F
Adam, John Quincy	XX	680522	F
Adams, John Robert	XX	671108	A
Adams, Lee Aaron	BB	660419	F
Adams, Oley Neal	BB	660617	F
Adams, Samuel	KK	651031	F
Adams, Steven Harold	XX	661018	F
Adkins, Charles Leroy	XX	680202	A
Adkins, Cloden	RR	680201	V
Adrian, Joseph Daniel	BB	670312	F
Adventio, Rudolpho Andres	AA	691101	N
Affel, Charles Andrew	ZR	771014	V
Agnew, Alfred Howard	RR	721228	N
Agosto-Santos, Jose	RR	670512	M
Ahlmeyer, Heinz Jr	BB	670510	M
Ahn, Hak Soo	–	670325	W
Aiken, Larry Delarnard	EE	690513	A
Albert, Keith Alexander	RR	700521	A
Alberton, Bobby Joe	XX	660531	F
Albright, John Scott II	XX	681213	F
Alcorn, Michael E	AA	700127	M
Alcorn, Wendell Reed	RR	651222	N
Aldern, Donald Deane	XX	700629	N
Aldrich, Lawrence Lee	BB	680506	A
Alegano, Vicente	RR	711108	W
Alexander, Fernando	RR	721219	F
Alford, Terry Lanier	XX	691104	A
Alfred, Gerald Oak Jr	XX	661211	F
Algaard, Harold Lowell	BB	710304	A
Allard, Michael John	BB	670830	N
Allard, Richard Michael	XX	670824	A
Allee, Richard Kenneth	XX	681221	F
Allen, Henry Lewis	XX	700326	F
Allen, Merlin Raye	BB	670630	M
Allen, Thomas Ray	XX	670731	F
Allen, Wayne Clouse	NR	700110	A
Alley, Gerald William	NR	721222	F
Alley, James Harold	BB	720406	F
Allgood, Frankie Eugene	BB	680326	M
Allinson, David Jay	XX	660812	F
Alloway, Clyde Douglas	BB	700607	F
Allwine, David Franklin	RR	710304	A
Alm, Richard Andrew	BB	660201	M
Almendariz, Samuel (NMN)	BB	670712	A
Alpers, John Hardesty Jr	RR	721005	F
Altizer, Albert Harold	BB	691008	A
Altus, Robert Wayne	XX	711123	F
Alvarez, Everett	RR	640805	N
Alwan, Harold Joseph	XX	670227	M
Amesbury, Harry Arlo Jr	BB	720426	F
Ammon, Glendon Lee	NR	660921	F
Amos, Thomas Hugh	XX	720420	F
Amspacher, William Harry J	NR	650602	N
Anderson, Denis Leon	BB	680111	N
Anderson, Gareth Laverne	RR	670519	N
Anderson, Gregory Lee	BB	700128	F
Anderson, John Stephen	BB	691104	A
Anderson, John Thomas	RR	680203	A
Anderson, John Wesley	RR	721227	F
Anderson, Martha	CC	750429	V
Anderson, Robert Dale	XX	721006	F
Anderson, Roger Dale	EE	680103	A
Anderson, Thomas Edward	BB	621006	M
Anderson, Warren Leroy	XX	660426	F
Andin, Fernando L	–	680131	W
Andre, Father	RR	710601	W
Andre, Howard Vincent Jr	BB	690708	F
Andrews, Anthony Charles	RR	671017	F
Andrews, Stuart Merrill	XX	660304	F
Andrews, William Richard	NR	661005	F
Angell, Marshall Joseph	BB	631212	A
Angstadt, Ralph Harold	XX	661018	F
Angus, William Kerr	RR	720611	M
Anh, San Lee	–	690727	W
Anselmo, William Frank	BB	680306	F
Anshus, Richard Cameron	RR	710308	A
Anson, Robert	RR	700803	V
Anspach, Robert Allen	BB	670911	A
Anton, Francis Gene	RR	680105	A
Antunano, Gregory Alfred	BB	710724	A
Anzaldua, Jose Jesus Jr	RR	700123	M
Apodaca, Victor Joe Jr	XX	670608	F
Appelhans, Richard Duane	XX	671016	F
Appleby, Ivan Dale	XX	671007	F
Archer, Bruce Raymond	RR	680328	M
Arcuri, William Youl	RR	721220	F
Ard, Randolph Jefferson	XX	710307	A
Arema, Kasem	–	660326	W
Armitstead, Steven Ray	XX	690317	M
Armond, Robert Laurence	BB	650618	F
Armstrong, Frank Alton III	BB	671006	F
Armstrong, John William	XX	671109	F
Arnaud, Jean Louis	RR	730822	W
Arndt, Delev	RR	740127	W
Arnold, William Tamm	XX	661118	N
Arnould, Marcel Leon	RR	720422	W
Arpin-Pont, Claude	–	700405	W
Arroyo-Baez, Gerasimo	KR	690324	A
Ashall, Alan Frederick	XX	680829	N
Ashby, Clayborn Willis Jr	BB	680217	N
Ashby, Donald Roberts Sr	BB	670119	N
Ashlock, Carlos	XX	670512	M
Asire, Donald Henry	NR	661208	F
Asmussen, Glenn Edward	BB	660205	N
Aston, Jay Steven	BB	710718	A
Astorga, Jose Manuel	RR	720402	A
Atkins, Eric	CC	750429	W
Atterberry, Edwin Lee	KR	670812	F
Austin, Carl Benjamin	BB	651202	N
Austin, Charles David	XX	670424	F
Austin, Ellis Ernest	XX	660421	N
Austin, Joseph Clair	XX	670319	F
Austin, William Renwick	RR	671007	F
Auxier, Jerry Edward	BB	680729	A
Avery, Allen Jones	BB	720406	F
Avery, Robert Douglas	XX	680503	M
Avolese, Paul Andrew	BB	670707	F
Avore, Malcolm Arthur	BB	650718	N
Ayers, Darrell Eugene	BB	700319	M
Ayers, Richard Lee	XX	700416	F
Ayres, Gerald Francis	XX	720618	F
Ayres, James Henry	XX	710103	F
Ayres, Timothy Robert	RR	720503	F
Ayres, Vicki	RR	750227	V

B

Name	Status	I-date	Service
Babcock, Ronald Lester	BB	710227	A
Babula, Robert Leo	XX	660828	M
Bacik, Vladimir Henry	XX	670827	M
Backus, Kenneth Frank	XX	670522	F
Bader, Arthur Edward Jr	NR	681130	A
Badley, James Lindsay	BB	680327	F
Badolati, Frank Neil	BB	660129	A
Badua, Candido Cardinez	RR	680201	W
Bagheri, (FNU)	RR	750310	W
Bagley, Bobby Ray	RR	670916	F
Bailey, Danial T	AA	691101	A
Bailey, James William	RR	670628	N
Bailey, John Edward	XX	660510	N
Bailey, John Howard	BB	670501	M
Bailey, Lawrence Robert	RR	610323	A
Bailey, Michael	CC	750429	V
Bailon, Reuben	MM	651225	V
Baird, Bill Allen	RR	680506	A
Baker, Arthur Dale	XX	650407	F
Baker, David Earle	RR	720627	F
Baker, Edric	–	750318	W
Baker, Elmo Clinnard	RR	670823	F
Baker, Jacky Doris	CC	750429	V
Baker, Veto Huapili	RR	721006	A
Balagot, Arturo Mendoza	RR	680201	W
Balamoti, Michael Dimitri	XX	691124	F
Balcom, Ralph Carol	XX	660515	F
Baldock, Frederick Charles	RR	660317	N
Baldridge, John Robert Jr	XX	691120	F
Ballard, Arthur T Jr	RR	660926	F
Ballenger, Orville Roger	RR	610422	A
Bancroft, William W Jr	BB	701113	F
Bankowski, Alfons Aloyze	BB	610323	F
Bannon, Paul Wedlake	XX	690712	F
Barbay, Lawrence	RR	660720	F
Barber, Robert Franklin	BB	650918	N
Barber, Thomas David	BB	680317	N
Barden, Howard Leroy	BB	670131	F
Bare, William Orlan	XX	670727	F
Barker, Jack Lamar	BB	710320	A
Barnes, Charles Ronald	XX	690316	A
Barnett, Charles Edward	NR	720523	N
Barnett, Robert Russell	BB	660407	F
Barnett, Robert Warren	RR	671003	F
Barr, John Frederick	BB	671018	N
Barras, Gregory Inman	XX	681218	F
Barrett, Thomas Joseph	RR	651005	F
Barrows, Henry Charles	RR	721219	F
Bartocci, John Eugene	BB	680831	N
Barton, Alan Keith	BR	700728	A
Bartsch, George		690427	W
Bates, Paul Jennings Jr	XX	710810	A
Bates, Richard Lyman	RR	721005	F
Batt, Michael Lero	XX	690316	A
Baudelet, Gaston	RR	710726	W
Bauder, James Reginald	XX	660921	N
Bauer, Richard Gene	BR	691104	A
Baugh, William Joseph	RR	670121	F
Bauhahn, Maurice Jonathan	CC	750429	V
Bauman, Richard Lee	XX	710317	A
Baxter, Bruce Raymond	BB	671109	A
Beach, Arthur James	BB	660320	M
Beals, Charles Elbert	BB	700707	A
Bean, James Ellis	RR	680103	F
Bean, William Raymond Jr	RR	720523	F
Beane, Douglas G.	AR	690601	M
Bebus, Charles James	NR	721221	F
Becerra, Rudy Morales	XX	700324	A
Beck, Edward Eugene Jr	XX	690809	M
Beck, Terry Lee	BB	691002	N
Becker, James Christof	BB	700815	A
Beckwith, Harry Medfor III	BB	710324	A
Bedinger, Henry James	RR	691122	N
Bednarek, Jonathan Bruce	NR	720518	F
Beecher, Quentin Rippetoe	XX	670611	A
Beekman, William David	RR	720624	F
Beeler, Carroll Robert	RR	720524	N
Beene, James Alvin	XX	661005	N
Beens, Lynn Richard	RR	721221	F
Begley, Burriss Nelson	XX	661205	F
Behnfeldt, Roger Ernest	NR	720819	F
Belcher, Glenn Arthur	XX	671231	F
Belcher, Robert Arthur	BB	690328	F
Belknap, Harry John	BB	660623	N
Bell, Holly Gene	NR	700128	F
Bell, James Franklin	RR	651016	N
Bell, Marvin Earl	BB	700630	F
Bell, Richard William	BB	691002	N
Bell, Steve	CC	740127	V
Bellindorf, Dieter	–	700408	W
Benedett, Daniel Andrew	BB	750515	M
Benge, Michael	RR	680128	V
Bennefeld, Steven Henry	BB	670729	M
Bennett, Harold George	KK	641229	A
Bennett, Robert Elwood III	BB	671213	F
Bennett, Sherman Henry	CC	750429	V
Bennett, Thomas Waring Jr	XX	721222	F
Bennett, William George	XX	670902	F
Benoit, Charles Edward Jr	CC	740122	V
Benson, Lee David	BB	680317	N
Benton, Gregory Rea Jr	XX	690523	M
Benton, James Austin	BB	670427	M
Berard, Aram Jules	CC	750429	V
Berdahl, David Donald	BB	720120	A
Beresik, Eugene Paul	BB	680531	F
Berg, Bruce Allan	BB	710807	A
Berg, George Phillip	BB	710218	A
Berg, Kile Dag	RR	650727	F
Berger, James Robert	RR	661202	F
Bergevin, Charles Lee	XX	680823	F
Berkson, Joseph Mike	BR	720502	A
Bernasconi, Louis Henry	RR	721222	F
Bernhardt, Robert Edward	BR	730205	F
Berry, John Alvin	BB	681205	A
Berube, Kenneth Allen	BB	670811	M
Bessor, Bruce Carleton	XX	690513	A
Beutel, Robert Donald	XX	711126	F
Beyer, Thomas John	XX	680730	F
Bezold, Steven Neil	XX	681029	A
Biagini, Frederick James	CC	750916	V
Bibbs, Wayne (NMN)	BB	720611	A
Biber, Gerald Mack	BB	610422	A
Bidwell, Barry Alan	BB	710618	N
Biediger, Larry William	NR	670129	F
Bifolchi, Charles Lawrence	XX	680108	F
Biggs, Earl Roger	NR	680116	A
Billipp, Norman Karl	XX	690506	M
Bingham, Klaus Jurgen	XX	710510	A
Birch, Joel Ray	BR	721221	F
Birchim, James Douglas	BB	681115	A
Bird, Leonard Adrian	BB	680713	M
Biscailuz, Robert Lynn	NR	670730	M
Bischoff, John Malcolm	BB	610422	A
Bishop, Edward James Jr	XX	700429	A
Bisz, Robert Irving	RR	661111	F
Bisz, Ralph Campion	XX	670804	N
Bittenbender, David Fritz	BB	670707	F
Bivens, Herndon Arrington	XX	700415	A
Bixel, Michael Sargent	BB	721024	N
Bizot, Francois	RR	711005	W
Black, Arthur Neil	RR	650920	F
Black, Cole	RR	660621	N
Black, Jon David	RR	671027	F
Black, Paul Vernon	BB	710301	A
Blackburn, Harry Lee Jr	NR	720510	N
Blackman, Thomas Joseph	BB	680510	M
Blackwood, Gordon Byron	NR	670527	F
Blair, Charles Edward	NR	680319	F
Blankenship, Charles Herma	BB	670707	F
Blanton, Clarence Finley	BB	680311	F
Blassie, Michael Joseph	BB	720511	F
Blessing, Lynn	BB	750515	M
Blevins, John Charles	RR	660909	F
Blevins, Lural Lee III	BR	680816	A
Blewett, Alan L	XX	620714	V
Bliss, Ronald Glenn	RR	660904	F
Blodgett, Douglas Randolph	XX	680419	A
Blood, Henry F	KK	680201	V
Bloodworth, Donald Bruce	XX	700724	F
Bloom, Darl Russell	BB	641113	M
Bloom, Richard McAuliffe	BB	660920	M
Bobe, Raymond Edward	XX	690316	A
Bodahl, Jon Keith	XX	691112	F
Bodden, Timothy Roy	XX	670603	M
Bodenschatz, John Eugen Jr	XX	660828	M
Boffman, Alan Brent	NR	710318	A
Bogard, Lonnie Pat	XX	720512	F
Boggs, Paschal Glenn	XX	670827	M
Bogiages, Christos C Jr	XX	690302	F
Bohlig, James Richard	BB	690819	M
Bohlscheid, Curtis Richard	BB	670611	M
Bois, Claire Ronald Alan	BB	670825	N
Boles, Warren William	BB	680118	N
Bollinger, Arthur Ray	BB	730205	F
Bolstad, Richard Eugene	RR	651106	F
Bolte, Wayne Louis	XX	720402	F
Boltze, Bruce Edward	BB	721006	M
Bomar, Jack Williamson	RR	670204	F
Bond, Ronald Dale	BB	680311	F
Bond, Ronald Leslie	XX	710930	F
Bono, Sterling Brian	ZR	870502	
Bonzon, R	RR	720409	W
Bookout, Charles Franklin	BB	700704	A
Booth, Gary Preston	BB	701223	A
Booth, James Ervin	XX	680623	F
Booth, Lawrence Randolph	XX	691016	A
Booze, Delmar George	XX	660124	M
Borah, Daniel Vernor Jr	XX	720924	N
Borden, Howard Alan	CC	750429	V
Borden, Murray Lyman	XX	661013	F
Borja, Domingo R S	BB	670221	A
Borling, John Lorin	RR	660601	F
Boronski, John Arthur	XX	700324	A
Bors, Joseph Chester	XX	680428	F
Borton, Robert Curtis Jr	XX	660828	M
Bosiljevac, Michael Joseph	NR	720929	F
Bossio, Galileo Fred	XX	660729	F
Bossman, Peter Robert	BB	660925	N
Boston, Leo Sidney	XX	660429	F
Bott, Russell Peter	XX	661202	A
Bouchard, Michael Lora	XX	681220	N
Bower, Irvin Lester Jr	BB	691006	M
Bower, Joseph Edward	BB	650803	F
Bowers, Richard Lee	XX	690324	A
Bowles, Dwight Pollard	BB	651103	F
Bowling, Roy Howard	NR	651117	N
Bowman, Frank (NMN)	BB	680616	N
Bowman, Michael Lee	BB	691002	N
Boyanowski, John Gordon	BB	711214	A
Boyd, Charles Graham	RR	660422	F
Boyd, Walter	BB	750515	M
Boyer, Alan Lee	XX	680328	A
Boyer, Terry Lee	RR	671217	F
Boyle, William (NMN)	BB	700228	A
Boyles, Howard H	BR	730209	V
Brace, Ernest C	RR	650521	V
Bracey, Lester Jr	BR	720503	F
Bradley, Ed	CC	731021	V
Bradshaw, Robert Samuel III	BB	700212	M
Brady, Allen Colby	RR	670119	N
Bram, Richard Craig	XX	650708	M
Branch, James Alvin	NR	650904	F
Branch, Michael Patrick	BB	680506	A
Brand, Joseph W	NR	660817	F
Brande, Harvey G	RR	680207	A
Brandenburg, Dale	BB	730205	F
Brandt, Keith Allan	NR	710318	A
Brashear, William James	XX	690508	F
Brasher, Jimmy Mac	BB	660928	A
Brassfield, Andrew Thomas	BB	700406	A
Braswell, Donald Robert	EE	670823	A
Brauner, Henry Paul	XX	720329	F
Brazelton, Michael Lee	RR	660807	F
Brazik, Richard	XX	670726	F
Breckner, William J Jr	RR	720730	F
Breeding, Michael Hugh	BB	700212	M
Breiner, Stephen Eugene	BB	680924	M
Bremmer, Dwight Amos	BB	711214	A
Brennan, Herbert Owen	XX	671126	F
Brenneman, Richard Charles	RR	671108	F
Brenning, Richard David	BB	690726	N
Brett, Robert Arthur Jr	XX	720929	F
Breuer, Donald Charles	XX	721120	M
Brewer, Lee	EE	680107	A
Brice, Eric Parker	BB	680604	N
Brice, Gabriel Paul	RR	720422	W
Brickman, Joseph	CC	750429	V
Bridger, Barry Burton	RR	670123	F
Bridges, Jerry Glen	XX	681020	A
Bridges, Philip Wayne	BB	710630	A
Briggs, Ernest Frank Jr	XX	680105	A
Briggs, Ronald Daniel	XX	690206	A
Brigham, Albert	BB	661214	M
Brigham, James W	RR	680913	A
Brinckmann, Robert Edwin	NR	661104	F
Brinton, Keith	CC	750429	V
Brodak, John Warren	RR	660814	F
Broms, Edward James Jr	XX	680801	N
Brookens, Norman J	RR	680204	V
Brooks, John Henry Ralph	XX	690513	A
Brooks, Nicholas George	BR	700102	N
Brooks, William Leslie	XX	700422	F
Brotz, Danny Ray	BR	670430	M
Brower, Ralph Wayne	BB	671109	F
Brown, Benny Richard	CC	750429	V
Brown, Charles A Jr	RR	721219	F
Brown, Donald Alan	XX	700730	F

Name	Status	I-date	Service
Brown, Donald Hubert Jr	NR	650812	N
Brown, Earl Carlyle	XX	691124	F
Brown, Edward Dean Jr	BB	650729	N
Brown, Frank Monroe Jr	BB	660919	N
Brown, George Ronald	XX	680328	A
Brown, Harry Willis	XX	680212	A
Brown, James Auston	BB	700812	A
Brown, James William	BB	660405	M
Brown, Joseph Orville	BB	660419	F
Brown, Paul Gordon	RR	680725	M
Brown, Robert Mack	XX	721107	F
Brown, Thomas Edward	BB	660429	N
Brown, Wayne Gordon II	XX	720717	F
Brown, Wilbur Ronald	XX	660203	F
Brown, William Theodore	XX	691103	A
Browning, Ralph Thomas	RR	660708	F
Brownlee, Charles Richard	XX	681224	F
Brownlee, Robert Wallace	XX	720425	A
Bruch, Donald William Jr	BB	660429	F
Brucher, John Martin	XX	690218	F
Brudno, Edward Alan	RR	651018	F
Brunhaver, Richard Marvin	RR	650824	N
Brunson, Cecil H	RR	721012	F
Brunson, Jack Walter	BB	710531	A
Brunstrom, Alan Leslie	RR	660422	F
Buchanan, Hubert Elliot	RR	660916	F
Bucher, Bernard Ludwig	BB	680512	F
Buck, Arthur Charles	BB	680111	N
Buckley, Jimmy Lee	NR	670821	N
Buckley, Louis Jr	XX	660521	A
Buckley, Victor Patrick	BB	691216	N
Budd, Leonard R Jr	RR	670821	M
Buell, Kenneth Richard	XX	720917	N
Buerk, William Carl	BB	710411	F
Bugarin, Arellano	RR	750310	W
Bullard, William Harry	BB	660825	N
Bullock, Larry Alan	BB	670101	A
Bundy, Norman Lee	BB	660906	N
Bunker, Park George	BB	701230	F
Burd, Douglas Glenn	BB	690801	F
Burdett, Edward Burke	KR	671118	F
Burer, Arthur William	RR	660321	F
Burgard, Paul E	BR	680606	M
Burgess, John Lawrence	BB	700630	A
Burgess, Richard Gordon	RR	660925	M
Burkart, Charles Willia Jr	XX	660613	F
Burke, Michael John	XX	661019	M
Burnes, Robert Wayne	BB	700105	M
Burnett, Donald Frederick	BB	680206	N
Burnett, Sheldon John	XX	710307	A
Burnham, Donald Dawson	XX	680202	A
Burnham, Mason Irwin	XX	720420	F
Burns, Donald Ray	RR	661202	F
Burns, Frederick John	KK	671225	M
Burns, John Douglas	RR	661004	N
Burns, John Robert	NR	660804	F
Burns, Michael Paul	XX	690731	A
Burns, Michael Thomas	RR	680705	F
Burris, Donald Deane Jr	BB	691222	A
Burroughs, William David	RR	660731	F
Burton, Niel	AA	710104	M
Busch, Jon Thomas	NR	670608	F
Bush, Elbert Wayne	XX	730108	A
Bush, John Robert	XX	680724	F
Bush, Robert Edward	NR	660324	F
Bush, Robert Ira	BB	660609	F
Bushnell, Brian Lee	BB	700409	N
Butcher, Jack M	RR	710324	F
Butler, Dewey Renee	BB	690714	A
Butler, James Edward	XX	700320	A
Butler, Phillip Neal	RR	650420	N
Butler, William Wallace	RR	671120	F
Butt, Richard Leigh	NR	661111	F
Byars, Earnest Ray	NR	670730	M
Bynum, Neil Stanley	XX	691026	F
Byrd, Hugh McNeil Jr	XX	690109	A
Byrne, James Sylvester	–	651018	W
Byrne, Joseph Henry	BB	680313	F
Byrne, Ronald Edward Jr	RR	650829	F
Byrns, William G	RR	720523	F

C

Name	Status	I-date	Service
Cadour, Jean Yves	MM	700200	W
Cadwell, Anthony Blake	BB	671017	A
Caffarelli, Charles Joseph	BB	721121	F
Cairns, Robert Alexander	BB	660617	F
Calderon, Benjamin	MM	670110	W
Caldwell, Floyd Dean	BB	711214	A
Calfee, James Henry	BB	680311	F
Calhoun, Johnny C	XX	680327	A
Call, John Henry III	BB	720406	F
Callaghan, Peter A	RR	720621	F
Callahan, David Francis Jr	BB	680923	N
Callanan, Richard Joseph	BB	660107	F
Callies, Tommy Leon	BB	690801	F
Calloway, Porter Earl	XX	680311	A
Camacho, Issac	EE	631124	F
Cameron, Kenneth Robbins	KR	670518	N
Cameron, Virgil King	XX	660729	N
Camerota, Peter P	RR	721222	F
Campbell, Burton Wayne	RR	660701	F
Campbell, Clyde William	BB	690301	F
Campbell, William Edward	XX	690129	F
Candungog, Alejandro	–	680131	W
Caniford, James Kenneth	XX	720329	F
Cannon, Frances Eugene	KR	680108	A
Cantel, Felix C	RR	711108	W
Canton, Suzan	CC	750429	V
Canup, Franklin Harlee Jr	BB	670114	N
Capling, Elwyn R	NR	680919	F
Cappelli, Charles Edward	NR	671117	F
Capron, Veronique Brigitte	ZR	840722	W
Caras, Franklin Angel	NR	670428	F
Carat, Paul Henry Jean	RR	720422	W
Carey, David Jay	RR	670831	N
Carlock, Ralph Lawrence	BB	670304	F
Carlson, Albert E	RR	720407	A
Carlson, John Werner	BB	661207	F
Carlson, Paul Victor	BB	670212	N
Carlton, James Edmund Jr	XX	670417	M
Caron, Gilles	–	700405	W
Carpenter, Allen Russell	RR	661101	N
Carpenter, Howard B	BB	670306	A

Name	Status	I-date	Service
Carpenter, Joe V	RR	680215	F
Carpenter, Nicholas Mallor	NR	680624	N
Carpenter, Ramey Leo	BB	690331	N
Carr, Donald Gene	XX	710706	A
Carreon, Armando D	MM	670110	W
Carrier, Daniel Lewis	NR	670602	F
Carrigan, Larry Edward	RR	670823	F
Carroll, John Leonard	BB	721107	F
Carroll, Patrick Henry	XX	691102	F
Carroll, Roger William Jr	XX	720921	F
Carter, Dennis Ray	XX	660828	M
Carter, George Williams	BB	720424	A
Carter, Gerald Lynn	BB	710126	N
Carter, James Devrin	BB	680613	A
Carter, James Louis	XX	660203	F
Carter, William Thomas	BB	661110	N
Cartwright, Billie Jack	XX	651222	N
Cartwright, Patrick G	BB	710131	N
Carver, Harry Franklin	BB	680410	A
Carver, Robert Charles	–	701103	W(A)F
Case, Thomas Franklin	NR	660531	F
Casey, Donald Francis	XX	680623	F
Cassell, Harley M	RR	680717	A
Cassell, Robin Bern	BB	670715	N
Castillo, Richard	NR	720329	F
Castro, Alfanso Rogue	BR	691104	A
Castro, Reinaldo Antonio	BB	670427	M
Causey, John Bernard	BB	660225	F
Cavaiani, Jon R	RR	710605	A
Cavalli, Anthony Frank	BB	660628	F
Cavender, Jim Ray	XX	691104	A
Cavierlo, Eric	CC	750429	W
Cavil, Jack W	BR	730209	V
Cayce, John David	BB	671112	N
Cayer, Marc Odilon	RR	680201	W
Cecil, Alan Bruce	BB	690921	A
Cerak, John P	RR	720627	F
Certain, Robert G	RR	721218	F
Cestare, Joseph Angelo	BB	680420	M
Chae, Kyu Chang	MM	680120	W
Chambers, Carl Dennis	RR	670807	F
Chambers, Jerry Lee	XX	680522	F
Champion, James Albert	XX	710424	A
Chan, Peter	BB	720925	N
Chandler, Anthony Gordon	BB	680616	N
Chaney, Arthur Fletcher	BB	680503	A
Chapa, Armando Jr	BB	680206	N
Chapman, Harlan Page	BR	651105	M
Chapman, Peter Hayden II	BB	720406	F
Chapman, Rodney Max	BB	690218	N
Charles, Norris Alphonzo	RR	711230	N
Charoenpong, Amnaj	–	680101	W
Charvet, Paul Claude	XX	670321	N
Chauncey, Arvin Ray	RR	670531	N
Chavez, Gary Anthony	XX	700730	F
Chavira, Stephen (NMN)	BB	710528	A
Cheney, Joseph C	BB	630905	V
Cheney, Kevin J	RR	720701	F
Chenoweth, Robert Preston	RR	680208	A
Cherry, Allen Sheldon	BB	670809	F
Cherry, Fred Vann	RR	651022	F
Chesley, Larry James	RR	660416	F
Chesnutt, Chambless M	NR	650930	F
Chestnut, Joseph Lyons	XX	701013	F
Chevalier, John R	RR	680717	A
Chiarello, Vincent Augustu	NR	660729	F
Ching, Yee Leon	CC	750429	V
Chipman, Ralph Jim	XX	721227	M
Chirichigno, Luis Genardo	RR	691102	A
Cho, Joon Bun	–	720323	W
Chomel, Charles Dennis	BB	670611	M
Chomyk, William (NMN)	BB	680422	F
Chorlins, Richard David	BB	700111	F
Christensen, Allen Duane	XX	720403	A
Christensen, John Michael	XX	720413	M
Christensen, William Murre	XX	660301	N
Christian, David Marion	NR	650602	N
Christian, George Palmer	CC	750327	V
Christian, Michael Durham	RR	670424	N
Christiano, Joseph	XX	651224	F
Christiansen, Eugene F	XX	690206	A
Christie, Dennis Ray	BB	670611	M
Christophersen, Keith Alle	BB	730121	N
Chubb, John Jacobsen	BB	710320	A
Chung, Yen Binh	CC	750429	V
Churchill, Carl Russell	BB	700503	F
Chwan, Michael D	NR	650930	F
Cichon, Walter Alan	XX	680330	A
Cius, Frank E	RR	670603	M
Clack, Cecil James	BB	690101	A
Claflin, Richard Ames	XX	670726	F
Clapper, Gean Preston	XX	671229	F
Clark, Donald E Jr	NR	660323	F
Clark, James William	ZM	780421	V
Clark, Jerry Prosper	XX	651215	A
Clark, John Calvin II	XX	691205	F
Clark, John Walter	RR	670312	F
Clark, Lawrence	XX	661018	F
Clark, Phillip Spratt Jr	NR	721224	N
Clark, Richard Champ	XX	671024	N
Clark, Robert Alan	XX	730110	N
Clark, Stanley Scott	XX	690214	F
Clark, Stephen William	BB	680503	M
Clark, Thomas Edward	XX	690208	F
Clarke, Fred Lee	XX	681213	F
Clarke, George William Jr	XX	671016	F
Claudel,	MM	700500	W
Claxton, Charles Peter	XX	671229	F
Clay, Eugene Lunsford	BB	671109	F
Clay, William Clifton III	BB	670412	M
Cleary, Peter McArthur	XX	721010	F
Clem, Thomas Dean	XX	680503	M
Clements, James Arlen	RR	671009	F
Cleve, Reginald David	BB	710322	A
Cline, Curtis Roy	XX	690918	A
Clinton, Dean Eddie	XX	670611	A
Clower, Claude Douglas	RR	671119	N
Clydesdale, Charles Fredri	BB	650315	N
Coady, Robert Franklin	XX	690118	F
Coakley, William Francis	NR	660913	N
Coalston, Echol W Jr	XX	680121	A
Coates, Donald Leroy	BB	660201	M
Cobbs, Ralph Burton	BB	660617	N

Name	Status	I-date	Service
Cobeil, Earl Glenn	KR	671105	F
Cocheo, Richard Newell	PP	680131	V
Cochran, Isom Carter Jr	BB	680523	A
Cochrane, Deverton C	XX	700617	A
Cody, Howard Rudolph	BB	631124	F
Coen, Harry Bob	XX	680512	A
Coffee, Gerald Leonard	RR	660203	N
Cogdell, William Keith	BB	670117	F
Cohron, James Derwin	XX	680112	A
Coker, George Thomas	RR	660827	N
Cole, Legrande Ogden Jr	NR	670630	N
Cole, Richard Milton Jr	XX	720618	F
Coleman, Jimmy Lee	XX	690306	A
Collamore, Allan Philip Jr	XX	670204	N
Collazo, Raphael Lorenzo	NR	680317	A
Collette, Curtis David	BB	660617	N
Collins, Arnold	BB	671204	M
Collins, Guy Fletcher	BB	680313	F
Collins, James Quincy	RR	650902	F
Collins, Peter	CC	740127	V
Collins, Richard Frank	XX	691122	N
Collins, Theothis	BB	680819	M
Collins, Thomas Edward III	RR	651018	F
Collins, Willard Marion	BB	660309	F
Colne, Roger	–	700531	W
Colombo, Gary Lewis	BB	680306	M
Coltman, William Clare	XX	720929	F
Colwell, William Kevin	XX	651224	F
Comer, Howard Brisbane Jr	BB	691124	A
Compa, Joseph James Jr	BB	650610	A
Compton, Frank Ray	BB	660321	N
Conaway, Gary Lee	BR	671024	N
Conaway, Lawrence Yerges	BB	700503	F
Condit, Douglas Craig	NR	671126	F
Condit, William Howard Jr	BB	690623	F
Condon, James C	RR	721228	F
Condrey, George Thomas III	BB	680508	A
Confer, Michael Steele	BB	661010	N
Conger, John Edward Jr	XX	690127	A
Conklin, Bernard	NR	660729	F
Conlee, William W	RR	721222	F
Conley, Eugene Ogden	BB	670121	F
Conlon, John Francis III	XX	660304	F
Connell, James Joseph	KR	660715	N
Conner, Edwin Ray	BB	700516	N
Conner, Lorenza (NMI)	XX	671027	F
Connolly, Vincent J	NR	661104	F
Connor, Charles Richard	XX	681028	M
Consolvo, John Wadswort Jr	XX	720507	M
Conway, James Bennett	BB	660412	A
Conway, Rosemary A	RR	750604	V
Cook, Dennis Philip	BB	660406	N
Cook, Donald Gilbert	KK	641231	M
Cook, Dwight William	XX	720921	F
Cook, Glenn Richard	XX	691021	F
Cook, James R	RR	721226	F
Cook, Joseph Francis	BB	680510	M
Cook, Kelly Francis	XX	671110	F
Cook, William Richard	XX	680428	F
Cook, Wilmer Paul	NR	671222	N
Cooke, Calvin C Jr	BB	720426	F
Cooley, David Leo	XX	680422	N
Cooley, Orville Dale	BB	680116	N
Coons, Chester Leroy	BB	680217	N
Coons, Henry Albert	XX	680228	N
Cooper, Daniel Dean	BB	720204	N
Cooper, Richard Waller Jr	XX	721219	F
Cooper, William Earl	XX	660424	F
Cooper, William G	CC	750429	V
Copack, Joseph Bernard Jr	NR	721222	F
Copeland, HC	RR	670717	F
Copenhaver, Gregory Scott	BB	750515	M
Copley, William Michael	XX	681116	A
Copp, James	ZM	881003	V
Corbitt, Gilland Wales	XX	670727	F
Cordier, Kenneth William	RR	661202	F
Cordova, Robert James	BB	680127	M
Cordova, Sam Gary	NR	720826	M
Corfield, Stan Leroy	BB	670501	M
Corle, John Thomas	BB	651208	M
Cormier, Arthur	RR	651106	F
Cornelius, Johnnie Clayton	BB	680626	F
Cornelius, Samuel Blackmar	XX	730616	F
Cornevin, Jean	–	700509	W
Cornthwaite, Thomas Guy	KK	681105	W
Cornwell, Leroy Jason III	XX	710910	F
Corona, Joel (NMN)	BB	701108	A
Corriveau, Robert D	AA	681118	M
Cortez, Ernesto N	–	680131	W
Coskey, Kenneth Leon	RR	680906	N
Cota, Ernest Keno	BB	680514	N
Cotten, Larry William	BB	700309	F
Cotton, James Paul	ZR		V
Cowan, Kenneth	CC	750429	V
Cozart, Robert Gordon Jr	NR	700320	A
Craddock, Randall James	NR	721221	F
Crafts, Charles	RR	641229	A
Craig, Phillip Charles	NR	670704	N
Crain, Carroll Owen Jr	XX	670308	A
Cramer, Donald Martin	XX	710105	A
Crandall, Gregory Stephen	NR	710218	A
Craner, Robert Roger	RR	671220	F
Craven, Andrew Johnson	XX	680512	A
Crayton, Render	RR	660207	N
Creamer, James Edward Jr	XX	680421	A
Crear, Willis Calvin	BB	710215	A
Crecca, Joseph	RR	661122	F
Creed, Barton Sheldon	XX	710313	N
Cressey, Dennis C	BR	720512	F
Cressman, Peter Richard	BB	730205	F
Crew, James Alan	XX	671110	F
Crews, John Hunter III1	XX	680522	F
Cristman, Frederick Lewis	XX	710319	A
Crockett, William James	BB	720822	F
Crody, Kenneth Lloyd	BB	720711	M
Crone, Donald Everett	BB	710215	A
Cronin, Michael Paul	RR	670113	N
Crook, Elliott	XX	710516	A
Cropper, Curtis Henry	BB	700405	N
Crosby, Bruce Allen Jr	BB	720330	A
Crosby, Frederick Peter	BB	650601	N
Crosby, Herbert Charles	XX	700110	A
Crosby, Richard Alexander	XX	671202	A

Name	Status	I-date	Service
Cross, Ariel Lindley	XX	680717	M
Cross, James Emory	BB	700424	F
Crossman, Gregory John	XX	680425	F
Crosson, Gerald Joseph Jr	XX	680516	F
Crow, Frederick Austin	RR	670326	F
Crow, Raymond Jack Jr	BB	720327	F
Crowe, Winfred D	RR	680717	A
Crowley, John Edward	BB	700810	A
Crowson, Frederick H	RR	700502	A
Croxdale, Jack Lee II	BB	671119	A
Crumm, William Joseph	BB	670707	F
Crumpler, Carl Boyette	RR	680705	F
Cruz, Carlos Rafael	XX	671229	F
Cruz, Raphael (NMN)	BB	630902	F
Cudlike, Charles Joseph	BB	690518	A
Cunningham, Carey Allen	BB	670802	F
Cunningham, Kenneth Leroy	XX	691003	A
Curlee, Robert Lee Jr	BB	650610	A
Curran, Patrick Robert	XX	690929	M
Curry, Keith Royal Wilson	BB	710108	N
Curtis, Thomas Jerry	RR	650920	F
Cushman, Clifton Emmet	XX	660925	F
Cusimano, Samuel B	RR	721228	F
Cuthbert, Bradley Gene	RR	681123	F
Cuthbert, Stephen Howard	NR	720703	F
Cutrer, Fred Clay Jr	BB	640806	F
Cutter, James D	RR	720217	F
Cyawr, Roger A	–	670915	M
Czerwiec, Raymond George	XX	690327	A
Czerwonka, Paul Steven	BB	680510	M

D

Name	Status	I-date	Service
Daffron, Thomas Carl	XX	700218	F
Dahill, Douglas Edward	XX	690417	A
Daigle, Glenn Henri	RR	651222	N
Dailey, Douglas Vincent	XX	681213	F
Dale, Charles Alva	XX	650609	A
Dallas, Richard Howard	BB	670427	M
Dalton, Randall David	BB	710724	A
Daly, James Alexander Jr	RR	680109	A
Daniel, Leon	CC	750429	V
Daniel, Stella Jean	CC	750429	V
Daniels, Verlyne Wayne	RR	671026	N
Danielson, Benjamin Frankl	XX	691205	F
Danielson, Mark Giles	XX	720618	F
Dano, Lucille Mai	CC	750429	V
Dao, Thi Huong	CC	750429	V
Darcy, Edward Joseph	XX	671229	F
Dardeau, Oscar Moise Jr	NR	671118	F
Darr, Charles Edward	NR	721221	F
Dat, Nguyen Quoc	RR	660514	W
Daugherty, Lenard Edward	RR	690511	A
Daughtrey, Robert Norlan	RR	650802	F
Daves, Gary Lawrence	RR	680201	V
Davidson, David Arthur	BB	701005	A
Davies, John Owen	RR	670204	F
Davies, Joseph Edwin	XX	680519	F
Davis, Brent Eden	XX	660318	M
Davis, Charlie Brown Jr	XX	700422	F
Davis, Daniel Richard	XX	690818	F
Davis, Donald Vance	BB	670725	N
Davis, Edgar Felton	XX	680917	F
Davis, Edward Anthony	RR	650826	N
Davis, Francis John	XX	720614	N
Davis, Gene Edmond	XX	660313	F
Davis, James Woodrow	BB	680311	F
Davis, Ricardo Gonzales	XX	690320	A
Davis, Robert Charles	XX	690323	F
Davis, Thomas James	RR	680311	A
Dawes, John James	BB	660505	A
Dawson, Alan	CC	750429	V
Dawson, Clyde Duane	NR	660323	F
Dawson, Daniel George	BB	641106	A
Dawson, Donald	RR	650401	V
Dawson, Frank Arthur	BB	680217	N
Dawson, James Vernon	BB	690716	F
Day, Dennis Irvin	BB	701103	A
Day, George Everette	RR	670826	F
Dayao, Rolando Cueva	BB	691002	N
Dayton, James Leslie	BB	680508	A
De Herrera, Benjamin David	BB	671119	A
De Soto, Ernest Leo	XX	690412	F
Dean, Charles	XX	740910	V
Dean, Donald Chester	BB	691002	N
Dean, Michael Frank	BB	700630	F
Dean, Ronald Keith	ZM	781124	W
Deane, William Lawrence	XX	730108	A
Deblasio, Raymond Vince Jr	BB	710618	N
Debruin, Eugene H	PP	630905	V
Decaire, Jack Leonard	BB	711103	A
Decoudu, Veronique	RR	730100	W
Deeds, Michael Scott	ZM	781124	V
Deere, Donald Thorpe	BB	660517	A
Deering, John Arthur	RR	680203	M
Degnan, Jerry L	MM	670828	V
Deichelmann, Samuel Mackal	XX	680906	F
Deitsch, Charles Edward	XX	681020	A
Delance, Christopher Edwar	ZM	781124	V
Deleidi, Richard Augustine	BB	690207	M
Dellenbaugh, Cornelia	ZR	771014	V
Delong, Joe Lynn	KK	670518	A
Deluca, Anthony J	RR	700205	N
Demmon, David Stanley	XX	650609	A
Dempsey, Jack Ishum	BB	660617	N
Demsey, Walter Edward Jr	BB	710218	A
Dengler, Dieter	EE	660201	N
Dennany, James Eugene	XX	691112	F
Dennis, William Roy	XX	680419	A
Dennison, James Richard	XX	680101	N
Dennison, Terry Arden	KR	660719	N
Denton, Jeremiah Andrew	RR	650718	N
Denton, Manuel Reyes	BB	631008	N
Derby, Paul David	BB	681117	M
Derrickson, Thomas G II	XX	671012	F
Desir, Roger	MM	700800	W
Despiegler, Gale A	RR	720415	F
Deuso, Carroll Joseph	BB	701215	N
Deuter, Richard Carl	XX	691122	N
Devers, David	BR	660813	A
Dewberry, Jerry Don	BB	680705	M
Dewhurst, John Dawson	ZM	781013	W
Dewispelaere, Rexford John	XX	691124	F
Dexter, Bennie Lee	KK	660509	F

Name	Status	I-date	Service
Dexter, Ronald James	KK	670603	A
Di Tommaso, Robert Joseph	XX	660729	F
Diamond, Stephen W	NR	660719	F
Dibble, Morris Frederick	BB	651205	A
Dibernardo, James Vincent	RR	680203	M
Dickens, Delma Ernest	NR	721221	F
Dickerman, Leeland	ZR	771014	V
Dickson, Edward Andrew	BB	650207	N
Diehl, Bernhard	RR	690427	W
Diehl, William C	KR	671107	F
Dierling, Edward A	EE	680203	A
Dilger, Herbert Hugh	BB	691002	N
Dillender, William Edward	BB	710320	A
Dillon, David Andrew	BB	660720	A
Dillon, Michael	RR	750227	V
Dinan, David Thomas III	BB	690317	F
Dingee, David B	RR	720627	F
Dingwall, John Francis	XX	650708	M
Dion, Laurent Norbert	BB	670817	N
Dix, Craig Mitchell	XX	710317	A
Dixon, David Lloyd	BB	680928	N
Doby, Herb	NR	670204	F
Doctolero, Rolando	RR	711108	W
Dodd, Joe Lee	EE	651010	V
Dodge, Edward Ray	XX	641231	A
Dodge, Ronald Wayne	NR	670517	N
Dodge, Ward K	KR	670705	F
Dodson, James	EE	660506	M
Dolan, Edward V	BB	750312	V
Dolan, Thomas Albert	XX	710810	A
Donahue, Morgan Jefferson	XX	681213	F
Donald, Myron Lee	RR	680223	F
Donato, Paul Nicholas	BB	680217	N
Donnelly, Verne George	NR	720917	N
Donovan, Leroy Melvin	BB	650519	A
Donovan, Michael Leo	XX	710930	F
Dooley, James Edward	XX	671022	N
Doremus, Robert Hartsch	RR	650824	N
Dority, Richard Clair	BB	701103	A
Doss, Dale Walter	RR	680317	N
Dotson, Jefferson Scott	XX	690809	F
Doughtie, Carl Louis	BB	650610	N
Doughty, Daniel James	RR	660402	F
Douglas, Thomas Evan	XX	651122	M
Dove, Jack Paris Sr	XX	670712	F
Downey, John T	RR	521129	V
Downing, Donald William	XX	670905	F
Doyle, Michael William	NR	720825	N
Drabic, Peter E	RR	680924	A
Draeger, Walter Frank Jr	BB	650404	F
Drake, Carl Wilson	BB	700618	F
Dramesi, John Arthur	RR	670402	F
Draper, Robert	ZR	800509	W
Dreher, Richard E	BB	720327	F
Driscoll, Jerry Donald	RR	660424	F
Driver, Clarence N	MM	730307	V
Driver, Dallas Alan	BB	691009	A
Drummond, David I	RR	721222	F
Duart, David Henry	RR	670218	F
Dubbeld, Orie John Jr	BB	710303	A
Ducat, Bruce Chalmers	NR	661202	F
Ducat, Phillip Allen	BB	660925	M
Duckett, Thomas Allen	XX	701212	F
Dudash, John Francis	NR	670426	F
Dudley, Charles Glendon	BB	660628	F
Dudman, Richard	RR	700507	V
Duensing, James Allyn	BB	730130	N
Duffy, Charles J	XX	610113	V
Duffy, John Everett	XX	700404	F
Dugan, John Francis	BB	710320	A
Dugan, Thomas Wayne	XX	681213	F
Duggan, William Young	XX	711231	F
Dujon, Leone	RR	720422	W
Duke, Charles R	MM	700530	V
Dumond, Yves M	RR	720408	W
Duncan, James Edward	BB	710303	A
Duncan, Robert Ray	XX	680829	N
Dunlap, William C	NR	691202	F
Dunlop, Thomas Earl	XX	720406	N
Dunn, John Galbreath	RR	680318	A
Dunn, John Howard	RR	651207	M
Dunn, Joseph Patrick	XX	680214	N
Dunn, Michael E	XX	680126	N
Dunn, Richard Edward	BB	720426	F
Dupont, Entienne	RR	720409	W
Duran, Elman	RR	711108	W
Dusing, Charles Gale	KK	651031	F
Dutton, Richard Allen	RR	671105	F
Duvall, Dean Arnold	XX	660313	F
Dyczkowski, Robert Raymond	XX	660423	F
Dye, Melvin C	XX	680219	A
Dyer, Blenn Colby	BB	670427	M
Dyer, Irby III (NMN)	BB	661202	A

E

Name	Status	I-date	Service
Eads, Dennis Keith	XX	700423	A
Earle, John Stiles	BB	700622	N
Earll, David John	XX	661021	F
Earnest, Charles M	BB	721128	N
East, James Boyd Jr	BB	690426	F
Eastman, Leonard Corbett	RR	660621	N
Eaton, Curtis Abbot	XX	660814	F
Eaton, Norman Dale	XX	690113	F
Eby, Robert Gino	XX	670821	V
Echanis, Joseph Ygnacio	XX	691105	F
Echevarria, Raymond L	XX	661003	A
Eckes, Walter W	EE	660510	M
Eckley, Wayne Alvin	XX	671229	F
Ecklund, Arthur G	XX	690403	A
Edgar, Robert John	XX	680205	F
Ediger, Max	CC	750429	V
Edmondson, William Rothroc	XX	660531	F
Edmunds, Robert Clifton Jr	BR	681027	F
Edwards, Harry Jerome	BB	720120	A
Edwards, Harry S Jr	XX	661020	N
Egan, James Thomas Jr	XX	660121	M
Egan, William Patrick	BB	660429	N
Egger, John Culbertson Jr	BB	671103	F
Ehrlick, Dennis Michael	BB	670119	N
Eidsmoe, Norman Edward	XX	680126	N
Eilers, Dennis Lee	XX	651224	F
Eisenberger, George Joe Bu	BB	651205	A
Eisenbraun, William F	KK	650705	A
Elander, William J Jr	RR	720705	F
Elbert, Fred	RR	680816	M
Elias, Edward K	RR	720420	F
Elkins, Frank Callihan	NR	661012	N
Ellen, Wade Lynn	BB	720424	A
Ellerd, Carl J	BB	691002	N
Elliot, Robert Malcolm	XX	680214	N
Elliott, Andrew John	XX	700609	A
Elliott, Artice W	RR	700426	A
Elliott, Jerry W	XX	680121	A
Elliott, Robert Thomas	NR	721221	F
Ellis, Billy J	XX	680103	A
Ellis, Jeffrey Thomas	RR	671217	F
Ellis, Leon Francis	RR	671107	F
Ellis, Randall S	XX	690418	A
Ellis, William Jr	XX	660624	A
Ellison, John C	XX	670324	N
Elm, Homer L	RR	731006	V
Elzinga, Richard G	XX	700326	F
Emberger, Collette	RR	650401	W
Emrich, Roger G	XX	671117	N
Engelhard, Erich C	BR	690622	F
Engen, Robert Joseph	NR	710218	A
Englander, Lawrence J	XX	680502	A
Ensch, John C	RR	720825	N
Entrican, Danny D	XX	710518	A
Erickson, David W	XX	680316	M
Erskine, Jack D	PP	681113	V
Erwin, Donald Edward	NR	681002	N
Escobedo, Julian Jr	BB	690901	M
Espenshied, John L	NR	691021	F
Esper, George	CC	750429	V
Estes, Edward Dale	RR	680103	N
Estes, Walter O	NR	671119	N
Estocin, Michael John	XX	670426	N
Etchberger, Richard Loy	BR	680311	F
Ettmueller, Harry L	RR	680203	A
Evancho, Richard	BB	680326	M
Evans, Billy Kennedy Jr	BB	681205	A
Evans, Cleveland Jr	XX	680313	M
Evans, James J	BR	650402	M
Evans, William Anthony	BB	690302	A
Eveland, Mickey Eugene	BB	711026	A
Everett, David A	RR	720827	N
Everette, Edward Love, Jr	AA	690618	M
Everson, David	RR	670310	F
Evert, Lawrence G	XX	671108	F

F

Name	Status	I-date	Service
Fallon, Patrick M	XX	690704	F
Fanning, Hugh M	NR	671031	M
Fanning, Joseph Peter	XX	681213	F
Fant, Robert St Clair	RR	680725	N
Fantle, Samuel	NR	680105	F
Farlow, Craig L	XX	710516	A
Farris, William F III	BB	680206	N
Featherston, Fielding W III	XX	691230	F
Fecteau, Richard	RR	521129	V
Fegan, Ronald James	BB	650409	N
Feigon, Larry	CC	750429	V
Feldhaus, John Anthony	XX	661008	N
Fellenz, Charles R	XX	691124	F
Fellowes, John Heaphy	RR	660827	N
Fellows, Allen E	XX	680320	F
Feneley, Francis James	BB	660511	F
Fenter, Charles Frederick	NR	721221	F
Fer, John	RR	670204	F
Ferguson, Douglas D	XX	691230	F
Ferguson, Walter Jr	KK	680823	A
Ferguson, Walter L	NR	721218	F
Ferguson, Willie C, Jr	BR	681011	M
Fickler, Edwin James	XX	690117	M
Fieszel, Clifford W	XX	680930	F
Filler, Fong Duong	CC	750429	V
Filloux, Marc	–	740410	W
Finch, Melvin W	NR	720330	A
Finger, Sanford IRA	BB	711026	A
Finlay, John Stewart	RR	680428	F
Finley, Dickie W	XX	681021	A
Finn, William Robert	XX	711224	F
Finney, Arthur Thomas	NR	660801	F
Finney, Charles E	XX	690317	M
Fischer, John Richard	BB	660909	M
Fischer, Richard William	XX	680108	M
Fisher, David John	–	690927	W
Fisher, Donald E	XX	671229	F
Fisher, Donald G	XX	700422	F
Fisher, Donald J. E.	–	–	W(A)A
Fisher, John B	RR	690212	A
Fisher, Kenneth	RR	671107	F
Fitton, Crosley J	NR	680229	F
Fitts, Richard A	NR	681130	A
Fitzgerald, Frances	CC	730401	V
Fitzgerald, Joseph E	XX	670531	A
Fitzgerald, Paul L Jr	XX	671017	A
Fevelson, Barry Frank	BB	710215	A
Flanagan, Sherman E Jr	BB	680721	F
Flanigan, John Norlee	XX	690819	M
Flecker, Michael David	ZR	840722	W
Fleenor, Kenneth Raymond	RR	671217	F
Fleming, Horace H III	RR	680510	M
Flesher, Hubert Kelly	RR	661202	F
Flom, Fredric R	RR	660808	F
Flora, Carroll E	RR	670721	A
Flynn, George Edward III	BR	640923	F
Flynn, John Peter	RR	671027	F
Flynn, Robert J	RR	670821	N
Flynn, Sean Leslie	PP	700406	V
Fobair, Roscoe Henry	XX	650724	F
Foley, Brendan Patrick	XX	671124	F
Foley, John Joseph III	BB	670611	M
Forame, Peter Charles	BB	711219	A
Forby, Willis Ellis	BB	650920	F
Ford, David Edward	RR	671119	A
Ford, Edward (NMN)	BB	681209	A
Ford, Randolph Wright	NR	680611	N
Forman, William S	XX	660122	N
Forrester, Ronald W	XX	721227	M
Fors, Gary Henry	XX	671222	M
Forsythe, Julia Bell	CC	750429	V
Fortner, Frederick J	NR	671017	N
Foster, Marvin L	XX	690316	A
Foster, Paul L	XX	671229	F
Foster, Robert Eugene	BB	660309	F
Foulks, Ralph Eugene Jr	NR	680105	N
Fowler, Donald R	XX	680801	A
Fowler, Henry Pope	RR	670326	F
Fowler, James Alan	XX	720606	F
Fowler, James Jewel	BB	691002	N
Fowler, Roy G	BB	691002	N
Frakes, Dwight Glenn	BB	650224	N
Francis, Richard L	RR	720627	F
Francisco, San Dewayne	XX	681125	F
Franco, Charles	BR	660607	F
Franjola, Matthew John	CC	750429	V
Frank, Martin S	RR	670712	A
Franke, Fred Augustus	RR	650824	N
Franklin, Charles E	NR	660814	F
Franks, Ian Jack	BB	680323	A
Fransen, Albert M Jr	BB	690702	N
Fraser, Kenneth J	RR	720217	F
Frawley, William D	XX	660301	N
Frazier, Paul Reid	BB	680903	A
Frederick, David Addison	NR	670730	M
Frederick, John William	KR	651207	M
Frederick, Peter J	XX	670315	F
Frederick, William V	NR	670705	F
Freng, Stanley John	BB	660617	N
Frenyea, Edmund Henry	XX	660122	N
Friese, Lawrence Victor	RR	680224	M
Frink, John W	XX	720402	A
Frishmann, Robert F	RR	671024	N
Frits, Orville B	BR	670520	A
Fritsch, Thomas William	BB	680510	M
Fritz, John J	RR	690208	V
Frosio, Robert Clarence	BB	661112	N
Fryar, Bruce C	XX	700102	N
Frye, Donald Patrick	NR	670719	N
Fryer, Ben L	NR	721228	F
Fryer, Charles Wigger	BB	660807	N
Fryett, George F	RR	611226	A
Fullam, Wayne E	NR	671007	F
Fuller, James R	NR	721221	F
Fuller, Richard Byron	RR	670714	N
Fuller, William O	XX	670826	F
Fullerton, Frank Eugene	XX	680727	N
Fulton, Richard J	RR	720613	F

G

Name	Status	I-date	Service
Gabriel, James	BR	620408	A
Gaddis, Norman Carl	R	670512	F
Gage, Robert Hugh	XX	660703	M
Gaither, Ralph Ellis	RR	651017	N
Galanti, Paul Edward	RR	660617	N
Galati, Ralph W	RR	720216	F
Galbraith, Russell D	XX	681211	F
Gallagher, Donald L	BB	680206	N
Gallagher, John Theodore	XX	680105	A
Gallant, Henry Joseph	BB	650713	A
Galvin, Ronald E	XX	670308	N
Gan, Leonardo M	BB	691002	N
Gande, Berman Jr	XX	700324	A
Ganley, Richard O	XX	691124	F
Garbett, Jimmy Ray	BB	691009	A
Garcia, Andres	BB	750515	M
Garcia, Ricardo Martinez	XX	710319	A
Gardner, Glenn Virgil	BB	661125	A
Gardner, John G	XX	670603	M
Garner, John Henry	BB	670529	N
Garrett, Maurice Edwin Jr	BB	711022	A
Garside, Frederick Thomas	NR	610323	F
Gartley, Markham Ligon	RR	680817	N
Garwood, Robert Russell	RR	650928	M
Gassman, Fred Allen	BB	701005	A
Gates, Albert Henry Jr	BB	700307	M
Gates, James W	XX	660406	A
Gatewood, Charles Hue	XX	680531	M
Gatwood, Robin F Jr	XX	720402	F
Gaudeul, E	RR	720407	W
Gaughan, Roger Conrad	BB	670501	M
Gauley, James Paul	BB	670110	F
Gauntt, William A	RR	720813	F
Gause, Bernard Jr	BB	750515	N
Gauthier, Dennis L	XX	691031	A
Gay, Arlo N	RR	750430	V
Gaza, Ofelia	RR	660624	W
Gaza, Vincente	KK	660624	W
Gee, Paul S	XX	680116	M
Gehrig, James M Jr	BB	650618	F
Geist, Stephen J	XX	670926	A
Geloneck, Terry M	RR	721220	F
Genslukner, Georg	–	700408	W
George, James E Jr	KK	680208	A
Gerber, Daniel A	PP	620530	V
Gerndt, Gerald Lee	RR	670823	F
Gerstel, Donald Arthur	XX	720908	N
Gervais, Donald Peter	XX	680501	A
Getchell, Paul E	XX	690113	F
Giammerino, Vincent F	XX	680627	A
Giannangeli, Anthony Rober	XX	720402	F
Gideon, Willard Selleck	RR	660807	F
Gierak, George Gregory Jr	BB	660613	N
Gilbert, Clarence E	AA	670628	M
Gilbert, Paul F	XX	720618	F
Gilchrist, Robert M	XX	661007	F
Gillen, Thomas Eldon	XX	700218	F
Gillespie, Charles R	RR	671024	N
Gillespie, John Francis	–	710417	W(A)A
Gillson, Peter Raymond	–	651108	W(A)A
Ginn, David Landrell	BB	701103	A
Giroux, Peter J	RR	721222	F
Gish, Henry Gerald	BB	680311	F
Gist, Tommy E	XX	680518	F
Glandon, Gary Alven	BB	660526	F
Glanville, John Turner Jr	BB	660613	N
Glass, Stuart	ZM	781013	W
Glasson, William Albert Jr	XX	660412	N
Glenn, Danny Elloy	RR	661221	N
Glenn, Thomas Paul	RR	700205	N
Glover, Calvin C	XX	680522	F
Glover, Douglas J	XX	680219	A
Godfrey, Johnny Howard	BB	660111	F
Godwin, Solomon Hughey	KK	780205	M
Goeden, Gene William	BB	670317	N
Goeglein, John Winfred	BB	700630	F
Goetsch, Thomas August	BB	720917	N
Goff, Kenneth B	XX	670824	A
Golberg, Lawrence H	NR	660808	F
Gold, Edward Frank	XX	651222	N
Gollahon, Gene Raymond	BB	650813	N
Golz, John Bryan	BB	700422	N
Gomez, Robert A	XX	700423	F
Gonzales, David	BB	700321	M
Gonzales, Jesus Armando	XX	680419	A
Gonzales, Jose Jesus	BB	670611	M
Goodermote, Wayne Keith	RR	670813	N
Goodman, Robert Oliver	RR	831204	N
Goodman, Russell Clemensen	BB	670220	F
Goodrich, Edwin R Jr	NR	670312	F
Goodwin, Charles B	XX	650908	N
Gopp, Thomas Alan	BB	670803	M
Gore, Paul Edwin	BB	691002	N
Gorsuch, William D	BB	691002	N
Gorton, Thomas Frederick	BB	631206	F
Gosen, Lawrence Dean	BB	680723	N
Goss, Bernard J	NR	660423	F
Gostas, Theodore W	RR	680201	A
Gotner, Norbert A	RR	710203	F
Gougelmann, Tucker P E	NR	750429	V
Gough, James W	RR	721228	F
Gouin, Donat Joseph	RR	680203	A
Gould, Frank Alton	XX	721221	F
Gourley, Laurent Lee	XX	690809	F
Goven, Robert A	XX	670401	F
Grace, James W	XX	690614	F
Graening, Bruce A	EE	670309	A
Graf, Albert Stephen	BB	690829	M
Graf, John George	XX	691115	N
Graffe, Paul L	XX	691003	A
Graham, Alan U	NR	721017	F
Graham, Dennis L	XX	680328	F
Graham, Frederick	ZR	830608	V
Graham, Gilbert James	BB	670928	N
Graham, James Scott	NR	670504	N
Grainger, Joseph W	KK	640808	V
Grammar, William M	BR	670520	M
Granger, Paul L	RR	721220	F
Graniela, Jose Antonio Jr	BB	680816	A
Grannec, Noel	–	700410	W
Grant, David B	RR	720624	F
Grantham, Robert Eugene	BB	710308	A
Grauert, Hans Herbert	BB	671103	N
Graustein, Robert S	NR	721221	N
Graves, Richard Campbell	BB	670525	N
Gravitte, Connie Mack	BB	660617	F
Gray, David Fletcher	RR	670123	F
Gray, Harold Edwin Jr	BB	650807	N
Grayson, William Ronald	BB	660401	N
Graziosi, Francis George	XX	700110	A
Green, Donald George	BB	651116	F
Green, Frank Clifford Jr	XX	720710	N
Green, George Curtis Jr	BB	701204	A
Green, Gerald (NMN)	BB	650912	N
Green, James Arvil	BB	700618	A
Green, Larry Edward	BB	680326	M
Green, Norman M	XX	680109	F
Green, Robert Bailey	BB	661025	F
Green, Sheldon H	ZR	800509	W
Green, Thomas Frederick	BB	711026	A
Greene, Charles E	RR	670311	F
Greenleaf, Joseph G	BB	720414	N
Greenley, Jon Alfred	BB	660107	F
Greenwood, Robert R Jr	XX	720902	F
Greer, Robert Lee	NR	640607	M
Gregory, Kenneth R	RR	680825	A
Gregory, Marie	CC	750329	V
Gregory, Paul Anthony	BB	700725	N
Gregory, Philippe	CC	750329	V
Gregory, Robert Raymond	NR	661202	F
Greiling, David Scott	XX	680724	N
Grella, Donald Carroll	BB	651228	A
Grenzebach, Earl W	XX	670512	F
Grewell, Larry I	XX	691124	F
Griffey, Terrence Hastings	BB	660526	F
Griffin, James Lloyd	KR	670519	N
Griffin, Rodney L	XX	700502	A
Griffith, John Gary	BB	680312	N
Griffith, Robert S	XX	680219	A
Grigsby, Donald E	RR	680717	A
Grissett, Edwin R Jr	KR	660122	M
Groom, George Edward	RR	620408	A
Grosse, Christopher A Jr	XX	680328	A
Groth, Wade L	XX	680212	A
Grubb, Peter Arthur	XX	670917	F
Grubb, Wilmer N	KR	660126	F
Gruters, Guy Dennis	RR	671220	F
Grzyb, Robert H	KK	671210	V
Guajardo, Hilario H	BB	670501	M
Guarino, Lawrence Nicholas	RR	650614	F
Guenther, Lynn	RR	711226	F
Guerra, Raul Antonio	BB	671008	N
Guffey, Jerry	EE	690304	A
Guggenberger, Gary John	RR	690114	A
Guiao, Feliciano	RR	711108	W
Guillermin, Louis F	XX	680430	F
Guillet, Andre R	XX	660518	F
Guillory, Edward Joseph	XX	670618	A
Guillory, Hubia Jude	BB	680425	A
Gulden, Frederick N	CC	750429	V
Gumbert, Robert William Jr	BB	700622	A
Gunn, Alan W	XX	680212	A
Gunther, Harry	XX	670821	W
Gurnsey, Earl F	RR	681127	A
Gutterson, Laird	RR	680223	F
Guy, Theodore Wilson	RR	680322	F

H

Name	Status	I-date	Service
Haas, Leon Frederick	BB	720717	N
Hackett, Harley B III	XX	680724	F
Hackett, James Edward	BB	720611	A
Hagan, John Robert	XX	690506	M
Hagen, Craig Louis	BB	650610	A
Hagerman, Robert W	NR	671106	F
Haifley, Michael F	NR	721228	N
Haight, Stephen Harold	BB	700509	A
Hail, William W	XX	650802	F
Haines, Collins Henry	RR	670605	N
Hale, John Douglas	BB	710308	A
Hall, Donald J	XX	670206	F

Name	Status	I-date	Service
Hall, Frederick M	XX	690412	F
Hall, Gary Lee	XX	750515	M
Hall, George Robert	RR	650927	F
Hall, Harley Hubert	XX	730127	N
Hall, James S	NR	660729	F
Hall, James Wayne	XX	721028	N
Hall, Keith Norman	RR	680110	F
Hall, Thomas Renwick	RR	670610	N
Hall, Walter Louis	BB	650610	A
Hall, Walter Ray	BB	710322	A
Hall, Willis Rozelle	BB	680311	F
Hallberg, Roger C	XX	670324	A
Halpin, David Paul	BB	680928	N
Halpin, Richard C	NR	720329	F
Halyburton, Porter Alex	RR	651017	N
Hamill, Kerry George	ZM	781013	W
Hamilton, Dennis C	XX	680105	A
Hamilton, Eugene D	XX	660131	F
Hamilton, John S	XX	670419	F
Hamilton, Roger D	XX	670421	M
Hamilton, Walter D	EE	651018	M
Hamm, James E	XX	680314	F
Hammond, Dennis Wayne	KK	680208	M
Handrahan, Eugene Allen	XX	681010	A
Hangen, Welles	NR	700531	V
Hanley, Larry James	XX	691104	F
Hanley, Terrence Higgins	XX	680101	N
Hanna, Kenneth	XX	680207	A
Hannoteaux, Guy	–	700406	W
Hanratty, Thomas Michael	BB	670611	M
Hansen, Lester Alan	XX	690813	A
Hanson, Gregg O	RR	720613	F
Hanson, Robert Taft Jr	NR	660203	N
Hanson, Stephen Paul	XX	670603	M
Hanson, Thomas Patterson	XX	670905	F
Hanton, Thomas J	RR	720627	F
Harber, Stephen J	XX	700702	A
Hardie, Charles David	BB	670727	N
Hardman, William Morgan	RR	670821	N
Hardy, Arthur Hans	BR	720314	F
Hardy, John C	BR	680403	F
Hardy, John K Jr	XX	671012	F
Hardy, William H	RR	670629	A
Hargrove, Joseph N	XX	750515	M
Hargrove, Olin Jr	XX	671017	A
Harker, David Northrup	RR	680108	A
Harley, Lee D	XX	660518	F
Harnavee, Chaichan	RR	650521	W
Harned, Gary Alan	XX	700324	A
Harper, Ralph Lewis	BB	680606	M
Harper, Richard K	BB	650519	A
Harris, Bobby Glenn	XX	710317	A
Harris, Carlyle Smith	RR	650404	F
Harris, Cleveland Scott	NR	680229	F
Harris, Gregory J	XX	660612	M
Harris, Harold Lee	BB	661022	A
Harris, Henry A	BR	700816	V
Harris, Jeffrey L	XX	720510	F
Harris, Jessie B	RR	690608	A
Harris, Paul Winiford	BB	670313	M
Harris, Reuben Beaumont	XX	660412	N
Harris, Stephen W	XX	700422	F
Harrison, Donald L	XX	681029	A
Harrison, Larry Gene	BB	710226	A
Harrison, Robert Heerman	XX	720618	F
Harrold, Patrick K	XX	691205	F
Hart, Joseph Leslie	BB	670225	F
Hart, Thomas Trammell III	NR	721221	F
Hartman, Richard Danner	KR	670718	N
Hartness, Gregg	XX	681126	F
Hartney, James C	NR	680105	F
Hartzheim, John Francis	BB	680227	N
Harvey, Jack Rockwood	XX	721128	F
Harwood, James Arthur	XX	710115	A
Harworth, Elroy E	NR	660531	F
Haselton, John H	BR	720511	F
Hasenbeck, Paul Alfred	XX	670421	A
Hassenger, Arden K	XX	651224	F
Hastings, Steven M	XX	680801	A
Hatch, Paul G	EE	690824	A
Hatcher, David Burnett	RR	660530	F
Hatley, Joel Clinton	NR	710305	A
Hattori, Masaki (NMN)	BB	680323	A
Hauer, Leslie J	NR	671118	F
Hauer, Robert D	XX	700905	F
Haukness, Steven	BR	680201	V
Haviland, Roy Elbert	BB	730130	N
Havranek, Michael William	BB	670611	M
Hawkins, Edgar L	XX	650920	F
Hawley, Edwin A Jr	RR	720217	F
Hawthorne, Richard W	XX	670912	M
Hayden, Glenn Miller	BB	680217	N
Hayhurst, Robert A	EE	680203	A
Heep, William Arthur	BB	680824	A
Heeren, Jerome D	RR	720911	F
Hefel, Daniel	RR	700205	A
Hegdahl, Douglas B	RR	670406	N
Heggen, Keith R	KR	721221	F
Heideman, Thomas Edward	BB	701024	F
Heilig, John	RR	660505	N
Heiliger, Donald Lester	RR	670515	F
Heiskell, Lucius L	XX	670206	F
Heitman, Steven W	XX	680313	A
Helber, Lawrence Neal	XX	660124	M
Held, John Wayne	XX	680417	F
Hellbach, Harold James	BB	670519	M
Helle, Robert R	RR	680424	M
Heller, Ivan Louis	BR	681011	N
Helmich, Gerald Robert	XX	691112	F
Helwig, Roger Danny	BB	690911	F
Hemmel, Clarence Joseph	BB	671021	F
Hempel, Barry Lee	BB	680510	M
Henderson, Alexander	RR	680201	V
Henderson, William J	RR	720403	F
Henderson, William R	BR	690123	A
Hendrix, Jerry Wayne	BB	720711	M
Henn, John Robert Jr	XX	720524	A
Henninger, Howard W	XX	660313	F
Henry, David Alan	BB	660919	N
Henry, Lee Edward	RR	680717	A
Henry, Nathan Barney	RR	670712	A
Hensley, Ronnie L	XX	700422	F
Hensley, Thomas Truett	XX	680317	F

Name	Status	I-date	Service
Hentz, Richard Jay	BB	710304	A
Hepler, Frank Monroe	BB	680512	F
Herbert, Michael Patrick	–	701103	W(A)F
Herlik, Querin E	RR	690212	A
Hernandez, Frank Sanchez	BB	700506	A
Herold, Richard Walter	BB	720902	F
Herreid, Robert D	XX	681010	A
Herrera, Frederick D	XX	690325	A
Herrick, Charles	BB	630905	V
Herrick, James W Jr	XX	691027	F
Herrin, Henry Howard Jr	XX	680101	N
Herrold, Ned R	XX	660531	F
Hertz, Gustav	KK	650202	V
Hesford, Peter D	XX	680321	F
Hess, Frederick William Jr	XX	690329	F
Hess, Gene Karl	BB	660617	F
Hess, Jay Criddle	RR	670824	F
Hessom, Robert Charles	BB	660305	N
Hestand, James Hardy	RR	710317	A
Hestle, Roosevelt Jr	XX	660706	F
Hetrick, Raymond Harry	BB	660224	F
Heubeck, Elmer Kerry	CC	750429	V
Heubeck, Nibrit Hican	CC	750429	V
Hewitt, Samuel Eugene	XX	660323	M
Heyne, Raymond Thomas	BB	680510	M
Hickerson, James Martin	RR	671222	N
Hickman, Vincent Joseph	BB	640114	F
Hicks, Prentice W	XX	690325	A
Hicks, Terrin D	XX	680815	F
Hiemer, Jerry Allen	BB	651117	A
Higdon, Kenneth H	RR	721221	N
Hilbrich, Barry W	XX	700609	A
Hildebrand, Leland	RR	711218	F
Hill, Arthur Sinclair Jr	BB	651229	N
Hill, Billy D	XX	680121	A
Hill, Charles Dale	BB	670515	N
Hill, Gordon C	XX	700630	F
Hill, Howard John	RR	671216	F
Hill, John Richard	BB	700427	A
Hill, Joseph Arnold	BB	680528	M
Hill, Rayford J	BB	691002	N
Hill, Richard Dale	BB	631206	F
Hill, Robert L	XX	661018	F
Hills, John Russell	BB	660214	F
Hilton, Robert Larie	BB	660314	F
Hinckley, Robert Bruce	RR	680118	F
Hines, Vaughn Maurice	BB	671108	A
Hirons, Alan	–	720426	W
Hise, James Hamilton	BB	670325	N
Hiteshaw, James Edward	RR	670311	F
Hivner, James Otis	RR	651005	F
Hockridge, James Alan	NR	721017	F
Hodges, David Lawton	BB	671007	N
Hodgson, Cecil J	XX	660129	A
Hoeffs, John Harvey	BB	661128	A
Hoff, Michael G	XX	700107	N
Hoff, Sammie Don	NR	660830	F
Hoffman, David Wesley	RR	711230	N
Hoffman, Terry Alan	BB	680819	M
Hoffson, Arthur Thomas	RR	680817	F
Hofrath, Dietrich	RR	730822	W
Hogan, Jerry F	XX	670121	N
Holdeman, Robert Eugene	XX	671125	M
Holden, Elmer Larry	BB	680609	F
Holguin, Luis Gallegos	XX	710103	A
Holland, Lawrence Thomas	BB	650612	F
Holland, Melvin Arnold	BB	680311	F
Holley, Tilden S	BB	680120	F
Hollinger, Gregg Neyman	BB	711214	A
Hollingsworth, Hal T	BB	660116	N
Holm, Arnold Edward Jr	BB	720611	A
Holman, Gerald Allan	BB	661214	N
Holmes, David Hugh	XX	660315	F
Holmes, Frederick Lee	XX	711230	N
Holmes, Lester E	XX	670522	F
Holt, Dewey Thomas	EE	670823	V
Holt, James W	XX	680207	A
Holt, Robert Alan	BB	680919	M
Holton, Robert E	XX	690129	F
Holtzman, Ronald Lee	BB	670824	A
Hom, Charles David	BB	670817	N
Homuth, Richard Wendal	BB	670523	N
Hopper, Earl Pearson Jr	XX	680110	F
Hopper, Joseph Clifford	BR	720503	F
Hopps, Gary Douglas	BB	660210	N
Horchar, Andrew Anthony J	BB	700409	N
Horinek, Ramon Anton	RR	671025	F
Horio, Thomas Teruo	RR	690511	A
Horne, Stanley Henry	NR	680114	F
Horsky, Robert Milvoy	BR	651211	F
Horton, Paul L	CC	750429	V
Hosken, John Charles	XX	700324	A
Hoskins, Charles L	XX	710216	F
Hoskins, Donald Russell	BB	720426	F
Hoskins, Thomas Reeve	CC	750330	V
Hoskinson, Robert E	XX	660729	F
House, John Alexander II	BB	670630	M
Housh, Anthony F	XX	680419	A
Howard, Lewis Jr	XX	700707	A
Howard, Luther Harris	BB	670630	A
Howell, Carter A	XX	720307	F
Howes, George Andrews	XX	700110	A
Hrdlicka, David Louis	XX	650518	F
Huard, James L	XX	720712	F
Hubbard, Edward Lee	RR	660720	F
Hubbs, Donald Richard	BB	680317	N
Huberth, Eric J	XX	700513	F
Hubler, George Lawrence	BB	680223	M
Huddleston, Lynn R	XX	670926	A
Hudgens, Edward Monroe	BB	700321	F
Hudson, Henry M	EE	651220	V
Hudson, Robert M	RR	721226	F
Huggins, Bobby Gene	BB	700604	F
Hughes, James Lindberg	RR	670505	F
Hughes, John David	CC	750429	V
Hughes, Richard Michael	CC	750429	V
Hughey, Kenneth Raymond	RR	670706	F
Huie, Litchfield Patterson	BB	670227	N
Hull, James Larry	BB	710219	F
Hume, Kenneth Edward	BB	650329	N
Hummel, John F	XX	710306	A
Humphrey, Galen Francis	BB	660201	M
Humphrey, Larry D	AA	701104	A

Name	Status	I-date	Service
Huneycutt, Charles J Jr	NR	671110	F
Hunsicker, James Edward	BB	720424	A
Hunsucker, James	RR	700205	N
Hunt, James D	XX	681013	N
Hunt, Leon Andrew	XX	720618	F
Hunt, Robert W	XX	680228	A
Hunt, William B	XX	661104	A
Hunter, James D	BB	681029	A
Hunter, Russell Palmer Jr	XX	660210	F
Hunting, Peter M	BR	651112	V
Huntley, Charles Paul	CC	750429	V
Huntley, John Norman	BB	690927	A
Hurst, John Clark	BB	680713	M
Huss, Roy Arthur	BB	680206	N
Huston, Charles G	XX	680328	
Hutton, James Leo	RR	651016	N
Hyatt, Leo Gregory	RR	670813	N
Hyde, Jimmy Don	BB	651205	N
Hyde, Michael Lewis	NR	661208	F
Hyland, Charles Keith	RR	680206	W
Hynds, Wallace G Jr	BB	670802	F

I

Name	Status	I-date	Service
Iandoli, Donald (NMN)	BB	671119	A
Ibanez, Di Reyes	XX	670605	M
Ichikawa, Yoshihiro	–	750300	W
Ichinose, Taizo	BR	731122	W
Ingram, Eric Stephen	ZR		V
Ingvalson, Roger Dean	RR	680528	F
Innes, Roger B	XX	671227	N
Intoratat, Phisit	EE	630905	W
Iodice, Frank C	EE	680530	M
Ireland, Robert Newell	XX	700422	F
Irsch, Wayne C	XX	680109	F
Irwin, Douglas	AA	680901	M
Irwin, Robert Harry	NR	720217	F
Ishii, Tomohara	KK	700531	W
Ishiyana, Koki	–	731122	W
Ivan, Andrew Jr	XX	710910	F
Iwashita, Fumio	–	741207	W

J

Name	Status	I-date	Service
Jablonski, Michael James	BB	690627	A
Jackson, Carl Edwin	BB	650627	F
Jackson, Charles A	RR	720624	F
Jackson, James E	RR	660705	A
Jackson, James Terry	BB	720323	F
Jackson, James W Jr	XX	690921	M
Jackson, Paul Vernon III	BB	721224	F
Jackson, William Braxton	NR	670719	N
Jacobs, Edward James Jr	BB	670825	N
Jacobs, John C	BB	660607	F
Jacobsen, Ellwood L	BR	630304	V
Jacobsen, Timothy J	XX	710516	A
Jacques, James J	BB	750515	M
Jacquez, Juan L	RR	690511	A
Jokovac, John Andrew	XX	670531	A
Jamerson, Larry C	XX	680421	A
James, Charlie Negus	RR	680518	N
James, Gobel Dale	RR	680715	F
James, Samuel L	XX	730418	F
Janousek, Ronald James	BB	690809	M
Jarvis, Jeremy M	XX	670725	F
Jayroe, Julius Skinner	RR	670119	F
Jefcoat, Carl H	RR	721227	F
Jefferson, James Milton	XX	670512	F
Jefferson, Perry Henry	XX	690403	F
Jeffords, Derrell B	XX	651224	F
Jeffrey, Robert Duncan	RR	651220	F
Jeffs, Clive G	XX	710312	F
Jenkins, Harry Tarleton	RR	651113	N
Jenkins, Paul Laverne	BB	700630	F
Jenne, Robert Earl	BB	680508	A
Jensen, George W	XX	660515	F
Jensen, Jay Robert	RR	670218	F
Jerome, Stanley Milton	BB	690218	N
Jesse, William C	BR	720502	A
Jewell, Eugene M	XX	650904	F
Jimenez, Juan Macias	BB	680511	A
Johns, Paul F	XX	680628	A
Johns, Vernon Z	NR	680203	A
Johnson, Allen L	NR	721228	F
Johnson, August David	BB	670203	N
Johnson, Bobby Louis	RR	680825	A
Johnson, Bruce G	XX	650610	A
Johnson, Buford Gerald	BR	680424	A
Johnson, Dale Alonzo	BB	661027	F
Johnson, Edward Harvey	NR	721221	F
Johnson, Edward Robert	RR	640721	A
Johnson, Frankie B Jr	XX	680421	A
Johnson, Gary Lee	BB	710218	A
Johnson, Guy D	NR	651220	F
Johnson, Harold E	RR	670430	F
Johnson, James Reed	BB	660821	A
Johnson, Joan	RR	750312	W
Johnson, Kenneth	RR	711219	F
Johnson, Norman	RR	750312	W
Johnson, Randolph L	XX	710220	A
Johnson, Richard E	RR	721218	F
Johnson, Richard Herman	BB	670729	M
Johnson, Robert Dennison	BB	670901	N
Johnson, Samuel Robert	RR	660416	F
Johnson, Sandra	RR	680201	V
Johnson, Stanley Garwood	BB	651203	M
Johnson, William D	XX	680119	A
Johnson, William Edward	BR	661006	M
Johnston, Steven Bryce	BB	730104	F
Johnstone, James Montgomer	BB	661119	A
Jones, Bobby M	XX	721128	F
Jones, Diane	RR	740122	V
Jones, Edwin D	EE	651220	V
Jones, George Emerson	BB	670707	F
Jones, Grayland (NMN)	BB	691123	A
Jones, James E	XX	661003	A
Jones, James Gradey	BB	661112	N
Jones, John Robert	XX	710605	A
Jones, Johnny Mack	BB	720424	A
Jones, Louis F	XX	671129	F
Jones, Murphy Neal	RR	660629	F
Jones, Orvin C Jr	XX	720416	F
Jones, Robert Campbell	RR	680118	F
Jones, Thomas N	RR	680825	A
Jones, Thomas Paul	BB	680206	N

Name	Status	I-date	Service
Jones, William E	NR	680105	F
Jordan, Larry M	XX	660412	N
Jourdenais, George Henry	XX	670401	F
Judd, Michael Barry	BB	670630	N
Judge, Darwin Lee	NR	750429	M
Judson, Lorenzo D	CC	750330	V
Jung, Joon Taek	–	670507	W
Jurecko, Daniel Edward	BB	680508	A

K

Name	Status	I-date	Service
Kahler, Harold	XX	690614	F
Kaji, Andrew Tsurugi	CC	750429	V
Kalil, Thomas E	KK	690208	V
Kane, Bruce Edward	BB	690809	M
Kane, Richard R	XX	670912	M
Kardell, David Allen	NR	650509	N
Karger, Barry Edwin	BB	680514	N
Kari, Paul Anthony	RR	650620	F
Karins, Joseph J Jr	NR	670311	F
Karst, Carl F	NR	681116	F
Kasch, Frederick Morrison	NR	670702	N
Kasler, James Helms	RR	660808	F
Kaster, Leonard Lee	BB	640806	F
Kato, Shojiro	PP	670729	W
Kaufman, Joseph	RR	730822	W
Kavanaugh, Abel L	RR	680424	M
Kay, Emmet James	RR	730507	V
Kearns, Joseph T Jr	XX	670603	F
Keefe, Douglas Oneil	BB	670520	M
Keesee, Bobby Joe	RR	700918	V
Keiper, John Charles	XX	661115	M
Keirn, Richard Paul	RR	650724	F
Keller, Jack Elmer	XX	660421	N
Keller, Wendell R	XX	690301	F
Kelley, Daniel Martin	BB	680425	A
Kemmerer, Donald R	XX	670806	F
Kemp, Clayton C Jr	BB	670112	N
Kemp, Freddie (NMN)	BB	660817	A
Kennedy, Alan Gordon	BR	691104	A
Kennedy, James Edward	XX	691222	A
Kennedy, John W	XX	710816	F
Kenney, Harry John	BB	681101	N
Kent, Robert D	XX	681220	M
Kerber, Marie Therese	KK	690427	W
Kernan, Joseph Eugene	RR	720507	N
Kerns, Arthur William	XX	661223	A
Kerns, Gail M	RR	690327	A
Kerr, Ernest Claney Jr	BB	680326	M
Kerr, Everett O	XX	660613	F
Kerr, John Creighton Gille	BB	670822	F
Kerr, Michael Scott	R	670116	F
Kertsengsre, Pratom	–	660326	W
Ketchie, Scott Douglas	XX	720409	M
Ketterer, James Alan	XX	680120	F
Key, Wilson Denver	RR	671117	N
Khamphanh, Nfi	MM	711227	W
Kibbey, Richard Abbot	XX	670206	F
Kiefel, Ernst Philip Jr	XX	660210	F
Kieffer, William L Jr	BB	700211	F
Kien, Cuong Trieu	CC	750429	V
Kien, Man Bao	CC	750429	V
Kien, Ngiep Trieu	CC	750429	V
Kientzler, Phillip A	RR	730127	N
Kier, Larry Gene	XX	700506	A
Kilcullen, Thomas M	XX	670826	F
Killen, John Dewey III	BB	670630	M
Killian, Melvin J	NR	650930	F
Kilpatrick, Larry R	XX	720618	N
Kim, Heung Sam	KK	680626	W
Kim, In Shik	–	710714	
Kim, Soo Keun	MM	671020	W
Kim, Sung Mo	KK	680626	W
Kimsey, William Arthur Jr	XX	680121	A
King, Charles D	XX	681225	F
King, Donald L	XX	660514	F
King, Gerald Eugene	BB	680510	M
King, John Dennis	CC	750429	V
King, Michael Eli	NR	710305	A
King, Paul Chester Jr	BB	680504	A
King, Ronald Runyan	BB	671003	F
Kinkade, William L	XX	680901	F
Kinsley, Anthony John	CC	750429	V
Kinsman, Gerald Francis	BB	710115	A
Kipina, Marshall F	XX	660714	A
Kirby, Bobby Alexander	NR	721221	F
Kirk, Herbert Arthur	BB	680311	F
Kirk, Thomas Henry	RR	671028	F
Kirksey, Robert Louis	BB	660101	A
Kistner, Mitchell	CC	750429	V
Kitchens, Perry Castellion	BR	701103	A
Kittinger, Joseph W Jr	RR	720511	F
Kjome, Michael H	RR	680131	V
Klassen, James	CC	750429	V
Klemm, Donald M	XX	670611	F
Klenda, Dean Albert	XX	650917	F
Klenert, William B	NR	661022	N
Klimo, James Robert	XX	691104	A
Klinck, Harrison Hoyt	NR	671119	F
Kline, Robert E	XX	661102	F
Klingner, Michael Lee	BB	700406	F
Klinke, Donald Herman	XX	720618	F
Klomann, Thomas J	RR	721220	F
Klugg, Joseph Russell	BB	701114	N
Klusmann, Charles F	EE	650606	N
Klute, Karl Edwin	BB	660314	F
Kmetyk, Jonathan Peter	BB	671114	M
Knabb, Kenneth Keith Jr	XX	681021	N
Knapp, Fredric Woodrow	BB	671102	N
Knapp, Herman L	XX	670424	F
Knebel, Thomas E	XX	680522	F
Knight, Billy M	–	651116	A
Knight, Henry C	XX	681020	A
Knight, Larry Coleman	BB	700409	N
Knight, Larry D	XX	661007	F
Knight, Richard	ZR	830608	W
Knight, Roy A Jr	XX	670519	F
Knochel, Charles Allen	BB	660922	N
Knuckey, Thomas William	NR	710527	A
Knutsen, Donald Paul	BB	710322	A
Knutson, Richard Arthur	XX	730108	A
Knutson, Rodney Allen	RR	651017	N
Kobashigawa, Tom Y	RR	700205	A
Koenig, Edwin Lee	BB	661214	N

Name	Status	I-date	Service
Kohler, Delvin Lee	BB	691002	N
Kollmann, Glenn Edward	BB	680312	N
Kolstad, Thomas C	NR	661022	N
Kommendant, Aado	XX	660808	F
Konyu, William Michael	BB	690416	A
Kooi, James Willard	BB	670611	M
Koonce, Terry T	XX	671225	F
Koons, Dale F	NR	711226	F
Kopfman, Theodore Frank	RR	660615	N
Kortmann, Hindrike	KK	690427	W
Kosh, Gerald E	RR	740119	V
Kosko, Walter	XX	650727	F
Koslosky, Howard M	BB	691002	N
Kott, Stephen J	NR	671031	M
Kowles, Alexander G	CC	750330	V
Kramer, Galand Dwight	RR	670119	F
Kramer, Terry L	RR	680717	A
Kraner, David S	BB	720605	N
Krause, Arthur E	RR	630608	V
Krausman, Edward L	XX	680316	M
Kravitz, James Stephen	BB	680217	N
Krech, Melvin Thomas	BB	660401	N
Krish, Claudia	CC	750429	V
Krobath, Alan J	RR	720707	M
Kroboth, Stanley Nea	NR	721221	F
Krogman, Alva Ray	BB	670117	F
Krommenhoek, Jeffrey M	XX	671025	N
Kroske, Harold W Jr	XX	690211	A
Krupa, Frederick	XX	710427	A
Krusi, Peter Herman	BB	671103	N
Kryszak, Theodore E	XX	660603	F
Kubley, Roy Robert	BB	670131	F
Kuhlman, Robert J Jr	XX	690117	M
Kuhlmann, Charles F	BB	680922	F
Kuhnnen, Marie Renate	RR	680304	W
Kula, James D	RR	720729	F
Kulland, Byron K	XX	720402	A
Kusaka, Ankira	–	700405	W
Kushner, Floyd Harold	RR	671130	A
Kusick, Joseph George	BB	671109	A
Kustigian, Michael J	XX	680505	N
Kuykendall, Willie Clyde	BB	710818	A
Kwortnik, John C	NR	660801	F

L

Name	Status	I-date	Service
Labeau, Michael H	RR	721226	F
Labhardt, Dominik	ZR	800509	W
Labohn, Garry Russel	NR	681130	A
Lacey, Richard J	XX	680131	A
Ladewig, Melvin E	XX	680824	F
Lafayette, John W	XX	660406	A
Laffie, George	CC	750429	V
Laffie, Kim Ngo	CC	750429	V
Laffie, Lina Marline	CC	750429	V
Lagerwall, Harry R	NR	721221	F
Lagrand, William John	BB	650905	A
Lahaye, James David	BB	650508	N
Laker, Carl John	BB	700617	A
Lamar, James Lasley	RR	660506	F
Lambton, Bennie Richard	BB	660613	N
Lamp, Arnold William Jr	BB	690412	F
Lancaster, Kenneth R	XX	680103	A
Lane, Charles Jr	XX	670823	F
Lane, Glen O	XX	680523	A
Lane, Michael Christopher	RR	661202	F
Lane, Mitchell S	XX	690104	F
Laney, Billy R	XX	670603	A
Lange, Mark Adam	ZR	831204	N
Lanie, Francois	CC	750429	V
Lannom, Richard Clive	XX	680301	N
Lapham, Robert Grantham	BB	680208	F
Laplant, Kurt Elton	BB	680606	M
Laporte, Michael Louis	XX	670905	N
Larson, Gordon Albert	RR	670505	F
Lasiter, Carl William	RR	680205	F
Latella, George F	RR	721006	F
Latendresse, Thomas B	RR	720527	N
Latham, James D	RR	721005	F
Latimer, Clarence Albert	XX	690330	A
Laureano, Lopez Ismael	BB	680220	A
Laurie, James Andrew	CC	750429	V
Lauterio, Manuel Alonzo	XX	730108	A
Lautzenheiser, Michael (NM)	BB	711026	A
Lavoo, John Allen	BB	680919	M
Lawrence, Bruce E	XX	680705	F
Lawrence, Edward George	CC	750429	W
Lawrence, Gregory Paul	BB	681005	F
Lawrence, William Porter	RR	670628	N
Laws, Delmer Lee	BB	660729	A
Laws, Richard Lee	BB	660403	N
Lawson, Karl Wade	BB	680409	A
Leabres, Josue A	RR	701017	W
Leaver, John Murray Jr	BB	720508	N
Lebert, Ronald Merl	RR	680114	F
Leblanc, Louis E Jr	RR	721222	F
Lecornec, John Gilbert	NR	750429	V
Ledbetter, Thomas Isaac	BB	640619	A
Lee, Albert Eugene	BB	720216	N
Lee, Chang Hoon	PP	670120	W
Lee, Charles Richard	NR	670709	N
Lee, Glenn Hung Nin	BB	700527	F
Lee, Kil Yung	PP	670120	W
Lee, Leonard Murray	XX	671227	N
Lee, Yong Sun	–	691102	W
Lee, Yoon Dong	–	720324	W
Leeper, Wallace Wilson	XX	671202	A
Leeser, Leonard Charles	BB	700128	F
Leet, David Leverett	XX	720413	M
Leetun, Darel D	XX	660917	F
Lefever, Douglas Paul	XX	691105	F
Lehnoff, Edward W	NR	671118	F
Lehnrn, Gary Robert	RR	700205	N
Lehrke, Stanley L	XX	720618	F
Lehrman, Ronald John	RR	680520	A
Lemcke, David Earl	BB	680521	A
Lemcool, Ernest F	AA	690612	M
Lemmons, William E	XX	670618	A
Lemon, Jeffrey C	XX	710425	F
Leng, Chay You	EE	700531	W
Lengyel, Lauren Robert	RR	670809	F
Lenker, Michael Robert	RR	680208	A
Leonard, Edward W	RR	680531	F
Leonard, Marvin Maurice	BB	710215	A
Leonard, Robert B	BB	691002	N
Leonor, Leonardo C	XX	721010	F
Leopold, Stephen Ryder	RR	680509	A
Lerner, Irwin S	XX	721220	F
Leroux, Pierre Emile	–	701009	W
Lerseth, Roger G	RR	720906	N
Lesesne, Henry D	RR	720711	N
Leslie, Jacques	RR	730100	W
Lester, Roderick B	XX	720820	N
Lestienne, F	RR	720407	W
Letchworth, Edward Norman	BB	670227	N
Levan, Alvin Lee	BB	661025	N
Levis, Charles Allen	XX	720402	F
Lewandowski, Leonard J Jr	XX	661019	M
Lewellen, Walter Edward	NR	710218	A
Lewis, Charlie Gray	BB	670517	A
Lewis, Earl Gardner	RR	671024	N
Lewis, Frank D	RR	721228	F
Lewis, James F	R	750416	V
Lewis, James W	XX	650407	F
Lewis, Keith H	RR	721005	F
Lewis, Larry Gene	BB	710227	N
Lewis, Merrill R Jr	NR	660720	F
Lewis, Robert	RR	680105	A
Ligon, Vernon Peyton	RR	671119	F
Liles, Robert L Jr	NR	721221	F
Lilland, William Allan	XX	671004	F
Lilly, Carroll B	XX	710409	F
Lilly, Lawrence Eugene	BB	710317	A
Lilly, Warren E	RR	651106	F
Lindahl, John Carl	BB	730106	N
Lindbloom, Charles David	BB	680820	N
Lindwald, Charles W	XX	680207	A
Lindland, Donald Frederick	NR	720906	N
Lindsey, Marvin Nelson	XX	650629	F
Lindstrom, Ronnie G	XX	700102	F
Lineberger, Harold B	XX	710129	F
Linh, Dam	CC	750429	V
Link, Robert C	XX	680421	A
Lint, Donald M	XX	700422	F
Lira, Jose Trinadad	AA	671209	A
Little, Danny Leonard	BB	700423	A
Livingston, Richard Allen	BB	691002	
Lloyd, Allen Richard	BB	710218	A
Locker, James D	BB	680609	F
Lockhart, George B	NR	721221	F
Lockhart, Hayden James	RR	650302	F
Lodge, Robert A	NR	720510	F
Logan, Donald K	RR	720705	F
Logan, Jacob Drummond	BB	651202	N
Loheed, Hubert B	XX	660201	N
Lollar, James L	RR	721221	F
Lomax, Richard Eugene	BB	680326	A
Loney, Ashton N	BB	750515	M
Long, Carl Edwin	BB	691220	M
Long, Donna	ZM	881003	V
Long, George Wendell	BB	680512	F
Long, John Henry Sothoron	XX	661018	F
Long, Julius Woolen Jr	RR	680512	A
Long, Rit	CC	750429	V
Long, Stephen G	RR	690228	F
Longanecker, Ronald Lee	BB	660708	M
Lono, Luther A	XX	690929	M
Lopez, Robert (NMN)	BB	680306	A
Lopez, Robert Charles	BB	680510	M
Lord, Arthur J	XX	680419	A
Louyrette, H	RR	720407	W
Lovegren, David Eugene	BB	690301	A
Low, James Frederick	RR	671216	F
Lowry, Tyrrell Gordon	BB	650618	F
Lucas, Larry Francis	BB	661220	A
Lucki, Albin E	XX	700423	F
Lukenbach, Max Duane	BB	651222	N
Luker, Russell Burt	BB	660201	M
Lull, Howard B Jr	XX	720407	A
Lum, David Anthony	BB	661220	F
Luna, Carter Purvis	XX	690310	F
Luna, Donald A	XX	690201	F
Luna, Jose David	RR	670310	F
Lundgreen, Kim Dung	CC	750429	V
Lundgreen, Kim Thoa	CC	750429	V
Lundy, Albro Lynn Jr	BB	701224	F
Lunsford, Herbert L	XX	670725	F
Lurie, Alan Pierce	RR	660613	F
Lusk, Andre	CC	750429	V
Luster, Robert L	BB	690123	A
Luttrell, James M	XX	710510	A
Lynn, Doyle Wilmer	BB	650527	N
Lynn, Robert R	NR	721221	F
Lyon, Donavan L	XX	680322	F
Lyon, James Michael	KK	700205	A

M

Name	Status	I-date	Service
Mac Laughlin, Donald C Jr	BB	660102	N
MacCann, Henry Elmer	XX	680328	F
Macdonald, George Duncan	NR	721221	F
Mackedanz, Lyle E	XX	680421	A
Macko, Charles	XX	690222	F
Macnamara, Lance	ZM	780421	V
Macphail, Don A	RR	690208	A
Madden, Roy Jr	RR	721220	F
Maddox, Notley G	XX	670520	F
Mader, Kurt	–	701018	W
Madison, Thomas Mark	RR	670419	F
Madison, William L	XX	660515	F
Madsen, Marlow Erling	BB	670118	N
Magee, Patrick Joseph	XX	710103	A
Magee, Ralph Wayne	NR	610323	F
Magers, Paul Gerald	BB	710601	A
Magnusson, James A Jr	XX	650404	F
Mahan, Douglas F	BR	700420	F
Mahoney, Thomas Patrick III	BB	680706	M
Mailhes, Lawrence Scott	BB	650810	N
Makel, Janie A	BR	630304	V
Makowski, Louis Frank	RR	661006	F
Mallaval, Gerald H	ZR	800509	W
Mallon, Richard J	Nr	700128	F
Malo, Isaako F	RR	710424	A
Malone, Jimmy M	XX	660504	A
Mamiya, John M	NR	660729	F
Mancini, Richard Michael	BB	680111	N
Mangino, Thomas Angelo	XX	670421	A
Mangus, Arlie Robert	BB	701103	A
Manhard, Phillip W	RR	680201	V
Mann, Robert Lee	BB	651022	F
Manning, Ronald James	BB	750515	N
Manor, James (NMN)	BB	720327	F
Manske, Charles Jerome	BB	690524	F
Mape, John Clement	BB	660413	N
Marchand, Wayne E	BR	620408	A
Marik, Charles Weldon	XX	660625	N
Mark, Kit T	MM	700530	V
Marker, Michael Wayne	BB	710304	A
Markham, James Morris	CC	740122	V
Marshall, Danny G	XX	750515	M
Marshall, James Alfred	BB	650618	F
Marshall, Marion A	RR	720703	F
Marshall, Richard Carlton	BB	650905	F
Martin, Aubrey Grady	BR	690719	N
Martin, David Earl	BB	670404	N
Martin, Donald Eugene	EE	680302	A
Martin, Douglas K	XX	730418	F
Martin, Duane Whitney	KK	650920	F
Martin, Earl	CC	750323	V
Martin, Edward Holmes	RR	670709	N
Martin, James Edward	BB	680217	N
Martin, Jerry Dean	BB	701103	A
Martin, John Bernard II	BB	701016	N
Martin, John M	XX	671120	F
Martin, Larry E	NR	680715	F
Martin, Richard Adam	–	700416	W
Martin, Richard D	XX	680501	A
Martin, Russell D	XX	660603	F
Martin, Sammy Arthur	BB	671227	F
Martinez-Mercado, Edwin Ju	BB	671111	A
Martini, Michael R	RR	721220	F
Marvel, Jerry Wendell	RR	680224	M
Marvin, Robert Clarence	BB	670214	N
Mascari, Phillip Louis	XX	690502	F
Maslowski, Daniel F	RR	700502	A
Mason, James Philip	BB	681017	A
Mason, William Hender	XX	680522	F
Massucci, Martin J	XX	651001	F
Masterson, Frederick J	RR	720711	N
Masterson, Michael John	XX	681013	F
Mastin, Ronald Lambert	RR	670116	F
Masuda, Robert S	XX	690513	A
Matagulay, Roque S	RR	620723	A
Mateja, Alan Paul	XX	720416	F
Matejov, Joseph A	BB	730205	F
Matheny, David P	RR	671005	N
Mathers, William Martin	ZR	840722	V
Matocha, Donald John	BB	680405	M
Matsui, Melvin K	RR	720729	F
Matteson, Glenn (NMN)	NR	610323	F
Matthes, Peter R	XX	691124	F
Mattix, Sam	RR	721027	V
Mauterer, Oscar	XX	660215	F
Maxwell, Calvin Walter	XX	691010	A
Maxwell, James R	BB	750515	M
Maxwell, Samuel C	NR	680912	F
May, David M	XX	710220	A
May, Michael Frederick	BB	690302	A
Mayall, William T	RR	721222	F
Mayer, Roderick Lewis	XX	651017	N
Mayercik, Ronald M	XX	671124	F
Mayhew, William John	RR	680817	N
Maysey, Larry Wayne	BB	671109	F
McAndrews, Michael William	BB	701223	A
McAteer, Thomas Joseph	BB	661110	N
McBride, Earl Paul	BB	661022	N
McCain, John Sidney	RR	671026	N
McCain, Marvin Raymond Jr	BB	680620	A
McCants, Leland S III	BR	681230	A
McCarty, James L	XX	720624	F
McCleary, George Carlton	NR	651105	F
McClellan, Paul Truman Jr	BB	651114	F
McClure, Claude D	RR	631124	A
McCombs, Phillip A	RR	740430	V
McConnaughhay, Dan Daily	BB	660205	N
McConnell, Jerry (NMI)	BB	680924	A
McCormick, Carl Ottis	BB	721006	F
McCormick, John Vern	NR	651201	N
McCormick, Michael T	XX	730110	N
McCoy, Meril Olen Jr	BB	701215	N
McCrary, Jack	XX	671229	F
McCubbin, Glenn Dewayne	XX	680519	F
McCuistion, Michael K	RR	670508	F
McCullough, Ralph W	RR	680717	A
McDaniel, Eugene Baker	RR	670519	N
McDaniel, John Lewis	BB	680426	F
McDaniel, Morris L Jr	XX	671004	F
McDaniel, Norman Alexander	RR	660720	F
McDonald, Emmett Raymond	XX	660531	F
McDonald, Herman	CC	750601	V
McDonald, Joseph William	XX	720503	M
McDonald, Kurt Casey	XX	641231	F
McDonell, R D (NFN/NMN)	BB	710325	A
McDonnell, John Terrence	XX	690306	A
McDonough, John Richard	BB	660620	N
McDow, Richard H	RR	720627	F
McElhanon, Michael Owens	XX	680816	F
McElroy, Glenn David	BB	660315	A
McElroy, John Lee	BB	680512	F
McElvain, James Richard	XX	721218	F
McEwan, James Arthur	BB	651022	F
McGar, Brian Kent	XX	670531	A
McGarvey, James Maurice	XX	670417	M
McGonigle, William Dee	BB	680510	M
McGouldrick, Francis J Jr	XX	681213	A
McGrane, Donald Paul	NR	670719	N
McGrath, James Patrick	BB	670803	N
McGrath, John Michael	RR	670630	N
McGrath, William Darrel	NR	671117	N
McIntyre, Scott Winston	BB	711210	F
McIntosh, Ian (NMI)	BB	701124	A
McIver, Alexander	BB	720503	F
McKain, Bobby Lyn	BB	680503	A
McKamey, John Bryan	RR	650602	N
McKay, Clyde William	AA	701104	V
McKay, Homer E	BB	680206	N
McKenney, Kenneth Dewey	XX	660515	F
McKinley, Gerald Wayne	BB	650331	N
McKinney, Clemie	NR	720414	N
McKinney, Neil Bernard	BB	630902	F
McKittrick, James C	XX	670618	A
McKnight, George Grigsby	RR	651106	F
McKnight, George Parker	BR	651211	F
McLamb, Harry Lawrence	BB	700618	F
McLaughlin, Arthur V Jr	XX	721220	F
McLaughlin, Olen Burke	BB	670707	F
McLean, James Henry	XX	650209	A
McLeod, Arthur Edward	BB	710212	A
McLeod, David Vance Jr	BB	730614	F
McMahan, Robert Charles	NR	680214	N
McMahon, Charles Jr	NR	750429	M
McManus, Kevin Joseph	RR	670614	F
McManus, Truman J	BB	680605	M
McMican, M D	NR	650602	N
McMillan, Isiah	RR	680311	A
McMorrow, John P	RR	610515	N
McMurray, Cordine	RR	670712	A
McMurray, Fred Howell Jr	XX	680407	A
McMurray, Frederick C	RR	720912	F
McMurry, William G	RR	680207	A
McNish, Thomas Mitchell	RR	660904	F
McPhail, William Thomas	XX	680522	F
McPhee, Randy Neal	BB	670430	M
McPherson, Everett Alvin	XX	660318	M
McPherson, Fred Lamar	BB	660128	F
McQuade, James Russell	BB	720611	A
McRae, David Edward	XX	661202	N
McRae, William Joseph	BR	670809	A
McSwain, George Palmer	RR	660728	N
McVey, Lavoy Don	BB	700302	M
McWhorter, Henry Sterling	NR	650829	N
Meadows, Eugene Thomas	XX	661013	F
Means, William Harley	RR	660720	F
Mearns, Arthur S	NR	661111	F
Mechenbier, Edward John	RR	670614	F
Mecleary, Read Blaine	RR	670526	N
Medaris, Rick Eggburtus	BR	691104	A
Meder, Paul Oswald	NR	721221	F
Mehl, James Patrick	RR	670530	N
Mehrer, Gustav Alois	RR	681225	A
Mein, Michael Howard	NR	681130	A
Meldahl, Charles H	XX	681020	A
Mellor, Fredric M	XX	650813	F
Melton, Todd M	BB	730205	F
Menges, George B	BR	670102	F
Mercer, Jacob E	XX	720618	F
Merch, Charles	CC	750429	W
Meroney, Virgil K III	XX	690301	F
Merritt, Raymond James	RR	650916	F
Metoyer, Bryford Glenn	BB	640118	A
Mettler, Willy	–	700416	W
Metz, James Hardin	NR	680415	F
Metzger, William John	RR	670519	N
Metzler, Charles D	BB	710621	N
Meyer, Alton Benno	RR	670426	F
Meyer, Lewis E	RR	680201	V
Meyer, William M	NR	670426	F
Meyers, Roger Allen	BB	690209	N
Mia, Felino	RR	711108	W
Michel, Etiene	–	700416	W
Mickelsen, William Emil Jr	BB	690810	N
Midgett, Dewey Allen	XX	671125	A
Midnight, Francis B	XX	670823	F
Mielke, Madelene Xuan Tran	CC	750429	V
Mielke, Misty Suong	CC	750429	V
Mielke, Richard Morris	CC	750429	V
Mikyo, Mai-Lan	CC	750429	V
Milikin, Richard M III	XX	660820	F
Milius, Paul L	XX	680227	N
Millard, Charles Worth	XX	680419	A
Miller, Carl D	XX	670905	F
Miller, Carleton Pierce Jr	BB	710106	N
Miller, Carolyn Paine	RR	750312	V
Miller, Curtis D	XX	720329	F
Miller, Edison Wainright	RR	671013	M
Miller, Edwin Frank	RR	680522	N
Miller, George C	BB	750312	V
Miller, Glenn Edwin	BB	680510	A
Miller, John Daniel	RR	750312	V
Miller, Luanne	RR	750312	V
Miller, Malcolm Thomas	BB	670510	N
Miller, Michael Andrew	BB	690328	F
Miller, Richard Arthur	XX	651122	M
Miller, Robert Charles	BB	680828	F
Miller, Robert Lester	BB	670307	N
Miller, Roger Alan	RR	700415	A
Miller, Wyatt Jr (NMN)	BB	700913	A
Milligan, Joseph Edward	RR	670520	F
Milliner, William Patrick	XX	710306	A
Millner, Michael	XX	671129	A
Mills, James B	XX	660921	N
Mills, James Dale	BB	680129	M
Mims, George J Jr	XX	651220	F
Min, Kyung Yoon	PP	670120	W
Minnich, Richard Willis Jr	NR	680104	N
Minor, Carrol William	BB	681209	N
Mirrer, Robert Henry	BB	710117	F
Mishuk, Richard E	XX	661019	M
Mitchell, Albert C	XX	680425	F
Mitchell, Archie Emerson	PP	620530	V
Mitchell, Betty Janet	RR	750312	V
Mitchell, Carl Berg	BB	640114	F
Mitchell, Donald Wayne	BB	680510	M
Mitchell, Gilbert L	XX	680306	N
Mitchell, Harry E	XX	680505	N
Mitchell, Thomas B	XX	680522	F
Mixter, David Ives	BB	710129	A
Miyazaki, Ronald Kazuo	BB	670131	F
Mobley, Joseph Scott	RR	680624	N
Moe, Harold John	BB	670926	M
Moe, Thomas Nelson	RR	680116	F
Molinare, Albert R	RR	720427	N
Monahan, Robert W	RR	660527	V
Mongilardi, Peter (NMN) Jr	BB	650625	N
Monlux, Harold Deloss	RR	661111	F
Monroe, Vincent Duncan	NR	680518	N
Montague, Paul Joseph	RR	680328	M
Montez, Anastacio (NMN)	BB	690524	A
Montgomery, Ronald Wayne	BB	691002	N
Moon, Walter Hugh	KK	610422	A
Mooney, Fred (NMN)	BB	710227	A
Moorberg, Monte Larue	NR	661202	F
Moore, Dennis Anthony	RR	651027	N
Moore, Ernest Milvin	RR	670311	N

Name	Status	I-date	Service
Moore, Herbert William Jr	XX	670903	F
Moore, James R	XX	670228	M
Moore, Jerry L	XX	690216	A
Moore, Maurice Henry	XX	680512	A
Moore, Ralph Edward	BB	670503	A
Moore, Raymond Gregory	BB	691009	A
Moore, Scott Ferris Jr	BB	700220	N
Moore, Thomas	KK	651031	F
Moore, William John	BB	660518	F
Moore, William R	BB	691002	N
Moorman, Frank D	BR	690123	A
Morales, Frank Adrian	XX	681206	V
Moran, Richard Allan	BB	660807	N
Moreau, Ron	RR	730503	V
Moreida, Manuel J	XX	671202	A
Moreira, Ralph Angelo Jr	NR	710305	A
Moreland, James L	XX	680207	A
Moreland, Stephen Craig	BB	680512	F
Moreland, William D	XX	680116	M
Morgan, Burke Henderson	BB	670822	F
Morgan, Charles E	NR	660706	F
Morgan, Charles V	BR	720502	A
Morgan, Edwin E	XX	660313	F
Morgan, Gary L	RR	721222	F
Morgan, Herschel Scott	RR	650403	F
Morgan, James S	XX	671110	F
Morgan, Thomas R	XX	670126	F
Morgan, William J	BB	720225	A
Moriarty, Peter Gibney	BB	710322	F
Morin, Richard G	XX	681220	M
Morley, Charles Frank	XX	700218	F
Morrill, David Whittier	BB	670318	M
Morrill, Merwin Lamphrey	NR	670821	F
Morris, George William Jr	XX	730127	F
Morris, Robert J Jr	NR	721226	F
Morrison, Glenn R Jr	XX	661026	F
Morrison, Joseph C	XX	681125	F
Morrissey, Richard Thomas	BB	690819	M
Morrissey, Robert D	XX	721107	F
Morrow, Larry K	XX	720529	A
Morrow, Michael	RR	700507	V
Morrow, Richard D	NR	671102	N
Mosburg, Henry Lee	BB	660926	A
Moser, D L	BR	661006	M
Moser, Paul Kierstead	BB	691002	N
Moshier, Jim Edwin	BB	670611	M
Mosley, Monique Cur	CC	750429	V
Moss, James	CC	750429	V
Mossman, Harry Seeber	XX	720820	N
Mossman, Joe Russell	BB	650913	N
Mott, David P	RR	720519	F
Mowrey, Glenn William	BB	680326	M
Mowrey, Richard Lynn	BB	661214	N
Mulhauser, Harvey	BB	670131	F
Mulkan, (FNU)	RR	750310	W
Mulleavey, Quinten Emile	XX	680403	A
Mullen, Richard Dean	RR	670106	N
Mullen, William Francis	XX	660429	M
Mulligan, James Alfred	RR	660320	N
Mullins, Harold E	XX	660603	F
Mundt, Henry G II	XX	690508	F
Munoz, David Louie	XX	690513	A
Murdock, Michael George	BR	680201	M
Muren, Thomas R	BB	720403	N
Murphy, Barry Daniel	BB	680318	A
Murphy, John S Jr	RR	720608	F
Murphy, Larron D	XX	700423	A
Murphy, Terence Meredith	BB	650409	N
Murray, Joseph Vaughn	BB	660218	N
Murray, Patrick Peter	NR	680119	M
Musetti, Joseph Tony Jr	BB	670928	N
Musil, Clinton Allan Sr	BB	710531	A
Musselman, Stephen O	NR	720910	N
Myers, Armand Jesse	RR	660601	F
Myers, David Gephart	BB	670608	M
Myers, Glenn Leo	RR	670809	F

N

Name	Status	I-date	Service
Nagahiro, James Y	RR	721221	F
Nahan, John Benedict III	BB	670803	M
Nakagawa, Gordon R	RR	721221	N
Nakajima, Teruo	XX	700529	W
Nakamura, Keijiro	–	741207	
Nash, John Michael	BB	660315	A
Nasmyth, John Herbert	RR	660904	F
Naughton, Robert John	RR	670518	N
Neal, Dennis Paul	XX	690731	A
Neco-Quinones, Felix V	RR	680716	A
Neeld, Bobby G	XX	690104	F
Neislar, David Phillip	BB	690220	N
Nellans, William L	XX	670917	F
Nelson, David Lindford	NR	710305	A
Nelson, James R	XX	670611	A
Nelson, Jan Houston	BB	700411	M
Nelson, Marjorie	RR	680201	V
Nelson, Richard C	NR	680306	N
Nelson, Steven N	EE	680107	M
Nelson, William H	NR	660720	F
Ness, Patrick Lawrence	NR	670823	N
Neth, Fred Albert	BB	660116	N
Netherland, Roger M	XX	670510	N
Neuens, Martin James	RR	660812	F
Neville, William Edward	BB	650618	F
Newberry, Wayne Ellsworth	BB	680929	F
Newburn, Larry Stephen	BB	670829	A
Newcomb, Wallace Grant	RR	670803	F
Newell, Michael Thomas	BB	661214	N
Newell, Stanley Arthur	RR	670712	A
Newingham, James A	RR	690208	V
Newman, James C Jr	BB	680206	N
Newman, Larry J	XX	720618	F
Newsom, Benjamin B	KR	660723	F
Newton, Charles V	XX	690417	A
Newton, Donald S	XX	660226	A
Newton, Warren E	XX	680109	A
Ngo, Thi Mau	CC	750429	V
Nguyen, Thi Chin	CC	750429	V
Nguyen, Thi Xuyen	CC	750429	V
Nguyen, Van Chien	CC	750429	V
Nguyen, Van Ho Lucien	MM	700626	W
Nguyen, Xuan Anh-Thu Richa	CC	750429	V
Nichols, Aubrey Allen	RR	750519	N
Nichols, Hubert C Jr	XX	660901	F

Name	Status	I-date	Service
Nickerson, William Brewste	BB	660522	N
Nickol, Robert Allen	BB	711026	A
Nicotera, Carl	–		A
–			
Nidds, Daniel R	XX	670421	A
Niedecken, William Clinton	BB	690215	N
Niehouse, Daniel Lee	KK	661125	V
Nightingale, Randall John	BB	680317	N
Nipper, David	BB	641121	M
Nix, Cowan Glenn	RR	661001	F
Nobert, Craig R	XX	660720	F
Nolan, Joseph Paul Jr	XX	710516	A
Nolan, McKinley	AA	671109	A
Nopp, Robert G	XX	660714	A
Nordahl, Lee E	XX	651220	N
Norrington, Giles Roderick	RR	680505	N
Norris, Calvin Andrew	BB	701103	A
Norris, Thomas Elmer	RR	670812	F
North, Joseph Jr	EE	651018	M
North, Kenneth Walter	RR	660801	F
Norton, Michael Robert	XX	691103	A
Nowicki, James Ernest	RR	691102	A
Nunez, Vicente	RR	711108	W
Nyhof, Richard E	XX	720618	F
Nyman, Lawrence Frederick	BB	660623	N
Nystrom, Bruce August	XX	661202	N
Nystul, William Craig	BB	750429	M

O

Name	Status	I-date	Service
O'Brien, John Lawrence	BB	661110	F
O'Brien, Kevin	XX	690109	A
O'Grady, John Francis	XX	670410	F
O'Hara, Robert Charles	XX	690206	A
Oakley, Linus Labin	BB	711029	F
Oca, Arcadio	–	680131	W
Ochab, Robert (NMN)	BB	700107	F
Oconnor, Michael Francis	RR	680204	A
Odell, Donald Eugene	RR	671017	F
Odom, Chester Randy II	AA	710425	A
Odonnell, Michael Davis	XX	700324	A
Odonnell, Samuel Jr	XX	720712	F
Odtone, Poom	–	640601	W
Offutt, Gary Phelps	BB	651001	F
Ogden, Howard Jr	BB	671018	M
Okamura, Akihiko	RR	650401	W
Okerlund, Thomas Richard	XX	710103	A
Olaughlin, Stephen M	BR	651225	V
Oldham, John Sanders	BB	670611	M
Olds, Ernest Arthur	XX	680311	F
Olmstead, Stanley E	XX	651017	N
Olsen, Betty Ann	KK	680201	V
Olsen, Floyd Warren	XX	680421	A
Olsen, Robert F	RR	680201	V
Olson, Barry Allen	XX	680926	A
Olson, Delbert Austin	BB	680111	N
Olson, Gerald E	XX	660313	F
Omelia, Dennis William	XX	710103	A
Oneil, James W	RR	720929	F
O'Neil, John J	BR	660813	A
O'Neill, Douglas Lee	XX	720403	A
Oppel, LLoyd	RR	721027	W
Orell, Quinlan Roberts	XX	681013	N
Orr, Warren Robert Jr	XX	680512	A
Ortiz-Rivera, Luis A	RR	661227	A
Osborn, Geoffrey Holmes	BB	650924	N
Osborne, Dale Harrison	RR	680923	N
Osborne, Edwin Nelms Jr	XX	671229	F
Osborne, Rodney Dee	BB	710304	A
Osborne, Samuel William Jr	BB	670427	M
Osburn, Laird P	RR	690212	A
Ostermeyer, William Henry	XX	720512	F
Ott, Edward Louis III	BB	670901	N
Ott, Patrick Lewis	BB	671002	M
Ott, William A	XX	701008	F
Overlock, John F	XX	680816	F
Overly, Norris M	RR	670911	F
Owen, Clyde C	BB	701215	N
Owen, Robert D	XX	680523	A
Owen, Timothy S	XX	680629	A
Owens, Fred Monroe	BB	650610	A
Owens, Joy L	XX	670607	F

P

Name	Status	I-date	Service
Pabst, Eugene M	XX	661007	F
Packard, Ronald L	XX	670731	F
Padgett, David E	XX	690206	F
Padgett, James P	RR	720511	F
Padgett, Samuel Joseph	BB	680410	A
Padilla, David Esequiel	BB	680518	M
Page, Albert L Jr	XX	670806	F
Page, Gordon L	XX	660307	F
Page, Jasper N	EE	651030	F
Page, Russell J	RR	680201	V
Paige, Gordon Curtis	RR	720722	N
Painter, John Robert Jr	BB	710618	N
Pak, Sung Yul	–	650303	W
Pak, Yang Chung	–		W
Palacios, Luis Fernando	BB	680606	M
Palen, Carl Anthony	XX	710103	A
Palenscar, Alexander J III	XX	670327	N
Pallard, Annick Louise	ZR	840722	W
Palmer, Gilbert S Jr	XX	680227	F
Palmgren, Edwin D	XX	680422	F
Panek, Robert J Sr	NR	700128	F
Pangilinan, Manuel	–	680131	W
Pannabecker, David Eric	BB	720327	F
Pantall, James Robert	BB	701103	A
Parcels, Rex Lewis Jr	BB	700309	N
Parish, Charles C	XX	680725	N
Parker, Charles Leslie Jr	BB	730121	N
Parker, David Wayne	BB	690206	A
Parker, Frank C III	XX	671229	F
Parker, John Jackson	BB	700304	N
Parker, Maxim Charles	BB	670318	M
Parker, Richard Harold	–	651108	W(A)A
Parker, Thomas Aquinas	BB	670405	N
Parker, Udon (NMN)	BB	660313	A
Parker, Woodrow Wilson II	XX	680424	F
Parks, Joe	KK	641222	A
Parks, Raymond F	XX	620714	A
Parra, Lionel	XX	680717	M
Parrish, Frank C	BR	680116	A
Parrott, Thomas Vance	RR	670812	F

Name	Status	I-date	Service
Parsels, John William	RR	700205	A
Parsley, Edward Milton	XX	660203	F
Parsons, Don Brown Jr	XX	660919	N
Parsons, Donald E	XX	690206	A
Parsons, Michael D	XX	710103	A
Partington, Roger Dale	BB	691101	M
Paschall, Ronald Page	XX	720402	A
Pasekoff, Robert E	XX	660313	F
Pastva, Michael James	BB	671206	M
Pate, Gary	XX	680522	F
Pattberg, Klaus	RR	730822	W
Patterson, Bruce Merle	BB	670727	N
Patterson, James Kelly	XX	670519	N
Pattillo, Ralph Nathan	XX	710216	F
Patton, Ian	RR	730628	W
Patton, Kenneth J	XX	680202	A
Patton, Ward Karl	BB	680727	N
Paul, Craig A	NR	721220	F
Paul, James Lee	BB	710205	A
Pauley, Marshall I	XX	660313	F
Paulson, Merlyn L	NR	720329	F
Pawlish, George F	XX	670308	N
Paxton, Donald E	XX	690222	F
Payne, John Allen	BR	691104	A
Payne, Kylis Therod	BB	720605	N
Payne, Norman	XX	681219	A
Peace, John Darlington III	XX	671231	N
Peacock, John Robert II	XX	721012	M
Pearce, Dale Allen	BB	710517	A
Pearce Edwin Jack	NR	720329	F
Pearson, Robert Harvey	NR	670611	F
Pearson, Wayne E	NR	690222	F
Pearson, William Roy	BB	720406	F
Pederson, Joe Palmer	XX	700623	A
Peel, Robert D	RR	650531	F
Pemberton, Gene T	KR	660723	F
Penakis, Elias	ZR	830629	W
Pender, Orland James Jr	XX	720817	N
Penn, Michael Gene Jr	RR	720806	N
Pennington, Ronald Keith	BB	670427	M
Pepper, Anthony John	BB	680406	M
Peralta, Benjamin Romane	AA	700830	A
Perisho, Gordon Samuel	XX	671231	N
Perkin, Vernon John	–	651018	W
Perkins, Cecil Carrington	BB	711214	A
Perkins, Glendon William	RR	660720	F
Perricone, Richard Robert	RR	670712	A
Perrine, Elton L	XX	670522	F
Perry, Otha Lee	BB	711214	A
Perry, Randolph Allen Jr	XX	721220	F
Perry, Richard Clark	NR	670831	N
Perry, Ronald D	NR	721221	F
Perry, Thomas Hepburn	XX	680510	A
Peters, Charles Henry	NR	660701	N
Petersen, Gaylord D	NR	670911	F
Peterson, Delbert R	XX	660309	F
Peterson, Dennis William	XX	670719	N
Peterson, Douglas Brian	RR	660910	F
Peterson, Mark Allen	XX	730127	F
Peterson, Michael T	RR	691102	A
Petri, Rudolf	RR	750811	W
Petrilla, John J Jr	BR	720502	A
Pettis, Thomas Edwin	BB	670523	N
Pfaffmann, Charles Brooks	BB	700409	N
Pfeifer, Ronald Edwin	BB	661006	M
Pfister, James F Jr	BR	680105	A
Phan, Trie Luc	CC	750429	V
Pharris, William Valrie	BB	660707	A
Phelps, Jesse Donald	BB	651228	A
Phelps, William	XX	711123	F
Phillips, Daniel R	XX	680207	A
Phillips, David Joseph Jr	BB	660703	F
Phillips, Elbert Austin	BB	680828	F
Phillips, Jon	ZR	850311	V
Phillips, Lillian Margueri	RR	750312	V
Phillips, Marvin Foster	BB	660926	A
Phillips, Richard Lee	RR	750312	V
Phillips, Robert Paul	XX	700623	A
Phipps, James L	XX	680109	A
Pick, Donald William	BB	680827	F
Piechaud, Phillipe	RR	720407	W
Pierce, Walter Mwelvin (MI)	BB	700610	A
Piersanti, Anthony J Jr	BB	701215	N
Pierson, William C III	XX	690413	A
Pietrzak, Joseph Ray	BB	710210	A
Pietsch, Robert E	XX	680430	F
Piittmann, Alan D	XX	661116	F
Pike, Dennis Stanley	XX	720323	N
Pike, Peter X	XX	690712	F
Pilkington, Thomas Holt	XX	660919	N
Pineau, Roland Robert	BB	671008	N
Pineda, Uldarico	RR	711108	W
Pirie, James Glenn	RR	670622	N
Pirker, Victor J	XX	651122	M
Pirruccello, Joseph S Jr	BB	681208	F
Pitchford, John Joseph	RR	651220	F
Pitman, Peter Potter	XX	670512	F
Pitt, Albert	XX	660124	M
Pittman, Robert Edward	BB	660928	A
Pitzen, John Russell	XX	720817	N
Pitzer, Daniel L	RR	631029	A
Plants, Thomas Lee	NR	650602	N
Plassmeyer, Bernard Herber	XX	700911	M
Platt, Robert L Jr	XX	670610	A
Pleiman, James Edward	NR	660314	F
Plowman, James Edwin	XX	670324	N
Plumadore, Kenneth Leo	BB	670921	M
Plumb, Joseph Charles	RR	670519	N
Pogreba, Dean Andrew	XX	651005	F
Polard, Perry	CC	750429	V
Polfer, Clarence	RR	720507	A
Pollack, Melvin	RR	670706	F
Pollard, Ben M	RR	670515	F
Pollin, George J	NR	670429	F
Polster, Harmon	XX	690715	F
Pond, Elizabeth	RR	700507	V
Pool, Jerry Lynn	XX	700324	A
Poole, Charlie S	XX	721219	F
Poor, Russell Arden	XX	670204	F
Port, William D	KR	680112	A
Porterfield, Dale K	BR	720502	A
Posey, George Ray	BB	680905	N
Posner, Gerald	CC	750429	V

Name	Status	I-date	Service
Potter, Albert J	EE	680530	M
Potter, William Joseph Jr	XX	671229	F
Potter, William Tod	XX	680205	F
Potts, Larry Fletcher	XX	720407	M
Powell, Lynn Kesler	NR	670821	F
Powell, William E	NR	680817	F
Powers, John Lynn	BB	710215	A
Powers, Lowell S	XX	690402	A
Powers, Trent Richard	NR	651031	N
Powers, Vernie Homer	BB	671224	A
Poynor, Daniel Roberts	BB	711219	F
Prantilla, Sarsenio	RR	711108	W
Prater, Roy Dewitt	BB	720406	F
Prather, Martin William	BB	670905	M
Prather, Phillip Dean	RR	710308	A
Preiss, Robert Francis Jr	BB	700512	A
Prentice, Kenneth M	BB	691002	N
Preston, James A	XX	660515	F
Prevedel, Charles F	XX	690417	A
Prevost, Albert Michael	BB	660201	M
Prewitt, William Roland	BB	670801	M
Price, Bunyan Durant	XX	700502	A
Price, David Stanley	BB	680311	F
Price, Donald E	RR	680717	A
Price, Larry D	RR	720730	F
Price, William Marshall	XX	721012	M
Pridemore, Dallas Reese	XX	680908	A
Primm, Severo J III	BB	730205	F
Pringle, Joe Harold	XX	680202	A
Profilet, Leo Twyman	RR	670821	N
Promsunan, Prasit	–	630905	W
Prudhomme, John Douglas	BB	651222	N
Pruett, William David	BB	700128	F
Pruner, William R	BR	660114	V
Pryor, Robert J	RR	690212	A
Puandej, Tanom	–	680201	W
Puentes, Manuel Rameriz	XX	710325	A
Puggi, Joseph D	XX	680202	A
Pugh, Dennis Gerard	XX	700319	F
Pugh, Kenneth W	NR	660412	N
Purcell, Benjamin H	RR	680208	A
Purcell, Howard Philip	BB	630902	F
Purcell, Robert Baldwin	RR	650727	F
Purrington, Frederick Raym	RR	661020	N
Putnam, Charles Lancaster	NR	670309	N
Pyle, Darrel Edwin	RR	660613	F
Pyle, Thomas Shaw	RR	660807	F
Pyles, Harley B	XX	651018	F

Q

Name	Status	I-date	Service
Quamo, George	BR	680414	A
Quinn, Francis	RR	620408	A
Quinn, Michael Edward	XX	691122	N
Quinn-Judge, Paul	RR	740122	W
Quinn-Judge, Paul	CC	750429	W
Quinn-Judge, Sophie	RR	740122	V
Quinn-Judge, Sophie	CC	750429	V

R

Name	Status	I-date	Service
Rackley, Inzar William Jr	XX	661018	F
Raebel, Dale V	RR	720817	N
Ragland, Dayton William	XX	660531	F
Ragsdale, Thomas	BR	680202	V
Ralston, Frank Delzell III	XX	660514	F
Ramirez, Armando (NMN)	BB	690523	A
Ramos, Rainier S	XX	680109	A
Ramos, Rodrigo	–	680131	W
Ramsay, Charles J	XX	680121	M
Ramsden, Gerald Lee	BB	680123	N
Ramsey, Douglas	RR	660117	V
Ramsower, Irving B II	NR	720329	F
Randall, Robert I	RR	720711	N
Rander, Donald J	RR	680201	A
Randolph, Clifford	CC	750429	V
Ransbottom, Frederick J	XX	680512	A
Rapin, Pierre	MM	710200	W
Rapp, Jeff	ZR	790515	V
Rash, Melvin D	XX	680522	F
Rattin, Dennis M	XX	691016	A
Ratzel, Wesley D	NR	720518	F
Ratzlaff, Brian M	RR	720911	F
Ratzlaff, Richard Raymond	RR	660320	N
Rausch, Robert E	XX	700416	F
Ravencraft, James A	BR	680618	A
Ravenna, Harry M III	XX	661115	A
Rawlings, James	XX	750103	V
Rawsthorne, Edgar Arthur	BB	651229	N
Ray, James Edwin	RR	660508	F
Ray, James Michael	KK	680318	A
Ray, Johnnie L	RR	720408	A
Ray, Michele	RR	670117	W
Ray, Ronald E	XX	691113	A
Rayford, King David Jr	RR	670702	A
Raymond, Paul D	XX	670905	F
Read, Charles Harold W Jr	XX	680824	F
Reaid, Rollie K	NR	721221	F
Reardon, Richard John	BB	690428	N
Reed, James William	XX	700724	F
Reed, Terry Michael	BB	690623	F
Reed, Theresa	CC	750429	V
Reeder, William S	RR	720509	A
Reedy, William Henry Jr	BB	680116	N
Reese, Gomer David III	BB	700424	F
Reeves, John Howard	BB	661223	M
Regan, John David	CC	750429	V
Regan, Lam Thi	CC	750429	V
Rehe, Richard Raymond	KK	680109	A
Rehmann, David George	RR	661202	N
Rehn, Gary Lee	BB	671109	M
Reich, William J	RR	720511	F
Reid, Harold E	XX	670913	M
Reid, John Eric	XX	710220	A
Reilly, Edward Daniel Jr	KR	660426	A
Reilly, Lavern G	XX	660515	F
Reinecke, Wayne C	BB	670112	N
Reiter, Dean Wesley	B	660925	M
Reitmann, Thomas E	XX	651201	F
Renelt, Walter A	XX	691120	F
Reno, Ralph Joseph	BB	660703	A
Rex, Robert A	XX	681208	F
Rex, Robert F	BB	690309	F
Rexroad, Ronald R	XX	680403	F
Reynolds, David Richard	BB	671121	A

Name	Status	I-date	Service
Reynolds, Jon Anzuena	RR	651128	F
Reynolds, Terry L	XX	720426	V
Rhodes, Ferris Ansel Jr	XX	710103	A
Riate, Alfonso Ray	RR	670426	M
Rice, Charles Donald	RR	671026	N
Rice, Thomas Jr (NMN)	BB	651228	A
Rich, Richard	XX	670519	N
Richardson, Dale W	XX	700502	A
Richardson, Floyd W	NR	670303	F
Richardson, Stephen Gould	BB	651130	N
Richtsteig, David J	BR	651208	M
Rickel, David J	XX	680516	F
Ricker, William Ernest	XX	681028	N
Rickman, Dwight G	XX	721225	M
Ridgeway, Ronald Lewis	RR	680225	M
Riding, Malcolm	BB	760312	W
Riess, Charles F	RR	621224	F
Rifaud, G	RR	720407	W
Riggins, Robert Paul	BB	680422	F
Riggs, Thomas F	XX	670611	A
Ringsdorf, Herbert Benjami	RR	661111	F
Riordan, John Michael	BB	661110	N
Rios, Jose	CC	750429	V
Rios, Noel Luis	BB	680306	F
Risner, Richard F	EE	680820	M
Risner, Robinson	RR	650916	F
Rissi, Donald L	NR	721218	F
Ritchey, Luther Edmond Jr	BB	631008	M
Ritter, George L	MM	711227	V
Rittichier, Jack Columbus	BB	680609	P
Rivenburgh, Richard W	BB	750515	M
Rivera, Fred John	CC	750429	V
Rivers, Wendell Burke	RR	650910	N
Roach, Marion L	BB	691104	A
Roark, Anund Charles	BR	680516	A
Roark, James David	BB	671112	N
Roark, William Marshall	NR	650407	N
Robbins, Richard Joseph	BB	660419	F
Roberson, John Will	BB	690622	A
Roberts, Gerald Ray	BB	651202	N
Roberts, Harold J Jr	BB	650618	F
Roberts, Michael Land	BB	680111	N
Roberts, Richard D	XX	690325	A
Robertson, John Hartley	XX	680520	A
Robertson, John L	XX	660916	F
Robertson, Leonard	XX	720707	M
Robertson, Mark John	BB	710210	A
Robinson, Edward (NMN)	BB	700309	A
Robinson, Floyd Henry	XX	690312	A
Robinson, Kenneth D	NR	660830	F
Robinson, Larry Warren	BB	700105	M
Robinson, Lewis Merritt	BB	670604	F
Robinson, Paul K	RR	720701	F
Robinson, William Andrew	RR	650920	F
Roby, Charles D	NR	670303	F
Rockett, Alton C Jr	XX	670602	F
Rodill, Daniel	CC	750429	V
Rodriguez, Albert E	NR	680311	F
Rodriguez, Ferdinand A	RR	680414	A
Roe, Jerry L	XX	680212	A
Roehrich, Ronald L	BB	680118	N
Rogers, Billy Lee	BB	691201	N
Rogers, Charles Edward	BB	670504	F
Rogers, Edward Francis	BB	680312	M
Rogers, Lyle Douglas	AA	700827	A
Roggow, Norman Lee	BB	671008	N
Roha, Michael R	EE	680107	M
Rollin, (FNU)	MM	700500	W
Rollins, David John	RR	670514	N
Rollins, James U	RR	680205	V
Romano, Gerald Michael	NR	650602	N
Romero, Victor	XX	680319	F
Romig, Edward Leon	BB	660617	N
Romine, Albert Wayne	BR	680516	A
Roraback, Kenneth M	KK	631124	A
Rosato, Joseph Frank	BB	660602	F
Rose, George A	RR	720621	F
Rose, Joseph	RR	660208	A
Rose, Luther L	XX	660603	F
Rosenbach, Robert Page	XX	700305	F
Ross, Douglas Alan	BB	690122	A
Ross, Jlynn Jr	XX	680317	A
Ross, Joseph S	XX	680801	F
Rossano, Richard Joseph	BB	710325	A
Roth, Billie Leroy	BB	650627	F
Rottmers, Peter Schrader	RR	690401	W
Rowe, James Nicholas	EE	631029	A
Rowley, Charles S	XX	700422	F
Rozo, James Milan	XX	700623	A
Rucker, Emmett Jr	BB	680524	F
Rudloff, Stephen A	RR	720510	N
Rudolph, Robert David	NR	650908	N
Ruffin, James Thomas	NR	660218	N
Ruhling, Mark John	RR	681123	F
Rumbaugh, Elwood Eugene	BB	750515	F
Rumble, Wesley L	RR	680428	F
Runnels, Glyn Linal Jr	BB	670630	M
Runyan, Albert Edward	RR	660429	F
Rupinsky, Bernard Francis	XX	680616	N
Rusch, Stephen A	XX	720307	F
Rushton, Thomas	RR	680201	V
Russell, Donald M	XX	671205	F
Russell, Kay	RR	670519	N
Russell, Peter J	XX	680801	A
Russell, Richard Lee	BB	720426	F
Rutledge, Howard Elmer	RR	651128	N
Ryan, William C Jr	BB	690511	M
Ryder, John L	XX	700609	F
Rykoskey, Edward Jay	BB	660818	M

S

Name	Status	I-date	Service
Saavedra, Robert	XX	680428	N
Sabog, Mateo	XX	700225	A
Sadler, Mitchell O Jr	XX	700630	F
Saegaert, Donald Russell	BB	650610	A
Sage, Leland Charles Cooke	BB	690623	N
Sahashi, Yoshihiko	RR	681228	W
Sakai, Kojiro	KK	700531	W
Sakamoto, Hideako	RR	731030	W
Salazar, Fidel G	BB	691002	N
Sale, Harold R Jr	XX	670607	F
Salinas, Mercedes Perez	BR	651211	F
Salley, James Jr	KK	710331	A
Salzarulo, Raymond Paul Jr	NR	660904	F
Sampson, Leslie Verne	NR	610323	F
San, Men Man	CC	750429	V
Sanchez, Florentino G	–	680131	W
Sanchez, Jose Ramon	BB	680606	M
Sanderlin, William D	NR	691202	A
Sanders, William Stephen	BB	700630	F
Sandner, Robert Louis	BB	660607	F
Sandoval, Antonio Ramos	BB	750515	M
Sands, Richard Eugene	BB	680512	A
Sandvick, Robert James	RR	680807	F
Sansone, Dominick (NMN)	NR	641210	A
Sansone, James J	BB	720810	N
Sargent, James Ray	BB	680510	M
Sather, Richard Christian	NR	640805	N
Sause, Bernard Jacob Jr	BB	670227	N
Savoy, M J	BB	660617	N
Sawhill, Robert Ralston	RR	670823	F
Sayre, Leslie Berkeley	BB	680320	A
Scaife, Kenneth D	BB	730103	N
Scales, Thomas R	RR	660527	V
Scarborough, Jay Ross	RR	750312	V
Schaneberg, Leroy Clyde	BB	700630	F
Scharf, Charles J	XX	651001	F
Schell, Richard J	XX	670824	A
Scherdin, Robert F	XX	681229	A
Scheurich, Thomas Edwin	XX	680301	N
Schiele, James F	XX	670712	A
Schierman, Wesley Duane	RR	650828	F
Schimberg, James Philip	BB	660109	A
Schimmels, Eddie Ray	BB	690218	N
Schmidt, Norman	KR	660901	F
Schmidt, Peter Alden	BB	700815	A
Schmidt, Walter R Jr	XX	680609	M
Schmittou, Eureka Lavern	BB	670523	N
Schoderer, Eric John	BB	661110	N
Schoeffel, Peter Vanruyter	RR	671004	N
Schoeppner, Leonard John	BB	700309	N
Scholl-Latour, Peter	RR	730822	W
Scholtz, Klaus D	NR	681130	A
Schoonover, Charles David	BB	660116	N
Schott, Richard S	XX	720407	A
Schreckengost, Fred T	NR	640607	M
Schroeffel, Thomas Anthony	BB	660218	N
Schrump, Raymond Cecil	RR	680523	A
Schuler, Robert Harry Jr	XX	651015	F
Schultz, Ronald James	XX	700721	A
Schultz, Sheldon D	XX	680105	A
Schulz, Paul Henry	RR	671116	N
Schumacher, James K	AA	691215	A
Schumann, John Robert	KK	650616	A
Schweitzer, Robert James	RR	680105	N
Schwertfeger, William R	RR	720216	F
Schwinn, Monika	RR	690427	W
Schworer, Ronald Paul	BB	670409	A
Scott, Dain V	XX	670821	N
Scott, David Lee	BB	680425	A
Scott, David Lloyd	ZM	781124	W
Scott, Martin R	XX	660315	F
Scott, Mike John	XX	690513	A
Scott, Vincent Calvin Jr	BB	690422	F
Scrivener, Stephen Russell	BB	710317	F
Scuitier, James J	–	680200	A
Scull, Gary Bernard	XX	700312	A
Scungio, Vincent Anthony	XX	661104	F
Scurlock, Leo D	XX	671221	A
Seablom, Earl Francis	BB	680718	A
Seagraves, Melvin D	BB	720430	N
Seagroves, Michael A	BR	690622	A
Searfus, William Henry	BB	671125	N
Seeber, Bruce G	RR	651005	F
Seek, Brian J	RR	720705	F
Seeley, Douglas Milton	BB	710317	F
Sehorn, James Eldon	RR	671214	F
Seidl, Robert	BB	750312	V
Seko, Masahiko	RR	671119	W
Sennett, Robert R	XX	660122	N
Serex, Henry Muir	XX	720402	F
Setterquist, Francis L	XX	680823	F
Seuell, John W	XX	720606	F
Seward, William Henry	BB	680306	M
Sexton, David Mason	BB	710315	A
Sexton, John C	RR	690812	A
Seymour, Leo E	XX	670703	A
Shafer, Philip R	XX	680419	A
Shanahan, Joseph Francis	RR	680815	F
Shank, Gary Leslie	NR	720723	N
Shankel, William Leonard	RR	651223	N
Shanks, James Lee	BB	680524	F
Shanley, Michael Henry Jr	NR	691202	A
Shannon, Patrick Lee	BB	680311	F
Shark, Earl E	KK	680912	A
Sharman, Neil	–	740910	W
Sharp, Samuel Arthur Jr	BB	670510	M
Shattuck, Lewis Wiley	RR	660711	F
Shaw, Edward Brendan	BB	650905	N
Shaw, Gary Francis	BB	671111	A
Shay, Donald Emerson Jr	XX	701008	F
Shea, James Patrick	BB	650420	N
Shea, Michael John	BB	750429	M
Shelton, Charles Ervin	PP	650429	F
Shepard, Vernon C	RR	691102	A
Sherman, John Brooks	BB	660325	M
Sherman, Peter W	NR	670610	N
Sherman, Robert C	KR	670624	M
Shewmake, John Daniel Sr	BB	711103	A
Shimek, Samuel Dale	BB	681209	A
Shimkin, Alex	MM	720712	V
Shin, Chang Wha	PP	701115	W
Shine, Anthony C	XX	721202	F
Shingaki, Tomotsu	RR	720819	F
Shingledecker, Armon D	XX	660531	F
Shinn, William Charles	BB	700128	F
Shively, James Richard	RR	670505	F
Shoneck, John R	XX	661018	F
Shorack, Theodore James Jr	BB	660609	F
Shore, Edward R Jr	RR	610515	A
Shriver, Jerry M	XX	690424	A
Shue, Donald Monroe	XX	691103	A
Shumaker, Robert Harper	RR	650211	N
Shuman, Edwin Arthur	RR	680317	N
Shumway, Geofrey Raymond	XX	720625	N
Siegwarth, Donald E	BB	660617	N
Sienicki, Theodore S	RR	720503	F
Sigafoos, Walter Harri III	XX	710425	F
Sigler, Gary Richard	RR	670429	F
Sijan, Lance P	KR	671109	F
Sikkink, Roy Dean	BR	690719	N
Silva, Claude Arnold	XX	670129	F
Silver, Edward D	XX	680705	F
Sima, Thomas William	RR	651015	F
Simmons, Robert E	NR	720329	F
Simmons, Willie E	RR	750816	V
Simms, Harold D	RR	680717	A
Simonet, Kenneth Adrian	RR	680118	F
Simpson, James Edward	KK	681105	V
Simpson, Joseph L	XX	680512	A
Simpson, Max Coleman	BB	670124	A
Simpson, Richard T	RR	721218	F
Simpson, Robert Lewis	BB	620828	F
Simpson, Walter Stephen	BB	670521	A
Singer, Donald M	NR	660817	F
Singleton, Daniel E	XX	690126	F
Singleton, Jerry Allen	RR	651106	F
Siow, Gale Robert	BB	680111	N
Sirion, Praphan X	RR	660326	W
Sisson, Winfield Wade	XX	651018	M
Sitek, Thomas Walter	BB	670823	N
Sittner, Ronald Nicholis	XX	670823	F
Sizemore, James Elmo	BB	690708	F
Skarman, Orval Harry	XX	680115	M
Skeen, Richard Robert	BB	700516	N
Skibbe, David William	RR	700302	M
Skiles, Thomas William	BB	711219	A
Skinner, Owen G	XX	701212	F
Skivington, William E Jr	XX	680512	A
Slater, Freddie Leon	BR	720503	F
Slattery, Mark Thomas	ZR	870125	W
Small, Burt Chauncey Jr	XX	670306	A
Smallwood, John J	XX	730616	F
Smiley, Stanley Kutz	BB	690720	N
Smith, Bradley Edsel	RR	660325	N
Smith, Carl Arthur	BB	670501	M
Smith, David R	XX	690316	A
Smith, Dean (NMN) Jr	BB	670315	N
Smith, Dewey Lee	RR	670602	F
Smith, Donald Glenn	RR	680513	A
Smith, Edward D Jr	NR	720329	F
Smith, Emmet Quimby	ZR	790515	V
Smith, Gene Albert	NR	660627	N
Smith, George Craig	XX	650403	F
Smith, George Edward	RR	631124	A
Smith, Hallie W	XX	680108	F
Smith, Harding Eugene Sr	XX	660603	F
Smith, Harold Victor	XX	660307	F
Smith, Harry W	XX	691112	F
Smith, Herbert E	NR	660729	F
Smith, Homer Leroy	KR	670520	N
Smith, Howard Horton	XX	680930	F
Smith, Joseph Stanley	BB	710404	F
Smith, Karen	ZR	790515	V
Smith, Lewis Philip II	XX	680530	F
Smith, Linda	EE	750310	V
Smith, Mark A	RR	720407	A
Smith, Maynard Lee	BR	680207	N
Smith, Michelle L	EE	750310	V
Smith, Philip E	RR	650920	F
Smith, Richard D	XX	650311	F
Smith, Richard Eugene	RR	671025	F
Smith, Robert Norman	XX	690819	M
Smith, Roger Lee	BB	681003	A
Smith, Ronald Eugene	BB	701128	A
Smith, Victor A	XX	690117	F
Smith, Warren Parker Jr	XX	660622	F
Smith, Wayne Ogden	RR	680118	F
Smith, William Arthur Jr	XX	680927	A
Smith, William J	CC	750429	V
Smith, William M	KK	690303	A
Smith, William Ward	BB	660723	F
Smoot, Curtis R	XX	710310	A
Snider, Hughie Franklin	BB	700428	A
Sooter, David William	RR	670217	A
Soucy, Ronald Philip Sr	BB	670523	N
Souder, James Burton	R	720427	N
Soulier, Duwayne	BB	670501	M
Southerland, Daniel Richar	CC	730401	V
Southwick, Charles Everett	RR	670514	N
Soyland, David Pecor	XX	710517	A
Sparenberg, Bernard J	BB	660205	N
Sparks, Donald L	XX	609617	A
Sparks, John G	RR	680424	A
Sparks, Jon M	XX	710319	A
Spaulding, Richard	RR	680201	V
Spencer, Dean Calvin III	BB	680607	A
Spencer, Larry Howard	RR	660218	N
Spencer, Warren R	NR	721220	F
Spencer, William A	RR	720705	F
Spengler, Henry Mershon III	NR	720405	A
Spilman, Dyke Augustus	XX	660927	F
Spindler, John Gates	BB	680421	M
Spinelli, Domenick Anthony	XX	680930	N
Spinler, Darrell John	BB	670621	F
Spitz, George R	BB	730205	F
Sponeyberger, Robert D	RR	721222	F
Spoon, Donald Ray	RR	670121	F
Spragens, John	RR	740430	V
Sprague, Stanley George	NR	660912	F
Sprick, Doyle Robert	XX	660124	M
Springman, Richard	RR	700525	A
Springsteadah, Donald K	BB	680311	F
Springston, Theodore Jr	XX	670603	F
Sprott, Arthur Roy Jr	BB	690110	F
Squire, Boyd E	XX	670712	F
Stackhouse, Charles David	RR	670425	N
Stacks, Raymond C	NR	681130	A
Staehli, Bruce Wayne	XX	680430	M
Stafford, Hugh Allen	RR	670831	N
Stafford, Ronald Dean	BB	721121	F
Stamm, Ernest Albert	KR	681125	N
Stancil, Kenneth Leon	BB	651228	A
Standerwick, Robert L	XX	710203	F
Stanley, Charles I	XX	690206	A
Stanley, Robert W	XX	670401	F
Stanton, Ronald	XX	681020	A
Stark, Lawrence J	RR	680201	V
Stark, William Robert	RR	670519	N
Stark, Willie E	XX	661202	A
Starner, Frances Lucille	CC	750429	V
Staton, Robert Milton Jr	BB	671111	A
Stavast, John Edward	RR	670917	F
Steadman, James E	XX	711126	F
Stearns, Roger Horace	NR	690911	F
Steen, Martin W	XX	660531	F
Stegman, Thomas	XX	680228	N
Steimer, Thomas Jack	BB	670508	N
Stephensen, Mark L	NR	670429	F
Stephenson, Henry John	KK	660913	W
Stephenson, Howard D	XX	720329	F
Stephenson, Richard Charle	BB	700205	N
Sterling, Thomas James	RR	670419	F
Stevens, (FNU)	CC	750429	V
Stevens, Larry James	XX	690214	N
Stevens, Phillip Paul	BB	680111	N
Stewart, Donald David	BR	651211	F
Stewart, Jack T	XX	670324	A
Stewart, Paul Clark	BB	710208	A
Stewart, Peter J	XX	660315	F
Stewart, Robert Allan	XX	670512	F
Stewart, Virgil Grant	BB	690517	F
Stickney, Phillip J	XX	660531	F
Stier, Theodore Gerhard	RR	671119	N
Stine, Joseph M	XX	660927	F
Stinson, William Sherrill	XX	730108	A
Stirm, Robert Lewis	RR	671027	F
Stischer, Walter Morris	RR	680413	F
Stockdale, James Bond	RR	650909	N
Stockman, Hervey Studdie	RR	670611	F
Stoddard, Clarence W Jr	BB	660914	N
Stolz, Lawrence G	NR	711226	F
Stone, Dana	PP	700406	V
Stone, James Marvin	BB	680107	A
Stonebraker, Kenneth Arnol	XX	681028	F
Storey, Thomas Gordon	RR	670116	F
Story, James Clellon	BB	690613	A
Storz, Ronald Edward	KR	650428	F
Stoves, Merritt III (NMN)	BB	670110	A
Stow, Lilburn Ray	BB	680426	F
Stowers, Aubrey E Jr	XX	680321	F
Stpierre, Dean Paul	XX	680522	F
Strait, Douglas F	XX	701018	A
Straley, John Leroy	BB	640118	A
Strange, Floyd W	XX	671202	A
Stratton, Charles W	XX	710103	F
Stratton, Richard Allen	RR	670105	N
Strawn, John Thomas	BB	710304	A
Strickland, James H	RR	680108	N
Stride, James Daniel Jr	BB	681005	AS
Stringer, John Curtis II	XX	701130	A
Stringham, William S	BB	730203	N
Strobridge, Rodney L	XX	720511	A
Strohlein, Madison Alexand	XX	710622	A
Strong, Henry Hooker Jr	XX	720525	N
Stroven, William Harry	XX	681028	F
Struharik, Paul Allen	RR	750310	V
Stuart, John F	XX	721220	F
Stubberfield, Robert A	NR	650506	F
Stubbs, William Wentworth	XX	691020	A
Stuckey, John Steiner Jr	BB	671111	A
Stuifbergen, Gene Paul	BB	681127	F
Stuller, John Charles	BB	680512	A
Stutz, Leroy William	RR	661202	F
Suber, Randolph Bothwell	XX	691113	A
Sulander, Daniel Arthur	BB	661202	A
Sullivan, Dwight Everett	RR	671017	F
Sullivan, Farrell Junior	NR	720627	F
Sullivan, James Edward	NR	721029	N
Sullivan, John B III	NR	660621	F
Sullivan, Martin Joseph	BB	670212	N
Sullivan, Robert Joseph	BB	670712	A
Sullivan, Timothy Bernard	RR	671116	N
Sumpter, Thomas Wrenne	RR	680114	F
Sutter, Frederick John	XX	711231	F
Sutton, William Carl	BB	700128	F
Suydam, James Lawrence	BB	691009	A
Swanson, John W Jr	XX	670615	F
Swanson, Jon Edward	BB	710226	A
Swanson, Roger W	XX	681031	A
Swanson, William Edward	BB	650411	N
Sweeney, Jon M	RR	690219	M
Swigart, Paul Eugene Jr	BB	690205	N
Swindle, Orson George III	RR	661111	M
Switzer, Jerrold Allen	BB	680318	M
Swords, Smith III	XX	671230	F
Sykes, Derri	KK	680109	A
Szeyller, Edward Philip	BB	670404	N

T

Name	Status	I-date	Service
Tabb, Robert Ernest	RR	700412	A
Tabor, John Walter	CC	750330	V
Tadios, Leonard Masayon	KK	641211	A
Tadtad, Gororedo	RR	711108	W
Takagi, Yujiro	–	700405	W
Talken, George Francis	BB	690802	N
Tallaferro, William P	EE	680206	M
Talley, Bernard Leo	RR	660910	F
Talley, James Lane	BB	640619	A
Talley, William H	RR	720511	F
Tamnyo, Arcadio Q	RR	701017	W
Tang, Yb	RR	740127	W
Tangeman, Richard George	RR	680505	N
Tanner, Charles Nels	RR	661009	N
Tapp, John Bethel	BB	660323	N
Tapp, Marshall L	XX	660515	F
Tatum, Lawrence B	XX	660910	F
Tavares, John R	MM	650518	V
Taylor, Danny Gene	BB	660928	A
Taylor, Edd David	BB	650829	N
Taylor, Edmund Battelle Jr	BB	720508	N
Taylor, Fred (NMN)	BB	650713	A
Taylor, James Harry	BB	710215	A
Taylor, James Lawrence	BB	660310	A
Taylor, Jesse Junior	NR	651117	N
Taylor, Neil Brooks	BB	650914	N
Taylor, Phillip Charles	NR	710527	A
Taylor, Ted James	BB	710715	A
Taylor, Walter Joseph Jr	BB	710206	A
Taylor, William B	EE	680320	A
Teague, James Erlan	NR	671119	N
Tellier, Dennis A	RR	690619	M

Name	Status	I-date	Service
Temperley, Russell Edward	RR	671027	F
Templin, Erwin Bernard Jr	XX	660122	N
Teran, Refugio Thomas	XX	700506	A
Terla, Lothar Gustav T	BB	700309	F
Terrell, Irby David	RR	680114	F
Terrell, Keavin Lee	BB	691002	N
Terrill, Philip B	KK	710331	A
Terry, Oral R	XX	680503	A
Terry, Ronald Terrance	BB	660129	A
Terry, Ross Randle	RR	661009	N
Terwillinger, Virgil Byron	BB	670313	M
Tester, Jerry Albert	RR	680520	A
Thackerson, Walter Anthony	BB	660521	A
Thani, Prasit	–	630905	W
Thomas, Daniel W	XX	710706	F
Thomas, Darwin Joel	BB	661014	N
Thomas, Fernando K	CC	750429	V
Thomas, Harry Eugene	BB	650813	N
Thomas, James Calven	XX	680403	M
Thomas, James R	XX	711125	F
Thomas, Kenneth D Jr	NR	660505	F
Thomas, Leo Tarlton Jr	BB	711219	F
Thomas, Robert J	NR	721218	F
Thomas, William E	RR	720519	M
Thomason, Ford Wilder	CC	750429	V
Thompson, Benjamin Arthur	BB	681025	A
Thompson, David Mathew	BB	720812	N
Thompson, Dennis L	RR	680207	A
Thompson, Donald E	XX	670204	N
Thompson, Fletcher	RR	730628	W
Thompson, Floyd James	RR	640326	A
Thompson, Fred N	RR	680320	F
Thompson, George W	XX	660515	F
Thompson, Melvin Carl	BB	680206	N
Thompson, Victor H	BR	670315	F
Thompson, William J	XX	680801	F
Thompson, William Joseph	BB	680116	N
Thongnuded, Thongdee	–	660326	W
Thoresen, Donald Nellis	BB	680111	N
Thorne, Larry Alan	BB	651018	A
Thornton, Gary Lynn	RR	670220	N
Thornton, Larry C	XX	651224	F
Thornton, William Dempsey	BB	670128	A
Thorsness, Leo Keith	RR	670430	F
Thum, Richard Cobb	NR	681125	N
Thurman, Curtis Frank	BB	680217	N
Thuy, Nhien Trieu	CC	750429	V
Tice, Paul Douglas	BB	660925	M
Tiderman, John Mark	BB	660321	N
Tiffin, Rainford	XX	660721	F
Tigner, Lee Morrow	BB	720822	F
Tik, Chui To	–	630905	W
Timmons, Bruce Allen	BB	661115	N
Tinsley, Coy R	RR	690209	A
Tipping, Henry Albert	XX	680702	F
To, Bao	CC	750429	V
Todd, Larry Richard	BB	680426	F
Todd, Robert Jacy	BB	670509	M
Todd, William Anthony	NR	720329	F
Tolbert, Clarence Orfield	NR	721106	N
Tolentino, Enrique	RR	750312	W
Tolentino, Lamberto A	RR	701017	W
Tomes, Jack Harvey	RR	660707	F
Toms, Dennis Leroy	BB	651121	N
Toomey, Samuel K III	NR	681139	A
Toop, Patricia	CC	750429	V
Torkelson, Loren H	RR	670429	F
Towery, Herman	BR	641022	A
Towle, John C	XX	700422	F
Townley, Roy F	MM	711227	V
Townsend, Francis Wayne	XX	720813	F
Trampski, Donald Joseph	XX	690916	A
Trautman, Konrad Wigand	RR	671005	F
Traver, John Grove III	BB	710322	A
Travis, Lynn Michael	BB	680206	N
Treece, James Allen	XX	661007	F
Trembley, J Forrest George	XX	670821	N
Trent, Alan Robert	XX	700513	F
Triebel, Theodore W	RR	720827	N
Trier, Robert D	NR	651220	F
Trimble, Jack R	RR	721227	F
Trimble, James Mitchell	BB	680406	M
Trimble, Larry Allen	NR	720415	F
Tritt, James Francis	BB	670707	N
Trivelpiece, Steve Maurice	BB	680404	A
Tromp, William Leslie	XX	660417	N
Trowbridge, Dustin Cowles	BB	691226	N
Trudeau, Albert Raymond	BB	711026	A
Trujillo, Joseph F	NR	660903	M
Trujillo, Robert S	XX	680107	A
Tschudy, William Michael	RR	650718	N
Tu, Anh Hoang	CC	750429	V
Tu, Thi Nhan	CC	750429	V
Tubbs, Glenn E	XX	700113	A
Tucci, Robert L	XX	691112	F
Tucker, Edwin Byron	NR	670424	N
Tucker, James Hale	XX	660426	F
Tucker, Timothy M	XX	711224	F
Tullier, Lonnie J	BR	680812	A
Tunnell, John Wallace	BB	660620	N
Turley, Morvan D	BR	670113	F
Turner, Frederick Ray	BB	681106	M
Turner, James Henry	BB	691009	A
Turner, John Douglas	–	651018	W
Turner, Kelton Rena	BB	650515	M
Turose, Michael Stephen	BB	720917	F
Tycz, James Neil	BB	670510	M
Tye Michael James	BB	691002	N
Tyler, Charles Robert	RR	670823	F
Tyler, George E	XX	681024	F
Tyszkiewicz, Arthur Kasimi	BR	670114	N

U

Name	Status	I-date	Service
Uhlmansiek, Ralph E	XX	670611	A
Underwood, (FNU)	CC	750429	V
Underwood, Paul G	XX	660316	F
Underwood, Thomas Wayne	BB	700321	M
Unger, Don Lee	BR	720503	F
Unidentified Frenchman 1	RR	750101	W
Unidentified Frenchman 2	RR	750101	W
Uom, Chem B	RR	640818	W
Uplinger, Barton John	BR	680219	M
Upner, Edward Charles	BB	651205	A
Urquhart, Paul Dean	BB	710528	A
Utecht, Richard W	RR	680204	V
Utley, Russel K	XX	690126	F
Uyeyama, Terry Jun	RR	680518	F

V

Name	Status	I-date	Service
Vaden, Woodrow Wilson	BB	641210	F
Van Artsdalen, Clifford Da	BB	680509	A
Van Buren, Gerald Gordon	XX	671229	F
Van Campden,Thomas Charles	BB	650624	A
Van Cleave, Walter Shelby	BB	690422	F
Van de Velde, Patrick	CC	750429	W
Van Dyke, Richard Haven	NR	680911	F
Vanbendegom, James Lee	KK	670712	A
Vanchong, Xiong	–	730507	W
Vandegeer, Richard (NMI)	BB	750515	F
Vanden Eykel, Martin D II	NR	691202	A
Vang, Leng Lor	–	730507	W
Vang, Pao Xiong	–	730507	W
Vanloan, Jack Lee	RR	670520	F
Vanputten, Thomas	EE	680211	A
Vanrenselaar, Larry Jack	NR	680930	N
Vanthi, Hoang Anh	CC	750429	V
Variyaphong, Tawatchi	–	640818	W
Varnadom Michael B	KR	700502	A
Vaughan, Robert Reddington	BB	671014	N
Vaughan, Samuel R	RR	711219	F
Vaughn, Christina Louise	CC	750429	V
Vaughn, Linda Sue	CC	750429	V
Vavroch, Duane P	RR	721226	F
Venanzi, Gerald Santo	RR	670917	F
Vennik, Robert Nicholas	BB	710826	A
Versace, Humberto Roque	KK	631029	A
Vescelius, Milton James	NR	670921	N
Viado, Reynaldo Rocillo	BB	691002	N
Vietti, Eleanor A	PP	620530	V
Villenponteaux, James H Jr	BB	660511	M
Vinson, Bobby G	XX	680424	F
Visconti, francis	XX	651122	M
Visot, Michel	–	700405	W
Vissotzky, Raymond Walton	RR	671119	F
Vitte, Raymond Jules	RR	720408	W
Vlahakos, Peter George	BB	660201	M
Vogel, Richard Dale	RR	670522	F
Vogle, Paul David	CC	750429	V
Vogt, Leonard Frederick Jr	BB	650918	N
Vohden, Raymond Arthur	RR	650403	N
Vollmer, Valentine Bernard	BR	680216	A

W

Name	Status	I-date	Service
Waddell, Dewey Wayne	RR	670705	F
Wade, Barton Scott	NR	721221	N
Wadleigh, Carl Dennis	AA	680621	A
Wadsworth, Dean Amick	BB	631008	F
Wagener, David Raymond	BB	661020	F
Waggoner, Robert Frost	RR	660912	F
Wagner, Raymond Anthony	BB	720327	F
Waku, Youshihiko	KK	700531	W
Wald, Gunther Herbert	XX	691103	A
Waldhaus, Richard G	RR	710804	V
Walker, Bruce C	XX	720407	F
Walker, Hubert C	RR	680114	F
Walker, Kenneth Earl	BB	641002	F
Walker, Lloyd Francis	BB	670131	F
Walker, Michael James	RR	700205	N
Walker, Michael S	XX	690715	D
Walker, Orien J	KK	650523	A
Walker, Samuel F Jr	XX	681213	F
Walker, Thomas Taylor	BB	660407	F
Walker, William John	BB	680420	M
Wall, Jerry Mack	BB	660518	F
Wallace, Arnold Brian	BB	670125	A
Wallace, Charles Franklin	BB	670828	M
Wallace, Hobart M Jr	XX	680119	M
Wallace, Michael J	XX	680419	A
Wallace, Michael Walter	NR	680328	N
Waller, Therman M	XX	660203	F
Walling, Charles Milton	XX	660808	F
Wallingford, Kenneth	RR	720407	A
Wallis, William Henry	–	650214	W
Walsh, Brian	MM	750425	V
Walsh, Francis A Jr	NR	721221	F
Walsh, James P	RR	720926	M
Walsh, Richard A III	XX	690215	F
Walters, Donovan K	NR	721221	F
Walters, Jack	KR	670519	N
Walters, Tim Leroy	BB	690309	A
Walters, William (NMN)	BB	690510	A
Waltman, Donald G	RR	660919	F
Walton, Lewis C	XX	710510	A
Walton, Wilbert	NR	700103	A
Wanat, George K Jr	RR	720408	A
Wangchom, Nophadon	RR	721017	W
Wann, Donald Lynn	BB	710601	A
Wanzel, Charles J III	NR	720329	F
Ward, Brian H	RR	721227	F
Ward, Neal C	XX	690613	F
Ward, Ronald J	XX	721218	F
Warte, John Alan	XX	691104	A
Warner, James Hoie	RR	671013	M
Warren, Arthur L	NR	661204	F
Warren, Ervin	XX	660603	F
Warren, Gray D	XX	691026	F
Washburn, Larry Eugene	BB	660617	F
Washington, Bobby	AA	690515	M
Waterman, Craig Houston	NR	670730	M
Waters, Samuel E	NR	661213	F
Watkins, Robert James Jr	BB	691008	A
Watkins, Willie A	RR	680109	F
Watson, Frank Peter	BB	650618	F
Watson, Jimmy L	XX	680313	A
Watson, Ronald Leonard	BB	710218	A
Watt, George	RR	670901	W
Wax, David J	NR	651220	F
Weaks, Melvin Lee	BB	710818	A
Weatherby, Jack Wilton	NR	650729	F
Weatherman, Earl Clyde	AA	671108	M
Weaver, Eugene	RR	680201	V
Weaver, George Robert Jr	BB	661101	N
Webb, Catherine M	RR	710407	W
Webb, Ronald John	RR	670611	F
Weger, John (NMN) Jr	BB	651022	F
Weimorts, Robert Franklin	BB	660422	N
Weisman, Kurt Frederick	BR	720426	F
Weisner, Franklin Lee	XX	691010	A
Weissenback, Edward J	XX	711227	V
Weissmueller, Courtney E	XX	670212	F
Weitkamp, Edgar Wilken	BB	601323	A
Weitz, Monek	BB	690525	M
Welch, Robert J	XX	670116	F
Wellons, Phillip Rogerson	BB	700817	F
Wells, Kenneth	RR	711218	F
Wells, Norman Louross	RR	660829	F
Wells, Robert James	BB	660722	A
Welsh, Larry Don	XX	690107	A
Welshan, John T	XX	680303	F
Wenaas, Gordon J	XX	671229	F
Wendell, John Henry	RR	660807	F
Werdehoff, Michael R	XX	680419	A
Weskamp, Robert L	KR	670425	F
West, John Thomas	XX	700102	F
Westbrook, Donald E	XX	680313	F
Westcott, Gary Patrick	BB	720330	A
Wester, Albert Dwayne	BB	681005	F
Weston, Oscar Branch Jr	BB	610323	F
Westwood, Norman Philip Jr	BB	700517	N
Wheat, David Robert	RR	651017	N
Wheeler, Eugene Lacy	XX	700421	M
Wheeler, James Atlee	BB	650418	F
White, Charles E	XX	680129	A
White, Danforth Ellithorne	BB	690331	N
White, James B	XX	691124	F
White, Richard	CC	750429	W
White, Robert Thomas	RR	691115	A
Whited, James Lafayette	BB	661119	A
Whitesides, Richard Lebrou	BB	640326	F
Whitford, Lawrence W Jr	XX	691102	F
Whitlock, Peter	RR	750310	W
Whitmire, Warren T Jr	XX	680501	A
Whitt, James Edward	BB	720323	F
Whitteker, Richard Lee	BB	680327	F
Whittemore, Frederick Herb	BB	680411	N
Whittle, Junior Lee	BB	660924	A
Wickham, David Wallace II	BB	651216	N
Widdis, James W Jr	XX	690323	F
Widdison, Imlay Scott	BB	680512	A
Wideman, Robert Earl	RR	670506	N
Widener, James Edward	BB	670611	M
Widener, Larry Allen	BB	680302	A
Widerquist, Thomas Carl	BR	720503	F
Widner, Danny L	XX	680512	A
Widon, Kenneth Harry	BB	680111	N
Wiechert, Robert Charles	BB681116		F
Wiehr, Richard Daniel	BB	730121	N
Wieland, Carl T	RR	721220	N
Wiggins, Wallace L	NR	680203	F
Wilber, Walter Eugene	RR	680616	N
Wilbrecht, Kurt Michael	BB	700607	M
Wilburn, John Edward	BB	680419	A
Wilburn, Woodrow Hoover	NR	670204	F
Wiles, Marvin Benjamin C	XX	720506	N
Wiley, Richard Dennis	BB	720612	A
Wilke, Robert F	XX	680117	F
Wilkins, Calvin Wayne	BB	690208	M
Wilkins, George Henry	XX	660711	N
Wilkinson, Clyde David	BB	710212	A
Wilkinson, Dennis E	NR	720510	F
Willett, Robert Vincent Jr	XX	690417	F
Williams, Billie J	NR	721209	F
Williams, Danny Huy	CC	750429	V
Williams, David Beryl	NR	720503	M
Williams, David R	XX	670401	F
Williams, Eddie L	XX	661003	A
Williams, Edward W	XX	720403	A
Williams, Howard K	NR	680318	F
Williams, James E	XX	660515	F
Williams, James R	XX	671229	F
Williams, James W	RR	720520	F
Williams, Leroy Christophe	BB	690525	M
Williams, Lewis Irvng	RR	670424	N
Williams, Richard F	KR	680108	A
Williams, Robert Cyril	BB	660701	F
Williams, Robert J	XX	720511	A
Williams, Roy C	XX	680512	A
Williams, Thaddeus Edward	BB	660109	A
Williamson, Don Ira	NR	650707	F
Williamson, James D	XX	680105	A
Willing, Edward Arlo	XX	680721	N
Willis, Charles E	RR	680201	V
Wills, Francis Desales	BB	660226	A
Wilmoth, Floyd A	RR	680717	A
Wilson, Claude David Jr	NR	661214	N
Wilson, Glenn Hubert	RR	670807	F
Wilson, Gordon Scott	NR	661122	F
Wilson, Hal K	RR	721219	F
Wilson, Harry Truman	BB	700604	M
Wilson, Marion Earl	BB	680203	A
Wilson, Mickey Allen	XX	730108	A
Wilson, Peter Joe	XX	701019	A
Wilson, Richard Jr (NMN)	BB	710614	A
Wilson, Robert Allan	XX	720618	F
Wilson, Roger E	NR	720611	M
Wilson, Wayne V	XX	670702	M
Wilson, William W	RR	721222	F
Wimbrow, Nutter J	NR	721226	F
Windeler, Charles Carl Jr	NR	720405	A
Winkler, John Anthony	BB	651122	N
Winn, David William	RR	680809	F
Winningham, John Q	NR	721221	F
Winston, Charles C III	NR	670801	F
Winters, Darryl Gordon	BB	660719	F
Winters, David M	XX	670421	A
Wiseman, Bain Wendell Jr	BB	701223	A
Wistrand, Robert C	XX	650509	F
Wogan, William M	XX	690216	A
Wolfe, Donald Findling	BB	671008	N
Wolfe, Thomas Hubert	BB	660628	F
Wolfkeil, Wayne B	XX	680809	F
Wolfkill, Grant	RR	610515	V
Woloszyk, Donald J	XX	660301	N
Wolpe, Jack	BB	670803	M
Womack, Lonnie Herman Jr	AA	671020	N
Womack, Sammie Norman	RR	661008	A
Wong, Edward Puck Kow Jr	XX	720327	A
Wong, Nancy Randy	CC	750429	V
Wonn, James Charles	BB	680217	N
Wood, Don C	XX	660116	F
Wood, Patrick Hardy	XX	670206	F
Wood, Rex Stewart	BB	670602	N
Wood, Walter Sutton	BB	660502	N
Wood, William C Jr	XX	720902	F
Woods, Brian Dunstan	RR	680918	N
Woods, David Walter	BB	701103	A
Woods, Gerald Ernest	BB	710218	A
Woods, Lawrence (NMN)	BB	641024	A
Woods, Robert Deane	RR	661012	N
Woods, Robert Francis	BB	680626	F
Woodworth, Samuel Alexander	BB	650417	F
Worcester, John B	XX	651019	N
Worley, Don Franklin	BB	680311	F
Worrell, Mark V	AA	681009	M
Worrell, Paul L	NR	661202	N
Worst, Karl Edward	BB	660302	F
Worth, James F	XX	720401	M
Wortham, Murray L	XX	671230	F
Worthington, Richard Charl	BB	700506	A
Wozniak, Frederick J	XX	670117	F
Wright, Arthur	XX	670221	A
Wright, Buddy	EE	680922	A
Wright, David Irvin	BB	701113	F
Wright, Donald L	XX	691124	F
Wright, Frederick Willisto	NR	721110	N
Wright, Gary G	XX	670117	F
Wright, James J	NR	671102	N
Wright, Jerdy Albert Jr	NR	660307	F
Wright, Thomas T	XX	680227	F
Writer, Lawrence Daniel	RR	680215	F
Wrobleski, Walter F	XX	670521	A
Wrye, Blair C	NR	660812	F
Wynne, Patrick E	NR	660808	F

X

Name	Status	I-date	Service
Xai, Da Ly	–	730507	W
Xai, Teng Yang	–	730507	W
Xai, Theng Thao	–	730507	W
Xavier, Augusto Maria	BB	660310	M

Y

Name	Status	I-date	Service
Yanagisawa, Takeshi	KK	700510	W
Yarbrough, William P Jr	NR	670119	N
Yeakley, Robin Ray	BB	720611	A
Yee, Leong-Ching	CC	750429	V
Yeend, Richard Carolinus J	BB	680609	F
Yim, John Sung	MM	750425	V
Yonan, Kenneth Joseph	NR	720424	A
Young, Barclay B	XX	720329	F
Young, Charles L	XX	680517	A
Young, Chi-Yeun	–	711221	W
Young, James Faulds	RR	660706	F
Young, Jeffrey Jerome	BB	700404	A
Young, John Arthur	RR	680131	A
Young, Myron A	RR	721012	F
Young, Robert M	KK	700502	A
Yuill, John H	RR	721222	F
Yurino, Yoshihiko	KK	700510	W

Z

Name	Status	I-date	Service
Zavocky, James John	BB	670825	N
Zawtocki, Joseph S Jr	KR	680208	M
Zempel, Ronald Lee	BB	670227	N
Zerbe, Michael R	BB	660415	N
Zich, Larry Alfred	XX	720403	A
Ziegler, Roy Esper II	RR	680208	A
Ziminske, Tom	CC	750429	V
Zimmer, Jerry Allen	BB	690829	M
Zissu, Andrew Gilbert	BB	671008	N
Zollicoffer, Franklin	BB	720424	A
Zook, David Hartzler Jr	XX	671004	F
Zook, Harold J	NR	660531	F
Zorn, Thomas O'Neal Jr	BB	720917	F
Zuberbuhler, Rudolph U	RR	720912	F
Zubke, Deland Dwight	XX	710301	A
Zuhoski, Charles Peter	RR	670731	N
Zukowski, Robert John	XX	690211	F
Zupp, Klaus H	RR	680717	A
Zutterman, Joseph A Jr	BB	680420	M

Total number of personnel were 3753

Index

Picture credits

The publishers would like to thank all the organisations, agencies and companies who have provided illustrations for this book. Photographs have been credited by page number, and by number on the page. Some references have, for reasons of space, been abbreviated as follows:

USAF : United States Air Force
USN : US Navy
USMC : United States Marine Corps
US DoD: US Department of Defense
ECPA : Etablissement Cinematographique et Photographique des Armees
DRVN : Democratic Republic of Vietnam
AP : Associated Press

Jacket front: AP. **Jacket back:** USN, US Army, USN, USAF, DRVN, US Army. **Front endpapers:** USAF. **Back endpapers:** USN. **Half-title page:** DRVN. **Title page:** ECPA. **Credits and contents page:** USN. **The authors page:** DRVN. **8:** US Army. **10-11:** US Army, DRVN, USN, US Army. **18-19:** US Army, USN. **47:** 1: DRVN. 2: US Govt. 3: DRVN. 4: Harlingue-Viollet. **48-49.** 1-5: US Govt. **50-51.** 1: Viollet. 2: DRVN. 3: DRVN. **52-53.** 1: US Govt. 2-3: ECPA. 4: DRVN. 5: Popperfoto. **54-55.** 2: US Govt. 3: DRVN. 4: ECPA. 5: Camera Press. **57.** 1 and 3: US Govt. **58-59.** 1-4: US Govt. 5-6: DRVN. **60-61.** All: DRVN. **62-63.** 1: Popperfoto. 2: US Govt. 4: Royal Laotian Army. **65.** 1: DRVN. 2: US Govt. 3: USN. 4: US Army. **66-67.** 1: US Army. 2-4: USAF. 5-7: US Army. **68-69.** 1: USAF. 2: US Army. 3: US Army. 4: DRVN. **70-71.** 1: USAF. 2: US Army. 3: DRVN. 4: US Army. 5-7: US Navy. **76-77.** 1-2: US Army. 3: DRVN. **74-75.** 2: Popperfoto. 3: DRVN. 4: US Army. 5-7: US Navy. **76-77.** 1-2: US Army. 3: DRVN. **78-79.** 1: US Govt. 2-4: US Navy. 5: US DoD. **81.** 1: US Army. 2: DRVN. 3: ECPA. 4: US Govt. **82-83.** 1: USN. 4: US Army. **84-85.** 1: US Govt. 2: USAF. 3: USN. 4: US Army. 5: USN. **86-87.** 1: USAF. 2-3: USN. 4: US DoD. **89.** 1: USN. 2-3: USAF. 4: DRVN. **90-91.** 1: DRVN. 2-3: US Govt. 4: USN. 5-7: USAF. **92-93.** 1: USAF. 2: USN. 3: USAF. 4-5: USN. 7: USAF. **97.** 1: US DoD. 2: USN. 3-4: DRVN. **98-99.** 1: US Army. 2: US Govt. 3-6: USN. **100-101.** 3: US Army. 4: USAF. **102-103.** 1-4: US Army. 5: USN. **104-105.** 1: US Govt. 2: US DoD. 3: DRVN. 4-6: USN. 7: USAF. **107.** 1: USN. 2: US Govt. 3: USMC. **108-109.** 1-2: US Govt. 3: USAF. 4: US DoD. 5: USN. 6: US Army. **110-111.** 2: USN. 3-4: US Govt. 4: US Army. 5: US Govt. **115.** 1: Australian Army. 2: USAF. 3: USAF. 4: US Govt. **116-117.** 1: US Army. 2: USAF.

3-5: US Army. **118-119.** 1: Popperfoto. 2-3: US Army. 4: USAF. **120-121.** 1: US Army. 2: USMC. 3: DRVN. 4: Australian Army. 5-6: USAF. 7-8: US Army. 9: USN. **123.** 1-3: DRVN. **124-125.** 1-4: DRVN. 5: US DoD. 6: USN 7: USAF. **126-127.** 1: DRVN. 2: USAF. 3: USMC. 4-5: DRVN. **128-129.** 1-7: DRVN. **131.** 1: USMC. 2-4: USN. **132-133.** 1-3: USN. **134-135.** 1-3: USN. 4: USMC. **136-137.** 1-4: USN. 5: DRVN. 6-7: USN. **138-139.** 1: USN. 2: USMC. 3-5: USN. 6: USMC. 7: USN. **141.** 1: USMC. 2-3: US Army. **142-143.** 1: USMC. 2-5: US Army. 6: USN. **144-145.** 1: USN. 2-3: USAF. 4-5: US Army. 6: USAF. **146-147.** 1: USMC. 2: DRVN. 3: USAF. 4: US Army. 5: Popperfoto. **149.** 1: USMC. 2: DRVN. 4: US Army. 5: USN. **150-151.** 1: US Govt. 2: US Army. 3: USAF. 5: US Govt. 4: US Army. 5: AP. 6: USN. **152-153.** 1-4: US Army. 5: DRVN. 6. US Army. **154-155.** 1: US Army. 3: US Govt. 4: US Army. 5: AP. 6: USN. **157.** 1: USAF. 2: Popperfoto. 3: DRVN. **158-159.** 2: US Army. 3: USAF. 4: DRVN. 5: US Army. **160-161.** 1-5: USAF. **162-163.** 1: USN. 2: USMC. 3: USAF. 4-6: USMC. 7: USAF. **165.** 1: USAF. 2: DRVN. **166-167.** 1: DRVN. 2-3: USAF. 5-8: USAF. **168-169.** 1-3: USAF. 4: USN. 5: USAF. 6: USN. 7: USAF. **170-171.** 1-7: USAF. **173.** 1: US Army. 2: US Govt. 3: USN. 4-5: USAF. **176-177.** 1-5: USN. 6: US Army. 7: USN. **178-179.** 1: USAF. 2: US Govt. 3: US Army. 4-5: USAF. 6: US Army. **180-181.** 1: AP. 2: DRVN. 3: USN. 4-5: US Govt. 6: US Army. **183.** 1: USN. 2: US DoD. 3: US Govt. **184-185.** 1: Govt of Kampuchea. 2-3: US Army. 4: USAF. 5: Govt of Kampuchea. 6-7: US Army. **186-187.** 1-2: DRVN. 3: US Army. 4: USAF. **188-189.** 1-2: USN. 3: Govt. of Kampuchea. 4: US Govt. 5-6: Govt of Kampuchea. **191.** 1: US Army. 2-3: DRVN. **192-193.** 1: USN. 2-3: US Army. 4: US Army. 5: USMC. 6: US Army. **195.** 1: USAF. 2: Popperfoto. **196-197.** 1: USAF. 2: US Army. 3-4: USMC. 5: DRVN. **198-199.** 1: USN. 2: USAF. **200-201.** 1-5: USAF. **202-203.** 1: USAF. 2: USN. 3–5: USAF. 6: DRVN. **204-205.** 1: DRVN. 2-5: USAF. **206-207.** 1-5: USAF. 6-8: DRVN. **208-209.** 1: USAF. 2: USN. 3: DRVN. 4: USAF. 5: US Army. **211.** 1: USMC. 2-3: USN. 4-5: US Army. **212-213.** 1: US Army. 4: US Army. 5: US Govt. 6: USN. **214-215.** 1: DRVN. 2-3: US Govt. 4: © 1971 by The New York Times Company. Reprinted by permission. 5: US Govt. **216-217.** 1: USN. 2: US Govt. 3: Popperfoto. **219.** 1: DRVN. 2: DRVN. **220-221.** 1: DRVN. 2: USN. 3: US Govt. 4: US Army. **222-223.** 1: USN. 3: US Army. 4: DRVN. 5: USAF. 6-7: USN. **224-225.** 1-3: US Army. 5-6: USN. **226-227.** 1-4: US Govt. 5: DRVN. 7: US Govt. 9-10: US Govt. **228-229.** 1: DRVN. 2: US Govt. 3: DRVN. **230-231.** 2-3: USN. 4: DRVN. 5: Popperfoto. 6-7: DRVN. **232-233.** 1: DRVN. 2: Popperfoto. 3: DRVN. 4-5: USN. **234-235.** 1: Popperfoto. 2-3: USN. 4: Popperfoto. 5: USN. 6: DRVN. **236-237.** 1-3: USAF. 4: DRVN. 5: USN. 6: DRVN. **239.** 1: USN. 2-4: DRVN. **240-241.** 1-2: DRVN. 4: Govt of Kampuchea. **242-243.** 1-3: DRVN. **244-245.** 1-3: Govt of Kampuchea; 4: DRVN. **246-247.** 1-2: Kingsway International Publications. 4-6: US DoD. **249-252.** US DoD. **252.** 1-2: League of Families. **253.** 3-5: US DoD.

"No nation should put the burden of war on its military forces alone."

*General
William C. Westmoreland,
US Army, retired*

"I don't see anyone wanting to get back into Vietnam. I see a lot of people wanting to get out."

*Richard M. Nixon,
former president of the United States,
speaking of the refugees from Vietnam,
Oxford Union, England,
November 30, 1978*

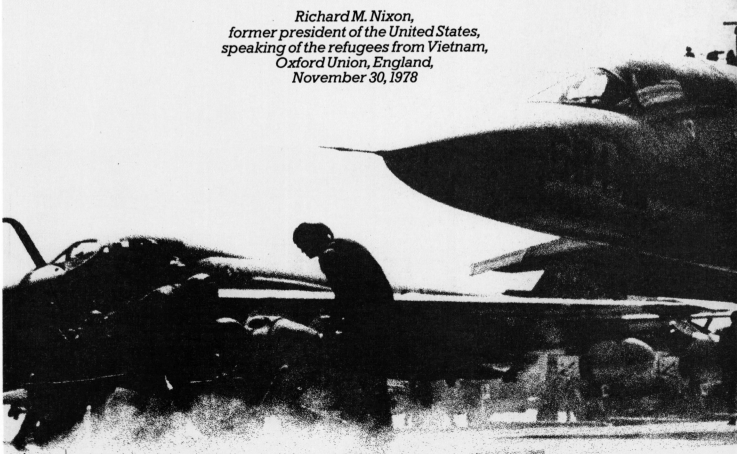